A Reader's Guide to the Social Sciences

The Free Press, New York

COLLIER-MACMILLAN LIMITED, LONDON

Copyright © 1970 by The Free Press
A DIVISION OF THE MACMILLAN COMPANY

1st edition © 1959 by The Free Press, a corporation

Printed in the United States of America

All rights reserved. No part of this book may be reproduced or transmitted in any form or by any means, electronic or mechanical, including photocopying, recording, or by any information storage and retrieval system, without permission in writing from the Publisher.

The Free Press
A DIVISION OF THE MACMILLAN COMPANY
866 Third Avenue, New York, New York 10022

Collier-Macmillan Canada Ltd., Toronto, Ontario

First Free Press Paperback Edition 1972

Library of Congress Catalog Card Number: 71-15373

printing number
1 2 3 4 5 6 7 8 9 10

A Reader's Guide to the Social Sciences

Edited by Bert F. Hoselitz

WITH CHAPTERS BY

Peter M. Blau & Joan W. Moore

Heinz Eulau, Norton S. Ginsburg

Gail M. Kelly, Walter R. Reitman

Bert F. Hoselitz

REVISED EDITION

[Fp]

Contents

Preface to the Revised Edition   xi

Preface to the First Edition   xiii

1 Sociology   PETER M. BLAU *and* JOAN W. MOORE   1

The Development of Sociology   3

  Early Social Philosophy   3
  The Separation of State and Society   5
  Inevitable Evolutionary Forces   7
  Concern with Social Reform   9
  History and Sociology   11
  The Scientific Study of Social Facts   14
  Implications and Reactions   17

Contemporary Sociological Literature in Selected Areas   20

  Social Theory   20
  Methods of Data Collection and Analysis   24
  Social Psychology   26
  Demography and Human Ecology   30
  Social Differentiation in Community and Nation   33
  Formal Organization   36

2 Anthropology   GAIL M. KELLY   41

Introduction   41

  The Subject Matter   41
  The Discipline   45

The Character of the Literature   47
   ETHNOLOGY   50
History of the Discipline   53
   EVOLUTIONISM   55
American Historical Anthropology   58

Contemporary Concerns   60

Culture Theory   60
   ARCHAEOLOGY   63
   CULTURE AND PERSONALITY   65
   ETHNOSCIENCE   68
   LINGUISTICS   69
Social Anthropology   71
   KINSHIP   73
   POLITICS   75
   ECONOMICS   76
   RELIGION   77
   CHANGES   78
Ethnography   80
   THE AMERICAS   82
   SUB-SAHARAN AFRICA   84
   THE MIDDLE EAST   85
   ASIA   86
   OCEANIA   88

3 Psychology   WALTER R. REITMAN   91

Introduction   91
Orientation   93
Sensation, Perception, Cognition, and Thought   94
   Cognition and Thought   97
Learning   100
The Individual   104
   Personality   106
   Motivation and Emotion   111
Social Psychology   116
On the Need to Apply What You Have Not Got   121
Statistics, Measurement, and Mathematical Models   123

4 Political Science   HEINZ EULAU   129

– I –

Introduction	129
Politics as Science: The State of Affairs	131
Political Theory: The Lost Frontier	135
The Core of Political Science: The Study of Government	143
Public Administration: Departure and Return	151
Beyond the Horizon: International Politics	158
The Party and the Vote: Behavioral Breakthrough	163

– II –

Political Theory: Rejuvenation	174
Political Man: Redivivus	182
American Laboratory: Politics	186
Federal Octopus: Law and Administration	194
Dynamics: Policy and Power	200
Comparative Politics: Method or Field?	210
International Politics: Urgency and Complexity	225
Conclusion: Quo Vadimus?	235

5 Economics   BERT F. HOSELITZ   239

Introduction	239
The General Scope of Economics	240
Early Works	242
Mercantilism	244
The Emergence of Scientific Economics	245
National Differences	253
Levels of Economic Writing	258
Methodology	263
Economic Theory	266
Theory of Value and Price and Theory of Production	266
Theory of Income and Employment	268
Monetary Theory	269

Theory of Economic Fluctuations	270
Theories of Economic Growth	271
Time and Space in Economic Theory	272
Theories of Consumption	273
Welfare Economics	274
International Economics	275
The Application of Economic Theories	275
Agricultural Economics	275
The Industrial Labor Force	276
The Economics of Trade Unionism	277
Labor-Management Relations	279
Theories of Management	279
Entrepreneurship	280
Invention and Innovation	281
Banking	282
Public Finance	283
Government Consumption	283
Economic Policy and Economic Planning	284
Balance of Payments and Foreign Trade	285
Economic History	286
Sources of Economic Data	290

6 Geography   NORTON GINSBURG   293

The Domain of Geography	293
Geography as a Compendium of Facts	294
Geography as the Study of Environmental Influences	295
Geography as the Study of Man-Nature Relationships	296
Geography as the Study of Landscape	297
Geography as Human Ecology	298
Geography as the Science of Distributions	298
Can There Be a Satisfactory Definition of Geography?	299
On Systematic Geography and the Regional Concept	300
Systematic Geography	301
Regional Geography and the Regional Concept	301

Systematic Subdivisions of Geography　　　　　　　　　304

 Physical Geography　　　　　　　　　304
 Historical Geography　　　　　　　　　305
 Cultural Geography　　　　　　　　　307
 Economic Geography　　　　　　　　　309
 Urban Geography　　　　　　　　　311
 Political Geography　　　　　　　　　312

The Map　　　　　　　　　314

Other Reference Materials　　　　　　　　　317

 Atlases and Gazetteers　　　　　　　　　317
 Research Aids and Publications　　　　　　　　　318

Bibliography and Author Index　　　　　　　　　319

Preface to the Revised Edition

Quite a few very crowded and eventful years have passed since the publication of the first edition of this book. Many persevering critics have continued to add important contributions to the social science topics that already existed. While the majority of the older studies still have a great deal to say that is valid, some of the newer criticism tends to temper the former views and therefore is preeminently worthy of examination. As more research accumulates, the individual scholar can narrow his field more and more, and thus become able to particularize with very meaningful detail. In addition, world events have managed to create new topics such as those brought about by the Cold War, the problems at the United Nations, the races for nuclear arms and outer space, and the population explosion.

Once more the listing cannot be complete, but it is sincerely hoped that it is altogether representative. The publishing explosion has been both a boon and a detriment, and if one must put the blame for a revised edition on any one thing, then the boom in books is the proximal cause. We have tried to be wisely selective in handling the burgeoning of the written word in social science, and to any with honest merit whom we may have overlooked, our distinct apologies.

This edition differs from the first edition in two major ways. It has proved impossible to prepare a revision of the History section without holding up the publication of the remaining sections and, secondly, there is, at the end of the work, a Bibliography of most titles mentioned in the separate essays. It was felt that the sheer volume of works referred to would make the Bibliography a welcome quick-reference addition.

B. F. H.

Preface to the First Edition

The idea for this volume on the literature of the social sciences was initially suggested by the requirements of library education. After World War II a tendency developed in library education to place less emphasis upon training in library practices as such and more upon providing the student with increased knowledge about the contents of books and the criteria of evaluating them. Among efforts to implement such objectives, a number of experiments were made with guides to the literature of the several disciplines, and one of these, dealing with the interpretation, evaluation, and use of library materials in the humanities has appeared under the title *The Humanities and the Library*, by Lester Asheim and associates (1957). That volume is based upon the content of introductory courses in the Graduate Library School of the University of Chicago and divides its attention between the literature of the humanities and the library's problems in organizing and servicing it. In the course of the experimentation with the present volume on the social sciences, the idea developed that a volume on the literature of the social sciences might be useful to a wider audience than librarians and at the same time might serve that group as well. Thus the focus finally adopted here centered on the task of presenting a general introduction to the literature of the social sciences that would deal with the differences in the literary output in the major disciplines and the nature of available tools, in the form of books, journals, pamphlets, and reference works, that are consulted and used by social scientists in their research and teaching. The present volume may serve, therefore, not only as a guide to librarians, but also as an introduction to the general reader interested in the literary output of the different social sciences, and even to social scientists in one discipline who wish to obtain a general overview of the literature of a sister discipline.

Although many books and quite a few journal articles are cited in this study, this is not a bibliography. An attempt has been made in each chapter to refer to the more important "classics" in each field, but beyond this the chief interest of each contributor has been to present a description of the type of literary output and its uses in a field of specialization, rather than a list of works. Some attention has been paid to including not only works incorporating substantive contributions, but also those discussing methodological questions, and each contributor has been free to add sections on popularized works in his fields and special items of interest in the literature of his specialty.

The books mentioned in each chapter are not necessarily selected because they are the worthiest titles in a field. In many instances, works have been cited because they present certain peculiarities worth discussion, and many of the titles are referred to mainly as examples of a type of writing or a kind of study, e.g., a "typical monograph" or a "typical textbook." Often some other titles—or, indeed, a dozen other titles—might have been put in the place of the works actually mentioned. In other words, this study is not a basic tool for the preparation of a reading list in general or specialized courses in any social science discipline. Although an effort was made to select "good" books for citation, the quality of a work has been only one of the criteria used for inclusion.

B. F. H.

A Reader's Guide to

the Social Sciences

1 Sociology

Peter M. Blau and Joan W. Moore

Sociology is often called the study of society or of social life. But such a simple definition in terms of subject matter does not distinguish it from the other social sciences. For they all study social life or, to put it more precisely, patterns of conduct that are common to groups of people. It is not their subject matter but their approach to it that differentiates the various social sciences. They ask different questions about social conduct, focus upon different regularities in it, and hence arrive at different explanatory principles for it. The economist, for example, is concerned with those patterns in a society that are produced by men's attempts to allocate means to ends rationally. And the psychologist analyzes how characteristics of the human personality or organism develop and give rise to patterns of behavior. In contrast, the sociologist is interested in the regularities in social conduct that are due neither to psychological traits of individuals nor to their rational economic decisions, but that are produced by the social conditions in which they find themselves.

There is, of course, an almost infinite number of social conditions that may influence the way people act, interact, and think, such as marital status, rural or urban residence, prestige, membership in a certain religious group, being an outcast who is discriminated against, sharing one cultural tradition rather than another, or living in a totalitarian or a democratic society, to name but a few. To bring order into this great variety of social factors, sociologists subsume them under two broad

1

categories: the social relationships between people and their common value orientations.

Every group of people is characterized by a complex network of social relationships. Strong attractions may develop between some members, whereas others do not particularly care for one another. Some members may be generally respected and others looked down upon or ignored. In one group, cooperative practices may prevail; in another, competitiveness. A leader whose suggestions are followed emerges in one group, while status relations remain egalitarian in a different one. Social relationships, then, define the individual's status in the group, and they distinguish groups from each other. In larger collectivities, moreover, group membership helps to define social status, and there are also patterns of relationships between groups. The social status of professionals differs from that of factory workers. One community may be little stratified; in a second, differentiation between social classes exists, but there is little conflict; whereas in a third, class conflict is acute. All these aspects of social relationships and their influence on patterns of conduct comprise the first type of factor with which the sociologist is concerned.

Differences in social status tend to become associated with differential role expectations. Once one member of the group has assumed the role of leadership, the rest will expect him to take the initiative and act like a leader and expect the others not to act like a leader. In addition to these different role expectations, normative expectations applying to all members usually develop in groups. Among factory workers, for example, there often exist informal standards of what constitutes a fair day's work, and the individual who exceeds these output standards will be penalized by his fellow workers. Other normative beliefs are shared by most members of an entire society or one of its major segments, such as the conviction that stealing is wrong, that one does not walk barefoot on the street, or that it is not proper to wipe one's mouth with the back of one's hand. Common beliefs not only define what is right and what is wrong but also which objectives are most valued. Thus, our society places a higher value on becoming an outstanding baseball player than on becoming an expert cook. In essence, the cultural tradition of a society consists of nothing but such shared beliefs that have been transmitted from one generation to the next. To be sure, these beliefs exist only in the minds of individuals: there is no group mind. But the crucial fact is that as far as any individual is concerned social values and norms constitute the shared basic convictions of the other members of the community in which he is born and socialized and among whom he must live and find social acceptance. Hence, common values and norms are social forces that exert a constraining influence upon the conduct of individuals; they are the second type of social factor with which the sociologist is concerned.

But what accounts for the differences in social relationships and common normative expectations between groups or societies? Although there is no simple answer to this question, it calls attention to the important problem of social change, since it is possible to explain why social structures differ by investigating their historical development. At any one time, the common orientations and social relationships in a community affect the way people act and interact. But in the course of social interaction, the beliefs and relationships of people change. Thus, when prejudiced white soldiers were compelled to fight shoulder to shoulder with Negroes, the need for cooperative interaction in combat produced changes in their relationships with Negroes and their beliefs about them. Only by taking social processes of change into account can an unrealistically static concept of social structure be avoided. Hence, sociology involves the scientific study of how social relationships and common normative orientations influence patterns of conduct, and how social conduct under various conditions in turn leads to modifications in the social structure.

This conception of sociology as a distinct science has gradually emerged only during the last century. The most conspicuous difference between earlier social philosophy and modern sociology is a methodological one. Earlier scholars primarily used historical sources to illustrate their theoretical conceptions. Contemporary sociologists, on the other hand, are much more prone to use systematic procedures of interviewing and observation to obtain data with which general hypotheses can be tested. Underlying this difference in method, however, are fundamental differences in objectives and in the formulation of problems to be investigated. It is in terms of these changes in focus and approach that we shall look at the historical development of sociology.

THE DEVELOPMENT OF SOCIOLOGY

EARLY SOCIAL PHILOSOPHY

Men have thought about social life and society and tried to explain them since ancient times. Two kinds of ancient thought about social life have been preserved—folk sayings and religious maxims, which often contain perceptive notions about the relationships between human beings, and the works of systematic philosophers, most of whom dealt extensively with society and its historical development.

Folklore and proverbs typically pertained to practical problems of everyday life. In general, the social thought of ancient philosophers was similarly concerned with finding solutions to the practical problems of society and not with a detached scientific analysis of social phenomena. In the *Ethics*, Aristotle made the classic statement of the distinction between "scientific knowledge" and the kinds of knowledge we can have of "things human." Since "things human" are variable, it is not possible to derive general principles about them but only to deliberate about them to arrive at a "true and reasoned opinion." This meant for Aristotle the attainment of practical and political wisdom, which enables a man to run his own life well, manage his household, and govern wisely and virtuously.

The Greek philosophers did not approach the study of society with a disinterested scientific attitude but with an interest in helping to create an ideal society. Plato, for example, developed his conception of an ideal society governed by philosophers in *The Republic*, and then he encouraged his pupils to institute such a political system in Syracuse. Aristotle's *Politics* is essentially a manual for statesmen to guide them in governing wisely and establishing a good society. These two works illustrate not only the utopian character of Greek social thought, but also that it did not distinguish the study of society and social institutions from the study of governments and political institutions.

These conceptions of an ideal state were related to theories of the origin and history of governments. Both Plato and Aristotle, although quite different in their approach, advanced evolutionary theories of historical development, and still another evolutionary theory was proposed by the Epicureans, whereas Polybius developed a cyclical theory of political change. In these theories, which suggest principles of social development and attempt to support them with historical data, the ancient philosophers came closest to what was later to become social science. But even here the approach was that of the philosophy of history rather than that of an analytical social science.

Three characteristics of ancient social thought are particularly pertinent for an understanding of the development of sociology. First, it failed to differentiate between the study of political systems and that of social structures. Second, interest in creating a utopian society discouraged a disinterested, objective approach to the study of social phenomena. Third, concern with explaining the origins of social or political institutions and the course of history focused attention upon unique historical occurrences rather than upon recurrent social patterns. To consider these three characteristic limitations is not to deny that some of the ancient social philosophers dealt very imaginatively with important problems of social life. Indeed, their profound insights were resurrected many

SOCIOLOGY 5

times in succeeding centuries; social thought followed closely in the footsteps of the great ancient philosophers until quite recently. Nevertheless, the development of sociology as we know it today was contingent on a change in orientation to the study of social life in these three respects.

THE SEPARATION OF STATE AND SOCIETY

Perhaps the earliest major break with traditional social philosophy was made by the social-contract theorists. The doctrine of social contract, first clearly set forth by Thomas Hooker in the sixteenth century, dominated social and political thought during the seventeenth and eighteenth centuries. Its two outstanding proponents, Thomas Hobbes and John Locke, used it in fundamentally different theories. Hobbes assumed that the state of nature is one of "war of all men against all men." To escape from this state, men enter into an irrevocable contract. Governments, Hobbes argued, are legitimated by this original contract and therefore do not require the consent of the governed. Locke, in sharp contrast, held that men are by nature sociable and that the state of nature is peaceful. Men enter into a social contract primarily to protect their rights, notably the right of private property. The consent of the governed is essential for legitimate governments, and if a government violates the social contract the people have not only the right but the moral duty to overthrow it. Jean Jacques Rousseau, who is best known for his glorification of the state of nature, also emphasized that the social contract is an expression of the consensus and common purpose of the people—"the general will" of the community.

In most respects, these theories are polemical arguments rather than scientific investigations. Their major objective is not to advance a detached analysis of society but to advocate a political philosophy, and their primary significance and influence have been political and ethical, not scientific. In attempts to bolster their political positions, these authors based their moral philosophies on theories of social origins. Their use of empirical material in support of these theories, however, indicates the limitations of this approach from a scientific standpoint. Since no direct evidence on social origins exists, concern with them encourages a tendency to use source materials to justify a priori assumptions rather than to test theoretical hypotheses. This tendency is strongly reinforced by an interest in defending a political position. Thus, both Hobbes and Locke cited the American Indians as examples of pre-political society, but Hobbes claimed that they "live at this day in [a] brutish manner," while Locke saw in their social life an illustration of the virtues of the state of nature.

Although the main concern of the social-contract philosophers was political, they did make an important contribution to the future development of sociology by stressing the distinction between society and its government. This distinction is implicit in Hobbes's argument that the foundation of political society is the social union of men in a country, not any particular form of government. It clearly underlies Locke's thesis that the preservation of organized society, without which "natural" rights cannot prevail, may even justify a revolution against the existing government. And Rousseau's concept of the general will, which he considered the root of the people's sovereign power and which he juxtaposed to the political government, anticipates the sociological concept of common value orientation.

It was not until the nineteenth century, however, that the difference between the political study of government and the sociological study of society was explicitly defined and became widely accepted. In a controversy with Heinrich von Treitschke, Robert von Mohl stated early in this century, "only quite lately have we arrived at a definite recognition that the life which men lead in common by no means has its existence in the state alone." Claude Henri de Saint-Simon proposed the establishment of a new science, devoted to the systematic study of the changes in social and economic conditions that have resulted from the industrial revolution and scientific advancements and aimed at discovering the general laws of the movement toward "social happiness." He also advocated that society should be ruled scientifically by social scientists. These ideas were elaborated, and the new science was given the name "sociology" by Saint-Simon's disciple, Auguste Comte.

Comte's *philosophie positive* (*Cours de Philosophie Positive*, 1830–42) rests on a conception of the organic nature of society and its progressive development. The social organism, just like that of the individual, consists of differentiated interdependent elements working together for common ends, but, in contrast to the biological organism, it is not immutable. Elaborating the formulations of Marie Jean de Condorcet, Saint-Simon, and others, Comte conceived of historical progress as advancing through three stages—the theological, the metaphysical, and the scientific or positive era. Each of the three basic parts of the human mind—feeling, action, and intellect—undergoes parallel development in three stages. Feelings also provide the motivating force for social progress, and intellect the guiding principle.

Methodologically, Comte set forth a hierarchy of the sciences, with mathematics at the base, followed in order by astronomy, physics, chemistry, and biology, and culminating in the new science of sociology. Since each science is a prerequisite for the higher ones, Comte held that sociology is the most complex. He differentiated it from the prevalent political philosophy by insisting that sociological investigations must use the objective or positive methods of observation, experimentation, and comparison characteristic of the natural sciences. The application of scientific knowledge about society would bring about the most advanced stage of human progress. Comte explicated in great detail the characteristics of this positivistic state, ruled by a sociological priesthood of positivism. It is, however, not this utopian vision, which was so dear to him, for which Comte has been remembered. His major contribution is methodological. Although he did not practice what he preached and did not conduct social research by scientific procedures, he was the first who explicitly defined sociology as the systematic empirical study of social phenomena rather than the abstract analysis of political principles and who delineated roughly the boundaries of this new discipline as encompassing investigations of social order and social progress or, as we would say today in less value-laden terms, social structure and social change.

INEVITABLE EVOLUTIONARY FORCES

Opposing Comte's notion that the application of scientific knowledge can hasten social progress were the increasingly influential Social Darwinists. They shared his assumption that social change is an evolutionary process but added the postulate that it is governed by unrelenting forces that cannot be modified by human action. Attempts to influence the inevitable course of evolutionary development, however well meant, only disturb the inherent social equilibrium and have necessarily ill effects. The aim of social science was held to be the discovery of the inevitable stages of social evolution analogous to Charles Darwin's tracing of the evolution of animal species.

The most influential proponent of the evolutionary doctrine was undoubtedly Herbert Spencer. It was he (and not Darwin) who originated the phrase "survival of the fittest," to describe the basic force underlying evolutionary progress, a conception influenced by Thomas R. Malthus' work on population pressure, *An Essay on the Principle of Population* (1798). The struggle for survival within and between societies produces a social equilibrium as it transforms incoherent homogeneity into coherent heterogeneity. Societies evolve from a state where all do the same kinds of things in disregard of one another into a state where specialization and mutual cooperation prevail. Early in the struggle for existence, militarism emerges. Organized warfare forces small isolated groups to combine into increasingly larger societies, and within these peace reigns. In time, "equilibration" between societies makes long periods of peace possible, and this gives rise to the industrial stage.

Evolutionary processes continue to operate within industrial societies, but criteria other than primitive force now govern the survival of the fittest. Spencer believed that "Evolution can end only in the establishment of the greatest perfection and the most complete happiness." But a prerequisite for the emergence of this utopia is that the natural processes of selection are not interfered with in any way. Spencer carried his laissez-faire position to the extreme of denying that the state has a right to assume responsibility for coining money, postal services, education, or sanitary measures. *First Principles* (6th ed., 1928) and *The Principles of Sociology* (3d ed., 1892) are representative works of Spencer.

Another interpretation of Social Darwinism focuses upon the conflicts between races and nationalities as the most fundamental processes of social life. It may well not be fortuitous that the two major proponents of this viewpoint—Ludwig Gumplowicz and Gustav Ratzenhofer—were both Austrians, that is, lived in a polyglot empire that was continually torn by strife between various nationality groups. This illustrates that the social conditions in which a scholar finds himself may influence the theories he advances (a thesis which was developed in detail much later by Karl Mannheim in his *Ideology and Utopia*, 1936). Similarly, the tremendous vogue that Social Darwinism and particularly the Spencerian evolutionary doctrine enjoyed in England and the United States at the end of the last century was probably partly due to their compatibility with existing social conditions. Evolutionary principles provided "scientific" sanction and justification for the cut-throat competition, the growing monopolies, the imperialistic wars, and other characteristics of this period of expanding capitalism.

The use of Social Darwinism to defend the capitalistic system is, perhaps, nowhere as evident as in the writings of William Graham Sumner, the outstanding follower of Spencer in the United States. Today, Sumner is best remembered among sociologists for his concepts of mores and folkways, the normative orientations and social usages that he analyzed and illustrated in his book *Folkways* (1906). In his lifetime, however, he was probably better known for his espousal of evolutionist and laissez-faire doctrines. The titles of his works are indicative of his orientation, for instance, "The Absurd Effort to Make the World Over," (in his *War, and other Essays*, 1933) or *What Social Classes Owe to Each Other* (1883).

Not all Social Darwinists, however, subscribed to its laissez-faire implications. Lester F. Ward, a contemporary of Sumner, was one who did not (*Dynamic Sociology*, 1883). He accepted the principle that conflicts between individuals and groups give rise to social evolution, although emphasizing that it is governed not so much by a struggle for sheer existence as by one for developing the optimum social structure.

But he argued that once social evolution reaches the stage where man can scientifically understand social phenomena, intelligent social action is possible. After this stage, sociological knowledge can and should be applied through legislation to accelerate social progress.

Most informed people today would tend to agree with Ward's position that the welfare of the community can be improved by deliberate social action and reject Sumner's thesis that legislation cannot be used as an instrument to guide social change. But even if in error, the notion that the social forces that govern society and its development are entirely beyond human control can be considered to have been, from the standpoint of the development of sociology, a "fruitful error." It helped to direct the efforts of sociologists away from constructing social utopias and toward the study of existing social conditions and the objective social forces that produced them. Although the writings of many Social Darwinists were far from detached in their defense of the *status quo*, the deterministic assumption underlying the evolutionary approach invites a detached orientation toward the study of social life. By inadvertence, as it were, Social Darwinism seems to have been instrumental in bringing about the kind of detached orientation toward social research without which a science of social life is not possible.

CONCERN WITH SOCIAL REFORM

Reformism was a current of thought that antedated Social Darwinism and continued parallel with it throughout the nineteenth century. In England, the misery-making potential of the new industrial system became glaringly evident at the beginning of the century. As early as 1802, advocates of reform raised their voices in Parliament, and their efforts were finally successful in the 1830's. The famous Factory Acts, regulating employment of children and correcting other abuses, were partly a response to the fact-finding endeavors of the reformers. Extensive inquiries into the state of affairs in the industries and cities of England were made during the first few years of the Reform Parliament. This survey movement was championed by Jeremy Bentham, who felt strongly that "scientific" legislation must be based on adequate knowledge about the actual conditions of social life. By the end of the century, not only government-sponsored surveys but also others not immediately concerned with policy had been conducted on a wide scale in England and on the Continent. Among the most famous are Pierre Frédéric Le Play's theoretically oriented *Les Ouvriers Européens* (1855) and Charles Booth's (ed.) monumental *Life and Labour of the People in London* (1829–97), which is a landmark in the development of empirical techniques of research.

The earliest large-scale empirical investigation of social conditions in the United States was Paul U. Kellogg's *Pittsburgh Survey* (1909-14). But the pioneering empirical studies of important theoretical as well as social problems were carried out at the University of Chicago shortly after World War I. William I. Thomas and Florian Znaniecki's *The Polish Peasant in Europe and America* (1918-20) is a five volume investigation of immigrants and their counterparts in the old country. By deriving a variety of theoretical conceptions from a detailed analysis of letters, life histories, and interviews, the authors gave considerable impetus to the growing conviction that sociological generalizations based on data collected specifically for this purpose can be as interesting as and are apt to be much more trustworthy than generalizations supported only with illustrative material from second-hand historical or ethnographic sources.

Robert E. Park, a journalist turned sociologist, stimulated research on a large variety of social problems, such as crime and minority groups. His interest in the problems of urban life led him, together with Ernest W. Burgess and Roderick D. McKenzie, to formulate a method for the systematic study of the social diversity and growth of cities, thereby creating a new branch of sociology—human ecology (Park, Burgess and McKenzie, *The City*, 1925; Burgess [ed.], *The Urban Community*, 1926). Park and Burgess also published what was for years the most influential text and source book in the field, *Introduction to the Science of Sociology* (1921).

Concern with social problems is not incompatible with an interest in fundamental theoretical questions. William F. Ogburn's *Social Change* (1923) is essentially a theory to account for the persistence of social problems. Ogburn suggested that value orientations, as well as social and political institutions, necessarily change more slowly than do technological and economic conditions; the resulting "cultural lag" is responsible for social problems.

In contrast to utopian visions, which encourage preoccupation with abstract conceptions of the ideal society, the reformer's zeal to improve existing social conditions motivated him to obtain more accurate knowledge about these conditions and the social forces that have produced them. Reform movements, therefore, helped to promote an interest in empirical social research and in the methodological problems of obtaining reliable information about social phenomena. Moreover, whereas the evolutionist's concern with social origins directed attention to unique historical data, the reformer's concern with prevailing problems indirectly had the effect of directing the attention of sociologists to recurrent social patterns, and it is only if data are conceptualized as recurrent phenomena that scientific generalizations can be derived from them.

SOCIOLOGY

HISTORY AND SOCIOLOGY

The principle that analytical social science conceptualizes historical conditions not as unique events but as recurrent phenomena became clarified in Germany in the course of theoretical and methodological controversies, notably that between the idealistic and the materialistic conception of social life, on the one hand, and the so-called *Methodenstreit*, centering on the difference between the historical and the analytical scientific approaches, on the other.

Karl Marx, accepting Georg Hegel's dialectic conception, juxtaposed his dialectical materialism to Hegel's idealistic interpretation of history. It is not spiritual forces but material conditions that underlie historical developments from thesis through antithesis to synthesis, and these material conditions can be scientifically studied. With technological advances, there arises a conflict between the state of technological knowledge and the traditional social organization of the economy. The reason for this conflict, and the form in which it finds expression, is the basic conflict of interest between social classes. The ruling class, in control of the means of production, is able to exploit the other classes for its own benefits and is, therefore, interested in preserving the status quo. The exploited classes are interested in fundamental changes in the social order that will bring an end to their exploitation. Once they recognize their interest, a revolution is inevitable, and this revolution permits further technological advances, heretofore prevented by the outmoded socioeconomic organization. For example, the productive potential of the Industrial Revolution could not be fully realized until the feudal order had been overthrown, and the fact that the other classes found themselves disadvantaged by the feudal aristocracy provided the motivating force for overthrowing it. Further technological progress makes the capitalistic system obsolete, and once the exploited working class becomes class conscious and realizes that their interests conflict with those of the capitalistic ruling class, the proletarian revolution will occur.

Three elements in Marx's writings are of particular sociological significance. First, by concentrating on objective "material" conditions instead of spiritual forces, he defines social phenomena in a way that makes their scientific study possible. Second, his emphasis on the relationships between social groups as central for explaining historical processes is more conducive to a sociological approach than the essentially biological concept of survival of the fittest. Third, he was perhaps the first scholar to anticipate what Talcott Parsons, a contemporary theorist, calls the voluntaristic theory of social action (in *The Structure of Social Action*, 1937). Marx's conception that revolution, although in an ultimate sense inevitable, occurs only when people are motivated to carry it out (when they have become "class conscious") implies that deterministic social forces exist, but that they become operative only through affecting voluntary action—an important insight made explicit and elaborated by Max Weber.

The haphazard use of historical material as evidence for "laws" of evolutionary progress evoked protests from many historians at the end of the nineteenth century. In the midst of this controversy, a number of German scholars, such as Wilhelm Windelband, Wilhelm Dilthey, and Heinrich Rickert, sought to clarify the nature of history by distinguishing it from the natural sciences. History, they held, is concerned with ideographic knowledge, that is, with understanding unique historical events and the particular conditions under which they occur. Science, on the other hand, is concerned with nomothetic knowledge, which means that it subsumes specific facts under general categories and derives generalizations about them. Many historians, such as Eduard Meyer, argued on the basis of this distinction that it is impossible to make generalizations about society and its development, since every historical event is unique. But other scholars used this distinction to formulate a new conception of sociology as an analytical science and to differentiate it from history.

Max Weber, the outstanding German social theorist and one of the fathers of modern sociology, was profoundly influenced in his thinking by these two controversies, the materialism-idealism and the history-science issue. His attempts to resolve them are illustrated in his most famous work, *The Protestant Ethic and the Spirit of Capitalism* (1893). Opposing a Marxist interpretation of historical change in terms of rational economic interests, he advanced the thesis that the ethic of Calvinism was a prerequisite for the development of modern capitalism. He showed how the various tenets of this religious dogma gave rise to "worldly asceticism," a moral devotion to disciplined hard work in one's own vocation. The Calvinist's religious duty is not to adjust to this world, which he considered corrupted by man's sinfulness, not to withdraw from it into a monastery, but to help transform it *ad majorem Dei gloriam* through unceasing effort in his secular job. The doctrine of double predestination, according to which good works cannot affect whether a man will be saved or damned, encourages an orientation to disciplined conduct and hard work, not as means to an ultimate end, but as intrinsic moral values. By elevating ceaseless effort and disciplined work in the mundane affairs of economic life into man's religious obligation, Calvinism produced a value orientation without which capitalism could not have come into existence. In support of this argument, Weber tried to show in his *Gesammelte Aufsaetze zur Religions-*

soziologie (1920–21), partly translated as *The Religion of China* (1951) and *Ancient Judaism* (1952) and in Hans Gerth and Wright Mills (eds. and trs.), *From Max Weber: Essays in Sociology* (1946), that socioeconomic conditions in other countries, such as China, were at least as favorable for the development of capitalism as those in Western Europe at the time of the Reformation, but that the modern form of capitalism did not emerge there because the religious system did not engender an orientation of worldly asceticism.

Weber's two most important methodological contributions to sociology are illustrated in this theory of the rise of capitalism. First, he held that it is not "material" economic conditions that are the major driving force in social life, but rather the spirit of a community. In contrast to the idealistic philosophers, however, he conceived of this spirit, not as a supernatural force, but as the common value orientation that prevails among the members of the community, which can be objectively ascertained and studied. The distinctive characteristic of sociological explanations is that they provide an understanding of how common value orientations motivate people's conduct. (Weber discusses this principle of *Verstehen* in *The Theory of Social and Economic Organization*, 1947.) It is not enough to show that social conditions produce, say, a certain economic organization; it is also necessary to demonstrate how these conditions give rise to a value orientation that motivates people's conduct in ways that find expression in that economic organization. Whereas in this respect sociology is different from the natural sciences, in another it is like the natural sciences and unlike history. That is the second methodological principle Weber emphasized—namely, that sociology is a generalizing science (*On the Methodology of the Social Sciences*, 1949). To be sure, every historical event is unique, but the sociologist ignores the unique aspects of events and treats them as social types in order to generalize about them. Even if there is only one modern capitalism, it is not conceptualized as a unique historical phenomenon, but as an "ideal type" that can be compared with other types of economic systems.

This methodological principle, which is related to the distinction between nomothetic and ideographic knowledge, is so important that it should be spelled out in some detail. Essentially, a scientific explanation involves reference to a generalization that can be empirically verified. To derive such explanatory generalizations, the scientist advances a hypothesis about what happened in a specific situation, and he tests this hypothesis by determining whether it holds true in other cases of the same kind. But this procedure is possible only if we arbitrarily decide to disregard the unique characteristics of each specific case and subsume it under a general category. Evidently, each relationship between two individuals is unique; but it is impossible to derive a scientific generalization about how this unique relationship influences the conduct of these two people. Only if we are willing to classify all kinds of otherwise different relationships into cooperative and competitive ones (or in some other way) can we derive a generalization about the effects of cooperation on, say, productive efficiency of workers. But what if there is only a single instance of a certain social structure, as in the case of modern capitalism? Then, in our opinion, you cannot derive scientific generalizations about it. In short, commitment to sociology as an analytical science requires a willingness to give up the study of all those very interesting historical phenomena that are unique, because no empirically verifiable generalizations about them are possible. Weber, although advancing the position that sociology is an analytical science, was not quite willing to pay the price such a commitment demands. He was too interested in the unprecedented characteristics of Western capitalism to forego studying them, and by defining his problem as explaining a unique historical occurrence, he made it inherently impossible, it seems to us, to find a scientific solution for it.

THE SCIENTIFIC STUDY OF SOCIAL FACTS

A few contemporaries of Weber arrived by quite different routes at a fundamentally similar methodological position. One of these was the German sociologist Simmel (Kurt H. Wolff [ed. and tr.], *The Sociology of Georg Simmel*, 1950). He stressed that sociology is not concerned with the substantive or psychological content of social life, but with the general form assumed by social associations. This means that the sociologist analyzes observed patterns of conduct in terms of the recurrent processes of social interaction that give human conduct its social form, such as competition, superordination and subordination, or conflict. He is not interested primarily in whether these observed patterns of conduct are part of the economic or political organization, nor in what kinds of psychological states motivate them.

Guided by this methodological conception, Simmel does not hesitate to tear social phenomena from their historical or situational context to use them in support of a general sociological principle. Thus, the role of the consumer in a competitive economy, the influence exerted by small third parties in German politics, and what happens in a group of three individuals if two of them struggle for leadership—all of these different social situations serve Simmel to illustrate his principle of *tertius gaudens*. It may be objected that he sometimes ignored important analytical distinctions, such as that between relations among groups and relations among individuals. In principle, however, the complete disregard of the unique features of the historical situation, of which Simmel's writings offer an extreme example, is a prerequisite for deriving testable generalizations about recurrent social phenomena, and thus for a science of sociology.

Emile Durkheim, a French contemporary of Simmel and Weber, has probably exerted a more profound influence in shaping modern sociology than any other man. Avowedly a positivist in the tradition of Comte, he conceived of sociology as the scientific study of the relationships between social facts. Social facts, he explained in *The Rules of Sociological Method* (8th ed., 1950), are general phenomena characterizing an entire community, such as laws; they exercise external constraint upon individuals; and they must be treated as objective "things," no less objective than the facts of any other science. Indeed, as a social realist Durkheim considered social facts to be more basic and objective phenomena than the variable psychological states of individuals. Later, however, he modified his position, claiming no longer that social facts are necessarily external to the individual, but that they are internalized as the "*conscience collective*," the common value-orientation of the community.

Durkheim was perhaps the first to draw the full implication of the conception of sociology as a generalizing social science and to translate it into systematic empirical research on recurrent social phenomena in support of theoretical principles. In his first major work, *De la Division du Travail Social* (1893), he tried to demonstrate that social facts must be explained in terms of other social facts, rather than in terms of psychological factors. He argued against the implicit psychologistic assumption of the evolutionists and utilitarians that social heterogeneity and specialization are the result of a striving for greater happiness and a higher standard of living. He suggested instead that the division of labor is generated by increasing population density—a social condition. Although he initially defined his problem as one of social origins, his major interest centered not on the origin of the division of labor, but on its significance for social solidarity. He showed that specialization destroys the homogeneity of outlook that provides the bond uniting the members of simple societies, but that it simultaneously produces a new basis for social solidarity by making the members of the society increasingly dependent on one another. Hence, the "organic solidarity" of complex societies is largely based on mutual dependence, and the "mechanical solidarity" of simple societies on common values.

The fundamental difference between Durkheim's approach and that of the evolutionists became fully evident only in his later works. Nineteenth-century anthropology was permeated by evolutionism. Ethnographic material on preliterate societies was used primarily to illustrate theories about the origins of modern social institutions and the evolutionary stages through which they have presumably progressed. This essentially historical and taxonomic orientation made anthropologists content with classifying societies on an evolutionary ladder. There was little interest in the systematic investigation of preliterate social life in its own right. In *The Elementary Forms of the Religious Life* (1915), Durkheim used ethnographic data on Australian aborigines in an entirely different manner. No longer concerned with social origins, he analyzed the religious life of these tribes to derive generalizations about the functions that religious beliefs and rituals serve for the community, theoretical generalizations that he considered relevant for the religious institutions of any society at any time. Although his research methods were not unexceptionable and his sources were of questionable reliability, the approach he charted to the systematic study of social structures helped to stimulate the development of reliable research methods in anthropology as well as sociology. Specifically, his conception of analyzing social structure, not in terms of social origins, but in terms of functional interdependence had a profound influence in both of these social sciences.

It is, however, an earlier work of Durkheim that exemplifies theoretical sociological research at its best—*Suicide*, published in 1897. At first sight, suicide might appear to be a purely individual phenomenon, best explained in psychological terms. Durkheim, however, observed that suicide rates differ from group to group, and he addressed himself to the sociological problem of explaining these social differences in suicide rates, not to the psychological question of what motivates an individual to take his own life. His main thesis was that social integration —the strength of the social ties that unite the members of a group— affects the likelihood of suicide, and he showed that this theoretical generalization, with some refinements, can explain a great variety of known facts about suicide rates. Catholicism leads to greater social integration than the individualistic faith of the Protestant; hostility and persecution create particularly strong integrative bonds among Jews; married people have integrative ties that single individuals lack; the unity of the community is greater in periods of war than in peace times; social integration is stronger in the rural villages than in the impersonal city. All these and many other differences in social integration are reflected in corresponding differences in suicide rates.

Profound theoretical insights and incisive analyses of source materials characterize all of Durkheim's works, but only in *Suicide* were his empirical data the kind that can support the theoretical generalizations advanced. Data from one religious system are obviously not sufficient evidence to test generalizations about the functions of religion in all societies. But how many religious systems can one man systematically investigate? One answer to this dilemma is to make information about many societies easily accessible to social scientists, as has been done recently in the Human Relations Area File. Durkheim found another solution for the same dilemma by defining his problem for investigation in *Suicide* in a way that assured sufficient empirical cases to test his theoretical generalizations. Scientific social research must confine itself to problems that deal neither with unique historical situations nor with social conditions about which information is so rare that they must be considered virtually unique, such as the emergence of the division of labor. The recognition of this basic limitation of social science has profoundly affected the course of sociology during the past half-century.

IMPLICATIONS AND REACTIONS

The new conception of sociology as an analytical science that emerged at the beginning of the twentieth century altered the character of sociological investigations substantively as well as methodologically. Concern with entire social systems and their historical development declined as it became increasingly apparent that finding enough cases that were reliably reported poses an almost insuperable obstacle to testing theoretical generalizations. More and more, sociologists devoted themselves to the study of recurrent social patterns that can be observed today—for example, how the power relations in a community influence its various institutions, how neighborhoods change as a city expands, how prestige is related to patterns of social association, how informal relations in work groups affect productivity, or how social status influences voting.

This change in substantive focus fostered a growing interest in quantitative methods of collecting and analyzing data. Once the sociologist turned from the study of historical materials to the investigation of patterns of conduct in contemporary society, the need for new methods of research became apparent. In response to this need, there developed a large body of methodological literature, particularly in the United States, dealing with problems of sampling, statistical techniques of analysis, reliable procedures for interviewing and questionnaire construction, systematic methods of observation, and the development of scales and other measuring devices. A variety of methodological controversies arose; for example, that between the advocates of complete life-histories—like those used in Thomas' and Znaniecki's study of immigrants previously cited—and the proponents of large-scale attitude surveys, such as Samuel A. Stouffer.

Another implication of the new focus in sociology was an increasing interest in social psychology. The study of how social conditions affect patterns of conduct raises the question of the psychological mechanisms involved in these social processes. The importance of understanding sociopsychological processes was emphasized by Max Weber, and although their significance for sociological investigations was explicitly denied by Durkheim, both he and Simmel implicitly recognized it in their psychologically perceptive analyses of social phenomena.

In the United States, a conception of social psychology peculiarly suited to the needs of sociology emerged, curiously, out of a philosophical tradition. The pragmatists Charles S. Peirce, James Baldwin, William James, and John Dewey were greatly interested in the human mind as a social product, and two of their followers, George Herbert Mead and Charles Horton Cooley, made outstanding theoretical contributions to the field of social psychology. Mead, a philosopher, advanced a theory of how the human mind and self develop in the course of social interaction, published posthumously from lecture notes as *Mind, Self and Society* (1934). The distinguishing characteristic of human beings is their ability to communicate with significant symbols, which arises in the process of social interaction. As the infant experiences that his meaningless noises elicit a social response—crying brings the mother with a bottle, he learns that crying is a sign with which he can communicate his need for food. More complex patterns of communication develop as the child advances to the stage where he can take the role of the other person and, thereby, anticipate the response his communications will elicit. By taking the role of the other, the child also learns to conform with the expectations of others. As he moves in wider social circles than his immediate family, the expectations of many different others are generalized and internalized. The "generalized other," as Mead calls it, is that part of the personality (or self) that governs human conduct in accordance with the moral precepts of the society. Without the restraints it imposes, social cooperation and, indeed, social life would not be possible. Although Mead's theory was not supported by empirical evidence, many of his insights have since been confirmed in empirical research, notably in Jean Piaget's studies of children's language, thinking, and moral standards.

Cooley was a sociologist with a special interest in social psychology. In *Human Nature and the Social Order* (1902), he argued against the twin fallacy of studying either individuals in isolation from society or social institutions as abstractions independent of human conduct. In his extensive treatment of the process of socialization, he coined the phrase, "looking-glass self," to refer to the influence a person's perception of how others view him has upon his self-conception. The social context in which the social nature of the individual is formed, Cooley elaborated in his *Social Organization* (1909), is the "primary group," a small group characterized by intimate face-to-face association and strong "we-feeling," notably the family, the play-group of children, and the close neighborhood. The concept of primary group, used somewhat more broadly than Cooley intended, has exerted much influence on recent empirical research.

Not all sociologists have accepted the scientific conception of sociology even today. In the struggle to gain acceptance for this new orientation, some extreme reactions against the older social philosophy developed. One form this reaction took has been a radical positivism, accompanied by almost total rejection of theory as a legitimate scientific concern. This extreme empiricism found expression in behaviorism in psychology, historicism in history, exclusive concern with ethnographic facts in anthropology, and operationalism in sociology. The operational approach, originated by the physicist Percy W. Bridgman, stresses that scientific concepts must be derived, not from theoretical frameworks, but from the empirical operations used in measurement. While this general position has not been widely accepted, most sociologists agree with its emphasis on using only concepts—albeit theoretically derived ones—that can be operationally defined. The operational approach is presented in George Lundberg's *Foundations of Sociology* (1939).

Another reaction against the earlier philosophy of history, especially its evolutionary version, has been an historical orientation in sociology, best exemplified by functionalism, a theoretical framework derived from Durkheim and elaborated by anthropologists such as Bronislaw Malinowski (*Magic, Science and Religion*, 1948) and Alfred R. Radcliffe-Browne (*Structure and Function in Primitive Society*, 1952), who exercised considerable influence among sociologists. Their dictum that social institutions should be explained on the basis of the present functions they serve in the social structure, rather than in terms of their historical development, is fully justified in preliterate societies, since any interpretation about social developments necessarily remains speculative in the absence of historical records. But when data about different time periods are available, there is no reason to ignore them. To state that sociologists are not concerned with unique historical events does not imply, of course, that they are not concerned with patterns of social change, and change can be studied only by examining relationships between social conditions at two or more different times. Indeed, the functional approach as originally conceived cannot cope with problems of social change. Many sociologists not committed to the functional viewpoint, however, have also neglected the study of social change, in large part because the systematic collection of data at several time periods is exceedingly costly and time-consuming.

20 PETER M. BLAU AND JOAN W. MOORE

Controversies between "empiricists" and "pure theorists" as well as between "functionalists" and those favoring a historical approach to sociology continue, but they appear to be waning. Recent years have seen an increasing emphasis on the integration of theory and empirical research. And even if the pious declarations that such integration is essential are often honored in the breach today, because many sociologists have been primarily trained either as theorists or as empirical researchers, the need to make these declarations may well be indicative of the future trend. Similarly, there has been an increasing interest in the study of social change and in adapting the functional approach to make it suitable for dealing with problems of change. To both of these trends, Robert K. Merton has made important contributions in *Social Theory and Social Structure* (1956). He was one of the first to emphasize that the only practical way to achieve an integration of theory and research in the near future is to concentrate on theories of the middle range—theories dealing with specific scientific problems rather than with the whole gamut of social life. He also reformulated the functional approach to make it applicable to the important problems of differential power and social change, particularly by emphasizing that dysfunctional as well as functional consequences of social patterns must be investigated—the disturbances they create as well as the contributions they make to stability.

CONTEMPORARY SOCIOLOGICAL LITERATURE IN SELECTED AREAS

SOCIAL THEORY

The growing interest in theories of the middle range has led to a closer connection between theorizing and empirical research in sociology. Increasing numbers of empirical studies are theoretically oriented, addressing themselves to problems posed by social theory and seeking to refine theoretical principles on the basis of empirical findings. An outstanding example is the investigation of union democracy by Lipset, Trow, and Coleman, which clarifies theoretical issues raised by Michel's "iron law of oligarchy" (see below). Several sociologists have carried out secondary analysis of the research results of others in explicit attempts to develop middle-range theories. The most important of these is *The Human Group* (1950) by George C. Homans. He analyzes five studies dealing with work groups and professional staffs in factories, street corner gangs, and small communities in Polynesia and New England, and subsumes their empirical results under a few basic generalizations about social interaction in small groups. Another illustration of the use of a variety of empirical studies to derive some theoretical principles is Seymour M. Lipset's *Political Man* (1960), which analyzes political processes and the conditions of democracy. A somewhat different approach to secondary analysis is illustrated in *Continuities in Social Research* (1950), edited by Robert K. Merton and Paul F. Lazarsfeld, in which empirical findings from one large project (Samuel Stouffer and others, *The American Soldier*, 1949) are reanalyzed from different theoretical and methodological viewpoints by a number of sociologists.

An interest in broader theories, however, continues to exist side by side with the prevailing emphasis on limited theoretical interpretations directly derived from systematic research. This interest reflects in part the influence of the sociological tradition; the great pioneers in sociology, such as Weber and Durkheim, developed encompassing theories that sought to explain the basic institutions of society, and several contemporary sociologists are inspired by the challenge of following in their footsteps and trying to improve on their theories. Pitirim A. Sorokin is a case in point (*Social and Cultural Dynamics*, 1937–41), and so is Talcott Parsons. But in part the interest in broad theory has another source; once limited theories that explain empirical findings have been developed, the challenge becomes one of discovering wider generalizations that can in turn explain the limited ones. This is the impetus that led Homans to move from middle-range to more general theory. Parsons and Homans are major proponents of the two dominant theoretical approaches in sociology today—structural-functional and exchange theory.

The basic conception of Talcott Parsons' structural-functional theory is that any social system, whether an entire society or one of its subsystems, consists of a structure of interrelated elements, and each element has the function of contributing to the adjustment and persistence of the social structure. Of particular importance is the maintenance of common-value intergration, which underlies social institutions. In collaboration with Edward A. Shils, Parsons developed a series of analytical distinctions between value orientations, such as that between universalism and particularism (*Toward a General Theory of Action*, 1951), and he analyzed the functions of specific value patterns for social life—for example, for the doctor–patient relation (*The Social System*, 1951). Subsequently, Parsons' theory concentrated on the way in which structural differentiation develops in response to the four fundamental functional imperatives of social systems (*Economy and Society*, 1956, with Neil J. Smelser). Every social system must meet four basic needs, and it becomes differentiated into subsystems that have the function of meeting these needs. The first problem that must be solved is that of mobilizing resources as means for adapting to existing conditions; for society as a whole, the economy serves this function. Second, the problem of goal attainment requires agreement on common objectives and allocation of resources to achieve them; a society's "polity" has this function. Third, differentiation creates problems of integration, and several institutions develop to reconcile conflicts and further integration, such as courts of law. Finally, the distinctive value patterns must be transmitted to new generations and tensions must be resolved, which are important functions of the family.

A major criticism that has been advanced against Parsons' highly abstract theory is that it consists essentially of an elaborate conceptual scheme of definitions and analytical distinctions rather than of substantive propositions from which testable hypotheses can be derived. Although George C. Homans has criticized Parsons on these grounds as well as others, his own general theory (*Social Behavior*, 1961), different as it is from Parsons', has been criticized on the same grounds (by James A. Davis, *American Journal of Sociology*, 67 [1962], 458). The fact that two outstanding modern social theories are subject to this criticism indicates that the broadest theoretical generalizations cannot as yet be formulated in sociology with sufficient precision to imply unequivocally testable hypotheses. Nevertheless, such broad theories are useful, since they help to integrate more limited ones from which testable hypotheses can be deduced. This is notably true for Homans' theory of elementary forms of social behavior. He starts with psychological propositions about individual behavior from Skinner's reinforcement theory and derives from them some principles of interaction among individuals conceived in terms of social exchange.

The fundamental assumption of the theory of social exchange is that not only economic transactions but other social interactions between individuals and groups entail the exchange of valuables. If a man does favors for others—for example, gives colleagues valuable advice—they are obligated to reciprocate by providing benefits for him in turn. Failure to discharge this obligation typically evokes the accusation of ingratitude, which shows that reciprocation is expected, and disinclines the man to do similar favors in the future, which indicates that self-interest demands reciprocation. What distinguishes noneconomic transactions is that the obligations incurred are diffuse rather than specified a priori by an (explicit or implicit) economic contract and that distinctly noneconomic valuables are most often used as the currency with which to discharge obligations, such as social approval, status, power, and authority. Thus, the development of differentiation of status in groups can be analyzed on the basis of the underlying processes of social exchange.

Exchange theory centers attention on the sociopsychological processes that characterize the interpersonal relations among individuals. It has been criticized, consequently, as involving psychological reductionism and ignoring the emergent social forces that distinguish complex structures and institutions in society and that cannot be reduced to psychological principles. Homans' answer to this criticism is that it refers not to a shortcoming but to the main virtue of his theory, since all propositions about social phenomena should be ultimately rooted, according to him, in more basic psychological propositions about human behavior. Other sociologists, however, do not accept this reductionist assumption. To be sure, Homans is not alone in favoring a psychological conception of social transactions. The application of game theory to the study of social interaction in dyads and triads by John W. Thibaut and Harold H. Kelley rests on a similar conception (*The Social Psychology of Groups*, 1959). But attempts have also been made to derive from principles of social exchange some sociological propositions about the emergent forces that govern complex social structures, for example, the development of legitimate organizations in society and opposition movements to them (Peter M. Blau, *Exchange and Power in Social Life*, 1964).

A number of sociologists have accused the dominant stream of modern social theory, particularly Parsonian theory, of ignoring the crucial social problems of today, overemphasizing integration and stability at the expense of conflict and change, and implicitly serving as a defense of the *status quo*. Before his premature death, C. Wright Mills became the main spokesman of this position (*The Sociological Imagination*, 1959). An explicit attempt to develop a social theory focused upon conflict rather than adjustment is Lewis A. Coser's *The Functions of Social Conflict* (1956), which uses Simmel's analysis of conflict as a point of departure. A different approach to the development of a dynamic framework for the study of social life is Walter Buckley's recent application of systems theory to the analysis of social structure (*Sociology and Modern Systems Theory*, 1967). Marx's thought, however, exerts little direct influence on American social theory, in contrast to its considerable influence in Western Europe as well as in the East.

Whereas sociologists use increasingly quantitative techniques in their research, most of their theories are not couched in quantitative terms and do not employ mathematical procedures. This is undoubtedly a weakness of contemporary social theory. But the primary reason for it is not, as is often thought, the lack of mathematical knowledge of theorists. It lies deeper than that. Most social theories are not formulated with sufficient precision to permit translation into mathematical formulae. Advances in theoretical concepts and formulations are required before mathematics can be applied successfully. There are, however, limited social theories that have been transformed into mathematical models. A survey of such mathematical models in sociology is provided in James S. Coleman, *Introduction to Mathematical Sociology* (1964).

METHODS OF DATA COLLECTION AND ANALYSIS

Research in sociology uses a variety of methods and techniques. Sociologists sometimes develop their own procedures of data gathering and analysis, and sometimes use those developed by other social scientists. For example, there has been growing interest in historical sociology in which the historians' techniques and canons of validity are employed in the service of collecting data to demonstrate general sociological propositions (see Werner J. Cahnman and Alvin Boskoff [eds.], *Sociology and History: Theory and Research*, 1964). And techniques developed in psychology, such as factor analysis, are used to investigate sociological problems that are remote from the individual behavior for which this procedure was orginally invented (see, for an application to urban analysis, Jeffrey K. Hadden and Edgar F. Borgatta, *American Cities*, 1965). Statistical techniques, such as multiple regression analysis, which have been more common in other fields than in sociology are increasingly utilized by sociologists, since the quantitative data needed for using them are more and more available in sociological research. Mathematical model building, mentioned above in the discussion of theory, is of course actually not a distinctive theory but a special method of formulating theories. Notwithstanding the growth of quantitative procedures, sociologists continue to use participant observation and case studies—techniques developed early in the discipline's empirical experience but now more highly regarded among anthropologists—to provide holistic views of complex phenomena, as in Herbert Gans, *The Urban Villagers* (1962).

Attempts to develop more systematic methods for directly observing and recording social interaction have been made, particularly by social psychologists. Perhaps the best known is Robert F. Bales's "interaction process analysis," which involves classifying each sentence and some nonverbal acts in group discussions into one of twelve categories, in addition to noting who makes the statement and to whom it is addressed. There is a growing body of research using this system, and a collection which includes representative studies has been published (A. Paul Hare, Edgar F. Borgatta, and Robert F. Bales [eds.], *Small Groups*, 1955). Used primarily in the analysis of interaction in small laboratory groups, the technique has also been employed in the study of natural groups, such as juries. The method and its theoretical rationale are described by Bales in *Interaction Process Analysis* (1950).

The interview survey deserves special mention in an overview of data collection techniques used by sociologists. In fact, interviewing surveys are often popularly assumed to be "the" sociological research procedure. Though this is far from being the case, it is probably the most widely used method of systematic social research and the one for which reliable techniques have been most fully developed. Its availability has also influenced the kind of substantive problems that have been most thoroughly investigated. Sociological texts on research methods typically devote most of their space to the discussion of procedures that pertain directly or indirectly to interviewing surveys. Well-known texts are William J. Goode and Paul K. Hatt, *Methods in Social Research* (1952); Marie Jahoda, Morton Deutsch, and Stuart Cook, *Research Methods in Social Relations* (1951); and, dealing with more advanced problems of analysis, Paul F. Lazarsfeld and Morris Rosenberg, *The Language of Social Research* (1955). Whereas these texts deal with a variety of issues, another is specifically devoted to survey methods (Herbert Hyman, *Survey Design and Analysis*, 1955). The various techniques of measurement and index-formation which have been developed, such as the Guttman scale and Lazarsfeld's latent attribute analysis, are also usually based on interviewing data (see Samuel Stouffer and others, *Measurement and Prediction*, 1950, for pioneering work on scaling). In fact, it is probably in the analysis of survey results that most technical innovations in sociology have been made. A recent discussion of statistical procedures for the analysis of survey and similar data is Hubert Blalock's *Casual Interferences in Nonexperimental Research* (1964).

The survey approach is best suited for the study of attitudes and their relation to social background factors, and this type of sociopsychological investigation has become particularly popular in sociology. A good illustration of such a study is Samuel Stouffer's *Communism, Conformity and Civil Liberties* (1955). One of the major criticisms that has been leveled against the survey approach is that the attitudes which a person expresses in a brief interview with a stranger, even if they reflect his honest beliefs at the moment, may not be directly related to his overt conduct. Thus, both Edward A. Shils and Seymour M. Lipset make the point that those individuals who make the most intolerant statements against a minority in an interview are not necessarily more antagonistic than others when personally confronted by a member of this minority. Uneducated people, for example, may well be particularly apt to express themselves in violent language and perhaps even say that all Communists should be executed, but they may be less intolerant toward Communists in actual life than better educated people who simply are not wont to make such extreme statements (see Richard Christie and Marie Jahoda [eds.], *Studies in the Scope and Method of "The Authoritarian Personality,"* 1954).

In the study of voting behavior, election results furnish a check on how realistic the attitudes obtained in an interviewing survey have been. Partly as the result of this reality check, the study of political behavior has advanced from superficial public opinion polling to sophisticated investigations of attitudes and their formation. Of particular significance in this respect was the pioneering study *The People's Choice* (1944), by Paul F. Lazarsfeld, Bernard Berelson, and Hazel Gaudet, in which the panel design was developed. Repeated interviews with the same sample ("panel") of respondents throughout the political campaign of 1940 made it possible to trace the processes by which people make political decisions and change their attitudes. Few people, it was found, change their vote intention in the course of the campaign, and those that do typically have little interest in the election. A systematic national survey of a presidential election is Angus Campbell, Gerald Gurin, and Warren E. Miller, *The Voter Decides* (1954).

Another criticism that has often been leveled against the survey method is that its focus on the attitudes and characteristics of a sample of unrelated individuals fails to provide the very information most needed for sociological analysis, namely, data on the relations between individuals and on the social structures of which they are a part. However, work has begun on adapting the survey method to meet this criticism. The way the opinions of friends and fellow workers affect a person's political attitudes is analyzed in Bernard Berelson, Paul F. Lazarsfeld, and William N. McPhee, *Voting* (1954), by the simple expedient of asking respondents what the opinions of their associates are. Other studies went one step further and obtained more reliable data by actually interviewing the associates of the original sample of respondents. Perhaps the most successful adaptation of the survey method to the study of a social organization has been made by Seymour M. Lipset, Martin Trow, and James S. Coleman in *Union Democracy* (1956), a very suggestive sociological investigation of membership participation in the International Typographical Union and the conditions that sustain democratic processes in unions. In recent years, contextual or milieu analysis has been used more frequently with survey data, as in Paul F. Lazarsfeld and Wagner Thielens, *The Academic Mind* (1958), and James A. Davis, *Great Aspirations* (1964). This approach permits the characterization of the social environment—for instance, in different universities or different cities—on the basis of survey data treated in the aggregate; the individual's responses are then analyzed in relation to his social milieu. Individuals with highly similar personal characteristics behave and feel differently if they find themselves in differing social surroundings, and sociologists are paying increasing systematic attention to this fact of life.

SOCIAL PSYCHOLOGY

The study of small groups has been one of the most rapidly growing fields of research in the decades since World War II. It is an interdisciplinary field, since both sociologists and psychologists are consumers as well as producers of research in this area. The study of small groups illustrates especially well the substantive implications of the new conception of sociology discussed previously. As long as sociologists were interested in explaining the "important problems" of human history or of society as a whole, it was only natural that they almost completely ignored the social structure of small groups, since its study did not seem relevant for their purposes. But once the focus shifted and the objective became to explain recurrent patterns of social conduct, the systematic study of social processes in small groups began to assume increasing significance. The very problems of social relations and social structure that tend to be neglected in interviewing surveys can readily be studied in small groups, and experimental situations can be created to investigate how various social conditions affect patterns of conduct and the development of a social structure.

Since small groups can easily be studied under controlled conditions, some investigators have used them to derive generalizations about larger social systems. They have, in effect, assumed that the processes observable in the small group are completely analogous to those operating in larger groups, or even in whole societies. Obviously, however, the small group is not a society in miniature, and this approach is no more justifiable than that of many of the earlier experimental psychologists, who attempted to derive generalizations about how children learn to read from observation of how rats learn to run through mazes. But although small groups undoubtedly do not replicate larger social structures, they pervade them. Since all large organizations and even societies consist, in one sense, of many small groups, an understanding of small groups and the social processes that occur in them is a prerequisite for an understanding of more complex social systems.

Most of the systematic methods used in the study of small groups are relatively new. The most widely used of these is the sociometric technique, developed by Jacob L. Moreno (*Who Shall Survive?*, rev. ed., 1953), originally for the purpose of group therapy. In essence, it consists of asking each member of a community—in Moreno's original study it was a girls' reformatory—with which others in the same group he or she would most like to be and engage in various activities with, and which ones would be least desirable as companions. The responses to these questions make it possible to trace the network of social relations in each group—choices, mutual choices, in-group choices, and so forth—and to determine the popularity of each member on a variety of dimensions.

We have briefly mentioned Bales's *Interaction Process Analysis* (1950) in the discussion of techniques of research. This is probably the most elaborate—technically and conceptually—of the many attempts made to find objective measures of the social interaction in groups. The first simple measure of interaction, a record of the amount of speaking activity and inactivity of each person in a group, was devised by Eliot D. Chapple. The method was later elaborated by Chapple and used outside the laboratory by Conrad Arensberg and William F. Whyte, for example, in the latter's perceptive *Street Corner Society* (1955).

Small-group research is one of the few areas in sociology where controlled experiments are conducted frequently. A famous series of early experiments is one in which Kurt Lewin, Ronald Lippit, and Ralph White explored the effects of authoritarian, laissez-faire, and democratic leadership. One of these studies, as well as many other small group investigations carried out by followers of Lewin, is reprinted in Dorwin Cartwright and Alvin Zander (eds.), *Group Dynamics* (1953). An early classic experiment is the one by Muzafer Sherif dealing with the effects of group norms on perception, *The Psychology of Social Norms* (1936).

In addition to systematic observation and experimentation, small-group research has also been subject to attempts at computer simulation and to formalization through mathematical models (see J. Berger, B. P. Cohen, J. L. Snell, and M. Zelditch, Jr. [eds.], *Types of Formalization in Small-Group Research*, 1962).

Despite differences in method, however, the substantive problems of research on small groups have remained roughly congruent with those of interest to the pioneers, with emphasis on development of social structure, differentiation of the roles of participants, emergence and significance of leadership, formation of coalitions and other subgroups, variations in networks of communication, and effects of size and other ecological constraints. Special attention has been focused on problems of deviance and control and those of decision-making and performance, even though these problems may be viewed quite differently in laboratory research from how they were conceived orginally, since it is not easy to reproduce the meaning of life experiences in the laboratory. Nevertheless, significant general theoretical contributions have emerged from this research, for example, in the work by Leon Festinger, *A Theory of Cognitive Dissonance* (1962). A. Paul Hare has edited *A Handbook of Small Group Research* (1962), which presents an overview of the field.

The study of small groups is, of course, only a small sector of social psychology. Indeed, social psychology is such a broad and pervasive branch of sociology that Amos Hawley and other sociologists have complained that the dominant sociopsychological orientation threatens to lead to the utter neglect of the systematic study of social structure itself. The wide range of sociopsychological concerns is exemplified in the *Handbook of Social Psychology* (1954), by Gardner Lindzey (ed.), as well as in Eleanor E. Maccoby, Theodore M. Newcomb, and Eugene

L. Hartley (eds.), *Readings in Social Psychology* (3d ed., 1958). Of central concern to the sociologist is the psychological aspect of the process of social interaction, in particular, the study of communication with significant symbols, to which George Herbert Mead made such great contributions. This so-called symbolic-interactionist approach is presented by Alfred Lindesmith and Anselm Strauss in their text *Social Psychology* (1956).

Symbolic interactionism has surged into sociological popularity once again with the writings of Erving Goffman, notably his original analysis of the process of managing the impression one makes on others in *The Presentation of Self in Everyday Life* (1959), and his more recent *Asylums* (1961) and *Stigma* (1963). Goffman and others have tended to blend the symbolic interactionist tradition with the philosophic tradition stemming from nineteenth-century German phenomenology, most notably the work of Axel Schuetz. The major proponent of the phenomenological approach in sociology is Harold Garfinkel (*Studies in Ethnomethodology*, 1967).

With the development and increasing acceptance of Freudian theories of personality development, a number of social scientists began to use psychoanalytic insights to reconceptualize their own fields. Harry S. Sullivan developed an implicit synthesis of Freud, as did George Herbert Mead, in *The Interpersonal Theory of Psychiatry* (1953). In sociology, his and Freud's direct influence have been particularly important in the study of socialization—the study of how personality develops in the course of interaction with others.

About a quarter of a century ago, anthropologists became interested in investigating the ways in which cultural differences in family structure and child-rearing tend to produce different "normal" personalities in different cultures. Ruth Benedict, in *Patterns of Culture* (1943), used data from several cultures to show how relative is the concept of a normal person, and Margaret Mead, in *From the South Seas* (1939), demonstrated how much cultural variation there is in the definitions of age and sex roles and in the practices of child-rearing. The most systematic elaboration of this insight that the institutional system affects the personality structure was made by two psychiatrists. Abram Kardiner, employing the concept of basic personality structure to refer to that aspect of personality common to all members of a culture, stresses that the primary institutions, notably the economic ones, govern the basic personality structure, which, in turn, affects the secondary institutions, such as the mythology (*The Individual and His Society*, 1939; *The Psychological Frontiers of Society*, 1945). Erich Fromm, in his *Escape from Freedom* (1941), does not assume that all members of a society are equally affected in their personality development by the institutional structure.

The socioeconomic conditions in which a group of individuals find themselves will shape their social character, which is similar for all members of a social class, but different for members of various classes in the same society. These conceptions of anthropologists and psychiatrists have influenced a variety of sociological investigations, particularly studies on the ways class and ethnic differences affect family structure, child-rearing, and, therefore, personality development (Allison Davis and Robert J. Havighurst, *Father of the Man*, 1947). It should be noted, however, that many conclusions of this early study were not confirmed by later research on American class differences in socialization (see Robert R. Sears, Eleanor E. Maccoby, and Harry Levin, *Patterns of Child Rearing*, 1957).

In the study of mass communication, the focus is not upon the process of communication per se, nor upon the development of the capacity to communicate, but upon the effects of various media of mass communication on attitudes and conduct. The extensive systematic research into the effects of Army orientation films and other media, reported by Carl I. Hovland, Arthur A. Lumsdaine, and Fred D. Sheffield in *Experiments on Mass Communication* (1949), showed that, while subjects learned new facts from these propaganda films, their attitudes were usually little affected by seeing them. Recent work has indicated that the group context in which communications are received exerts much influence on the meanings attributed to them and the effect they produce. Direct social contacts influence opinions and attitudes more than do mass media, but the latter do have some indirect effects. Elihu Katz and Paul F. Lazarsfeld demonstrate (in *Personal Influence*, 1955) that opinion leaders help to transmit the influence of the mass media; that is, the individuals most influential in shaping the opinions of others are in their own thinking considerably affected by the mass media. These authors also show that there are types of opinion leaders, and that political news, movie gossip, and homemaking information travel by different social routes to their ultimate audiences. Analysis of the process of diffusion of mass media messages is also the concern of the more recent theoretically oriented appraisal by E. M. Rogers, *Diffusion of Innovations* (1962).

DEMOGRAPHY AND HUMAN ECOLOGY*

Whereas the covert and subjective aspects of social conduct are at the focus of social psychology, its overt and objective aspects are at the focus of demography and human ecology. Demography is the study of population—its size, distribution, and composition. Traditionally, the

---

* We gratefully acknowledge the helpful suggestions for this section of Donald J. Bogue and Patricia Hodge.

emphasis has been upon developing precise quantitative methods for describing and analyzing population trends, such as changes in birth and death rates and migration patterns. Demographers have usually approached their research with an empirical orientation, and they have shown little concern with underlying sociopsychological processes. More recently, however, a number of studies have been undertaken that combine interviewing surveys with demographic analysis in order to investigate these sociopsychological processes associated with various overt characteristics of population, such as fertility (see Clyde V. Kiser (ed.), *Research in Family Planning*, 1962; Charles F. Westhoff, Robert G. Potter, and Philip C. Sagi, *The Third Child*, 1963; Roland Freedman, Pascal K. Whelpton, and Arthur A. Campbell, *Family Planning, Sterility, and Population Growth*, 1959; Lee Rainwater, *Family Design*, 1965; and Donald J. Bogue (ed.), *Mass Communication and Motivation for Birth Control*, 1967). Interest in developing theoretical generalizations from demographic findings has also become more pronounced (Joseph J. Spengler and Otis D. Duncan [eds.], *Population Theory and Policy*, 1956, a companion volume to their *Demographic Analysis*, 1957). Excellent overviews of the field are provided by the summary of demographic findings in the United Nations Department of Social Affairs Population Study No. 17, *The Determinants and Consequences of Population Trends* (1953); and by the collection of articles by Philip M. Hauser and Otis D. Duncan, *The Study of Population* (1959). Another summary is presented in the sophisticated textbook by William Petersen, *Population* (1968). Notable examples of demographic research are Dudley Kirk's *Europe's Population in the Interwar Years* (1946); Kingsley Davis' *The Population of India and Pakistan* (1951); the methodologically innovative Ansley J. Coale and Melvin Zelnik's *New Estimates of Fertility and Population in the United States;* and Hope T. Eldridge and Dorothy S. Thomas' *Population Redistribution and Economic Growth, United States, 1870–1950* (Vol. III, 1964). The policy concerns of demographers are well illustrated in the collection by Philip Hauser (ed.), *The Population Dilemma* (1963), and a policy-oriented general discussion is just being published (Bogue, *Principles of Demography*, 1968).

Demographers have long been interested in the areas of social life that overlap with the concerns of economists. Demographer-sociologists are as likely as labor economists to study the labor force, and demographers along with economists have been deeply interested in the phenomena of urbanization and urban growth and change. Philip M. Hauser and Leo F. Schnore's *The Study of Urbanization* (1965) represents the interdisciplinary nature of the concern with urbanization, including contributions by anthropologists as well as by economists and sociologists—demographers and others. The study of the ways in which cities grow and change has been a special concern of urban ecology as originally conceived by Robert E. Park. Human ecology has been defined as the "study of the spatial and temporal relations of human beings as affected by the selective, distributive, and accommodative forces of the environment." (See Robert E. Park, Ernest W. Burgess, and Roderick D. McKenzie, *The City*, 1925.) The procedure of urban ecology has been, fundamentally, to distinguish geographical areas in the city that are relatively homogeneous in economic or demographic respects and then compare the social characteristics of these areas, as illustrated by Harvey Zorbaugh's *Gold Coast and Slum* (1929). An early interest of ecologists in social problems was encouraged when researchers found that the incidence of a wide variety of "pathological" phenomena—such as juvenile delinquency, crime, divorce, mental illness, and suicide—is systematically distributed throughout the city, being highest in the so-called "area of transition" right around the central business district and diminishing gradually as one goes out toward the suburbs (Clifford R. Shaw and Henry McKay, *Juvenile Delinquency and Urban Areas*, 1942, and Robert E. L. Faris and Henry Warren Dunham, *Mental Disorders in Urban Areas*. 1939).

The greatest contribution of urban ecology to sociology is that it constitutes one of the earliest attempts to study systematically social structures rather than individual behavior. On the other hand, the ecological approach has been criticized for providing a basically economic interpretation of city growth which ignores other important social factors that affect it, such as the traditions that develop in a neighborhood and the common values that attach people to it (Walter Firey, *Land Use in Central Boston*, 1947, and Milla Alihan, *Social Ecology*, 1938). Recently, however, the field had broadened to encompass interests far wider than those of the original urban ecologists, and ecological research has taken into account some of the criticisms that have been made. New problems have been incorporated into ecology, such as that of the relations between cities, or that of the relations between a metropolis and its hinterland (Bogue, *The Structure of the Metropolitan Community*, 1949). (The overlap with the concerns of economists—in this case with the regional economists—is particularly evident in this field. For an illustration, see Otis Dudley Duncan and others, *Metropolis and Region*, 1960.) Amos Hawley has carried the ecological perspective further than most of its other proponents, developing a framework for a general sociological theory based on the ecological approach. He conceived of ecology very broadly as the study of "the nature of community structure in general, the types of communities that appear in different habitats, and the specific sequence of change in community development" (*Human Ecology*, 1950). The most recent important systematic advance in the field is Otis Dudley Duncan's analysis of "Social Organization and the Ecosystem" in Robert E. L. Faris (ed.), *Handbook of Modern Sociology* (1965).

SOCIAL DIFFERENTIATION IN COMMUNITY AND NATION

A totally different orientation to research on communities is that of the social anthropologists, a number of whom became interested in the study of contemporary society and started to conduct community studies around 1930. Their approach is to take the community as a whole and not to attempt to break it down into segments for analysis, as do the ecologists. Furthermore, in contrast to the ecological focus on material economic and geographical conditions, anthropologists place primary emphasis on the cultural values of the community. Finally, they are not as committed to the use of quantitative methods as the ecologists are. A good example of an anthropological community study is Conrad Arensberg and Solon Kimball's *Family and Community in Ireland* (1940).

The central concern of many anthropologically oriented studies of modern American communities, including the two pioneering series, is the social stratification of the community. Robert S. and Helen M. Lynd, in *Middletown* (1929), and particularly in their follow-up of the same Midwestern community during the depression, *Middletown in Transition* (1937), are primarily interested in differences in economic power and their implications for the life chances of individuals and for the institutional structure of the community as a whole. W. Lloyd Warner's Yankee City series, taking quite a different view of stratification, analyzes class differences in style of life and patterns of associations in an old New England community (Vol. I, *The Social Life of a Modern Community*, with Paul S. Lunt, 1941). A number of later community studies concentrated on specific aspects of stratification; thus, August Hollingshead's *Elmtown's Youth* (1949) deals with class differences among adolescents and their significance for education, and Floyd Hunter's *Community Power Structure* (1953) is an investigation of institutional leadership in a southern metropolis.

Another major interest of community studies is the investigation of the relations among ethnic groups and the emerging patterns of ethnic differentiation. The third volume of the Yankee City series (Warner and Leo Srole, *The Social Systems of American Ethnic Groups*, 1945) exemplifies this, as do Elin Anderson's study of another New England city, *We Americans* (1937), and Everett C. Hughes's research on a Canadian town, *French Canada in Transition* (1943). Particular attention has been paid to the semicaste relations between Negroes and whites in Southern communities (see Allison Davis, B. Burleigh, and Mary R. Gardner, *Deep South*, 1941; John Dollard, *Caste and Class in a*

Southern Town, 1937; Hortense Powdermaker, *After Freedom,* 1939). Research into the social structure of ethnic subcommunities is illustrated by Louis Wirth's *The Ghetto* (1928) and St. Clair Drake and Horace R. Cayton's *Black Metropolis* (1946).

A simple and optimistic assimilationist view of the future of racial and ethnic groups has largely been abandoned by sociologists. Some see evidence of a future of pluralism (Milton Gordon, *Assimilation in American Life,* 1964; Nathan Glazer and Daniel Patrick Moynihan, *Beyond the Melting Pot,* 1963), though the viability of such a structure is debated by those who see the climactic Negro struggle for equality as challenging its assumptions. Sociologists have not predicted the increasing momentum of the Negro movement against segregation and for greater "black power" but only followed it by studying some of its repercussions (Lewis Killian and Charles Grigg, *Racial Crisis in America,* 1964). It has been only recently that other ethnic groups have been extensively studied as well. A research project on the nation's second-largest minority, the Mexican-Americans, is in the process of completion (Leo Grebler, Joan W. Moore, Ralph Guzman, and associates, *America's Second Minority: Los Chicanos,* forthcoming), just as their struggles for equality begin to compete for headlines with the Negroes'. And the highly visible Puerto Ricans, located primarily in research-conscious and ethnic-conscious cities, also have their chroniclers (Patricia C. Sexton, *Spanish Harlem,* 1965). The studies of ethnic groups like these three is far from an ivory-tower exercise, as is indicated by the account of the political controversy stirred by one semi-academic government report (Lee Rainwater and William L. Yancey, *The Moynihan Report and the Politics of Controversy,* 1967).

Ethnic and race relations have also been studied outside the community setting. Gunnar Myrdal's *An American Dilemma* (1944), a collaborative work of great scope, and Edward Franklin Frazier's *The Negro in the United States* (1949) are comprehensive investigations of the social situation in which the American Negro finds himself. A great deal of research has been devoted to the problems of prejudice and discrimination. One approach has been to study the personality and social background of prejudiced people (Theodor W. Adorno and others, *The Authoritarian Personality,* 1950; Bruno Bettelheim and Morris Janowitz, *Social Change and Prejudice,* 1964). Another approach has been to analyze intergroup relations (Everett C. and Helen M. Hughes, *Where Peoples Meet,* 1952). Robin M. Williams, Jr., made an inventory of existing knowledge on prejudice and discrimination in *The Reduction of Intergroup Tensions* (1947), and more recently he and his associates have reported an extensive study of interethnic contact in a variety of American communities (Robin M. Williams and associates, *Strangers Next Door,*

1964). However, there is a growing need for studies of institutionalized racism, in contrast to individual prejudice and discrimination, as pressures for change become increasingly desperate and find expression in both social movements and organized opposition to them.

Class differentiation is, to an even greater extent than ethnic differentiation, a society-wide phenomenon. Generalizations about stratification based on studies of single communities have been criticized not only for using an inadequate sample but also because the aspects of stratification most relevant in the study of the status system of a community are different from those most pertinent for the analysis of the class structure of the society. In particular, it has been emphasized that prestige and social associations, conspicuous as they may be in differentiating the members of a local community, are not as important in the investigation of a society's stratification system as power relations, economic differences, and occupational mobility.

A number of investigations are concerned with various problems of the American stratification system rather than that of a single community. Thus, Cecil C. North and Paul K. Hatt conducted a national survey of the prestige associated with different occupations, reprinted in Reinhard Bendix and Seymour M. Lipset's collection of studies on stratification, *Class, Status and Power* (1966). Several studies have explored the extent of "class consciousness" in America; examples are Alfred W. Jones's *Life, Liberty and Property* (1941) and Richard Centers' *The Psychology of Social Classes* (1949), a national survey which shows that political attitudes and class identification are related to occupational position. C. Wright Mills's *White Collar* (1951) and *The Power Elite* (1956) present intensive studies of single strata, and which pose a number of political as well as theoretical issues. A recent attempt to develop a broad theory of stratification is Gerhard E. Lenski's *Power and Privilege* (1966).

One of the earliest works on the important subject of social mobility was Pitirim A. Sorokin's *Social Mobility* (1927). Nationwide studies of social mobility, typically defined as the difference in occupational status between father and son, have been carried out in a number of countries, including England (David V. Glass, *Social Mobility in Britain*, 1954), Sweden (Goesta Carlsson, *Social Mobility and Class Structure*, 1958), and Denmark (Kaare Svalastoga, *Prestige, Class and Mobility*, 1959). S. M. Miller presents a systematic secondary analysis comparing occupational mobility in more than a dozen different societies in "Comparative Social Mobility" (*Current Sociology*, 9, 1960), and Lipset and Bendix use some of these cross-national comparisons in their theoretical analysis, *Social Mobility in Industrial Society* (1959).

This series of national studies has only recently been complemented by a nationwide study of occupational achievement and mobility in the

United States (Peter M. Blau and Otis Dudley Duncan, *The American Occupational Structure*, 1967). The influences exerted on the chances of occupational success by various conditions are examined—for example, the handicaps from which Negroes suffer are analyzed—and so are some consequences of social mobility, such as its influence on fertility. Two important questions previous studies have raised are how occupational opportunities in America today compare with those at earlier times and with those in other countries. Limited studies of social mobility in Indianapolis (Natalie Rogoff, *Recent Trends in Occupational Mobility*, 1953) and into the business elite (W. Lloyd Warner, *Occupational Mobility in American Business and Industry*, 1928–1952) did not confirm earlier predictions that social mobility would decline in this country. The nationwide study confirms these conclusions: opportunity for upward mobility has not declined and may even have increased in recent decades. Moreover, opportunity for social mobility from the working class into one of the top occupational strata seems to be better in the United States than in other countries.

FORMAL ORGANIZATION

Since sociology can be considered the study of the social processes by which the activities and interactions of people become organized into an integrated whole, the formal organization provides a particularly good "natural laboratory" for social research. In the army or factory, the government office or hospital, we find a clearly circumscribed social situation that has the special advantage of being, unlike the controlled conditions in the experimental laboratory, a natural social product rather than the artificial creation of the investigator.

Early students of formal organizations tended to focus on the requirements any organization must meet to persist and to operate efficiently, and on the social implications of these requirements. Thus, Weber, in his classic essay on bureaucracy (in Gerth and Mills [eds. and trs.], *From Max Weber: Essays in Sociology*, 1946) systematically analyzed the characteristics of the bureaucracy and its personnel that are associated with maximum efficiency in the administration of large-scale tasks. Robert Michels in *Political Parties* (1915) suggested that the inevitable bureaucratization of large democratic political parties or unions, because of the need for administrative efficiency, perverts their original egalitarian principles of organization; and he argues that, therefore, oligarchy is inevitable, and no democratic organization can survive for long periods. Adolf A. Berle, Jr., and Gardiner C. Means (*The Modern Corporation and Private Property*, 1933) show that the bureaucratic organization of the giant business corporation, in effect, contradicts the American values of private property and profit as an incentive.

In the thirties, empirical research in industry led to the concept of the "informal organization" that exists within the formal organization—the networks of social relationships and the common norms that arise in work groups. For example, factory workers often develop informal production standards of what constitutes a "fair day's work," and most individuals conform to this group norm, pay-incentive systems not withstanding. Since these social norms and the interpersonal relations that develop in the work groups affect the operating practices and patterns of social interaction of workers, their social conduct cannot be explained in terms of the formal organization alone; it is also shaped by their informal organization. Operating efficiency as well as morale suffer if the latter is ignored by management (Elton Mayo, *The Social Problems of an Industrial Civilization*, 1945; Fritz J. Roethlisberger and William J. Dickson, *Management and Worker*, 1939; Chester I. Barnard, *The Functions of the Executive*, 1938).

The effects of the informal organization on productivity, performance quality, work satisfactions, absenteeism, and turnover made the investigation of it important for management and stimulated the development of the so-called "human relations" approach in industry. Daniel Katz, Robert L. Kahn, and others of the Survey Research Center at the University of Michigan published a number of studies exploring the significance of informal relations for supervision. The theoretical and practical implications of this research tradition are examined by Rensis Likert in *New Patterns of Management* (1961). Along similar lines, Charles R. Walker and Robert Guest investigated the social conditions and special problems created by the assembly line in *The Man on the Assembly Line* (1952) and, with Arthur N. Turner, *The Foreman on the Assembly Line* (1956).

There have been several studies of how emergent informal patterns mold and even transform the formal organization. One of these examines the social structure of a hospital (Alfred H. Stanton and Morris S. Schwartz, *The Mental Hospital*, 1954). Another deals with the repercussions of a change in management on the organization of a factory (Alvin W. Gouldner, *Patterns of Industrial Bureaucracy*, 1954). William F. Whyte analyzes the cross-pressures created by conflicts between authority relations and the flow of work in a service industry (*Human Relations in the Restaurant Industry*, 1948). Several investigators have been concerned with the sources and processes of change in government agencies (Philip Selznick, *TVA and the Grass Roots*, 1949; Peter M. Blau, *The Dynamics of Bureaucracy*, 1963).

Most of these are case studies of a single organization, and this fact calls attention to a fundamental methodological problem in organizational research. The more rigorous an empirical investigation is in its methods, the less it tends to deal with questions of organizational life. Samuel A. Stouffer's *The American Soldier* (1949), for example, is based on reliable quantitative data on a larger scale, namely, interviews with samples of thousands of soldiers. This approach, however, permits him to make only sociopsychological generalizations about soldiers, not to generalize about the social organization of the army. Interviews with a sample of isolated individuals cannot furnish reliable information about the organizational context. But even if many members of an organization are not only interviewed but also systematically observed in their organizational setting where they interact with one another, the data obtained pertain only to one organization, and scientific generalizations cannot be based on a single case.

This is not a new dilemma. It is the same one that faced sociologists at the end of the last century when they attempted to make scientific generalizations about the development of modern capitalism or the origin of the division of labor. And sociologists resolved the dilemma, as we have pointed out, by resigning themselves to the fact that social phenomena that are so rare as to be virtually unique are simply outside the realm of a generalizing science. But formal organizations are not quite that rare—surely not in our age of bureaucratization. As case studies of single organizations accumulate, sufficient systematic data for testing generalizations about organizational life will become available. Moreover some recent empirical studies of one formal organization have made comparative analyses of various organizational segments within it, and this, too, makes it possible to derive tentative generalizations about social organization. Finally, a number of investigators have recently started to conduct research in which comparable data on large numbers of organizations—several hundred of them—are obtained, providing a basis for the systematic analysis of the interrelations between organizational characteristics, and thus for refinement of the theory of organization.

On one hand, then, formal organizations are neither as rare nor as complex as entire societies, and this facilitates their systematic investigation. On the other hand, research on formal organizations deals with complex social structures, not merely with small groups or with individuals in isolation from their social relations and structural context, as attitude surveys, as well as demographic analyses, tend to do. It is for these reasons that the systematic study of formal organizations appears to us to be a particularly fruitful field in which to advance scientific knowledge about the ways in which human conduct becomes socially organized.

This preference for a specific field is, of course, based on a value judgment in which not all sociologists would concur. The conception of sociology as outlined in this chapter has been as an analytical science. Although it has only recently emerged out of divergent traditions and continues to be refined and modified, it is a conception that most sociologists today share, however different their specific interpretations and emphases might be. The persistence of conflicting theoretical viewpoints combined with the growing agreement on fundamental methodological issues promises to stimulate research that will increase the body of scientific generalizations in sociology.

* * *

Three types of general references which have not been discussed should be briefly illustrated—introductory texts, histories of sociology, and periodicals.

Two popular simple texts are John F. Cuber's *Sociology* (3d ed., 1955), and William F. Ogburn and Meyer F. Nimkoff, *Sociology* (1940). Introductory texts on a somewhat more advanced level are illustrated by Robert M. MacIver and Charles H. Page, *Society* (1949); Kingsley Davis, *Human Society* (1949); and Robin M. Williams, Jr., *American Society* (1951), which is focused on a discussion of American institutions. The integration of selected readings into an introductory text, made famous by Robert E. Park and Ernest W. Burgess, *Introduction to the Science of Sociology* (1921), has recently been revived in Leonard Broom and Philip Selznick, *Sociology* (1955). A recent popular text is Everett Wilson's *Sociology: Rules, Roles, Relationships* (1966), and a comprehensive source book is the *Handbook of Sociology* (1964), edited by Robert E. L. Faris.

Histories of the development of sociology include the following: Harry E. Barnes (ed.), *An Introduction to the History of Sociology* (1948); Harry E. Barnes and Howard Becker, *Social Thought from Lore to Science* (2d ed., 1952); Floyd N. House, *The Development of Sociology* (1936); Pitirim A. Sorokin, *Contemporary Sociological Theories* (1928). An excellent overview and assessment of American sociology during the first half of this century is provided by Edward A. Shils, *The Present State of American Sociology* (1948), and developments in the various branches of sociology during the last decade are covered in two volumes, one sponsored by UNESCO and edited by Hans Zetterberg, *Sociology in the United States of America* (1956), and the other edited by Joseph B. Gittler, *Review of Sociology* (1957). A highly critical appraisal of recent theories is presented in Pitirim A. Sorokin's *Sociological Theories of Today* (1966).

The two major sociological journals are the *American Sociological Review* (1936–), the official publication of the American Sociological Society, and the *American Journal of Sociology* (1895–). Other important journals in sociology are *Social Forces* (1922–), *Sociometry* (1937–), the *British Journal of Sociology* (1950–), *Sociological Abstracts* (1952–), *Sociology and Social Research* (1916–), *Rural Sociology* (1936–), and *Social Problems* (1953–). Periodicals in related fields that often contain sociological studies include *Human Relations* (1947–), *Public Opinion Quarterly* (1937–), *Human Organizations* (1941–), and the *Administrative Science Quarterly* (1956–).

2 Anthropology

Gail M. Kelly

INTRODUCTION

THE SUBJECT MATTER

The literature of anthropology is more diffuse and fragmented than that of any other social science discipline. Anthropology is not exclusively a social science. It has substantial numbers of its practitioners working on subjects closely allied with the natural sciences and others who are nearer the humanistic disciplines. These specialize in subfields that all contribute to anthropology as the general study of man, but have little to do with one other. This introduction to the literature will concentrate on the social science fields to the virtual exclusion of the others. It is, therefore, necessary at the outset to make it clear that humanistic and natural scientific activities within the anthropological discipline are extraordinarily important in influencing the overall character of the subject. The preoccupation of this bibliographical essay with the social science related concerns of anthropology ought not to mislead the reader into supposing that the structure of the subject is fairly represented by the selection.

The term anthropology evokes disparate images in the minds of the literate public. Special areas or topics are sometimes emphasized to the exclusion of the more general unifying ones. Thus, to some readers, anthropology is the study of arrowheads, to others, old bones, while still others with limited exposure to academic anthropology may identify it with the study of totemisms or cross-cultural studies of child-rearing practices. None of these is a false impression, but they are merely aspects of a larger whole.

For the general public and sometimes for anthropologists as well, the central concerns are of lesser importance than are the delights of the minutia of one or the other special subjects. National differences in the organization of the subject exacerbate this problem of identity. General anthropology as it has grown up in the United States has insisted that exposure to a range of subjects from human biology to language to archaeology and the customs of primitives past and present are essential to the perpetuation of what it feels to be the distinctive contribution of anthropology to human knowledge. On the other hand, different terminological designations have been used in England and on the continent to refer to this activity, included under the rubric "anthropology" in the United States.

For the nonspecialist, the constituent subject matters of general anthropology hold a fascination which is, perhaps, uniquely characteristic of anthropology among the social sciences. Interest in the "exotic" is always strong, and accounts of travels among strange peoples with curious customs have had a constant popular following at least since the fifteenth century in Europe. The field of anthropology by its incorporation of, and identification with, such pleasant and exciting subjects has had a receptive public for its findings since it began to emerge as a distinct and serious field of study in the nineteenth century.

A somewhat difficult distinction ought to be made early between writings of professional anthropologists, which are referred to here as the "literature" of anthropology, and the kinds of data in diverse form on which anthropologists themselves rely in their own researches. A center of theoretically relevant literature by anthropologists will be held in common by all of the practitioners of a major anthropological subfield, for example, social anthropology, but the data in terms of which anthropological problems are explored will be collected from sources in large part quite outside the writings of professionals from other fields of scholarly activity, such as history, politics, geography, or biography.

Thus, to talk about the literature is to emphasize its theoretical center. The data utilized in research are often peripheral to the discipline's organization. They are the raw material for anthropological inquiry. The seventeenth century, in this as in most fields of intellectual endeavor, marked a turning point in thinking about the subject that we now consider anthropology. The increased interest in travel, developing as it did contemporaneously with a general acceptance of new ideas about the scientific method, stimulated the development of critical attitudes toward societal customs and institutions that shaped the intellectual milieu in which the social sciences appeared. New, reflective, acquaintance with the non-Western world was especially important for the emergence of "proto-anthropology." As experience with the non-Europeans developed, and with the publication of significant descriptions in Europe, a public eager for such information was formed that has continued to this day. The problem of how this interest developed and persists is more relevant to the intellectual history of Western Europe than it is to the history of anthropology. However, the mere existence of a body of concerned amateurs has been an invaluable support to the development of scientific anthropology and continues to be important to the field's organization, though less so as professionalization and specialization increase. Travelers, administrators, traders, and adventurers writing on related topics are seldom distinguished from anthropologists by some members of the amateur public. Films and pictorial magazines have popularized subjects close to anthropology, especially in their exploitation of anthropologically relevant locales and customs. Popularized literature on para-anthropological subjects are often among best sellers and mold opinions about the work of anthropologists.

Anthropological findings have played a role in the history of other social science and humanistic studies by providing them with comparative data from the non-Western world, though they do not always employ these systematically. Sometimes quite out of spirit with the prevailing trend in anthropological interpretation in the early twentieth century, the nonanthropologists have viewed primitives as representing types of social or cultural adaptation ancestral to our own. They have looked to anthropology and to anthropological archaeology for the reconstruction of institutions of the Western past. Other nonevolutionists' use of anthropological data for extending our knowledge of the range of human experience has attracted the interest of other scholars. To the humanist, some anthropological material is of immediate importance. In the routine description of primitive cultures, the traditional ethnographer commonly records myths and folktales, describes artifacts, music, and art forms, of all sorts, which may be the subject of analysis for humanists using their own conceptual tools. Especially important are those instances in which the primitive world has influence or has a counterpart in Western art. When there is widespread interest in some aspect of primitive culture, it may become a relatively autonomous field of study or it may be partially incorporated into a traditional humanistic field. Thus, primitive plastic and graphic arts have increasingly become subjects in which art historians have an interest and folklorists, who consider material collected by anthropologists and of their own collection, are semiautonomous with respect to the main body of anthropology. The anthropologists have seldom concentrated on exclusively aesthetic aspects of primitive art. They have rather been concerned with art in the context of cultural interpretation or social function.

Social scientists outside of anthropology have rarely made anthropological data or the theoretical formulations of anthropology central to their own formulations. Anthropological findings have on the whole been used in peripheral ways to explore possible human social variation in basic institutions or to suggest the types of social arrangements from which contemporary institutions have developed. Only in the heyday of unilineal evolutionists' studies did anthropology intrude fundamentally on other social science theory. Perhaps the new popularity of large-scale comparative developmental and evolutionist study will again make anthropology an important source of data for allied subjects, though this is less likely as other nonanthropological social scientists begin themselves to do extensive field work in non-Western countries. It is the case that at least one of the distinctive contributions of the field to the fund of human knowledge, the description of primitive institutions, is no longer exclusively the concern of the anthropologist. The demands that interests in non-Western economic and social development make on the anthropological records, and the extent to which the anthropological literature cannot fill the needs of other social and applied sciences, as these move into closer contact with the non-Western world, will call forth an examination by anthropologists of the fundamental contribution and orientation of their subject. Indeed, to some extent, this reevaluation of the contribution of anthropology has already begun. Sociologists, economists, political scientists, community developers, and historians immersed in the study of the new nations of Africa and Asia provide an interesting contrast to the characteristic approaches of anthropology to the same allied subject matter. It is bound to be the case that this competition, to the extent that it is such, will challenge anthropology. Though these specialists ordinarily have recourse to the literature of anthropology as a background to the study of modern institutions, they will necessarily compete with anthropology in the description of modern institutions at the level of the village or the tribe, where anthropology has up to now felt most confident. This is not to say that the wealth of anthropological description is valueless to kindred social scientists. Quite the contrary, anthropological findings, or more specifically the ethnographic record, is usually the only corpus of data, the only serious detailed social scientific descriptive work available in an area where nothing exists aside from government description, census data, and the like. The nonanthropologist academicians preparing to do field work will familiarize themselves with whatever data exists of whatever quality in the anthropological tradition. It is ordinarily the case that the remote areas in which anthropologists have worked have been the areas neglected until recently by other serious scholars. The fact that by contemporary standards much of this information is unsatisfactory because of its fragmentary character does not detract from the very real achievement of ethnographers who because of the conditions under which they work, are fortunate to be able to provide information at all in some circumstances. It is inappropriate to contrast a scant ethnographic survey of a remote area out of contact with administrative centers where conditions of work are arduous, and where no written record is available, with comparable coverage of a community at the fringe of a literate society. That there are gaps in the record that may surprise the nonspecialists will come as no surprise to the anthropologist. The number of professional anthropologists until the end of World War II was very small and the number of those who had done extensive field work was smaller still. The impossiblity of anything like world ethnographic coverage with the limited resources available to the professional is apparent.

THE DISCIPLINE

The constitution of the discipline is a matter of national traditions and, within these, of the relative emphases of schools of theory. Roughly, while Americans have sustained the broadest possible vision of the "science of man: with all wide-ranging concern for the biological and historical conditions of his development," the British tradition has not been so broad in their statement of the anthropological mission. Rather than being branches of the same subject, physical anthropology and folkloristic and linguistic studies are seen as, at best, allied subjects to what is here termed the "social science" part of anthropology, social or cultural anthropology. (As I have noted, by no means would all social anthropologists choose to identify their subject with social science, but it is convenient so to group them here.) However inadequate this may be as a definition of its present activities, it tends to be the case that *social anthropology* describes social organizations or relational systems primarily, and cultural anthropology has specialized in the analysis of symbolic behavior. These lines are not clearly drawn and, in fact, despite the programmatic distinctions, there is considerable similarity in the work done by these "schools."

(Because this distinction no longer seems especially crucial and in order to avoid the awkwardness of "sociocultural," social and cultural anthropology will be used as synonyms in this chapter.)

American anthropology, with its concentration on both cultural and social objects, refers to either "cultural" or "social" anthropology as the specialization nearest social science, while the British, denying an interest in the concept of "culture," prefer "social" anthropology.

Whatever the designations, there is a division based on objectives or goals that gives rise to the major categories of relevance to social scientific anthropology: the so-called "descriptive-historical" fields and the "social-analytic" fields.

More simply stated, there is a distinction between the espousal of a natural historical, or of a scientific, model for anthropological inquiry. The descriptive emphasis is characteristic of both *ethnography* (the description of customs or the way of life of a single culture) and *anthropological archaeology* (the description of the material remains of past cultures and their interpretation). This contrasts with the aims of *social anthropology*, which seeks to establish general propositions about social life like those at which other social sciences aim. It also contrasts with *ethnology*, which may, through use, mean very much the same thing or may be larger in scope, referring to the theoretical and comparative study of human custom that includes both social anthropology and all other theoretical approaches to the understanding of man and his works. Social anthropology historically was said to be synonymous with "comparative sociology" or sociology of primitive people.

Anthropologists have spent an inordinate amount of time in defining their discipline; they continue to do so. Though it lacks rigor, one of the conventions of the definition is to contrast anthropology with the subjects with which it is most closely connected intellectually: history and sociology. It differs from the former in having been concerned primarily with people without the written tradition that provides the material for historical work and, from the latter, by being interested in peoples who lack the technological and organizational complexity of those urban societies that have interested sociologists. In short, anthropology has, in the past, primarily studied primitives and groups on the periphery of sophisticated cultures. This situation is changing both in response to the transformation of the non-Western world and because of the willingness of anthropologists to try their techniques on more complex systems. When they have shifted their attention to contemporary Western society, anthropologists have tended to approach it as they would a primitive field, with a close study of an isolate—a village or a community. W. Lloyd Warner's Yankee City series is a pioneering attempt at the application of anthropology to modern society. Robert and Helen Lynd's *Middletown* (1956; 1959), Carl Withers' *Plainville, U.S.A.* (1945), Evon Vogt's *Modern Homesteaders* (1955), and Charles Keil's *Urban Blues* (1966) all employ anthropological method for the study of contemporary communities and subcultures in the United States. A small but impressive list of ethnographies of modern European communities illustrates the reward to be derived from the anthropological study of communities long in contact with complex, urban society. Julian Pitt-Rivers' *The People of the Sierra* (1954), Ronald Frankenberg's *Village on the Border* (1957), L. Wylie's *Village in the Vaucluse* (1957), Conrad Arensberg's *Irish Countrymen* (1959), and Michael Kenny's *A Spanish Tapestry: Town and Country in Castile* (1961) are within the tradition of anthropological community studies.

Anthropology's claim to exclusive concentration on the primitive world has been challenged for a very long time by persisting interest in enclaves in touch with civilizational centers, but maintaining their traditional character. Most of these are included in the domain of studies of *peasant life*. Within anthropology, the importance of these studies has grown enormously. In the total corpus of ethnographic material published each year, those devoted to the study of peasants from all parts of the world would constitute surely more than half the total. Oscar Lewis' *Village Life in Northern India* (1958), the same author's *Tepoztlán: A Village in Mexico* (1960), S. Mintz' *Worker in the Cane* (1960), Robert Redfield's *Folk Culture in Yucatan* (1941), and E. R. Leach's *Pul Eliya: A Village in Ceylon* (1961) present a varied sample of books based on work with peasants.

All disciplines have conventions about the form in which the publication of findings and speculations reaches the relevant public. Those of anthropology, though they differ only slightly from those of other social sciences, are, as forms of communication, in themselves instructive of the discipline's organization. To the novice, the most unusual of these is the use of the term "monograph" and the diversity of publications included in this genre. A treatise on a single subject, a monograph has a special place in anthropology as the form in which ethnographic information is typically conveyed to the anthropological public in its most polished state as the definitive report in full detail on the life of a people or some aspect of it. In the major monographs on the subject, social anthropologists find not only data, but interpretations of great theoretical import as well and, on the whole, the contributions on which anthropological reputation rest. Thus, the monographs are the center of anthropological literature, and not just repositories of data.

THE CHARACTER OF THE LITERATURE

The reader who is introduced to anthropology in the second half of the 1960's finds a literature that is substantially different in scope and emphasis, and especially as to quantity and form of publication from that of a decade earlier. Though a survey of anthropological writings would elicit very few selections of topics without precedent in the 1950's, the sheer numbers of writers and consumers and the attendant bulk of publication are sufficient to have transformed a subject largely caught up in its own technical and methodological problems into one that has close contact with worldly concerns affected more by political changes in the non-Western world than by development in the discipline. The vastly increased possibilities for anthropological research and of publications reporting on the findings are one area in which expansion of the literature is obvious. The increasing number of anthropologists who have done field work, their obligations to publish, and the trend toward earlier publication of major monographs than was the case at an earlier period, and the fact of less elapsed time between field work and appearance of results, have importantly altered the corpus of ethnographic literature in most accessible sections of the non-Western world. Increased interest in the nonanthropological social scientists and other scholars, as well as governments, has produced a public which supports markedly improved bibliographical tools, synopses, and the like, of great importance in facilitating anthropological studies and research. The number and quality as well as the availability of bibliographical guides to nearly all regions and for all subjects have been greatly improved over the last decade. For the beginner, and for the small library desiring to improve the quality of its anthropological collection, American Anthropological Association Memoir 95, *Resources for the Teaching of Anthropology* (1963), edited by Mandelbaum, Lasker, and Albert, is a valuable source listing standard works by topic and area. The Royal Anthropological Institute of Great Britain and Northern Ireland now publishes a quarterly *Index to Current Periodicals* (1963–) indexing the periodical articles in its large collection, chiefly by area. UNESCO's *International Bibliography of Cultural Anthropology* (1955–) surveys both books and periodical contributions.

Also for the library, the recent publication of the catalogues of special collections (by the G. H. Hall Co.) is an event worthy of special note. The facsimile catalogues of the Peabody Museum, the Bishop Museum, and the Northwestern University Africa collection are invaluable tools for advanced research students and, of course, for scholars. For readers with some anthropological knowledge, the *Biennial Reviews of Anthropology*, edited by B. Siegel, (1959–) are an important source of reference to the periodical literature in English. These volumes, containing bibliographical essays on topics which vary slightly from volume to volume, maintain a high standard of cogency and selectivity. Essays on physical anthropology, linguistics, and archaeology as well as standard social organizational topics, are included.

Another sort of change in the composition of anthropological literature in recent years has been brought about by the demand for quality instructional materials specifically written for students. The standard textbooks of Kroeber (1948), Forde (1934), Boas (1938), Herskovits (1948), Beals and Hoijer (1965), as these have inevitably become dated, have been replaced not so much by other texts as by books of readings and selections of monographs written specifically for pedagogic purposes. *Readings in Anthropology* by E. A. Hoebel, J. D. Jennings, and E. R. Smith (1955) and M. H. Fried's *Readings in Cultural and Physical Anthropology* (1959) in two volumes are both widely used, as is Peter Hammond's collection *Cultural and Social Anthropology: Selected Readings* (1964). The Prentice Hall Foundations of Modern Anthropology series publishes comprehensive introductions to anthropological subfields written by specialists for undergraduates. Recently, under the general editorship of George and Louise Spindler, a series of original *Case Studies in Cultural Anthropology* has provided the instructor with a quantity of usually excellent, brief, original monographs of use to both introductory and more advanced students. Much that is marketed for classroom use is, encouragingly, sufficiently good to count as important to the discipline in its own right. These monographs might supplement collections of essays presenting theoretical materials or an introductory text.

While there seem to be few attempts to write textbooks for general anthropology, texts introducing social anthropology have appeared in surprising numbers. Paul Bohannan's *Social Anthropology* (1963) is the most eclectic of these attempts to survey the anthropologists' contribution to the study of social organization. R. Firth's *Elements of Social Organization* (1956), J. Beattie's *Other Cultures* (1964), G. Pocock's *Social Anthropology* (1961), and Peter Lienhardt's *Social Anthropology* (1964), though all directed to nonanthropological audiences, are presentations of more systematic personal statements than views of the work of the discipline. This is also true of M. Gluckman's *Politics, Law and Ritual in Tribal Society* (1965) which contrasts with the others by reason of its emphasis on the importance of political and legal process in the understanding of social organization.

Books of readings, of both original and collected papers, reports of seminars and conferences, important papers collected from periodicals and series to describe an area or to illuminate a problem or concept are now the characteristic form of publication in anthropology as in the other social sciences. The paperback revolution has played a role in this change. Such series as the American Museum of Natural History Sourcebooks in anthropology, containing papers by contemporary and historical figures in the discipline on such topics as economics, witchcraft, and war have radically altered the way in which anthropological reading is undertaken.

Books devoted exclusively to lengthy, sustained analyses of theoretical issues by single authors are rare in anthropology. Theoretical contributions are normally made in papers focused on problems that require the introduction of new data or the interpretation of existing data in the light of new ideas. Collections of papers on allied subjects published as books have a long history in anthropology, but books of collected essays of the work of eminent contemporary theoreticians are far more numerous than in the past. To such important collections as Franz Boas' *Race, Language and Culture* (1940), Alfred Kroeber's *Nature of Culture* (1952), Alfred Radcliffe-Brown's *Structure and Function in Primitive Society* (1952), a number of books of collected theoretical essays have been added in the past few years: E. E. Evans-Pritchard, *Essays in Social Anthropology* (1962) and *The Position of Women in Primitive Societies and Other Essays* (1965), B. Firth, *Essays on Social Organization and Values* (1964), C. Kluckhohn, *Culture and Behavior* (1962), E. R. Leach, *Rethinking Anthropology* (1961), C. Lévi-Strauss, *Structural Anthropology* (1963), R. Lowie, *Selected Papers in Anthropology* (1960), G. P. Murdock, *Culture and Society* (1965), and M. P. Redfield, *Human Nature and the Study of Society* (1962) and *The Social Uses of Social Science* (1963).

ETHNOLOGY. Ethnographic studies, though not labeled as such, go back very far in time. A concern with the explanation of custom and mores marks the antecedents of contemporary ethnography. The account of Herodotus of the customs of the people he visited is the first ethnographic description of which we have record. Subsequent, particularly post-fifteenth-century, accounts of travelers, mercantile explorers and missionaries, as well as accounts of voyages of discovery, constitute basic source materials for social anthropological and ethnological studies. Expeditions were typically charged with responsibility for gathering ethnographic materials to aid governments in the task of evaluating the nature of peoples contacted and their resources, but the standards fell far short of those of modern scientific anthropology. Occasionally observers were sent by governments to accompany parties for the purpose of gathering ethnographic materials to aid in conquest or administration and, for the most part, such ethnographic material is incidental to the reports of other aspects of expeditions. These reports appear either separately or in some notable collections. Of particular interest are the works issued by the Hakluyt Society, founded in 1846 for the purpose of publishing. The series of publications following James Cook's famous voyages is also of interest to anthropologists. Such works usually provide only brief, sketchy accounts of any one tribe or group of tribes. (An exception is provided by the *Jesuit Relations* [73 vols., 1896–1901], an invaluable collection of ethnographic materials covering the period from 1610 to 1791 in northeastern North America which is an account of extended contact with the aborigines of one area.)

ANTHROPOLOGY 51

Another source for these accounts is Edward Godfrey Cox's *A Reference Guide to the Literature of Travel, Including Voyages, Geographical Descriptions, Adventures, Shipwrecks, and Expeditions*, published in three volumes—*The Old World, The New World*, and *England*—by the University of Washington (1935-49). These accounts by travelers, discoverers, and conquistadores, however, were not systematic expositions of culture; their authors were more interested in recounting daring feats or describing quaint and exotic customs than in furthering the knowledge of the varieties and similarities of human culture. The influence of contact with the West on the best cultures and on Western civilization as well has attracted the attention of professional historians in increasing numbers. Records of these cultural encounters are outside anthropological literature, but close to the interests of anthropologists. Examples are D. Lach's (1965) *Asia in the Making of Europe* and P. Curtin's *The Image of Africa: British Ideas and Action, 1780-1850* (1965).

Modern anthropological works began to appear in the middle of the nineteenth century. Prior to that time there had been various attempts to systematize the history of man in universal developmental frameworks, or to study single institutions for the purpose of reconstructing their origins. Some of these were of a high order of scholarship and provided arguments (for example, Grotius' defense of the comparative method) still considered valid. More frequently, they were simply speculative accounts of origins or stages of development which have ceased to have importance for anthropological thought. The data available were used in support of a priori developmental schemes, and, where data were not available, rational conjecture filled the lacunae.

Sir Henry Maine, John F. McLennan, and Edward B. Tylor in Britain; Johann Bachofen in Switzerland; Lewis H. Morgan and John W. Powell in the United States; Philipp W. A. Bastian, Gustav F. Klemm, and Friedrich Ratzel in Germany; and Emile Durkheim in France may be regarded as the founders of contemporary social and cultural anthropology. The distinctiveness of the new approach which characterizes the work of these "founders" of the discipline, as compared with earlier writers on anthropological or ethnographic topics, lies in their search for generalizations about the evolution and growth of human culture, or some part of it, in the manner of natural scientific investigation. The belief that man could be studied scientifically was basic to the development of ideas of social evolution. Maine, who dealt chiefly with legal and political institutions, attempted to explain the changes in social relations, from simple to complex societies, in terms of the gradual replacement of status by contract relationships. Morgan developed a theory to describe various stages of cultural evolution from savagery to barbarism and, further, to civilization. His field researches with the Iroquois (*League of the Iroquois*, 1904) and his treatise on kinship (*Consanguinity and Affinity*, 1870) advanced the subject in its scientific aims. Bachofen attempted to show the historical primacy of matriarchy over patriarchy, and McLennan's work centered on an attempt to formulate a natural history of the family.

Generalizations in earlier writings were based chiefly on common sense rather than on reliable empirical data, or they were static associations between certain given traits and given conditions, rather than attempts to explain why and in what manner cultural traits or institutions change under the impact of external or internal factors. But in the course of the nineteenth century, some empirical confirmation was provided for the theory of progress, which had dominated much of the thinking of social scientists during the eighteenth and nineteenth centuries. This was accomplished by the final destruction of the belief in the history of creation related in Genesis, and the gradual development of evolutionary ideas in biology, which found empirical verification in paleontological and geological data. The result of these developments was to induce social scientists to turn to the development of theories of social change and social evolution, similar to biological and geological theories.

The impact of the idea of biological evolution, therefore, was of the greatest importance to the development of anthropology; moreover, although modern cultural anthropologists view the theories of such writers as Lewis H. Morgan (*Ancient Society*, 1877, 1959) and (*Primitive Marriage*, 1865, 1870) and Johann Bachofen (*Das Mutterrecht*, 1861, 1948) as antiquated, they acknowledge the profound value which the work of these men had in furthering the study of social anthropology (see the section on evolutionism below). At the same time, there are many parts of the work of Sir Henry Maine (*Ancient Law*, 1861, 1917) or Edward B. Tylor (*Researches into the Early History of Mankind and the Development of Civilization*, 1865, 1878, and *Primitive Culture*, 1871, 1958), and particularly Emile Durkheim and Friedrich Ratzel (*Völkerkunde*, 1885), which are considered largely valid by many modern students of social anthropology. With the exception of Morgan, these were "armchair" theorists who collated data from various sources. Much of the criticism directed toward these students has pointed out the relatively uncritical use of available source materials. The critical approach to data has largely been characteristic of twentieth-century anthropology, particularly American anthropology.

In its early years, in the 1840's and '50's, anthropological interests were carried on by associations of amateurs. These displayed the same variety of interests and approaches to the study of man which has characterized later anthropology. Anthropology continued primarily as an avocational pursuit until late in the century. However, by the early

1900's, much of the present structure of the academic discipline of anthropology had come into being—chairs of anthropology and anthropology departments were created. Museums, government agencies (interested in colonial or aboriginal peoples), and universities were all contributing to anthropological researches.

A great many schools of anthropological thought have existed since the 1850's. Some of these have ceased to be significant, but a surprising number have survived in only slightly modified form to the present day.

HISTORY OF THE DISCIPLINE

The recent interest in the history of science has produced some writing about the historical development of anthropology, especially about the evolutionists and their critics, but despite the apparent need for a first-rate treatment of its development, there does not seem to be a history of anthropology of intellectual merit relevant for understanding the present state of the discipline. Here, as elsewhere, the differences between schools and national traditions in their understanding of the nature and goals of the subject at this time suggest that sectarian accounts promoting the ascendency of one set of ancestors over another is the best that can be hoped for. Of the early history or the prehistory of the subject, sufficiently remote to render most readers neutral, if not disinterested, there is the greatest potential for the writing of a generally acceptable account. Alfred C. Haddon's *History of Anthropology* (1910) continues to be of interest. Robert Lowie's *History of Ethnological Theory* (1937) remains the standard text, though its deficiencies for an understanding of the antecedents of most problems relevant to contemporary anthropology are apparent. Glyn Daniel in *A Hundred Years of Archaeology* (1950) and in *The Idea of Prehistory* (1963), surveying the development of prehistory, writes on the emergence of the study of man's past and the changes in the conception of man that were prerequisites and consequences of scientific anthropology. E. E. Evans-Pritchard's *Social Anthropology* (1952), though it does not claim to be an introduction to the subject, is one of the most valuable accounts of the traditions contributing to social anthropology. A large number of writers on theoretical topics have reason to review aspects of the field in constructing their own theories. Lévi-Strauss's *Structural Anthropology* (1963) has some especially noteworthy passages on history important to the understanding of his own work, especially American historical anthropology. There are a few histories directed toward student and popular audiences. H. R. Hays's *From Ape to Angel* (1958) is a lively, if somewhat inaccurate, account of the development of modern anthropology. Its strengths lie in the anecdotal accounts of nineteenth-century practitioners; anthropology as a social science is scarcely discussed. Stanley Edgar Hyman's *The Tangled Bank* (1962) contains chapters analyzing the writings of Darwin, Frazer, and Freud. *The Golden Age of American Anthropology* (1960), Margaret Mead and Ruth Bunzel (eds.) is a reader in the development of American ethnology that contains, in its brief introduction to its constituent sections, much material of interest for the understanding of the recent past of American anthropology. Edward Preble and Abram Kardiner's *They Studied Man* (1961) concentrates on the theoretical advances by recent major contributors to social and cultural anthropology, emphasizing the relevance of anthropology to other social sciences. This book is primarily an exposition of theory rather than a history of the science.

Anthropological interest in its own history and the recognition of anthropology by historians of science are both detectable trends. At present, a reevaluation of the recent past of the discipline is evident. The new journal *History of the Behavioral Sciences* is further proof of the new legitimation of concern for history within the part of anthropology modeling its work on science. This follows a period when concern for history or history of theory was thought to contradict scientific aims.

One of the consequences of the outpouring of paperback books in the social sciences is the new availability of large numbers of heretofore inaccessible, out of print, "classics" of the field. The bond of common concern with descriptive ethnography perhaps makes "classical" contributions more attractive to anthropologists than to other branches of the social sciences. One by one, many of the most famous writings of nineteenth- and early twentieth-century anthropologists appear. The University of Chicago Press Classics in Anthropology series under the editorship of Paul Bohannan has republished James Mooney's *The Ghost-Dance Religion and the Sioux Outbreak of 1890* (1965), a remarkable piece of field ethnography—one of the most important accounts of nativistic movement; *Kwakiutl Ethnography* (1966), the major report of Boas' extensive Kwakiutl studies; Morgan's *Houses and Houselife of the American Aborigines* (1965), and E. B. Tylor's *Researches Into the History of Mankind* (1878). Basic Books also has a Classics in Anthropology series, edited by Stanley Diamond, concentrating on a more recent period of anthropology's growth. Robert Lowie's *Culture and Ethnology* (1917) and Paul Radin's *The Method and Theory of Ethnology* (1933) have been published, with new introductions underlining the significance of the classic to the development of the field.

Social anthropology has a more theoretically important line of republished classics in the series of newly translated monographs from the French sociological–anthropological tradition of the Durkheim school, translated and introduced by social anthropologists at the

Institute of Social Anthropology at Oxford. Marcel Mauss, *The Gift* (1954), R. Hertz, *Death and the Right Hand* (1960), and Durkheim and Mauss, *Primitive Classification* (1963), among others, have more than historical interest. As is the case with sociological theory, American anthropology has been changed by the belated realization of the significance of the writings of European sociologists in the early part of the century, especially, of course, Durkheim and Weber. Durkheim, because of his obvious importance to British social anthropology, is much better known in general anthropology, but there is evidence that the younger generation of American anthropologists, familiar with and influenced by American sociological theory, are making greater use of Weber's writings as interest in problems of religion, politics, and modernization challenge kinship as the focus of social anthropological attention.

EVOLUTIONISM. It was stated above that some variety of evolutionistic thought seemed to pervade the anthropological theorizing of the nineteenth century. The intellectual biases and predispositions toward evolutionistic theory antedated Charles Darwin, but notions of biological evolution did change the view of social evolutionists somewhat. The radical rationalist view gave way to the notion that man might have little to do with influencing the shape of some kinds of institutions which evolve independently, according to laws of social evolution.

In general, the theory of cultural evolution was focused on gross developments in the succession of simple types of institutions by complex types, all of them being categorized according to their presumed central function. Herbert Spencer's list is typical: domestic, ceremonial, political, ecclesiastical, professional, industrial. Evolutionists at the end of the century placed a high value on ethnographic fact. The difficulty with the earlier theories, so they thought, was that they were much too speculative. They, on the other hand, could make use of accumulated data furnished by an assortment of reporters. In the sense that they took these statements of fact and arranged them in huge compendia, according to some classification or other, they were more empirical than their eighteenth-century prototypes.

In addition to the idea of progress and the assumption of an inevitable, determined development, most anthropologists assumed the "psychic unity" of mankind. In simplest terms, this theory holds that all men, other than the pathological, have the same general instincts or drives, and all are capable of the same processes of cognition. In both cases, the assumption has to do with capabilities, not with cultural modifications and the content of cognition under specific circumstances. If, however, the specific societies are taken to be the essential or typical aspects, then the working assumption may lead one astray. Similarly, if capabilities are taken as actualities, then one is bound to misinterpret. The latter situation led to the interpretation of primitive religion in purely intellectualistic terms by Tylor (*Primitive Culture*, 1871, 1958), and of magic by Frazer (*The Golden Bough*, 1894, 1951). Some of these concepts have been found useful in modified form. The latter work has had tremendous influence in creating interest in anthropology among educated laymen.

All Victorian anthropologists were not equally evolutionistic in orientation. Some assumed the evolutionist framework, but without explicit concern for its major outlines. Edward A. Westermarck (*The History of Human Marriage*, 1889, 1921) and Maine (*Ancient Law*, 1917) both questioned the unilineal scheme of the evolution of the family which postulated primitive promiscuity as the first and monogamy as the final stage of the development of that institution.

In the United States, cultural evolution was challenged by the American school associated with Franz Boas, with its advocacy of an extremely cautious, empirical anthropology firmly rooted in field ethnography and avoiding premature theorizing, large-scale generalizing, or interpretive frameworks of the sort identified with cultural evolution. The most famous schemes of unilineal evolution, like that proposed by Morgan in *Ancient Society* (1877, 1959), were rejected because they did not stand up in the opinion of critics, when challenged methodologically by the growing corpus of ethnographic fact. Whatever the reasons, outside of archaeology and popular anthropology, few anthropologists favorable to the idea of cultural evolution or cultural cumulation were conspicuous in the second quarter of the twentieth century. Though it has its own national history, separate from that of the United States, British anthropology too abandoned cultural-social evolutionism along with all large-scale speculation about the stages in the progress of man, preferring specialized, close studies of particular problems or particular peoples. The important exception to this is to be found in the work of Leslie White, who has written extensively on his own view of evolutionism. The interest in evolutionism has recently grown on several fronts and the number of young scholars sharing White's views, in whole or in part, has made an important impact on the discipline's thought on this subject in the past decade.

White's central concept is culture and he defines the discipline, anthropology, as "culturology," the science of culture. The essence of culturology is the assumption of the superorganic view: that culture has its own laws of development which neither individuals nor groups can control. For White, man's past unfolds as a history of advancing control over sources of energy, and the course of history is marked by the differences in the ways and magnitudes "in which energy is harnessed and expended." This implies that the proper study of culture will place technology, the culturally ordered used of energy, at the center of its interests as the determinant of cultural systems. White considers his theory of culture to be the same as that of his predecessors, Morgan and Tylor, but to be a more fully articulated theory. The unique capacity of man to engage in symbolic processes, "to symbol," is, for White, man's distinctive property that brought culture into being. These views on cultural evolution are presented in *The Science of Culture* (1949) and the *Evolution of Culture* (1959), and in the Festschrift volume, *Essays in the Science of Culture* (1960), G. E. Dole and R. L. Carneiro (eds.).

A controversial contribution to cultural theory, influenced by White, is M. D. Sahlins and E. R. Service (eds.), *Evolution and Culture* (1960). These essays suggest hypotheses and concepts that supplement and modify White's evolutionary theory.

The view of evolution represented by the work of Julian Steward and his students is an alternative to White's. Steward stresses the importance of the ecological factors interacting with social arrangements rather than cultural (technological) capacities alone (*Theory of Culture Change*, 1955).

The current evolutionism is multilineal rather than unilineal. It admits the possibility of various lines of cultural development, positing no necessary stages of cultural achievement through which all societies must pass. Multilineal evolution postulates, rather, that similar social forms having like functions have developed through similar, though independent, adaptational processes and sequences. Steward believes that through a detailed analysis of such instances we may be able eventually to formulate universal laws of cultural development. The data used in the formulation and testing of these hypotheses of multilineal evolution concerning cross-cultural regularities are taken both from ethnological and archaeological sources. In *Irrigation Civilizations: a Comparative Study* (1955), edited by Steward, an interesting attempt is made to bring together both New and Old World archaeological materials in an attempt to test one of the hypotheses relating to the conditions of the development of civilization.

Both White and Steward provide the kind of ethnological thought that has relevance for archaeologists in their work of reconstructing long-range cultural changes.

The centennial observance of the publication of Darwin's *Origin of Species*, 1959, was the occasion for the publication of a number of significant appraisals of the present state of anthropology's interest in evolution. The three volumes of Sol Tax (ed.), *Evolution after Darwin* (1960), with the third volume specifically concerned with the evolution of man, provided a major reappraisal of the state of evolutionary ideas. The Anthropological Society of Washington published an unusually stimulating set of papers in its *Evolution and Anthropology: A Centennial Appraisal* (1959), B. J. Meggars (ed.), discussing the status and prospects of evolutionary thought in all phases of general anthropology.

The subject of the evolution of human social behavior has developed markedly in this decade. Largely due to new theoretical directions in physical anthropology, old questions concerning the emergence of culture have been revived. Significantly, the role of culture as a factor in human evolution has been the subject of lively speculation and study. The papers in S. L. Washburn (ed.), *The Social Life of Early Man* (1961) treat the problems of the emergence of early man and speculate about his early social arrangements from a variety of points of view. The symposium papers, *The Processes of On-Going Human Evolution* (Lasker [ed.], 1960), considered culture in the selective process, and Howell and Washburn in their contribution to *The Evolution of Man* (Tax, [ed.], 1960) discussed the importance of technology in man's development.

Increasing anthropological interest in primatology is closely related to renewed concern for some of the puzzling features of the evolution of human social life. The "ethnography" of infrahuman primates is surely one of the exciting developments of the past decade and it has stimulated thought concerning the protohominid phase of evolution. A useful collection of the behavioral studies of primates with a foreword characterizing their relevance to anthropology is Irven DeVore's *Primate Behavior: Field Studies of Monkeys and Apes* (1965).

AMERICAN HISTORICAL ANTHROPOLOGY

American anthropology has a diverse origin. Though Lewis H. Morgan is one of the acknowledgedly great figures of early theoretical anthropology, his influence was probably greater elsewhere than in his own country, the United States. The early American anthropologists were not as much interested, on the whole, in ethnology as in ethnography, particularly in the study of American Indians. By the later part of the nineteenth century, the Indians no longer posed a threat to the whites. Many persons were beginning to romanticize the "vanishing Americans," and were eager for detailed information about their pre-contact mode of life. There was, in general, a growing interest in ethnographic subjects; new museums were founded, and in 1879, largely through the work of Major John Welsley Powell, the Bureau of American Ethnology was established. This Bureau continued to publish a sizable proportion of the available ethnographic materials dealing with aboriginal American subjects. The famous Zuñi studies by Frank Cushing and the studies of the prairie Indians by Fletcher and La Flecheare were published in the BAE annual reports. The text of publication of ethnographical materials was later taken over by the Smithsonian Institution.

The school of anthropology developed under the guidance of Franz Boas, called the American Historical School, has been most significant in shaping American anthropological thinking. It has been viewed as stemming primarily from a reaction against ideas of social and cultural evolution, though it bears no resemblance to the cultural diffusionist schools discussed above (which were also reacting against evolutionism). Boas contended that it was essential to control knowledge of the specific historical past of the peoples studied, that primitive peoples as well as great civilizations had histories which were important to the understanding of present cultural situations. This led Boas and some of his followers to seek increasingly refined techniques for reconstructing the histories of nonliterate cultures.

Boas' influence on the development of American anthropology has been immense, though he did not himself write a major book. Some of his articles and essays have been collected in *Race, Language, and Culture* (1940). An earlier collection of technical papers, *The Mind of Primitive Man* (1911, 1938) is a slightly more popular presentation of Boas' views. These views are not amenable to concise presentation. The influence of Boas is felt mostly through his students. He is not identified with a single "cause" in anthropology, unless his emphasis on the importance of field work would be so considered. Boas' own field work was done with the Central Eskimo and with the Kwakiutl Indians of Vancouver Island. His work is highly regarded for the accuracy and thoroughness with which he studied those aspects of culture which he thought relevant for anthropological inquiry. Boas is most frequently criticized for his choice of subject matter—i.e., for omissions from field study—and more importantly, for his reluctance to generalize on the basis of his work. Appraisals of the influences of Boas are available in the Melville Herskovits biography, *Franz Boas*, and the AAA publication, *The Anthropology of Franz Boas* (1959), edited by W. Goldschmidt. Leslie White has been sharply critical of the influences Boas exerted over American Anthropology. His criticisms have been published in *The Ethnography and Ethnology of Franz Boas* (1963).

Historical reconstruction both inside and outside the anthropology framework has been a continuing concern of some American anthropologists. It is the field of cultural anthropology which is most closely allied with archaeology. Some anthropologists have contended that anthropology is basically a historical discipline whose business is to test laws formulated by those who are "foolish" enough to present them; it is not the business of anthropology to formulate such laws.

It is easily seen how reconstructing the history of nonliterate peoples should have become such an important part of anthropology. Sociologists dealing with the Western world, or with other societies (though this is infrequent) that had writing, could take advantage of a variety of records available for these societies and of the research of historians. For the most part, they did not have to do sociological and historical analysis (in the sense both of descriptive integration and chronological work) at the same time, and prehistorical research was not a part of their training or interest.

Techniques and literature of both linguistics and archaeology are available to the anthropologist in his attempts at reconstruction. Following Edward Sapir, American anthropologists have been particularly sensitized to the potential value for cultural reconstruction of linguistics techniques. Linguistic reconstruction, which is a part of linguistics proper, is based on comparative techniques and provides formulations of the degree of relationship between languages, and thus of the relationship between peoples speaking related languages. Linguistic analysis, particularly comparison of lexical items, has been used as a basis for the reconstruction of earlier features of a culture, i.e., by comparing vocabulary the cultures share, it is possible to make inferences about the character of the culture at the time the languages diverged. Recently there have been added refinements in the field of linguistic reconstruction which are of considerable importance to anthropologists.

Archaeology has been the primary anthropological subfield concerned with the problems of reconstruction of the cultural past. Archaeologists have, of course, devised techniques for dating their findings, both in relative terms, e.g., by stratigraphy, and absolute, e.g., using dendrochronology and carbon 14 techniques. The reconstruction work of the archaeologist and the ethnologist have ordinarily been carried on as independent researches. Very recently, in line with the general trend toward interdisciplinary area work, there have been attempts to integrate archaeological and historical researches with ethnography and cultural geography, in an effort to provide a more comprehensive picture of man's relationship to the environment within a given area (see the following section).

CONTEMPORARY CONCERNS

CULTURE THEORY

The general result of the work in which almost all American students participated in some fashion during the last fifty years was the development of a particular set of theories, perhaps most conveniently summed up in Ralph Linton's *The Study of Man* (1936) and in Alfred Louis Kroeber's essays, *The Nature of Culture* (1952). The theory is somewhat eclectic, and there is not complete unanimity of definition among all its students. It is neither evolutionist nor rigidly functionalist. Culture elements or factors are considered, in the main, to be independent of each other, but it is freely acknowledged that for the participants in any culture the cultural elements have meaning and internal consistency. This view is summed up by Robert Redfield in a passage in his work, *The Folk Culture of Yucatan* (1941):

> In speaking of "culture" we have reference to the conventional understandings, manifest in act and artifact, that characterize societies. The understandings are the meanings attached to acts and objects. The meanings are conventional and therefore cultural insofar as they have become typical for the members of that society by reason of intercommunication among the members.

This definition clearly establishes the relationship between the reality of culture elements and the values and beliefs of the human group. Thus, even if two cultures have similar or identical institutions or artifacts, if different meanings are attached to these elements, the cultures are clearly different. The distinction among cultures chiefly consists of sets of culturally determined values and beliefs, rather than of objects and acts of man.

As it has developed, this conception of culture fits very well into the wider framework of "social relations" (including cultural anthropology, sociology, and social psychology) as it is presented by, for instance, Talcott Parsons and Edward A. Shils, editors of *Toward a General Theory of Action* (1951). It should be noted that the main stress is on interaction and mutual communication. Moreover, the emphasis on the meaning of the various cultural elements and their integration in a value system clearly implies that whatever independence is postulated for the elements is due chiefly to the method of investigation. We may analyze any one element by itself, assuming the others remain unchanged. If, however, the existence of a reasonably integrated system of values, which is necessary for a tolerable degree of social stability, is assumed, then the mutual interdependence of the various culture elements must be postulated. This mutual interdependence of the components of a culture arises from their subordination to a common system of values.

The acceptance of this conception has promoted the mutuality of interest between sociologists of the structural–functional persuasion and social anthropologists of this stamp. Additionally, it has focused anthropological interest on the crucial position of the concept of value in anthropological research. Perhaps the most useful review of the anatomy of cultural systems for the anthropologist is found in Parsons' *The Social*

System (1951). This outlines the areas of general agreement within the social sciences concerning the concept of culture: that it is shared, learned, and transmitted by symbols. Anthropology is considered to be, in this division of labor, the discipline charged with the investigation of cultural systems: ideas, beliefs, and values. These interests are pursued traditionally under headings such as primitive religion, comparative values, cultural history, and cultural personality.

The history of the use of the concept culture is a history, on the one hand, of definitions sharpening and refocusing observations and statements of problems and, on the other hand, of observations and immediate problems demanding the redefinition of concepts. Therefore, it is not surprising to find that anthropologists seem to mean different things when talking either of a culture or of culture in general, or that they use these concepts in different ways. Anthropological uses of the "culture" concept are not always informed by general theories of cultural systems. Clyde Kluckhohn and Alfred L. Kroeber compiled and ordered anthropological and other definitions of culture and have discussed culture theory in their excellent monograph, *Culture; A Critical Review of Concepts and Definitions* (1952).

Edward B. Tylor was the first to emphasize the concept of culture in English (*Primitive Culture*, 1871, 1958) as the central concept around which a new branch of knowledge was to form. (Klemm had used it much in the same fashion in Germany thirty years earlier.) For Tylor, culture is "that complex whole which includes knowledge, belief, art, law, morals, custom, and other capabilities and habits acquired by man as a member of society." Culture has been thought to consist of traits and institutions which can be subjected to historical (evolutionistic) investigation. In consequence of this view, several important studies were written which made comparative analyses of particular culture traits in several societies or tried to trace the evolution and changes of a single culture trait through time. One of the most famous comparative studies of a set of culture traits is Sir James G. Frazer's *The Golden Bough* (1894, 1951), which deals with certain aspects of religious belief. Later, such comparative studies were challenged on the grounds that the things compared were not of meaningful content. Whether or not such studies are methodologically admissible depends, of course, upon whether culture traits are considered sufficiently separable from one another to make possible the full examination of each in isolation from others. Interest in the reassessment of Frazer's method and reputation is represented in several recent papers by anthropologists on Frazerian anthropology and in I. C. Jarvie's *Revolution in Anthropology* (1964).

Questions of the place of origin of various aspects of culture were of particular concern to ethnological theorists in the early part of the twentieth century. The so-called diffusionist schools assumed the noninventiveness of man, which meant that aspects of human culture either have a common origin or have been invented only a small number of times and were then transmitted from culture to culture. The proof which representatives of the diffusionist school provide for their view is that certain culture traits are common to several societies, or that certain ornamental forms, or tools, or other aspects of culture are found in otherwise unrelated societies. The chief representatives of the view (heliocentricism) that the common origin for human cultural traits is to be found in ancient Egypt have been William J. Perry (*The Children of the Sun*, 1923, 1927) and Grafton Elliott Smith (*The Migrations of Early Culture*, 1915). A less one-sided, but still essentially diffusionist, theory is held by the culture-historical school, the main representative of which is Father Wilhelm Schmidt (*The Culture Historical Method of Ethnology*, 1939). This school sees its intellectual ancestor in Friedrich Ratzel, whose *Anthropogeographia* (1882-94, 1911) had a tremendous influence not only on anthropology but also on the development of human geography in Germany. The main adaptation to anthropology of Ratzel's ideas was undertaken by Fritz Graebner, who, in his *Methode der Ethnologie* (1911), outlined the program of the school which is called *Kulturkreise* (culture circles) process—i.e., geographically deployed complexes of culture are identified and converted into culture strata, which gives a chronology of events. The main object of this school was clearly antievolutionary. Many of its chief adherents were Roman Catholics, whose efforts, in essence, may be viewed as an attempt to reconcile ethnographic findings with the history of humanity outlined in the Scriptures. In contrast to some other anthropological schools, notably the functionalists, who were either nonhistorical or antihistorical in orientation, the cultural historical school and the diffusionists emphasize historical relationships and developments.

ARCHAEOLOGY. In the past two decades, archaeological awareness of the possible value, or relevance, of ethnological theory for interpretation of archaeological finds has grown. During the same period, social anthropologists and sociologists have become more interested in longterm social change, whether on an evolutionary model, or in terms of some other scheme of long-range development. Parsons' *Societies* (1966) and Eisenstadt's *Political Systems of Empire* (1963), formulating a new theory of social evolution, make use of archaeological accounts in their expositions. Eric Wolf, in *Sons of the Shaking Earth* (1959), includes a synthesis of Middle American archaeological data, freely interpreted, in his stimulating survey of the "people of Mexico and Guatemala: their land, history, and culture" for the past 20,000 years.

The archaeological approach associated with Professors Robert Braidwood and G. Willey has produced several volumes of real interest for the social anthropologist. The innovation of this "school" is in its methodology as well as interpretation. This entails a broad conception of the task of the archaeologist and his participation as a member of a team of scholars and scientists (paleobotanists, zoologists, geochronologists, and other nonarchaeological specialists in ancient culture) in aid of a broader understanding of cultural process. The emphasis of this approach is on archaeology as a technique providing data for the understanding of the major social and cultural transformations in man's history. The origins of agriculture and of cities and the interrelationship between these processes are problems of preeminent importance. Animal and plant domestication, food surpluses, specialization of labor, and the changes in human settlement patterns are topics of special interest. *Courses Toward Urban Life* (Robert J. Braidwood and Gorden R. Willey, 1962) presents the findings of a symposium surveying the transition from food gathering to agriculture in several parts of the world from the Ice Age to the rise of urban civilization and the common features of these transitions. In *The Evolution of Urban Society* (1966), Robert Adams presents a "comparative study of the processes of urbanization in Mesopotamia and Prehispanic Mexico." Taking his material from the development of the ancient Sumerian kingdoms and from urbanization in the valley of Mexico, Adams demonstrates that the processes that led from animal domestication to urbanization in both areas present underlying similarities in the conditions precipitating the processes, leading toward parallel developments, similar, but not necessarily following the same steps. The emphasis in the Braidwood-Willey volume is on the process of relationship of man to his environment as a result of animal and plant domestication. Adams' discussion, on the other hand, is largely in terms of social organization or relations. Cultural and social factors are more significant in this volume. Adams also describes the process leading to food production as an essential precondition to the "Urban Revolution." Other recent books that employ social science understandings for interpretation are Willey's *Introduction to American Archaeology*, Vol. I (1966), which presents with straightforward archaeological descriptions a cogent summary of the social significance of current knowledge of the archaeology of Middle and North America; K. Chang's *Archaeology of Ancient China* (1965), intellectually close to Braidwood's work, describes the autochthonous development of agriculture and urbanization in China, in the Huang-Ho (Yellow River) Valley, and the controversial *The Island Civilization of Polynesia* (1960) by R. Suggs with its account of the migration of Polynesians to their present area and the subsequent development of Polynesian society. (Suggs is sharply critical of the work of Heyerdahl's hypothesis of New World Polynesian contact.)

Though they do not themselves attempt to relate their discussions to the problems of social science, two recent works on ecological subtects are of potential interest to social anthropologists concerned with jhe evolution of human behavior. Karl W. Butzer in *Environment and Archaeology: An Introduction to Pleistocene Geography* (1964) discusses the impact that the Pleistocene had on the social life of early man. Butzer's concern is that of prehistoric geography, with an analysis of the Pleistocene environment, attempting to integrate it with cultural-historical perspective. A symposium paper on the ecological background relevant to the advent of early man is published in Howell and F. Bourliére, *African Ecology and Human Evolution* (1963) and in S. L. Washburn's *Social Life of Early Man* (1961).

CULTURE AND PERSONALITY. The field of culture-personality has occupied the attention of many able theoretically orientated American anthropologists. These investigators have examined various phases of the relationship between the two orders. In this research, anthropologists have been chiefly, but not exclusively, influenced by psychoanalytic thinking. The application of psychoanalytic and related psychological theories to the explanation of behavior in relatively simple groups promised to be particularly useful in explaining the aspects of the personality system that were shared by a plurality of the culture's members. Edward Sapir, in a series of programmatic papers reprinted in his *Selected Writings in Language, Culture and Personality* (1949), edited by David Mandelbaum, brought the possibilities to the attention of cultural anthropology. Several attempts were made to explain behavior patterns in a given culture by appeal to psychological types which were directly or indirectly derived from Freud's psychoanalytic concepts and theories. For example, one of the early works in this field, Ruth Benedict's *Patterns of Culture* (1934), uses the terminology of Carl G. Jung. Abram Kardiner, in *The Psychological Frontiers of Society* (1945), attempts to provide a general outline of the procedure and potential results of this method for studies of personality development. These are pioneer contributions to the field. Margaret Mead's *Coming of Age in Samoa* (1961) was an important test of the universality of psychoanalytic assumptions concerning adolescence. Subsequent contributions attempt to evaluate and measure the actual contribution made by psychological and psychiatric theories to anthropological and social relations research, and to restate the theoretical assumptions of this work afresh. Examples of these efforts can be found in a number of summary accounts, readers, and texts. For the total area, perhaps the most complete summary and bibliography of contributions before 1955, are to be found in Clyde Kluckhohn's "Culture and Behavior," in Gardiner Lindzey (ed.), *Handbook of Social Psychology* (1954).

The field of culture-personality covers a wide variety of types of work, including the analysis of the process of socialization and enculturation of children in different environments, the consequences of socialization for adult behavior, and its extension into standard behavior patterns (sometimes also called " national character"), as well as attempts to describe an entire culture in terms of the personality patterns of the individuals embraced by it. Since the earliest of these studies in the early 1930's, methods and theories in the field of culture and personality have been much refined, relying heavily on techniques from fields in psychology.

It is difficult for the amateur to detect the direction in which the culture-personality field is currently tending. Despite the pessimism expressed by many practitioners and observers in the 1950's, some aspects of this speciality show considerable vitality and, while older attempts to typify the model or basic character of populations are not much in evidence, more differentiated accounts of the relationship of aspects of personality to aspects of culture are. Academic psychologists have assumed a more significant role in the intellectual collaboration. F. K. Hsu's *Psychological Anthropology* (1961) and B. Kaplan's *Studying Personality Cross-Culturally* (1961) are important recent collections of articles that survey current research in the field. The latter (Kaplan) includes a major critical review of the field by Milton Singer. For the student, new books of readings and essays on culture-personality, like Robert Hunt's *Personalities and Cultures: Readings in Psychological Anthropology* (1966), are available, and an impressive eclectic view of all of the literature is to be found in Victor Barnouw, *Culture and Personality* (1963).

The field is no longer dominated by psychoanalytic approaches: A. F. C. Wallace's *Culture and Personality* (1961) especially stresses a cognitive and physiological approach to anthropology and suggests ways of viewing personality that may be more congenial to anthropologists averse to Freudian theory. Wallace is critical of the turn culture-personality thought has taken in considering culture to be an "external environment" pressed upon, and perceived by, individuals uniformly. In this pluralistic emphasis, denying that normal members of a society must have the same personality, Wallace returns to considerations that sparked Sapir's initial interest in the field. The view of culture-personality of M. G. Spiro differs from that of Wallace in generally accepting the significance of the findings and formulations of his predecessors in culture-personality and their model of culture learning. Spiro (Hsu, editor, 1961) argues for the importance of studies of personality and social system to explain the articulation of these two orders. This interest converges with that of social psychology.

The approach to ethnography through use of life histories has common intellectual origins with culture-personality, but, as a mode of gathering descriptive data, is separate from it and theoretically neutral. In a period when anthropology was concerned with reconstructing the past, life histories were gathered routinely since memory of informants was the only ethnographic way of knowing about the past of nonliterate peoples in detail. Interest in personality psychology gave added impetus to this task. L. L. Langness in *The Life History in Anthropological Science* (1965) surveys the history and development of the field. Of the many biographies now available, Paul Radin's *Crashing Thunder, The Autobiography of an American Indian* (Winnebago) (1926) is not only one of the first truly rigorous works of "ethnobiography," but also one of the best. Walter Dyk's *Son of Old Man Hat* (Navaho) (1938), Clellan Ford, *Smoke from Their Fires: the Life of a Kwakiutl Chief* (1941), and Lee Simmons, *Sun Chief* (Hopi) (1942) are other examples from the period when interest in this approach was strong in American Indian studies. Two more recent biographical works from Africa are M. F. Smith's *Baba of Karo, a Woman of the Muslim Hausa* (1955) and E. H. Winter, *Beyond the Mountains of the Moon: the Lives of Four Africans* (1959).

Cross-cultural studies of child-rearing practices from psychoanalytic and other psychological points of view have been especially identified with culture-personality. The contributions to this study by John and Beatrice Whiting are sufficiently distinctive to be termed "Whiting-type" studies. These are statistical studies of socialization practices and their correlations with cultural institutions. J. W. M. Whiting and I. L. Child, *Child-training and Personality Development: a Cross-Cultural Study* (1953) and F. W. Moore (ed.), *Readings in Cross-Cultural Methodology* (1961) are the seminal studies in this field. A number of subsequent studies have illustrated the value of the approach, e.g., Beatrice B. Whiting (ed.), *Six Cultures: Studies of Child-Rearing* (1963) which compares the results of the findings of six teams of researchers, I. L. Child, T. Storm, and J. Veroff, "Achievement Themes in Folklore Related to Socialization Practice," in J. W. Atkinson (ed.), *Motives in Fantasy, Action, and Society* (1958); and in the same volume J. Whiting, "Totem and Taboo—a Re-evaluation," correlating the presence of totemism with sleeping arrangements. A review of the methods for the field study of child-rearing by J. W. M. and B. B. Whiting is to be found in P. H. Mussen (ed.), *Handbook of Research Methods in Child Development* (1960).

The culture-personality development was stimulated by the interest of American anthropologists in cultural theory. It has been a controversial subject and is one of the enthusiasms that British social anthropology has not shared with its American counterpart. The Durkheimian derivation of British social anthropological theory with its rejection of psychological determinants for social behavior is as important a determinant of this attitude of disinterest in psychological anthropology as the rejection of the concept culture.

A new direction in anthropology's relationship with psychology is emerging in a variety of ways, with the exploration of cognitive, rather than personality, considerations as its focus. Interest in this field of inquiry is shared by social anthropologists on both sides of the Atlantic to the extent that both have been influenced by the writings of the renowned French ethnologist, Claude Lévi-Strauss, especially his *Totemism* (1963), and *The Savage Mind* (1966). In these remarkable books and in his essays, Lévi-Strauss reopens the discussion of the character of primitive thought processes that had remained closed by anthropologists for some years because of the problematic nature of the distinctions that had been made between (prelogical) primitive and (logical) civilized man. Lévi-Strauss holds that "the savage mind is logical in the same sense and the same fashion as ours" and that savage thought continues in modern man supplemented by scientific thought. Lévi-Strauss stresses the intellectuality of the primitive mind that demands and generates cultural order, or structure, through systems of classification. The significance of the thought of Lévi-Strauss in its influence on the anthropological world can only be noted here. *Mythologiques: le cru et le cuit* (1964), as yet unavailable in an English translation, is the first of three proposed volumes that examine the structures of New World mythologies, in the light of his structuralist theory.

Another trend in American anthropology with strong affinities to Lévi-Strauss's structuralism, sharing with it a common heritage of influence from structural linguistics and a complex history of cross-fertilization, is the approach called the "new ethnography," or "ethnoscience."

ETHNOSCIENCE. This approach differs from Lévi-Strauss's in being much less concerned with philosophical, specifically epistemological, issues. The new ethnography seeks to describe aspects of the cognitive culture, equated with culture as a whole, if this definition is accepted: "A culture itself amounts to the sum of a given society's folk classifications, all of that society's ethnoscience, its particular way of classifying its material and social universe" (Davenport in Romney and D'Andrade). The new ethnography proposes a method for processing ethnographic observation in such a way as to permit the ethnographer to discover those classificatory schemes and distinctions that are held by the culture's participants, reflecting the culture's cognitive system. The ethnographers who have experimented in this technique aspire to provide the subject with a means of describing culture that will be both replicable and accurate to facilitate the task of ethnographic comparison. There are a number of interesting papers by practitioners of this procedure on such subjects as disease categories, color categories, kinship terminology, ethnozoology, and weddings. Romney and D'Andrade's *Transcultural Studies in Cognition* is an excellent introduction to the approach. *Explorations in Cultural Anthropology* (1964), Ward Goodenough (ed.), contains a number of relevant papers in this tradition.

LINGUISTICS. While anthropological linguistics is too specialized to be surveyed in this bibliographical guide, some of its methods and findings have inspired changes in American social anthropology that require brief description. The advances in linguistics have given new direction to anthropologists interested in culture theory, who see in the success of linguistic techniques possibilities for improving culture theory generally. The new ethnography is the most obvious example. Some of its founders are themselves able linguists.

"Language and culture" is a name given the various studies that have attempted to examine the relationship between language and other cultural systems. In the recent past, language and (or *in*) culture studies primarily consisted of attempts to refine and/or test the hypotheses of Edward Sapir and Benjamin Lee Whorf concerning the interrelationship of the structure of language and the world view of its speakers. These formulations ranged from those which assert that linguistic categories determine thought processes to those contending that the language, to some extent, reflects the world view of the speaker. Readers who choose to approach this subject historically might begin with *The Selected Writings of Edward Sapir*, D. Mandelbaum (ed.) (1949), or with the volume in which Whorf presents his ideas on the role of language in organizing human experience, with examples from his own work with the Hopi Indians, *Language, Thought and Reality* (1956). Some criticisms and discussions as well as a resume of the researches stimulated by the Sapir-Whorf hypothesis are available in Harry Hoijer (ed.), *Language in Culture* (1954).

Facility in linguistics was very much a part of the American historical anthropologists of the Boas school, but in the post–World War II period, descriptive or structural linguistics was internally increasingly differentiated and on the whole was removed from general anthropological discourse as it became more specialized in its techniques and more sophisticated in its theory. Ideas on the role of language in culture were put aside because, while the linguists perfected their approaches, the social anthropological audience for this writing admired and despaired of being able to render descriptions of other aspects of the cultural system as elegant as those produced by linguists. A rapprochement of linguistics and social anthropology is much discussed at present, especially in the stimulating programmatic work of Dell Hymes, who foresees a new role for linguistics within the social sciences, made attractive by powerful, intellectually successful work in formal systems. His *Language in Culture and Society* (1964), compiled as a reader for instructors and university students, represents in one volume the full range of present social anthropological interest in language. Hymes contends that linguists in their field research and analysis should consider the social and cultural contexts of language as well as its specifically linguistic aspects. The readings included are organized by topic and suggest direction for research as well as surveying findings: (1) the scope of linguistic anthropology, (2) the evaluation of the differences and similarities between languages, (3) the relationship of world view to grammatical categories and of vocabulary to cultural focus, (4) the function of language in social structure and expressive speech, and (5) linguistic change. In another publication, *The Ethnography of Communication* (1964, John Gumperz and Dell Hymes [eds.]), Hymes discusses the place of language within the culture's total communication system. The writings of the sociologist Erving Goffman have aroused considerable interest among anthropologists interested in nonlinguistic forms of interpersonal communication in such books as *Presentation of Self in Everyday Life* (1956) and *Behavior in Public Places* (1963). For a less advanced treatment of the potential of linguistics as a social science, the essay, "A Perspective for Linguistic Anthropology," in *Horizons in Anthropology* (Tax, 1964), can be recommended as a lucid introductory treatment. An interesting set of papers on communications describing areas of mutual relevance to cultural anthropology, linguistics, psychology, and psychiatry is *Approaches to Semiotics* (1964, T. Sebeok, Alfred S. Hayes, and Mary Catherine Bateson [eds.]). The paper by Hayes on "Paralinguistics and Kinesics: Pedagogical Perspectives," usefully surveys these intriguing subjects bearing on cross-cultural understanding.

Cultural change, cultural contact, and political development all have implications for linguistic behavior. The rigorous treatment of language in its social setting is in its infancy, but several contributions to special problems in this area might be mentioned: Uriel Weinreich's *Languages in Contact* (1953), C. A. Ferguson and Gumperz (eds.), *Linguistic Diversity in South Asia Survey: Studies in Regional, Social and Functional Variation* (1960), and R. B. LePage, *The National Language Question* (1964). Bilingualism and multilingualism are discussed in F. A. Rice (ed.), *Study of the Role of Second Languages* (1959) and in papers in the journal *Anthropological Linguistics*, especially Vol. IV (1962).

Anthropological Linguistics, The International Journal of American Linguistics, Word, and *Language* regularly publish articles and reviews in anthropological linguistics, the latter publishing excellent comprehensive biennial bibliographical essays. The significance and nature of the transformational movement associated with Professor Noam Chomsky is reviewed and evaluated in Archibald Hill's *The Promises and Limitations of the Newest Type of Grammatical Analysis* (1965).

SOCIAL ANTHROPOLOGY

Social anthropology developed in the latter half of the nineteenth century as a subject concerned with the development of general theories of the evolution of human social arrangement. It was in some respects the product of interests in translating evolutionary formulations into the social realm, but its history is more complicated than this and was importantly an outgrowth of, or a descendant of, theories of economic, political, and social institutions that come from the Enlightenment. The most cogent account of the history of social anthropology may be found in E. E. Evans-Pritchard's *Social Anthropology* (1952). Religion and the family were institutions of particular interest to the major figures of nineteenth century theoretical anthropology, many of whom were lawyers or, if professional scholars, comparative religionists. Early social anthropology was primarily concerned with the nature and evolution of religion, family, and kinship. Recording of kinship terminologies and descriptions of family life were necessary adjuncts to traditional ethnographic works. Morgan's *Systems of Consanguinity and Affinity of the Human Family* (1870) stands as the first important effort to systematize and compare knowledge of kinship systems found in various parts of the world, and it is to Morgan that most American social anthropologists look as the intellectual ancestor of their subject. There were few empirical attempts to subject the internal structure of family and kinship relations to intensive study but the work of Fustel de Coulanges on the institutions of ancient society, *The Ancient City* (1901), was a seminal account in what later came to be called social structural terms of the relationship of family to religion. Durkheim, influenced by Coulanges, was, for the development of modern anthropology, as important as Morgan. Shortly before the turn of the century, social anthropology flourished in France, mainly under his aegis. Durkheim, and his students, Mauss, Hubert, Granet, were as important to the establishment of contemporary sociological analysis as to anthropology, but the two disciplines have interpreted this tradition in slightly different ways. Durkheim, his followers, and those who have been influenced by him have worked with ethnographic data, not as an afterthought, but as a basis of their investigations.

Few of the Durkheim school were field workers themselves, but this in no way has limited the influence of the school on anthropological theory.

Through his analysis of values and beliefs, Durkheim was concerned with the problem of how a social system achieves stability and conformity. In several of his works, but most notably in *The Elementary Forms of the Religious Life* (1915, 1957) he stipulates as the unit of culture the "collective representation" or "shared idea" which arises unconsciously in the minds of the members of a society and forms the vehicle by which they develop their thought. Our ideas of space, time, and logical order are examples of such representations. According to Durkheim, these function to maintain the solidarity of the group. Durkheim and his followers saw the significance of comparative research for their problem areas, and most of his students did comparative studies of institutions. Preoccupation with the persistence of social groups tended to emphasize social statics rather than dynamics; problems of social change, with social change viewed as the common phenomenon, were not the focus of Durkheim's work nor that of his followers.

For contemporary anthropology, the primary impact of Durkheim's theories on the cohesiveness of the social system has been in the development of what has come to be known as structural-functional theory, particularly through the work of two British anthropologists, A. R. Radcliffe-Brown and Bronislaw Malinowski. (For some American anthropologists the term "structural-functional theory" has been associated more closely with Parsonian sociology.) Radcliffe-Brown's reputation was established by a publication of a study of peoples on an island in the Indian Ocean, *The Andaman Islanders* (1922, 1948). What is of importance in this context, however, is Radcliffe-Brown's contribution to social theory rather than ethnography. This contribution is fairly represented in *Structure and Function in Primitive Society* (1952), a series of essays published separately over a period of years, and in *A Natural Science of Society* (1957), a publication of a lecture series presenting Radcliffe-Brown's theoretical ideas of the 1930's.

He accepted from Durkheim the interpretation that cultural (though he preferred the term "social") phenomena may be accounted for by their contribution to the solidarity of the group. He rejected psychological explanations. The most convincing case study of solidarity from this perspective is his own *The Andaman Islanders*.

The influence of Radcliffe-Brown on anthropology in the United States and Britain has been enormous. His stress on the functional relations of the structures of society promoted the exhaustive study of the social structures of a number of primitive societies, especially in Africa and Australia. Outstanding examples of monographs influenced by the

Radcliffe-Brown conception of anthropology are Evans-Pritchard, *The Nuer* (1940), W. L. Warner's *Black Civilization* (1958), Meyer Fortes' *The Dynamics of Clanship Among the Tallensie* (1945), and Fred Eggan's *Social Organization of the Western Pueblos* (1950) (all ethnographic monographs in this essay cited as examples of social anthropology are influenced to a greater or lesser extent by Radcliffe-Brown's work). Bronislaw Malinowski's functionalism, though different from Radcliffe-Brown's, converged with it in its emphasis on detailed descriptions of the organization of single cultures.

Like Radcliffe-Brown, Malinowski advocated a "functionalist" approach to the study of primitive society, though his focus was cultural rather than social. All parts of a culture were, in his view, functionally related to one another. Malinowski's conception of function stressed the manner in which the culture takes account of the motivations and physiology of the individual and manages to mold and provide for his needs.

Radcliffe-Brown's was a more purely sociological approach, analyzing the contribution of institutions and beliefs to the maintenance of the social system. Malinowski's views of culture are summed up in his article, "Culture," in the *Encyclopedia of the Social Sciences* (1930-35), and in a collection of his essays, *Magic, Science, and Religion* (1948). Malinowski and Radcliffe-Brown emphasized many of the same aspects of anthropological investigation, particularly the need for detailed, intensive field study and theoretical analysis by the same investigator, and the focusing of theoretical attention on the internal processes of a society. Malinowski's own field work was done with the Trobriand Islanders, and led to a series of notable monographs—e.g., *Argonauts of the Western Pacific* (1922, 1961). Malinowski's contributions to anthropology are examined in a volume of critical essays written by former students, *Man and Culture* (1957), edited by Raymond W. Firth.

KINSHIP. Social anthropology is associated with the study of the social structure of simple societies. These societies, by definition, lack integrative systems mechanisms at a higher level of organization than those of units based on common acknowledgment of genealogical bonds. "Genealogical" connectedness in such societies ought not to be construed as being the same thing as our own reckoning of kinship affiliation. Societies differ in their concern for tracing and maintaining relationships. Kinship in almost all societies of interest to anthropologists is of equal interest to people in the society studies. Thus, the prevalence of monographs dealing with kinship and related subjects is not a fortuitous or arbitrary fact of theoretical preoccupation of a discipline apart from the empirical material with which they are dealing.

Social anthropology has pursued two basic lines of inquiry in its consideration of the domain of kinship. Evolution and its descendants have emphasized the terminological systems and the morphology of kinship systems in order to reconstruct the past of societies, viewing kinship as the best—or at least one—of the indicators of the prior state of a development. An alternative is to suppose that the network of kinship relations is the key to understanding the present state of the integration of a society, providing, as it were, a map of the crucial relationship among the groups constituting the social order. The "doing" of kinship generates its own extremely technical language and literature.

For the novice perhaps the best introduction is found in one of the good textbooks on social anthropology. Paul Bohannan's *Social Anthropology* (1963), John Beattie's *Other Cultures* (1964), and Raymond Firth's *Elements of Social Organization* (1956) all introduce the subject in a comprehensible fashion. John Barnes contributed a general article on the field of kinship for the fourteenth edition of the *Encyclopaedia Britannica* that is a good introduction to the subject. Because of the importance of kinship study in social anthropology, no one treatment, no set of terminological conventions, will meet with universal approval by specialists. These presentations are perhaps sufficiently eclectic to prepare the reader for more technical papers. It is also the case that most of the exciting contributions to the field of kinship analysis are published in anthropological journals and therefore are not included in this list. Anthropology's preoccupation with kinship is sometimes difficult for the lay audience to understand. The significance that the subject assumes in the lives of the kind of people regularly studied by anthropologists may be better appreciated when encountered in the detailed exposition of a kinship system in the social structure of a single society, for example, in Firth's remarkable monograph of Polynesian society, *We, the Tikopia* (1936), or Evans-Pritchard's *Kinship and Marriage among the Nuer* (1951). More technical surveys of a variety of approaches to the study of kinship organized by types of societies or types of kinship systems are available for the student familiar with the rudiments of the subject. Radcliffe-Brown in the introduction to *African Systems of Kinship and Marriage* (1950) summarizes the state of the field to that time. D. M. Schneider and K. Gough (eds.), *Matrilineal Societies* (1961), describing the distinctive characteristics of social systems where descent is traced through females; Rodney Needham's *Structure and Sentiment* (1962), discussing explanations for cross-cousin marriage, Edmund Leach's *Pul Eliya* (1961), placing kinship in the context of the land tenure system; and Meyer Fortes' *Dynamics of Clanship* (1945) and *Web of Kinship* (1949), exploring the potentials of formal social structural techniques—all are examples of major anthropological writing with the kinship focus representing variations in British social anthropological approaches to the subject. Many American scholars write in the same tradition. For a view of kinship and a review of the literature from the perspective of a scholar concerned with historical reconstruction, the famous *Social Structure* (1949) by George Peter Murdock provides one coherent account with its own terminology. For the student, E. Shusky has written a manual for kinship study largely employing the Murdock definitions.

POLITICS. In the introduction to their second series of papers, *Philosophy, Politics, and Society* in 1962, the editors complain of the failure of anthropologists to recommend for inclusion suitable materials in political anthropology, except for the famous *African Political Systems* (1940, Evans-Pritchard and M. Foster [eds.]):" We are convinced that the political anthropologists have further developed their ideas since that time, but we are forced to record that it does not seem to be in directions which they are yet anxious to report to political theorists and philosophers" (P. Laslett and W. G. Runciman, 1962, x). This reluctance to further the study of political anthropology has changed. Lately, the anthropologists interested in political system and process have been much in evidence. This recent upsurge in social anthropological concern for political process has come from stimulus provided by encounters with self-conscious modernization or from anthropological contact with large-scale societies for which the familiar kinship level of analysis is conceptually inadequate, whether modernizing, or simply changing. If there could be said to be polarities in contemporary social anthropology, they might be represented by formal structural analysis on the model of linguistics on the one hand and political anthropology on the other, with characteristic methods and interpretations coming from sociology and political science. Influence from the anthropology associated with the University of Manchester is strong in this development. Max Gluckman's *Politics, Law and Ritual in Tribal Society* (1965) serves as an introduction to this field. Two collections of papers on politics by anthropologists illustrate the approaches and problems of contemporary interest, as does Lucy Mair's *Primitive Government* (1962); Michael P. Banton (ed.), *Political Systems and the Distribution of Power* (1965); and Swartz, Turner, and Tuden (eds.), *Political Anthropology* (1966), which defines the field and attempts to clarify its concepts in the comprehensive introduction by the editors. The theoretical framework of this political anthropology is derived from behavioral political science. The bibliographical essay by David Easton (Siegel's *Biennial Review*) surveys the subject through the 1950's and provides valuable abstracts of the most important work of the years 1955–57. Easton's whole discussion is designed to be useful in orienting the thinking of anthropologists on political topics. Monographs focusing on such subjects as group conflict, decision-making, bureaucracy factionalism, political structure, and social control have been appearing with greater frequency. Lloyd Fallers, *Bantu Bureaucracy* (1956), investigating traditional and modern realms of political behavior among the Soga of East Africa, and F. G. Bailey's *Politics and Social Change: Orissa in 1959* (1963), studying the relation of levels of government, are examples of this sort of approach. A. Beals and B. Siegel's *Divisiveness and Social Conflict* (1966) offers a comparative study of intra-group conflict among Pueblo Indians and in a community in southern India. E. N. Eisenstadt's *Political Systems of Empires* (1963) is an ambitious, comparative study examining a large number of historical empires to explain the causes of the rise of centralized bureaucratic empires. In the famous *Political Systems of Highland Burma* (1954), E. R. Leach is closer to social structural analysis than to the examples of dynamic political anthropology enumerated above. Leach describes the transformation of political systems through a series of political organizational forms characterized by ideologies ranging from egalitarian to autocratic.

ECONOMICS. The economic life of primitive societies has been of continual interest to social anthropologists. Malinowski's classical monograph, *Argonauts of the Western Pacific* (1961), one of the most important reports in the history of ethnography, was conceived of by its author as a contribution to the understanding of primitive economic life challenging prevailing European opinion of the economic philosophy of primitive man. Ethnographers have invariably included descriptions of the academic organization of groups studied. M. J. Herskovits, in *The Economic Life of Primitive People* (1940), generally surveyed the topic, attempting to give direction to anthropology's concern with economic life. This was criticized in an important review article by the economist, Frank Knight. The original work, Knights' criticisms, and Herskovits' rejoinder are published together in the revised edition (1952). In its earliest phase, economic anthropology was concerned to establish the existence of analytical separate economy in simple society and unique or unusual properties of the institutions of primitive economics which put them outside the competence of the discipline of economics.

Anthropologists are currently interested in being able to describe and analyze academic processes and institutions encountered in the non-Western world in ways comprehensible to other students of economic life. This entails much greater economic sophistication on the part of anthropologists than was true in the recent past. As anthropologists study complex societies in the process of social and economic modernization, they must necessarily become familiar with economic institutions that exceed the descriptive powers of the vocabulary of ordinary social structural analysis. K. Polanyi, C. M. Arensburg, and H. W. Pearson (eds.), *Trade and Market in the Early Empires* (1957), brought institutional economics to the attention of the anthropological audience, and the subsequent course of anthropological discussion was much influenced by its publication. The market has become the focus of special interest: Alice Dewey's *Peasant Marketing in Java* (1962), P. J. Bohannan and G. Dalton's *Markets in Africa* (1962) and S. Mintz' study of the peasant markets are examples. Sol Tax's *Penn Capitalism: Guatemalan Indian Economy* (1953) is one of the best detailed descriptions of a primitive economy.

The economic development of non-Western societies has, of course, engaged the interest of anthropologists. Cyril Belshaw's fine monograph, *Traditional Exchange and Modern Markets* (1965), pulls the field of economic anthropology together in a fashion that makes accessible to the general reader his data drawn from primitive, peasant, and modernizing economies. R. Firth and B. S. Yamey have edited a series of papers, *Capital, Saving, and Credit in Peasant Societies* (1964), of relevance to development economics and anthropology. They describe the difficulty found in translating basic economic concepts from Western to non-Western materials and, in nineteen reports from the non-Western world, provide a wealth of data on the operation of capital and savings. A recent reader in economic anthropology reviewing the field has been edited by G. Dalton—*Tribal and Peasant Economics* (1966).

RELIGION. The anthropological study of religion might be considered central to social anthropology. Certainly most of the major contributors to the historical development of social anthropological theory, Durkheim, Radcliffe-Brown, and Malinowski, for example, have discussed the relationship of religious belief to social structure, and all general ethnographies include substantial accounts of religious beliefs and behavior. Nevertheless, theories of religious behavior and the analysis of religious symbol systems have not shown the degree of intellectual improvement that is obvious in studies of kinship, marriage, politics, or economy. Max Weber's famous studies in the sociology of religion have only lately come to influence anthropologists' thinking, probably because anthropologists are more and more working on the kind of archaic societies that are a part of Weber's comparative studies. Clifford Geertz's *Religion of Java* (1960) is the most thorough examination of a complex religious scene by an anthropologist. In this work, Geertz describes three variants of religious persuasion in Java and the contributions of the three groups of believers to the social structure of a Javanese town.

Philip Newman's *Knowing the Gururumba* (1965), though a short study aimed at an undergraduate audience, is an exceptionally able attempt to analyze the religious system of a primitive society (New Guinea). The renewed interest in religious subjects is also seen in the important analysis of *Nuer Religion* (1956) by Evans-Pritchard and G. Lienhardt's *Divinity and Experience: Religion Among the Dinkas* (1961), both providing close analyses of religious belief systems.

W. A. Lessa and E. Z. Vogt's *Reader in Comparative Religion* (1958) reprints much of the important article-length literature in the anthropological study of religion. Anthony F. C. Wallace's interesting *Religion: An Anthropological View* (1966) is an original work in the study of religious behavior more attentive to psychological literature than are most anthropological discussions of this subject. This book, on the other hand, neglects important contributions in the sociology of religion. An impressive series of essays on religious subjects appears in the monograph *The Anthropological Study of Religion*, of the Association of Social Anthropology, with essays by younger anthropologists illustrating the state of anthropological thought in this area.

CHANGE. The concern of social and cultural anthropologists with the nature of the process of change in simplest societies has altered dramatically in recent years. In one form or another, concern with change is as old as the subject. The founders of sociological and anthropological theories, the evolutionists, ancient and modern, the functionalists, and the scholars attempting to treat sociology as an aspect of history, were all studying social change. The questions that concerned these scholars had to do with whether to look for internal or external factors to account for change in social and cultural systems and to ascertain general sequences of changing variables for all—or for certain—classes of social systems which would account for transformations.

A history of anthropology like Robert Lowie's *History of Ethnological Theory* (1937) catalogues the sequence of prevailing explanation for change in ethnological theory. The problem of whether change originates within the culture or is imposed upon it is discussed under the topic heading "Invention versus Diffusion." This problem gave rise to a group of theories which contended that the process of invention is generally freakish and that an innovation occurs only once, or at least very rarely; therefore the main process by means of which new procedures and beliefs are learned is by diffusion from a single center of origin. This is a position of the *cultural diffusionists*. This area of concern, once so dominant, is now largely a problem of the intellectual past, except where it survives as an interpretative problem in culture history or as a topic in popular anthropology. In social anthropology itself, the problems of change have been entirely recast. The modernization of much of the non-Western world necessarily reorients the anthropological study of change.

The field of acculturation or culture contact (both synonyms for diffusion-in-process) received extensive treatment by anthropologists from the earliest times, in which there was an identifiable social anthropological field-work tradition, to the 1950's. Herskovits, *Acculturation* (1938), and Tax (ed.), *Acculturation in the Americas* (1952), summarize the knowledge of this subject as it was conceptualized at these periods. Felix Keesing compiled a comprehensive annotated bibliography of studies of change extending over nearly a century of scholarly attention to transformation in primitive societies, *Culture Change; An Analysis and Bibliography of Anthropological Sources to 1952* (1953).

In the preceding description of social anthropology and cultural theory, works primarily concerned with change have been treated under institutional headings. For example, Manning Nash's *Machine Age Maya* (1958) or Geertz's *Peddlers and Princes* (1963) might be discussed either as economic anthropology or as studies of change. The notable lack of quality presentations of the whole or aspects of the theoretical framework of social anthropology is apparent in the absence of general treatments of change in the literature. It is the nature of contemporary anthropology to prefer the examination of an illustrative single case to a general theory. There is a further difficulty in describing anthropological studies of change in that increasingly, as the subject of modernization has become a focus of research rather than a programmatic concern, anthropologists in the field of development publish with sociologists, political scientists, and economists who share an interest in allied topics. A cultural approach to the problems of development is evident in some of the literature written by specialists in other disciplines. For an introduction to the field of modernization, the papers in Geertz (ed.), *Old Societies New States* (1963) provide an instructive guide to the theoretical direction of research on new nations. The illustrations in some of these papers are by now dated but the subject is well reviewed. I. Wallerstein's *Social Change: The Colonial Situation* (1966) is a reader containing a more than usually large number of papers of interest to anthropologists. The periodicals *Economic Development and Culture Change* and *Comparative Studies in Society and History* regularly publish articles on change in traditional society.

Applied anthropology is the subfield concerned with facilitating change in traditional societies by employing thoughts of scientific anthropology. The publication of the Association for Applied Anthropology, *Human Organization*, is devoted to studies of aspects of change. In response to the active participation of anthropologists in consultative capacities and the demand of governmental agencies and programs like the Peace Corps for anthropological counsel in cross-cultural programs, a number of new books and manuals have been published that make use of anthropological insights. Charles Erasmus' *Man Takes Control: Cultural Development and American Aid* (1961), Ward Goodenough's *Cooperation in Change* (1963), and George Foster's *Traditional Cultures* (1962) are examples.

Few monographs published in the past ten years have neglected the study of change. At an earlier time anthropologists were strongly criticized for their failure to acknowledge the intrusion of modern institutions on the communities they study. This criticism has no validity now. Numerous examples of studies directed at an understanding of change in microcosm are available. Redfield's *Chan Kom, The Village That Chose Progress* (1950) is a famous account of modernization. Both Firth's *Social Changes in Tikopia* (1959) and Mead's *New Lives for Old* (1956) show the advantages of the study of a recent condition of peoples studied earlier by the same anthropologist. Margaret Stacey's *Tradition and Change* is a stimulating attempt to deal with a complicated form of change in more or less traditional structural terms.

ETHNOGRAPHY

Anthropological material for the study of culture, society, and the individual is derived from ethnographies which describe data gathered by the anthropologist in the field.

Ethnography occupies a central position in anthropological research. Adequate cultural descriptions are a prerequisite for historical or sociological interpretation. Adequacy, for these purposes, is determined by the completeness of the coverage and the quality of the data for the problem at hand. Obviously, the ethnographer cannot anticipate in advance the variety of uses to which his description may be put. Sometimes descriptions are made without explicit problem frameworks; others focus on specific theoretical problems or on gathering information to fill gaps in data previously acquired. Recent ethnography, on the whole, has been more concerned with this kind of problem orientation. It includes a much narrower range of materials, usually dealt with more intensively, than did the early general monographs.

A major consideration in the late nineteenth and early twentieth century was to gather the necessary descriptive materials before the indigenous culture (and its bearers) died out. This is a problem for the anthropologist, and it is still thought desirable to obtain information from and about those persons who have been least contaminated by contact with Western civilization, though this consideration has ceased to have the priority it once had. Related to this is the aim of reconstructing the cultures of people who have been changed through contact with other cultures, especially Western culture. The social anthropologists, though not historians themselves, have increasingly felt the need of taking historical materials into account in various phases of their work. Contemporary anthropologists usually approach field work with a series of questions to be answered, and they publish monographs, when possible, which attempt to answer these questions. Since there is some prior ethnographic knowledge of the people available to him, the anthropologist will not ordinarily feel compelled to describe all the aspects of the culture which were thought essential by earlier workers. The monograph which deals in greater or lesser detail with the whole cultural and social life of a people, from their gods to their pots and pans, is a genre of the past.

Though some do continue to describe the primitives of their study without mention of the effects of modernization on traditional life, increasingly ethnographers have been taking change into account. This new perspective may require the ethnographer to take cognizance of the work of fellow social scientists: political scientists and economists especially, to handle the variables of more complex situations of change.

The tradition of field work by trained anthropological investigators is a product of the late nineteenth century, further developed in the twentieth. With few exceptions, ethnologists up to that time had been content to rely on data gathered by all varieties of collectors, but had not themselves worked with non-Western peoples. There was a sudden florescence in the final decades of the nineteenth century which produced a number of what are now deemed classic ethnographic accounts. These reflected the increasing interest and proficiency in techniques of data gathering and introduced a flood of new concepts (native words) which constitute the core of the present anthropological vocabulary. Some of these monographs have had influence far beyond anthropological circles. Baldwin Spencer and F. J. Gillen's *The Native Tribes of Central Australia* (1899) is particularly notable in this respect, since these data figured importantly in the formulations of Frazer, Durkheim, and Freud. The field work that an anthropologist must do today is almost always preceded by a detailed examination of the materials already available on the peoples and cultures which he is to study. He may consult documents in the government records or the minutes of the tribal council, but ordinarily he will still be primarily dependent on the work of his anthropological predecessors. Though anthropologists were not traditionally much concerned with providing guides to the available materials, a number of excellent bibliographic works have appeared recently, and reference sources in general seem to be improving.

Because of the wealth of ethnographic data and because of the specialized nature of much of this writing, the citations in the paragraphs that follow will be minimal and introductory. On the whole, the compiler has chosen to include bibliographies, books, and periodicals containing significant bibliographical materials, and readers representing a range of available sources in preference to a listing of significant monographs. Ethnographies, where they do appear, are meant to illustrate the types of work and the names of important anthropologists identified with these specific areas. All of the monographs cited in this essay could, obviously, be sorted and included under topic designations. Only sources in English are included.

The choice of areas for organizing this ethnographic information is arbitrary. Asia, for example, comprises the ethnographic areas of Southeast Asia, Southwest Asia, India, China, and Japan, each of which is separate and would be subdivided in a more extensive presentation. Anthropologists treat civilizational materials from the perspective of the little communities, or closed communities, within them. Typically, monographs from such areas will bear titles such as "A Village Study of," "The Hill Peoples of." No attempt is made here to list sources for civilizational study except insofar as they are necessary to introduce the areas to the reader.

THE AMERICAS. The study of American Indians was the principal, though not the exclusive, concern of American ethnography to the end of World War II. For this reason, the aboriginal peoples of North America are the best known in the world.

Franz Boas' students worked mostly on this continent. Outside academic anthropology, the government publications of the Bureau of American Ethnology are the richest single source of descriptive materials on the American Indian in the late nineteenth and early twentieth century. Combined academic and governmental resources in ethnography provide an outstanding record. Ordering this great mass of data has occupied many of the most talented workers. Clark Wissler's *The American Indian* (1917) was a pioneering codification of the culture areas of North American aborigines. A. L. Kroeber's *Cultural and Natural Areas of Native North America* (1939) was an outstanding early attempt to correlate cultural and ecological features of traditional American Indian societies. Harold Driver has done a valuable job of organizing ethnographic data for students in his *Indians of North America* (1961) and in his *The Americas on the Eve of Discovery* (1964) he has brought together an interesting short book of accounts of American Indian life at the time of contact by both contemporary anthropologists and by eyewitness observers. Ruth Underhill's *Red Man's America* (1953) also introduces the continent to the beginning student from the perspective of cultural anthropology.

Because of the longer period of intensive study, there tend to be proportionally more monographs, and fewer books of readings in American Indian studies than in other ethnographic areas. Collected papers suggesting important areas of ethnographic research in North America are Fred Eggan (ed.), *Social Anthropology of North America* (2d ed., 1955) and E. Spicer's *Perspectives in American Indian Culture Change* (1961).

G. P. Murdock's *Ethnographic Bibliography of North America* (3d ed., 1960) is an essential reference guide to North American ethnography. F. Hodge's *The Handbook of American Indians North of Mexico* is an old (1907–10) but valuable reference guide, recently reprinted (1959). Swanton's *The Indian Tribes of North America* (1952) is especially useful as a guide to names of groups.

The number of excellent monographs in North American Indian studies is so vast that it is impossible to do justice to the range. Several of the most famous are now available in paperbacked editions. R. Lowie's *The Crow Indians* (1935) is a famous example. Within the United States, the cultural area of the Plains and the Southwest are the best known in ethnography. *The Southwestern Journal of Anthropology*, *The American Anthropologist*, and *Ethnology* are periodicals publishing significant articles on American Indian research.

* * *

Much ethnographic research of high quality is currently being conducted in Mexico and will influence the way this literature is discussed in the future. At present, most of this new work is not, unfortunately, represented in books. The famous studies of urban poverty by Oscar Lewis, in the tradition of an older urban sociology have attracted much favorable attention outside Mexico and stimulated public interest in the potential of anthropological technique to illuminate modern problems. *Five Families: Mexican Case Studies in the Culture of Poverty* (1959) and *The Children of Sanchez* (1961) suggest new techniques and themes for social anthropological research. Dwight Heath and Richard Adams have assembled a series of essays on contemporary Latin America that give some sense of the relevance and limitations of the social anthropological approach to the study of modern Latin-American societies (1965).

Four volumes of a projected eleven volume *Handbook of Middle American Indians* R. Wauchope (ed.), to cover geography, archaeology, and social and cultural anthropology have recently been published; these will be helpful in an area without, at present, major generally available reference sources.

The contributions of the late Robert Redfield to Central American ethnology are well-known, especially *Folk Culture of Yucatan* (1941). His *Tepoztlan, a Mexican village; A Study of Folk Life* (1930), was later studied by Oscar Lewis: *Tepoztlán, Life in a Mexican Village Restudied* (1951).

The seven volume *Handbook of South American Indians* (1946-59), edited by Julian Steward, is the single most valuable source on South American ethnology available in English. Though it is uneven in its coverage, this is the fault of the state of the ethnographic information. Steward and L. C. Faron have written a good single-volume account of the ethnology of the area, *Native Peoples of South America* (1959), that makes it possible to introduce the area in an undergraduate course. The monographs of South America are commonly unavailable, or not in English. Timothy J. O'Leary has lately published an *Ethnographic Bibliography of South America* for the Human Relations Area Files (1963).

SUB-SAHARAN AFRICA. For breadth of coverage and excellence of individual contributions, sub-Saharan African ethnography is outstanding, equaled only by the literature on aboriginal North America. The research with American Indians differs from that in Africa in important ways, but chiefly because the former concentrated on the reconstruction of the societies of Indians before, or in the early stages of, contact while the latter has worked with integrated and viable societies. Before World War II, African ethnography was chiefly the work of British and French investigators. American anthropologists have been increasingly in evidence in African studies in recent years, but the bulk of the work is European. There has, perhaps, been greater anthropological concern with problems of modernization in Africa than elsewhere.

The monographic series, Ethnographic Survey of Africa, is publishing, in outline and summary form, social and cultural data for, ultimately, all of the nonliterate peoples of sub-Saharan Africa. There are few general, modern books on Africa to serve as introductions. G. P. Murdock's *Africa: Its Peoples and Their History* (1959) is an exception stressing the reconstruction of the history of the native populations. The accuracy of the ethnographic data in this book has been questioned and this form of presentation of African data, though it has value, obscures distinctive features of the societies and cultures that fall outside Murdock's analytic and conceptual vocabulary.

Africa and Africans (1964) by Paul Bohannan is one of the few popular introductions to African ethnology. James Gibbs has edited a book of brief original ethnographies, *Peoples of Africa* (1965), written by investigators who have worked in various parts of the continent, that is an exceptionally useful book for introductory purposes. Simon and Phoebe Ottenberg's *Cultures and Societies of Africa* (1960) presents a sample of professional writings on aspects of African research for a more advanced audience.

The books *African Political Systems* (1940), *African Systems of Kinship and Marriage* (1950) and *African Worlds* (1954) are earlier collections of original papers by eminent Africanists that continue to be of methodological and substantive interest, since they represent the mature phase of social structural analysis.

The select International African Institute ethnographic bibliography edited by C. D. Forde, is an excellent source book, essential to African studies courses. Joseph Greenberg's revised linguistic classification of Africa is another reference document necessary to courses surveying the continent. The African bibliographic center publishes special and general bibliographies bimonthly. The periodicals *Africa*, *Modern African Studies*, and *The Journal of African History*, are standard sources for keeping abreast of Africanist research.

THE MIDDLE EAST. The Middle East is sporadically represented in recent ethnography. Wherever a major civilizational complex exists, traditional anthropology has tended to specialize in minority or marginal peoples and allocated the remainder to humanistic scholarship. In the case of the Middle East, this means to culture historians and to Islamicists. The new orientation of anthropology toward peasants as well as tribes introduces new possibilities for work in areas like the Middle East, but even with peasant studies, the output is relatively small.

Bernard Lewis' *The Arabs in History* (1960) introduces the area in an especially helpful way for anthropologists. H. A. R. Gibb's short *Mohammedanism* (1949) is the standard introduction to Islam essential to even beginning students. The works of G. V. Von Grunebaum: *Unity and Variety in Islam* (1955), *Studies in Islamic Cultural History* (1954), *Islam, Essays in the Nature and Growth of a Cultural Tradition* (1961), and *Medieval Islam* (1953) are basically historical works, but with such awareness of the dimensions of social and cultural analysis that they can be readily used by social scientists interested in comparison.

For the modern Middle East, Hamed Ammar's *Growing Up in an Egyptian Village* (1954), Frederik Barth's work—especially *Nomads of South Persia* (1960), Carleton Coon's famous *Tribes of the Rif* (1931), John Gulick's *Social Structure and Culture Change in a Lebanese Village* (1955) and Gavin Maxwell's *People of the Reeds* (1957) are good monographic sources.

Though outside anthropological literature, Doreen Warriner's studies on land tenure, *Land and Poverty in the Middle East* (1948) and

Land Reform and Development in the Middle East (1957) have clear relevance for students of Middle Eastern social structure. For Iran, Ann Lambton's *Landlord and Peasant in Persia* (1953) is an essential source on this same topic.

For bibliography, Richard Ettinghausen has compiled *A Selected and Annotated Bibliography of Books and Periodicals in Western Languages* (1954) and Henry Field has collected a six volume *Bibliography on Southwestern Asia* (1953–). A catalogue of articles on Islamic subjects in periodicals and other collective publications, *Index Islamicus* (1960), has been compiled by J. D. Pearson and J. F. Ashton of the School of Oriental and African Studies. The *Middle Eastern Review* regularly publishes articles of interest to students of this area.

ASIA. Anthropological interest in Asia since World War II has been strongest in Southeast Asia and India. The inaccessibility of large areas of Asia and the growing political barriers to conducting research will influence the quality of ethnography produced in the coming year. Overall, the student of Asia is well served by general introductions and bibliographies. In its September issue each year, the *Journal of Asian Studies* publishes an excellent bibliography of the whole of the Far East, available in most libraries. E. Reischauer and J. Fairbank's *History of East Asian Civilization* (1960–65), in two volumes, provides a more than adequate introduction to the area for students with anthropological interest.

For Southest Asia, the publications of the Yale University Southeast Asia Cultural Report Series have been an important source of research findings. F. M. Lebar, G. C. Hickey, and J. K. Musgrave compiled a summary of writing, containing data on a large number of ethnolinguistic groups of mainland Southeast Asia. *Social Structure in Southeast Asia*, (1960) edited by G. P. Murdock, reports on aspects of social structure, largely kinship, for a number of groups. Anthropology is conventionally primarily interested in marginal peoples, and Peter Kundstadter (ed.) has brought together a series of essays on groups in the two volume *Southeast Asian Tribes, Minorities, and Nations* (unpub.).

Among the monographs published during the past few years, G. Kickey's *Village in Vietnam* (1964), Geetrz's *Social History of an Indonesian Town* (1965), and Nash's *Golden Road to Modernity: Village Life in Contemporary Burma* (1965) are of special interest.

C. A. Fisher's *Southeast Asia* is one of the most comprehensive introductions to this area (1964). The bibliography by J. F. Embree and L. O. Dotson, *Bibliography of the Peoples and Cultures of Mainland Southeast Asia* (1950), is a standard work. Raymond Kennedy's *Bibliography of Indonesian Peoples and Cultures* (1955; rev. ed.), and the

Human Relations Area File bibliography compiled by the Philippine Studies Program of the University of Chicago are useful research tools.

* * *

India, like Japan, has its own professional cultural and social anthropologists and its journals, in English, devoted to publication of research findings. Substantial numbers of American and British anthropologists have specialized in India. The community, or village, is the characteristic focus of recent studies. *Village India* (1955), edited by McKim Marriott, is a sampler of village studies. Gerald Berreman's *Hindus of the Himalayas* (1963) is the report of research in a relatively isolated and unknown area.

From 1957 to 1964, *Contributions to Indian Sociology,* edited by Louis Dument and David Pocock, published structural studies of India. *Man in India* is the general anthropology journal published in Bihar, containing articles of social anthropological interest. Several guides and syllabi introducing American undergraduates to Indian studies are in print. For example, the college of the University of Chicago published a syllabus, *Introduction to the Civilization of India: Changing Dimension of Indian Society and Culture* (1957), which is useful for orientation. A similar work is William de Bary (ed.), *Sources of Indian Tradition* (1958). One special number of the *Journal of American Folklore*, edited by Milton Singer, *Traditional India: Structure and Change* (1959) is a helpful introduction to the research interests of India specialists.

The sociological problem in India of the greatest universal significance is the study of caste groupings. A few examples of the extraordinarily rich literature on this subject are M. H. Srinivas, *Caste in Modern India and Other Essays* (1962), Adrian Mayer's *Caste and Kinship in Central India* (1960), M. Marriott's *Caste Ranking and Community Structure in Five Regions of India and Pakistan* (1960), E. R. Leach (ed.), *Aspects of Caste in South India, Ceylon, and Northwest Pakistan* (1960), and Harold Isaacs' *India's Ex-Untouchables* (1965).

* * *

The excellence of recent social science work on Japan, largely recent historical Japan, stands as an example for workers in other geographic areas of the potential value of social scientific inquiry. Japanese scholars are active participants in social science research. The history and present state of Japanese anthropology are interestingly reviewed in an essay by Takao Sofue in Siegel (ed.), *Biennial Review of Anthropology* (1961).

Twelve Doors to Japan (1965) edited by Hall and Beardsley, is an unusually helpful introduction adapted from a university survey course. B. S. Silberman has compiled a reader of Japanese studies, *Japanese Character and Culture* (1962). John Embree's study, done in the 1930's, *Suye Mura, a Japanese Village* (1939), is one of the most famous ethnographic works on Japan of the prewar period. *Village Japan* (1959), by R. K. Beardsley, J. W. Hall, and R. E. Ward, reports on the present state of village studies. A number of interesting studies on modernizing Japan, not all by anthropologists, are available: R. Dore's *City Life in Japan* (1958), D. Plath's *The After Hours* (1964), and M. Jansen (ed.), *Changing Japanese Attitudes toward Modernization* (1965) are accounts of more complex situations of change than those with which anthropologists are ordinarily concerned.

Because of its significance in the alteration of societal institutions prerequisite to the nineteenth-century modernization of Japan, the Tokugawa period (1603–1847) has attracted particularly detailed scholarly attention. For social anthropologists Robert Bellah's *Tokugawa Religion* (1957) and Dore's *Education in Tokugawa Japan* (1965) are especially notable surveys of the period.

China is currently beyond the reach of foreign social science research for the most part. The exigencies of the political situation have directed social science's interest increasingly to those subjects that can be studied at a distance: historical problems and ideologies and belief systems. A singular exception to the anthropological exclusion from contemporary China is the report of a four day survey by the Australian social anthropologist, W. Geddes (*Peasant Life in Communist China* [1963]), of a village studied by Fei Hsiao-t'ung in the 1930's.

Older studies of anthropological relevance and examinations of data collected in the pre-Communist period in China of value are L. Hsu's *Under the Ancestor's Shadow; Chinese Culture and Personality* (1948), Marion Levy's *The Family Revolution in Modern China* (1949), and Olga Lang's *Chinese Family and Society* (1946).

W. T. de Bary, Wing-tsit Chan, and Burton Watson compiled a *Sources of Chinese Tradition* (1960), for students. Arthur F. Wright's *Studies in Chinese Thought* (1953), originally a monograph of the American Anthropological Association, was compiled to introduce anthropologists to the problems in sinology relevant to their work.

OCEANIA. The ethnographic designation Oceania includes the island groupings of the Pacific: Melanesia, Micronesia, Polynesia, and the aboriginal peoples of Australia. Oceania has been fortunate in attracting some of the most important anthropological talent of this century. The field work monographs by such eminent researchers as Margaret Mead,

Bronislaw Malinowski, Raymond Firth, Gregory Bateson, and Cyril Belshaw are among the notable contributions to the recent ethnographic record of the area. The literature introducing the area as a whole is, with the exception of some historically important but out-of-date surveys, not so distinguished. Douglas Oliver's *The Pacific Islands* (1962) is perhaps the best general introduction for the student to the historical and ethnological background of the island peoples, and C. R. A. Taylor's *A Pacific Bibliography* (1965) is an essential tool for directing anthropological reading on the Pacific.

The recent interest in millenarian movements has emphasized the importance of cargo cult movements, largely located in Melanesia. One of these is described historically and areally by Peter Lawrence in *Road Belong Cargo* (1964). Peter Worsley's *The Trumpet Shall Sound* (1957) is a theoretical account of cargo cults throughout Melanesia.

For New Guinea, James Watson's *New Guinea: The Central Highlands* (1964) contains recent professional papers of interest. The work of Malinowski on the people of the Trobriand Islands is one of the fullest descriptions of a primitive people of which we have records. The most famous reports of this expedition are *Argonauts of the Western Pacific* (1922) and *Coral Gardens and Their Magic* (1935). R. Fortune's *Sorcerers of Dobu* (1963) analyzes the magical systems and social structure of a closely related people. A. P. Elkin's *Social Anthropology in Melanesia* (1953) reviews research in the area.

The famous writings of Dr. Margaret Mead are based on field work conducted in Melanesia (*Growing Up in New Guinea; New Lives for Old*) and Polynesia (*Coming of Age in Samoa*). Firth's *We, the Tikopia* (1936) and subsequent writings on the Tikopia provide an extraordinarily lucid and detailed account of the lives of one Polynesian people. A review of the whole area in historical and archaeological perspective is to be found in R. Sugg's *Island Civilizations of the Pacific* (1960). F. Keesing reviews the state of research in the area in *Social Anthropology of Polynesia* (1953).

The ethnographic interest on the part of Americans in Micronesia at the end of World War II and since has produced several publications of note. H. Barnett's *Being a Palauan* (1969), T. Gladwin and S. B. Sarason's *Truk: Man in Paradise* (1953), W. Goodenough's *Property, Kin, and Community on Truk* (1961), and E. G. Burrows and M. Spiro's *An Atoll Culture* (1957) are especially worthy of note.

R. M. and C. H. Berndt in *The World of the First Australians: an Introduction to the Traditional Life of the Australian Aborigines* (1964) have put together a much needed general account of what is known of the life of Australian aborigines, relying on their own field work and that of their many illustrious predecessors, including Spencer and Gillan,

Radcliffe-Brown, Elkin, Warner, Howitt, and others. The wealth of data collected by anthropologists and others is described in John Greenway's *Bibliography of the Australian Aborigine and the Native Peoples of the Torres Straits in 1959* (1963). The present state of aboriginal studies is reviewed in W. E. H. Stanner and Helen Sheils' *Australian Aboriginal Studies; A Symposium of Papers Presented at the 1961 Research Conference* (1963).

Research in Oceania is centered at universities in the Pacific as well as departments of major American universities. The University of Hawaii and the Australian National University are especially important centers of research and publication for the area. In addition to papers published in general anthropological periodicals, the reader will want to see the journal *Oceania* for the whole area, and *Mankind*.

3 Psychology

Walter R. Reitman

INTRODUCTION

Psychology may not be the oldest profession, but surely it was the earliest hobby. Most men turn amateur psychologist, pure or applied, at some time in their lives, and the best of these amateurs have made contributions whose importance may not be discounted even in our own very much more organized day and age. Sometimes such concern with psychological phenomena grows out of pressing societal or environmental problems. The recent Supreme Court decisions on civil rights, for instance, have stimulated a great deal of interest in the psychological consequences of constrained interracial contact, much of it realistic and entirely appropriate in view of the far-reaching potential effects. The same may be said of the recurring reexaminations of our educational system, and more broadly, of the fundamental social and psychological incentive systems which determine the distribution of effort in the United States.

It is more difficult in other cases to discover situational alterations which account for increased public concern over psychological problems. There is little evidence, for example, to suggest that the marked upsurge of concern for mental health follows upon any corresponding increase in the proportional incidence of mental illness. Quite the contrary, after careful study of some of the most complete records available, Herbert Goldhamer and Andrew W. Marshall conclude in *Psychosis and Civilization* (1953) that the relative frequency of psychoses for age groups under fifty in their sample had shown no increase at all over the past 100 years. Here we may be dealing less with any specific situational alteration than with a change in the popular orientation toward mental well-being. The present-day growth of large-scale management training programs and of business support for studies of industrial psychology poses somewhat similar problems of interpretation. Big industrial organizations, presupposing a high level of functional organization, have existed in quantity for a good number of decades. Aside from a limited number of pioneering investigations conducted prior to World War II, however, the growth of interest in collaborative effort—"teamwork" and team products, systems engineering applied to organizational problems, and particularly in the group dynamics of management—is a recent phenomenon.

Whatever the sources of popular interest and concern for specific problems, the cumulative result has been a marked expansion of the literature of psychology. *Psychological Abstracts* (1927–), a monthly journal summarizing most of the material of psychological interest published in the Western world, in 1966 alone reviewed over 500 periodic sources, and in this single twelve-month period abstracted almost 14,000 articles and books, about three-fifths again as much as in a comparable period a decade ago.

Of these numerous periodicals, the group published by the American Psychological Association probably enjoys the widest circulation among psychologists. Besides *Psychological Abstracts*, there are, first of all, eight journals distinguished principally by the content areas they serve. These include *Journal of Applied Psychology* (1917–), *Journal of Counseling Psychology* (1954–), *Journal of Educational Psychology* (1910–), *Journal of Personality and Social Psychology* (1965–), *Journal of Comparative and Physiological Psychology* (1921–), and *Journal of Consulting Psychology* (1937–), which contains contributions primarily on clinical psychology. The *Journal of Abnormal Psychology* (1965–), publishing studies of many facets of human psychology, and *Journal of Experimental Psychology* (1916–), reporting research on sensation, perception, learning, and other aspects of general psychology, also fall under this heading. *Psychological Bulletin* (1904–) publishes research methodology, while *Psychological Review* (1894–) specializes in theoretical articles and interpretations of research in all areas of psychology. *Contemporary Psychology* (1956–), finally, contains reviews of current books in psychology. In addition to these publications of the American Psychological Association, there are a good many other journals serving the many areas of special interest to psychologists.

The extent of the literature on psychology precludes a comprehensive review, and this chapter does not do justice to the full scope of psychology. Instead it focuses mainly upon certain areas presumably of more immediate interest to other social scientists. Representative classics, reference works, and surveys are cited where further detail may be desirable, and instances of important trends are discussed to indicate the underlying orientations of academic psychology and the problems it must face in realizing its potentialities. Those who desire more comprehensive coverage may wish to examine one of the several general texts now available, for example, the fourth edition of Ernest R. Hilgard and Richard C. Atkinson's excellent *Introduction to Psychology* (1967).

ORIENTATION

The focus of psychological concern is the individual in interaction with his environment. So bald a definition would seem to encroach upon the preserves of other specialities, and yet the overlap is less an artefact of the definition or a portent of imperialistic aspirations than an evidence of the extensive frontiers which psychology holds in common with other social sciences. It is just these shared boundaries which provide a firm foundation for psychological participation in the broad interdisciplinary enterprises which have become so popular in recent years.

But if psychology is a social science, it is also a behavioral science, information processing science, and a biological science. Interaction of organism and environment is observed on all of these levels, and findings at one point regularly are taken over and reappear in rather different settings as explanatory principles. Individual function provides hypotheses for studies of groups. Elaborate expositions of the principles of complex human organization take as their source the mazes and alleys of rat psychology. And no psychologist can ignore the implications of the amazing progress now being made in understanding the molecular bases of heredity (see "The Genetic Code: III," by F. H. C. Crick, *Scientific American*, 1966) and the ways in which genetic determinants interact with other factors in determining behavior (see, for example, "Hormones and Genes," by Eric H. Davidson, *Scientific American*, 1965). The intent of this volume argues against the systematic inclusion of aspects of psychology which seem so distant from the common core of social science, but numerous critical developments are nonetheless occurring in what might seem to be unlikely places, and an adequate presentation of the direction of modern psychology must include some reference to them.

The scope of psychology has not always been so broad. As recently as 1929, Edward B. Titchener argued, in his *Systematic Psychology: "Prolegomena*, that psychologists should confine themselves to the study of conscious experience as it related to the organism." To be sure, Titchener acknowledged the legitimacy of studies of behavior, but he just as surely defined them out of psychology.

The rallying cries of thirty years ago are without current effect upon our present efforts, however; the martial triumphs of earlier generations are as little known to modern psychologists as the knightly encounters of a thousand years before. Nowadays, references even to such acknowledged masterpieces as William James's two-volume *Principles of Psychology* (1890) are rare. And if we today are indifferent to our immediate antecedents, we must be accounted quite ignorant of relevant but not explicitly psychological writings of earlier periods, even though many of the basic concepts of modern psychologists are direct if unwitting descendants of such earlier prepsychological ideas.

Psychologists are therefore most fortunate in having available a number of valuable histories of psychological thought and of the development of their speciality as a separate entity. Gardner Murphy's *Historical Introduction to Modern Psychology* (1949) nicely details the descent of our modern concepts and displays the interconnections between psychological speculation and the more general history of ideas. Edwin G. Boring, well-known for his insistent attempts to broaden the temporal and geographic range of the discipline, has contributed not only *Sensation and Perception in the History of Experimental Psychology* (1942), but also a second edition of his *A History of Experimental Psychology* (1950). Both volumes are scholarly and exciting delineations of the men and the times which advanced the field, with constant reference to the movements of the intellectual climate over the years.

SENSATION PERCEPTION, COGNITION, AND THOUGHT

Lack of food will kill an organism, but so will lack of information. Adaptation to an environment is impossible without information about it, and the limits of access to such information are defined by the organism's capacity to sense energy changes about him. The organism is sensitive also to many stimuli arising from internal adjustments and alterations, but these modalities have been studied less extensively than the externally oriented apparatus. The latter, particularly vision, has been the object of more than 100 years of systematic investigation.

It is misleading, however, to think of sensations as entirely within sensory organs. On the contrary, the peripheral alterations are simply one of several components of a continuous chain of excitation proceeding stepwise centrally to the cortex; the changes initiated within the sensory organs interact with the ongoing activity of the intermediate elements of the neuronal net; and the resultant pattern of cortical activity is the product of all of these combinations and transpositions and bears an extremely complex and indirect relation to the initial sensory input from which it is so many steps removed. And as the attention of the psychologist turns from the original stimulation, the partial and indirect cause of the subsequent activity, to events that occur further and further along the neuronal network, the psychological problem gradually changes from a concern for the organism's capacity to obtain information to an analysis of the organization and patterning of the complex sequences of neural activity; at this point the poorly defined boundary dividing sensation from perception has been crossed.

Among the interesting books dealing with this general area are *Perception* (1966) by Ronald H. Forgus, and *Sensory Communication* (1961) edited by Walter A. Rosenblith. Another important source book is *Vision and Visual Perception* (1955) edited by Clarence H. Graham. Many of the most important classical theories of sensation and perception are well described in Floyd H. Allport's *Theories of Perception and the Concept of Structure* (1955).

One of the most interesting new approaches to sensation and perception involves viewing these processes in terms of the decisions that have to be made in recognizing or classifying patterns of environmental stimulation. Two excellent volumes written from this viewpoint are *Signal Detection and Recognition by Human Observers* (1964) edited by John A. Swets, and *Signal Detection Theory and Psychophysics* (1966) by David M. Green and John A. Swets.

A good example of the progress now being made in analyzing through experiments the complex chain of neurophysiological events involved in the sensation-perception continuum may be found in "The Visual Cortex of the Brain" (*Scientific American*, 1963) by David H. Hubel. Although not easy reading for the layman, this authoritative account nonetheless provides a clear and thoughtful presentation of the state of our knowledge of the neurophysiological processes underlying perception.

No psychological theory arising from the study of perception can compare in the scope and importance of its influence with Gestalt theory, which has provoked invaluable research upon everything from the electrophysiology of the cerebral cortex to the dynamics of social groups. Prior to Max Wertheimer's memorable demonstration in his "Experimentelle Studien über das Sehen von Bewegung" in the *Zeitschrift für Psychologie* (1912) that, under proper conditions, apparent motion might be perceived even though there was absolutely no stimulus movement to which it corresponded, psychologists tended to believe that careful analysis would prove all percepts to be composed of elemental sensations, each of which corresponded to some specific physical energy. Complex percepts were explained in accordance with "laws of association" as aggregates of simpler percepts bonded together through association due to similarity, contrast, or contiguity. Wertheimer's experiments demonstrated conclusively that a theory dealing with mere aggregates of associated elements could not account for phenomena of perceptual patterning and organization, and the principles of Gestalt psychology were shortly thereafter applied to problems in every area of psychology, preeminently by Kurt Koffka in his *Principles of Gestalt Psychology* (1935). Although the Gestalt position not infrequently appeared to American environmentalists as a kind of nativistic crusade, this evidently was not the crucial point for at least some of the pioneers of the movement; Wolfgang Köhler's *Gestalt Psychology: an Introduction to New Concepts in Modern Psychology* (1947), a far more accessible if less comprehensive volume than Koffka's, seems mostly intent upon demonstrating that the empiricist, associationist, "bricks and mortar" theories of psychological organization are "quite unable to do justice to the nature of sensory experience." And it is one of the oddities of psychological history that the Gestaltists, who began with a "field" theory of psychological organization which seemed almost aphysiological in its neglect of the then accepted principles of neurological function, have actually forced a predominantly associationist American psychology into critical debate over the adequacy of the basic innate apparatus it postulates. No current theory of psychology which attempts to include a discussion of underlying neurophysiology can avoid acknowledging a tremendous debt to the Gestalt psychologists for having made explicit the complex patternings and interactions of psychological processes that are implied by our simplest perceptions.

Köhler has observed that relatively greater familiarity with the raw materials of psychology frequently makes new psychological findings seem less exciting and important than comparable advances in the physical sciences. Outstanding exceptions to this rule, however, are the discoveries of unsuspected effects due to monotonous environmental stimulation recently reported by Woodburn Heron and his associates in the *Canadian Journal of Psychology*, and summarized by Heron in an article on "The Pathology of Boredom" in the *Scientific American* (1957). Marked reduction in sensory variation produced not only motivational and emotional disturbances, but also pronounced alterations in perceptual and intellectual functioning, as well as hallucinatory experiences and alterations in brain-wave patterns. While attempts made by others to utilize these findings as explanations for the effectiveness of "brain-washing" remain speculative, they undoubtedly demonstrate, as Heron concludes, that "a changing sensory environment seems essential for human beings."

COGNITION AND THOUGHT

Plato believed cognition to be one of the three primary faculties of the human mind. In that light, the modern psychological edifice until recently would seem to have been as shaky as a two-legged stool. This was due in part to a preference among many American psychologists for investigations dealing with peripheral rather than central variables, the former appearing to be more accessible and amenable to control. There also is a substantial overlap between cognition and perception, and much that might seem to involve thinking or knowing has been analyzed in perceptual terms. Then, too, some who are ill at ease at the idea of thought often have been willing and able to deal with "problem solving behavior." Certainly this area in the course of its development has seen a good deal of interesting work, much of it summarized by George Humphrey in *Thinking: An Introduction to Its Experimental Psychology* (1951), a sustained and scholarly analysis of the issues and experiments that gradually evolved into our modern psychology of thought. In general, however, the psychology of cognition and thought was for a long while one of the weaker sisters among psychological areas.

Lately, however, there has been a marked and sustained change for the better. One of the first harbingers of this new era was *A Study of Thinking* (1956), by Jerome S. Bruner, Jacqueline J. Goodnow, and George A. Austin. This book deals mainly with human concept formation and is interesting particularly because of its emphasis on the importance of the strategies people use in the course of complex mental activity. Concept formation and utilization continues to be a lively area for investigation, as will be evident from Earl B. Hunt's *Concept Learning* (1962), Edwin J. Martin's article on "Concept Utilization," in Vol. III of the *Handbook of Mathematical Psychology* (1965), edited by R. Duncan Luce, Robert R. Bush, and Eugene Galanter, and *Experiments in Induction* (1966), by Earl B. Hunt, Janet Marin, and Philip J. Stone.

One of the most significant innovations for the area of cognition and thought, as for psychology generally, has been the development mainly by Allen Newell, Herbert A. Simon, and their associates, of an approach employing techniques variously referred to as heuristic programs, dynamic models, and information processing models. The simplest way to grasp this new development is in terms of an example.

Imagine you knew nothing of how automobiles worked, and wanted an explanation. One very useful kind of explanation would be in terms of the significant structures involved, the functions they play, and the ways in which these functions interrelate. For example, there is the engine, the transmission, and so on. Each of these structural components plays some function in the overall operation of the automobile depending upon the ways in which these components are related. Similarly, a more detailed explanation would require a discussion of the organization of any particular component into subcomponents, their subfunctions, and the interrelations among them. If you wanted to be sure that you really understood how the automobile worked, one way to convince both yourself and others would be to build one. Were you able to construct something which behaved as an automobile does, that would be a pretty good sign that you had a good grasp of the structures and functions involved. Note that explanations in biology often are of this form. We analyze the organism into such significant structures as the heart, the liver, and so forth, and then investigate the functions these structures play and the substructures comprising any particular organ.

Newell, Simon, and others have attempted to investigate human information processing in thinking, learning, concept attainment, and other areas by analyzing these activities in terms of the hypothetical information processing organs and functions involved. As a test of the adequacy of their explanations, and as a means of investigating the implications of their theories, they frequently express these theories as computer programs. Now it becomes possible to investigate just what their models imply by running the program on the computer to see what behaviors it produces and how these behaviors compare with those of humans engaged in comparable activities. This is the strategy that underlies all of their work, including such fundamental theories as those embedded in the problem solving and learning programs described in *Computers and Thought* (1963), edited by Edward A. Feigenbaum and Julian Feldman.

One of the most widely influential treatments of the human being as an information processing system is to be found in *Plans and the Structure of Behavior* (1960), by George A. Miller, Eugene Galanter, and Karl H. Pribram. A good discussion of the advantages and limitations of information processing models, the ways in which they are constructed, and their applications in various areas of psychology is contained in *Cognition and Thought* (1965), by Walter R. Reitman.

Information processing models constitute only one of the several important directions of growth in the area of cognition and thinking. Another is well represented in a recent book by Adriaan D. de Groot entitled *Thought and Choice in Chess* (1966). De Groot begins from the theoretical framework provided by Otto Selz and goes on to present a detailed and careful empirical study of the thought processes of chess masters. In particular he shows that chess skill is not a matter of thinking faster or of instantaneous exploration of many alternatives but rather of selective search procedures based on the master's vast knowledge of the possibilities of the game. De Groot's careful investigation nicely shows what can be accomplished by detailed analyses of complex thinking in real situations. His more recent work pursues the problem utilizing both naturalistic and experimental techniques.

Another fascinating line of development is represented by the current widespread interest in the growth of cognitive processes. Much of this work takes its origins from research by Jean Piaget and his associates. John H. Flavell's *The Developmental Psychology of Jean Piaget* (1963) gives an excellent introduction to his work and the background from which it derives. A number of interesting recent studies in the same area, but from a somewhat different point of view, are presented in *Studies in Cognitive Growth* (1966), by Jerome S. Bruner, Rose R. Olver, and Patricia M. Greenfield, and others.

Still another closely related area of current interest has to do with language. Most of the impetus here has come from a group of linguists associated with Noam Chomsky at the Massachusetts Institute of Technology. This group begins with the proposition that any adequate model of language must be generative: that is, it must be able to account for the production and comprehension of new sentences, sentences that the human being has never heard or produced before. To achieve this, the MIT group treats what the human knows of his language as a system of rules capable of mediating the comprehension and production of language. There is an evident relation between this approach and that of the information processing modelers. In both cases the theory is stated as a system of functions capable of doing something. In both cases also the concepts used are related to, though not limited by, the structure and process concepts that have evolved over the past two decades to describe and deal with the complex information processing systems we now can implement on digital computers. A good introduction to the basic point of view of the MIT group is presented in Jerry A. Fodor and Jerrold F. Katz (eds.), *The Structure of Language* (1964), and *Aspects of the Theory of Syntax* (1965) by Chomsky gives an account of his recent work. For discussions of the implications and application of these ideas in research on human language behavior, see Ursula Bellugi and Roger Brown (eds.), *The Acquisition of Language* (1964), and the chapter on "Psycholinguistics" by Susan M. Ervin-Tripp and Dan I. Slobin in Vol. XVII of the *Annual Review of Psychology* (1966), edited by Paul R. Farnsworth, Olga McNemar, and Quinn McNemar.

Because it is in the middle of a period of rapid development and change, the area of cognition and thinking is not easy to summarize. One of the first to attempt to provide a general picture of the psychology of cognition and thought in the light of these new developments was J. McVicker Hunt, in *Intelligence and Experience* (1961). Daniel Berlyne tries, in his *Structure and Direction in Thinking* (1965), to discuss most of these recent developments and to relate them to a broad range of experimental research, thus preserving continuity with earlier work by learning theorists and others on simpler forms of information processing in humans and in lower organisms. The most balanced picture of the field is the superb and stimulating treatment provided by Ulric Neisser in *Cognition* (1967). Beautifully organized and written, this volume includes detailed discussions of all of the subjects briefly referred to here, as well as many others that could not be considered. The book is very highly recommended to readers who wish an up-to-date understanding of the present status of this field of psychology.

LEARNING

Whatever we may think of it, we live in an age which has reified conviviality and institutionalized the coffee break. Even if we did not, however, one somehow doubts that many students of learning, having tired for the moment of the condensed and detailed journal articles which are their daily fare, would turn for their respite to Burrhus F. Skinner's little novel of life, *Walden Two* (1948). Yet this volume by a respected learning theorist convincingly portrays a near future in which a science of learning will both educate the utopian social man and also make possible his complete totalitarian control. *Walden Two* is hardly a subtle book, but its speculations brilliantly evoke the latent potentialities that make the psychology of learning so fascinating and fundamental a subject.

The amazing development and preeminence in America of learning psychology, particularly compared with its insignificant position abroad, has been ascribed to the peculiar importance the dominant values of the American culture attribute to adaptability to change. Ours, we are told, was an open, expanding society, with trails to break, foreigners to integrate. What was important were progress and change, and little attention was given to the stable things handed down from generation to generation. It was William James who popularized pragmatism, an American philosophy of the *usefulness* of truth, in which the truth of a belief was judged by its results. Certainly the disinclination to accord a significant role to nativistic factors, characteristic of behaviorist learning theory, also was long evident throughout American psychology as a whole, and although we now are in the early phases of a reconsideration of the importance of one's innate endowments, it is easy to see why the first empirical and environmentalist formulations of the sources of behavior and behavior change took firm root here and grew rapidly.

It was a German, Hermann Ebbinghaus, who took the first significant step toward an empirical science of learning, reporting in his *Uber das Gedächtnis* (1885) the use of nonsense syllables to study the formation of associations without reference to meaning. In 1898, Edward L. Thorndike published *Animal Intelligence,* and in it he set forth an early formulation of a systematic but empirical theory of learning which was to maintain its preeminence in America for more than thirty years. Deriving in large part from the intellectual tradition of the English associationist philosophers, Thorndike's system replaced the notion of associations among ideas with the concept of connections between sensory inputs and response outputs which were determined by subsequent rewards or punishments following the response in this situation. His later writings had extensive practical influence upon pedagogical practice. More recent experimentation has made necessary extensive alterations in Thorndike's position, but his experimental orientation, his associationist predilections, and his emphasis upon the consequences of behavior as determinants of learning have remained dominant characteristics of American learning theory to this day.

The concern for a psychology of *behavior* and its modifications, so evident in Thorndike's writings, was made the cornerstone of "behaviorism," a movement determinedly promoted by John B. Watson and described in detail in his *Behavior: An Introduction to Comparative Psychology* (1914). Watson attacked the mentalistic and the introspective, but instead of discarding higher mental processes, he tried to incorporate them into his psychology of overt behavior by reconceptualizing them as potential peripheral behavioral mechanisms. Thought, for example, became "implicit speech." Attractive because they seemed to offer new means of getting at elusive psychological functions, these reconceptualizations failed to distinguish adequately between peripheral behaviors as causes and as correlates, and so in themselves were improvements really only by fiat.

Ivan P. Pavlov's *Conditioned Reflexes* did not appear in English translation until 1927, but news of his work reached America over a decade earlier, and Pavlovian principles were incorporated in several places into theories of learning. Since both the neutral stimuli associated with natural stimuli and the responses they came through association to elicit were amenable to observation and control, Pavlovian formulations proved congenial to behaviorist theories, and conditioning became a fundamental learning paradigm. According to Pavlov, however, contiguity was a sufficient condition for learning, whereas Thorndike considered reward and punishment to be more important determinants. Despite the innumerable experimental attempts to decide this issue, there still remain wide divergences among learning psychologists as to the necessary and sufficient conditions.

Clark L. Hull's principal conceptual contribution to learning theory was a nicely integrated conceptual scheme which incorporated the findings of both Thorndike and Pavlov into a single theory of learning grounded in a principle of reinforcement not very different from Thorndike's ideas about the effects of reward and punishment. But modern learning psychology is even more indebted to Hull, for in large part it was his influence which moved it in the direction of a systematic postulational science striving to derive quantitative predictions of behavior change. Hull's *Principles of Behavior* (1943), *Essentials of Behavior* (1951), and *A Behavior System* (1952) were basic reading for learning theorists for much of the last decade.

Quite apart from whatever intrinsic value Hull's theoretical notions may have possessed, his systematic approach seemed to have one basic and incontrovertible merit: it would premit the deduction of hypotheses which could be tested precisely. Furthermore, since tests of these rigorously deduced hypotheses were strict tests of the entire theory, Hull's procedure appeared to make possible the quick and efficient acceptance or rejection of the underlying postulates. For a time a major portion of the literature on learning was devoted to tests of aspects of Hullian theory.

Two considerations have prevented Hullian theory from becoming the very first formulation of principles of learning to be either strictly verified or strictly rejected. As numerous psychologists have suggested, and as Sigmund Koch exhaustively demonstrates in his chapter on "Clark L. Hull" in *Modern Learning Theory* (1954), by William K. Estes and others, the theory contains important gaps, inconsistencies, and indeterminacies that render it, in fact, untestable *in toto*. Secondly, too many theorists have worked with isolated concepts, ignoring the conditions imposed by the total theoretical context. This is hardly a reflection on the theory, of course, but it remains true nonetheless that many of the specific concepts have been employed to "explain" what are plainly contradictory results. As Harry F. Harlow protested in his survey, "Learning," in the *Annual Review of Psychology* for 1952, "... the present-day rubber band theoretical systems can stretch to encompass any data regardless of how opposed they may be to the original predictions of the theorist."

Oddly enough, however, the tremendous volume of research inspired by Hullian theory, for all its failure either to confirm or invalidate its conceptual bases, has nonetheless had a lasting effect on the psychology of learning. For, at a time when many learning theorists were content with programmatic definitions and gross verbal "laws," as Ernest R. Hilgard puts it in a review of *A Behavior System* (*Psychological Bulletin*, 1954), "This is the novelty Hull contributed: a system at once fertile in its predictions, and precise enough to be vulnerable to experimental attack." Even though the models learning theorists now use—for example in studies such as those described in Richard C. Atkinson, Gordon H. Bower, and Edward J. Crothers' *An Introduction to Mathematical Learning Theory* (1965)—employ concepts quite distinct from those to be found in Hull's work, the overall cast of the enterprise continues to bear his mark.

Hull's was by no means the only behaviorism. Edwin R. Guthrie worked out another, and his *The Psychology of Learning* (1935; revised, 1952) is famous for its contention that the complexities of learning phenomena reduce to a single proposition: "A combination of stimuli which has accompanied a movement will on its reoccurrence tend to be followed by that movement." The very antithesis of cumbersome hypotheticodeductive theories, Guthrie's simple principle of stimulus and response association through contiguity would seem to assert nothing more radical than that you will do again exactly what you did last time in the same situation. From the viewpoint of reinforcement theorists, however, this prosaic postulate generates some astounding hypotheses, and it has provoked a number of important experimental investigations.

While Skinner's novels are unlikely to insure immortality for him, his experimental investigations of behavior, such as those reported in *The Behavior Organisms* (1938), rank as basic contributions to the psychology of learning. Notoriously averse to formal theories, including those of his fellow behaviorists, Skinner has sought instead to determine empirically, by manipulation of parameter values, the relationship between such important aspects of the environment as the schedule of reward and the behavior emitted by organisms existing in it. Skinnerian ways of thinking about behavior change remain very much with us in such diverse fields as the investigation of language behavior, the treatment of behavior disorders, and the new field of programed instruction (see, for example, *The Analysis of Behavior* (1961), by James G. Holland and Burrhus F. Skinner).

At first blush it is difficult to imagine how any of the basic principles of Gestalt theory ever could be incorporated into a behaviorist theory of learning. Yet this is probably not an inaccurate characterization of Edward C. Tolman's position as he has set it forth in his *Purposive Behavior in Animals and Men* (1932) and in subsequent statements, such as those to be found in his *Collected Papers in Psychology* (1951). Less formally worked out than Hull's position, Tolman's cognitive constructs have proven attractive to many psychologists who prefer central to peripheral constructs but who do not wish to sacrifice the indisputable methodological superiorities of explicitly behavioristic approaches to the study of learning phenomena. Kenneth MacCorquodale and Paul E. Meehl have utilized Tolman's constructs as the bases for a formalized expectancy theory of learning in their chapter on "Edward C. Tolman" in *Modern Learning Theory* (1954), edited by William K. Estes and others. For many psychologists, such cognitively oriented presentations have become acceptable alternatives to the stimulus-and-response constructions of more orthodox behaviorists, particularly now that we have in the information processing models of Newell, Simon, and others examples of how the concepts of goal, purpose, and expectancy may be incorporated into psychological theories in objective and well-specified ways. Kurt Lewin's orientation, quite similar to that of the original Gestalt theorists, has also had some influence upon recent positions. Lewin has had relatively little effect upon experimental investigations of learning, however, and his ideas are better discussed in connection with social psychology.

The current research on learning is almost always reported in individual journal articles. There are, however, a number of up-to-date comprehensive discussions. *Hilgard and Marquis' Conditioning and Learning* (2d ed., 1965) is a revision made by Gregory A. Kimble of the classic account of the experimental literature by Ernest R. Hilgard and Donald G. Marquis. Perhaps the best survey of recent tendencies may be found in the last six chapters of the newly revised *Theories of Learning* (3d ed., 1966), by Hilgard and Gordon H. Bower. Although the entire volume is at a consistently high level, it is interesting to note that, in contrast to the organization of the earlier chapters about principal theorists, the last sections are oriented about relatively specific problems and approaches. Perhaps this reflects a current disenchantment with research intended as a crucial test of a formal theory and a preference instead for empirical investigations of specific problems in the light of more limited formulations. If this is the case, it may make for more confusion, but it also seems to be resulting in a sustained body of new work. Other important aspects of the field are reflected in *Categories of Human Learning* (1964), edited by Arthur W. Melton, and in current issues of the *Journal of Verbal Learning and Verbal Behavior* (1962-   ).

THE INDIVIDUAL

The most widely known of the psychologist's tools is the psychological test, the systematic sampling of an individual's behavior. The results of investigations of psychological processes such as learning, perception, or thinking are obtained either as disparities in average performance on some psychological measure between groups distinguished by some antecedent difference, or else as relationships between the scores individuals obtain on one test and the scores they make on another. Firmly established associations among test scores, or between test scores and antecedent variables, really form the bedrock of experimental psychology.

An individual's test score has other uses as well. Compared with the scores of others on the same test, it measures relative standing. Contrasted with the individual's score on the same test at some other time, it denotes the degree of change. Evaluated together with the individual's scores on other tests, it yields a profile of strengths and weakness in the traits or abilities presumed to underlie the obtained test scores. The utilization of test scores to provide information about individuals, or groups of individuals, rather than about psychological processes, is the basis of the psychology of individual differences.

A great many of the most important psychological tests developed as solutions for specific practical problems. Although the amazing investigations of Sir Francis Galton and his *Inquiries into Human Faculty and Its Development* (1883) are a treasure trove for test makers, the first great standardized tests—the measures of complex intellectual functions—resulted from a need to identify subnormal children in order to investigate the suitability of certain educational techniques for them. The early Binet-Simon scales prepared for this purpose subsequently were revised several times, and in 1916, with the appearance of *The Measurement of Intelligence*, Lewis M. Terman's famous revision of the Binet-Simon scales, the Stanford-Binet, became available. Despite recent attempts at the analysis of intelligence into several more specific factors, the latest revision of the Stanford-Binet Test (3d, 1960) and the measure of general intelligence devised by David Wechsler, described in *The Measurement and Appraisal of Adult Intelligence* (4th ed., 1958), are easily the most widely employed of the individual general classification tests in current usage.

Following the wide acceptance of general classification tests, increased attention was paid to measures intended to assess particular aptitudes. The rapid proliferation of specific measures to meet the growing need for efficient selection and training of industrial specialists was accelerated still further by world war and cold war; the prompt and efficient selection of individuals who could learn the indispensable specialized military and technological skills became vital for national survival. But as the flood of new tests increasingly threatened to swell beyond all control, important new handbooks and compendia appeared to maintain order and to channel the mounting confusion. The most notable of these are the *Mental Measurements Yearbooks*, by Oscar K. Buros (ed.). Appearing in 1938, 1940, 1949, 1953, 1959, and 1965, successive *Yearbooks*, although they covered of necessity only tests widely used or newly appearing in the interim periods, included critical reviews and evaluations by test experts and thereby made an important contribution to the technical improvement of psychological tests. Anne Anastasi's *Psychological Testing* (2d ed., 1961) is a comprehensive and excellent survey of the applications of the most important kinds of measuring instruments, as is Frank S. Freeman's somewhat more critical *Theory and Practice of Psychological Testing* (rev. ed., 1955). Up-to-date information on specific tests and on test usage is available in current issues of the *Journal of Applied Psychology* (1917–), *Journal of Consulting Psychology* (1937–), and *Educational and Psychological Measurement* (1941–).

Closely associated with differential psychology are investigations of classes or groups of individuals distinguished by particular characteristics, or by age, sex, or intelligence. Leona E. Tyler's *The Psychology of Human Differences* (3d ed., 1966) includes a good general introduction to this area. The extensive literature on child and developmental psychology is treated in detail in the *National Society for the Study of Education Yearbook: Child Psychology* (1963), by Harold W. Stevenson (ed.), and in a two volume *Review of Child Development Research* (1964 and 1966), both volumes by Martin and Lois Hoffman (eds.). These volumes include an excellent survey of the fascinating and suggestive if less quantitative studies reported by Jean Piaget in such books as *The Language and Thought of the Child* (1926) and *The Moral Judgment of the Child* (1932). Another noteworthy study is Lewis M. Terman's invaluable collaborative investigation of genius, described in the series *Genetic Studies of Genius* (1925–) and in articles in the thirty-ninth *Yearbook* of the National Society for the Study of Education (1940). These contributions of Piaget and Terman are also outstanding in the attention given to the social consequences of the attributes under consideration.

PERSONALITY

"Personality," writes Raymond B. Cattell in his *Personality: A Systematic, Theoretical, and Factual Study* (1950), "is that which permits a prediction of what a person will do in a given situation." So defined, the study of personality has much in common with the psychology of individual differences, and in fact differential psychologists use the term to refer to such nonintellectual attributes as temperament, emotionality, and rigidity. Investigations of these attributes form but a limited segment, however, of the spectrum of writings on the psychology of personality.

The simplicity of Cattell's definition is deceptive and conceals a very considerable implication. It suggests that far from forming a corner of differential psychology, personality not only totally comprehends that area, but also presupposes the laws of perception, learning, and motivation; for the successful prediction of behavior presumes an adequate knowledge of all psychological principles. Despite these implications, many personality theorists would quite willingly subscribe to the substance of the definition; in the absence of broad and experimentally validated psychological principles, they postulate their own. And if, on occasion, they seem to be "talking about things which everybody knows in language which nobody understands," it seems no less difficult to prefer instead the *ad hoc* studies of *ad hoc* variables which line the opposite shore. As Dan L. Adler summarizes the situation in his review of "Some Recent Books on Personality" in the *Psychological Bulletin* (1954),

> The experimentalists' efforts are now all too often vitiated by absorption in details and specious variables . . . they seem to have narrowed rather than broadened the breadth of their conceptualization and pursuits. There is a danger that the hypothetico-deductive method will be lost to them for lack of a theoretical vehicle to carry it. The clinical group presents the problem differently. They have not forsaken scientific method—principally because they have never adopted it. Although their explanatory systems have rarely lacked breadth, they have continuously lacked evidence.

To a certain extent the uninspiring condition of the psychology of personality today is a consequence of its diverse origins. The clinic must be credited with the major continuing impetus to its development, and most of the principal personality theories developed out of intimate contact with the treatment of patients suffering from ailments which gradually were perceived to be psychological in nature. Academic psychology, however, also has made extensive contributions to the study of personality, not only through individual theorizing and experimentation, but also through university clinics that were intended as much for the exploration of personality as for therapeutic purposes. Finally, a third major source of contributions has been the increasingly frequent studies making use of entirely objective test batteries and sophisticated techniques such as factor analysis. Results from these three areas of endeavor are at the present time almost entirely isolated and unintegrated.

There is a further obvious reason for the relative lack of any real progress in this area. Whatever their theoretical persuasion, personality psychologists are primarily interested in organismic variables; they lack the relatively greater opportunities for rigor available to students of learning or perception, where important stimulus and response variables are far more amenable to measurement and control; their concepts must be derived from data which are alternately manifested, imperfectly perceived, and multiply determined.

In addition to its varied origins, the numerous close affiliations of personality psychology with social and motivation psychology, with sociology and anthropology, and most important of all, with psychoanalytic theory preclude even a superficial attempt at comprehensiveness. There is, however, a unique and invaluable set of five volumes, *The Index of Psychoanalytic Writings* (1956-   ) compiled by Alexander Grinstein, which is claimed to list "every book, article, monograph, abstract and review published by over 5000 psychoanalytic writers in the last 60 years." The availability of this monumental reference work makes it somewhat less difficult to omit in this survey extended references to the important psychoanalytic influences on personality theory and research.

Sigmund Freud, of course, may not be omitted; there is probably no branch of the psychological literature on personality which is not immeasurably in his debt. He is the unique exception to the otherwise accurate characterization of earlier psychological writers as men who today go honored but unread. His *Psychopathology of Everyday Life* (1914), which first appeared in German in 1901, remains a compelling introduction to the psychoanalytic orientation, while such classics as *The Interpretation of Dreams* (1913, trans. from the 3d German ed.) continue to appear in new editions and to enjoy wide readership among psychologists and nonpsychologists alike. While all of Freud's works are now available in a recently completed *Standard Edition of the Complete Psychological Works* (1953-   ), James Strachey (ed.), it may be that the most convincing evidences of Freud's ability to arrive patiently and carefully at meaningful analyses of his patients' behavior are contained in the five volumes of his *Collected Papers* (1948-50), works which deal with individual case histories and with specific concepts and problems. Written with characteristic clarity and felicity of expression, these papers convey the excitement at new discoveries and the cautious reserve which Freud evinced as he mulled over tentative formulations about the genesis and organization of personality.

The works of Carl G. Jung, considered by some to be second in importance only to those of Freud, have had a relatively limited effect upon contemporary psychology. Only a few of Jung's concepts have been adopted for general use, and even in these cases the use is far less systematic than is the case with terminology borrowed from Freud. The publication of Jung's *Collected Works* (1953-   ) undoubtedly makes his ideas more accessible, but even if contemporary psychologists become more familiar with Jung's thought, it is doubtful that a system so distinctly different in tenor and in basic assumptions will find much acceptance among them.

Continued contact with the id, ego, and superego has established a certain tolerance for the familiar tripartite model of personality structure, and the center of gravity of American psychology most surely has undergone a pronounced shift toward interest in the irrational dynamics of human behavior as a consequence of the substantive merits of Freud's work. On the other hand, the more optimistic "American" view of man as a creative organism with a potential for rational, healthy self-realization (evident in such works as Carl R. Rogers' *Client-centered Therapy; Its Current Practice, Implications, and Theory*, 1951) has undoubtedly had a reciprocal influence, so that recent psychoanalytic theory shows signs of more limited concern with the forces of the id and a greater interest in the constructive aspects of the ego. The appearance of Ernest Jones's excellent three volume biography, *The Life and Work of Sigmund Freud* (1953-57), a measured analysis of Freud's work within the context of the intellectual influences of the day, of Calvin S. Hall and Gardner Lindzey's clear and concise expositions in their chapter on "Psychoanalytic Theory and Its Applications in the Social Sciences" in Lindzey's (ed.) *Handbook of Social Psychology* (1954), and of Hall's lucid if uncritical introductory volume, *A Primer of Freudian Psychology* (1954), have also materially contributed to the rapprochement between Freudian and academic psychologies of personality.

The contributions of colleagues and disciples who attempted to develop psychoanalytic theory further within the Freudian framework, as well as those of one-time associates who broke with Freud and developed theories of their own, are summarized in Gerald S. Blum's *Psychoanalytic Theories of Personality* (1953), in which the stages of psychosexual development form multiple foci for the exposition of similarities and contrasts, and in Ruth Munroe's *Schools of Psychoanalytic Thought* (1955), a volume notable for its thoughtful and well-balanced presentations.

Four full decades were to pass after Freud began his investigations before contributions by academic psychologists to the study of personality appeared in any significant number. Gordon W. Allport's *Personality; A Psychological Interpretation* (1937) attracted considerable attention for its indictment of what Allport claimed was an historical or genetic bias in psychoanalytic theory and for its determined insistence upon the importance of the contemporary motivation of the unique and cardinal individual. A second important volume by a Harvard author was Henry A. Murray's collaborative *Explorations in Personality* (1938). In addition to the yeoman's service it performed by freely introducing psychoanalytic notions into academic settings, this work made popular a number of novel diagnostic techniques, among them the Thematic Appreception Test (TAT), and opened important new possibilities for the empirical assessment of personality variables. Other contributions in this general tradition include David C. McClelland's *Personality* (1951), Julian B. Rotter's *Social Learning and Clinical Psychology* (1954), and George A. Kelly's two volumes on *The Psychology of Personal Constructs* (1955).

The chief argument of advocates of an objective, factor analytic approach to personality is the great potential superiority of the method over the usual intuitive alternative as a taxonomic tool for the identification of primary personality dimensions. The point is forcefully advanced in Raymond B. Cattell's *The Scientific Analysis of Personality* (1965), and Cattell presents considerable evidence for several personality factors which show "reasonable stability" in a report on "The Principal Replicated Factors Discovered in Objective Personality Tests," published in the *Journal of Abnormal and Social Psychology* (1955). Hans J. Eysenck, author of *The Scientific Study of Personality* (1952) and *The Structure of Human Personality* (1953), is another strong proponent of the technique, and his article on "The Logical Basis of Factor Analysis" in the *American Psychologist* (1953) is an outstanding exposition of its possibilities.

The advent of multivariate and multidimensional statistical techniques initially seemed to hold great promise for social and clinical psychology as well as for research on personality. They appeared to afford rigor and precision to analyses of the patterns and manifolds with which investigators in these areas had to deal. At the present time, it is doubtful that these objectives have been attained. While it is difficult to find agreement on the relative merits of factor analytic contributions to the study of personality, however, they have probably had two permanent and very beneficial negative effects. In the first place, they have by contrast focused attention on the ideological rather than scientific status of most of the more popular speculations which currently are classified as personality "theory." In the second place, they have made imperative renewed efforts to come up with alternate solutions to the basic measurement problems which many would suggest are being mistakenly finessed by the assumptions required for the factor analytic model, and for the powerful but stringently demanding linear statistical models in general use at the present time.

A well-balanced and representative selection of currently focal orientations to personality is contained in *Theories of Personality* (1957), by Hall and Lindzey, including sympathetic presentations of several important positions which could not be considered here. The appropriate chapters of recent numbers of the *Annual Review of Psychology* are also strongly recommended, however, for their considered and detailed if distinctly less cheery analyses of current theorizing and research on personality and its assessment.

MOTIVATION AND EMOTION

Many overtones resulting from the varied origins and comprehensive aspirations of personality psychology find echoes in the literature of the even more recent and less well-defined area of motivation. Best understood as a collection of theory and research drawn from several distinct areas, the literature of motivation psychology is frequently the work of men who principally were learning, physiological, social, or personality psychologists and who viewed motivation as a limited topic, each within the context of his own primary frame of reference. The generalized, interrelated problems of the intensity, direction, and maintenance of behavior, which today form the focus for a growing interest in motivation per se, have only recently come to be conceptualized in this unitary fashion and investigated with the integrated resources of the older areas of research. Despite increased interaction among the several approaches to motivational problems, however, there exists no generally accepted single orientation as yet, and so it may be best to eschew Procrustean methods here and to review representative contributions with reference to the original points of view.

Psychologists have generally considered emotion and motivation closely related. The two are generally associated in modern theories, but no more so than in the very much earlier *Outlines of Psychology* (1902), in which Wilhelm Wundt argued that "all feelings, even those of relatively indifferent character, contain in some degree an effort towards or away from some end." Perhaps because of their preoccupation with the description of conscious content, most early investigators were concerned primarily with feelings and emotions; relatively little attention was devoted by academic psychology to the dynamics of striving. *The Psychology of Pleasantness and Unpleasantness* (1932), by John G. Beebe-Center, and *Feeling and Emotion* (1937), by Harry N. Gardiner, Ruth C. Metcalf, and Beebe-Center summarize the generally inconclusive history of these investigations and also contain excellent accounts of prepsychological analyses of these phenomena. David Rapaport's *Emotions and Memory* (1942) is notable for its very careful and closely reasoned examination of the extensive literature of this somewhat more delimited area of endeavor. Discouraged, perhaps, by the meager returns obtained for the effort expended on them, psychologists have turned in other directions, and experimental studies of feeling and emotion in the traditional contexts have disappeared almost completely from the current literature.

The persistent probings of physiological psychologists, on the other hand, have frequently been well rewarded, and considerable importance is now quite generally attached to investigations of the biological bases of emotion and motivation. Knowledge of the physiological changes accompanying motivational stages such as hunger and thirst has advanced considerably, and its significance is well recognized. To a somewhat lesser extent, psychologists also are now aware of the extent to which the primary motivational mechanisms can be conceptualized almost entirely at the physiological level; Eliot Stellar, in an article on "The Physiology of Motivation" in the *Psychological Review* (1954), actually goes so far as to theorize that the amount of motivated behavior can be viewed as in large part an immediate function "of the amount of activity in certain excitatory centers of the hypothalamus." Finally, some of the most provocative and exciting attempts to analyze the complexities of psychological organization and behavior, as for instance, Karl S. Lashley's chapter on "The Problem of Serial Order in Behavior" in Lloyd A. Jeffress' (ed.) *Cerebral Mechanisms in Behavior; The Hixon Symposium* (1951), or Donald O. Hebb's discussion of "Drives and the C.N.S. (Conceptual Nervous System)" in the *Psychological Review* for 1955, have been based to a considerable extent upon thoughtful extrapolations from neurophysiological discoveries. Physiological psychology necessarily must receive relatively short shrift in an essay such as this, but the broad importance of a number of recent physiological developments for any general behavioral science cannot be overemphasized, and social scientists of whatever persuasion who are watching for new breakthroughs could do worse than to keep an occasional eye cocked in this direction.

Walter B. Cannon's *Bodily Changes in Pain, Hunger, Fear and Rage* (2d ed., 1929) must be counted among the classical contributions to the physiological psychology of emotional states. Cannon also has contributed to the basic concepts of modern motivational theory. His concept of homeostasis, postulating the maintenance of bodily equilibria at optimal levels as a principal basis for behavior, is set forth in *The Wisdom of the Body* (1932), and has since been elaborated by some more recent authors who argue for the utility of regarding all motivated behavior as homeostatic in a broader sense. Donald B. Lindsley's chapter on "Emotion" in S. Smith Stevens' (ed.) *Handbook of Experimental Psychology* (1951) also makes excellent use of physiological findings as bases for some far-reaching propositions about motivation and emotion. An outstanding analysis of a wide range of physiological data, together with a number of promising hypotheses about the physiological concomitants of an equally wide range of important psychological processes, is to be found in Ernst Gellhorn's *Physiological Foundations of Neurology and Psychiatry* (1953).

This volume also provides considerable support for the increasing tendency to accept physiological mechanisms as possible alternative sources of many motivational and emotional pathologies which quite recently were to be interpreted only in developmental, dynamic, or interpersonal terms. None of the recent neurological discoveries are of greater potential importance to the progressive improvement of the understanding of the brain mechanisms underlying emotion and motivation, however, than the striking behavioral results of direct electrical stimulation obtained by James Olds and reported in his description of "A Physiological Study of Reward" in David C. McClelland's (ed.) *Studies in Motivation* (1955), and in his chapter on "Physiological Mechanisms of Reward" in Marshall R. Jones's (ed.) *Nebraska Symposium on Motivation* (1955), which is the third volume of *Current Theory and Research in Motivation, A Symposium* (1953-) issued by the Psychology Department of the University of Nebraska.

Learning psychologists and social psychologists also have gradually produced extensive literatures on motivation. Learning theorists have varied considerably among themselves for several decades on the relative utilities of several plausible conceptualizations of motivational variables, but these differences have provoked an impressive body of experimental studies which have increasingly served to refine and sharpen recent formulations. Many of these studies are discussed in Leo J. Postman's scholarly critique of "The History and Present Status of the Law of Effect" in the *Psychological Bulletin* (1947). Much of the most recent material relevant to the motivational assumptions inherent in current views on learning is analyzed with comparable care and discernment in *Modern Learning Theory* (1954), by William K. Estes and others.

A number of learning psychologists have become quite interested in certain classes of environmental parameters as important determinants of behavior. A series of stimulating papers from the laboratories of Harry F. Harlow, Kay C. Montgomery, Edward L. Walker, and others have proven conclusively that such factors as environmental novelty, variability, and complexity can account for major portions of behavioral variance. Good discussions will be found in *Functions of Varied Experience* (1961), by Donald W. Fiske and Salvatore R. Maddi (eds.), and in *Curiosity and Exploratory Behavior* (1965), by Harry Fowler.

Several European ethologists, studying comparative behavior as a function of habitat, agree on the importance of environmental stimuli for the maintenance and direction of behavior, but nonetheless accord them a radically different role, that of releasers for innate patterns of activity. Although these scientists have been reporting their findings for more than two decades, the body of work came to the general attention of American psychologists only with the publication in English of Nikolaas

Tinbergen's *The Study of Instinct* (1951) and of a slender and charmingly written if scarcely less provocative volume, *King Solomon's Ring* (1952), by Konrad Z. Lorenz. For a short time thereafter, the ethologists' findings created a series of obvious disturbances in American thinking about motivation and learning which were given voice in papers such as William S. Verplanck's "Since Learned Behavior Is Innate, and Vice Versa, What Now?" in the *Psychological Review* (1955).

The ethologists' investigations have no doubt resulted in a more general awareness of the elaborate possibilities for innate patterning of behavior in lower species. They also very likely have contributed, together with the work of Donald O. Hebb and his associates, to a renewed interest in studies of environmental interaction with early learning and development, such as those discussed by Frank A. Beach and Julian Jaynes in their review of "Effects of Early Experience upon the Behavior of Animals," in the *Psychological Bulletin* (1954), and by William R. Thompson's paper on "Early Environment—Its Importance for Later Behavior," in Paul H. Hoch and Joseph Zubin's (eds.) *Psychopathology of Childhood* (1955). There has, however, been no marked increase in psychological investigations of the implications of the ethological position to date, perhaps because of a lack of shared underlying orientations, and it would be premature to conclude that the ethologists' studies additionally have had anything but a very restricted effect upon the fundamental concepts of American motivation psychology.

Emphasis on the major importance of environmental determinants of motivation, a recent tendency in learning theory, has traditionally been a central feature of social psychological formulations, where present and past situational cues, their perception, and their communication are principal antecedents of behavioral direction. Learning theorists, ethologists, and social psychologists all have been concerned with somewhat different aspects of the environment, of course, and it is particularly difficult to deal with current social psychological concepts relevant to motivation apart from the context of group dynamics and interaction. While consideration of these concepts will therefore be deferred until the general consideration of social psychological literature, their influence upon much current motivation theory must be emphasized at this point.

Donald O. Hebb's examination of the various capacities in which environmental stimuli may determine behavior is but one of the outstanding features of his remarkable investigation of *The Organization of Behavior* (1949). Hebb's thoughtful integration of fundamental components of Gestalt theory into an associationist framework which itself incorporated many of the most important neurophysiological discoveries and speculations of the time resulted in a creative theory of behavior with far-reaching implications for the study of motivation. The really unique merit of this book, however, may well be its admittedly speculative but systematic and integrated approach to the diverse and complex functions of the organism in terms of a unified and comprehensive quasi-neurological theory of behavior. Even when compared with such established orientations as the Freudian and Hullian prototypes, there is good reason to consider an expectancy formulation such as Hebb's, particularly after its modification in his recent paper (cited above), as one of the most promising bases for the further development of our knowledge of human motivation and behavior.

If the literature of our time be considered *in toto*, there are many reasons to select as its most important source of motivational notions the writings of the psychoanalytic theorists, from Freud to the present time. This influence is illustrated in other chapters in this volume as well as in our previous consideration of the psychology of personality. In addition to the several psychoanalytic models and the many specific insights into personality structure and development which Freud bequeathed to posterity, he also gave wide currency to two basic assumptions which have since become fundamental tenets for many students of human motivation. First, Freud conceived of elemental motives which were in some sense inaccessible to deliberate observation, and the wide dissemination of his persuasive and convincing arguments for this position no doubt have mutually reinforced the now quite popular tendency to question the value of introspective examinations of conscious motivational content. In the second place, Freud insisted that all behavior was motivated. The effects of this position have probably been at least as important. It makes the study of motivation in many ways synonymous with the operational study of behavior, much as the psychology of personality has been conceived on occasion; the position has no doubt considerably increased the importance attributed to studies of human motivation, since interest in the measurement of human motivation gradually has differentiated out of a more diffuse clinical and academic concern for the structure and dynamics of personality.

If a Freudian interest in basic and unconscious motives is one of the dominant notes of modern motivation psychology, the recent appearance of an increasing number of investigations of rational and probabilistic choice behavior seems a promising contrapuntal theme. The interested hearing accorded this work may in part be due to the affiliation with promising new mathematical developments which is noted in *Mathematical Thinking in the Social Sciences* (1954), Paul F. Lazarsfeld (ed.), and in *Decision Processes* (1954), Robert M. Thrall, Clyde H. Coombs, and Robert L. Davis (eds.). Ward Edwards' "The Theory of Decision Making" in the *Psychological Bulletin* (1954) is an excellent review of the relevant psychological material. A good introductory discussion is

"Emerging Technologies for Making Decisions" by Edwards, Harold Lindman, and Lawrence D. Phillips, in Frank Barron and others, *New Directions in Psychology II* (1965). A representative sample of current approaches is contained in *Human Judgments and Optimality* (1964), Maynard W. Shelly, II and Glenn L. Bryan (eds.). An interesting sampling of other approaches to motivational theory and research may be found in John W. Atkinson's *Introduction to Motivation* (1964), Charles N. Cofer and Mortimer H. Apley's (eds.) *Motivation: Theory and Research* (1964), and Ralph N. Haber's (ed.) *Current Research in Motivation* (1966). Detailed presentations of many other current lines of investigation which could not be considered here are contained in recent volumes of the annually appearing *Nebraska Symposium on Motivation* (1953–), Marshall R. Jones (ed.).

SOCIAL PSYCHOLOGY

Although a few psychologists principally interested in perception, learning, personality, or motivation have attempted to expand their conceptual frames of reference into general theories of behavior, most limit their investigations typically to the particular aspect of the total interaction of organism and environment with which they are immediately concerned. While much the same thing is true of many social psychologists as well, social psychology as a whole really involves all aspects of this interaction, but only when it occurs among objects having some social significance. The perception of lines differing in length, for example, is hardly of concern to a social psychologist unless, as in Solomon E. Asch's investigation of the "Effects of Group Pressure upon the Modification and Distortion of Judgments," reported in Eleanor Maccoby, Theodore M. Newcomb, and Eugene L. Hartley's (eds.) *Readings in Social Psychology* (3d ed., 1958), the perceptual problem is made the focus of a situation with interpersonal implications. In analogous ways, and when other socially relevant objects are concerned, the social psychologist also investigates problems in learning, cognition, motivation, development, and personality. He therefore is subject to influences in almost all other areas in psychology, as well as being more likely than most psychologists to interact with sociologists, anthropologists, and other social scientists.

The earliest works on social psychology, as far back as Gabriel Tarde's *Les Lois de l'imitation* (1890) or Gustave LeBon's *The Crowd* (2d ed., 1897), bear more than a taste of the clinic. While Tarde ascribes social behavior to "imitation" rather than to "suggestion," which is regarded by LeBon as the critical concept, the two are largely agreed on the impulsivity and almost pathological irrationality of group behavior.

A decidedly different orientation marked William McDougall's *An Introduction to Social Psychology* (1908). Inspired by the Darwinian cosmogony, McDougall impressed the concept of instinct and founded upon it a theory of social behavior. Nativism now became the popular basis for a decade of systematic social psychology. Lists of instincts proliferated without modesty, and the term increasingly came to be applied to all supposed uniformities of human conduct, with benign disregard for the presence or absence of evidence of their innateness.

The spectacle of so massive an accord upon such slender foundations proved too tempting. "Are There Any Instincts?" Knight Dunlap asked in the *Journal of Abnormal and Social Psychology* (1919), and amidst resounding "noes!" from the new environmentalists and from anthropologically inspired adherents of cultural relativism, the idol toppled and was heard from no more. For as Edwin B. Holt, himself no mean defender of the opposite extreme, was to exclaim somewhat later in his *Animal Drive and the Learning Process* (1931):

... man is impelled to action, it is said, by his instincts. If he goes with his fellows, it is the "herd instinct" which actuates him; if he walks alone, it is the "anti-social instinct"; if he fights, it is the instinct of "pugnacity"; if he defers to another, it is the instinct of "self-abasement"; if he twiddles his thumbs, it is the thumb-twiddling instinct; if he does not twiddle his thumbs, it is the thumb-not-twiddling instinct. Thus everything is explained with the facility of magic-word magic.

An associationist orientation to the objective study of behavior, increasingly becoming characteristic of the psychology of learning, made considerable headway among social psychologists with the publication in 1924 of Floyd H. Allport's *Social Psychology*, which borrowed concepts from individual learning theory and then extrapolated from them to explanations of group phenomena in terms of multiperson aggregates. In addition to many valuable hypotheses about group behavior, Allport also contributed to the growing awareness among social psychologists of the potentialities of empirical investigation. Somewhat later, Neal E. Miller and John Dollard, substituting concepts derived from Hullian learning theory for the principles used by Allport, made another interesting attempt in their *Social Learning and Imitation* (1941) to analyze such social psychological phenomena as the transmission of complex social behaviors from a somewhat similar point of view.

Although concepts from learning theory have found extensive employment in certain areas of social psychology, the field is no doubt far more indebted in its current theoretical and reseach orientation to the work of Gestalt psychologists and of others associated with the essentials of the Gestalt position. Muzafer Sherif's *The Psychology of Social Norms* (1936), which pointed out the influence of cultural factors upon social perception, emphasized the restructuring of cognitive organization which occurred as previously external social norms were internalized and became organizing frames of reference for behavior. Such concepts as cognitive restructuring are far more frequently invoked to explain the acquisition and manifestation of new forms of social behavior than principles of conditioning.

Like Sherif and the Gestalt psychologists, Kurt Lewin also believed that behavior was best understood in terms of the conceptualization of the total psychological situation or field. In volumes such as *A Dynamic Theory of Personality* (1935) and *Field Theory in Social Science* (1951), Lewin's arguments against theories of behavior framed with reference to historical rather than contemporary causation and acts instead of intentions were made known to American psychology. The extraordinary influence of his writings made them vehicles for what amounted to a drastic reformulation of the metatheory of much of social psychology. It was Lewin, furthermore, who made explicit and convincing the motivational propositions inherent in Gestalt and field-theoretic thinking about dynamic, self-equilibrating psychological systems, and the vectorial terminology he developed to describe such motivational processes not only incited a great deal of research on such now classic problems as the recall of interrupted tasks (the Zeigarnik effect) and the level of aspiration, but also remains a clear antecedent of many of the interactional formulations of current social psychology. One recent introductory presentation of social psychological theory and research sympathetic to Gestalt and field-theoretic ideas is David Krech, Richard S. Crutchfield, and Egerton L. Ballachey's *Individual in Society* (1963).

Since the psychoanalytic literature typically is concerned with the history and present status of the needs of the individual in interaction with the external, primarily social, pressures affecting his development, there might seem to be little there which is not of immediate interest to social psychologists. This was the position Sigmund Freud himself took in the most explicitly pertinent of his writings, *Group Psychology and the Analysis of the Ego* (1922). Freud felt that individual and group psychology were being divided on the basis of the size of the units considered, a factor he held to be quite trivial, and he went so far as to suggest that large group phenomena which in his day were being explained by concepts such as "herd instinct" or "group mind" might be understood far more adequately and parsimoniously in terms of concepts derived from the study of the smallest and most primary group, i.e., the family.

In the few instances however where psychoanalytic thinking is incorporated into presentations of social psychology in an integrated and detailed fashion, as in Theodore M. Newcomb's *Social Psychology* (1950), it typically derives from the more socially and culturally oriented analysts, such as Erich Fromm, Karen Horney, or Harry S. Sullivan, presumably because these theorists have discarded the biological bases of orthodox psychoanalytic theory and therefore are more easily translated into social psychological terms.

A good part of the major impact created by Theodor W. Adorno, Else Frenkel-Brunswik, Daniel J. Levinson, and R. Nevitt Sanford's *The Authoritarian Personality* (1950) may be traced back to its psychoanalytic orientations and to the far-reaching implications of the hypotheses they inspired. Undertaken as an investigation of anti-Semitism and prejudice, the study attempted to demonstrate the dependence of ideologies and fundamental attitudes upon specific patterns of personality structure and child-rearing practices. Because of the profound social importance of the subject, it drew much attention; a number of careful and thorough methodological critiques were made public in *Studies in the Scope and Method of "The Authoritarian Personality"* (1954), Richard Christie and Marie Jahoda (eds.). Although generous to a fault in their praise of the "importance" and "impact" of the earlier work, the contributors tended to conclude after their methodological evaluations that, as one said, "almost nothing stands up of the original study."

Mortimer Brewster Smith, Jerome S. Bruner, and Robert W. White have studied a series of case histories for clues to the relationships between the attitudes men hold and their underlying personality dynamics and structure in *Opinions and Personality* (1956). Somewhat less inclined to strictly psychoanalytic interpretations of the antecedents of attitude than *The Authoritarian Personality*, these analyses resemble more the admirable didactic portraits of White's *Lives in Progress* (2d ed., 1966).

As is evident from its central position in the studies just discussed, the concept of attitude has maintained its vitality despite changes in the interests of social psychologists which have long since retired contemporaries like "instinct" and "imitation" to pasture. Although it has never attained the exclusive position implied by William I. Thomas and Florian Znaniecki, who in their classic five volume study of *The Polish Peasant in Europe and America* (1918–20) defined social psychology as "the scientific study of attitudes," it remains, as Gordon W. Allport writes in his chapter on "The Historical Background of Modern Social Psychology" in Gardner Lindzey's (ed.) *Handbook of Social Psychology* (1954), "probably the most distinctive and indispensable concept on contemporary American social psychology."

The reasons for this popularity are easy to discern. Allport points out that the term is sufficiently flexible so as to presuppose no systematic position on the origins of attitudes, on the extent of genetic determination, or on limitations as to the kinds of objects to which they may apply. On the other hand, one wonders about the real utility of a concept which lumps together so diverse a range of phenomena. The putative similarities not only are not demonstrated thereby, but on the contrary become practically inaccessible to investigation just because they have been assumed. The cheery applicability of the term to everything from motor sets to life philosophies occasionally smacks of the successful political candidate who derives his popularity from those freely pledged commitments to every local interest which collectively make it impossible for him to satisfy any one of them.

While the numerous surveys, polls, and attitude studies of recent decades have not been distinguished for the permanent value of their contributions to the foundations of social psychology, one set of volumes, *Studies in Social Psychology in World War II*, must be accounted an outstanding exception to the general rule. Three of these volumes, *The American Soldier: Adjustment During Army Life* (1949), *The American Soldier: Combat and Its Aftermath* (1949), and *Measurement and Prediction* (1950) are by Samuel A. Stouffer and his collaborators; the fourth, *Experiments on Mass Communication* (1949), is the work of Carl I. Hovland, Arthur A. Lumsdaine, and Fred D. Sheffield. In addition to providing a fund of data about important practical problems of military existence, these volumes also made significant contributions to knowledge of fundamental importance about such topics as the problem of leadership in a democracy, as well as to various branches of research methodology.

Social psychology, like general psychology, has analyzed its variables predominantly in terms of effects upon individuals. Studies of social perception, cognition, and attitude traditionally have found the individual a convenient unit of study. Recently, however, a number of psychologists have turned to the group, and have tried to analyze group formation, stability, communication, conflict, and change in terms of group laws, largely without reference to individual variables. The effect of Lewinian influences upon many of these investigations is evident throughout *Group Dynamics* (2d ed., 1960), Dorwin Cartwright and Alvin Zander (eds.).

The reader who wishes a broader introduction to social psychology, including many topics omitted from the present discussion, should consult Roger Brown's *Social Psychology* (1965) or Edwin P. Hollander's *Principles and Methods of Social Psychology* (1967). At a more advanced level, the new revision of the *Handbook of Social Psychology* (1967), edited by Gardner Lindzey and Elliot Aronson also will prove very useful.

ON THE NEED TO APPLY WHAT YOU HAVE NOT GOT

It is customary to divide psychology into the "pure" and the "applied," although the result is precious little light and a really uncomfortable amount of heat. There is little controversy about the very considerable experimental literature on practical problems concerning efficient design of industrial and military apparatus and the like, since the experimental manipulations are hardly different from those encountered in other laboratory investigations. Good references here are *Human Factors in Technology* (1963), Edward Bennett, James Degan, and Joseph Spiegel (eds.), Ernest J. McCormick's *Human Factors in Engineering* (2d ed., 1964), and *Human Engineering Guide to Equipment Design* (1963), Clifford T. Morgan, Jesse S. Cook, III, Alphonse Chapanis, and Max W. Lund (eds.). But many other areas of applied psychology are less well situated.

It has been held that even were scientific rigor attainable in these other applied activities, it would be misdirected, if not positively harmful, to require that the applied psychologist adhere strictly to the usually prescribed procedures. The engineer who knows his physics still tinkers, and the corpus of knowledge which academic psychology offers as aid frequently looks rather closer to alchemy than to physics.

Several considerations weaken this analogy. In the first place, the engineer's tools are more valid and reliable than those of the applied psychologist. The best of the objective psychological measuring instruments are relatively crude, and there also is a pronounced tendency, particularly among clinical psychologists, to rely heavily on the so-called "projective tests," notably the Roschach inkblot test and the TAT. These presume that responses to the unstructured test stimuli will be based on the attitudes and underlying feelings which the individual "projects" into them. The resulting responses are analyzed for putative insight into the dynamics of the individual, the ultimate rationale for the procedure frequently deriving from the clinician's subjective convictions about its utility. So employed, these measures are at best diagnostic aids, without scientifically demonstrated validity in the overwhelming majority of cases.

In the second place, engineers get more feedback. If the clinician plays a hunch, and utilizes a given technique at a certain point, it is he who has to decide whether the final outcome should be characterized as a success or a failure. If the engineer plays a hunch in building a bridge, it is somewhat easier to outline objective techniques to determine whether the bridge will perform to some objectively defined criterion. And published analyses of clinical predictions, such as *The Prediction of Performance in Clinical Psychology* (1951), by E. Lowell Kelly and Donald W. Fiske, and Paul E. Meehl's very fine survey and evaluation of *Clinical Versus Statistical Prediction* (1954), hardly provide any reason to believe that clinical hunches are in any way improvements over entirely objective test estimates. Comparable assessment procedures in other applied areas presumably fare no better. E. Lowell Kelly writes in his survey of "Theory and Techniques of Assessment," in the *Annual Review of Psychology* (1954):

> The curious state of affairs wherein the most widely (and confidently) used techniques are those for which there is little or no evidence of predictive validity is indeed a phenomenon appropriate for study by social psychologists. This reviewer can only assume that in the absence of evidence of their predictive validity, such techniques must serve an important function other than assessment. Is it that they serve primarily to reduce threats of anxiety for persons confronted with the necessity of making significant decisions in the lives of individual clients or patients? Lacking dependable validated techniques for making the predictions essential to wise decisions, it should not be surprising if persons responsible for professional decisions were to gravitate to the use of techniques which yield a relatively large amount of information concerning the subject, regardless of how irrelevant most of the information may be. Add to extensity of information provided by the technique a theoretical orientation sufficiently flexible to permit using the information in a manner which seems "to explain" any subject, and we have what would seem to be the necessary ingredients for an anxiety-reducing prescription!

Edward J. Shoben, Jr., points out much the same syndrome of social demand, the necessity for critical decisions in the absence of requisite knowledge, and the consequent but unfortunate result in his review, "Some Recent Books on Counseling and Adjustment," in the *Psychological Bulletin* (1955). As he puts it, the "... psychologist himself often is motivated to seize desperately on any idea or technique that has the appearance of usefulness. When the chips are down, as they generally are in professional practice, scepticism about one's own resources is a luxury that few can afford."

We have a paradox. How are you to apply what you have not got? The interim solution is clear, if unsatisfactory. The work must be done, and certainly there are no people better qualified, by dint of their experience and training, to accomplish whatever we currently are capable of doing than those now engaged in this work. In the long run, as has been happening in medicine, intensive research will gradually improve the situation. The primary interim consideration is well stated by Shoben. "To say that professional practice must rely on hunch and accumulations of uncontrolled experience is to say nothing derogatory *so long as one knows what is happening*."

Intensive work now is under way in several applied areas, with the twin aims of evaluating and shoring up current practice and also of developing and validating new procedures. Educational psychology, a field well described in Lee J. Cronbach's *Educational Psychology* (2d ed., 1963), furnishes several examples. Cognitive psychologists are among those with recently reawakened interests in education. Jerome S. Bruner, for instance, has become heavily involved in this area, contributing among other things two widely read books, *The Process of Education* (1960) and *Toward a Theory of Instruction* (1966). *Learning by Discovery* (1966), Lee Shulman and Evan R. Keislar (eds.), reports on a broad range of efforts to develop and evaluate new classroom teaching procedures. A good discussion of the current roles of ability and achievement tests in education is presented in Henry Chauncey and John E. Dobbin's *Testing* (1963). Finally, new developments in programmed learning and its applications in education are treated in detail in *Learning and Programmed Instruction* (1965), by Julian I. Taber and others, in *Programmed Learning and Computer Based Instruction* (1962), by John E. Coulson (ed.), and in *Teaching Machines and Programmed Learning* (1965), by Robert Glaser (ed.).

Recent volumes of the *Annual Review of Psychology* also attest to the scientific merit of a growing number of applied psychological investigations. A great portion of the applied literature does not fall in this category, however, and so rather than attempt an inadequate summary of its principal features, the present essay recommends consideration of the appropriate chapters of the *Annual Review of Psychology* volumes. For an introduction to applied psychology as a whole, see Anne Anastasi's *Fields of Applied Psychology* (1964).

STATISTICS, MEASUREMENT, AND MATHEMATICAL MODELS

When in 1940 Jerome S. Bruner and Gordon W. Allport published their survey, "Fifty Years of Change in American Psychology," in the *Psychological Bulletin*, the most striking alteration they reported was the marked increase in the use of statistics as an adjunct to psychological research. At present, in fact, no major American journal of experimental psychology normally will print a research report which lacks as a bare minimum descriptive statistical summaries of the results. As Bruner and Allport suggest, this value which modern American psychologists attach to numbers undoubtedly "reflects the preoccupation with quantitative standards of excellence characteristic of most American cultural activities." But at least as important, one imagines, is the real increase in scientific efficiency which results from the rational utilization of descriptive and test statistics. All scientific knowledge is probabilistic, "best guess" knowledge. The future direction not only of the individual scientist but also of the whole scientific enterprise must be determined by best guesses from past research. In imprecise sciences such as psychology, with their large uncontrolled sources of error variance, the accurate estimation of the best guess can only be described as crucial.

The research psychologist is a gambler. He wants to maximize his chances of coming out ahead. Where the design of the next experiment hinges upon the results of the last one, the most accurate guess as to what is associated with what is most likely in the long run to lead to the most fruitful results. Since all psychologists profit from the sharpening of best guesses, it is not hard to see why attention to measurement theory and statistics has increased phenomenally; it seems a most rational and appropriate form of behavior.

The bases and psychological applications of statistics are very well summarized in an excellent recent text, *Statistics for Psychologists* (1963), by William L. Hays. The power of any particular kind of statistics derives from the assumptions inherent in the underlying mathematical models. When these assumptions may justifiably be referred to data, the use of these statistics lends precision and generality to the conclusions drawn. The more stringent the assumptions, however, the more likely it becomes that in one or more respects the model departs from the real population parameters.

In addition to such widely used statistics as analysis of variance and product-moment correlation, measurement theorists have developed a variety of "nonparametric" techniques. These forego the precision of conventional statistics on order to make possible best guesses more appropriate to the data. Keith Smith's treatment of "Distribution-Free Statistical Methods and the Concept of Power Efficiency" in *Research Methods in the Behavioral Sciences* (1953), Leon Festinger and Daniel Katz (eds.), is an excellent introduction to these techniques and the problems which gave rise to them.

Factor analysis in America is intrinsically associated with Louis L. Thurstone. Thurstone's use of the technique in studies of mental abilities has yielded one of the principal collections of information in this area, and his text, *Multiple-Factor Analysis* (1947), remains one of the key volumes on the statistical bases of the method. Despite its wide acceptance as an aid to research in some areas, many applications of factor analysis continue to excite controversy. The current debate over the place of factor analytic methods in the overall strategy of psychological investigation has, however, persuaded many psychologists to examine carefully the underlying assumptions of popular techniques of multi-dimensional measurement. More and more frequently we are reminded that all psychological theory about measurable variables necessarily implies a complete antecedent theory of psychological measurement, specifying in detail all assumptions and operations required in going from raw behavior to general assertions about associations among variables.

Awareness of the importance of such antecedent conditions no doubt has been intensified still further by an increasingly frequent tendency in methodologically more advanced areas to make explicit the underlying mathematical bases of psychological theory, as for instance in *Stochastic Models for Learning* (1955), by Robert R. Bush and Frederick Mosteller. Learning theory continues as one of the favorite targets for mathematical modeling, as for example in Richard C. Atkinson, Gordon H. Bower, and Edward J. Crothers' *An Introduction to Mathematical Learning Theory* (1965).

But efforts to utilize the power of mathematics are now to be found throughout psychology. In addition to those already cited in this chapter in connection with specific content areas, we may mention as further examples Lawrence E. Fouraker and Sidney Siegel's *Bargaining Behavior* (1963), the fascinating and illuminating combination of societal, mathematical, and psychological concerns Anatol Rapoport displays in *Fights, Games, and Debates* (1960) and *Strategy and Conscience* (1964), and Wendell R. Garner's excellent treatment of psychological applications of information theory in *Uncertainty and Structure as Psychological Concepts* (1962). For stimulating discussions of mathematical models underlying the sorts of data one gets from scales, questionnaires, and other instruments of psychological measurement, see Warren S. Torgerson's *Theory and Methods of Scaling* (1958), and Clyde H. Coombs' *A Theory of Data* (1964). Other recent developments in mathematical psychology are well described and illustrated in two recent multivolume series, *The Handbook of Mathematical Psychology* (1963-65), R. Duncan Luce, Robert R. Bush, and Eugene Galanter (eds.), and *Readings in Mathematical Psychology* (1963-65), also edited by Luce, Bush, and Galanter. Finally, a first rate introduction to the role of mathematics in psychology which presumes a minimum of mathematical knowledge is George Miller's *Mathematics and Psychology* (1964).

A brief consideration of current issues of *Psychometrika* (1936-) and of relevant chapters of recent volumes of the *Annual Review of Psychology* provides convincing evidence of the present importance and real potential of these newer approaches; Lincoln E. Moses' chapter, "Statistical Theory and Research Design" (1956) actually utilizes an organization deriving from the concepts of decision theory, and there are underway several efforts at reorganization of experimental methodology in the light of these developments. As Edward L. Walker observes in his survey, "Learning," in the *Annual Review of Psychology* (1957),

"Psychologists, even old ones, had better accelerate their study of mathematics."

IN CONCLUSION

Readers of this essay should keep its limitations in mind. It is not a comprehensive or representative review of the psychological literature. Psychology abroad has not been discussed (see relevant chapters in recent volumes of the *Annual Review of Psychology*), and many areas, including sensory, applied, developmental, and comparative psychology are mentioned only in passing or omitted altogether. The topical arrangement of the essay, furthermore, suggests a neater organization of the field of psychology than is the case. In many places psychology resembles in structure less a nicely compartmentalized department store than a sprawling oriental bazaar. As Charles W. Eriksen points out in his review of "Personality" in the *Annual Review of Psychology* (1957),

Research . . . in psychology as a whole shows many of the characteristics of a fad. There will be a virtual flood of studies on a problem for a couple of years and then a new era or idea catches the fancy of Ph.D. candidates. . . . All too often the work is mainly demonstrational in nature. . . . And when the wave of enthusiasm moves on, there are frequently too few experimenters left to weed out and consolidate that which is theoretically useful and reproducible. . . .

With some notable exceptions, research tends to be characterized by one-shot experiments rather than programmatic attacks on a problem. While this leads to suggestive hypotheses, failure to follow up in many instances leaves uncertainty as to the reproducibility of the results and unclarity as to the relevant parameters. . . . there also seems to be a decrease in scholarship. Too little effort is made by researchers to relate their findings to those of other investigators.

The net effect is a literature which in many important areas is almost totally confused, congested, and nonadditive. The proverbial wheels of progress spin all right, but the gears don't mesh. And this increasingly overloaded and inefficient vehicle today faces imminent and unprecedented challenges to its limited effectiveness as a medium of communication. Today there are more psychologists than ever before; they have more money available to them for research than ever before; and with academic advancement determined by productivity, they are certain to produce more than ever before. Remember, too, the computers which revolutionize the kind of research we can do (see, for example, William R. Uttal's *Real Time Computers*, 1967 in press) also geometrically increase our capacity to do it.

For all this bewildering array of activity, however, several trends stand out. Physiological psychologists, together with those other disciplines concerned with the biological bases of human activity, are making steady progress. One cannot help but come away impressed with what we have been learning in this area when one compares a good modern text, for example Richard F. Thompson's *Foundations of Physiological Psychology* (1967) with comparable texts of a decade or two ago. Another obvious development is the increasing computerization and formalization to be found throughout psychology. We have discussed examples of this in research on cognition and psycholinguistics, but there are other examples to be drawn from every part of the field. Finally, we may note the amazing growth of the various fields of applied psychology. Clinical, educational, and industrial psychology, human engineering, and a variety of related fields are developing rapidly, with the result that psychology as a whole now has a very different flavor from that it possessed as a largely academic discipline a generation ago. For other views on the present state and likely trends of the field, see the ambitious multivolume series *Psychology: A Study of a Science* (1959-), edited by Sigmund Koch.

Some may prefer to consider the rather mixed and uneven stream we call psychology less a science than a series of attempts to build a science, and the present shape of the field is likely to alter as much over the next few decades as it has in the past thirty years. But at its best, psychology already has found out a good deal about human behavior, and it promises to continue to do so.

4 Political Science

Heinz Eulau

– I –

INTRODUCTION

Like all literature, writings on politics follow fashion. New styles, topics, aims come to dominate the creative imagination of successive generations. Fashions, of course, are not arbitrary. They are themselves symptoms of temporary predispositions and orientations stemming from and being responses to new conditions. The dilemma faced by the writer on politics is obvious. Politics—whether as vocation or hobby—is absorbing, and rarely does it permit that aloofness from fashion, if not passion, that is the ideal of scientific inquiry. Karl Mannheim, in *Ideology and Utopia* (1936), went further than any other contemporary writer in tackling the problem of interest and disinterest in political knowledge. He succeeded in opening our eyes to the complexity of the dilemma, making us perhaps more humble in our aspirations, but he hardly led us out of our predicament.

Yet, in politics at least, predicaments need not be counsels of despair. In fact, if politics means anything, it means making choices and taking sides, even though, as Mr. Justice Holmes once put it, we may have to wager our salvation on some unproved hypothesis. This, perhaps, is the fashion of our own day: that, at last, political inquiry has been freed from "the quest for certainty," and that we are willing to settle for what is hypothetical or, at most, probable. Within such a frame of reference, there is nothing doctrinaire or dogmatic about inclusions or exclusions from what one may declare to be the limits of a field of knowledge.

For the body of literature, past and present, dealing with government and politics, past and present, is huge, and selections must be made. This review of some of the literature—and it does not pretend to anything more than a review—is intended to be suggestive rather than exhaustive. It is not a bibliography of politics. It is not a report on all the problems, issues, and trends in political literature. It is almost wholly confined to American writings, with references to foreign literature only if influences on American thinking can be traced. It ignores the rich mass of periodical writing which, in some areas, may be more important than books. This essay, then, is just one political scientist's appraisal of some works which, it seems to him, are crucial in surveying the state of the literature on politics. While some of these books are mentioned because they appear to be outstanding contributions to the continuing reorientation of political thinking and research, others are cited only because they may be typical of some major tendency in the literature, and still others are introduced because they may serve the purpose of further reference. Excluded are political novels, journalistic writings, biographies, and autobiographies, not because they necessarily fail to convey important insights into political behavior, to present keen analyses of political phenomena, or to enrich our political wisdom, but because they are not political science.

This limitation does not mean that the author pretends to know what the nature of political science is—for he is admittedly allergic to a statement of essences. But it is also not to be implied that he embraces an operational definition of the discipline—to the effect that political science is what those calling themselves political scientists do. As a reader is entitled to knowledge of a writer's observational standpoint, candor requires the author to suggest that his own commitments are to what is usually referred to as the "political behavior approach." The characteristics of this approach were summarized by the author and two colleagues, Samuel J. Eldersveld and Morris Janowitz, in *Political Behavior: A Reader in Theory and Research* (1956), as follows:

1. It specifies as the unit or object of both theoretical and empirical analysis the behavior of persons and social groups rather than events, structures, institutions, or ideologies. It is, of course, concerned with these latter phenomena, but only as categories of analysis in terms of which social interaction takes place in typically political situations.

2. It seeks to place political theory and research in a frame of reference common to that of social psychology, sociology, and cultural anthropology. This interdisciplinary focus follows inevitably from a concern with behavior—overt or symbolic. Even though the particular transactions studied are limited

to those carried out in pursuit of political roles and political goals, political behavior is assumed to be a function of personality, social organization, and society.

3. It stresses the mutual interdependence of theory and research. Theoretical questions need to be stated in operational terms for purposes of empirical research. And, in turn, empirical findings should have a bearing on the development of political theory. Its empiricism is, therefore, quite unlike the "brute facts" approach of an earlier descriptive empiricism. It is self-consciously theory-oriented.

4. It tries to develop rigorous research design and to apply precise methods of analysis to political behavior problems. It is concerned with the formulation and derivation of testable hypotheses, operational definitions, problems of experimental or *post-facto* design, reliability of instruments and criteria of validation, and other features of scientific procedure. It is in this respect that the political behavior approach differs most conspicuously from the more conventional approaches of political science. Yet, it does not assume that the procedures of the scientific method can be simplistically and mechanically applied to the analysis of the political process.

POLITICS AS SCIENCE: THE STATE OF AFFAIRS

Although politics is probably as old as social man himself, political science as an academic discipline is a relatively recent and predominantly American phenomenon. Most preliterate forms of social organization required some sets of norms, rules, or customs which were of binding decisional character or could serve as bases for communal decisions. There were systems of social ordering, involving superior-subordinate or, perhaps, equalitarian relationships. Even customary social relations, not evidently depending on explicit rule-making, probably called for authoritative interpretations by men. Sanctions of one kind or another, in the form of rewards or punishment, were likely to be present in the simplest political relationships. Decisions had to be made, accepted, and enforced, if the social life of the community was to survive the hazards of an environment whose control was often beyond the technological know-how of the community. Indeed, politics, like primitive religion, was probably a part of man's efforts to come to grips with the environment.

Whether one prefers to trace political science back to Plato and Aristotle, or to the more empirically-minded Machiavelli, or to the establishment of independent academic departments of political science in the late nineteenth century, or to Charles Merriam's *New Aspects of Politics* (1925), is largely a matter of taste. Unfortunately, political scientists have expended an inordinate amount of time and effort disputing the origins and nature of their discipline. And the colloquy is likely to continue for some time to come. If, therefore, at mid-century, political scientists are agreed on anything, it is probably on the muddled state of their science. Political scientists are riding off in many directions, evidently on the assumption that if you don't know where you are going, any road will take you there. One need only consult the volume entitled *Contemporary Political Science, A Survey of Methods, Research and Teaching*, published in 1950 by UNESCO's Department of Social Sciences, with contributions by scholars from many countries; or the report entitled *Goals for Political Science* (1951), prepared by the American Political Science Association's Committee for the Advancement of Teaching (which, in due course, was properly raked over the coals by another set of political scientists in the Association's official journal); or a good many books and articles concerned with the scope and methods of political science, a body of literature that since World War I has reached formidable proportions, but which, in general, reverberates with the same old arguments, no matter what side a writer may be on.

This is not a plea for further efforts to define the "scope" of political science—efforts which, hindsight suggests, have occupied the attention of the profession more than the harvest warranted. For "scope" is a deceptive term which seems to imply that the topics to be handled under a given title can be clearly delimited by simply drawing boundaries. But a scientific enterprise cannot be located in space, for it is a series of ever-changing methods of inquiry and sets of data which are being tested in the solution of problems, theoretical and practical. As problems, observational standpoints, and sought-after solutions change, the discipline will also appear differently, and boundaries and methods tend to shift with such changes, more or less swiftly, subject only to cultural lags and, more often than not, the resistance of vested disciplinary interests.

One might argue, paradoxical as it may seem, that the health of a discipline can be judged by the concern it shows with its unsolved problems. To admit one's difficulties and weaknesses is not proof of infirmity, but a prerequisite of youth and growth. Unlike economics, equipped with a central instrument of analysis—the price system—which enables the economist to develop useful theorems explaining a few of the facts of economic life, political science has been unable to evolve a central model that could serve as a reasonably stable point of departure into political inquiry. In its 1951 report, the Association's Committee for the Advancement of Teaching recommended that "increased attention be given to conceptual and systematic political science as the factor around which all other elements should adhere," but to date relatively little work has been done toward what, it seems clear, is by no means an acceptable goal for political scientists.

There are those who find the scientific enterprise obnoxious and take the position that the proper study of politics is concerned with ideal values, and that, on the practical side, politics is an art. Their point of departure may be justification of the State, in capital letters, perhaps well exemplified by Bernard Bosanquet's *The Philosophical Theory of the State* (1899); or it may be a defense of the individual and his associations against the State, such as the earlier work of Harold J. Laski, best expressed in *A Grammar of Politics* (1925). Poles apart in their moral predispositions, monist and pluralist idealists agree that politics is a matter of values, immune to any laws of cause and effect.

At the other extreme in modern political science are those whom, for want of a better name, one may call "brute empiricists." Baconian in orientation, physical science of an earlier time serves them as a model. Their method is inductive inference of the causal effects of political phenomena. They insist on the observation of uniformities as a necessary condition of prediction and experimental verification. Representative of this tendency is Stuart A. Rice's *Quantitative Methods in Politics* (1928), which is distinguished by the great care taken in the application of investigatory techniques, something which cannot be said for many other studies of a similar orientation. Yet, the results of this kind of inquiry have been rather limited sets of discontinuous low-level generalizations, of little theoretical use, or, in its more enthusiastic phase, the premature statement of dubious "laws," such as William B. Munro's "law of the pendulum" in *The Invisible Government* (1928), at most a return to Aristotle's observation of the cyclical movement of governmental forms.

It may be that earlier failures to find receptivity in the profession for systematic models agitate against renewed efforts in this direction. A work such as George E. G. Catlin's *The Science and Method of Politics* (1927), perhaps the only systematic attempt to investigate the assumptions of political science as science, had no influence whatsoever on the course of the discipline, possibly because its strongly individualistic and Hobbesian premises did not square with immediate realities as experienced by most political scientists. Harold D. Lasswell and Abraham Kaplan's *Power and Society* (1950), while in sympathy with the aim of developing systematic models for political science, is largely concerned with formulating empirically usable sets of interdependent definitions and mutually reinforcing operational hypotheses.

More recently, in *The Political System* (1953), David Easton has critically analyzed political science from the point of view of the need for a comprehensive conceptual framework which would permit the simultaneous, systematic ordering of both institutional data and facts of political behavior, but his proposal for an equilibrium theory of politics—by no means a new idea—has been received with some skepticism. In fact, even those who fancy themselves as belonging to the avant-garde of political scientists, often called "political behaviorists," are prone to advise against what they evidently consider premature system-building. As stated in *Political Behavior: A Reader in Theory and Research* (1956), Heinz Eulau, Samuel J. Eldersveld, and Morris Janowitz (eds.), "the political behavior approach has been essentially catholic and eclectic. Although the ultimate objective of some of its practitioners may be the construction of 'systematic theory,' it has remained eminently pragmatic in application."

There are, of course, persuasive reasons for caution. A systematic theory must not only be internally consistent, but it must be in keeping with the accepted record of facts which it presumably brings into meaningful relationship. Yet, the record of political facts that is known resembles a jigsaw puzzle in which many pieces are missing. Moreover, existing empirical studies are fragmentary, often cast in contradictory frames of reference, and produced at intervals of time over many decades. The task of system-building with materials of such heterogeneous origin and substance is precarious. But if he ignores the hard facts, the systematizer is likely to be lost out of sight by his more drudging colleagues. As will be seen later on, the estrangement of theory and empirical research, even on lower levels of investigation, has been and still largely is the most fatal flaw of contemporary political science.

It has come to be realized, therefore, that the choice is not one between system-building, unencumbered by research, and empirical inquiry, unencumbered by theory. Rather, it is more and more recognized that systematic formulation and empirical research must go hand in hand. And while theory-building may be more difficult than empirical investigation, research is more time-consuming. In other words, systematization must adjust itself to the pace set by research, just as research must seek continuing theoretical enlightenment. Fortunately, one can point to a number of recent enterprises which seem to heed this injunction. It is also interesting to note that many of these undertakings have been cooperative ventures, evidently on the realization that no single scholar, working alone, can come to grips with the complexities of politics. But one must also name in this connection the work of individual scholars, such as David Apter's *The Gold Coast in Transition* (1955), a self-consciously interdisciplinary structural-functional analysis of "political institutional transfer." On the other hand, research not consciously fertilized by theory, no matter how grandiose in design or number of collaborators, is likely to be disjointed. As an example, one might mention the work carried out by a team of scholars at the Brookings Institution, in cooperation with political scientists throughout the country, and reported in five massive volumes edited by Paul T. David, Malcolm Moos, and Ralph Goldman, *Presidential Nominating Politics in 1952*

(1954). While these volumes are full of much interesting information, they are devoid of theoretical significance from the point of view of a systematic politics.

All this does not mean, of course, that political science has not progressed in the last sixty years or so. Actually, the record is impressive, and recent developments suggest the vitality of the discipline. But this should not be cause for self-satisfaction. The history of political science as an independent field of inquiry can be written as a history of successive emancipations from earlier limitations and false starts. Yet, these successive emancipations have been additive rather than cumulative: the old survives with the new, and the old acquires new defenders as the new relies on old apostles. It is impossible to say, therefore, that anything has been disproven as long as conventional tests of proof—the requisites of scientific status in any field of knowledge—are not commonly accepted by political scientists, or, in fact, are rejected by some as altogether irrelevant in political inquiry.

There are those impatient with "method." Given the aridity and the scholasticism of much methodological discussion, their impatience is understandable, though not justified. What they are saying, in effect, is that the results matter, and not the processes of inquiry by which the results are obtained. But if political science as disciplined discourse is to differ from other forms of political communication, the processes by which findings are made and conclusions reached must be replicable, either logically or empirically. There are, admittedly, standards of excellence for political philosophy, for political polemics, for political fiction, or for political guidance. But they differ from those canons of scientific method by which a political science must be judged.

POLITICAL THEORY: THE LOST FRONTIER

Perhaps the most pervasive feature of political science as it emerged in the late nineteenth century from its age-old marriage with moral philosophy, history, and public law is the separation of theory and empirical research. With positivism already regnant in both history and law since the second quarter of the century, the mid- and late-Victorian complacency, characterized by an easy and naive belief in the inevitability of progress and liberty under law, was congenial to the eschewal of ethical sentiments. This development is understandable. Positivism is the response of men living in an era (and aura) in which problems of ultimate ends are believed to be rooted in man himself or his natural and social environment. Moreover, the social order may seem stable and be taken for granted, so that, when decisions must be made for the community, they appear to involve choices of means rather than ends. But with the elimination of questions of value from political disquisitions, positivism also exorcised empirically relevant theory. What now went as theory was largely a combination of imported abstract German ideas about the nature of the State, a concept really alien to the American experience, Austinian notions of sovereignty that their exponents found troublesome to reconcile with federal institutions and other facts of American life, and evolutionary doctrines about races and nations. Yet, the study of political institutions was quite unencumbered by these "theoretical" excogitations, being concerned with descriptive, historical, formalistic analyses of governmental structures and constitutional principles. Works such as Woodrow Wilson's *The State* (1889) or John W. Burgess' *Political Science and Comparative Constitutional Law* (1890–91) are of interest today mainly to antiquarians.

But the stage was set for making theory peripheral to the core enterprise. Theory in American political science, as elsewhere, came to mean the history of political philosophies. William A. Dunning's three volumes—*A History of Political Theories, Ancient and Mediaeval* (1902), *A History of Political Theories, from Luther to Montesquieu* (1905), and *A History of Political Theories, from Rousseau to Spencer* (1920)—set the tone for a long series of similar works, of more or less originality, describing the contents of the classical texts and avoiding critical assessment. In due time, similar histories were written for particular countries, notably the United States, England, France, and Germany. Or the precedents were traced for particular concepts, such as Charles E. Merriam's *A History of the Theory of Sovereignty since Rousseau* (1900) or Francis Cokers' *Organismic Theories of the State* (1910). To this may be added a still growing body of studies on particular political philosophers, with a strong dose of biography and historical-environmental data added to make textual exegesis more palatable. But once the pragmatic reaction set in against the empty formalism and legalism of the earlier political science, theory was left hanging in mid-air, with neither its feet firmly rooted in contemporary political facts, nor its head in the frankly speculative heaven of metaphysics.

This is not intended to suggest anything said about politics before 1800 or 1900 is not relevant for present investigation. To commit the classics to oblivion—if that were possible—would only mean a reversal of the attitude of those who believe that nothing significant has been written about politics since Plato, Aristotle, and Thomas Aquinas. The issue is certainly not one of the moderns versus the ancients. The real issue is the uses to which classical as well as modern political writings are to be put. It is for this reason that study of the classics must necessarily take account of the state of the discipline within which these writings find their problematic focus, theoretical status, and methodological apparatus. Otherwise it is impossible to specify criteria needed to determine whether or not a literary production falls within a designated critical orbit.

For those able and willing to give the classics another try—for whatever reason—most of them are available in cheap editions. The "spell of Plato" may best be caught in the *Republic*, written about 380 B.C., a weird mixture of utopian writing, elitist predilections, and metaphysical speculation about human purposes from which, by an admittedly rigorous logical procedure, an ethical absolutism is derived. The *Republic* represents a genre of idealist political writing which has survived to the present day and which sees the definition of the ideal political community as the major task of political thinking. This type of political literature undoubtedly provides important data for political science, but it is not political science unless the notion of "science" is deprived of all meaning. It supplies data for political science not because of the eternal verities to which it aspires, but rather because it is symptomatic of the reactions of highly sensitive and intelligent men to times of stress and strain. It is of importance in understanding the history of the political intellect, and it is important because it symbolizes the aspirations of men for a better life and because it has driven men on to action, no matter how mistaken their assumptions and how dangerous their behavior.

More profitable from the point of view of modern political science is Aristotle's *Politics* which dates from about 350 B.C. Aristotle combined logic with empirical observations in creating the method of comparative analysis of political institutions. There is, of course, much that is nonsense in the *Politics* and even more that is irrelevant except for antiquarian interest, but the modern political scientist finds here a first classification of government structures, a theory of governmental change, an appreciation of custom and tradition as powerful forces in political behavior, the beginnings of social class analysis, and an ethics of political responsibility.

In Thomas Aquinas' *Summa Theologica*, written about 1250 A.D., the natural law doctrine of the Stoic philosophers was integrated into the Christian teaching of divine order, combined with the Aristotelian emphasis on customary norms or common law, and supplemented by a just regard for the sound legal positivism of the Roman jurists. The resulting synthesis represented a *tour de force* of considerable intellectual achievement and influence, notably on the emergence of constitutionalism.

The intellectual ferment of the Renaissance produced, in Niccolò Machiavelli, the first of the modern political theorists. His *Prince*, which first appeared in 1513, is one of the most controversial books in political theory and remains a monument to the liberation of man's mind from medieval preoccupations with metaphysics and religion. Often denounced as a work of an amoral charlatan, it is a dispassionate analysis—except for the last, possibly forged, chapter—of the political style of the Renaissance, a clear-headed appraisal of the role of political power in human affairs, and a keen dissection of the problem of means and ends in political conduct. The book oozed the spirit of a changing times. The *Prince* represents a kind of political writing that has come in for much criticism, by both idealists and empiricists, but its propositions are neither purely descriptive nor dogmatically absolute, Rather, as close reading will show, they usually are cast in terms of hypothetical statement—"if you want this, then do that," and the success of action is made dependent on a great many conditions which might interfere with desired consequences. In other words, the statements made by this genre are not only tentative, subject to verification in practice, but the probability that expected results will occur is made contingent on the presence or absence of specified circumstances. It is for this reason that Machiavelli's *Prince*, on the surface so little sanguine about the possibilities of an ethics of responsibility, may be considered a precursor of the theoretical-empirical method of our own day.

By comparison with the *Prince*, Jean Bodin's *Republic* of 1576 seems unduly cryptic, but Bodin freed political theory from its bondage to theology and presented a secular conception of natural law and its ethical premises. His concept of sovereignty would become a central notion in political science and plague political theory down to the recent past; yet, if one appraises his theory of sovereignty, it appears eminently rooted in human reality, whereas later formulations seem depersonalized and metaphysical.

If Machiavelli's *Prince* was modern in that it represented the first truly empirical approach to the problem of power, Thomas Hobbes's *Leviathan* (1651) was modern in that it treated politics from the methodological standpoint of the new physical sciences. Deductive, logical, schematic, and comprehensive in his method, Hobbes related his "political system" to human behavior in general, approximating the structural-functional conceptions of recent social science. The fact that Hobbes ignored empirical observations may account, in part at least, for the relatively small influence of his work on the later course of political science. Instead the *Leviathan* fell in disrepute as an argument in favor of absolute monarchy, though it is often noted that the *Leviathan* stimulated John Locke to write in 1690 his *Second Treatise of Civil Government*, which became the bible of eighteenth-century liberalism.

Both Hobbes's and Locke's works, like the third of what constitutes the great trilogy of the age, Jean Jacques Rousseau's *Social Contract*, which first appeared in France in 1762, are cast within the framework of natural law philosophy, with its assumptions about the omnipotence of human reason, its speculations about the contractual origins of civil society, and its contemporarily congenial individualism. If they cannot serve any longer as viable theories, they continue to be important polemical tracts of the times—Hobbes as the father of absolutism, Locke as the father of liberalism, and Rousseau as the father of nationalism.

Much neglected by historians of political theory is the work of Giovanni Battista Vico, whose *Principii d'una Scienza Nuova* (1725; 2d ed., 1730) is an expression of revolt against the ahistorical, speculative methods and findings of the natural law philosophers. Vico's approach impressed the Baron Charles Louis de Montesquieu, whose great *De l'esprit des loix* (1748) marks the modern revival of Aristotle's empirical, historical, and comparative analysis. Montesquieu is, of course, best known for his formulation of the principle of the separation of powers. His influence on American political thought is evident in *The Federalist* (1787-88), a series of essays by Alexander Hamilton, James Madison, and John Jay in favor of the new American Constitution. In England, Edmund Burke's subtle mixture of guarded liberalism in economics and equally guarded conservatism in politics is well expressed in his *Reflections on the Revolution in France* (1790).

Political thought in the outgoing eighteenth and nineteenth centuries moves along many roads. Conservatism, romantic and reactionary; liberalism, constitutional and utilitarian; socialism, utopian and "scientific"; nationalism, idealist and historical; individualism, anarchic and democratic; and other ideological formulations compete in the struggle for men's minds. Jeremy Bentham's *An Introduction to the Principles of Morals and Legislation* (1789) and later works postulated reform in terms of the principle of utility based on "pain and pleasure" as its "two sovereign masters." Georg W. F. Hegel's *Grundlinien der Philosophie des Rechts* (1821) marked the apotheosis of the "state." Liberalism found its most distinguished spokesman in John Stuart Mill, whose *On Liberty* (1859) and *Considerations on Representative Government* (1861) remain to this day unequaled as expressions of constitutional sanity. Karl Marx and Friedrich Engels, in *The Communist Manifesto* of 1848, combined the dialectic method and historical analysis in their theory of the inevitable class struggle. Everywhere change was in the air, and men everywhere sought to control the change in line with their preferences and predilections. Political theory was, above all, man's response to a rapidly changing world of industrialization, urbanization, and colonization. The Enlightenment's idea of progress was given powerful impetus by the discoveries of Darwin, and progress and evolution became almost synonymous in usage. The tremendous strides made in the natural sciences spurred on those dedicated to the study of human affairs. The time had come for the emergence of the social sciences as independent disciplines. And with it also came the decline of political theory.

Dunning's descriptive historicism dominated the scene for a generation, and it was not until 1937, when George H. Sabine published *A History of Political Theory*, that some fresh air would ventilate the moldy caves of historical scholarship. Before Sabine, Charles H. McIlwain, in a sophisticated introduction to *The Political Works of James I* (1918), had shown the possibilities of creative theoretical activity in the writing of the history of ideas, but his later *The Growth of Political Thought in the West* (1932) was more conventional. McIlwain tended to view political philosophies as rationalizations rather than as determinants of political action, but unlike Sabine he was not clear as to just what the important problems of a political theory really are. Instead, it was Sabine who reversed the trend in the study of political theory by reintroducing methodological rigor into the analysis of political ideas. As he pointed out in the preface to the revised edition of his book in 1950, "... any clear-headed theory of politics requires discrimination between states of fact, causal connections, formal implications, and the values or ends that a policy is designed to achieve. In any political philosophy all these factors are combined, but no combination can alter the fact that they are logically different and that conclusions about them are differently warranted." Yet, even after Sabine, most of those who call themselves "political theorists" seem to ignore this methodological injunction. They continue to present the work of a classical writer without discriminating between the various dimensions of theory—value statements, causal hypotheses, empirical data, epistemology, and techniques of obtaining political goals. When, in the early fifties, David Easton came to write his *The Political System* (1953) subtitled "an inquiry into the state of political science," he did not find wide acceptance of the Sabinian view among his colleagues.

The trouble with the classics is not that they are studied, for they should be studied, but rather it is the way they are studied. Unless the student of historical writings approaches his subject with some notion of just what he is after, and with some methodological sophistication, his work must necessarily remain without significance. If it is his attitude that all the really important things which need to be said about politics have already been said by the classics, his scholarship, no matter how erudite, will be uncreative from the point of view of theoretical progress. Historical scholarship is an activity essentially different from theory construction, be it concerned with value theory or casual theory.

The objective of history-writing is narrative, either to tell us "how things have actually been," or to tell us "how things have come to be what they are." The objective of theory is either to clarify values and goals of public policy, or to advance causal propositions which can be empirically verified. Little has been done along these lines by political theorists who have taken the historical road. As an example of the former, one might mention William Y. Elliott's *The Pragmatic Revolt in Politics* (1928), with which one may partly disagree, but which does not pull its punches in its critique of pluralism; or Leo Strauss's masterful *The Political Philosophy of Hobbes: Its Basis and Its Genesis* (1952). As an example of the latter, there is Robert A. Dahl's recent *A Preface to Democratic Theory* (1956), which is an acute analysis of the causal propositions and functional hypotheses implicit in various historical formulations of democracy. A masterpiece of historical-theoretical writing is Otto von Gierke's *Das Deutsche Genossenschaftsrecht* (1868–73), part of which is available in an English translation by Frederic W. Maitland, *Political Theories of the Middle Ages* (1900).

The prevailing mode of dealing with theory is still either rejection of the premises on which propositions are based, or criticism of the logical procedures used in making deductions from major theoretical propositions, or, perhaps worse, selective quotation with the implicit attempt at ridicule. Articles and book reviews in the journals are still full of these kinds of diatribes. The technique is literary, and as one reads these tracts or articles of the critics, one is struck by the use of metaphor, loose assertion, flowery language, and often invective.

Of course, logical analysis and conceptual clarification are important ingredients of a viable political theory. A notable example is Thomas D. Weldon's analysis of classical political theory, *The Vocabulary of Politics* (1953). The book is a critique of classical styles of thinking with their real essences, absolute standards, and geometrical methods, as well as a plea for attention to meanings which change with changes in institutions, problems, and human aspirations. But the final test of a theory's validity does not lie either in polemical exegesis or even in logical analysis. It lies in the ability of the theory to withstand the rigorous test of empirical proof. This kind of test requires ingenuity, patience, and much drudgery. In part, of course, theorists must blame themselves if their work arouses nothing but verbal excoriation. Theories devoid of operational definitions and testable hypotheses are difficult to defend in the absence of proof. And, admittedly, the burden of proof lies with the theorist rather than with the critic. It is for this reason that, if political theory is to be freed from the jungle war of polemical disputation, political theorists have an obligation to be explicit about the character of the statements they make— whether they are propositions of fact or of value—and to remain within a range of factual data or value problems to which their theories presumably refer, as well as to provide for those lines of empirical inquiry which alone can prove or disprove their assertions.

And if academic political theory in its historical garb contributed little to a science of politics, it contributed even less to the reformulation of political values or the creation of new ones. Academic political theorists, though insistent on the need for a normative political philosophy, have not produced a single major piece of writing that might be considered a contribution to a political value system. Until recently, what creative value theory was produced was more likely to be the work of philosophers and intellectuals generally than of academic political theorists. Perhaps the most persistently creative political theorist on the American scene, whose work spans almost two generations and an ever-changing orientation, has been Walter Lippmann, by profession a journalist, but at heart a teacher. From *A Preface to Politics* (1913), a hopeful plea for reform, through *A Preface to Morals* (1929), in search of a new political ethics, *An Inquiry into the Principles of the Good Society* (1937), an assessment of the problem of freedom and control, to the recent *Essays in the Public Philosophy* (1955), Lippmann articulated some of the major value problems of the century. John Dewey, a philosopher, in *The Public and Its Problems* (1927), *Individualism, Old and New* (1930), and *Liberalism and Social Action* (1935), reconceptualized democratic liberalism in terms of pragmatic assumptions. Thomas V. Smith, another philosopher, contributed *The Democratic Way of Life* (1926), *Beyond Conscience* (1934), and *The Promise of American Politics* (1936). Max Lerner, though trained as a political scientist, formulated a program for liberals in *It Is Later Than You Think* (1938), *Ideas Are Weapons* (1939), and *Ideas for the Ice Age* (1941). Recently, two political scientists, Louis Hartz, in *The Liberal Tradition in America* (1955), and Clinton Rossiter, in *Conservatism in America* (1955), have written creative reappraisals of the American political tradition.

There has been some change, notably since World War II, under the impact of the fascist and communist challenges. An increasing number of political scientists have come to devote themselves to problems of public policy. Yet, those interested in the formulation of policy alternatives have not been political theorists, but students of public administration, international relations, or judicial processes. And while some of them may consciously see themselves as the descendants of the great classical theorists, their work hardly supports Leslie Lipson's assertion, in *The Great Issues of Politics* (1954), that "indispensable for understanding politics are the classic works of eminent thinkers which have stood the test of time."

THE CORE OF POLITICAL SCIENCE: THE STUDY OF GOVERNMENT

The early separation of political theory from the main body of political science had profound effects on the formulations which were given the new discipline. Not only was the "state" accepted as the basic unit of analysis, eliminating from the focus of political science many political phenomena which did not fit its arbitrary definition, but the works which made some claim on comprehensiveness were little more than compilations of abstract principles, descriptions, and classifications of governmental institutions, powers, and tasks. Raymond G. Gettell's *Introduction to Political Science* (1910) or James W. Garner's *Introduction to Political Science* (1910) codified the early lore and proverbs. They are of little use because they were not based on careful analysis of the facts of political life and were, at best, syntheses of a wide and often contradictory assortment of concepts, ideas, and "data." Westel W. Willoughby, in a series of works including *An Examination of the Nature of the State* (1896), *The Fundamental Concepts of Public Law* (1924), and *The Ethical Basis of Political Authority* (1930), struck a more sophisticated note, combining legal analysis with the search for origins, structural description with normative assessment, and statement of principles with supporting data. Willoughby's trilogy probably represents the most consistent and comprehensive statement of political science as conceived by the founding fathers of the discipline. Francis G. Wilson's *The Elements of Modern Politics* (1936), a latecomer of this genre of general works, brought the tradition up to date but also heralded its departure.

A more realistic approach was Harold J. Laski's *Grammar of Politics* (1925) which, however, was looked on in America more as a work in pluralist political theory than as a statement of political science. The pluralist standpoint is also present in the works of Robert M. MacIver, *The Modern State* (1926) and *The Web of Government* (1947), but in contrast to Laski's philosophical-speculative perspective, MacIver's orientation is rooted in sociological and anthropological institutional data. Arthur N. Holcombe's *Foundations of the Modern Commonwealth* (1923) and Edward M. Sait's *Political Institutions* (1938), still describing political principles and institutions, were frankly critical, though unable to transcend the traditional limitations set by acceptance of "the state" as the basic concept of analysis. Sait's book, in particular, was sensitive to "methods of approach," but it did not offer alternatives to description.

Of somewhat different caliber are two works which appeared in the thirties, Herman Finer's monumental two-volume *The Theory and Practice of Modern Government* (1932) and Carl J. Friedrich's *Constitutional Government and Politics* (1937). Though both retained the concept of the "state" to circumscribe the central object of political analysis, they drew on a broad range of data derived from what by then had become the subfield of "comparative government" and skillfully integrated them into the theoretical formulations of the classics as handed down by the historians of political thought. There was still historical narration and legal description in these two works, but both took cognizance of the existence of pressure groups and public opinion phenomena as important ingredients of the political process.

Within the framework set by this tradition, political science in the first forty years of this century produced an abundance of historical, constitutional, and institutional studies on almost every conceivable subject related to government, whether on the local, state, national, or international level. The problems of constitution-making, constitutional interpretation, and constitutional change constituted the center of political investigation. They were supplemented by descriptive analyses of governmental structures, notably accenting the difference between the presidential and parliamentary systems of government and the difference between the unitary and federal forms of territorial organization. In later years, the differences between democratic and authoritarian governmental systems were given attention. Studies on the origin, nature, and structure of representation, the history and activities of political parties, the organization and procedures of legislative bodies and the functions of administrative departments circumscribed the other limits of this literature. Avoiding theory, the studies were often informative, sometimes insightful, rarely systematic, and never dynamic in character. Pretending to freedom from value judgments, they were nevertheless shot through with normative assumptions, depending on the writer's orientation. In due course, each of these concerns would become a specialization.

When in the late forties UNESCO undertook its survey of the state of political science, it was a basic assumption of the project that the development of political science has been very uneven in different parts of the world, and that, therefore, an international accounting might "bring to light causes of international as well as internal tension which might otherwise have remained unknown." Indeed, perusal of the UNESCO volume reveals that whereas American political science traveled the pragmatic route with little theoretical enlightenment ever since World War I, continental scholarship in political science remained historical, legal, and, above all, philosophical in orientation. Yet, from the beginning it had been realized that a political science that would not permit comparison of either political institutions or political behavior patterns would necessarily remain culture-bound and parochial. But at its worse, comparison became comparison of uncomparables, tending to reinforce preference for one's own traditional institutions; while at its best, comparison amounted to little more than parallel description of institutions in terms of low-level empirical concepts which were foisted on more or less systematic observations. In spite of lip service to the contrary, the study of comparative government, so-called, was a seriatim presentation of national institutions or organizational problems. The texts, from Abbott Lawrence Lowell's *Government and Parties in Continental Europe* (3d ed., 1897) through James Bryce's *Modern Democracies* (1921) to Taylor Cole's well-edited *European Political Systems* (1953), to name only a few in a long list of books, are comparative in name only. This is not to imply that they were of inferior scholarship, but that scholarship treated foreign institutions within a methodological frame of reference that was largely set by concepts derived from English or American constitutional experience. There were, of course, exceptions, such as the works of Finer and Friedrich already mentioned. But students of comparative government were, more often than not, specialists on a single country, and the proliferation of works on particular countries, too extensive for citation here, is apt testimony of the continued attractiveness of the country-by-country approach. Or they produced a rich body of specialized works on the functioning of presumably unique institutions in a foreign country, such as Walter Sharp's *The French Civil Service* (1931), William Ivor Jennings' *Cabinet Government* (1936), or Arnold Brecht's *Federalism and Regionalism in Germany* (1945), to mention only a few works that are typical. More recently, under the impact of an interdisciplinary "area approach," political scientists have come to deal with foreign institutions in a more multidimensional setting, relating political forms and processes to the social structure and culture of a given country, such as Robert Scalapino's *Democracy and the Party Movement in Prewar Japan* (1953) or Merle Fainsod's *How Russia Is Ruled* (1953), but even these studies fall short of the requirements of comparative analysis.

There is today much ferment among students of comparative government. Under the auspices of the Social Science Research Council, a Committee on Comparative Politics has recently begun to specify major types of research needs, delimit areas of ignorance, and concern itself with theoretical and methodological problems. These tendencies have been summarized and evaluated by Roy C. Macridis in his critical *The Study of Comparative Government* (1955).

It was in the nature of the American experience that constitutional law should claim the attention of political scientists bent on specialization. The great political conflicts in American history had been conflicts over the Constitution. And even if not really legal but political in character, conflicts between the President and Congress, or between the federal government and the states, were seen in a constitutional perspective. Constitutional problems arising out of the due process, equal protection of the laws, and contract clauses of the Constitution, as well as such constitutional grants as the commerce power and taxing power, were of interest to political scientists. Yet, if one expected a treatment of these matters by political scientists different from that of the lawyers, such as Walter Bagehot had undertaken in *The English Constitution* (1867), the literature, at least until recently, does not reveal it. This is true even of the most political of American constitutional issues, the problem of judicial review. Justice Marshall's denial of the politically creative role of the courts in *Marbury v. Madison* (1803), still defended over a hundred years later by Justice Roberts in *United States v. Butler* (1936), had been codified in Kent's, Story's, and Cooley's nineteenth-century commentaries, and their authority seemed insurmountable. The pervasiveness of the classical legal approach is evident in an early work of Edward S. Corwin, *The Doctrine of Judicial Review* (1914) and Charles G. Haines's *The American Doctrine of Judicial Supremacy* (1914; 2d ed., 1932).

When the breakthrough came by way of "sociological jurisprudence" and the new "legal realism," it was led by lawyers rather than by political scientists. Justice Benjamin Cardozo took a close look at what the judges really do when they interpret the law in *The Nature of the Judicial Process* (1921), which was followed by such works, all by lawyers, but of interest to political scientists, as Thurman Arnold's *The Symbols of Government* (1935) and *The Folklore of Capitalism* (1937), or the more psychologically oriented work of Jerome Frank, in *Law and the Modern Mind* (1930) and *Courts on Trial* (1949). The spirit of the Rooseveltian attack on the judiciary is probably best expressed in the work of a participant observer, Robert H. Jackson's *The Struggle for Judicial Supremacy* (1941). But political scientists contributed little to the new orientation. An exception is Robert K. Carr's *The Supreme Court and Judicial Review* (1942), and Fred V. Cahill summarized and evaluated the ferment of a generation in *Judicial Legislation; A Study in American Legal Theory* (1952). Charles Herman Pritchett, in *The Roosevelt Court* (1948) and *Civil Liberties and the Vinson Court* (1954), among political scientists, dissected the semantics, political issues, and judicial attitudes of the Supreme Court personnel. More recently, a young political scientist, Victor G. Rosenblum, in *Law as a Political Instrument* (1955), has broken new ground in delineating the political and the legal in what is admittedly a matter of interdisciplinary concern.

Within the framework set by the historical approach and constitutional categories, political scientists specializing in "national government," "state government," and "local government" produced a formidable body of either descriptive or, in some cases, frankly remedial literature. The problems associated with federalism loomed large. Earlier writers took the defensive view in favor of what they considered the "historic balance" between the federal government and the states. Beginning with the nineteen thirties, description and diagnosis were supplemented by engineering efforts to improve state-federal relations, the writers evidently recognizing that little was to be gained from posing concrete problems in terms of abstract "centralization versus decentralization" dichotomy. Typical of the new approach were Jane Perry Clark's *The Rise of a New Federalism* (1938) and George C. S. Benson's *The New Centralization* (1941). Two recent volumes, *Studies in Federalism* (1954), Robert R. Bowie and Carl J. Friedrich (eds.), and *Federalism: Mature and Emergent* (1955), Arthur W. Macmahon (ed.), present sophisticated analyses of the political aspects of federalism throughout the world.

Second only to the problems arising out of the territorial division of powers in interest to political scientists were the problems stemming from the functional separation of powers between the President and Congress, particularly the President's role in legislation. James Hart discussed executive orders in *The Ordinance Making Powers of the President of the United States* (1925), but the leading book dealing generally with the President's influence on legislation was a broadly-gauged study by Edward S. Corwin, *The President, Office and Powers* (1940). Lawrence H. Chamberlain's *The President, Congress and Legislation* (1946) is suggestive, and Wilfred E. Binkley's *President and Congress* (1947) traced the relations of the two agencies through history. One may also mention two recent books which attest to the continuing interest in the office of the President, Edward S. Corwin and Louis W. Koenig's *The Presidency Today* (1956) and Clinton Rossiter's *The American Presidency* (1956).

In addition to the works on federalism and presidential politics, political scientists have produced an enormous body of monographic studies on almost every conceivable institutional and problematic area of American government and politics. In particular, studies of Congress have been abundant. If the earlier of these studies, such as Robert Luce's *Legislative Procedure* (1922) and *Legislative Assemblies* (1924), were concerned with description of legal powers and the procedural maze of the legislative process, interest has gradually shifted toward the need for organizational reforms, as in George B. Galloway's *Congress at the Crossroads* (1946), and, even more recently, to the political dimensions of the legislative process, as in James M. Burns's *Congress on Trial* (1949) or Bertram Gross's *The Legislative Struggle: A Study in Social*

Combat (1953). Gross interpreted the legislative process as a struggle among groups in conflict, as did Stephen K. Bailey in *Congress Makes a Law* (1950), a detailed study of how the Full Employment Act of 1946 progressed through the legislative maze from theoretical conception to final passage. Yet these studies are more concerned with the group nature of political conflict generally than with how legislators actually behave. A stab toward such explanation was made by Julius Turner, in *Party and Constituency: Pressures on Congress* (1952), who correlated roll call votes on crucial issues with the character of Congressmen's constituencies. Few, if any, of these studies advance a systematic theory of legislative behavior. Bailey, for instance, referred to his method as a "vector analysis," but this turns out to be at most a convenient metaphor to circumscribe "the interaction of ideas, institutions, interests, and individuals" as components of the policy-making process.

The literature on American state and local government is similar in approach to that on national government. Constitutional questions and the role of the governor as administrator and policy-maker are treated as if they were microscopic cases of the national pattern. State administrative reorganization, legislative reform, as well as the relations between the state and its municipalities appear as proper concerns of academic study. The literature is too extensive to be mentioned here.

The more specialized political scientists became, the greater also became the alienation of theory from research, and the less able were students of such subfields as constitutional law, comparative government, public administration, or international relations to take cognizance of significant theoretical and methodological formulations at what had become the fringe rather than the core of their discipline. The fate of Arthur F. Bentley's *The Process of Government* (1908), one of the most creative works in American political science, is symptomatic. Bentley, equally dissatisfied with the structural formalism, metaphysical theory of the state, and cant about civic virtue of what he called "a dead political science," had suggested as the "raw materials" of politics the activities and relationships of those social groups whose unending interactions constitute the political order. But Bentley's realism made no impact on the thinking of his contemporaries and had to be almost independently rediscovered by hard work twenty years later in the work of specialists on administrative and legislative politics. Such works as Peter Odegard's *Pressure Politics* (1928), Edward Pendleton Herring's *Group Representation Before Congress* (1929), or Elmer E. Schattschneider's *Politics, Pressures and the Tariff* (1935) were applications of Bentley's thought, but there is little indication that these authors drew directly on his subtle discussion of action and interaction, of functional relations and group processes as objects of inquiry. Moreover, the internal politics of the great associations whose activities impinge on the political system remained unexplored. Oliver Garceau's *The Political Life of the American Medical Association* (1941) broke new empirical ground in this respect, but it was not until David B. Truman's *The Governmental Process* appeared in 1951 that Bentley's theoretical contributions were rewoven into the central fabric of political science.

Similarly, a work of the English political scientist Graham Wallas, *Human Nature in Politics*, which, like Bentley's book, appeared in 1908, remained unheeded, in spite of the fact that such classical theoretical works as Machiavelli's *Prince*, Hobbes's *Leviathan*, or Mill's *On Liberty* have been explicitly based on psychological premises concerning the nature of man. Here, too, the separation of theory and research proved costly. When, in 1922, Walter Lippmann published his *Public Opinion*, there was nothing in the literature of political science he could utilize other than Wallas' work, with the exception, perhaps, of Abbott Lawrence Lowell's *Public Opinion and Popular Government* (1913). But it is in the nature of the scientific enterprise that its different departments cannot coexist forever in splendid isolation. The separation of politics from the study of personality, just as its separation from the study of group processes, was bound to be ended. It was primarily due to the restless spirit of Charles E. Merriam that political science would, in due time, again become a "behavioral science" rather than remain a taxonomic undertaking. In *New Aspects of Politics* (1925), Merriam outlined what amounted to a major research program for a generation of political scientists. Merriam reasserted the propriety and desirability of applying psychological and sociological concepts and techniques to political investigation. He insisted on the need for minute inquiry and microscopic studies of political behavior carried on by advanced scientific methods. And, above all, he called for a rejuvenation of political theory as a guide in research and the verification of hypotheses through empirical proof.

Merriam's influence on the subsequent course of American political science was less a function of his many writings than of his teaching. Along with colleagues and a group of brilliant students Merriam founded in the twenties and thirties what may well be called a "school," but which was both something more and something less than a "school" in the narrow sense of the term. For Merriam was much too freewheeling a scholar to hamstring independent efforts. What the members of the "Chicago school" had in common was a revolt against the prevailing formal, legal, historical, and descriptive tradition. But each of its members charted his own course without being tied to a master's "line." Yet, they carried the "message" of revolt into a variety of subfields in which they became specialists. In the field of public administration,

Leonard D. White was always sensitive to new trends, and Herbert A. Simon would add new dimensions to the discipline. In the field of international relations, Quincy Wright and Frederick L. Schumann contributed new approaches. Harold F. Gosnell, using voting statistics, showed the possibilities of rigorous treatment of such data as well as of experimentation, to be followed in due time by Valdimer O. Key, Jr. Charles Herman Pritchett would come to study the attitudes of Supreme Court justices by scrutinizing their decisions more systematically than had ever been done before. David B. Truman, Avery Leiserson, Alfred De Grazia, and others would make important contributions toward a more behavioral orientation in political science.

Last, but by no means least, the most imaginative among the Chicago renovators is Harold D. Lasswell. His influence has steadily grown since his *Psychopathology and Politics* (1930), with its unashamed Freudian premises, dazzled an almost disbelieving profession. Once again, after many years of denial, the problems of human nature were reintroduced into the study of politics. Speaking in a language strange to most political scientists, Lasswell's analytical schema, even if not totally accepted, has come to be widely used in behavioral studies of the political process. One might mention here as an example a book by Alexander L. and Juliette L. George, *Woodrow Wilson and Colonel House* (1956), whose authors skillfully apply categories of personality analysis in a study of two important decision-makers.

While Lasswell is best known for his contribution to a psychology of politics, his active mind continued to extend the frontiers of political science in other respects as well. In *World Politics and Personal Insecurity* (1935), he elaborated his conception of "configurative analysis," pleading for a multidimensional approach. In *Politics: Who Gets What, When, How* (1936), influenced by Vilfredo Pareto and Gaetano Mosca, he elaborated what remains probably the sharpest nonlegal and non-normative definition of politics:

> The study of politics is the study of influence and the influential. The science of politics states conditions; the philosophy of politics justifies preferences. This book, restricted to political analysis, declares no preferences. It states conditions.
>
> The influential are those who get the most of what there is to get. Available values may be classified as *deference, income, safety*. Those who get the most are *elite;* the rest are *mass*.

In spite of strong positivistic leanings, Lasswell recognized early the central significance of values in political inquiry. In *Psychopathology and Politics*, he advanced the notion of a "preventive politics" as a kind of medical approach to the attainment of democratic values. And in

Democracy Through Public Opinion (1941), he began the effort to relate statements of fact to statements of value which led to the conception of political science as "policy science." His continuing interdisciplinary and methodological interests are best expressed in the volume of articles entitled *The Analysis of Political Behavior: An Empirical Approach* (1948), notably an essay on "General Framework: Person, Personality, Group, Culture." Decision-making as both a procedural and substantive problem is given further attention in *Power and Personality* (1948), which also brings Lasswell's psychopolitical approach up to date. Decisional processes and attempts at their systematization, as well as researches into the policy aspects of law, are to be found in a number of recent articles, as yet not brought together in book form. In the introduction to *Power and Society* (1950), Lasswell, in cooperation with Abraham Kaplan, outlined his conception of a "framework for political inquiry." Finally, one must mention the work of Lasswell and many associates in the area of symbolic political behavior, chiefly by way of content analysis, some of which may be found in *Language of Politics* (1949).

PUBLIC ADMINISTRATION: DEPARTURE AND RETURN

Among the subfields of political science, public administration was the first to break loose from its moorings in the mother discipline, but it seems also destined to be the first to return to the womb. In fact, it looks as if public administration is serving as a main channel through which a new body of knowledge, transcending disciplinary boundaries, is being funneled into the central current of political science. From psychology comes what is often referred to as the "human relations" approach, and from sociology comes a systematic orientation best characterized as "organizational theory." At the same time, the new tendencies were bound to encounter the ticklish problem of value. One may speculate on why this is so. One reason may well be that among those specializing in various branches of political science, students of public administration were most likely to participate in governmental activities. Hence, they were more likely to test their concepts and principles against the harsh realities of political life than were students of government in general or international relations, not to mention the historians of political theory. Both the New Deal and World War II attracted political scientists into government service to a degree not previously known, and here they were brought into closer contact with social scientists from other disciplines than in the faculty clubs of their universities.

Public administration is eminently concerned with the relationship between means and ends, between facts and values, between conduct and the goals of action. The basic model is one of rational action predicated on the correct calculation of those alternatives of conduct which are most conducive to the attainment of a given set of ends and with a minimum loss of other goals. The model clearly specifies the necessity of weighing both alternate goals as well as alternate means. In spite of the relative simplicity of this model, the history of public administration has been tortuous—a case of either too little or too much. In particular, the apparent discrepancy between the rational aspect of administrative structure and the "irrational action" of human beings is a source of bewilderment to many students of public administration.

Because, perhaps, the problem of values looms so large in public administration, the "founders" of the field developed a sharp division between policy and administration at the very beginning of the discipline. There were, of course, plausible reasons for this: in part, an independent study of public administration was the outcome of the demand for an impartial civil service and other governmental reforms unencumbered by politics; and, in part, it was a corollary in government of the scientific management movement in private business, with its emphasis on economy and efficiency; finally, it was possessed by the spirit of the progressive movement of the first decade which took progress for granted as the goal of human endeavor and inquired little into other possibilities. The most explicit statement of the desirability of separating politics from administration is one of the classics of American political science, Frank G. Goodnow's *Politics and Administration* (1900). Administration, Goodnow argued, should be separate not only from partisan politics, but also from policy-making in general. One might also mention an early essay by Woodrow Wilson, "The Study of Administration," which appeared in the *Political Science Quarterly* for 1887. The preoccupations of the scientific management movement are best caught in Frederick W. Taylor's *The Principles of Scientific Management*, first published in 1911 and reprinted many times since.

The general acceptance of the notion of progress, with its predilection for Jeffersonian ends which now, in the age of increasing urbanization, industrialization, and mechanization, could be best realized by Hamiltonian means, is best expressed in another classic, Herbert Croly's *The Promise of American Life* (1909), a book of some influence on the later course of American liberalism. Goodnow's distinction between politics and administration was further elaborated by William F. Willoughby who, in *The Government of Modern States* (rev. ed., 1936), conceived of administration as a "fourth branch," independent of the executive power but to be controlled by the legislature. This "theory" was never widely accepted. Yet, the early texts in the field, especially Leonard D. White's *Introduction to the Study of Public Administration*

(1926)—a widely used book, continued to reflect the direction set by Goodnow.

The question, "administration for what?" was largely ignored. If not ignored, values were taken for granted. The lack of interest in the policy objectives of public administration was probably both cause and effect of the separation of politics and administration. Policy formation was considered a function of politics and its execution a matter of administration. It was apparently assumed that because means and ends could be separated logically, they could also be separated in practice. Politics was "dirty business," and "taking administration out of politics" meant progress. The model failed to meet either the realities of policy or those of administration. It provided a fragmentary view of the administrative process, as if administration could be removed from its political context. The research emphasis was on the formal structural aspects of administration, or on rather vague "principles" of desirable administrative conduct which, if only properly applied, would make for efficient performance.

Yet, it must be pointed out that those who first advanced the dichotomy of politics and administration were not political conservatives. Many of them were in the forefront of political reformers who advocated the city manager form of government, regulatory agencies, and such devices of direct democracy as the initiative and the referendum. It was only after their post-World War I descendants had left reform behind that administration was considered an end in itself, with its corresponding neglect of the political problems of representation and party responsibility.

A gradual shift in thinking about public administration, perhaps first heralded by Felix Frankfurter in *The Public and Its Government* (1930), did come with the advent of the New Deal, to be consummated only after World War II. The problems created by the depression shattered the easy assumption that the ends of government could be taken for granted and that policy considerations could be strictly excluded from administration. Pragmatism, notably as expounded in John Dewey's *The Public and its Problems* (1927), penetrated the consciousness of students of public administration. Moreover, the old maladies of corruption had been largely remedied, and it was no longer to be feared that contact with politics and policy-making would besmirch the good name of public administration. The new tendencies were noted by Leonard D. White in *Trends in Public Administration* (1933).

In general, writers on public administration continued to discuss structural matters throughout the thirties, and an influential volume edited in 1937 by Luther Gulick and Lyndall Urwick, *Papers on the Science of Administration*, once more restated the traditional approach and its magic summary term of administrative functions, POSDCORB, i.e., planning, organizing, staffing, directing, coordinating, reporting, and budgeting. The verbal scholasticism of public administration is also evident in Schuyler Wallace's *Federal Departmentalization: A Critique of Theories of Organization* (1941), which reviews in great detail the arguments for and against administrative centralization. But other writers began to place public administration in its political context by emphasizing the nature of policy-making. Administrative matters were now consciously dealt with in the framework of specific governmental programs. Administration came to be viewed as a means to an end which could not be properly evaluated apart from the uses to which it was being put. John M. Gaus and Leonard O. Wolcott's *Public Administration and the United States Department of Agriculture* (1940) is conceived in terms of the newer approach. In a later theoretical work, *Reflections on Public Administration* (1947), Gaus referred to this orientation as "an ecological approach," for it builds "quite literally from the ground up; from the elements of a place—soil, climate, location, for example—to the people who live there—their numbers and ages and knowledge, and the ways of physical and social technology by which from the place and in relationship with one another, they get their living." The new orientation was given a near-manifesto form in a series of essays by John M. Gaus, Leonard D. White, and Marshall E. Dimock, *The Frontiers of Public Administration* (1936). Policy-making as a central facet of public administration is most explicitly admitted in a post–World War II volume of essays by Fritz Morstein Marx (ed.), *Elements of Public Administration* (1946), written mostly by younger political scientists who had some kind of governmental experience during the war. It is given its most complete formulation in Paul H. Appleby's *Policy and Administration* (1949). The various developments in the field from Goodnow on are ably discussed by Dwight Waldo in *The Administrative State: A Study of the Political Theory of American Public Administration* (1948).

Two problems in particular have continued to occupy the attention of students of public administration. One is the problem of "bureaucracy," the other the problem of the "public interest." The problem of bureaucracy, as seen by political scientists, involved the issues of administrative discretion and administrative responsibility. Administrative supremacy was first bitterly attacked in England, in Gordon Hewart's *The New Despotism* (1929), and in this country by James M. Beck in *Our Wonderland of Bureaucracy* (1932), but both substituted polemics for analysis. Early works such as Cecil T. Carr's *Delegated Legislation* (1921) or Frederick F. Blachly and Miriam E. Oatman's *Administrative Legislation and Adjudication* (1934) were primarily concerned with legislative specification of discretionary limits. John Dickinson's *Administrative Justice and the Supremacy of Law in the United States* (1927) is still an excellent work on the control of bureaucracy by the judiciary, and it was supplemented by James M. Landis' *The Administrative Process* (1938). Robert E. Cushman wrote a broad, historical study in *The Independent Regulatory Commissions* (1941), but Marver H. Bernstein's *Regulating Business by Independent Commission* (1955) is a more critical analysis of the problem of administrative control. Charles S. Hyneman favored democratic political control of the bureaucracy in a somewhat nostalgic *Bureaucracy in a Democracy* (1950), in contrast to the position taken by Carl J. Friedrich, in *Constitutional Government and Democracy* (rev. ed., 1950), that bureaucrats are ultimately subject only to a degree of self-limitation. That bureaucrats reflect the dominant political elite is essentially the argument of John D. Kingsley in a study of the British civil service, *Representative Bureaucracy* (1944). And that bureaucracy is never better or worse than the men who fill administrative positions seems to be the underlying theme of two works using the biographical approach, Edward Pendleton Herring's *Federal Commissioners: A Study of Their Careers and Qualifications* (1936) and Arthur W. Macmahon and John D. Millett's *Federal Administrators: A Biographical Approach to the Problem of Departmental Management* (1939).

In recent years the problems of bureaucratic behavior, and notably its pathology, have also come to occupy sociologists, whose point of departure has usually been the keen observations on bureaucracy of the German Max Weber, now available in English in a collection by H. H. Gerth and C. Wright Mills (eds.), *From Max Weber: Essays in Sociology* (1946), as well as in a translation by A. M. Henderson and Talcott Parsons, *The Theory of Social and Economic Organization* (1947). In this connection, a *Reader in Bureaucracy* (1952), Robert K. Merton and associates (eds.), brings together in handy format the best theoretical and empirical work done on the sociology of bureaucracy. Other excellent studies are Reinhard Bendix' *Higher Civil Servants in American Society* (1949), Peter M. Blau's *The Dynamics of Bureaucracy* (1955) and *Bureaucracy in Modern Society* (1956), as well as a research study by a political scientist, Dwaine Marvick's *Career Perspectives in a Bureaucratic Setting* (1954).

How the "public interest"—a vague and ambiguous concept—comes to be formulated by administrators and legislators has given rise to a lively body of literature. Arthur F. Bentley's rather pessimistic conception of special interest groups pressing on one another was modified in terms of a "reconciliation" conception in Edward Pendleton Herring's now classical *Public Administration and the Public Interest* (1936), while

Avery Leiserson, in *Administrative Regulation: A Study in Representation of Interests* (1942), suggested acceptance of administrative action by interest groups as the standard of whether or not the "public interest" has been met. More recently, Earl Latham, in *The Group Basis of Politics* (1952), and David B. Truman, in *The Governmental Process* (1951), have dealt with the problem of how policy-makers accommodate themselves to conflicting group pressures. But no systematic theory has as yet been evolved, though a supplementary "Note on Conceptual Scheme" in Martin Meyerson and Edward C. Banfield's *Politics, Planning, and the Public Interest* (1955) is suggestive.

The tendencies which came to dominate public administration thinking in the middle thirties not only questioned the possibilty (and desirability) of separating policy from administration, but also indicated that the so-called "principles of administration"—especially "economy" and "efficiency"—were wanting as criteria of good administration in the face of the urgent problems that needed to be solved in depression America.

But it is easier to talk about the relationship between means and ends than to specify just how they are related. Any step in the direction of a solution to the problem of facts and values, even if incomplete, could be expected to have far-reaching consequences for administrative theory. The step was taken, in a frontal attack, by Herbert A. Simon in *Administrative Behavior: A Study of Decision-Making Processes in Administrative Organization* (1947). Although published after the war, Simon's book had been conceived in the early forties and represented by far the most radical critique of traditional public administration. Strongly influenced by logical empiricism, with its exclusion of statements of value as researchable topics, Simon once more seemed to introduce the separation of policy and administration. But this interpretation is incorrect. Rather, it was Simon's objective to bring logical clarity into what had been confused notions, in both the older approach as well as in the newer trends. Simon argued that while statements of value, at least at present, are beyond the pale of empirical proof, goals of policy can be translated into statements of fact which can be tested. And as the goals of public administration are mainly immediate rather than remote, the possibility of a science of administration was once more asserted. Indeed, statements of ultimate ends—freedom, justice, welfare, and other values of democratic ideology—are meaningless unless connected with relevant means propositions. Simon's work represented, therefore, a theoretical orientation which had been lost in the years since Goodnow made the distinction between policy and administration. While critical of what he called the "proverbs of administration," Simon offered a series of hypothetical propositions of empirical relevance. In particular, the concepts of "economy" and "efficiency" are shown to be serviceable as criteria of administrative effectiveness in the context of theoretically demonstrable means-ends "chain" constructs.

Simon's book represented a departure and new beginning in another respect. It brought administrative thinking into line with a psychology of human relations. Students of public administration had been aware of Mary Parker Follett's plea for attention to the motivations of individuals and groups in organizations, but her *The New State* (1918) was more likely to be cited than read, and her suggestive papers, collected by Henry Metcalf and Lyndall Urwick in *Dynamic Administration* (1942), had been heeded more by students of private than public administration. The "human relations" approach proper had been developed at the Harvard Business School by Elton Mayo and his associates, had been stated first in Mayo's *The Human Problems of Industrial Civilization* (1933), and was subjected to rigorous empirical research in the Hawthorne experiments, reported in Fritz J. Roethlisberger and William J. Dickson's *Management and the Worker* (1939). Meanwhile, in 1938, an enlightened business executive, Chester Barnard, in *The Functions of the Executive*, had drawn on his rich personal experiences in pointing to the importance of what since has come to be called "informal organization." These and other developments were exploited by Simon and his associates, Donald W. Smithburg and Victor A. Thompson, in a lively text, *Public Administration* (1950).

In recent years, too, students of other disciplines have begun to concern themselves with administrative and organizational problems, and they have brought to the study of administration a good deal of theoretical and methodological sophistication. One might mention Alexander H. Leighton's participant-observational *The Governing of Men* (1945), a study of a Japanese relocation camp by an anthropologically-trained psychiatrist; Philip Selznick's sociological *TVA and the Grass Roots* (1949), with its concept of "cooptation"; or Laura Thompson's *Culture in Crisis: A Study of the Hopi Indians* (1950), based on the findings of the "Indian Personality and Administration Research" sponsored by the Office of Indian Affairs and the Committee on Human Development at the University of Chicago. Edward C. Banfield, in *Government Project* (1951), a study of a federal government-sponsored cooperative farm in Arizona, demonstrated how documentary materials, combined with *postfacto* interviews, can be used in behavioral analysis. Seymour M. Lipset, Martin Trow, and James Coleman, in *Union Democracy* (1956), have shown the possibilities of organizational analysis for an understanding of political processes in private associations. The implications of the great increase in number, size, and complexity of organizations in modern times is treated by Kenneth E. Boulding, an economist, in *The Organizational Revolution, A Study in the Ethics of Economic Organization* (1953).

At present, two trends are noticeable in public administration. There is first an effort to reconstruct and report administrative experience in its historical dimension. This may take the form of comprehensive history writing, such as Leonard D. White's *The Jeffersonians* (1951) and *The Jacksonians* (1954), or it may take the form of history writing at a relatively low level of abstraction, represented by the volume of "cases" edited by Harold Stein, *Public Administration and Policy Development* (1952). Designed primarily for teaching purposes, these cases are detailed descriptions of complex administrative situations, but limited in time and scope.

The other trend, "organizational theory," is characteristic of the attempt to develop empirically-testable theoretical models of organizational behavior. In this connection, communication theory and the theory of games have become of interest to students of public administration and political science in general. Richard C. Snyder, H. W. Bruck, and Burton Sapin present a comprehensive model which takes account of motivation as an important variable in *Decision-Making as an Approach to the Study of International Politics* (1954). A volume of lectures given at the Brookings Institution and collected in *Research Frontiers in Politics and Government* (1955) includes essays by Herbert A. Simon on "Recent Advances in Organization Theory" and by Richard C. Snyder on "Game Theory and the Analysis of Political Behavior." Robert A. Dahl and Charles E. Lindblom, a political scientist and an economist, respectively, in *Politics, Economics and Welfare* (1953), explore different types of decision-making—polyarchy, hierarchy, bargaining, and the price system—from the point of view of both organizational control and policy consequences.

BEYOND THE HORIZON: INTERNATIONAL POLITICS

The study of international politics has been in almost constant ferment for a number of years. Part of the ferment is the gradual shift that occurred in transferring the study of international politics from the domains of history and law to that of political science. And part of the ferment probably is the fact that with this transfer the study of international politics, while getting rid of some of the compulsions of the historians and the lawyers, has inherited many of the headaches of the political scientists.

Before World War I one can hardly speak of there having been an independent study of international politics. The relations among states were, of course, of interest to historians and international lawyers, but whereas the former were primarily concerned with diplomatic history, the latter were preoccupied with the legal agreements existing between "sovereign nations," their rights and duties under the body of international law, customary and positive, that had evolved since the dawn of the modern era. And if the lawyers built comprehensive and abstract legal systems which postulated a "family of nations," the historians dealt with concrete diplomatic events and sought after, in a hit-or-miss fashion, the "causes" of war, but seldom peace. Typical of the diplomatic approach was David J. Hill, *A History of Diplomacy in the International Development of Europe* (1905-14). The leading treatise of international law in the United States was John B. Moore's eight volume *A Digest of International Law* (1906). The historical method employed by both historians and lawyers did not make for generalizations, not to mention theories of international intercourse. What theory there was, Frank M. Russell has shown in *Theories of International Relations* (1936), was largely of a normative, philosophical, or apologetic character.

The study of international relations proper began only after World War I. With the aims and functions of the League of Nations as its main focus, the between-wars approach was motivated by a hopeful moralism which, in the face of recurring disasters, was stubbornly intent on formulating and implementing the goals of the international society, largely through organizational and legal means. Great emphasis was placed on formal structures, techniques of peaceful adjustment of international conflicts, and legal commitments. Information from geography to economics, from history to ethics, was harnessed into service, but lack of methodological rigor tended to confuse untestable assertions with statements of fact. The huge literature of the period ranged from comprehensive texts such as Raymond Leslie Buell's *International Relations* (1925) or Clyde Eagleton's *International Government* (1932) to formal studies of the League, such as Sir Alfred Zimmern's *The League of Nations and the Rule of Law, 1918-1935* (1936), to specialized treatises on the judicial settlement of disputes, such as Hersh Lauterpacht's *The Function of Law in the International Community* (1933), to historical treatments of wars, such as Sidney B. Fay's two-volume *The Origins of the World War* (1928), and to particular problems, such as Parker T. Moon's *Imperialism and World Politics* (1926). Most of these books, in addition to special pleading in favor of some preferred remedy for the world's ills, showed great technical competence and were singularly free of nationalistic obsessions.

There was, of course, dissent from what to some scholars appeared to be an undue preoccupation with institutional gadgets by which presumably rational men would bring the international house into order. Frederick L. Schumann published his brilliant *International Politics* in 1933, treating the politics among nations in a "state system" lacking a common government as a struggle for power, emphasizing cultural and historical antecedents as well as the attitudes and behavior patterns of nationalism and imperialism, critically reviewing the foreign policies of the major powers in terms of alternatives open to policy-makers, but not neglecting the possibilities of international law, organization, and diplomacy. Charles A. Beard, long in the forefront of the iconoclasts, subjected the vague notion of "national interest" to ironic scrutiny in *The Idea of National Interest* (1934). Nicholas Spykman's *America's Strategy in World Politics*, opening up the problems of national security, was not published until 1942, though its author had cried out for more rigorous methodological procedures in the study of international politics throughout the thirties. Finally, in *Britain and France Between Two Wars* (1940), Arnold Wolfers not only interpreted the activities of the League of Nations in terms of the foreign policies of its two dominant members, but also related their foreign policies to the political interests and ideologies of the major political groups in the two nations.

The changing focus of research in international politics was characterized by an increasing tendency to emphasize the motivations of nations and their policy-makers, their capacity to carry through on commitments, and those internal psychological, industrial, geographic, and demographic variables which determine that capacity. Moreover, with the ascendancy of political scientists among students of international relations, very much the same questions came to be asked about international politics as are asked about domestic politics: what modes of behavior are common to all states, rather than what is unique in the foreign policy of a single state? What are the conditions requisite to what types of foreign policy? What makes for repetition in the behavior of nations? What are the processes of decision-making? How does domestic politics interact with foreign politics? In other words, the shift was one from description of formal governmental structures and philosophical speculation about the ends of policy to closer observation of political processes and decision-making situations. The tendency to break down the separation of international from domestic affairs, even in the treatment of international law, is evident in Philip C. Jessup's *A Modern Law of Nations* (1948), and the close relationship between domestic ideologies and foreign policy is at the heart of Charles Micaud's *The French Right and Nazi Germany, 1933–1939* (1943).

With this new orientation came a greater reliance on the interview, either of the intensive or the sample survey variety, and on quantitative content analysis of mass communications, as tools of inquiry, rather than on official documents, papers of state, or newspaper accounts. Thomas A. Bailey's *The Man in the Street* (1948) and a volume by Lester Markel and others, *Public Opinion and Foreign Policy* (1949), are more or less tendentious in that the former took an optimistic, the latter a pessimistic view of public opinion as a formative force in foreign policy-making. On the other hand, Gabriel A. Almond's *The American People and Foreign Policy* (1950) is free of such biases and a keen analysis of the sociological and psychological factors influencing public opinion on foreign policy. It describes the environment in which foreign policy decisions must be made, traces historic trends in the development of American culture and character-making for possible prediction of responses, and conceptualizes attitudes in terms of "moods" which contribute to the shifting quality of American foreign policy. As an example of the uses of content analysis in the study of foreign policy, perhaps most suggestive is *The "Prestige Papers"* (1952) by Ithiel de Sola Pool and others, a refined treatment of the editorial comment of some of the world's leading newspapers over a span of fifty years. Of course, the older approaches continue to be pursued with some tenacity.

Unfortunately, the reaction to the reformist orientation in international relations literature of the interwar years resulted, first, in a rather futile and sterile debate over "realism versus idealism" in approaches to the study of international politics, and, second, in a tendency to ignore values altogether. As in other fields of human behavior, so in the study of international politics, the approach which ignores or denies the relevance of values and prides itself on its factual hard-headedness tends to smuggle in its values by the back door, with the difference that it is blind to its own value judgments. The "built-in" danger of what one may call "vulgar realism" may be exemplified by the work of an influential Englishman, Edward H. Carr. In *The Twenty Years' Crisis, 1919-1939* (1939) Carr succeeded in presenting a reasonably critical diagnosis of the international situation. But in the following *Conditions of Peace* (1942), the "naturalistic fallacy" of his realism appears as an unadulterated "wave-of-the-future" doctrine, with its justification of appeasement and appraisal of Hitler as a twentieth-century Napoleon. The implicit value scheme is that "what is, is good," and it is not only good, but will last. From a methodological point of view, this approach makes for great flexibility. In *The Soviet Impact on the Western World* (1947), a little book full of otherwise suggestive insights, Carr easily switched from Hitler to Stalin as the new savior: "The missionary role which had been filled in the first world war by American democracy and Woodrow Wilson had passed in the second world war to Soviet democracy and Marshal Stalin."

Carr's work indicates the danger of treating data without a scheme of clearly specified values. Fortunately, not all realist interpretation eschews the problem. As Thomas D. Weldon has shown in *States and Morals* (1947), a concern with values, as long as values are clearly distinguished from facts, does not necessarily mean lack of precision in systematic knowledge, but, on the contrary, contributes to the clarification of policy alternatives as they are circumscribed by the facts of the situation. In other words, given the existence of an international state system, national goals are a legitimate point of departure in the study of those forces and tendencies which shape the behavior of nation states. Outstanding proponents of this type of "realism" are William T. R. Fox, *The Super-Powers* (1944), and Hans Morgenthau, *Politics Among Nations* (1948). More recently, George F. Kennan's *American Diplomacy, 1900–1950* (1951) has been hailed as an example of this realism. Yet, in accepting "power" as the goal toward which foreign policies are oriented, this modified realistic approach tends to hypostatize a single value into a principle of interpretation which may not find general acceptance. Moreover, as John H. Herz has pointed out in a fine theoretical study, *Political Realism and Political Idealism* (1951), implicit in both the realist and idealist views of international politics are hypotheses about human nature which come to be treated as if they were analytical models. The difficulty with either a model which postulates an ideal world system without conflict, or a power model which is predicated on the assumption of continued conflict, is that neither comes to grips with those expectations concerning the foreseeable future in terms of which policy-makers must make their decisions.

But "realistic" need not refer to a model that makes certain assumptions about the nature of men and nations. It may refer merely to the observational position of the investigator, and in that sense the model does not either specify the preferences of the inquirer or postulate characteristics of the object of inquiry. Rather, the observer formulates alternate expectations about the shape of things to come and assesses these expectations in terms of a variety of values, among which maximization of power may be only one value. Such models were first suggested by Lasswell in *World Politics and Personal Insecurity* (1935) under the name of "developmental constructs," and some such models were presented in his *The World Revolution of Our Time, A Framework for Basic Policy Research* (1951). Hence, analysis of international politics comes to concern itself with the study of those forces and conditions which shape national expectations and values. This approach assumes that orientations toward power differ from culture to culture, and it avoids the assumption of "realism" that all men everywhere are equally power-motivated. On the level of research this approach traces changes in the distribution of crucial social and political characteristics of world elites and counter-elites which serve as indices of social and political change affecting the distribution of top political power in world society. One should consult in this connection Harold D. Lasswell, Daniel Lerner, and C. Easton Rothwell, *The Comparative Study of Elites* (1952).

International politics, as a field of scientific study, has come to mean, then, investigation of the influences that bear upon the shaping of foreign policies, the process of policy formulation and execution, as well as of the techniques required to adjust the differing foreign policies to each other. The focus of research, as in Quincy Wright's *A Study of War* (1942), has become both more systematic and interdisciplinary than it had previously been. A good index of the newer trends is the type of research articles which have been published in the journal *World Politics* since 1948. A theoretical application of the multi-dimensional method in the area of international organization is Werner Levi's excellent *Fundamentals of World Organization* (1950). The vast range and complexity of the problems facing foreign policy-makers is well documented in the series of volumes published between 1947 and 1954 by the Brookings Institution under the title *Major Problems of United States Foreign Policy*. Legislative and administrative aspects of American foreign policy-making are treated, respectively, in Robert A. Dahl's *Congress and Foreign Policy* (1950) and James L. McCamy's *The Administration of American Foreign Affairs* (1950). An increasing number of studies are concerned with the ideological dimensions of foreign policies. An excellent example is Nathan Leites's *A Study of Bolshevism* (1953).

Accompanying the trend toward more systematization has also been a wider recognition that international political behavior cannot be understood in terms of rational decision-making models alone, but that it is affected by largely unconscious, culture-bound preconceptions and the emotional flavor of the total political environment. Otto Klineberg, a social psychologist, in *Tensions Affecting International Understanding* (1950), surveyed and summarized the relevant literature, and increasing attention is paid by students of international politics to the "personality-in-culture" formulations of the cultural anthropologists. Gabriel A. Almond's *The Appeals of Communism* (1954) or Gardner Murphy's *In the Minds of Men* (1953) are particularly valuable from this point of view. Karl Deutsch, in *Nationalism and Social Communication* (1953), applied recent developments in communication theory to international analysis. The most ambitious effort to present a systematic, interdisciplinary model of interactional behavior in terms of a theory of action is *Decision-Making as an Approach to the Study of International Politics* (1954), by Richard C. Snyder, H. W. Bruck, and Burton Sapin.

THE PARTY AND THE VOTE: BEHAVIORAL BREAKTHROUGH

The problem of how governments are empowered was at the heart of much classical political theory. Whether the power of some men to rule over others was derived from divine authorization, customary legitimization, violent usurpation, or popular consent constituted central issues of different theories of representation. Harold F. Gosnell, in *Democracy, The Threshold of Freedom* (1948) and Alfred De Grazia, in *Public and Republic: Political Representation in America* (1951), have perceptively traced the course of theories of representation and their institutionalization in different electoral systems.

It is anomalous, therefore, that the study of the role of political parties in the representative process did not come into its own until fairly recently. Why this should be so is a matter of speculation. One reason might be that preoccupation with the extension of the franchise during the nineteenth and early twentieth centuries deflected students of democratic politics from attention to the role of political parties in popular government. Moreover, the reform movement's efforts to introduce the devices of direct democracy—initiative, referendum, and recall—were partly based on the biased assumption that parties were detrimental to a truly democratic politics. Finally, unlike in the case of governmental processes, neither constitutional nor other formal models were at hand to serve at least as initial points of departure in empirical study, and the construction of theoretical models was not thought of as a proper concern of political science.

In England, the emergence of Parliament during the eighteenth century as the locus of political power which was shared by Whigs and Tories enabled Henry Bolingbroke and Edmund Burke to sense the central significance of parties in the political process. Yet, the founders of the American Republic, though aware of the importance of parties, or factions, as they called them, did not cherish their development, even if they could not long avoid their manipulatory potentialities. To Alexis de Tocqueville, observing American politics in the early nineteenth century and reporting on his experiences in *Democracy in America* (1835-40), parties appeared as part and parcel of democratic life. The first extensive treatment of parties is to be found in the work of an Englishman, James Bryce's classical *American Commonwealth* (1888), followed in 1898 by Henry Jones Ford's *The Rise and Growth of American Politics*. The tradition set by foreigners, such as de Tocqueville and Bryce, in observing American politics has been continued by the Englishman Denis W. Brogan in *Politics in America* (1954). Systematic analysis of party solidarity by way of study of roll-call votes in selected sessions of Parliament, Congress, and some American state legislatures was first undertaken by Abbott Lawrence Lowell in *The Influence of Party upon Legislation in England and America* (1901). In 1902 appeared the Russian Moisei Ostrogorskii's critical treatise, *Democracy and the Organization of Political Parties*, which interpreted party as a means of expressing and manipulating mass public opinion in a democracy.

But with the turn of the century and the concurrent separation of political theory from the study of political institutions, with its attendant emphasis, first on formal-legalistic, and later on reformist approaches, party politics, if not misunderstood or even denounced, practically disappeared from scientific discourse. An acute, critical diagnosis of American politics, such as James Allen Smith's *The Spirit of American Government* (1907), just as the books of Arthur F. Bentley and Graham Wallas, did not cut the academic ice, and Charles A. Beard's *An Economic Interpretation of the Constitution of the United States* (1913), treating the interplay of factional politics and class interests in the creation of the basic American law, came to influence the study of contemporary party politics only in the twenties.

Without empirically relevant theoretical models available, the study of party politics proved elusive. Ostrogorskii had treated parties as organizational artifacts, and in 1915, in *Political Parties*, Robert Michels, taking as a premise the hierarchical ordering of all organizations, including even parties which, like the Social Democrats, prided themselves for their egalitarianism, had taken a dim view of their democratic potential. The subsequent course of the study of political parties has recently been traced and evaluated by Neil A. McDonald in an excellent little volume, *The Study of Political Parties* (1955). Whether conceptualized as groups, associations, organizations, or institutions, parties seem to defy pertinent analytical categories, or, if such categories are employed, they seem to do violence to some pertinent facts of party.

Arthur N. Holcombe's *Political Parties of Today* (1924) is the pioneering work in the recent study of American parties. By the time Holcombe came to write his book, studies of aggregate voting behavior had been undertaken, and they suggested the possibility of treating sectional groupings as units in the analysis of party politics. Though avoiding generalizations, Holcombe carefully specified sectional party shifts of power and examined their relationship to the functioning of the party system as a whole. In 1940, Edward Pendleton Herring, in an empirically attractive, but theoretically inconclusive, *The Politics of Democracy*, put the accent on the personal relations of party leaders. Valdimer O. Key, Jr. in *Politics, Parties and Pressure Groups* (1942), the best available text (which has gone through several editions), noted the psychological attachment of partisans to their party, while Elmer E. Schattschneider. in his imaginative *Party Government* (1942), considered party "the property of organization." None of these formulations are mutually inconsistent, but rather complementary, sustaining the hope for a systematic theory of party politics.

Fortunately, theoretical difficulties have not stood in the way of a fruitful body of empirical work which, hopefully, will fertilize future theoretical development. In fact, as the work on parties, unlike the work on government, was not bound to a rigidly legal model, it has shown greater flexibility in formulating middle-range hypothetical propositions. Moreover, in spite of sometimes strongly normative components in most interpretations, classification in terms of party functions and doctrinal differentiations has facilitated comparative analysis, as is attempted, though not completed, in a recent volume edited by Sigmund Neumann, *Modern Political Parties* (1956). Comparison has been most fruitfully executed by Valdimer O. Key, Jr., in *Southern Politics in State and Nation* (1949), a monumental effort to trace in great detail the variations of the Southern one-party system from state to state, utilizing interviews, voting statistics, and other social data. If *Southern Politics* was primarily descriptive, its recent—but partial—sequel for the North, *American State Politics: An Introduction* (1956), contains many hypotheses about the working of the American party system which are subjected to empirical test and contribute to a more systematic and less generalizing view of American party politics. Key's two books are, in many respects, testimony to David B. Truman's expression of frustration attendant on efforts to come to grips with party phenomena, in *The Governmental Process* (1951):

The behavior patterns [of parties] are fluid and inconsistent. The term does not have the same meaning at the national, State, and local levels of government; it may not have the same meaning in two States or in two localities; finally, in the nation, in a single State, or in a single city the term may not have the same meaning at one point in time as at another, in one campaign year and in the next. It usually means in election campaigns something very different from what it means when applied to activities in a legislature.

In the absence of a systematic theoretical framework for the study of political parties, the historical approach continues to be attractive. Wilfred E. Binkley's *American Political Parties: Their Natural History* (1943) is a lively account of American party history. Malcolm Moos, in *The Republicans* (1956), recently demonstrated the vitality of historical interpretation in a detailed study of one of the two major parties. Richard F. Hofstadter, a historian, in *The American Political Tradition and the Men Who Made It* (1948), utilized the life histories of the great presidents in an interpretation of the unfolding drama of American political history. Descriptive case studies of the big-city political machines, such as Harold F. Gosnell's *Machine Politics: Chicago Model* (1937) or Roy V. Peel's *The Political Clubs of New York City* (1935), have been abundant. Life histories have been used by Harold Zink in *City Bosses in the United States* (1930), and by Dayton D. McKean in a study of Frank Hague, *The Boss: The Hague Machine in Action* (1940). William

Foote Whyte, a sociologist, presented a realistic study of the relationship between organized crime and politics in *Street Corner Society: The Social Structure of an Italian Slum* (1955). Other community studies, notably William Lloyd Warner's *Democracy in Jonesville* (1949) and Floyd Hunter's *Community Power Structure* (1953), contain valuable data on the relationship between local social structures and political behavior.

Abroad, notably in England and France, there has been renewed interest in the study of political parties since the last war. In France, Maurice Duverger, Georges E. Lavau, François Goguel and Georges Dupeux have published insightful works on party politics and voting behavior. Unfortunately, only Duverger's work, *Political Parties* (1954), has been translated among the more general treatises. It is of interest because Duverger stresses the effect of different structural patterns of party systems as independent variables on both modes of leadership and public opinion phenomena. In England, which for decades had taken her party system for granted to such a degree that it was given relatively little scholarly attention, a series of detailed electoral studies were carried on since 1945 at Nuffield College in Oxford by Ronald B. MacCullum, Alison Readman, Herbert G. Nicholas, and David E. Butler, culminating in the latter's *The Electoral System in Britain, 1918-1951* (1953). Also noteworthy is a study by James F. S. Ross, *Elections and Electors; Studies in Democratic Representation* (1955).

Valuable aid in understanding party politics and the role of parties in the political process has come and is likely to continue to come from the increasing number of investigations into the voting behavior of the electorate. This is particularly true of the studies published after World War II. The tone of the earliest studies, using aggregate voting statistics, had been set by sociologists, and when, after about 1924, political scientists undertook similar studies, the main concern was with voter turnout at the polls and voting preferences, which data were correlated with such other available demographic data as age, sex, race, education, income, religion, occupation, ethnic origin, or urban-rural residence, to test isolated, low-level hypotheses about the behavior of aggregate groupings. Other studies were satisfied with simple tabulations to permit broad generalizations and comparisons. While some of these studies were more pretentious than either methods employed or findings warranted, others exhibited great ingenuity in the use of classificatory and statistical techniques but were innocent of theoretical considerations.

Best known among these investigations is the pioneer work on political participation by Charles E. Merriam and Harold F. Gosnell, *Non-Voting* (1924). An experiment in the stimulation of voting was subsequently reported by Harold F. Gosnell in *Getting Out the Vote* (1927), and Gosnell continued these interests in *Why Europe Votes* (1930) and

Grass Roots Politics (1942). Other works in the same or similar vein were Stuart A. Rice, *Farmers and Workers in American Politics* (1924) and *Quantitative Methods in Politics* (1928), James K. Pollock, *Voting Behavior: A Case Study* (1939) and, in cooperation with Samuel J. Eldersveld, *Michigan Politics in Transition* (1942). Trend analysis for the purpose of prediction is most frequently associated with the name of Louis H. Bean, *Ballot Behavior* (1940) and *How to Predict Elections* (1948). A broad canvass of national voting behavior through time is presented in two books by Cortez A. M. Ewing, *Presidential Elections, From Abraham Lincoln to Franklin D. Roosevelt* (1940), and *Congressional Elections, 1896-1944* (1947). This literature has been constructively criticized by Samuel J. Eldersveld in a sophisticated appraisal, "Theory and Method in Voting Behavior Research," reprinted in *Political Behavior: A Reader in Theory and Research* (1956), Eulau, Eldersveld, and Janowitz (eds.).

Few of these earlier studies were of direct help in assessing the functioning of the American party system. Arthur N. Holcombe, as already mentioned, had examined sectional tensions in American party politics in his *Political Parties of Today* (1924). In his later *The Middle Classes in American Politics* (1940), Holcombe described the changing balance of power between urban and rural areas from the point of view of its effect on the party system. But it was not until Valdimer O. Key, Jr., revived the use of aggregate voting data that this type of analysis was purposefully used as a tool to gain insight into the structural and functional patterns of the American party system.

Aggregate voting studies were inherently incapable of either explaining the individual voter's motivations and perceptions or the effect of party activities on his behavior. If the dynamics of the party system were to be understood, the role of the voter in the functioning of the system and his behavior in the context of party activities had to be ascertained. This kind of study was made possible by the appearance of the representative sample survey, or "poll," from about 1936 on. By interviewing voters, students of electoral behavior were now able to reconstruct the motivational, attitudinal, and perceptual context in which voting as a decisional activity took shape. Moreover, the introduction of the so-called "panel method" of repeated interviews at various points in time permitted conceptualization of voting as a decisional process rather than as a simply momentary act.

Unfortunately, political scientists for some time not only failed to recognize the scientific potentialities of the interview survey and to acquire the skills necessary for its execution, but some of them were frankly hostile to the new technique, as evidenced by Lindsay Rogers' ill-advised attack, in *The Pollsters* (1949). Of course, the "failure" of the commercial polls in 1948—associated with the names of George Gallup, Elmo Roper, and Archibald Crossley—did not help matters, but quick action by a Committee on Analysis of Pre-election Polls and Forecasts of the Social Science Research Council in publishing its constructively critical report, *The Pre-election Polls of 1948* (1949) by Frederick Mosteller and others, tended to restore confidence in survey techniques. Perhaps more important is the fact that due to this initial hostility of political scientists, the study of voting behavior, temporarily at least, slipped out of their hands into those of sociologists and social psychologists. The result was, however, that while these studies derived their significance from the sociological or social psychological theories in terms of which they were conceived, they tended, as Key has remarked, "to take the politics out of the study of electoral behavior."

The pioneering study of Paul F. Lazarsfeld, Bernard Berelson, and Hazel Gaudet, *The People's Choice* (1944), reporting the results of panel-type interviews during the 1940 presidential campaign in Erie County, Ohio, seemed, it is true, unduly sociological in its crass assertion that "social characteristics determine political preference." But the Erie study, as well as its successor of 1948, the Elmira study, reported in Bernard Berelson, Paul F. Lazarsfeld, and William N. McPhee, *Voting* (1954), contain much of value for an understanding of the political party system and its operation—notably on the tendency of campaign activities to activate the voter and reinforce his preferences rather than convert him; on the operation of "cross-pressures" in the voting situation; on the role of the mass media of communication; on the nature of the decisional process as one of slow crystallization rather than of rational choice; or on the political consequences of primary-group relationships.

The most comprehensive study of the influence of party, party-related issues, and candidates on voting behavior was a national probability sample survey conducted both prior to and after the 1952 presidential election by the Survey Research Center of the University of Michigan, and reported by Angus Campbell, Warren E. Miller (a political scientist), and Gerald Gurin in *The Voter Decides* (1954). By examining how the voter relates himself to politics in terms of identifications, preferences, interests, and expectations, Campbell and his associates succeeded in presenting an image of the American party system, at least on the national level, as it is perceived by the electorate and seems to influence the electorate's behavior. Samuel A. Stouffer, using data collected by the Gallup and Roper organizations, has demonstrated the advantages of sample survey analysis for the study of mass phenomena in *Communism, Conformity and Civil Liberties* (1955).

It is also interesting to note that the 1952 Michigan design was flexible enough to permit treatment of the data by a number of political scientists in terms of their own preoccupations, setting a precedent for the wider use of such data. Alfred De Grazia used the Michigan data in portraying in detail western voting patterns in *The Western Public, 1952 and Beyond* (1954). Morris Janowitz, a sociologist, and Dwaine Marvick, a political scientist, reanalyzed the Michigan data on the basis of a competitive theory of democracy in *Competitive Pressure and Democratic Consent* (1956).

A recent summary and appraisal of voting studies, of the aggregate and survey type, both American and European, is an article, "The Psychology of Voting: An Analysis of Political Behavior," by Seymour M. Lipset and others, published in *Handbook of Social Psychology* (1954), Gardner Lindzey (ed.).

EPILOGUE

In a moment of euphoric exultation, a distinguished political scientist and former president of the American Political Science Association, Peter H. Odegard, recently took "A New Look at Leviathan" (in a volume of essays, *Frontiers of Knowledge in The Study of Man*, 1956, Lynn T. White, ed.):

There is a new look in the study of politics; an increasing awareness of the baffling complexity of what since Aristotle has been called the queen of the sciences—the science of politics. No longer a hostage to history, and freed at last from its bondage to the lawyers as well as from the arid schematism of the political taxonomists, political science is in the process of becoming one of the central unifying forces for understanding why we behave like human beings. As the dominant mood of the interwar period was one of specialization and isolation among the major disciplines, so the mood of this postwar generation is one of specialization and integration.

Perhaps Professor Odegard is unduly hopeful. Certainly, those laboring in the vineyards of political behavior research can take heart from such acclaim. Certainly, too, it is true that much progress has been made in political science in recent years. But a sober, second look also suggests that Professor Odegard's picture is still more in the nature of a snapshot of a possible future than of a richly painted current canvas. In fact, there is no surer way to kill the newer trends than to "coopt" the label "political behavior" without reservations. As one considers the requisites of behavioral research, one must recognize a continuing need for intellectual humility. For few are those who can say that they have fully mastered these requisites.

The qualifications for advancing a science of politics are exacting, and there is only small indication that political scientists even now receive the kind of research training necessary to meet them. On the contrary, there are those who, entranced by interview schedules, scales, indices, and statistical devices, undertake research without being aware of the many epistemological and methodological assumptions they make in using these techniques; there are those who, immersing themselves in just these assumptions, never come around to doing empirical research and substitute for it a new verbal scholasticism; and there are, finally, those who, though adequate technicians, are not sufficiently trained in political theory or acquainted with past institutional research, with the result that they do not ask any really significant questions. Yet, the future for a science of politics is bright, and Professor Odegard may have caught some of the rays.

— II —*

In the third quarter of the twentieth century the world of government and politics had become an ever expanding multiverse. The multiplication of independent nation-states, the growth of governmental services, the political activation of mass publics, the diversification of governmental institutions and the resulting complexity of political relationships, within and among nations, had brought about fundamental changes in the world political order. No longer was it possible to think of politics in the simple terms of the previous century that pitted man against the state, class against class, or nation against nation. No longer was it feasible to speak of political goals such as freedom, justice, equality, or security as eternal verities discoverable by right reason and realizable if only right reason were applied to the task of governance. No longer was it viable to agree with Jefferson that "the government is best that governs least," though it was equally meaningless to assert the opposite. Much political discourse was still conducted in terms that contrasted liberalism and conservatism, capitalism and socialism, democracy and communism as meaningful political alternatives. But in the real world of national and international politics the tasks of government had become more complicated than the inherited vocabulary could satisfy.

Political science as a learned discipline had reacted only slowly to the changing multiverse of politics, but react it finally did. In 1956, a sensitive observer and distinguished political scientist, the late Peter H.

* This essay is a continuation and not a revision of the earlier essay on "Political Science" in *A Reader's Guide to the Social Sciences* (1959). The earlier essay covered the literature through 1956. With a few exceptions, therefore, the present essay is devoted largely to books that appeared in the United States after 1956.

Odegard, reviewed the wondrous things that seemed to be happening in the study of politics:

> There is a new look in the study of politics; an increasing awareness of the baffling complexity of what since Aristotle has been called the queen of sciences—the science of politics. No longer a hostage to history, and freed at last from its bondage to the lawyers as well as from the arid schematism of political taxonomists, political science is in the process of becoming one of the central unifying forces for understanding why we behave like human beings.

Indeed, it was commonplace to speak of a "behavioral revolution" in political science and a "behavioral movement," as if a new scientific ideology had been born, carried forward by an army of single-minded "Young Turks" zealous upon overthrowing an "establishment." Strangely, this image was not propagated by the innovators themselves but rather by the rear guard of an ancestral order that, its own protestations notwithstanding, had lost its groundings in the past. An English scholar, Bernard Crick, in *The American Science of Politics* (1959), and a relay team of American "political philosophers" whose anchor man was Professor Leo Strauss, in *Essays on the Scientific Study of Politics* (1962), Herbert J. Storing (ed.), contributed to the myth of behavioral invincibility. In seeking to slay the behavioral dragon, these antagonists of the new political science harmed themselves more than their imagined enemies.

A more sober look at what has happened in political science would characterize the new tendencies not as a revolution but as a renaissance. It is in the nature of a renaissance to look both forward and backward, to seek out what seems worthwhile in the past in order to shape a more promising future. This is as true of science as it is true of the arts and letters. In *The Political System: An Inquiry into the State of Political Science* (1953), David Easton, speaking for the generation of political scientists who had come of age during World War II and after, had deplored the current state of the discipline and suggested new scientific horizons. Ten years later, in *The Behavioral Persuasion in Politics* (1963), Heinz Eulau wrote for a new generation that all too readily seemed to forget its roots in classical political theory:

> The return to the behavior of man as the root of politics is a new beginning. For in dealing with the conditions and consequences of man's political conduct, the behavioral persuasion represents an attempt, by modern modes of analysis, to fulfill the quest for political knowledge begun by the classical political theorists. The behavioral persuasion in politics, as I understand it, is a return to the bases of man's political experience in which the great theorists

of the past found nurture and sustenance.... The modern political scientists who adapt the new theories, methods, and techniques of behavioral science to political analysis are in the tradition of the classical political theorists.

And four years later, a group of the renaissance men addressed themselves to the question of "what relevance, if any, does the 2000-year heritage of political theory have today?" In *Contemporary Political Science: Toward Empirical Theory* (1967), Ithiel de Sola Pool (ed.), the contributors showed how modern behavioral research has shed light on some of the great questions which political theorists have asked through the centuries, and how the classical theories could fertilize modern research.

Like any renaissance, the period was characterized by much soul-searching about the scope and methods of political science. In a UNESCO-sponsored trend-report, Dwight Waldo presented a perhaps all too self-consciously balanced appraisal, *Political Science in the United States of America* (1956). The rumblings of discontent which contributed much to the new political science could be heard in *Approaches to the Study of Politics* (1958), edited by Roland Young. Political theorists, along with sociologists and social psychologists, gave testimony that the study of politics, rooted in the past, could no longer ignore developments at the frontiers of the behavioral sciences. And only a few years after, in *Essays on the Behavioral Study of Politics* (1962), edited by Austin Ranney, the vitality of the new political science in the study of elections, legislative institutions, international politics, and other fields was impressively demonstrated.

Meanwhile, Charles S. Hyneman, in *The Study of Politics: The Present State of American Political Science* (1959), had presented a rather noncommittal overview of the discipline, and Vernon Van Dyke, in *Political Science: A Philosophical Analysis* (1960), had probed into the epistemological assumptions of a field undergoing rapid change. But it was the oldest of the "Young Turks," Harold D. Lasswell, who once more, in *The Future of Political Science* (1963), presented a blueprint of the discipline's challenges. And as Lasswell looked forward to the twenty-first century, William Anderson, in *Man's Quest for Political Knowledge: The Study and Teaching of Politics in Ancient Times* (1964), took a long look back to ancient Mesopotamia, Egypt, Israel, Greece, and Rome to discover the when, where, and why of the quest for empirical political knowledge.

Not surprisingly, political scientists also turned the spotlight of the empirical method on themselves. In *American Political Science: A Profile of a Discipline* (1964), Albert Somit and Joseph Tanenhaus reported on the responses of a random sample of the profession called upon to appraise the quality of research and teaching in political science and its subfields. Subsequently, in *The Development of American Political Science* (1967), the same authors reviewed the intellectual and institutional growth of the discipline from its founding in the late nineteenth century to the present. Finally, in *Contemporary Political Analysis* (1967), James C. Charlesworth (ed.), scholars of different persuasions articulated their differences and testified to the continued intellectual heterogeneity of political science.

But books about books and research about research do not make a renaissance. They are symptomatic of a discipline's search for identity, but they do not really give it purpose and direction. To appreciate the new political science as an experience in creativity, the works of creation themselves and not programmatic pronouncements or critical commentaries must bear witness. However, a bibliographical essay is inevitably an exercise in current history. Like all current history, therefore, it is likely to be prone to those misjudgments that the unavoidably myopic view of the present entails. The explosion in publications about politics in the last decade makes the task of the bibliographer especially hazardous. To take the long view in the short time perspective is not only difficult but perhaps foolish. Yet, if there is a common need, it is to provide from time to time a synoptic view of the bits and pieces that an explosion invariably leaves about.

POLITICAL THEORY: REJUVENATION

Politics, Albert Einstein once observed, is more difficult than physics. For politics as an aspect of human behavior is probably more complicated, more intricate, and more elusive than any other aspect. In part this is because the number of variables directly or indirectly relevant to politics is enormous, and because they are related to each other in manifold ways. Politics is both organized and unorganized complexity. Robert MacIver once spoke of "the web of government" as something more than a simple analogy. Yet, even a web has pattern, and it is the search for pattern that makes political theory the heart of the enterprise.

In part, also, the elusiveness of politics as a subject of inquiry is due to the fact that politics in the real world is conducted in terms of a code that is difficult to decipher. For politics involves both deception and self-deception, straight talk and double-talk, promises and compromises, bluffing and calling the bluff. Assertions that something is nonpolitical or nonpartisan are often strategies of playing the political game. But, paradoxically, once the code of politics is broken, the "language of politics," as Murray Edelman showed in *The Symbolic Uses of Politics* (1964), may be highly conducive to political understanding. Indeed, what has come to be called "ordinary language analysis" was fruitfully applied to political problems. Works such as Richard E. Flathman, *The Public Interest: An Essay Concerning the Normative Discourse of Politics* (1966), or Hanna F. Pitkin, *The Concept of Representation* (1967), came to breathe fresh air into the study of political discourse.

As one might expect in a multiverse of actors and actions, efforts to understand and explain the complexities and intricacies of political life have given rise to a great variety of theoretical approaches. The oldest of these is, of course, the philosophical tradition that goes back to Plato and Aristotle. For Plato and Aristotle politics was the search for justice and the good life. For Hobbes it was the control of men who, if left to their own devices, would live in a state of nature where life is brutish, nasty, and short. For Bentham and the utilitarians, politics was the means by which men could improve their private and collective interests in line with the pleasure principle. For Marx, it was the instrument by which a class of exploiters could maintain its domination of the exploited.

Not the least significant consequence of the impact of empirical behavioralism on political science was the rejuvenation of political theory whose "decline" David Easton, in *The Political System* (1953), had characterized as a "malaise." Although much of the new theorizing was being done in the context of empirical inquiry, where it properly should be done, theorizing about theory as an autonomous endeavor contributed fruitfully to the rejuvenation of political theory. Sorting out the normative and empirical components of political theory from an analytic point of view, yet seeking to link them because political philosophers have a concern for reality and political scientists a concern for values, Arnold Brecht, in *Political Theory: The Foundations of Twentieth-Century Thought* (1959), made an impressive contribution to the clarification of the role of theory in political science.

While political theorists no longer practiced purely historical or exegetical analysis of other theorists' theories, the spell of the classical tradition continued to cast a long shadow on the study of political theory. Yet, the emphasis shifted to *using* the ideas of the past in the solution of contemporary intellectual, ethical, and practical problems rather than cultivating them for their own sake. Although attacking positivism, scientism, and historicism and chiding political science for not concerning itself with the problem of the "best" political order in the tradition of the Greeks, Leo Strauss, the leading spokesman of that tradition, raised important questions about the problem of valuation in *What Is Political Philosophy?* (1959). The view of the political as the most general and integrative order of human associations was presented by Sheldon S. Wolin in a critical historically oriented, but by no means historical, treatise, *Politics and Vision* (1960). An attempt to link classical theories and contemporary empirical research was made by Andrew Hacker in

The Study of Politics: The Western Tradition and American Origins (1963). Perhaps the most laborious effort to make classical political theory relevant to contemporary concerns was Carl J. Friedrich's *Man and His Government: An Empirical Theory of Politics* (1963). Combining his wide theoretical and historical knowledge with his long-term study of comparative institutions, Friedrich provided a broad-gauged synthesis that is likely to serve a generation of scholars as a point of theoretical departure. By way of contrast, an equally ambitious attempt at synthesis, George E. G. Catlin's *Systematic Politics: Elementa Politica et Sociologica* (1962), was largely a failure.

The classical tradition is less concerned with describing and explaining political behavior and institutions than with speculating about the goals of political action and prescribing the modes of conduct for the achievement of these goals. The problem of democracy and related questions about equality, freedom, and obligation were of continuing interest to political theorists. The outstanding general work was Giovanni Sartori's *Democratic Theory* (1962). Drawing not only on the Anglo-American but also on the European experience with democracy, Sartori succeeded in harmonizing modern research on democratic behavior with normative considerations of democracy. More limited in focus but especially stimulating were C. W. Cassinelli, *The Politics of Freedom: An Analysis of the Modern Democratic State* (1961), David Spitz, *Democracy and the Challenge of Power* (1958), and Thomas L. Thorson, *The Logic of Democracy* (1962). Joseph Tussman, in *Obligation and the Body Politic* (1960), dealt with the foundation of education in a self-governing community, and Edmond Cahn, in *The Predicament of Democratic Man* (1961), raised the issue of the citizen's moral involvement in the decisions of his government. Christian Bay's *The Structure of Freedom* (1958) brought to bear the findings of modern behavioral science on the traditional issues of liberty, and Felix Oppenheim, in *Dimensions of Freedom* (1961), subjected relevant concepts to rigorous logical analysis. Sanford A. Lakoff, in *Equality in Political Philosophy* (1964), critically examined changing conceptions of a central term in political theory. John H. Schaar's *Loyalty in America* (1957) was a historical and philosophical inquiry into a difficult problem facing democracy in the modern age.

Under the impact of the sociology of knowledge, textual exegesis gave way to more contextual treatment of important figures in the history of political thought. Increasingly, historians of political theory drew on a variety of documents other than the texts themselves—parliamentary debates, correspondence, newspapers, and so on—in dealing with political ideas. Among the best of these studies were Joseph Hamburger's *James Mill and the Art of Revolution* (1963) as well as his *Intellectuals in*

Politics: John Stuart Mill and the Philosophical Radicals (1965), both of which were as much concerned with the utilitarians' political practices as with their intellectual pursuits. Melvin Richter, in *The Politics of Conscience: T. H. Green and His Age* (1964), sought to discover the reasons for the popularity of an obsurantist idealism in an age of predatory materialism. David Kettler's *The Social and Political Thought of Adam Ferguson* (1965) examined the conflicting orientations and roles of a neglected figure in eighteenth-century thought. Harvey C. Mansfield, Jr., in *Statesmanship and Party Government—A Study of Burke and Bolingbroke* (1965), provided a keen analysis of the clairvoyant conceptions of party by one and the confused conceptions of party by another influential statesman. Michael Walzer, in *The Revolution of Saints* (1965), studied the origins of modern radical politics in the sixteenth century and sought to construct a general model of radical politics.

Historical knowledge of political thought was enriched by numerous other works that, for reasons of space, cannot possibly be enumerated here. But the influence of the sociology of knowledge was evident in several works that took a critical stance toward the consequences of political ideas in contemporary politics. James H. Meisel, in *The Myth of the Ruling Class: Gaetano Mosca and the Elite* (1958), provided a long-needed commentary on an important figure in the Machiavellian tradition of political theory. Peter Bachrach's *The Theory of Democratic Elitism: A Critique* (1967) addressed itself to related contemporary problems. William Kornhauser's *The Politics of Mass Society* (1959) raised important theoretical questions about the psychological and sociological foundations of modern political movements. Seymour M. Lipset concerned himself with the prerequisites of democracy in a volume of essays, *Political Man* (1959). Glendon Schubert, in *The Public Interest* (1960), dissected various versions of a particularly mushy concept of political theory. Robert W. Tucker's *The Just War: A Study in Contemporary American Doctrine* (1960) analyzed the maxim that war is justified only in response to aggression. And Henry S. Kariel, in *The Decline of American Pluralism* (1961), attacked familiar interpretations of the American social order.

The problem of how past political theory can be made relevant to contemporary theorizing and how contemporary social science can be used in the study of past political theory was self-consciously tackled, with more or less success, in two ambitious works. With a sure grasp of modern behavioral science knowledge, Alvin W. Gouldner, in *Enter Plato: Classical Greece and the Origins of Social Theory* (1965), applied notions derived from game theory, conflict theory, communication theory, stratification theory, and so on, to a less than sure analysis of Athenian political thought. *Theories of the Political System: Classics of*

Political Thought and Modern Political Thought (1965), by William T. Bluhm, was a clever if malformed attempt at juxtaposing certain classical and contemporary writers that failed to be convincing because, in stressing continuities, it neglected to take account of the profound discontinuities that make for a very conspicuous separation of the ancients and the moderns.

Although the contemporary study of politics continued to include philosophical, legal, and historical components, the main trend in political theory was empirical, behavioral, and scientific. This is not to say that there was much agreement. On the contrary, an abundance of models and theories testified to the elusiveness of the subject matter. In a first reaction to the speculative, formal-legal, and historical traditions that spawned the centuries, one group of modern political scientists sought to explain politics in terms of the groups that constitute the multiverse of politics and the processes of interaction that occur among them as they struggle to maximize their interests. This "theory," if it can be called a theory, had been given authoritative formulation by David B. Truman in *The Governmental Process* (1951) and Earl Latham's *The Group Basis of Politics* (1952). But "group theory" failed to have empirical payoffs, and it seemed to come to a theoretical dead end. When, in 1960, E. E. Schattschneider published *The Semisovereign People*, he felt constrained to emphasize that "the concepts formulated here constitute an attack on all political theories, all research techniques and concepts tending to show that American politics is a meaningless stalemate about which no one can do anything." Schattschneider's book was, in many respects, a valedictory of the group theorists. Group theory was not represented in *Varieties of Political Theory* (1966), by David Easton (ed.), a collection of essays representative of the new approaches to political theory. And it was summarily dismissed as inadequate in another overview of contemporary theoretical postures, Eugene J. Meehan's *Contemporary Political Thought: A Critical Study* (1967).

Just as empirical political science injected new life into critical political theory, though often only to draw blood, so a number of behavioral theories developed in related disciplines came to influence empirical political science. Whether this influence would, in due time, give rise to an autonomous positive theory of politics was more a matter of promises than those engaged in the enterprise perhaps cared to admit. For though their formulations were *in principle* testable, the gap between theoretical promise and empirical performance was by no means closed. Indeed, much positive theory, like critical theory, seemed to come to rest on the comfortable assumption that theory is the same thing as knowledge, or that having provided an empirical *illustration*, empirical *proof* was surely just around the corner. But in the crucible of research, it often turned out, positive theories were something less than harbingers of self-evident or easily discoverable truths.

Nevertheless, exciting steps were taken in the development of positive or empirical political theories. They ranged from microtheories about the behavior of individual actors to macrotheories about the behavior of whole political systems. They involved theories that, once more, elevated individual rationality and self-interest into causal principles of action, and theories that postulated rationality as a consequence of unintended social processes. They included theories that proceeded analytically and deductively, in the manner of mathematics, and theories that proceeded synthetically and inductively, in the tradition of natural science. All in all, it was a time of intellectual fermentation and hope. Even though political scientists in the aggregate perhaps continued not knowing where they were going, at least some of them were on roads with clear destinations. That there seemed to be many roads was no longer experienced as disturbing.

While empirical research was chiefly influenced by formulations derived from the behavioral sciences proper, political theory came to lean heavily on economics. Economics, by all odds the most successful of the social sciences from a practical point of view, had always been envied by those political scientists who saw their discipline as a "policy science." For economics was practical without surrendering its parsimonious assumptions or rigorous modes of analysis. When Anthony Downs, in *An Economic Theory of Democracy* (1957), developed a positive theory of voter and party action, political scientists were both alarmed and pleased by the forceful simplicity of the argument. Downs's theory was based on simple behavioral assumptions about rationality, ordered preferences, and utility maximization, and it included predictive statements as to what would happen under certain conditions, such as varying degrees of uncertainty or information costs. Downs showed that politics, like economics, was not immune from axiomatic theorizing.

Unlike Downs, who stressed the behavior of parties more than of individuals, James M. Buchanan and Gordon Tullock, in *The Calculus of Consent: Logical Foundations of Constitutional Democracy* (1962), presented an unabashedly individualistic model of the constitutional process. Distinguishing between constitutional and operational decisions as well as between external and decision-making costs, these authors derived from a model of the rational, utility-maximizing actor propositions about how collective decisions are made under a variety of constitutional rules. Finally, another economist, Mancur Olson, Jr., in *The Logic of Collective Action* (1965), drawing on group theories developed in political science, extended the "economic" type of analysis to the behavior of large collectives.

But doubts remained, and though political scientists could not ignore the work of the economists in their domain, the conventional bias in favor of centrally coordinated rather than market-directed political action was not easily shaken. Had not the most sophisticated among them, Herbert A. Simon, in *Models of Man: Social and Rational* (1957), advised in favor of a middle course between the rationalistic and maximizing assumptions of the economists and the assumptions about human irrationality of the psychologists? Simon's notion that political behavior is "satisficing" rather than optimizing, that political man is prepared to replace relatively better outcomes by less preferable ones, had not been lost on political scientists. Simon's conception of rationality in decision-making, it seemed, was closer to empirical reality than the excessively rational models of strict economic analysis.

More persuasive to political scientists, therefore, was the model of "partisan mutual adjustment" presented by another economist, Charles E. Lindblom in *The Intelligence of Democracy* (1965). Drawing on the economist's conception of the market system as a method of coordinating economic decisions, but also on the pluralistic conception of the polity as a system of dispersed power, Lindblom argued that political decision-making involves processes of bargaining and exchange that achieve governmental rationality and efficiency better than do central coordination and authority. Along with an earlier work on "disjointed incremental problem solving," *A Strategy of Decision* (1963), coauthored by David Braybrooke, Lindblom's theory of decision-making through mutual adjustment seemed destined to have a lasting impact on contemporary political theory. Moreover, notions of exchange were becoming fashionable in sociology. Peter M. Blau, in *Exchange and Power in Social Life* (1964), sought to link micro- and macro-processes of human action by applying such concepts as exchange, reciprocity, imbalance, and power to problems of social conflict and change.

Although political scientists had been acquainted with the economic theory of games, little use other than theorizing by analogy had been made of it in the study of politics until William Riker, in *The Theory of Political Coalitions* (1962), presented a model of n-person games that dealt with three critical principles of coalition formation—the size principle, the strategic principle, and the disequilibrium principle. Mathematical models were also used by Duncan Black in a study of voting, *The Theory of Committees and Elections* (1958), that construed voting in elections as an extension of voting in small committees.

An altogether different tradition of theorizing was evident in works that were influenced, on the one hand, by "general systems theory," and, on the other hand, by the sociological theory of social systems developed by Talcott Parsons. The latter's general formulations and particular contributions to the study of politics were set forth by William C. Mitchell in *Sociological Analysis and Politics: The Theories of Talcott Parsons* (1967). General systems theory seemed to have influenced the excruciatingly complex conceptual scheme for the analysis of political systems developed by David Easton. In *A Framework for Political Analysis* (1965), Easton presented a structure of concepts thought useful for political analysis. Political life was seen as an "adaptive, self-regulating, and self-transforming system of behavior." Easton's basic units were the interactions among system members rather than actors or institutions. Politically relevant interactions were those that contribute to the "authoritative allocation of values" for a whole society. Easton elaborated his framework in a massive volume, *A System Analysis of Political Life* (1965), which presented the political system as a vast "conversion process" of political inputs into political outputs, and which concerned itself with the problems of stability and change in systems. A tour de force of monumental synthesis, Easton's work puzzled rather than fired the imagination of political scientists. The complexity of his definitions and constructions seemed to make it difficult to falsify whatever concrete research hypotheses might be derived from it. As in the case of most synthetic theories, there was a good deal of metatheorizing and reification in Easton's work. As with game theory, systems notions seemed to be more acceptable in the study of international than of intranational politics.

Another systems approach, derived from engineering models of communication and cybernetics rather than from the organic models of biology, was developed for application in the study of politics by Karl W. Deutsch in *The Nerves of Government: Models of Communication and Control* (1963). Despite its emphasis on strategies of control, Deutsch's model, like Easton's, seemed to be more useful as an organizing and heuristic device, more a tool for mapping uncharted areas of inquiry than a tool for prediction and explanation. Another work of this genre, concerned with the conditions under which men obey and control the remote environment, yet attempting to get away from concepts like "power" and "authority," was Neil A. McDonald's *Politics: A Study of Control Behavior* (1965).

More immediately influential in empirical research was Robert A. Dahl's modest, if incisive, *Modern Political Analysis* (1963). Dahl had come by his theoretical formulations in a slow and incremental way. Collaborating with Charles E. Lindblom in *Politics, Economics and Welfare* (1953), Dahl had explored different types of decision-making—polyarchy, bargaining, and the price system—from the point of view of both organizational control and policy consequences. In *A Preface to Democratic Theory* (1956), he had presented an acute analysis of the causal propositions and functional hypotheses implicit in various historical formulations of democracy. *Modern Political Analysis* was firmly grounded in the tradition of political theory, cognizant of modern conceptions of system and related terms, and closely attuned to the empirical work of contemporary behavioral research. As a result, Dahl's formulation of the political system as "any persistent pattern of human relationships that involves, to a significant extent, power, rule, or authority," proved more attractive from a political standpoint than "weak" models borrowed from general systems or communication theory. While the latter were useful in suggesting that the specifically political in human behavior is only a special case of the generic, knowledge of the generic is no substitute for knowledge of the specific. For what may be true in general need not be true in specific circumstances. Moreover, unlike more global theorists, Dahl remained close to the scientific tradition that sees causal analysis as the main challenge of the scientific enterprise, in the field of politics as elsewhere.

POLITICAL MAN: REDIVIVUS

The "great men" of history, movers and shakers of human destiny, have always fascinated the political imagination. Whether for good or evil, empire builders and conquerors, fanatics and revolutionaries, political philosophers and ideologues, famous statesmen and legislators, and many other types of *homo politicus* have left their mark on the course of political history. Their motivations and ambitions have been chronicled in biographies. Their lives, and often their deaths, are powerful reminders that politics with its human actors left out of it would be a very barren politics indeed.

Although the classics of political philosophy from Plato to Mill had been "peopled systems," modern political science, at least until very recently, neglected the human actors that make political institutions and processes tick. "Human nature in politics" had no place in the usual curriculum of political science. This has drastically changed. And not only the "great men" of political history, but also the "forgotten men" of modern mass society have become suitable subjects of political inquiry.

Investigations of political behavior at the level of the individual have ranged from the intensive study of political personality, pioneered by Harold D. Lasswell in *Psychopathology and Politics* (1930) and *Power and Personality* (1948) to extensive attitude surveys across nations as those utilized by Gabriel A. Almond and Sidney Verba in *The Civic Culture* (1963). The intensive study of personality remained especially difficult, for any number of reasons, but especially because political scientists lacked the analytical know-how of clinical psychiatry which is a necessary condition for access to "political patients." As a result, political scientists had to rely on documentary evidence in reconstructing the political personalities of their subjects. Of the few studies in this genre, none measured up to *Woodrow Wilson and Colonel House* (1956), by Alexander L. and Juliette L. George, which skillfully applied categories of personality analysis in a study of two important decision-makers. Perhaps the most successful of subsequent works was a study of a German socialist leader by Lewis J. Edinger, *Kurt Schumacher: A Study in Personality and Political Behavior* (1965). Others were more in the nature of political biography than personality analysis, such as James M. Burns's *Roosevelt: The Lion and the Fox* (1956), Alex Gottfried's *Boss Cermak of Chicago: A Study of Political Leadership* (1962), or Arnold A. Rogow's *James Forrestal: A Study of Personality, Politics and Policy* (1963).

The most significant work in the field of political personality was Robert E. Lane's *Political Ideology: Why the American Common Man Believes What He Does* (1962), a study of the ideologies of fifteen working- and lower middle-class men from the perspective of their personalities. Categories of personality analysis also served Lucian W. Pye in *Politics, Personality and Nation Building: Burma's Search for Identity* (1962), an interview study with selected elites that probed into the anxieties and self-doubts of political leaders confronting the task of nation building. Erwin C. Hargrove, in *Presidential Leadership: Personality and Political Style* (1966), traced the effect of personal predispositions and styles on the choices made by recent American presidents.

A few other works pursued psychological themes from a more theoretical point of view. John H. Schaar, in *Escape from Authority* (1961), criticized the ambiguous psychoanalytic speculations of Erich Fromm and presented a revised vision of society. James C. Davies, in *Human Nature in Politics* (1963), sought to develop a more broadly gauged psychological interpretation of politics that speculated about the relevance of "human needs" as generating forces. And Rogow and Lasswell, in *Power, Corruption, and Rectitude* (1963), tried to show that the public behavior of individual politicians is directly related to both personality development and institutional context. But apart from these and possibly a few other efforts, the intensive study of political personality remained open.

However, once the individual person had become an acceptable unit of political analysis, the floodgates were opened for an almost infinite range of inquiries that was bounded only by the individual's own finite mortality. Children as well as senior citizens became subjects of inquiry.

Herbert Hyman, a social psychologist, in *Political Socialization* (1959), stimulated much subsequent research by inventorying earlier studies of children's political attitudes and the sources of these attitudes. Fred I. Greenstein, in *Children and Politics* (1965), studied the developing orientations of elementary school children and how these orientations varied by status and sex. Robert D. Hess and Judith V. Torney, in *The Development of Political Attitudes in Children* (1967), reported on political attitude formation of 12,000 children in terms of influences of family, peer group, sex, class, intelligence, teacher attitudes, and so on. At the other end of the life continuum, Frank Pinner, Paul Jacobs and Philip Selznick, in *Old Age and Political Behavior* (1959), a study of an interest group devoted to the aged, examined the group's membership characteristics, leadership, and organization, shedding new light on the political aspirations of a growing sector of the population.

Citizen behavior, studied in institutional contexts, became an area of independent concern. Robert E. Lane, in his broadly conceived *Political Life: Why People Get Involved in Politics* (1959), synthesized much scholarly writing and suggested new avenues of inquiry. Lester W. Milbrath, updating Lane's work in *Political Participation* (1965), further explored how and why people get involved in politics, providing a propositional inventory and an assessment of propositions about citizen political activity in terms of available evidence. Eugene Burdick and Arthur J. Brodbeck edited a volume of critical essays, *American Voting Behavior* (1959), that brought to bear on the analysis of political behavior a strong dose of sociological and psychoanalytic insights. Leila A. Sussmann, in *Dear FDR: A Study of Political Letter Writing* (1963), explored a medium of communication between President and people that had not been previously acknowledged as a political device of mass action.

The political behavior of ethnic and religious groups became the subject of specialized inquiry. Religious minorities were studied by Lawrence H. Fuchs, in *The Political Behavior of American Jews* (1956), and by John H. Fenton, in *The Catholic Vote* (1960). But it was the problem of the American Negro in North and South that became a major focus of inquiry. Hugh D. Price, in *The Negro and Southern Politics* (1957), was the first to deal with the voting behavior of Negroes, and Herbert Garfinkel's *When Negroes March* (1959) set the pace for work on the politics of protest. James Q. Wilson, in *Negro Politics: The Search for Leadership* (1960), interpreted the political organization of the urban Negro community as a response to problems arising out of the metropolitan environment in which most northern Negroes live. Robbins L. Gates's *The Making of Massive Resistance* (1964) was a clinical case study of what happened in Virginia between 1954 and 1956 in connection with public school desegregation. Everett C. Ladd, Jr., in *Negro Political*

Leadership in the South (1966), dealt with the problem of recruiting a capable corps of native leaders. By far the most important work on Negro politics was Donald R. Matthews and James W. Prothro, *Negroes and the New Southern Politics* (1966), which carried on the work on America's number one unsolved problem and made their volume a distinguished successor to V. O. Key's *Southern Politics in State and Nation* (1949). Relying on diverse research strategies, including a population survey, intensive community studies, aggregate election statistics, and census data, Matthews and Prothro made excellent use of the most recent methods of multivariate analysis and other techniques. They succeeded in deepening scientific understanding of both the manifold causes of the Negro's inferior political and social status in the South and the possible consequences of the more recent changes in Negro activity and power.

Between the intensive study of individual personality and the extensive study of large populations, an increasing number of inquiries were conducted into the behavior of the men who occupy the leading positions in government—legislators, judges, administrators, and executives. Of particular interest was the question of how politicians become politicians. The recruitment process was treated in many works dealing with particular institutions, but it also became an area of independent inquiry. Dwaine Marvick, in *Political Decision-Makers: Recruitment and Performance* (1961), brought together a number of pioneering studies made at home and abroad. Joseph A. Schlesinger, in *How They Became Governor* (1957), traced the career lines of American state executives from 1870 to 1950, and in a subsequent work of great merit, *Ambition and Politics: Political Careers in the United States* (1966), outlined the political opportunity structure in America and examined how this structure constrains the ambitions of politicians. Two studies of British parliamentarians dealt with recruitment, Philip W. Buck's modest *Amateurs and Professionals in British Politics* (1963), and Austin Ranney's sophisticated *Pathways to Parliament: Candidate Selection in Britain* (1965). Morris Janowitz, in *The Professional Soldier* (1960), presented an elaborate statistical as well as qualitative profile of the military profession and its responses to technological change, while Heinz Eulau and John D. Sprague, in *Lawyers in Politics: A Study of Professional Convergence* (1964), analyzed the complementary career roles of the lawyer and the legislative politician. The relationship between career development and bureaucratic behavior was treated in two volumes, *The Image of the Federal Service* (1964), by Franklin P. Kilpatrick, Milton C. Cummings, Jr., and M. Kent Jennings, and in *The Higher Civil Service* (1964), by David T. Stanley. Following earlier works on the same topic, Dean E. Mann and James W. Doig studied federal political appointees of the second level in *The Assistant Secretaries: Problems and Processes of Appointment* (1965).

Political behavior research, beginning with intensive personality study but not limited to it, had an enormous impact on political knowledge. It freed the student of politics from exclusive reliance on documentary evidence and opened for him the doors of courts, legislatures, agencies, private associations, and even that castle of privacy, the home. Quantitative data came to supplement qualitative appraisals of political things, making possible the rigorous testing of hypotheses as well as exploration of areas of politics that, only twenty years ago, seemed forever doomed to remain matters of speculation. Not the least important among the newer studies, along with the study of individuals, were studies of small political groups. These groups are of political interest partly because they influence the political outlook and behavior of their members, and partly because they may be important centers of political decision-making.

Two works, Sidney Verba's *Small Groups and Political Behavior: A Study of Leadership* (1961), and Robert T. Golembiewski's *The Small Group: An Analysis of Research Concepts and Operations* (1962), critically assessed the small-group literature developed by sociologists and psychologists and made suggestive recommendations for the study of small political groups. But these works did not stimulate much empirical research, except in the legislative arena, where political scientists had come to recognize the importance of cliques but also of the informal behavioral patterns of legislative committees. The one significant exception that treated small political groups in their own right was James D. Barber's pioneering *Power in Committees: An Experiment in the Governmental Process* (1966), a study based on intensive observations of twelve local boards of finance brought into an experimental laboratory setting and directly concerned with the group properties of political behavior. Out of the mainstream of political science but of all the more interest and importance was a research project on a "therapeutic community" reported by Robert Rubenstein and Harold D. Lasswell in *The Sharing of Power in a Psychiatric Hospital* (1966). This microanalysis of the hospital as a decision-making institution in which staff as well as patients were observed and analyzed in terms of Lasswell's well-known value-personality categories was likely to have a long-range effect on the study of political behavior in small groups.

AMERICAN LABORATORY: POLITICS

Despite the variety of possible theoretical approaches to the study of politics, it is possible to specify, if not define, what politics is about.

Minimally, politics is concerned with decisions by which a community distributes its resources (but of course not all resources) and regulates its collective life. By community is meant not only a territorial unit like a nation-state or one of its subdivisions, but also a nomadic tribe, a church organization, a business corporation, a voluntary association, or an international body like the International Postal Union. From this perspective a small group like a troop of boy scouts or even a family can be viewed as a political community. For what all of these collectivities, large or small, have in common is the making of decisions that enable them to pursue their objectives and contribute to their maintenance. To do so, they will develop more or less formal norms, rules or customs—constitutions—which are binding on all members so that collective decisions can be made and their enforcement guaranteed. More often than not, these rules or customs validate and legitimize the prevailing social order, making for superior-subordinate or, perhaps, equalitarian relationships among the members. To maintain the rules, roles, and relationships, there are usually sanctions of one kind or another, in the form of rewards or penalties, of more or less authoritativeness and severity. But sanctions are only the ultimate means by which a community maintains itself and seeks its collective goals. Decisions as to what the goals should be and how to attain them are made in a variety of ways that rarely activate sanctions. Precisely because a community is an aggregate of persons who are joined by a consensus to belong together and who interact with each other in generally approved ways, much of political conduct involves persuading and compromising, bargaining and deferring, promising and adjusting, trusting and representing, obeying and ruling. These verbs, better than the familiar nouns such as power, authority, or law, describe what goes on in politics. Of course, there are other patterns of behavior too. Where communal consensus is low, as in many of the new nations or in nations undergoing rapid social change, or in the world community, there is a great deal of threatening, bribing, fighting, fearing, and killing. But because politics involves diverse forms of violence, it would be a mistake to see it in these terms alone. Eulau, in *The Behavioral Persuasion in Politics* (1963), tried to develop this behavioral conception of the political process. Lewis A. Froman, Jr., in *People and Politics: An Analysis of the American Political System* (1962), applied a similar conception of American politics.

It was in the context of the United States and in connection with American political processes that the new empirical ways of looking at politics in behavioral terms developed most rapidly and extensively. America became the laboratory, both subject and object of research, at all levels of the governmental system. Because direct observations of political behavior are difficult to come by in the real world, most of this research used political attitudes and roles as handles for coming to grips with reality. In general, whether researchers preferred attitude or role formulations seemed to vary with the population that was studied. Where, as in research on elections, the population was a random sample, attitudes provided the preferred topics. Where, as in studies of legislatures, a finite population was available, role conceptions proved most useful. Where, as in community studies, both a population sample and a more or less well defined elite were included in the research design, both attitudinal and role analysis were put into service.

The attitudinal parade continued to be led, not surprisingly, by a major work on voting and elections, long a playground of political research. In their remarkable *The American Voter* (1960), Angus Campbell, Philip E. Converse, Warren E. Miller, and Donald E. Stokes not only brought to bear on their subject all the sociological and sociopsychological insights of mass survey research, but they also utilized the data gathered at the level of the individual to develop a suggestive theory of elections at the system level of analysis. In *Elections and the Political Order* (1966), the same authors extended their inquiries in space and time, giving both historical and comparative depth to the study of electoral behavior. The related theme of the relationship between public opinion and government action was treated in *Public Opinion and American Democracy* by Key, who, unafraid of normative judgments about the quality of American political life, boldly marched on grounds where more data-bound empirical researchers would fear to tread. Combining survey data with his rich general knowledge of political processes, Key made a major contribution to the theory of democracy and pluralistic politics. In a posthumous volume, *The Responsible Electorate* (1966), he argued the basic rationality of the voter in his electoral choices.

Paradoxically, the very success of the national probability survey tended to discourage research on elections at the level of the individual. The complexities and costs of such surveys were major obstacles to its wider application. Although more limited, local studies, permitting inquiry into highly specific aspects of voting behavior, were reported, as in a volume by M. Kent Jennings and L. Harmon Zeigler (eds.), *The Electoral Process* (1966), electoral research outside the confines of Michigan's Survey Research Center declined. A few investigators, like Eulau, in *Class and Party in the Eisenhower Years* (1962), undertook secondary analyses of the data collected by the Michigan group. But the general tendency was to harness available survey findings for institutional interpretation rather than to extend the frontiers of electoral research. A number of works successfully integrated voting behavior research into the study of political parties. Among the best were Avery Leiserson, *Parties and Politics: An Institutional and Behavioral Approach* (1958),

Nelson W. Polsby and Aaron B. Wildavsky, *Presidential Elections* (1964), Frank J. Sorauf, *Political Parties in the American System*, Fred I. Greenstein, *The American Party System and the American People* (1963), and Allan P. Sindler, *Political Parties in the United States* (1966).

On the other hand, fresh research, utilizing both survey methods and aggregate statistics, fertilized a number of state and regional studies. The deviant case of California was treated by Eugene C. Lee in *The Politics of Nonpartisanship* (1960), and the special case of Wisconsin by Leon D. Epstein in *Politics in Wisconsin* (1958). A number of works, such as John H. Fenton's *Politics in the Border States* (1957) and *Midwest Politics* (1966), or Duane Lockard's *New England State Politics* (1959), intensified knowledge of particular regions, but none matched the pioneering and politically sophisticated *American State Politics* (1956) by Key. In general, the study of political parties as behavioral systems did not progress as much as one might have expected. The outstanding exception, and a work of broad scope, though geographically limited, was an intensive study of party organizations in the Detroit area by Samuel J. Eldersveld, *Political Parties: A Behavioral Analysis* (1964). Attacking the simplistic view of the party as a hierarchy, and focusing on the characteristics, perceptions, attitudes, communications, and intraorganizational relationships of party leaders on all levels, Eldersveld examined the impact of party organizations on the electorate. The party appeared as an enormously complex structure of horizontal and vertical relationships—a "stratarchy" of sometimes conflicting, sometimes competing, and sometimes cooperating interests.

Few other studies of party politics matched Eldersveld's work in depth of analysis. James Q. Wilson, in *The Amateur Democrat* (1962), studied the conflict between the new-style "amateur" and the old-style "professional" as well as the implications of the former's rise for the American political process. Paul T. David, Ralph M. Goldman, and Richard C. Bain, in *The Politics of National Party Conventions* (1960), provided a more systematic analysis of the subject than had been found in an earlier work by placing more emphasis on patterns of delegate behavior and the factors making for these patterns. Alexander Heard's *The Costs of Democracy* (1960) was a thorough examination of the impact of campaign finance on the nominating and electoral process, of the sources of campaign finance, the ways of raising funds, and the problem of equalizing and regulating the expenditure of political funds. A number of more limited works also delved into the process of presidential nominations and elections. Hugh A. Bone's *Party Committees and National Politics* (1958) was followed by Cornelius P. Cotter and Bernard C. Hennessy's *Politics Without Power: The National Party Committees* (1964), which stressed the various roles of party chairmen, analyzed membership composition, and dealt with the committees' manifold activities. Gerald Pomper, in *Nominating the President: The Politics of Convention Choice* (1966), and Lucius Wilmerding, Jr., in *The Electoral College* (1958), provided broad overviews of other aspects of the presidential selection process.

A perhaps unanticipated consequence of the behavioral renaissance in political science was the reemergence of interest in the history of American politics, and especially of the American party system. While most of the earlier works had been largely histories of presidential elections and the shifts of coalitions from election to election, the newer work began to penetrate the structural and interpersonal relationships that make the major parties bastions of organizational complexity. Manning Dauer's *The Adams Federalists* (1953), an ecological study of Federalist decline and Jeffersonian rise, had shown the contribution that a well-done historical approach can make to political science. But the temper of the times did not inspire many political scientists to follow Dauer's lead. Rather, it was the interest in comparative development that, in the sixties, directed attention to a reexamination of the American experience in nation building. William N. Chambers' *Political Parties in a New Nation* (1963) and Seymour M. Lipset's *The First New Nation* (1963) were symptomatic of the new concern. Noble E. Cunningham, in *The Jeffersonian Republicans* (1958) and in *The Jeffersonian Republicans in Power* (1963) reviewed the changing patterns of early party organization. Clinton Rossiter, in *1787: The Grand Convention* (1966), covered familiar ground in novel fashion. Content analysis of colonial newspapers permitted Richard L. Merritt to provide more intensive understanding of the American political background in *Symbols of American Community, 1735–1775* (1966). By all odds the most exciting of the new historical studies, however, was James S. Young's *The Washington Community, 1800–1828* (1966), a rich contextual study of the Washington "establishment" that deftly probed, in the author's own words, into "the governing group as entity: legislators, executives, judges, and all who gather around them at the seat of power; their inner life as a group; their special world as a governing fraternity; the lifeways and workways, the outlooks and values, the organizational patterns, that distinguish this unique group in American Society." With this work Young ended, for once and all, the alleged conflict between historical and behavioral inquiry.

Legislatures in state and nation became happy hunting grounds for the new generation of political scientists. Regardless of whether the interest was in legislatures for their own sake, or because they perform important governmental tasks in the polity, or whether the legislature was considered a convenient research site for exploring and testing hypotheses about political behavior and processes, the end effect was the same:

hardly any facet of legislative operations escaped scholarly attention. Studies included research on individual legislators; legislative roles in general; small informal groups; legislative socialization and recruitment; norms, rules, and sanctions; structure and tasks of committees; party behavior and coalition formation; legislative oversight and executive relations; representation and constituency relations; staffing; particular policies and issues; and many other topics. Much of this research was reported in journal articles, and the best found their way into such compendia as John C. Wahlke and Eulau (eds.), *Legislative Behavior: A Reader in Theory and Research* (1959) or Robert L. Peabody and Nelson W. Polsby (eds.), *New Perspectives on the House of Representatives* (1963). Two good textbooks reflected the new learning: Malcolm E. Jewell and Samuel C. Patterson, *The Legislative Process in the United States* (1966), and William J. Keefe and Morris S. Ogul, *The American Legislative Process* (1964).

Research on legislatures is blessed by an abundance of materials. There is rich documentation, though much more in the case of Congress than of the state legislatures; there are recorded roll-call votes that, if properly handled, provide much information, and there are legislators and their staff who are game, if elusive game, for the persistent interviewer. The confrontation of diverse data and methods of inquiry in the legislative field contributed to shattering the myth that behavioral and institutional analysis are necessarily opposed to each other. Two works, in particular, broke new ground. Donald R. Matthews, in *U.S. Senators and Their World* (1960), probed into the patterns of behavior, folkways, and effectiveness of a unique institution. Wahlke, Eulau, William Buchanan, and LeRoy C. Ferguson, in *The Legislative System: Explorations in Legislative Behavior* (1962), undertook a comprehensive and comparative analysis of the variety of attitudes and roles, norms and relationships, that make the legislature a highly patterned system of political behavior and contribute to its operation in predictable ways. In addition to this four-state study there were others dealing with single state legislatures, such as Frank J. Sorauf's *Party and Representation: Legislative Politics in Pennsylvania* (1963), William Buchanan's *Legislative Partisanship: The Deviant Case of California* (1963), and several others. James D. Barber, in *The Lawmakers: Recruitment and Adaptation to Legislative Life* (1965), explored patterns of recruitment into and adjustment to the Connecticut legislature of a group of freshman Solons.

The Congress, and especially the House of Representatives, received more attention than any other legislative chamber. Roland Young's *The American Congress* (1958) was the last of the old-time institutional studies, and George B. Galloway, dean of congressional students, gave a historical overview in *History of the House of Representatives* (1962).

But most works of the decade dealt with special aspects of the congressional operation. That the political party has greater impact on congressional behavior than commonly believed was demonstrated by David B. Truman in *The Congressional Party* (1959). An intensive study of partisan behavior during the Eighty-first Congress, based on bloc analysis of roll-call votes, this work was especially sensitive to the different roles played by the majority and minority leadership. David R. Mayhew continued Truman's work in *Party Loyalty among Congressmen* (1966), a study of the differences between the parties between 1947 and 1962. Duncan MacRae, Jr., in *Dimensions of Congressional Voting* (1958), experimented with scale analyses of roll-call votes to determine Congressmen's positions on vital issues. Holbert N. Carroll dealt with a single issue area in *The House of Representatives and Foreign Affairs* (1958), and LeRoy N. Rieselbach, in *The Roots of Isolationism* (1966), probed further into the relationship between Congress and President in the foreign policy field. Milton C. Cummings, Jr., in *Congressmen and the Electorate* (1966), and Lewis A. Froman, Jr., in *Congressmen and their Constituencies* (1963), were concerned with problems of representation. Froman subsequently dealt with internal strategies, rules, and procedures in *The Congressional Process* (1967). And David J. Rothman, in *Politics and Power: The United States Senate, 1869–1901* (1966), studied the transformation of the Senate during the last quarter of the nineteenth century.

The veracity of the statement that "congressional politics is committee politics" was given credence by a number of studies that probed into the behavioral patterns and activities of committees. The intricacies of congressional appropriations politics were investigated by Richard F. Fenno, Jr., in a path-breaking and exhaustive study, *The Power of the Purse* (1966). Rich in descriptive detail, Fenno's book was one of the best intensive case studies ever written in any field, and though it was a self-consciously functional analysis, with all the scientific difficulties that this type of analysis entails, its broad systemic framework sensitized the researcher to the many problems of a complex political organization. By concentrating on committee behavior as its object of study, Fenno's work contributed to uncovering the links that connect the individual decision-maker to the decision-making institution as a whole.

The often arbitrary power of the House Rules Committee, and especially of its chairman, was the main focus of James A. Robinson's *The House Rules Committee* (1963) that examined both the internal structure of the Committee and the effects of its decisions on the political life of the House. In *Congress and Foreign Policy-Making* (1962), the same author harnessed numerous case studies prepared by different researchers for the purpose of generalization concerning congressional foreign-policy making. A variety of other works treated different aspects of congressional life. How Congressmen themselves perceive and interpret their work was recorded in a report of round-table conferences among three dozen Congressmen by Charles L. Clapp, *The Congressman: His Work as He Sees It* (1963). Congressional staff operations were described by Kenneth Kofmehl in *Professional Staffs of Congress* (1962). Congressional oversight was the concern of Joseph P. Harris, *Congressional Control of Administration* (1964). And interviews with Congressmen provided much of the material for a reform-oriented study by Roger H. Davidson, David M. Kovenock, and Michael K. O'Leary, *Congress in Crisis: Politics and Congressional Reform* (1966).

Congress may play second fiddle to the Presidency as a policy innovating institution, but the Presidency and not Congress has been neglected by political science research. There are any number of reasons for this neglect, the most important probably being the difficulty of gaining access to an institution that is highly self-protective and secretive in its operations. Only "insiders" are likely to get the necessary "feel" for, if not access to, information that the study of the Presidency requires. But insiders are rarely political scientists. Richard Neustadt was an exception, and his book, *Presidential Power* (1960), was an exceptional book. In Neustadt's influential analysis the President does not simply sit somehow at the apex of a submissive hierarchy of political appointees and bureaucrats. Rather, he is at the center of a complex net of power relationships that require him to husband or spend his resources more like an honest broker than a haughty commander if he wishes to achieve his legislative and administrative goals. Only Theodore C. Sorensen's *Decision Making in the White House* (1963)—a lawyer's inside view of President Kennedy's short incumbency—came close to Neustadt's perceptive interpretation of the decision-making process at the presidential level. However, insider Roger Hilsman's *To Move a Nation* (1967)—a report on and analysis of the politics of foreign policy during the Kennedy administration—represented an important contribution to knowledge of the Presidency as a living institution.

This is not to say that some other works on the Presidency were of inferior quality. But they lacked the empirical vitality of the congressional studies, and they did not convey the same sense of immediacy. The fourth edition of Edward S. Corwin's *The President: Office and Powers* (1957) remained the standard work in the institutional tradition, and Glendon A. Schubert's *The Presidency in the Courts* (1957) examined the judiciary's control over the Presidency—in general ineffective. Wilfred E. Binkley's *The Man in the White House: His Powers and Duties* (1959) provided historical perspective. Richard F. Fenno's *The President's Cabinet* (1959) and Stephen Horn's *The Cabinet and Congress* (1960) were careful studies of institutional relationships. Laurin L. Henry, in

Presidential Transitions (1960), dealt with the problem of administrative changes in the wake of presidential turnover. Nelson W. Polsby's *Congress and the Presidency* (1964), a short text, included suggestive ideas. The role of the President as a national "opinion leader" was explored by Elmer E. Cornwell, Jr., in *Presidential Leadership of Public Opinion* (1965). Of course, these and some other works by political scientists did not exhaust what was written about the Presidency and particular Presidents. Historians, journalists, biographers and even novelists continued to find in the Presidency a rich mine of materials for their own particular uses. But as a research site for the study of political behavior, the White House and the network of related institutions proved elusive.

FEDERAL OCTOPUS: LAW AND ADMINISTRATION

Public administration as a semiautonomous field of political science never recovered from the postwar shock of recognition of its own intellectual sterility. The sterility had been engendered by the notion that politics and administration were separate domains, each with laws of its own, but the reintroduction of political variables into the study of administrative processes and behavior turned out to be a more formidable task than expected. The failure of students of public administration to heed Herbert A. Simon's injunctions, in *Administrative Behavior* (2d ed., 1957), led to research atrophy in a field that, in the interwar years, had been led by some of the finest minds in political science. Symbolically, perhaps, one of these leaders, Leonard D. White, completed his history of administration with *The Republican Era, 1869–1901* (1958). A volume of essays in honor of another leader, Paul H. Appleby, *Public Administration and Democracy* (1965), edited by Roscoe C. Martin, was more nostalgic than hopeful. Perhaps the clinical stance of the field prevented its practitioners from being research innovators or theoreticians.

Although "public administration" continued to be taught in separate courses of political science, the field ceased to exist as an autonomous theoretical enterprise. Instead, public administration was increasingly seen as merely an arena of public action where, just as in private arenas, it was possible to study generic processes of bureaucracy, decision-making, and organizational behavior. But most of the interesting work along these lines was not done by political scientists but by sociologists and social psychologists as well as by a new species of specialists called "organization theorists." When James G. March and Herbert A. Simon published their inventory of relevant hypotheses, *Organizations* (1958), only a handful of political scientists were listed in their comprehensive bibliography.

Since then, a number of political scientists have dealt with generic issues of organization. Victor A. Thompson, in *Modern Organization* (1961), argued in favor of perceiving organizational behavior in terms of its bureaucratic context rather than in terms of individualistic psychology. Robert Presthus, in *The Organizational Society* (1962), emphasized the psychological adjustments to organizational setting that successful action seems to require. Robert T. Golembiewski, in *Behavior and Organization* (1962), stressed the importance of the small group in the organizational network. Two volumes of essays, Sidney Mailick and Edward H. Van Ness (eds.), *Concepts and Issues in Administrative Behavior* (1962), and William J. Gore and J. W. Dyson (eds.), *The Making of Decisions* (1964), testified to the interdisciplinary character of the new approaches. William J. Gore, in *Administrative Decision-Making: A Heuristic Model* (1964), advocated the inclusion of political considerations generated by conflicts over goals in models of rational choice. Gordon Tullock, in *The Politics of Bureaucracy* (1965), and Anthony Downs, in *Inside Bureaucracy* (1967), developed models of rational behavior based on assumptions of individual self-interest. A few books, like Peter Woll's *American Bureaucracy* (1963) or William W. Boyer's *Bureaucracy on Trial* (1964), presented overviews of administrative problems and practices. Frederick C. Mosher and Orville F. Poland, in *The Costs of American Governments: Facts, Trends, Myths* (1964), dispelled false notions about governmental costs and fiscal policies. And Bertram M. Gross, in a magisterial two-volume work, *The Management of Organizations* (1964), presented what was likely to remain the *magnum opus* of the field. But again, perusal of Gross's extensive bibliography on both research and general studies revealed the same poverty of political science writing noted by March and Simon.

Empirical research on administrative behavior and decision-making was primarily done by students in fields other than political science. Among the few exceptions of note were Herbert Kaufman's *The Forest Ranger* (1960), a study of the tensions that arise out of the paradoxical need for both fragmentation and integration in large-scale organizations; Robert L. Peabody's *Organizational Authority: Superior-Subordinate Relationships in Three Public Service Organizations* (1964), which examined the empirical viability of four different types of authority—of position, competence, person, and legitimacy; or Aaron Wildavsky's *The Politics of the Budgetary Process* (1964), which demonstrated that budget makers are more concerned with incremental changes at the margins than with using the budget as a tool of global planning. W. Lloyd Warner, Paul P. Van Riper, Norman H. Martin, and Orvis F. Collins reported on the social and personal characteristics of federal personnel in *The American Federal Executive* (1963).

The atrophy of public administration as a field of research also affected research on the potentially fascinating problems of governance arising out of the American federal system. William Anderson's *The Nations and the States: Rivals or Partners?* (1955) was the last but perhaps best work on American federal relationships in the tradition of the late thirties and early forties. W. Brooke Graves's belated *American Intergovernmental Relations* (1964), similarly, articulated the faith of public administrators in governmental reform through structural reorganization. A series of refreshing essays speculating on the areal distribution of power and its consequences, *Area and Power: A Theory of Local Government* (1959), edited by Arthur Maas, failed to be followed up by relevant research. Alpheus T. Mason, in *The States Rights Debate: Antifederalism and the Constitution* (1964), reviewed again the often ambiguous and conflicting ideas of the makers of the American Constitution. But, as a genre in its own right, the constitutional and administrative treatment of the issues of American federalism largely disappeared.

However, a new interest in federal problems developed among some scholars who took as their point of departure not the constitutional or administrative but the political aspects of federal relationships. A new model of the American federal system as functionally analogous to a marble cake of shared activities and services evolved out of a variety of empirical studies that were launched in the "federalism workshop" at the University of Chicago in 1955 under the guidance of Morton Grodzins. His posthumous *The American System* (1966) presented "a new view of government in the United States" as one of antagonistic (and hence intrinsically political) cooperation between the different governmental levels. In Grodzin's judgment this view testified to both the apparently chaotic complexity but also to the fundamentally decentralized, responsible and responsive nature of the American system—evidence of its health and vigor rather than of decline or decay. The book demonstrated the possibility and desirability of empirically grounded policy research. Another member of the Chicago workshop, Daniel J. Elazar, in *The American Partnership* (1962), provided historical depth for this new conception of American federalism. In a subsequent work, *American Federalism: A View from the States* (1966), Elazar emphasized the implications of different "state political cultures" for federal relations. A volume by Robert A. Goldwin (ed.), *A Nation of States* (1963), presented a variety of views, and the emergence of the city as a further "partner" and the pervasiveness of the new federalism were appraised by Roscoe C. Martin in *The Cities and the Federal System* (1965). Other political aspects of cooperative federalism were treated historically and analytically by Glenn E. Brooks, *When Governors Convene: The Governors' Conference and National Politics* (1961).

Another novel view of federalism from the perspective of empirical political theory was introduced by William H. Riker in *Federalism: Origin, Operation, Significance* (1964). Less deferential to formal constitutional and administrative preconceptions than the conventional writers, Riker approached federalism from the vantage point of modern theories of political bargaining. Both the "mature" federal systems of the West and the "transitional" systems of the developing nations served as foci of theoretical attention. Although not directly focused on federalism, the interpenetration of national and state policies in a variety of issue areas was treated in a suggestive volume edited by Herbert Jacob and Kenneth N. Vines, *Politics in the American States: A Comparative Analysis* (1965). The issue of education, increasingly affected by the federal system, was explored in a study of three states by Nicholas A. Masters, Robert H. Salisbury, and Thomas H. Eliot, *State Politics and the Public Schools* (1964).

If political scientists had reason to be chagrined by the demise of public administration as a creative field of research, they were delighted by the lively intellectual rumblings in the oldest of the discipline's subfields—the study of public law. Indeed, it became questionable whether "public law" was in fact what the new generation of political scientists were studying. For their focus of attention shifted from the substantive aspects of public law—well taken care of in the law schools—to the courts as political institutions that performed political tasks very much like legislatures and executive agencies, though under characteristically judicial rules of decision-making; and it shifted to the social and attitudinal attributes of judges and the effects of these attributes on judicial outputs, as well as to the internal interactions of judges and juries as intrinsically political phenomena. Of course, the importance of the policy-making role of the United States Supreme Court had long been recognized even by conventional public law scholars; but there had been much discomfort about the court's political role. That the whole judicial establishment is a political institution engaged in political practices or having political goals was a notion that only a few political scientists had dared to even think about. There had been, within the legal fraternity itself, dissent from the arid formalism of "positive" jurisprudence; the "sociologists" and "realists" had prepared the ground for a "judicial politics." But it was not until a postwar generation of political scientists had been trained in the behavioral sciences that the study of public law was gradually transformed into a political science of judicial institutions and judicial behavior.

In the middle of the fifties, two books were noted as symptomatic of the break with the past, C. Herman Pritchett's *The Roosevelt Court: A Study of Judicial Politics and Values* (1948), and the same author's

Civil Liberties and the Vinson Court (1954). Pritchett's innovations were twofold: first, he saw the Court as a decision-making group whose voting and opinion behavior could be explained in terms of the individual justice's attitudes toward issues of public policy; and second, through quantitative analysis of many cases, Pritchett could scrutinize the nature of the coalitions among the justices with respect to particular issues. This new orientation came to be carried forward by a small, courageous band of young political scientists led by prolific Glendon Schubert whose *Quantitative Analysis of Political Behavior* (1959) not only extended Pritchett's bloc-analysis method, but gave examples of the uses that could be made of game-theoretical models and of scalogram techniques. In *Constitutional Politics: The Political Behavior of Supreme Court Justices and the Constitutional Policies That They Make* (1960), Schubert combined old and new ways of studying public law and the courts in a major treatise. In *Judicial Decision-Making* (1963), Schubert and other "judicial behaviorists"—S. Sidney Ulmer, Stuart S. Nagel, Harold J. Spaeth, Joseph Tanenhaus, Fred Kort, Herbert Jacob, and Kenneth N. Vines—presented further examples of how a variety of social science techniques could be useful in dissecting the courts as political institutions, including graph theory, interviewing, factor analysis, and content analysis. In *The Judicial Mind* (1965), a study of eighteen Supreme Court Justices between 1946 and 1963, Schubert studied the relationship between judicial attitudes and policy-relevant law cases to discover the patterns that make the court a consistent institution. Finally, in *Judicial Behavior: A Reader in Theory and Research* (1964), also edited by Schubert, what had now become the "judicial behavior movement" erected its own monument. The volume's chapter headings showed the range of the movement's concerns—"Cultural Anthropology and Judicial Systems"; "Political Sociology and Judicial Attributes"; "Social Psychology and Judicial Attitudes"; or "Mathematical Prediction of Judicial Behavior."

Somewhat different in approach, but equally intent of demonstrating the political nature of judicial institutions, was the work of those who took a more contextual view of what the judges are doing when they interpret or declare the law. In particular, the judges' relationships outside the court system became topics of inquiry. Victor G. Rosenblum, in *Law as a Political Instrument* (1955), and Jack W. Peltason, in *Federal Courts in the Political Process* (1955), broke new ground. A lawyer, Alexander M. Bickel, in *The Least Dangerous Branch: The Supreme Court at the Bar of Politics* (1962) ignited fires of controversy. Herbert Jacob's *Justice in America* (1965) extended this type of analysis to state courts and to all participants in the judicial process, including interest groups, bar associations, judges, and public attorneys. Interest-group litigation in the Supreme Court was treated by Robert A. Horn in *Groups and the*

Constitution (1956), and by Clement Vose in *Caucasians Only; The Supreme Court, the NAACP, and the Restrictive Covenant Cases* (1959). John R. Schmidhauser, in *The Supreme Court as Final Arbiter in Federal-State Relations, 1789-1957* (1958), suggested the political role of the court in the politics of the federal system. In *The Supreme Court: Its Politics, Personalities, and Procedures* (1960), Schmidhauser examined the social and political backgrounds of the justices, the external forces operating on the court, and the effects of changes in the court's internal procedures and customs. The impact of the American Bar Association on judicial selection and the ro'es that judges play was the subject of Joel B. Grossman's *Lawyers and Judges: The ABA and the Politics of Judicial Selection* (1965). David J. Danelski, in *A Supreme Court Justice Is Appointed* (1964), scrutinized in detail the political circumstances surrounding the appointment of Justice Butler and the consequences of the appointment for the court's doctrinal development. Samuel Krislov's *The Supreme Court in the Political Process* (1965) was a sober overview based on behavioral as well as organizational considerations. Walter F. Murphy, in *Elements of Judicial Strategy* (1964), and Martin Shapiro, in *Law and Politics in the Supreme Court* (1964), analyzed by both traditional and novel concepts the roles of judges, their discretionary capabilities, their personal objectives and bargaining strategies. Finally, Harry Kalven and Hans Zeisel reported the findings of the famous "Chicago jury project" in *The American Jury* (1966).

More traditional students of the judicial process continued to make lucid contributions though they often had an ax of their own to grind. Walter Berns, in *Freedom, Virtue and the First Amendment* (1957), attacked the Supreme Court; and Milton R. Konvitz, in *Fundamental Liberties of a Free People: Religion, Speech, Press, Assembly* (1957), defended it. David Fellman explored a vital issue in *The Defendant's Rights* (1958). Loren P. Beth provided a disinterested analysis in *The American Theory of Church and State* (1958). Robert J. Harris looked at the equal protection clause of the Constitution and its interpretation in *The Quest for Equality* (1960), and Robert G. McGloskey reexamined the history of judicial review in *The American Supreme Court* (1960). Glenn Abernathy studied another aspect of civil liberties in *The Right of Assembly and Association* (1961), and Charles S. Hyneman, in *The Supreme Court on Trial* (1963), while admitting the ambiguity of interpretation that must necessarily accompany the court's exercise of power, adjudged the court as an effective instrument of democracy. Harry Kalven, examining the impact of the civil rights movement on the First Amendment in *The Negro and the First Amendment* (1965), insisted that judges react to political challenges not simply in terms of their own political predispositions, but also in terms of acceptable doctrinal development. In a work of a somewhat different genre, Otto Kirchheimer, in *Political Justice: The Use of Legal Procedure for Political Ends* (1961), unmasked the political misuses of justice by totalitarian governments.

DYNAMICS: POLICY AND POWER

Looking at politics in terms of institutional structures is to take a rather static view of governmental complexity. Another way is to analyze the processes that seem to be characteristic of particular institutions. In this perspective politics appears as a developing sequence of actions and events through time, a matter of becoming rather than being. The accent is put on the changing nature of political life, regardless of whether the changes are fast or slow, easily identifiable or more difficult to trace. When the emphasis is on processes, many factors are seen as influencing the course of political events, but they are separated only for analytical convenience. In reality, typically political processes—electoral, legislative, judicial, administrative, and so on—are highly interrelated as the focus of attention shifts from one to the other. This is most evident when the issues involved are spectacular as in the contemporary movement of the American Negro for civil rights. The arena of politics in which the battle for civil rights is waged shifts from the courts to the legislature, from the legislature to the administration, from the administration to the streets and back again to the courts, and so on.

Looking at politics in terms of process has introduced a good deal of realism into political knowledge. According to the static model of American government as one of separated powers, one branch of government makes the laws, another interprets them, and a third carries them out. But if we look at the "carrying out" process, for instance, it soon becomes evident that the administrative process violates the constitutional model. In the modern administrative process, the same agents make rules that have the force of law, interpret these rules in controversial cases and issue binding decisions, and see to it that these decisions are obeyed by citizens, associations, corporations, or unions. Moreover, the participants in this process are not only executives and bureaucrats but also interest groups seeking special favors, disinterested "outside" experts whose advice is sought, legislators who carry on an oversight function or intervene on behalf of constituents, or judges who are called upon to redress grievances.

There are some difficulties in viewing politics as process. One of these is the limited capacity of the approach to transcend description of single "cases," and hence a limited capacity for generalization. Cases are rich in descriptive detail of the factors that have gone into particular policy outcomes, and they provide a very realistic picture of the sequence of actions across the different institutional arenas in which a policy was hammered out. But because such cases are usually selected precisely because they deal with spectacular or "interesting" situations, they cannot tell us much about the political process in general. An attempt to generalize concerning a particular policy arena, made by James A. Robinson in *Congress and Foreign Policy-Making* (1962), was only partially successful because the thirty-odd cases at the author's disposal had been prepared by different scholars using different concepts and attending to different aspects of the processes involved.

Nevertheless, approaching politics from the point of view of process calls attention to the formulation, promulgation, and application of policies by which a community distributes its resources and regulates its collective life. The study of public policies has long been a concern of political science, but a science of public policies does not as yet exist. The myriad studies that have been made of public policies—foreign, educational, labor, agricultural, and so on—are largely historical, descriptive, or legal analyses of particular cases. Usually addressed to the solution of "problems" and, therefore, prescriptive in their conclusions, many of these studies make fascinating and sometimes even enlightening reading. They undoubtedly aid the citizen as they aid the statesman in orienting himself in a given policy area. But almost no systematic comparative treatment of public policies has been attempted and generalizations about the causes or consequences of public policies are likely to be of low validity. A notable exception was Thomas R. Dye's *Politics, Economics, and the Public* (1966) which, using financial and census data, systematically related policy outputs in education, health, highways, and other policy areas of the American states to properties of both the political and surrounding social environment. Although this work was by no means free of difficulties that the types of data used engender, it was likely to stimulate efforts along similar lines.

This is not to say that the policy-*making* process has not been thoroughly or even scientifically studied. In a pioneering work, *Congress Makes a Law* (1950), Stephen K. Bailey has probed deeply into the great variety of influences that shaped the Full Employment Act of 1946—the influence of public opinion, interest groups, economists, the President, and members of Congress. In *The Political Process and Foreign Policy* (1957), Bernard Cohen systematically investigated most of the factors and considerations relevant to the Japanese peace treaty as a statement of American foreign policy. In *Dixon-Yates: A Study of Power Politics* (1962), Aaron Wildavsky dissected the great variety of circumstances that muddled this famous controversy in the field of water resources. *American Business and Public Policy* (1963), by Raymond A. Bauer, Ithiel de Sola Pool and Lewis A. Dexter, was an examination of the American political process as a whole and of the contribution made to it by all those who were concerned with trade legislation—the business world, vitally affected local communities, organized interest groups, and Congress. Harold P. Green and Alan Rosenthal, in *Government of the Atom: The Integration of Powers* (1963), gave a careful historical and analytic account of the complexities of policy-making in the matter of atomic energy, its uses and control. Gilbert Y. Steiner, in *Social Insecurity: The Politics of Welfare* (1966), examined the political process in the making of public assistance policies. Other works of this genre were Glenn H. Snyder, *Stockpiling Strategic Materials: Politics and National Defense* (1966), Murray Edelman and R. W. Fleming, *The Politics of Wage-Price Decisions: A Four Country Analysis* (1965), Demetrios Caraley, *The Politics of Military Unification: A Study of Conflict and the Policy Process* (1966), and Edward A. Kolodziej, *The Uncommon Defense and Congress, 1945-1963* (1966).

The scientific question of why policies come about and why they are what they are has proved elusive. The question is elusive because facts never speak for themselves; and, as a result, different and often conflicting policy alternatives can be deduced and suggested from the same set of facts. But the problem of developing a science of public policy goes beyond this difficulty. It requires categories of analysis of a sufficiently abstract order that would permit the policy scientist to overcome the rich historical and descriptive detail that usually preoccupies the student of a particular case. For this purpose, "policy" must be conceived of as the total relationship of government to its environment, as expressed in its concrete programs and specific decisions. Thus conceived, public policy is a response of government to challenges or pressures from the physical and social environment—wars, famines, depressions, population movements, technological advances, clashing private interests, and so on. Changes in public policy, then, occur in response to changes in the environment, and they can be of two kinds: either the policy adjusts and adapts the political system to environmental changes, or it brings about changes in the environment. Which alternative is chosen, or whether both are chosen, depends potentially on a great variety of factors—the structure of the political system itself, its rigidity or flexibility; the vitality and diversity of the interests that have a stake in the policy; the functions which the system is seen to perform traditionally, which may encourage or discourage new policies; the resources that the political system is capable of mobilizing to deal with changes in the environment; and last but not least, the values which policy-makers seek in formulating policy—their conceptions of the good life.

The problem of policy analysis is complicated by the fact that policy can be a response to the environment without particular decisions having been made. In other words, no government can be without a policy, even if government officials refuse or fail to make decisions regarding a policy. Their failure to decide and its consequences constitutes a policy in the sense that it is a response, if a negative one, to environmental challenges. Indeed, many of the "problems" that today face the United States—the Negro revolt, the crisis in education, the issue of poverty and unemployment, for instance—are largely due to inadvertent policies.

It is for all of these reasons that the systematic study of public policy and of the policy process is high on the agenda of political science. Needless to say, perhaps, the continued need of a society for policies appropriate to meet the challenges of the environment cannot await the discovery of scientific solutions. But the enlightened citizen, in turn, should understand and appreciate the difficulties of policy analysis that confront the political scientist. He should not expect more from political science in the field of public policy than the current status of the field allows him to expect.

One of the most common roads into the labyrinth of policy-making has been the study of interest groups whose pervasiveness in the American political process has long fascinated the imagination of journalists and political scientists alike. Yet, little more is known about the dynamics of interest group politics from a *scientific* perspective than when, in the late fifties, Samuel J. Eldersveld, in a cogent essay on "American Interest Groups: A Survey of Research and Some Implications for Theory and Method"—in Henry W. Ehrmann (ed.), *Interest Groups on Four Continents* (1958)—reviewed the field. In part, this lag in scientific development is due to the nature of the subject. Interest groups are highly diverse and proliferate to such an extent that, even if the number of case studies were increased manyfold, generalizations would have to remain highly tentative. Harmon Zeigler's overview of the literature, in *Interest Groups in American Society* (1964), was theoretically inconclusive.

The few studies published immediately before and after the appearance of Zeigler's book, while often insightful in their own right, contributed little to theoretical understanding. One might mention Phillip O. Foss, *Politics and Grass* (1960), which showed that public ownership of grazing lands is largely a fiction; Robert Engler, *The Politics of Oil* (1961), which indicated that the petroleum industry is a private government that uses public government to promote its goals of more economic power and larger profits; Joseph R. Gusfield, *Symbolic Crusade: Status Politics and the American Temperance Movement* (1963), which suggested that moral reform movements are not easily understood by models of economic class conflict; Michael D. Reagan, *The Managed Economy* (1963), which examined the role of business in national policy-making;

Martha Derthick, *The National Guard in Politics* (1965), which developed but did not apply a conception of group power as a ratio of achievements to goals; or Alice K. Smith, *A Peril and a Hope: The Scientists' Movement in America, 1945-1947* (1965), which described how scientists came into government and sought to influence public policy. How "science" became a power and major function of government was treated more philosophically in Don K. Price's *The Scientific Estate* (1965). Two sociologists, William A. Glaser and David L. Sills edited a volume, *The Government of Associations* (1966), which included studies about the internal and external dimensions of modern associational life.

Even if the empirical net was cast more widely, as in Corinne L. Gilb's *Hidden Hierarchies* (1966), a study of the relationships between a variety of professions and government, the very complexity of the description stood in the way of meaningful generalization. By all odds the most successful work of the period was Grant McConnell's *Private Power and American Democracy* (1966), which attributed the influence of interest groups in penetrating the public agencies, presumably designed to regulate them as to their success in manipulating and controlling their own particular clienteles. The myth of pressure group power suffered a setback, however, in a thorough study of reciprocal trade legislation in Congress by Raymond A. Bauer, Ithiel de Sola Pool and Lewis A. Dexter, *American Business and Public Policy* (1963). Though they concentrated on a single area of legislation, the authors transcended the limitations of a case study and developed generic conceptions about the relationship between interest groups and Congress, generating fresh hypotheses for independent and systematic testing. That interest groups have less influence than often supposed was also the finding of Lester Milbrath's *The Washington Lobbyists* (1963), a study based on interviews with some one hundred group agents and an assortment of Congressmen and their staff. The legal aspects of lobbying were treated in Edgar Lane, *Lobbying and the Law* (1964).

That a broader policy perspective might be useful in leading studies of influence out of their quandary was suggested by a small number of works that focused attention on policy processes. In *The Politics of Distribution* (1955), Joseph C. Palamountain had rejected the simplicity of the "group approach" that sees policy as a confluence and balance of competing interests. But few empirical studies continued this line of inquiry. The paradox that governmental decision-making requires both secrecy and publicity was the subject of Francis E. Rourke's *Secrecy and Publicity Dilemmas of Democracy* (1961). The pervasiveness of political considerations in the sacrosanct arena of public education was demonstrated in a comparative study by Nicholas A. Masters, Robert H. Salisbury, and Thomas H. Eliot, *State Politics and the Public Schools* (1964).

Different policy-making processes and policy outcomes in the American states were treated by a team of writers in a well-edited volume by Herbert Jacob and Kenneth N. Vines, *Politics in the American States: A Comparative Analysis* (1965).

Despite the kaleidoscopic quality of politics, men from earliest times on have sought to discover a single principle that could bring order into the great diversity of things political. What seemed to stand out in politics, more than anything else was the existence of relationships that involved the control of one person by another, of one group by another, of the many by the few, and possibly of the few by the one. The Romans had a word for it, *potestas*, and medieval as well as early modern writers called it "sovereignty." Often identified with monopoly, legitimate or illegitimate, of the means of physical coercion, power seemed to be the political equivalent of wealth as the crucial means of economic production. Indeed, in an epoch such as our own, in which governments are able to mobilize national resources for control of internal opposition and territorial conquest, power seems to be the pervasive reality of political life.

Yet, obvious and self-evident as power appears to be in the governance of men, the phenomenon has proved elusive. Just as in the case of the search for the "sovereign" in political systems with separated and divided branches of government, the search for power seems to involve infinite regression. There always seems to be a power behind power—a Madame Pompadour behind Louis XIV, a Colonel House behind President Wilson—and the end of the search is never in sight. Power, some have speculated, may be more myth than reality.

This is not to say that power may not be a useful myth, either for those who can use it to their own advantage or those who seek to overthrow presumed power-holders. In its legal cloth—sovereignty—the notion that power was ordained by God or nature to be lodged in monarchs and princes held sway for centuries, and monarchs used it to legitimize their claims to rulership and punish those who would contest their claims. Even after the downfall of monarchies and the advent of republics, democratic or not, the sovereignty of parliaments was declared to be the primary justification of why the laws should by obeyed. The alleged sovereignty of nations—their power to control their own territories —was claimed to absolve them from responsibility in international conduct, on the implicit principle that might is right.

But power has also been a convenient object of attack for those who sought to displace occupants of governmental positions. Marx viewed the state and its power apparatus as the instrument by which the capitalistic bourgeoisie controlled and victimized the proletariat; and though he envisaged a utopian society in which there would be no state, and therefore no power, he advocated a proletarian dictatorship as a necessary prerequisite to emancipate the working class and guarantee its victory. In the history of the United States, the "power" of Wall Street was the target of the populist movement in the 1890's, and in the 1950's an insurgent sociologist, C. Wright Mills, in *The Power Elite* (1956), tried to identify those, who in his view, occupy the "command posts" of the American political system. More recently, the cry of "black power" has taken hold in one sector of the Negro movement in its quest for equal rights as a counterweight to something called "white power."

While power remains a slogan of political warfare, modern research has increasingly challenged the viability of the concept as a means to understanding political reality. If there is an "establishment" of the high and mighty in Washington, London, or Moscow, the notion that it is a monolithic concentration of power does not square with the diversity and often the contradictoriness of its decisions. If there is such a thing as power, it is highly dispersed, and if it is dispersed, it is questionable whether the concept of power is really descriptive of the relationships of control that characterize complex political systems. Robert A. Dahl, in *Pluralistic Democracy in the United States: Conflict and Consent* (1967), presented an historical and analytical account of this vision of American politics. On the highest levels of government, of course, the existence of power cannot be readily proved or disproved because the making of governmental decisions, and especially of the most important ones, is likely to be secret and not accessible. But this difficulty is considerably lessened in the study of local communities, and power as an explanatory concept for understanding politics has been most thoroughly investigated in these communities.

So neglected and obsolescent was the study of local politics in the middle fifties that one writer could speak of "the lost world of municipal government." Yet, as if to make this indictment a self-denying prophecy, political scientists countered it with vengeance. The local arena soon became a lively research site for a great variety of theoretically oriented empirical studies. And it proved to have its own methodological advantages. Better than in larger political systems, it was possible to pursue at the local level a variety of interests that, in the larger systems, were more elusive. Not only questions concerning the nature and distribution of power, but also questions concerning the "integration" of political units or the "functions" of government could be more easily examined here than in the larger settings. Of course, that the local community once again became a center of research interest was not just due to these scientific concerns. By the late fifties, the urgent social and political problems of urban and metropolitan life had forced themselves to the attention of political scientists and, from this policy perspective, reawakened their interest in local government.

Much heat but also much light was shed on the perplexing problem of power in a series of studies implicitly or explicitly attacking the theoretically exaggerated and methodologically doubtful thesis, advanced by sociologist Floyd Hunter in *Community Power Structure* (1953), that local public affairs are dominated by a closely knit elite whose influence extends to all important areas of community-wide decision-making. Hunter's dubious methods, his failure to deal with actual decisions, and his neglect of formal government in the political life of the city he studied—Atlanta—invited attacks. Once the battle was over, all that could be said of Hunter's work was that its very weaknesses had the salutary effect of stimulating more viable research. And if, for a time, there had been the lingering doubt that his findings, even if not true elsewhere, were true of Atlanta, this doubt was dispelled by a follow-up study, M. Kent Jennings' *Community Influentials: The Elites of Atlanta* (1964), which did not find the city to be governed by an exclusive, monolithic elite.

The great variety of urban decision processes and the multiplicity of participants taking diverse roles were examined, with reference to concrete issues, by Edward C. Banfield in *Political Influence* (1961). Banfield found that Chicago's structure of political influence largely reflected the decentralized formal structure of the city's government. Political fragmentation resulting from multiple and overlapping jurisdictions was seen as intensified by competition between political parties and interest groups so that, on particular issues, quite different persons or organizations were found to influence the decision process. Similarly, in *Governing New York* (1960), Wallace S. Sayre and Herbert Kaufman discovered a "multi-centred system" in which separate and numerous "islands of power" compete and make public policies. A pluralistic system of noncumulative and dispersed inequalities was also found to characterize the politics of New Haven, Connecticut, in Robert A. Dahl's theoretically sophisticated *Who Governs? Democracy and Power in an American City* (1961). Historical analysis of elite transformation, case analyses of several policy-making arenas, and a cross-sectional analysis of resource distribution among citizens were combined to provide a complex, conceptually elegant portrait of competitive politics, and to liberate the study of political influence from its excessive dependence on the single-peaked notion of social stratification.

Most of the studies that followed were anticlimactic—studies such as Robert Presthus, *Men at the Top: A Study of Community Power* (1964), dealing with two small up-state New York communities, or Aaron Wildavsky, *Leadership in a Small Town* (1964), a study of Oberlin, Ohio. New analytic ground was broken, however, by combining comparative with longitudinal analysis, in a study of decision-making in four communities, *The Rulers and the Ruled* (1964), by Robert A. Agger, Daniel Goldrich, and Bert E. Swanson. Stability and change were treated as functions of convergent and divergent tendencies in the preferences, demands, and expectations of both community leaders and ordinary citizens. This work perhaps represented the most extensive and most catholic empirical study in the well-researched field of community power.

How diverse research approaches can lead to different findings about the nature and distribution of political power was evident in a collection of research papers by Morris Janowitz (ed.), *Community Political Systems* (1961). And a critical appraisal of the "stratification approach" to the study of community power and elucidation of the pluralist alternative were provided by Nelson W. Polsby in *Community Power and Political Theory* (1963).

What all of these studies suggest is that even if power is not a myth, it is a mystery—an "appearance" that can be found if one wishes to find it, a "disappearance" that vanishes if one does not wish to find it. As a result, there has been much controversy among scholars of community politics about proper procedures of inquiry. It seems that whether power is found or not found is related, in part at least, to the investigator's predispositions which, in turn, influence his choice of research procedures. If one proceeds from the admitted fact that a community's resources are unequally distributed, so that some people have more wealth or status than others, and if one assumes that those with wealth and status alone make all the important decisions, then, indeed, power is "found." But do the rich and respected really make the decisions—all decisions or only some decisions? What decisions do they make? In contrast to the "stratification school" of power analysis, the "pluralists" do not begin their inquiry by assuming the existence of a power elite but rather by searching for those who in fact participate in the making of important decisions.

There is much to be said in favor of the pluralist approach. Concerned less with the social backgrounds and identities of would-be participants in the political process and more with the actual roles of those who actively participate in local decision-making, the pluralists find a wide dispersion of effective decision-making centers that vary from issue area to issue area. On some issues only small groups of interested persons may participate in making community-wide decisions; on other issues, elected or administrative officials may in fact make the decisions; on still other issues the local electorate may have the final say-so. But, on most decisions, the policy-making process is likely to be carried on in many arenas at once, involving a great variety of actors from humble petitioners to the boss of a political machine, from apathetic voters to the executive director of a chamber of commerce, from isolated individuals to the leader of a disciplined labor union. The outcome of this multifaceted political process may in part be determined by the position of the actors in the hierarchy of valued positions, as the stratification theorists assume; but it may also be determined by actors' strategies, their bargaining skills, unanticipated opportunities—in short, by the kaleidoscopic quality of the political game. The pluralists do not find that these actors overlap from one issue area to the next. Some perhaps do, but rarely often enough to deserve being called "men of power." If power there is in this pluralist image of the community, it is fragmented, dispersed, and noncumulative. But if this is so, power is surely of limited use in explaining the political process, and it cannot serve as the central organizing concept of politics as wealth does in the study of economics.

Related to the pluralist studies were a number of other works which, however, were less concerned with the problem of power and more with the "functions" that the community political process serves. Martin Meyerson and Edward C. Banfield had pioneered this genre in *Politics, Planning and the Public Interest* (1955), a study of public housing in Chicago. The same city was the locale for Peter H. Rossi and Robert A. Dentler's *The Politics of Urban Renewal* (1961). Four functions of the policy process—promoting economic growth, providing life's amenities, maintaining traditional services, and arbitrating conflicting interests—were formulated by Oliver P. Williams and Charles R. Adrian in *Four Cities: A Study in Comparative Policy Making* (1963). That "managing conflict in matters of public importance" is the major function of local government was the central thesis of the first text synthesizing the new research findings, Edward C. Banfield and James Q. Wilson, *City Politics* (1963). That policy innovations are made by the minority, or rather the "majority-in-the-making," was the argument of Theodore J. Lowi in a historical study, *At the Pleasure of the Mayor: Patronage and Power in New York City, 1898-1958* (1964).

For social scientists, the "metropolitan problem" is composed of innumerable substantive issues—from traffic congestion to air pollution and crime on the streets. For political scientists, the problem is largely the fragmentation of responsibility due to lack of integration among the metro-area's sometimes competing, sometimes conflicting, sometimes overlapping, sometimes cooperating, and sometimes merely coexistent jurisdictions. If an earlier literature had been more concerned with the question of governmental reform, the recent literature was more likely to explain why reform efforts had failed, and why and how, despite all the difficulties, the metro-area manages to survive as a viable system of sorts. John C. Bollens and Henry J. Schmandt, in *The Metropolis, Its People, Politics and Economic Life* (1965), wrote a broad survey of the problems besetting the modern metropolis that took account of both recent empirical research and the older reformist propositions Most other works dealt with particular areas. Robert C. Wood, after pioneering a study of the suburban phenomenon from a political perspective, *Suburbia: Its People and Their Politics* (1959), analyzed the working of the New York metropolitan region—"one of the great unnatural wonders of the world" —in *1400 Governments* (1961). Roscoe C. Martin and Frank J. Munger edited a series of case studies of metropolitan decision-making, *Decisions in Syracuse* (1961). Edward Sofen, in *The Miami Metropolitan Experiment* (1963), and Brett W. Hawkins, in *Nashville Metro: The Politics of City-Council Consolidation* (1966), described two of the successful instances of metropolitan reorganization to date. Few of these works contributed much to modern political theory. A notable exception was *The Integration of Political Communities* (1964), a collection of papers by Philip E. Jacob and James V. Toscano (eds.), which sought to develop theoretical propositions about areal integration by juxtaposing international and metropolitan problems.

COMPARATIVE POLITICS: METHOD OR FIELD?

Only a generation ago it was still common to think and speak of forms of government in terms of the constitutional charters that formally ordered political relationships in most political systems. Indeed, having a written constitution was considered the defining characteristic of modern government (though even then the case of England, with its unwritten constitution, created some difficulties). Constitutionalism had become, in the outgoing eighteenth and throughout the nineteenth centuries, the dominant ideology of government-makers, and it was identified with liberalism, democracy, and progress. Man's liberation from the bondage of feudalism and monarchic absolutism was sought through constitutional safeguards, notably some kind of separation of powers and a bill of rights. In an era in which there was infinite hope for a better future, forms of government that did not conform to constitutional standards and the rule of law—say Russian Czardom, Chinese feudalism, or Latin-American dictatorship—were largely considered deviant. In due time, it was expected, the inevitable pressure toward progress would surely bring these deviant forms into line with Western standards of constitutionalism.

The course of political history in the years after World War I did not fulfill the optimism of the constitutionalists. Forms of government variously called totalitarian, fascist, authoritarian, or communist rather than liberal or democratic, appeared, not only in the constitutionally "backward" nations but also, as in the case of Germany or Italy, in nations that had been on the road toward constitutional government. And after World War II, while constitutional government acquired a new hold in the defeated Axis nations, various forms of communist government spread from the Soviet center to the Soviet periphery in countries as far apart as Yugoslavia and China. In the "new nations" of Asia and Africa, moreover, varieties of bureaucratic-autocratic or charismatic-autocratic governmental forms rather than liberal and democratic forms emerged as political realities. True, many of these nations, as previously the nations of Latin America, formally adopted constitutions patterned on Western models, but the reality behind these formal constitutions was quite different.

The great variety of governmental forms makes it both difficult to develop meaningful classifications and hazardous to propose valid generalizations. For, whatever the formal arrangements, a country's "living constitution"—its actual governmental practices—does not necessarily conform to the formal document. This is true even in the Western nations like the United States or Great Britain with their long constitutional traditions. Yet, underlying all forms of government seem to be two basic views which, in different mixes, define a country's constitutional stance and style. On the one hand, society is looked on as being made up of competing interests that generate demands and, therefore, conflicts which government is instituted to satisfy and resolve. On the other hand, society is looked upon as a rather inchoate and purposeless aggregate of individuals and groups which must be molded, through governmental activity and governmental leadership, into a viable social system. In the first view, government appears as the servant of the people and as the broker of conflicting interests that themselves articulate their needs and demands. In the second view, these needs and demands must be stimulated by government to bring about social change and development.

The increasing nationalization of politics contributed powerfully to the expanding multiverse of politics and, as we shall see, to a fundamental reorientation in the study of what had been called "comparative government." As people after people asserted their independence, it became evident that the models of government structures and functions based on the historical experiences of the Western nations were inadequate to cope with the problems of nation building in the developing countries. In these countries of Africa and Asia, cultural, social, and economic conditions made for problems which Western models of government under law, of peaceful change through the processes of representation and legislation, were unable to handle. Revolutions and coups d'etat, insurgency and civil war, charismatic and military regimes rather than democratic or parliamentary institutions accompanied the new nationhood. Recognition that highly diverse political cultures constitute political reality has enormously expanded the horizons of the multiverse of government. The boundaries of this multiverse are as yet little explored and only a few of its subdivisions have been thoroughly investigated.

Changes and circumstances in the real world, then, made for a renaissance in the study of comparative politics. The need to come to grips with new types of polity, and the concomitant need to develop new concepts in order to do so, were reflected in a number of single-country studies which, like the earlier institutional works of traditional "comparative government," were not really comparative, yet which strained for comparison by suggesting common theoretical departures. Among the best of these were David E. Apter, *The Gold Coast in Transition* (1955) and *The Political Kingdom of Uganda* (1961); James S. Coleman, *Nigeria: Background to Nationalism* (1958); Myron Weiner, *The Politics of Scarcity: Public Pressures and Political Response in India* (1962); Leonard Binder, *Religion and Politics in Pakistan* (1961) and *Iran: Political Development in a Changing Society* (1962); Aristide R. Zolberg, *One Party Government in the Ivory Coast* (1964); Robert E. Scott, *Mexican Government in Transition* (1959); and several others. But if single-country studies were to be more than descriptive accounts of particular political units, if they were to serve as bases for genuine comparison as a method of inference across national boundaries, the study of comparative politics, to deserve its name, seemed to require at least minimum agreement among researchers on empirically reliable and theoretically valid concepts.

The movement to advance comparative method by theoretical means was institutionalized in the early fifties in a "Committee on Comparative Politics" of the Social Science Research Council that, under the initial leadership of Gabriel A. Almond, came to have considerable influence on subsequent work. Beginning with a volume edited by Almond and James S. Coleman, *The Politics of the Developing Areas* (1960), which in an introductory essay presented a system-relevant, functional model of the polity, the initiative of the committee led to a series of books that at once pinpointed the advantages and difficulties of the new approaches, including *Communications and Political Development* (1963), Lucian W. Pye (ed.); *Bureaucracy and Political Development* (1963), Joseph La Palombara (ed.); *Political Modernization in Japan and Turkey* (1964), Robert E. Ward and Dankwart A. Rustow (eds.); *Education and Political Development* (1965), James S. Coleman (ed.); *Political Culture and Political Development* (1965), Pye and Sidney Verba (eds.); and *Political Parties and Political Development* (1966), Palombara and Myron Weiner (eds.).

While the studies included in these volumes were largely characterized by a common vocabulary that relied on structural-functional categories and concepts, and while these usages certainly provided new *bases* for comparison, they were still essentially case studies that do not permit those generalizing inferences that the comparative method presumably makes possible. Comparison requires more than common conceptual tools and functionally equivalent categories of analysis; it requires similar data collected by sufficiently similar techniques to make comparison genuinely comparative. This is not to say that the new studies did not yield new insights into political processes across nations. Influenced as they often were by historical sociology in the tradition of Max Weber, especially as that tradition had been forwarded in the theoretical work of Talcott Parsons, they were concerned with topics which the older institutional approach had neglected—problems of authority and legitimacy, cleavage and consensus, and those problems that, under names such as modernization, political development, or nation building, were of immediately topical interest. Indeed, one could come to the conclusion that "comparative politics" was less an empirical science than a modern version of classical political theory—more given to "understanding" than to testing propositions about reality. The flood of researches reported from all continents and conducted on all levels of analysis, from the individual to the nation, could neither be easily cumulated and codified nor evaluated.

As a result, like Aristotle, students of comparative politics sometimes resorted to classifications and typologies or to theoretical formulations of such extraordinary complexity that empirical testing became difficult, if not impossible. In the competition of classifications and theories, the latter chiefly concerned with the problems of change, none emerged persuasive enough to find universal scholarly consent. Hence the quest for a common vocabulary had the paradoxical and inadvertent effect of creating an almost Babylonic confusion. Comparative politics as a theoretical enterprise—in contrast to the empirical study of national systems, subnational institutions, or political behavior—threatened to become a scholastic game of definitions. A valiant effort to provide a comprehensive framework for comparative analysis that would accommodate both structural-functional and developmental categories of analysis was made by Almond and G. Bingham Powell in *Comparative Politics: A Developmental Approach* (1966). A volume of articles presenting diverse perspectives was Harry Eckstein and David Apter (eds.), *Comparative Politics* (1963).

Studies of "development" or "modernization" set the major tone of the work on comparative politics in the decade under review. These studies ranged from sweeping historical accounts, such as Rupert Emerson's *From Empire to Nation* (1960), to sweeping analytic treatises, such as Apter's *The Politics of Modernization* (1965) or Marion J. Levy's *Modernization and the Structure of Societies* (1965); from intensive studies of colonialism as a point of departure for modernization, such as J. S. Furnivall's *Colonial Policy and Practice: A Comparative Study of Burma and Netherlands India* (1956), to theoretically oriented works on particular problems of nation building, such as Clifford Geertz (ed.), *Old Societies and New States: A Quest for Modernity in Asia and Africa* (1963), Karl W. Deutsch and William J. Foltz (eds.),*Nation-Building* (1963), J. Roland Pennock, *Self-Government in Modernizing Nations* (1964), Reinhard Bendix, *Citizenship and Nation Building* (1964), or T. H. Marshall, *Class, Citizenship, and Social Development* (1964); from descriptive accounts of the experience in new states, such as Marver H. Bernstein's *The Politics of Israel: The First Decade of Statehood* (1957), to analytic studies of old states, such as Seymour M. Lipset's *The First New Nation* (1963), a book on the emergence of the United States; from case studies of purposive planning for modernity, such as Charles T. Goodsell's *Administration of a Revolution: Executive Reform in Puerto Rico under Governor Tugwell, 1941–1946* (1965), to broad prescriptive treatments, such as Edward W. Weidner's *Technical Assistance in Public Administration Overseas: The Case for Development Administration* (1964). Analytic problematics were treated in A. F. K. Organski, *The Stages of Political Development* (1965), and in Robert T. Holt and John E. Turner, *The Political Basis of Economic Development* (1965), which reversed to good effect the conventional ordering of the political and economic variables in this type of theory and research. Perhaps the most lucid account of the problems involved was a slender volume by Pye, *Aspects of Political Development* (1965), that identified a number of "crises"—of identity, legitimacy, penetration, participation, and integration—on whose successful resolution political development presumably depends.

The ever increasing scope of governmental activities in the Western and Communist worlds and the corresponding quest for the good life in the new nations—their "rising expectations"—has brought about an interpenetration of politics and economics, of public and private affairs, previously unknown in the history of mankind. Nations continue to differ a great deal in the degree to which the satisfaction of human needs is handled by the public and private sectors of society. But the responsibility of government to provide for the public welfare has become universally accepted. People everywhere expect government, whatever its structure, to meet their minimum demands for health, housing, education, jobs, and security. As a result, even in a highly developed country like the United States, where the private sector still satisfies a wide variety of human interests, various forms of government ownership, control, regulation, aid, advice, and stimulation have become integral parts of the political process. Men are disagreed as to whether the increased role of government in human affairs has limited or widened any one individual's range of opportunities; but most men are probably agreed that, under modern conditions of economic and technological complexity, the problem of basic human needs will in the end be decided by pragmatic rather than by ideological considerations. Moreover, the ever increasing demands made by men freed from feudal bondage have not only contributed to governmental expansion and complexity; they have also enormously increased the domain of the private sector, to such a degree that one has come to speak of the "domain of private governments." Although public government remains at the apex of the political multiverse, it has its rivals in the private sector for the loyalties of men. Huge industrial and financial corporations, giant labor unions, farmer organizations, professional associations, and a myriad of other collectivities increasingly "govern" the conduct of their members, not only within these organizations, but also in relation to public government. Private organizations and associations not only intervene between the individual citizen and his public government, but also carry a considerable part of the governing burdens and of all the responsibilities this involves.

Interest or pressure groups as carriers of private demands on government on the subnational level had long been studied in the United States. Only slowly and often reluctantly did students of comparative politics proceed with similar analyses in other countries. Comparative work on interest or pressure groups was stimulated by a symposium edited by Henry M. Ehrman, *Interest Groups on Four Continents* (1958). Ehrman had pioneered the kind of work proposed in this volume in *Organized Business in France* (1957), and in due time was followed by Harry Eckstein's *Pressure Group Politics: The Case of the British Medical Association* (1960), Joseph La Palombara, *Interest Groups in Italian Politics* (1964), and Samuel H. Beer, *British Politics in the Collectivist Age* (1965). These studies tended to put in sharp relief the culture-bound character of American theoretical formulations about group politics.

Increasingly in Western nations the government comes to set national policies quite independently of the wishes or demands of social or individual interests. In the Western nations, because of its control over resources through taxation, the government is in a strong position to manipulate the economy through its spending policies, taxing policies, setting of interest rates, and so on, quite independent of the particular preferences of the interests affected by these policies. On the other hand, in developing nations government cannot afford to be altogether unresponsive to the articulation of important interests, should such articulation occur. Even in totalitarian societies like the Soviet Union where centralized national planning is at the heart of the "living constitution," the government is likely to be sensitive to the preferences of particular interests that have emerged since the revolution and occupy high status positions in Soviet society—say the professions, the military, or the bureaucracy.

Not unexpectedly, given the normative interest in "development," a good deal of work centered in work on administrative structures and processes in the developing nations. This work served to raise important questions about the relevance of theories of bureaucracy in non-Western settings. Morroe Berger, in *Bureaucracy and Society in Modern Egypt* (1957), pioneered the study of a higher civil service in a transitional society. Henry F. Goodnow's *The Civil Service of Pakistan: Bureaucracy in a New Nation* (1964), Robert O. Tilman's *Bureaucratic Transition in Malaya* (1964), and above all, Fred W. Riggs's *Administration in Developing Countries: The Theory of Prismatic Society* (1964), pointed up the weakness of attempts to apply Western principles of public administration in non-Western countries. Riggs, in particular, argued that the "prismatic" society reacts to its own problems in its own characteristic ways, and that it is perhaps more stable than the "traditional-transitional-modern" typology of development allows for. Noteworthy also in this connection is Karl A. Wittfogel's *Oriental Despotism: A Comparative Study of Total Power* (1957); S. N. Eisenstadt's impressive historical-sociological account of past bureaucracies, *The Political Systems of Empires* (1963); and Barrington Moore's *Social Origins of Dictatorship and Democracy: Lord and Peasant in the Making of the Modern World* (1966).

The interest in non-Western bureaucratic phenomena seemed to have revived a concern with administrative institutions in the West, with special emphasis on historical development. For instance, Herbert Jacob, in *German Administration since Bismarck: Central Authority vs. Local Autonomy* (1963), dealt with the problem of bureaucratic responsiveness to public demands; or Robert C. Fried, in *The Italian Prefects: A Study in Administrative Politics* (1963), analyzed the circumstances under which local administrative institutions developed. The modern political invention of the "ombudsman"—a commissioner appointed by the legislature to investigate and, if necessary, redress individual grievances about administrative abuses, prominent in some Scandinavian countries and elsewhere—was discussed in a volume edited by Donald C. Rowat, *The Ombudsman: Citizen's Defender* (1965). Local administrative problems of the metropolitan area were treated in Frank Smallwood's excellent *Greater London: The Politics of Metropolitan Reform* (1965).

Party politics in particular nations continued to be of specialized scholarly concern. Among the best of these studies were Richard L. Sklar, *Nigerian Political Parties: Power in an Emergent African Nation* (1963), which delved into the crisscrossing interests and loyalties of a highly pluralist society; Clement H. Moore, *Tunisia since Independence: The*

Dynamics of One-Party Government (1965), which examined the ability of a regime given to the cult of personality to build durable institutions; Robert W. Anderson's *Party Politics in Puerto Rico* (1965), which suggested how a party can become an identifiable unit through identification with its leader and founder; or two comprehensive works, Ruth S. Morgenthau's *Political Parties in French-Speaking West Africa* (1964), and a volume edited by James S. Coleman and Carl G. Roseberg, *Political Parties and National Integration in Tropical Africa* (1964). The peculiar relationship between racial tensions and party politics was treated by Gwendolyn M. Carter in *The Politics of Inequality: South Africa Since 1948* (1958). One of the few books that studied politics abroad at the local level was Kurt Steiner's *Local Government in Japan* (1965). The frustrations of a party leadership deprived of contact with its mass following was the subject of Lewis J. Edinger's *German Exile Politics: The Social Democratic Executive Committee in the Nazi Era* (1956). The tendency of parties in a two-party system to become more and more alike was analyzed by Robert T. McKenzie in *British Political Parties: The Distribution of Power within the Conservative and Labour Parties* (1964). A few books concerned themselves with the working of legislatures, such as Gerhard Loewenberg's *Parliament in the German Political System* (1966), Duncan MacRae's methodologically sophisticated *Parliament, Parties, and Society in France, 1946–1958* (1967), and Allan Kornberg's *Canadian Legislative Behavior* (1967), which made explicit comparisons with similar studies of legislatures in the American states.

These and other national or subnational studies suggested that the study of comparative politics still contained a highly idiographic component that could not easily be erased by a common vocabulary. Moreover, the common vocabulary was by no means as common as the terms used might have suggested. As is so often the case in the study of man and society, a concept like "function"—found in almost all of the recent works on comparative politics—has different meanings and was used in different ways. Quite often, function was simply used to describe the activities or tasks of an individual or organization. But this usage did not prove useful because not only do similar structures perform different tasks or functions, but similar functions (tasks) may be performed by different structures. The latter realization led to a search for "equivalent functions," protecting the analyst from comparing things that were not comparable and bringing more realism to the study of political institutions.

Somewhat different was another approach that used the concept of function in a deductive manner. This approach was largely cultivated by those who perceived politics in terms of "system." "Functional requisite analysis" would ask, initially, what functions *must* be performed if the political system was to be maintained. This approach seemed to have the virtue of universal applicability, equally useful in the study of primitive or highly developed politics, and it seemed to be promising from a comparative point of view. But its weaknesses soon became manifest. Often certain functions were not performed or only unsatisfactorily performed, yet the system seemed to be working reasonably well. Moreover, in its search for system-maintaining functions, this approach tended to neglect the needs of individuals or groups which were possibly opposed to the interests of the system as a whole, making for political conflict—certainly as much an aspect of politics as harmony.

Finally, the concept of function was used to refer to the consequences of political action—but in two senses. In one sense, it asked whether a given political activity in fact served the purpose that it was intended to serve. Rather than assuming that a function must be performed, it assumed that political action is in part purposive and inquired whether the sought-after end is being attained. This usage had another payoff. It directed attention to consequences that were not contemplated—consequences that might be functional or dysfunctional for the political system as a whole or for particular individuals or interests, depending on the observer's valuational standpoint. But, in another sense, functions as consequences were treated as "effects" in the fashion of causal analysis. The distinction between these two uses was often obscured, but it is an important one because it presumes quite different research strategies. If one thinks of functions as effects, research begins with these effects and searches for sufficient or necessary conditions (causes), or both. If one treats functions as consequences, one assumes that the causes are known and proceeds heuristically. Whatever the merits of this approach, it was unlikely to make for a nomothetic science of politics. This is quite evident if one contrasts the single-nation or subnational studies with those that were designed to test hypotheses across national boundaries in order to arrive at generalizations that can withstand the proof of cross-national falsification. In an important work, *Political Oppositions in Western Democracies* (1966), the editor, Robert A. Dahl, utilized to good effect a variety of individual national contributions in developing cross-national hypotheses about the causes and consequences of political opposition.

Hypotheses and variables familiar in the American context gave guidance to a survey research study, based on interviews with both voters and party officials in selected communities, *Political Parties in Norway* (1964), by Henry Valen and Daniel Katz. Studies like these, more often reported in journal articles than in books, eschewed the tendency to develop comprehensive conceptual schemes for the analysis of whole systems and preferred to test hypotheses of the middle range in selected contexts. Similarly, Leon D. Epstein, in *British Politics in the Suez Crisis*

(1964), suggested and tested a variety of propositions about the role of the parties in a crisis situation. James L. Payne, in *Labor and Politics in Peru: The System of Political Bargaining* (1965), examined the conditions under which violence may be rationally used as an instrument of political bargaining over economic issues. Morris Janowitz, in *The Military in the Political Development of New Nations* (1964), suggested generic propositions about the capacity of the military to rule, modernize, and build mass support. In a study based on secondary analyses, *Party and Society: The Anglo-American Democracies* (1963), Robert R. Alford concerned himself with the integrative and adaptive effects of cleavages evident in class, regional, and religious voting patterns in a number of "advanced" nations. Fresh research from many nations, focusing on questions of consensus and cleavage, was reported in a volume by Seymour M. Lipset and Stein Rokkan (eds.), *Party Systems and Voter Alignments* (1967).

Hypothesis-testing studies, unlike studies cast in various functional formulations, are predicated on the availability of mass statistical data. The need for "data-making" to facilitate internation comparison was only recently recognized in a field that traditionally relied on governmental and other documents, newspapers and more or less casual observations. One step in the direction of making gross characterizations of countries around the globe in terms of institutional, functional, behavioral, and other variables available for quantitative analysis was Arthur Banks and Robert Textor's *A Cross-Polity Survey* (1963). Although the reliability and validity of the "data" presented in this volume was marred by the subjective-judgmental nature of the procedures used, the book employed bivariate analysis as at least initial indications of relationships that may be significant features of the world's national political systems. Bruce M. Russett, Hayward R. Alker, Karl W. Deutsch, and Harold D. Lasswell (eds.), in a *World Handbook of Political and Social Indicators* (1964), stated systematic estimates of probable error margins in census and other quantitative data and used refined statistical methods of summarization. Data evaluation and suggestions for the use of quantitative data were presented in a volume by Richard L. Merritt and Stein Rokkan, (eds.), *Comparing Nations: The Use of Quantitative Data in Cross-National Research* (1965).

Efforts at comparative analysis in a cross-cultural perspective through studies of the individual actor—whether ruler or ruled—as the empirical unit of analysis remained limited if suggestive. This was probably due, in part, to the disrepute into which the earlier "national character" studies (of the anthropologists) had fallen; in part, to the fact that large-scale studies of individuals in foreign countries required resources that were not readily available; and in part, to failure in training young students of comparative politics in the methods of modern behavioral science. If one compares studies done abroad on individual behavior with those of American politics, the retarded development of "comparative political behavior" analysis is evident.

A great deal of previously unavailable information about political behavior at the citizen level in the Soviet Union was provided in a massive study based on interviews with several hundred Soviet refugees, written questionnaires solicited from several thousand emigrees, and intensive life histories: *How the Soviet System Works: Cultural, Psychological and Social Themes* (1956), by Raymond A. Bauer, Alex Inkeles, and Clyde Kluckhohn, and *The Soviet Citizen* (1959), by Alex Inkeles and Raymond A. Bauer. How and why communism proves appealing in an underdeveloped country was examined by Lucian Pye in a pioneering study, *Guerilla Communism in Malaya: Its Social and Political Meaning* (1956), which was based on intensive interviews with sixty Malayan Chinese who had joined and left the communist movement. In a subsequent work, *Politics, Personality and Nation Building: Burma's Search for Identity* (1962), Pye again made use of interviews with selected elites to probe into the anxieties and self-doubts of political leaders confronting the task of nation building. An interesting, semipsychoanalytic study covering a seven-day period in the politics of a nation was Constantin Melnik and Nathan Leites's *The House without Windows: France Selects a President* (1958). Cultural analysis guided Edward Banfield's *The Moral Basis of a Backward Society* (1958), a study of a retarded Italian community, and Leites's *On the Game of Politics in France* (1959). Anthropologist G. William Skinner contributed a study relevant to comparative political behavior in *Leadership and Power in the Chinese Community in Thailand* (1958). A book of interest in this connection was *Political Anthropology* (1966), by Marc J. Swartz, Victor W. Turner, and Arthur Tuden.

Only two major works based on mass sample surveys across national boundaries were reported. The first, *The Passing of Traditional Society: Modernizing the Middle East* (1958), by Daniel Lerner, emphasized the "mobile personality" as the agent of modernization in six Middle Eastern countries. The second, *The Civic Culture: Attitudes and Democracy in Five Nations* (1963), by Gabriel Almond and Sidney Verba, gave vitality to the study of comparative political behavior. Using a typology of "parochial," "subject," and "participant" styles of political culture, Almond and Verba sought answers to questions about the functioning and viability of democratic political systems related to and finding expression in the political beliefs, aspirations, and participation of citizens. The foreign policy attitudes of government leaders and other members of national elites were the subject of Lloyd A. Free's *Six Allies and a Neutral* (1959).

Studies of elites and their transformation at the level of the individual were continued in a number of countries. Frederick W. Frey's *The Turkish Political Elite* (1965) and William L. Guttsman's *The British Political Elite* (1963) used both quantitative and qualitative data to provide relevant insights into the political behavior of British politicians. Morris Janowitz, in *The Professional Soldier* (1960), though primarily dealing with the changing profile of the military in the United States, introduced comparative data from European nations that illuminated his analysis. Dwaine Marvick edited a volume, *Political Decision-Makers: Recruitment and Performance* (1961), that included treatments of elites in different nations on different levels of government.

Men move other men and nations, but men are possessed by ideas and ideals that give impetus and direction to their movements. Modern politics, in a comparative perspective, can be written as a history of political ideologies. Ideologies—more or less coherent and consistent sets of beliefs, values, opinions, and aspirations—serve as sources of obedience or consent, or they serve as sources of revolt. They are justifications for deeds done and promises of deeds to be done. They seek to unmask the pretensions of political enemies and to mask the real intentions of their advocates. But, above all, they give meaning to what men do in politics. Even a politics that eschews ideology is ideological. Such avoidance is itself an ideological posture in the arena of politics.

The "age of ideology" was ushered in by the American and French Revolutions, but many earlier movements were ideological. The Crusades, military operations at the borders of medieval Christendom, were fought in the name of the Christian religion, and the Crusaders conquered or died as missionaries for their beliefs. Similarly, the religious wars of the sixteenth and seventeenth centuries, fought in reality more to protect or expand dynastic interests than to carry on the Protestant and Catholic missions, were yet deeply influenced by the competing Christian faiths. Military exhaustion rather than ideological victory or defeat brought an end to combat in the name of religion.

But religious were soon replaced by secular ideological movements. Social class and later national interests rather than religious affiliation provided the bases of ideological conflict. Liberalism became the ideology that, from the sixteenth century on, aided the rising bourgeoisie in breaking down the fetters of feudalism, resisting monarchical absolutism, and ushering in modern capitalism and constitutionalism. Liberalism, associated with industrial and commercial capitalism as the new mode of economic production and distribution, and with individualism as the new mode of defining societal goals, provided the ideological underpinnings of the American and French Revolutions and, in the nineteenth century, triumphed throughout the Western world.

No matter how pervasive an ideology may be as an item of political culture, it is invariably challenged by counterideologies. How effective these counterideologies are seems to depend, in large part, on their existential roots. Liberalism was successful because it was the ideology of a class that, due to its increasing control of the economy, was bound to become dominant. Nineteenth-century conservatism, occasionally successful, ultimately failed because it was the ideology of a class that sought to revive an ancestral order out of step with the march of events. Not so with socialism which, freed from its earlier utopian moorings, was formulated by Karl Marx and Friedrich Engels into the ideology of the growing working class of the nineteenth century. It became an effective ideology in two ways. Initially, Marxian socialism was, in many respects, a continuation of the humanistic tradition of liberalism. Although Marxian economic theory predicted the collapse of the capitalist order, it derived from classical economic theory; and Marxian political theory sought to liberate the working class from the shackles of bourgeois domination, just as liberalism had sought to free the bourgeoisie from feudal and absolutist oppression. In its social-democratic version, therefore, the Marxian ideology was a continuation of the liberal quest for freedom, equality, and human dignity, and democratic socialism was liberal in temper and outlook. In its communist version, as developed by Lenin, Marxism was derailed from its humanistic bases and became the ideology of a movement that demanded a degree of loyalty and commitment never before known in the world of politics.

Soviet Communism as an ideological phenomenon suggests that ideology not only molds political action, but is molded by it. The particular circumstances that surround the victory of the Soviets in Czarist Russia, still more feudal than capitalist in economic organization, and the tradition of state omnipotence in Russia gave the socialist-communist ideology its peculiar format. More than either liberalism or democratic socialism, communism was both profoundly nationalistic and internationalistic. Moscow became the center of a world revolutionary movement more than Paris had ever been. The nationalism of the French Revolution, initially expansionist, was effectively contained by the nationalisms of the states that rose to defeat Napoleon. The nationalism of Soviet Communism, though also contained, was international. Today, of course, it is being contained not only by Western resistance, but also by the varieties of new national communisms that have evolved in Yugoslavia, Romania, China, and elsewhere. Like Western liberalism, Soviet Communism is being adapted to national exigencies and conditions.

Conventionally, the study of ideology has been limited to the study of the written vocabulary and the history of political movements. It largely neglected the important problem of just how it happens that ideological thinking so strongly influences the behavior of individuals, not only of leaders but of followers as well. If the compelling force of ideology is to be understood, its roots in the personality of the "true believer" require scientific inquiry. In regard to communism, Almond pioneered this type of analysis in *The Appeals of Communism* (1954), but most works were in the literary tradition, combining the analysis of texts with historical study. The spread of communism to China occasioned two noteworthy books, Franz Schurmann's *Ideology and Organization in Communist China* (1966), and Arthur A. Cohen's *The Communism of Mao Tse-Tung* (1964). Of the numerous books on the Soviet Union, Adam Ulam, in *The Unfinished Revolution* (1960), interpreted communism as an industrializing and modernizing movement. Z. Brzezinski and Samuel Huntington, in *Political Power: USA/USSR* (1963), presented a broadly conceived comparison of ideological patterns, elite transformations, and policy-making processes.

The peculiar conditions surrounding the success of the communist ideology in nations which, had Marx's predictions been correct, would have been the last rather than the first to be communized, have made it difficult to sort out the humanistic and totalitarian components of communism. Whether totalitarian techniques of oppression were essential ingredients of communism has always been a controversial question. There is little such disagreement with respect to the ideology of National Socialism which, for a score of years, made Germany a totalitarian nightmare and threatened to usher in a totalitarian world order. German fascism was an ideology that unequivocally reversed both liberal and communist values. Hate rather than love, inequality rather than equality, superiority rather than fraternity, slavery rather than freedom, unreason rather than reason were the values at the core of the national socialist ideology. It was an ideology of destruction rather than of construction, of nihilism rather than humanity. All ideologies are based on deeply felt emotions, but National Socialism elevated emotion to the status of philosophy. Carl J. Friedrich and Brzezinski, in *Totalitarian Dictatorship and Autocracy* (1956), wrote an epitaph to the traditional and abundant literature on totalitarianism.

All modern ideologies, though transnational because of the universality of their claims to righteousness, have been closely associated with nationalism which, over the long run, has proved to be the most effective force in modern politics. In an age in which the national state is the predominant form of political organization and in which there is reason to believe that the national state may well be an obsolete institution in the face of needs for more global forms of integration, it is important to remember that nationalism once was a revolutionary ideology. It was revolutionary in the sense that it defined as the objective of any political community the welfare of the nation as a whole as against the welfare of those who had ruled in the name of God, dynasty, or social class. Once equality and fraternity had been recognized as the values that, along with liberty, best served the interests of all men, liberalism found in nationalism its most potent ally for the realization of these values. For nationalism was capable of mobilizing the masses of men by appealing to their deepest emotions and by satisfying their most profound longings. Nationalism gave men a sense of mutual identification hitherto unknown in the annals of mankind; it gave them an object of love and affection that could be widely shared; and it gave them a sense of sacrifice. By rallying men to the banners of the nation, nationalism introduced a new sense of the heroic into the American and French, and later into the nineteenth- and twentieth-century revolutions, including those that, after World War II, led to the end of colonial rule. To this day, though repeatedly challenged by the counterideology of internationalism as a more inclusive human ideal, nationalism remains the most powerful ideology of the modern world.

The vitality of nationalism as an ideological weapon was attested by a number of works dealing with the phenomenon on different continents. In a loosely constructed but suggestive volume, *The Conflict Society: Reaction and Revolution in Latin America* (1961), Kalman H. Silvert probed into the perplexing ideological patterns of Latin America. Gerhard Masur, in *Nationalism in Latin America* (1966), provided further evidence. The special case of an apparently genuinely native socialist ideology with strong nationalist tinges was the subject of Harry Kantor's *The Ideology and Program of the Peruvian Aprista Movement* (1966). Leonard W. Doob, in *Patriotism and Nationalism: Their Psychological Foundations* (1964), examined the significance of nationalism to political and economic development, with particular reference to tiny South Tyrol. Leonard Binder, in *The Ideological Revolution in the Middle East* (1964), suggested that Arab nationalism has never become a truly secular movement, thus retarding the process of change from the traditionalist religious model of the state to the modern nation-state. John H. Kausky edited a volume stressing the ideological factor in political change, *Political Change in Underdeveloped Countries: Nationalism and Communism* (1962). Two volumes bringing together a variety of empirical studies concerning the relationship between ideology and political behavior were noteworthy: *Ideology and Discontent*, David Apter (ed.), and *Cleavages, Ideologies and Party Systems: Contributions to Comparative Political Sociology* (1964), Erik Allardt and Yrjo Littunen (eds.).

No limited survey of the literature can do justice to the vast number of works dealing with foreign nations. An attempt was made here to present outstanding as well as typical contributions.

INTERNATIONAL POLITICS: URGENCY AND COMPLEXITY

Of the events that contributed to the changed nature of politics in the middle of the twentieth century, none has probably been more crucial than man's experience of two world wars and the intervening totalitarian holocaust. For, as a result of this experience, our easy assumptions about "progress" in a well ordered and rational universe of politics have been shattered. No longer can it be assumed that it is man's inevitable destiny to be free from corporate bondage—be the corporation the state, the church, the party, or the firm. No longer can it be taken for granted that world organizations like the United Nations will inevitably yield to stronger international or even perhaps supernational government. Whatever forces may exist making for global integration, they are offset by forces making for national or regional dispersion. It has become clear that progress is forever accompanied by decay, and that under certain conditions men may cherish security more than freedom, or uncontrolled government more than wide citizen participation in the political process.

The critical problems of international politics stem from the very simple fact that the system of nation-states that evolved in the last three hundred years lacks a common supreme authority with a preponderance of legitimate force. It is true that this system has developed an intricate machinery of institutions and processes by which many of the difficulties arising out of the existence of independent nations can be and are adjusted by peaceful means—through diplomacy, treaties, international organizations, mediation, arbitration, and other modes of political settlement. But each nation, no matter how large or small, reserves for itself the right to be the ultimate judge of its own interests and to act on behalf of these national interests as it sees fit, subject only to its own calculations, correct or not, of its capacity to sustain and defend its interests by military force. "Power politics" is based on the coercive capabilities of individual nations or coalitions of nations.

The very nature of the system of nation-states makes this outcome inevitable. For, rather than striving for the creation of transnational instrumentalities that would integrate its diverse units into a cohesive whole, just as lesser territorial units had been integrated into the nation-state, the Western and now the world system of sovereign states encouraged the aspirations of peoples for national independence and made national self-determination the supreme value of international conduct. Even though, in fact, a nation's actual ability to define its goals and run its foreign affairs as it sees fit may be severely limited by its resources and the prevailing pattern of the world system of states which may be controlled by "great powers," as immediately before and after World War I, or by "superpowers" as after World War II, the principle of national sovereignty contains within itself the seeds of its own destruction.

This is not to say that the system of nation-states is altogether chaotic. In the first place, within this system has developed a body of international law, relevant to the conduct of international relations, by which most nations abide even in time of war. The possibility of attaining a more peaceful international order through extending the rule of law to conflicts not presently regulated by international law was suggested by Grenville Clark and Louis B. Sohn in *World Peace Through World Law* (1960). Second, the world community, if such it can be called, has in fact developed a network of international economic cultural, technical, and social organizations which, even if their decisions are not binding because not backed by force, serve to reduce many of the causes of international conflict and alleviate, through voluntary consent, many common problems such as poverty, disease, unequal education, and so on. And while such international organizations as the old League of Nations and the present United Nations have not been effective in preventing the use of force in conflicts between the powers, and indeed often serve as instruments of power politics as much as instruments of pacification, they have provided some bases for international integration. Inis L. Claude's *Swords Into Ploughshares: The Problems and Progress of International Organization* (1964) was an excellent introduction into the subject.

The compelling urgency and exasperating complexity of the problems involved has made for an almost schizophrenic orientation in the academic study of "international politics." On the one hand, there was the continuing policy-oriented search for both immediate and remote "solutions" of the perplexing and threatening conditions that give rise to international tensions, conflicts, and wars. On the other hand, there was an increasingly abstract preoccupation with frameworks, theories or models which, at times, seemed to introduce more complexity than there is in reality, and which tended to take the study of international politics out of the domain of empirical investigation. There was also, of course, a huge amount of writing that was mainly descriptive, historical, or legal, and there was a perhaps even larger literature of a speculative character that was long on opinion but short on analysis. Only in the last few years did students of international politics come to realize that fresh "data-making" was as necessary a component of the scientific enterprise as the construction of models and theories.

The most ambitious theoretical attack on the complexity of international politics was made by scholars who, taking a global view, sought guidance in "general systems theory." The objective was to discover those self-regulative properties of the international system that were thought to make for international stability. Morton Kaplan, in *System and Process in International Politics* (1957), identified six types of international system—balance of power, loose bipolar, tight bipolar, universal, hierarchical, and unit veto. Best known, of course is the balance-of-power pattern in which each nation seeks to maximize its own power by seeking to thwart the efforts of another nation or coalition of nations to control the entire international system. Although this pattern has been effective as a stabilizer, its tendency to make for competitive arms races has time and again upset the international equilibrium and led to armed combat. The bipolar pattern of two coexisting superpowers may similarly make for temporary stability in the international system, but its durability seems to require the presence of a "third force" to prevent its transformation into what has become known as "cold war."

Kaplan's analysis was rigorous and closely reasoned, if compulsively deductive and unduly abstract. In a later work, jointly authored with Nicholas deB. Katzenbach, *The Political Foundations of International Law* (1961), Kaplan speculated about the differences in international law that might correspond to particular theoretical systems. Working on a lower level of abstraction, being less committed to deduction and relying more on historical experiences, Richard N. Rosecrance, in *Action and Reaction in World Politics: International Systems in Perspective* (1963), was concerned with factors making for international stability and disturbance.

A systems approach influenced by the sociological theory of Talcott Parsons was articulated in George Modelski's analysis of *The Communist International System* (1960), while in *A Theory of Foreign Policy* (1962) the same author presented a "balance sheet theory" of the foreign policy process. Other system models were based on explicit or implicit conceptions of equilibrium. A direct approach was George Liska's *International Equilibrium: A Theoretical Essay on the Politics and Organization of Security* (1957) that examined the multiple meanings of the equilibrium concept and its uses in explaining stability and change in international relations. Many of the theoretical issues involved in system and equilibrium formulations of international politics were treated by several authors in Klaus Knorr and Sidney Verba (eds.), *The International System: Theoretical Essays* (1961).

Opposed to the abstract theorizing in terms of system and equilibrium were those theoreticians who sought guidance in history and preferred inductive treatment and comparison of historical situations. This position was articulated in a volume edited by Stanley H. Hoffman, *Contemporary Theory in International Relations* (1960). Adda B. Bozeman, in *Politics and Culture in International History* (1960), examined the course of foreign relations in ancient China, India, the Islamic world, and ancient and medieval Europe down to about 1500 A.D. F. H. Hinsley, in

Power and the Pursuit of Peace: Theory and Practice in the History of Relations between States (1963), stressed the history of diplomacy but had little to say about ideological and psychological factors. In an interesting work, *Imperialism: The Story and Significance of a Political Word, 1840–1960,* Richard Koebner and Helmut Dan Schmidt developed a "semantic approach to history" that examined the interrelationship of political action and political vocabulary.

Different in theoretical orientation was the approach of those who proceeded, in more philosophical fashion, from central problems and sought to answer them in speculative ways. Kenneth N. Waltz, for instance, in *Man, the State, and War: A Theoretical Analysis* (1959), one of the best books in this genre, sought the causes of war in the nature of man, the nature of the state, and the nature of international politics. More restrictive was the approach of Hans J. Morgenthau who, proceeding from assumptions about power motivations of rational actors, continued to espouse his position in *Dilemmas of Politics* (1958) and a revised edition of *Politics Among Nations: The Struggle for Power and Peace* (1960). Finally, reacting in part to the tendency of the more abstract theories to personify states or reify systems, Harold and Margaret Sprout developed an "ecological approach" in *The Ecological Perspective on Human Affairs, with Special Reference to International Politics* (1965), concerned with the relationship between the perceived and operational environments within which international political processes take place.

The difficulty of coming to empirical grips with the international political system as a whole directed students of international politics to the study of the influences that bear upon the shaping of foreign policies and the processes of policy development. The theoretical aspects and methodological problems of approaching international affairs from the foreign policy perspective were discussed in Richard C. Snyder, H. W. Bruck, and Burton Sapin, *Foreign Policy Decision Making: An Approach to the Study of International Politics* (1962), a reissue of an earlier, privately published volume. But few empirical studies followed the broad-gauge interactional model of Snyder and his associates. In general, studies of foreign-policy-making either dealt with its institutional aspects or they were case studies of particular policy-making situations. The best and most broadly conceived work was Burton M. Sapin's *The Making of United States Foreign Policy* (1966).

Among the case studies, by far the most thorough and enlightening, because conceived as a special case of the more general problem, was Bernard C. Cohen's *The Political Process and Foreign Policy: The Making of the Japanese Peace Settlement* (1957), which examined the role of the Senate, informal advisers, interest groups, public opinion, and the press in the making of the treaty with Japan. R. H. Dawson, in *The Decision to Aid Russia, 1941: Foreign Policy and Domestic Politics* (1959), paid particular attention to the role of public opinion. Also noteworthy was A. S. Whiting, *China Crosses the Yalu: The Decision to Enter the Korean War* (1960).

Institutional studies, interestingly, dealt more with the role of Congress than of the President in foreign-policy-making, probably because the Congress is more accessible than the White House. An important exception was Roger Hillsman's *To Move a Nation* (1967), a study of the politics of foreign policy during the Kennedy administration. The Congressional arena was explored by Holbert N. Carroll in *The House of Representatives and Foreign Policy* (1958), but no work similar in scope and depth dealt with the Senate. D. N. Farnsworth treated several aspects of senatorial participation in *The Senate Committee on Foreign Relations* (1961), and James A. Robinson brought together numerous case studies in order to generalize about foreign-policy-making in *Congress and Foreign Policy-Making: A Study of Legislative Influence and Initiative* (1962).

The ambiguous role of public opinion in foreign-policy-making did not receive the kind of attention that one might have expected in view of the refinement of the sample survey instrument in recent years. Alfred O. Hero, Jr., in *The Southerner and World Affairs* (1965), reviewed southern opinion on international affairs between 1936 and 1962, and James N. Rosenau, in *Public Opinion and Foreign Policy* (1961), presented an overview. The mediating function of the press in the foreign policy process was treated by Bernard C. Cohen, *The Press and Foreign Policy* (1963), and the emergence of an "attentive public" in connection with foreign aid legislation was analyzed by James N. Rosenau in *National Leadership and Foreign Policy: A Case Study in the Mobilization of Public Support* (1963).

More concerned with the content of foreign policy decisions were a number of general and special works utilizing different modes of analysis. Norman A. Graebner, in a tendentious book, *The New Isolationism: A Study of Politics and Foreign Policy Since 1950* (1956), studied the relationship between party politics and foreign policy since the outbreak of the Korean War. Cecil V. Crabb, Jr., raised disquieting questions in *Bipartisan Foreign Policy: Myth or Reality?* (1957). American relations with particular foreign nations were examined in a spate of books such as Russell H. Fiefield, *Southeast Asia in United States Policy* (1963), Frank C. Darling, *Thailand and the United States* (1965), or Henry A. Kissinger, *The Troubled Partnership: A Reappraisal of the Atlantic Alliance* (1965). Among these books, only one, Bruce M. Russett's *Community and Contention: Britain and America in the Twentieth Century* (1963), presenting a theory of capability and response as well as employing new methodological approaches, was likely to fascinate the scientifically oriented student of foreign affairs. A general behavioral analysis of negotiations in international conduct was Fred C. Iklé's *How Nations Negotiate* (1964).

In addition to country-specific studies, other works dealt with function-specific areas of foreign policy. Charles Wolf, Jr., in *Foreign Aid: Theory and Practice in Southern Asia* (1960), dealt with the multiple ends of foreign aid programs. Robert T. Holt and Robert W. van de Velde, in *Strategic Psychological Operations and American Foreign Policy* (1960), examined propaganda as an instrument of foreign policy. Harold L. Nieburg, in *Nuclear Secrecy and Foreign Policy* (1964), studied the policy process from the perspective of the requirement for secrecy. American interests and values as they affect space exploration policy were analyzed by Vernon Van Dyke in *Pride and Power: The Rationale of the Space Program* (1964). The relationship between international politics, the United Nations, and American foreign policy was the subject of Lincoln P. Bloomfield's *The U.N. and U.S. Foreign Policy* (1960). Hans J. Morgenthau, with his usual vigor, deplored the increasing purposelessness of American foreign policy and the tendency toward conformity in *The Purpose of American Politics* (1960). Rosenau, in a book of readings, *International Politics and Foreign Policy* (1961), pinpointed many of the research dilemmas facing the student of international relations and foreign politics.

Foreign policy decision-making affects the international political system, and its study may serve as a handle to understand it, but it is no substitute for describing or explaining policy-making *in* the international system *for* the system. Regional and international organizations have long been foci of scholarly interest in order to come close to the decision-making process in the international arena, but most of these studies have been historical, formal, and legal. A variety of such studies continued to be published—such as Lincoln B. Bloomfield's *Evolution or Revolution? The United Nations and the Problem of Peaceful Territorial Change* (1957), Walter R. Sharp's *Field Administration in the United Nations System* (1961), or Arthur L. Burns and Nino Heathcote's *Peace-keeping by U.N. Forces from Suez to the Congo* (1963), and numerous others. Also directly concerned with international processes were J. David Singer's *Financing International Organization: The United Nations Budget Process* (1961) and John Stoessinger's *Financing the United Nations* (1964). Few of these studies were either theoretically or methodologically interesting, as was also the case with studies of regional organizations or security systems. One might list Charles G. Fenwick, *The Organization of American States* (1963); Alvin J. Cottrell and James E. Dougherty, *The Atlantic Alliance* (1964); or Robert W. Macdonald, *The League of Arab States: A Study in the Dynamics of Regional Organization* (1965).

But there were also some notable exceptions. A theory of integration, substantiated by references to historical cases, was advanced by Karl W. Deutsch and others in *Political Community and the North Atlantic Area* (1957). New vistas along the same theoretical lines, derived from comparison of problems arising in the international and national-metropolitan arenas, were opened up in a volume to which Deutsch made major contributions, *The Integration of Political Communities* (1964), Philip E. Jacob and J. V. Toscano (eds.). An important theoretical contribution to the problems of regional unification was made by Joseph S. Nye, Jr., *Pan Africanism and East African Integration* (1965). Z. K. Brzezinski's *The Soviet Bloc* (1960) was a theory-relevant work on the politics of Eastern Europe.

The theoretically most convincing and empirically most solid contributions to the study of international organization were made in two volumes by Ernst B. Haas. In *The Uniting of Europe: Political, Social and Economic Forces, 1950-1957* (1958), Haas presented rich evidence as to how international questions of a functional kind—concerning coal and steel, atomic energy, customs and tariffs, and defense—became matters of international decision-making and were disposed of through international arrangements. In his second book, *Beyond the Nation-State: Functionalism and International Organization* (1964), a study of the International Labor Organization and perhaps the best of all the studies on international relations in the period, Haas examined the close relationship between international integration and the emergent functional needs of the international community. Also relevant in this connection were L. N. Lindberg's *The Political Dynamics of European Economic Integration* (1963), and James P. Sewell's *Functionalism and World Politics: A Study Based on United Nations Programs Financing Ecomonic Development* (1966).

International law remained a special subfield but more cultivated by lawyers than by political scientists. Of the less technical treatises, Philip C. Jessup's *Transnational Law* (1956) was critical of the distinction between domestic and international law and demanded recognition of individuals, corporations, and international organizations as well as of states as "subjects" of international law. New ideas were produced in Myres S. McDougal, Harold Lasswell, and I. A. Vlasic, *Law and Public Order in Space* (1963). International law "in the making" was treated by Werner Feld in *The Court of European Communities: New Dimensions in International Adjudication* (1964), which studied the effect of judges' professional backgrounds and qualifications on their decisions.

As long as the international order remains a "power system" of one kind or another, its understanding requires the analysis of the factors or determinants of national power. Klaus Knorr, in *The War Potential of*

Nations (1956), dealt with many of these determinants. Of course, the relative impact of the bases of power varies with changing circumstances. During the nineteenth century, a nation's geographical location enabled it to control important gateways of possible conquest; or its natural resources and population size were crucial in building up its military forces. In the two world wars, though both ultimately concluded by virtue of superior military power, such factors as the loyalty and sense of purpose of the population, though difficult to measure, were important ingredients of survival, as in the cases of Great Britain and Soviet Russia. Today the size and morale of the population is probably less important than a nation's technological progress, its ability to manipulate its economy, and its administrative know-how in managing men and machines.

In the wake of these changes, an ever increasing tide of books dealt with national—usually American—defense policies, the problem of deterrence, and the problem of developing appropriate controls. In fact, it was not uncommon to speak of "national security affairs" as an emerging subfield of political science. Perhaps no work received as much publicity as Herman Kahn's magisterial—for some tantalizing—study of deterrence, *On Thermonuclear War* (1960), although Henry A. Kissinger's *Nuclear Weapons and Foreign Policy* (1957), investigating limited atomic war as a deterrent, sounded equally ominous. Bernard Brodie's *Strategy in the Missile Age* (1959) dealt with air power, and Glenn H. Snyder's *Deterrence and Defense* (1961) with alternate strategies for deterring nuclear attacks. The problem of dealing with deterrence of lesser aggressions was treated by Robert E. Osgood in *Limited War: The Challenge to American Strategy* (1957), and Morton H. Halperin, in *Limited War in the Nuclear Age* (1963), searched for rational standards of conduct in military policy.

There was a great variety of other books whose titles convey the preoccupations of their authors: Paul Y. Hammond, *Organizing for Defense: The American Military Establishment in the Twentieth Century* (1961), was concerned with the factors affecting the organization and control of the armed forces; Harry H. Ransom, *Central Intelligence and National Security* (1958), and Roger Hilsman, *Strategic Intelligence and National Decisions* (1956), studied the relation between foreign policy and the intelligence services; Charles J. Hitch and Roland McKean, in *The Economics of Defense in the Nuclear Age* (1960), dealt with relevant economic problems. From the perspective of political science and in the tradition of pluralist politics, by far the most sensible of the writings on defense was Samuel P. Huntington's *The Common Defense: Strategic Programs in National Politics* (1961), which carefully weighed the relative influence of different actors and factors on defense policies, and which wisely appraised the potential for conflict between national security needs and other social values. Soviet orientations concerning security were explored by Raymond L. Garthoff in *Soviet Strategy in the Nuclear Age* (1958), and by V. D. Sokolovsky in *Military Strategy: Soviet Doctrines and Concepts* (1963). That "national security affairs" is, indeed, a "field" was substantiated by Gene M. Lyons and Louis Morton in *Schools for Strategy: Education and Research in National Security Affairs* (1965). Morton Berkowitz and Peter G. Bock brought together a variety of relevant writings in *American National Security: A Reader in Theory and Policy* (1965).

The increasing role of the military in national decision-making also became a subject of scholarly concern. In *The Soldier and the State: The Theory and Politics of Civil-Military Relations* (1957), Samuel P. Huntington raised the dilemma of civilian control, exploring it in terms of attitudes and behavior patterns from an historical perspective. While Huntington advocated restricting the military to strictly military functions, John W. Masland and Lawrence I. Radway, in *Soldiers and Scholars: Military Education and National Policy* (1957), explored and seemed to approve the role of the military in general national decision-making. The policy orientations of the military and related matters were also studied by Morris Janowitz, in *The Professional Soldier* (1960), and in a volume of essays edited by Samuel P. Huntington, *Changing Patterns of Military Politics* (1962).

Disarmament or arms control as an alternative to conflictual means for warding off international aggression remained on the agenda of scholarly interest, if less so than in earlier periods. Post–World War II efforts were treated by Bernard C. Bechhoefer in *Postwar Negotiations for Arms Control* (1961), and by John W. Spanier and Joseph L. Nogee in *The Politics of Disarmament* (1962). The problem of inspection was dealt with, from a technological standpoint, in Seymour Melman (ed.), *Inspection for Disarmament* (1958), and, from a legal standpoint, in Louis Henkin, *Arms Control and Inspection in American Law* (1958). Emile Benoit and Kenneth Boulding discussed the economic implications of disarmament in *Disarmament and the Economy* (1963). The problematics of "arms races" were treated, with reference to the two world wars, by Lewis F. Richardson in *Arms and Insecurity* (1960), a comparative, quantitative analysis.

In recent years, theorizing about international politics by way of analogy to behavioral systems other than the polity itself became prominent. Game theory, in particular, proved attractive. Thomas C. Schelling, in *The Strategy of Conflict* (1960), presented a theory of bargaining, and Kenneth E. Boulding, in *Conflict and Defense* (1960), treated war as a special case of conflict, using economic models as a point of departure.

Critical of this approach as too restrictive was Anatol Rapoport's *Fights, Games and Decisions* (1960) which advocated a more eclectic approach. In short, because the processes of international politics seem to be guided by principles of conduct quite different from those that are characteristic of political behavior within a nation, increasing attention is now being paid to the behavioral aspects of international politics. The long-held assumption that if states were only democratically organized and democratic procedures were introduced into international conduct then world harmony would improve has proved to be a pious wish. For this assumption was not only counter to the reality of a state system in which man's primary loyalty is to his own nation and in which national security is the primary goal of foreign-policy-makers, but it was also extraordinarily naive and parochial. It ignored the great variety of cultural norms and orientations that are deeply rooted in the national consciousness, the psychological attributes and perceptions of available strategies of policy-makers, and the complex intra- and inter-national settings in which foreign policy decisions are made. Much contemporary research is therefore devoted to the analysis of international behavior on the level of the individual, be he an important national policy-maker or the proverbial man on the street. Herbert Kelman collected many of the best of these studies in *International Behavior: A Social-Psychological Analysis* (1965), and J. David Singer provided additional materials in *Human Behavior and International Politics* (1966).

Empirical studies of behavior in the international arena only slowly penetrated the barriers of access that can be blamed for the retarded development of behavioral studies in the field. However, three works, in particular, stood apart as proof that international behavior is not immune to quantitative and empirical analysis. Thomas Hovet, Jr., in *Bloc Politics in the United Nations* (1960), and in *Africa in the United Nations* (1963), as well as Hayward R. Alker, Jr., and Bruce M. Russett, in *World Politics in the General Assembly* (1965), pioneered new approaches and arrived at significantly novel findings about the behavior of international actors. A variety of behavioral studies that pioneered in "data-making" were brought together by Singer in *Quantitative International Politics: Insights and Evidence* (1968). As a result of these developments, many of them reported in journal articles rather than in books, the study of international politics has shifted away from blueprints for a better international order toward clarifying and explaining national policies. The foreign policy behavior of states came to be explained in terms of the perceptions of national policy-makers, their motivations and objectives. Attempts were made to bring international politics into the laboratory where international situations, such as armament races or decisional crises, could be imitated, with individual "subjects" taking the roles of statesmen or nations. Presumably, the "controls" possible in the laboratory setting would permit the experimenter to vary conditions that cannot be varied in the real world, and to identify the crucial factors that determine policy outcomes. The uses of this technique were exemplified in a volume of essays, *Simulation in International Relations* (1963), by Harold Guetzkow, Chadwick F. Alger, Richard A. Brody, Robert C. Noel, and Richard C. Snyder.

In general, then, the study of international politics moved away from a preoccupation with "power" and "national interest" in the direction of discovering the conditions, environmental and human, that give rise to the manifold patterns of national conduct and international behavior. Attention has been shifted away from the overt declarations of national policy-makers to the circumstances that, at any one time, define policy alternatives, including a nation's position within the national community, its concrete goals, its behavior patterns and strategies, and so on. While it is much too early to say whether these approaches will have more practical and salutary payoffs than earlier "idealist" or "realist" interpretations of world politics, they are certainly more firmly grounded in the knowledge about human behavior that the behavioral sciences have made available to national policy-makers.

CONCLUSION: QUO VADIMUS?

In the years 1957–67, the review of the literature suggests, political scientists were navigating the multiverse of politics on many vessels, with differently gauged compasses, and in many different directions. What was written of an earlier period, with some amendments, still holds:

The history of political science as an independent field of inquiry can be written as a history of successive emancipations from earlier limitations and false starts. Yet, these successive emancipations have been additive rather than cumulative: the old survives with the new, and the old acquires new defenders as the new relies on old apostles. It is impossible to say, therefore, that anything has been disproven as long as conventional tests of proof—the requisites of scientific status in any field of knowledge—are not commonly accepted by political scientists, or, in fact, are rejected by some as altogether irrelevant in political inquiry.

But there was change in these years, and the change consisted in an increasing acceptance by a growing cadre of researchers at the discipline's frontiers of that methodological self-consciousness without which the quest for a science of politics cannot be fulfilled. Until the most recent period, concern with methods had not been a hallmark of political science. This has drastically changed. Not that political scientists "invented" many new methods. Rather, they borrowed liberally from the other behavioral sciences and from statistics, but applied them creatively to the complex and elusive problems of political research. Nevertheless, there remained much confusion about methodology which such books as Eugene J. Meehan's *The Theory and Method of Political Analysis* (1965) or Fred M. Frohock's *The Nature of Political Inquiry* (1967) only tended to exacerbate. For books about methodology rarely aid the progress of empirical science. That progress is more likely to come in the crucible of empirical research.

More useful were some works on certain techniques more often used by political scientists than by other social scientists, such as *Content Analysis* (1963), by Robert C. North and associates, or *Legislative Roll-Call Analysis* (1966), by Lee F. Anderson and others. Kenneth Janda, in *Data Processing: Applications to Political Research* (1965), and Robert E. Ward, collaborating with colleagues, in *Studying Politics Abroad: Field Research in Developing Areas* (1964), provided useful handbooks for the novice investigator. Perhaps the most stimulating of these books was Hayward R. Alker's *Mathematics and Politics* (1965) which, by way of examples drawn from politics, introduced the student to the notions of probability, multiple causation, and multivariate analysis. The possibilities of computer simulation were suggested by Ithiel de Sola Pool, Robert P. Abelson, and Samuel L. Popkin, in *Candidates, Issues, and Strategies—A Computer Simulation of the 1960 and 1964 Presidential Elections* (1965).

If, at the beginning of the period, there was still much concern with the "scope" of political science, by its end these attempts at "boundary-drawing" by largely arbitrary definitions (as against theoretical efforts at disciplinary closure) had largely abated. Indeed, boundaries were no longer seen as something to be respected, but as something to be explored and extended. A new generation of scholars, schooled in the methods and theories of the behavioral sciences, seemed to fret at the idea that their intellectual vistas should be limited by the traditional academic frontiers. This breaking through departmental boundaries made, perhaps, for some turmoil at the discipline's core, but it made, in a very real sense, for "breakthroughs" at the cutting edges of political knowledge. If the strain toward interdisciplinary catholicity threatened the discipline's unity, the new generation appeared to be quite unconcerned. And if many difficulties and dilemmas of observation, analysis, and influence remained, they were seen as challenges rather than as causes of despair.

In general, the core and the periphery of political science were no longer defined by subject matter but by modes of attack. No longer could one think of "political theory" as being core and of "behavioralism" as being periphery. Political theorists themselves moved to the periphery as they experimented with linguistic and contextual analysis, and behavioralists moved to the core as they applied historical and institutional methods of inquiry to old problems and new. If the intellectual processes involved made for tension between tradition and innovation, they were symptomatic of scientific movement and development. No longer, at last, was true the bitter comment that David Easton had made in 1953— "however much students of political life may seek to escape the taint, if they were to eavesdrop on the whisperings of their fellow social scientists, they would find that they are almost generally stigmatized as the least advanced." Political scientists did eavesdrop, and what happened is now history. Political science has taken its place as a behavioral science alongside the other "sciences of man." Not that this has made the world a better place to live in. But it has given new hope that it might be a better place if political ignorance can someday yield to political knowledge.

5 Economics

Bert F. Hoselitz

INTRODUCTION

In few other fields of social science are the varied modern uses of print so fully exemplified as that of economic analysis and practical economic activity. The importance of efficient economic activity to the individual and to the community is not new; from the beginning of time man has had to devote most of his waking hours to the task of getting his livelihood. Yet for many centuries these activities remained sufficiently uncomplicated to be easily learned through simple instruction and early participation. Improvements came slowly and were easily absorbed into existing habits of work. The economic environment was limited almost entirely to the small, self-contained community, and familiarity with its conditions was gained through the normal experiences of living in it. Under such circumstances, the necessary communication among individuals working together or assuming responsibility for different tasks could be most effectively carried on orally. Even in primitive communities, the available methods of earning a living were influential in determining patterns of social organization, and changes in these methods brought about social changes; but again the adjustment was so "natural," and frequently so slight and so gradual, that the participants may scarcely have been aware of the relationship between the two.

While literature dealing with practical economic activities appeared in very early historic periods, it was not ubiquitous, and dependence upon it was very slight. Only in modern times have the increasing complexity of economic activities and the accompanying expansion of the economic environment necessitated the development of a variety of specialized forms of literature. At the same time, the difficulty of social and political adjustment to accelerating changes and the widespread awareness that the welfare of all is involved in decisions concerning economic policy have instigated a flood of publications discussing the desirability of various policy decisions. Such publications are usually intended for the general reader and hope to influence his attitudes and actions in relation to economic questions.

The relation of economics as a field of scientific investigation to these manifold economic activities is different from that of the natural sciences to the various technological fields, in that the advancing knowledge of the economist is not "applied" to practical life in the same way. His attempts to develop and to validate generalizations concerning economic behavior create no new products or industries, but may be used to predict what will happen if certain economic policies are pursued. Thus, the innumerable decisions which must be made by governmental agencies, by corporate bodies, by labor unions, and other professional interest groups, and, ultimately, by individuals, may be affected by their knowledge of economists' work.

THE GENERAL SCOPE OF ECONOMICS

There are almost as many definitions of the scope and subject matter of economics as there are writers on the topic. Definitions originating in the 1770's, the 1880's, and 1940's exhibit in quasi-epigrammatic form the progress of economics as a social science since the middle of the eighteenth century. Adam Smith defined it as "the science of wealth"; for him its scope was limited to the study of the nature, causes, and external aspects of the wealth of nations. Alfred Marshall defined economics as "the study of men in the ordinary business of life," and more recently an American economist is reputed to have said "that economics is what economists do."

In attempting to derive a somewhat narrower definition which will fit at the same time the total output of economic literature, a distinction should be made according to whether the primary emphasis of a work is ethical, political, or scientific. The first category includes works which aim to exhibit the ways and means by which a particular moral imperative can be achieved in the realm of economic activity. The most obvious examples are works emanating from religious groups, such as the famous Encyclical of Pope Leo XIII, *Rerum Novarum* (1891), but many of the writings of various reform groups partake of this character.

Political economic writings, in the narrower sense, are works written for the purpose of discussing the economic aspects of particular political measures. Political economic writings predominated in the seventeenth and eighteenth centuries and continue to form an important part of the literature of economics today. As a consequence, during most of the nineteenth century, economics was usually called political economy.

Economics, as it is conceived of in institutions of higher learning, may be described as the study of the economic system—the study of the production, distribution, and consumption of material goods and services destined to fulfill the needs of persons and groups in human societies. Exploration of the economic system can proceed in four main directions: (1) economic theory, which is concerned with the general principles of human behavior in the realm of the economic system; (2) methodology and measurement, which is concerned with ways and means of measuring more or less accurately the performance of an economic system and the magnitude of changes within the economy; (3) economic policy, which is concerned with the steps which should be taken by governments or by private groups and individuals to bring about certain desired results within the realm of economic activity; and (4) economic history, which is concerned with the equalization or explanation of the current state of the economy as a result of developments in the past.

These four directions are not independent. For example, methodology and measurement may be necessary as a tool for the study of economic history, and economic history may be used to test the validity of economic theory. Further, any scientific economic study must be based on some economic theory, and thus the writings in any economic field always include, explicitly or implicitly, some theoretical portions. The degree of theoretical content differs among the different economic fields. In international economics or monetary economics some very extensive theoretical works have been published, whereas in the field of business administration the bulk of the writing has been in applied economics. Some of the other fields occupy an intermediate position between these extremes. In a field like labor and industrial relations, for example, one can find such predominantly theoretical works as Paul H. Douglas' *The Theory of Wages* (1934) and such purely institutional and descriptive writings as Sidney and Beatrice Webb's *Industrial Democracy* (1897).

One central feature of all economic problems, theoretical and applied, is that they all involve a process of maximization (or minimization) in the realm of social action. This may be expressed differently by saying that an economic problem exists if some social end is given and has to be achieved with a minimum of expenditure of means, or if a set of means is given and a maximum result is to be achieved. Thus, an economic problem arises whenever scarce resources must be allocated among alternative uses.

Such economic problems appear in the simplest daily experiences of choice-making, requiring no elaborate analyses. The consumer shopping in the market is engaging in economic behavior as truly as is the large corporation deciding to cut production costs in order to meet lower prices. The former may use only the *Consumer Reports* (1936–) for guidance, while the latter calls upon an entire battery of experts, both in the flesh and in print.

Much specialization exists nowadays in economics. Some sense of it can be obtained by consulting the list of special fields in economics drawn up by the American Economic Association. After citing some special subfields of economic theory and economic history, the following main areas of applied economics are mentioned: money, banking, and business finance; public finance; international economics; labor and industrial relations; land and agricultural economics; business organization; and public utilities and transportation. To these should be added perhaps the growing field of consumer economics.

EARLY WORKS

Though comprehensive treatments of economics did not appear before the late eighteenth century, economic problems were the subject of literary efforts long before that time. The catalogue of the Kress Collection, for example, mentions several hundred tracts and pamphlets, as well as books, which appeared long before Adam Smith's *An Inquiry into the Nature and Causes of the Wealth of Nations* (1776). Some of these publications are extremely interesting, not merely from an antiquarian standpoint, but also as contributions to history, to the development of theoretical ideas, and—in some instances—even as guides for policy.

The development of towns devoted chiefly to trade and the beginnings of industry in the thirteenth century made empirical study of several economic problems imperative. A society based overwhelmingly on agricultural production in the manor, with only a rudimentary division of labor and with very little trade, was not conducive to the investigation of basic economic questions. By the thirteenth and still more by the fourteenth century, progress had been made in Western Europe toward the establishment of centralized power. In attempting to strengthen their own position and to weaken that of the nobility, monarchs extended privileges to the towns, thus stimulating trade and industry.

An important prop to royal power was the control of fiscal and monetary matters by the king. Trade required money and credit as indispensable instruments. And so it is not surprising that, from the fourteenth century until well into the eighteenth, economic thinking and the literature dealing with economic questions concentrated chiefly on the following topics: (1) the value and role of money and coinage; (2) the problem of "usury" or interest; (3) the question of revenue, taxes, and public debt; and (4) the regulation of internal and international trade. Only slowly did the notion arise that these problems were really subsidiary to questions of manpower (population), resources, capital formation, production, and the general mechanisms for achieving the distribution of resources and income among the various economic units.

The problem of money and coinage was made acute by the frequent and arbitrary depreciation of coinage by princes for their personal enrichment. Here was a topic which offered an opportunity to voice moral judgments, as well as views on the economic aspects of inflation. And this opportunity was grasped avidly by writers, among whom—as could be expected in the Christian Middle Ages—ecclesiastics were especially prominent. A considerable number of such tracts on monetary problems have been preserved. The most famous among them are probably Nicolas Oresme's tract on the change in the value of money, composed in the fourteenth century, and Gabriel Biel's *Treatise on the Power and Utility of Moneys* (1930), which was published first in the middle of the sixteenth century. At that time the inflow of precious metals which followed upon the discovery of America had begun to play havoc with the value of standard coins and the stability of prices. Thus, soon after Biel had written his work, which is still steeped in medieval thought and language, Jean Bodin composed his famous essay on the impact of the importation of American treasure on European prices, *The Response to the Paradoxes of Malestroit* (1947, from the 2d ed., 1578). The difference in spirit from Biel's treatise (and Malestroit's work, to which Bodin's tract was an answer) is striking. Biel's and Malestroit's efforts are predominantly moral and hortative, whereas Bodin's book is distinctly analytical. It has, not undeservedly, been called the "first modern work on economics."

Treatises on public revenues, trade, and usury appear almost as frequently as those on money, but there is no need to discuss this literature in detail. The best of it is described in such modern pieces as William James Ashley's *An Introduction to English Economic History and Theory* (2d ed., 1892–93) and in the Richard H. Tawney's Introduction, written in 1925, to Thomas Wilson's *A Discourse upon Usury*, which was first published in 1572.

MERCANTILISM

Whereas in political and religious history the break between the medieval and the modern eras is fairly sharp, in economic history, and above all in the history of ideas on economic subjects, there is little change from the late Middle Ages until well into the eighteenth century. By that time Western Europe was on its way toward industrialization, and the great powers had begun their expansion into colonial regions. Governments had developed the deliberately planned economic policies and practices which we call "mercantilism." Standing midway between the moralism of the Middle Ages and the scientism of the post-Smithian era, the outstanding characteristic of mercantilism is its moralistic pragmatism. Almost all works of the period can be grouped in two classes: (1) tracts of the day, concerning some immediate problem of economic policy; or (2) handbooks for princes and their ministers, compilations of rules and advice on how to govern and how to regulate economic affairs.

Another element which the writings of the mercantilists have in common is their political nature. This is understandable, in view of the practical and topical nature of the tracts, the lingering traces of moralism, and the lack of any general theory. The authors of most economic tracts were spokesmen either for the government or for some group, class, church party, or faction which had an ax to grind. A third common characteristic of the mercantilist literature was its loose terminology. The cumbersome language employed by some writers often caused their works to remain all but unknown for a long time. Mercantilist literature was, and probably still is, a gold mine for the discovery of new, and often not insignificant, forerunners of later theories. A case in point is Isaac Gervaise's *The System or Theory of the Trade of the World* (1720), which was "rediscovered" in the 1920's by Professor Jacob Viner. The fact that Gervaise's very original tract remained unappreciated for more than two hundred years may be attributed in part to its rarity and slight outward appearance, but in part also to its awkward and inelegant language.

Obviously, the economic works of the mercantilist writers present a serious bibliographic problem. Many were pamphlets which appeared anonymously. Many others were pirated, varying from edition to edition, and almost of all of them quickly became scarce. The most extensive collections of English mercantilist writings are those in the Library of the British Museum and in the Goldsmith Library of the London School of Economics. Three excellent bibliographies exist: *The Literature of Political Economy: A Classified Catalogue*, compiled by John R. McCulloch in 1845 and reprinted by the London School of Economics in 1938; Henry Higg's *Bibliography of Economics*, 1751–75 (1935–); and Joseph Massie's *Bibliography of the Collection of Books and Tracts on Commerce, Currency and Poor Law, 1557–1763*, reprinted in 1937 by G. Harding's Bookshop, London.

In the United States, there are three extensive and valuable collections of mercantilist works. The most comprehensive is the Kress Collection at Harvard University; the two others are the Wagner Collection at Yale and the Selig Collection at Columbia. The catalogue of the Kress collection is an important reference tool for economic writings antedating 1776.

In view of the undoubted value and the scarcity of some of the mercantilist tracts, a number of them have been reprinted. The most notable enterprises along these lines are an Italian collection of reprints edited by Pietro Custodi, entitled *Scrittori Classici Italiani di Economia Politicia* (50 vols., 1803–16) and a series of reprints of classical and mercantilist English writers published by the Johns Hopkins University Press. To these collections should be added the reprints of the works of some of the most interesting and curious mercantilist writers, as, for example, William Petty's *Economic Writings*, which were published in two volumes in 1889, and again in 1963, or Richard Cantillon's *Essai sûr la nature du commerce en général* (1755), which has been reprinted several times, most recently in an authoritative annotated edition in 1952. A good work about this period is Eli F. Heckscher's *Mercantilism* (1955).

THE EMERGENCE OF SCIENTIFIC ECONOMICS

In Western Europe the age of mercantilism came to an end by the middle of the eighteenth century. In Germany and parts of Italy it lingered on, but by the beginning of the nineteenth century mercantilism was largely extinct there as well. The transition from mercantilist economics to what may be called modern economics was characterized by a profound change. Beginning with the Physiocrats in France and with Adam Smith in Britain, economics attains the status of an empirical science. This should not be interpreted to mean that all moralistic and ethical reasoning is foreign to Smith and his followers. In fact, part of the appeal of the *Wealth of Nations* lies in the occasional excursions into philosophy, in its frequent epigrammatic observations, and in the injection of casual observations on topics unrelated to its main argument. This is a characteristic the *Wealth of Nations* shares with other great works in economics, for example, Marx's *Das Kapital*, Alfred Marshall's *Principles of Economics* (1890), Karl Menger's *Principles of Economics* (1950), and John Maynard Keynes's *The General Theory of Employment, Interest and Money* (1936). But in spite of the frequent asides on philosophy, morals, and politics, the distinguishing quality of modern economics is that in method, structure, and general outlook it is scientific. Modern economists tended to develop a general systematic theory whose propositions and theorems are derived from, or are reducible to, empirical observation. To the extent that this occurs in any field, the writers and the audience tend to become specialized, and the resulting publications are seldom read by anyone but specialists. Popular thinking and scholarly thinking tend to draw apart unless there is a constant flow of communication, sometimes in the form of "popularizations," sometimes incidental to the discussion of practical issues.

Even though a common characteristic of all modern economics is its scientific nature, it cannot be said that a uniform and generally accepted body of economic theory was developed from the first. In fact, the period from 1750 to 1920 saw the rise and decline of several schools of economics whose members often vehemently opposed one another's theories. These disagreements were based sometimes on differences concerning the data or initial assumptions considered as appropriate foundations for economic analysis; sometimes they turned on differences regarding the methods used or on the relationships established between variables. In the nineteenth century, sharp disagreements split the various schools of thought over rival theories or rival methods in economic analysis. The battle of socialism *versus* its critics, of free-traders *versus* protectionists, and the famous *Methodenstreit*, in which the relative merits of the historical against the analytical method in economics were argued, are examples.

Classical economics, which placed the theories of value and production in the center of economic analysis, arose when the central figures in the economic process became more and more clearly the individual commercial and industrial entrepreneurs. It was in industry and trade that the bulk of the wealth of England was produced, and the decisions of the many thousands and later millions of independent entrepreneurs determined to an increasing extent the form and the amount of wealth produced. The philosophical basis of a hedonist utilitarianism and the political basis of a laissez-faire state show through classical economics in many places. Thus, Smith's *Wealth of Nations* set the stage for the rising liberalist generation in the nineteenth century: it displayed the vicious effects of mercantilism and the beneficial objects of laissez-faire.

A laissez-faire system is one of free competition and free trade, in which economic forces are permitted to find expression without compulsion and in which the self-interest of all individuals achieves a better solution of economic problems than regulation by the state.

But the reality of the early nineteenth century did not conform fully to the picture evolved by the philosophers and theorists. The problem of poverty arose in an acute form. Thomas R. Malthus' famous *An Essay on the Principle of Population* (1798) was concerned with the means of alleviating poverty and distress. He found that the interference with the natural processes of the free market would lead only to worse evils than those which such measures were designed to remove, and he advocated "moral restraint" or delayed marriage and chastity as the most effective and indeed the only means of improving the condition of the poor. The entire economic literature of the early nineteenth century, although profoundly concerned with the problem of poverty and the means of its alleviation, regarded relief by political authorities and legislation designed to lessen poverty not only as futile, but sometimes as positively evil. For example, David Ricardo, who scarcely favored the landed interest, fully accepted Malthus' conclusions on population growth in his *On the Principles of Political Economy and Taxation* (1817).

The alternative to the policy of laissez-faire was the advocacy of measures to be taken by the government for the purpose of regulating the "anarchic" conditions created by a free market system. It is probably not incorrect to say that the fundamental difference between various schools of thought in economics since the middle of the nineteenth century can be reduced to the conflict between advocates of traditional liberal policies and advocates of various degrees of "planning." Even the socialists, who have traditionally been regarded as advocates of the most complete system of regulation and planning, do not present a united front in this respect. Karl Marx, for instance, was never very specific about the bases for the economic organization of a socialist society: as to its political future, he predicted that the means of production would become the property of society (not the "state"), and that at this stage the functions of the state as a monopoly of power would come to an end, the function of government consisting purely of administering the socially owned resources—the picture of an anarchist utopia.

John Stuart Mill who, in his *The Principles of Political Economy* (1848), represented classical economic theory, and Karl Marx, who exemplified socialist economic theory, thus can be said to stand at a crucial point in the history of economic thought. From their time on, various assaults were made on the freely functioning, unregulated economy, some from the right and some from the left. Protectionist theories, theories of a modified paternalism by the state, theories supporting government-fostered economic development, theories embracing a large sector of legislation and regulation for purposes of social reform, and theories stipulating the nationalization of sectors of the economy were the various alternatives to classical economic theory. Among the chief representatives of these theories were Henry George, *Progress and Poverty* (1879); Henry Charles Carey, *Principles of Social Science* (1858–59); Friedrich List, *The National System of Political Economy* (1856): and Adolph H. G. Wagner, *Theoretische Sozialokonomik* (1907–09).

List and Wagner are representatives of the German historical school and Carey and George of the American social-reform movements. They laid the foundations for institutional economics, which drew strength in part from the work of Thorstein Veblen, chiefly his *Theory of the Leisure Class* (1899). Veblen himself cannot properly be called an economist. His works are stimulating and often satirical studies of sociological topics, with economic implications. The major contribution made by the dominant school of American institutionalism is doubtless the work of John Rogers Commons, whose chief works, *Legal Foundations of Capitalism* (1924) and *Institutional Economics: Its Place in Political Economy* (1934), are probably the most profound writings issuing from the institutional school. Yet the contribution they make to the main body of economic theory is minute; their value consists in a discussion of the social relations and the legal forms and framework of governmental regulation affecting economic processes, rather than in a new or original analysis of these processes themselves. Appealing, as they so frequently do, to the hope for a better society, the works of such men as George, Carey, and Veblen have been the bestsellers among economic works.

The strong influence of institutional thought in America has led to attempts to combine traditional economic theory with institutional theory. This approach was begun by Wesley C. Mitchell, the founder of the National Bureau of Economic Research. The bureau is one of the chief private agencies in the United States collecting data of economic importance and publishing monographic studies reporting the results of this research. Mitchell's main role consisted in recognizing that in order to bring the more empirically minded institutional approach closer to the more theory-oriented neoclassical approach, it was of foremost importance to determine by careful, often detailed research what were the actual forms and patterns in which such economic institutions as firms, households, government departments, markets, and others functioned. Only on the basis of such empirical knowledge could a marriage between the institutional and the theoretical approaches be achieved. The position of Mitchell has thus been one of intermediary, and he has been claimed both by the traditional school as one of their followers and by the institutionalists as an institutionalist. In fact, Mitchell's writings covered large areas of economic topics, and he was not afraid to discuss some of the philosophical and ethical problems relevant for economics. His most characteristic work, containing essays of various hues, is *The Backward Art of Spending Money* (1937). His position as an empiricist and theorist is expressed in a book which he wrote jointly with Arthur F. Burns under the title, *Measuring Business Cycles* (1944).

Finally, a new approach to what might best be called institutional economics has recently appeared in the United States. So far, it has not yet led to a widespread literature, but a few basic contributions have been published. This new kind of "institutionalism" starts not from dissatisfaction with classical or neoclassical economic doctrines, but from the attempt to determine the place and function of economic activity within the framework of society as a whole and to ascertain the wider social determinants of economic actions. The general theoretical framework for this approach is set down by and in the work of Talcott Parsons and Neil J. Smelser, *Economy and Society* (1946).

While writers of the social-reform, historical, and institutional schools were at work, economic theory was developed further on the basis of its original classical formulation. The chief centers where most of the work was done were at first England and Austria, and a little later Sweden and Italy. The vigorous cultivation of economics in the first-named countries was due to the presence in each of a man of outstanding genius who attracted around himself a series of talented younger men and capable older co-workers. These two men were Alfred Marshall and Karl Menger. In England, the light of pioneer research in economic theory had never been quite extinguished, and, after the death of Mill, John Elliott Cairnes and William Stanley Jevons had continued the tradition. Jevons shares with Menger and the French economist Leon Walras the honor of having first stated the principle of marginal analysis in a systematic and integrated form. The circle of scholars who were associated with Marshall includes some of the most eminent names in British economics. An interesting picture of the later days of this "Cambridge group" is given in Roy F. Harrod's *The Life of Maynard Keynes* (1951). Both Harrod and Keynes were members of the group, along with Arthur Cecil Pigou, Dennis Holmes Robertson, John R. Hicks, Jean and Edward A. G. Robinson, Ralph G. Hawtrey, and many others. It would be futile to attempt even a cursory analysis of the contributions of these writers. Together, they have done more than any other group to restate economic theory, in all its branches, in the form in which it has become generally accepted today.

The circle of men who assembled around Menger or were inspired by him was hardly less numerous or eminent than the Cambridge circle of Marshall. In fact, the Austrian doctrine had initially a wider international reputation and found more ready acceptance than the Cambridge school. Its chief early spokesmen were Eugene Bohn von Bawerk and Friedrich Wieser; its doctrines were introduced into Sweden by Knut Wicksell, into Italy by Maffeo Pantaleoni and Luigi Cossa, and into Holland by Nikolaas G. Pierson. In France, Charles Gide and others spread the new doctrine, and in the United States, Simon N. Patten and Richard T. Ely received it with sympathy.

By the end of World War I, the synthesis of the American and English branches of economics based firmly on marginal analysis had been achieved, but it was not long before a new approach was developed which at first seemed to tear asunder the laboriously built edifice of economic theory. This new approach has often been designated as Keynesian economics, since John Maynard Keynes's *The General Theory of Employment, Interest, and Money* (1936) appeared to put forth a set of entirely new ideas and to lift discarded and heretical theories to a new level of respectability. In reality, the important contribution made by Keynes was essentially along the traditional lines of the Cambridge school, but the immediate impact of the new approach on economic theory was profound, because of the attention drawn by Keynes to macroeconomic relationships.

Since the two alternative theoretical approaches, microeconomics and macroeconomics, parallel the opposing points of view in the most important practical problem of the day, i.e., the extent of freedom or of planning desirable in the economic sphere, the difference should be clearly understood. An economic system such as that of any modern capitalist country can be viewed as being composed of a large number of decision-making units, which for convenience may be classified into two groups, firms and households. The firms buy productive resources and sell finished products to other firms and to households; the households sell productive resources and buy finished products. The firms make decisions with the purpose of maximizing money profits, the households with the aim of maximizing satisfaction. Now, the analysis of how these units will act if put under certain constraints, the grouping of firms into industries, and so on, presents us with a simplified model of economic analysis following a microeconomic approach. The term "microeconomic" is applied because the smallest significant entity, the firm or household, is chosen as the starting point. In order to gain a full picture of the economic structure and process of a society, various methods of aggregating the behavior of these entities have to be applied.

The macroeconomic approach begins, so to speak, at the other end of the scale. Instead of starting with the activity of the smallest decision-making unit, this approach commences with the examination of the major aggregate variables relevant to economic analysis, such as national income, national savings, total consumption, and total investment. It disregards in its first approximation the distributive aspects of these variables and the effect of various policy measures on them. The macroeconomic approach can be more directly related to governmental regulatory practices than can the microeconomic approach, since emphasis in the latter is placed on the independent manipulation of major variables, an obvious device. In practice, economists who advocated a high degree of government regulation adopted the macroeconomic approach, whereas economists favoring a minimum of governmental interference in economic life favored the microeconomic. In American economic literature, the two approaches are represented by such works as Alvin H. Hansen's *Fiscal Policy and Business Cycles* (1941) for macroeconomics and Henry C. Simons' *Economic Policy for a Free Society* (1948) for microeconomics.

Since the latter part of World War II, the conflict over Keynesian economics has died down to a considerable degree, becoming resolved through a division of economic analysis into two related parts, usually designated as price analysis and national income analysis. This trend had begun in England before the war and was given considerable impetus by the work of John R. Hicks, who had attempted such a relation in *Value and Capital* (1939), and whose more popular work was adapted to the American scene by Albert G. Hart in *The Social Framework of the American Economy* (1945). Although the battle over Keynesian economics was resolved by the recognition of different but equally valid and mutually related approaches to economic theory, the conflict over the degree and kind of regulatory activity in which the government should and could engage has not been resolved. But this is primarily a political rather than an economic issue.

The economic literature of that period has been dealt with descriptively and analytically in a number of ways. First, there is a series of general histories of economic thought. Many of these productions are textbooks and were occasioned by the fact that courses in this field are common in American colleges and universities. A good example is Reich Roll's *A History of Economic Thought* (1939). A brief survey can also be found in the article, "Economics," in the *Encyclopedia of the Social Sciences* (1930–35). But we also have some highly original works in this field. The books range from compilations of titles scarely more than annotated bibliographies to highly original analyses. Some treat the whole sweep of economic history, from its earliest manifestations in the writings of some authors of antiquity to the present century. Examples are Joseph A. Schumpeter, *History of Economic Analysis* (Elizabeth B. Schumpeter, ed., 1954); Henry W. Spiegel (ed.), *The Development of*

Economic Thought: Great Economists in Perspective (1952); Joseph J. Spengler and William R. Allen (eds.), *Essays in Economic Thought: Aristotle to Marshall* (1960); and Bert F. Hoselitz and others, *Theories of Economic Growth* (1960).

Other works deal with special periods or "schools" in economics. Here the most valuable efforts cover a broader area than merely technical economics. In tracing through the development of economic ideas, it is often necessary to include the general political and philosophical thought of a period. Some of these works, though principally in economics, should be considered general intellectual histories of a particular period or movement: Edwin Cannan, *A History of the Theories of Production and Distribution in English Political Economy from 1776 to 1848* (1924); Joseph Dorfman, *The Economic Mind in American Civilization* (1946-50); Eli Halevy, *The Growth of Philosophic Radicalism* (1949); Lionel Robbins, *The Theory of Economic Policy in English Classical Political Economy* (1952); Leslie Stephen, *The English Utilitarians* (1900); and Georges Weulersse, *Le mouvement physiocratique en France* (1910).

All these works are secondary sources: i.e., although they discuss the development of economic ideas and theories, they present only excerpts from the works of the authors of these ideas, and in many cases they discuss, question, alter, and interpret these ideas in ways which would have surprised or even shocked the original writers. Yet the continuing concern with these works resulted, in large measure, from the challenge which these older writers presented and the many instructive lessons which could be learned from them. Hence, it is not surprising that, at various times, the collected writings of the great economists were published in order to provide as full and comprehensive a documentation as possible of their own words and reasoning. In some instances, nationalistic or other political considerations played a role. For example, the publication of the writings of Friedrich List was motivated, in part, by the urge to present to the German public the challenging ideas of a great German economist, and the plan to bring out a complete edition of the works of Karl Marx and Friedrich Engels was plainly motivated by the need, on the part of the intellectual leaders of the Soviet Union, to present the full corpus of the works of their messiahs. Yet many of these editions are produced on thoroughly scholarly lines, and several of them may be regarded as constituting the *editio princeps* of the writings of several great economists. We list here a series of the most interesting sets of these collected works. All of them contain the writings of great and important economists, and some have brought to light various previously unknown manuscripts, letters, and other ephemera and thus have greatly enriched our knowledge of the writings of these authors. For Jeremy Bentham, see *Jeremy Bentham's Economic Writings* (1952-

54), W. Stark (ed.); for John Law, *Oeuvres, complètes* (1934), Paul Harsin (ed.); for Friedrich List, *Schriften Reden, Briefe* (1932-35), Erwin V. Beckerath and others (eds.); for Karl Marx and Friedrich Engels, *Historischkritische Gesamtausgabe: Werke, Schriften, Briefe*, (1927-32), D. Raizanov and others (eds.); for Carl Menger, *The Collected Works of Carl Menger* (1934-36); for Francois Quesnay, *Oeuvres économiques et philosophiques de F. Quesnay* (1888), August Oneken (ed.); for David Ricardo, *The Works and Correspondence of David Ricardo* (1953-55), Piero Staffa and M. H. Dobb (eds.); and for Anne R. J. Turgot, *Oeuvres de Turgot et documents la concernant* (1913-23), Gustave Schelle (ed.).

In addition to making available for the general student the works of the masters in convenient new editions, some of the scarce older tracts have been collected and reprinted. Here again, some antiquarianism, some pride in the early achievements of a national culture, some search for intellectual origins, and some competition for finding priorities of theories have played a role. But as is the case with the reprints of collected works, the republication of older tracts and other books in economics had the additional advantage of making more readily available to the general student works which attracted his interest and which were often of great scarcity. It is eloquent testimony to the utility and value of these reprints that several series are again out of print and that more than one printing had to be made of some items. Among the more interesting collections and series of this kind are A. Dubois (ed.), *Collection des économistes et des réformateurs sociaux de la France* (1911-13); Jacob H. Hollander, *Reprints of Economic Tracts* (1903 and later years); John R. McCulloch (ed.), *Old and Scarce Tracts on Money* (1933); and John R. McCulloch (ed.), *Early English Tracts on Commerce* (1952).

NATIONAL DIFFERENCES

It has become commonplace to point to the differences between the economic literature of the U.S.S.R., on the one hand, and that of the West, on the other. It is similarly well-known that the German economic literature of the Nazi period and some Italian economic literature of the fascist period often displayed aspects that are clearly attributable to the political predilections of those countries. What is less often recognized is that the American or British economic literature is influenced by similar factors, and that the entire form of exposition, argument, and validation of propositions contained in these works is contingent upon the value structure generally acknowledged in these countries.

This last factor can perhaps best be exhibited by a comparison of the economic literature of the last fifty years in the English, German,

French, and Italian languages. Englishmen have always exhibited a practical sense in their scholarly work; the elaborate conceptualization common in German social science is foreign to them. They prefer a rough but adequate empiricism; and, as often as not, their approach and their propositions are justified by appeal to pragmatic value. Alfred Marshall's definition of economics as "the study of men in the ordinary business of life" is typical of this attitude. Although American social science has been strongly affected by German scholarship, notably in history and sociology, American economics displays the same pragmatic and common-sense features as British economics. This may be explained chiefly by the profound influence exercised on American economic writing by classical English economics.

French and also Italian economics is colored by the tradition, common in Romance countries, of rigorous abstract logical reasoning. Although other countries have had their share of outstanding mathematicians and logicians, in France the cult of pure mathematics is more generally practiced and enjoys more prestige than anywhere else. It is more than coincidence that the "big names" in the history of mathematical economics, at any rate before 1914, are predominantly those of Frenchmen, Italians, or Romance Swiss—Christoph Bernouilli, Jules Dupuit, Antoine A. Cournot, Leon Walras, Vilfredo Pareto, Maffeo Pantaleoni, Enrico Barone, and Luigi Amoroso, to name but a few. It is perhaps typical of the French and Italian approach to economics that the epoch-making work of Leon Walras remained almost unknown outside the limited circle of mathematical economists who had read it. It was more than seventy-five years before an English translation, *Elements of Pure Economics* (1954), appeared.

In contrast to both the Anglo-Saxon and the Romance approaches to economics, the German is "philosophical." This word is used in a special sense, designating the fact that the ultimate validity and appropriateness of any piece of economic writing is judged by whether or not it fits into a larger system embracing, often, not only all social science, but law and parts of philosophy as well. In addition to this property of being part of a wider system, German economic works are also distinguished by the elaborate erudition usually displayed. Many pieces are copiously documented with numerous references, often to obscure and scarce sources. This tendency to present exhaustive and elaborate documentation was furthered by the bias in favor of historical and descriptive rather than analytical economics prevailing in Germany for a large part of the nineteenth century. The characteristics of German works on economics were therefore threefold: (1) they tended to throw light on the development of economic institutions and relations; (2) they succeeded in establishing elaborate categorizations of economic institutions and in this fashion contributed significantly to the greater clarity of concepts, indeed drawing attention to several neglected factors whose presence became obvious when classification and subclassification were carried to extremes; and (3) because of the emphasis on economic institutions rather than economic variables, German work focused clearly on the social nature of economic processes. This last emphasis has resulted in an economic literature of a wider generality and more profound applicability than the work of analytical economics predominant in the Anglo-Saxon countries or in France and Italy. Max Weber's *The Protestant Ethic and the Spirit of Capitalism* (1930) or his *The Theory of Social and Economic Organization* (1947), Werner Sombart's *Der moderne Kapitalismus* (1902), and Karl Bucher's *Industrial Evolution* (1901) are examples of this breadth of German economics and of the fact that economic processes are seen and interpreted within their wider social context.

But to preclude an exaggerated impression of the differences between economic studies as carried on in various countries, it should be pointed out that in recent decades the national peculiarities in economic research have tended to become less pronounced. In part, this has been due to the emergence of pressing economic problems of worldwide impact, such as the economic consequences of the two world wars and the Great Depression of the 1930's. In part it has resulted from improved international collaboration and the impact of economic research carried on by international agencies, such as the United Nations, UNESCO, the International Labor Office, the World Bank, and others, and the exchange of views of scholars from many countries at international conferences dealing with topics in the social sciences.

The impact of these agencies on the diminution in international differences in the approach and study of economics, at least in the non-Communist countries, has been threefold. In the first place, they have published, as already mentioned, factual data and research reports which were distributed all over the world and which are regarded as authoritative source materials. Second, they have set up international associations, as, for example, the International Economic association, which have held international conferences attended by persons from all countries and which also have sponsored the publication of translations of economic works of importance, especially those appearing in the less widely known languages. A periodical publication, *International Economic Papers*, was inaugurated in 1951 and has brought to the attention of English-speaking economists articles and essays in various languages, notably Italian, Dutch, the Scandinavian languages, and the Slavic languages. Another publication, the *Handbook of Latin American Studies* (1936–), gives some idea of the progress in economics that has been made by Latin Americans in the past two decades. The *Index Trans-*

lationum, published from 1932 to 1940 by the International Institute of Intellectual Cooperation, and since 1949 continued under the auspices of UNESCO, gives some idea of the extent and kinds of translations now being produced.

Third, the United Nations and the World Bank have undertaken studies of the economies of various underdeveloped countries. Although these studies were made primarily as a service for the setting up of economic development policies and plans in these less advanced countries, they were carried out by teams of economists—and other social scientists—coming from different countries and, hence, reflecting different approaches to economics. The concentration upon a common problem has forced these economists, with often varying viewpoints, to find ways and means of adjusting their approaches to one another. Some efforts, especially those of the International Bank for Reconstruction and Development, have been published and present valuable evidence not only of how well international teams of social scientists can work together, but also of the economic conditions or problems of particular underdeveloped countries. Among its studies, the works on *The Economic Development of Kenya* (1943) and *The Economic Development of Morocco* (1965) are representative examples.

A final word must be said about the relation between economics in the West and economic writings in the Soviet orbit. Among the various countries in the Communist portion of the world, Russia and China have long traditions of economic thought and practice. The Chinese traditions, in particular, go back some 2500 years; and although one of the earliest economic works on China, the Kuan-Tzu, has given rise to a good deal of controversy regarding its authorship and date of composition, there exist in English translation two economic works which date back to the first century B.C. and the first century A.D., respectively. Part of the former was published in a translation by Esson M. Gale under the title *Discourses on Salt and Iron* by Huan K'uan (1931), and the latter was translated in its entirety by Nancy Lee Swann under the title *Food and Money in Ancient China* by Pan Ku (1950). Both contain numerous passages which appear remarkably "modern" in character. The later pre-Communist economic literature of China is based on treatises such as these, and only in the last thirty years has Western economics made any inroad into Chinese economic thinking. Contemporary Chinese economic scholarship has taken on most of the characteristics of Soviet Russian scholarship and employs most of the methods and techniques practiced in contemporary Russian economics.

In Russia itself, the indigenous tradition of economic speculation goes back much less far than in China. Although a few Russian mercantilist writers have been discovered, economics as a field of interest was introduced in Russia during the nineteenth century. Even then, Russian writers were under the influence of Western thought, but adapted the lessons they learned to their own problems. In the late nineteenth century Russia produced a number of outstanding economic historians, as well as some very competent economic theorists. Some basic work was done in Russia in quantitative and mathematical economics and economic statistics. The economic historians Maksim M. Kovalevskii and Paul Vanogradoff, the statistician Aleksandr A. Chuprov, and the economic theorist Ladislaus von Bortkiewicz gained international fame.

At the same time, however, Marxism began to take firm root in Russian economics. By the turn of the century, a large part of Russian economic writings were produced by men with more or less socialist persuasion. Writers like Peter Struve or Mikhail Tugan-Baranovsky, who were both Marxists, though opposed to Lenin, also attained an international reputation. With the Revolution, the "orthodox" theories of Marxist economics attained a victory. In the first years after the revolution, there had not yet been elaborated a line from which deviations were not tolerated. Thus, the early issues of the main Soviet economic periodicals contain lively discussions of a number of economic problems. But this changed with the consolidation of the power of Joseph Stalin.

Hence, as concerns more recent economic works, those published since about 1930, two types must be distinguished. One group comprises the major official compendia on economic history and structure, programmatic statements, and textbooks. These works are all characterized by their strict adherence to Marxian language and ideas, although the latter are modified from time to time so as to suit the official line of the Communist Party at any one time. These works abound with quotations from Marx, Engels, Lenin, and, since about 1932, Stalin. On the whole, these works are of little value, since the doctrine is laid down in the speeches and other declarations of the Soviet leaders, and the texts supply the supporting evidence and historical justification.

The second group of economic writings is essentially on a technical level. In conformity with the dominant pattern of publications in the U.S.S.R., these works also begin with references to the Marxian classics, notably to the opinions of Stalin. But this is a mere formality. Russian economic planning requires the publication and distribution of technical works on such problems as industrial economics, production policies, accounting systems, money management, and the like. Thus, this kind of literature is little different in its general aspects from the corresponding literature in the West.

Unfortunately, most of the technical writings are available only in Russian. They consist chiefly of articles in learned journals and occasional monographs. Since the old saying, "Russica non leguntur," is still largely true, only a small part of the output of Russian economic scholarship is accessible to most Western students, although translations of such economic works as the *History of the National Economy of Russia to the 1917 Revolution* (1949), by Peter I. Liaschenko, have been made available through the cooperation of the American Council of Learned Societies.

In the last few years, other services have been opened which supply Russian and other East European materials in English. For example, the National Committee for a Free Europe publishes a monthly magazine, *News from behind the Iron Curtain* (1952–   ), which contains occasional articles from the Eastern European press in translation and which also carries digests of laws and newspaper articles from these countries. Another similar service on the Russian press is published weekly by the Joint Committee on Slavic Studies of the American Council of Learned Societies and the Social Science Research Council, entitled *Current Digest of the Soviet Press* (1949–   ).

This has been imitated for the Indian press by the Bureau of International Relations of the Department of Political Science at the University of California at Berkeley, which publishes a quarterly magazine entitled *Indian Press Digests*. These digests are, of course, highly selective in their coverage, but they present very adequate materials and summaries of the main political and economic developments as reported in the press of countries whose languages are understood and read by only a few Americans. Since the selection and digesting is very well done, they have great value, even for scholars who read these languages, in providing a quick overview of the most important developments in the public-opinion-forming organs of these countries.

On the whole, scholars who do not read Russian can obtain more exact and better information from the writings of non-Russian scholars who have devoted themselves to a study of Russian economics than from the available translations of Russian works. More specifically, the writings of Eugene Varga, or even of Joseph Stalin, are less revealing than such studies as Gregory Bienstock, Solomon M. Schwarz, and Aaron Yugow, *Management in Russian Industry and Agriculture* (1944); Abram Bergson (ed.), *Soviet Economic Growth* (1953); Abram Bergson and Simon Kuznets (eds.), *Economic Trends in the Soviet Union* (1963); and D. Shimkin, *Minerals: Key to Soviet Power* (1953).

LEVELS OF ECONOMIC WRITING

In the past twenty years, doubtless as a consequence of the impact of the great depression and the economic complexities resulting from the war, the general public has become more aware of and more interested in the effects of major economic changes upon daily life and activities. But not only has popular interest in economics increased; activities of central and local governments requiring the services of economists have been greatly extended, and as a consequence of these developments, more people have been motivated to acquaint themselves with the rudiments and foundations of economics. In other words, economics as a discipline in colleges and universities has gained in popularity; more students are enrolled in courses; more and more varied curricula are being offered. Many high schools now offer courses in elementary economics, and even elementary schools with well-rounded social studies programs incorporate some economic topics. The past twenty years, therefore, have brought considerable growth to one form of popularization, the issuing of more and more varied textbooks.

Not all textbooks are popularizations. For example, Alfred Marshall's *Principles of Economics* has been used often as a text; yet no one would regard this work as a popularization. Marshall's book is written not with the purpose of providing the beginning or even the more advanced student with a foundation in economics, but rather with the aim of providing a summary of economics in its most advanced stage at the time the book was written. Thus, the book contains a large amount of original material and by its very nature is more a treatise than a text.

The college text, although a popularization in the widest sense of the term, usually has several distinguishing marks which other forms of popularization do not have. For the most part, texts are written by competent scholars, sometimes even by men who have made pioneering contributions to their field. Second, texts are organized so as to be systematic and comprehensive accounts of the fields they deal with. Third, texts are often theoretical in orientation—though not always; for example, John Ise's *Economics* (1946) is mainly descriptive and attempts to familiarize the student with economic institutions, rather than with theoretical relationships. Even when they deal with practical or policy problems, they base the exposition upon underlying theoretical propositions. Fourth, texts usually contain, explicitly or implicitly, an exposition of the methods by which the propositions set forth are attained.

The reader should not infer that there are no qualitative differences among textbooks. On the contrary, they vary greatly in quality, so much so that one is constantly surprised to find that several of the poorer texts apparently compete successfully with the better ones. But whatever their quality, even the poorest texts display some of the characteristics indicated, and this fact justifies a separate consideration of them.

A few words should be said concerning the authorship of texts and of popular economic literature in general. The fact that the author of a popular work is a competent scholar is, of course, no guarantee of its quality. But if a text or other popular work is written by a scholar of high repute, it has certainly the probability of exhibiting the thinking of an original and fertile mind and usually also of making a significant contribution accessible to a public wider than the narrow circle of scholars. Examples of successful texts that have been written by men of high competence are Kenneth Boulding's *The Economics of Peace* (1945) and *Economic Analysis* (4th ed., 1966); Paul Samuelson's *Economics* (7th ed., 1967); and Richard G. Lipsey and Peter O. Steiner, *Economics* (1966).

Apart from textbooks, one can distinguish three kinds of popularizations of scholarly works: digests, popular accounts in the narrow sense, and vulgarizations. The author of a digest uses his skill not primarily to present his own thought, but to interpret in a more generally accessible form the work of another. It goes without saying that digests, like any other form of literary production, may vary greatly in quality. Often the staunch adherence to an original produces a less useful digest than a freer treatment. An excellent example of how a very difficult technical book was digested in a form understandable to the average reader is A. P. Lerner's article, "Mr. Keynes' 'General Theory of Employment, Interest, and Money,'" which was published in the October 1936 issue of the *International Labour Review*.

Digests of scholarly books are rare, however. Most scholarly books do not lend themselves readily to digesting, and it is usually easier to write an independent account incorporating the views of an author or of a school. Hence, much of the popular economic literature consists of independently written works rather than digests. Thus, while the article mentioned above may be considered a digest of the volume by Keynes, a small book by Joan Robinson, *Introduction to the Theory of Employment* (1937), which came out a little later, is designed to be "a simplified account of the main principles of the Theory of Employment for students who find they require some help in assimilating Mr. Keynes' *General Theory*." Books of this kind are closely akin to textbooks, the chief difference being that they are not written specifically for use in a classroom, but are destined rather for the average nonspecialized reader who wants to gain a fuller understanding of the most recent advances in economic thinking. With the increasing technicality of scientific economic writing and the growing number of high school and college graduates who have had some elementary training in economics, the audience for this type of simplification is expanding.

More important from the standpoint of the general reader, however, are books which deal not with the popularization of a particular theoretical advance, but rather with the exposition and analysis of current economic problems and policies, for the purpose of informing and perhaps influencing the layman. The greater significance of these works consists in their advocating or defending some currently discussed measure of wide significance. Sometimes the immediate urgency of the policy discussed in such a book is obvious. An example is Seymour Harris' *The European Recovery Program* (1948). Sometimes it is more remote, as in Sir William Beveridge's *Full Employment in a Free Society* (1944) or in Friedrich A. von Hayek's *The Road to Serfdom* (1944). The mere fact that such a book is concerned with problems of policy means that the author takes sides and that he is advocating measures he regards as steps toward certain implicit or explicit values or goals. Works of this kind are the primary concern of the general reader, for in such, competent people discuss policies in terms comprehensible to him, yet on a basis of sound scholarship.

All the contributions in economics which have relevance for the general reader are in some applied field. But numerous writings in applied fields are produced primarily for specialists and are not even of interest to general economists or economists in other specialties. In economics, as in other fields of knowledge, specialization has been driven to a rather high degree, and for this reason a considerable portion of the literature which is commonly included among economic writings and is reviewed and discussed in economic journals and magazines is of interest to only a small proportion of the subscribers of these journals. For this reason, many economic works written "for the general public" also became one of the main sources of information in a special field for economists in other specialties. For example, the field of agricultural economics is one in which there exists a rather specialized literature which has its own clientele. In the United States, a special quarterly journal, the *Journal of Farm Economics* (1919–), is published which numbers among its subscribers few individuals whose research and teaching interests are not in the field of agricultural economics. In addition, the United States Department of Agriculture and many state agricultural departments publish numerous specialized reports on various aspects of agricultural economics which also have appeal for the same body of readers. However, at various times, agricultural economists publish more general works, writings with a much wider appeal which are read by economists in other special fields—and sometimes even persons who do not specialize in economics at all. Examples of such works are Theodore W. Schultz's article "Investment in Human Capital" (1960), or his book *Transforming Traditional Agriculture* (1964), or a book edited by him under the title *Food for the World* (1945).

Other specialized fields in economics present the same features, and it is only books like the ones listed by Schultz or corresponding ones in other fields which circulate among economists in general. By far the larger percentage of specialized publications have, therefore, a rather well defined and rigorously circumscribed readership. This also holds for periodical publications. In the United States, there are three scholarly journals in economics which contain contributions in all specialized subfields of economics and which, therefore, appeal to economists regardless of their field of special interest. Chief among them is the *American Economic Review* (1911–), the official journal of the professional association of American economists. The other two are distinguished both by their long history and their skillful editorship over many years. These two journals are published by the Economics Departments at Harvard University and the University of Chicago and, like the official journal of the American Economic Association, the *Quarterly Journal of Economics* (1886–), and the *Journal of Political Economy* (1892–) are read by economists in all fields and circulate over the whole world. Among more specialized journals, there are some devoted to regional interests, such as, for example, *Southern Economic Journal* (1933–) or, in Britain, the *Scottish Journal of Political Economy* (1954–); but the greatest number of periodical publications with less than general appeal are in specialized fields. Corresponding to the *Journal of Farm Economics*, there are published, for example, *Land Economics* (1925–), specializing in the fields of planning, housing, and public utilities; the *Journal of Finance* (1946–), which as its title indicates concentrates on problems of private finance. Some specialized journals are published by governmental or international agencies, as, for example, the *Monthly Labor Review* (1915–), published by the United States Bureau of Labor Statistics, or the *International Labour Review*, published by the International Labour Organization. Some journals contain contributions which often tend to go beyond economics or to discuss the interrelations between economics and other social sciences. For example, the *Canadian Journal of Economics and Political Science* (1935–) contains essays in economics as well as other social sciences. This is considered preferable to publishing small, separate journals in the various fields which would have difficulty maintaining a sufficient circulation. Since Canadian economists usually have easy access to American or British journals, this may be regarded as a wise policy. *Social Research* (1934–) also publishes articles in the various social sciences, but here a special viewpoint, i.e., the desire to present materials more on an interdisciplinary level, seems to be the prevailing reason for the inclusion of essays in various social science fields. Finally, a publication like *Economic Development and Cultural Change* (1952–) presents essays in the various social sciences, primarily because its editorial policy is based on the assumption that a thorough investigation and analysis of the problems of economic growth, to which it is devoted, requires a careful study not only of economic factors, but also of those customarily falling into other social disciplines.

In addition to these journals, which are all concerned with the need and requirements of the scholar or the student, there exists of course a large mass of periodical publications which are of social appeal, such as *Fortune* (1930–). They range to highly specialized periodicals, like *Time Sales Financing* (1936–), which deals exclusively with problems of instalment credit to consumers. Although many of the periodicals usually have little interest for the economist, and above all for the general economist, it should not be forgotten that some very important contributions to economics have sometimes been published first in journals or magazines which were specially oriented toward the needs of a particular group of businessmen or administrators. For example, a most important contribution to the economic theory of value, Jules Dupuit's "De la mesure de l'utilité des travaux publics," appeared for the first time in 1844 in the *Annales des ponts et chausées*, a periodical concerned primarily with the engineering and administrative aspects of roadbuilding and transportation facilities in general. Though only a few examples of this kind could be cited, it is nevertheless possible that ideas which, at a given time, do not find entrance in the more "orthodox" economic journals may appear first in specialized business publications, because they are considered either too limited or one-sided in approach. Sometimes such contributions are "rediscovered," and their full importance for general economics is recognized.

METHODOLOGY

The works described so far may be regarded as providing a general survey of economics and its problems as a field, the history of economic ideas, and the main components of the great corps of economic writings by the most famous and most widely reputed scholars in the field. These works are the backbone of any collection of books in economics, and it is on the basis of these volumes that more specialized aspects of the literature should be considered.

The first specialized topic to which we turn is the consideration of method in economics. Although there is a rather high degree of unanimity today on the most appropriate methods in economics, this has not always been the case. One of the most memorable quarrels in the history of economics was the so-called *Methodenstreit* or "battle of methods" between Carl Menger (*Untersuchungen über die Methode der Socialwissenschaften* (1883) and Gustav Schmoller, which turned around the primacy of generalizing theoretical versus particularizing historical method in economics. It also touched upon the degree of empirical support for economic propositions and emphasized the need for economists to either accept current psychological theories or make their own assumptions about relevant aspects of human behavior. Most of these conflicts have been resolved, although even today there are somewhat different approaches, and the "model-builders" do not always see eye-to-eye with the strict "simple-minded empiricists." But the conflicts have become greatly mitigated and must be regarded mainly as differences in emphasis rather than in basic approach.

Economists today tend to proceed in their research by a common method, which is in its chief aspects identical with the procedures of any empirical science, i.e., the testing of theories by relating them to empirically observable data. Economists go out to collect factual data or use those collected by others (e.g., statistical offices, census bureaus, and so on). They have developed methods of determining factual data from indirect evidence and have participated in adding greatly to the knowledge and sophistication of the statistical treatment of mass phenomena. On the basis of factual data, various generalizations are attempted, and sets of generalizations are built into theories. Until very recently, most of these theories were stated in ordinary language, but it has become customary to state theories in mathematical form.

Yet not all the progress of method has been in mathematical or semimathematical fields. There has been clarification in language and in specialized economic terms, and there has also been some clarification about the overall assumptions of human nature and human behavior on which economic propositions are built. Whereas the early economists were utilitarians, and later economists assumed an inbred hedonism and rationality, modern economics has dropped these restrictive assumptions about human nature and merely assumes that human beings act reasonably consistently, i.e., that they continue a given behavior pattern until they make an explicit change.

There has also been a third field in which economic method has progressed—the integration of historical and contemporary comparative study. Until very recently, economic history was regarded by many economists as a separate branch of study having scarcely any relationship with economics proper. This split is now disappearing. Economists discover that many facts which are true about the past of some societies are found in the present of some other societies. Certain institutions in historical settings have analogies or similarities in the present. It has thus become increasingly common to combine certain historical and comparative studies. At the same time, many of the statistical and mathematical procedures which were developed in economics have been applied to historical problems.

In brief the spirit impinging upon method in economics is strongly influenced by positivism. Economics has ceased to be speculative and based on a priori reasoning—though old habits die slowly, and every now and then a thoroughly speculative book does appear. In its theoretical formulations, economics is slowly giving up the less accurate, purely linguistic statements and replacing them with rigorously mathematical ones. In collecting its data, it applies the various forms of empirical method employed in the social sciences generally, and it processes the data by means of often quite complex statistical methods. Finally, it tends to encompass historical and institutional materials and treat them with a comparative approach. Thus, most of the differences between "schools" have diminished and, in large measure, been abolished.

Finally, economic method has become both narrower and broader as concerns its interrelation with other social sciences. In its assumptions about human behavior it has greatly reduced the emphasis on hedonistic or rational behavior. On the other hand, economists have become increasingly aware that interrelations with other fields of social research are in many instances indispensable for the furthering of adequate knowledge, and hence they look with more sympathy on interdisciplinary treatments of certain problems. The development, in the other social sciences, of methods similar to those in economics has helped greatly in this process. Although it is premature to expect that this interdependence will lead to a unified social science, a surer command of method in economics and a more modest interpretation of present achievements go a long way toward laying the groundwork for further elaboration of more refined methods in economics and the other social sciences.

Much of the literature on method is not contained in special monographs or treatises, but appears incidental to substantive contributions. However, we list here a number of works which concern themselves primarily with method in economics and which represent, on the whole, the present state of methodology in the field: Roy G. D. Allen, *Mathematical Analysis for Economics* (1939); Robert Dorfman and others, *Linear Programming and Economic Analysis* (1958); Trygve Haavelmo, *The Probability Approach in Economics* (1944); John M. Keynes, *The Scope and Method of Political Economy* (1891); Tjalling Koopmans, *Three Essays on the State of Economic Science* (1957); Lionel Robbins, *An Essay on the Nature and Significance of Economic Science* (1935); Paul Samuelson, *Foundations of Economic Analysis* (1947); Hans Theil, *Linear Aggregation of Economic Relations* (1954); and John von Neuman and Oskar Morgenstern, *Theory of Games and Economic Behavior* (1953).

The statistical approach to the evaluation of empirical observations —common in many sciences (e.g., biometrics, psychometrics)—has also been accepted by economists. The application of statistical methods by economists is called econometrics. When the economist studies a certain problem, he knows that there are many factors which affect the case under study; however, he wants to (and can) concentrate only upon a few factors, and he neglects all the others. Because of this neglect, he cannot expect to discover the precise relationship between the factors (or variables) upon which he concentrates his attention. But if it can be assumed that those variables which were neglected occur in a certain random way, then the econometrician is able to estimate the degree of error in his conclusions about the quantitative relationships which he found between the remaining variables.

There is a rapidly growing literature in econometrics, both in econometric theory and in the application of the theory to the measurement of quantitative relationships within economic systems. Examples are A. S. Goldberger, *Economic Theory* (1964); H. S. Houthakker and L. D. Taylor, *Consumer Demand in the United States, 1929–1970, Analyses and Projections* (1966); J. Johnston, *Econometric Methods* (1963); L. R. Klein, *Economic Fluctuations in the United States, 1921–1941* (1950); and H. Theil, *Economic Forecasts and Policy* (1961).

ECONOMIC THEORY

The literature on economic theory which appeared in the last two hundred years is quite wide in scope—and has undergone much specialization. Following are some of the main fields of economic theory.

THEORY OF VALUE AND PRICE AND THEORY OF PRODUCTION

One of the basic questions which appeared in early economic studies dealt with what determines the price of a certain commodity. One answer was the value to the user—the utility derived from the consumption of the commodity—which determines its price. However, some empirical observations seem to refute this explanation—e.g., the price of water is much lower than the price of diamonds, though water is much more useful. Another answer was that it is the cost of producing it which determines the price of a commodity. But again a difficulty arises: how can one explain, for example, the price of land, which is a gift of nature and which man did not have to produce? The answer finally reached is that price depends both on the utility derived from the commodity and on the cost of producing it. Further—and this is a crucial device in modern economic analysis—it is not total utility and total cost of a commodity, nor the average cost per unit of that commodity, that determines its price: the price is determined by the *marginal* utility and the *marginal* cost of that commodity. In other words, price is determined by the utility which was derived from the "last" unit or which would be derived from the consumption of one additional unit.

Whereas costs of production are, in a certain sense, something tangible and can be measured, utility is only a theoretical construct and cannot be observed empirically or measured directly. However, to some extent utility can be measured indirectly, through the observation of individual preferences among different commodities. If the consumer is confronted with the choice of either consuming a unit of one commodity or a unit of another commodity, then his choice should reveal which commodity yields more utility to him, or how many units of one commodity would yield as much utility as one unit of another commodity. This kind of experiment also brings up another central feature of economic analysis: it starts with the assumption that man has a limited amount of resources and therefore has to choose between alternatives; in the simplest case, he has to choose between commodity A and commodity B—he cannot have both A and B!

Once the mechanism of price determination is understood, the economist tries to explain and predict changes in the price and the quantity produced of a commodity as a result of such things as changes in consumers' incomes or the introduction of a sales tax.

Some of the basic works on the theory of value and price are Francis Y. Edgeworth, *Mathematical Physics* (1881); John R. Hicks, *Value and Capital* (1939); Nicholas Kaldor, *Essays on Value and Distribution* (1960); Frank H. Knight, *The Ethics of Competition and Other Essays* (1935); and Leon Walras, *Elements of Pure Economics*, translated by William Jaffe (1954).

The theory is applicable to any commodity. However, certain commodities or groups of commodities have drawn special attention, e.g., the prices of factors of production, such as the price of capital goods and the price of land; or the price paid for the services received from factors of production—the rent on land and other capital goods and the wages of labor. The rate of interest is also a price—the price received for postponing consumption—and hence can also be analyzed with similar tools. Rent, wages, and interest are closely related to the theory of production and the theory of capital. The following books discuss these subjects: Eugen Bohn von Bawerk, *Capital and Interest* (1890); Sune Carlson, *Study on the Pure Theory of Production* (1939); John M. Clark, *Studies in the Economics of Overhead Costs* (1923); Paul H. Douglas, *The Theory of Wages* (1934); Irving Fisher, *The Nature of Capital and Interest* (1906); John R. Hicks, *The Theory of Wages* (1932); Wassily W. Leontief, *The Structure of American Economy* (1951); Joan Robinson,

The Accumulation of Capital (1956); and John R. Hicks, *Capital and Growth* (1965).

The free play of the market forces of supply and demand (which, in the case of consumer goods, are a reflection of the above-mentioned marginal costs and marginal utility) usually achieves an efficient allocation of resources. This efficiency is impaired if "perfect" competition does not prevail. An extreme case of absence of competition is a monopoly (i.e., the presence of only one seller or one buyer in a given market); but usually the market structure is less extreme, and there is some competition, but only among few—which is called oligopoly. These problems are analyzed in Edward Chamberlin, *The Theory of Monopolistic Competition* (1956); Milton Friedman, *Essays in Positive Economics* (1953); Joan Robinson, *The Economics of Imperfect Competition* (1933); George J. Stigler, *The Theory of Price* (1946); and Robert Triffin, *Monopolistic Competition and General Equilibrium Theory* (1940).

THEORY OF INCOME AND EMPLOYMENT

The economy of a nation consists of many small economic units: firms and households. The behavior of these units can be analyzed with the aid of the theory of value and price and some other specialized theories—all falling under the heading of "microeconomics," the study of the small economic unit. But sometimes the economist is not interested in the behavior of a particular economic unit or in the price of a particular commodity and the quantity produced of it—he might be interested in the overall performance of the economy. The subjects he may investigate in this context—macroeconomics—involve not the output of a particular commodity, but rather the level of output of all commodities taken together, not the price of a single commodity, but rather some indicator of the price of all goods traded in the economy.

Among the main problems which macroeconomics discusses are the following. What determines the level of national output—and national income? What determines the level of employment—and unemployment? What determines the price level? What determines the allocation of national product between consumption and investment? As its name indicates, the theory of income and employment deals with the forces determining income and employment, but the boundary within macroeconomics between the theory of income and employment and other subjects is quite arbitrary. This arbitrariness actually reflects the stage of unification which macroeconomics has reached: income, employment, prices, and growth are all interdependent, and a theory which deals with one aspect of macroeconomics cannot ignore the other aspects. This unification of macroeconomics is due mainly to the work of Keynes.

Since macroeconomics is concerned with the level of welfare of the population as a whole, it is the foundation for more specialized studies which deal with government's economic policy, such as fiscal and monetary policy.

The Great Depression of the 1930's proved that economic theory did not then have adequate tools for dealing with the problems of national income and employment. Keynes's *The General Theory of Employment, Interest and Money* (1936) changed this situation and greatly advanced macroeconomics—both in its development as a theory and, no less important, in its implications for government policy.

The following are only a few of the many monographs which have appeared in this field: William J. Baumol, *Business Behavior, Value, and Growth* (1959); William H. Beveridge, *Full Employment in a Free Society* (1945); Raymond W. Goldsmith, *A Study of Savings in the United States* (1955–56); Simon Kuznets, *National Income and Its Composition, 1919–1938* (1941); Abba P. Lerner, *The Economics of Control* (1944); George L. S. Shackle, *Expectations, Investment, and Income* (1938); and Paul Studenski, *A Study of the Income of Nations: Theory, Measurement, and Analysis, Past and Present* (1958).

MONETARY THEORY

The invention of money was a most important step toward a more efficient economy of specialization and division of labor. But in order to fulfill its task efficiently, money has to preserve its value—something which it did not always accomplish. This loss of value—inflation—sometimes happens in extreme proportions (for example, the hyperinflation in Germany after both world wars); it sometimes takes on quite sizable proportions (in some South American countries, prices have doubled within a year or two); and it occurs often in many developed countries at more moderate rates (price rises of two to five percent a year). This loss in the value of money not only reduces its usefulness (and induces people to use substitutes which are less efficient), but also causes undesirable changes in income and wealth distribution and severe hardship to some parts of the population: to people who invested their savings in life insurance and in bonds, or to employees who get fixed pensions.

Inflation—especially high rates of inflation—can usually be attributed directly to changes in the quantity of money. Monetary theory is concerned with the relationship between the quantity of money and the price level.

Changes in the quantity of money affect not only the price level, but also the level of national output and employment. Further, in a modern economy, changes in the quantity of money are brought about by the banking system—the commercial banks and the central bank—and are closely associated with changes in interest rates. Monetary theory studies these interrelations between the quantity of money, the price level, interest rates, and national output. The following works contain extensive discussion of these various aspects of money: Morris A. Copeland, *A Study of Money Flows in the United States* (1952); Irving Fisher, *The Purchasing Power of Money, Its Determination and Relation to Credit, Interest, and Crises* (1925); Keynes's *Monetary Reform* (1924) and *A Treatise on Money* (1958); Arthur W. Marget, *The Theory of Prices* (1939–42); Don Patinkin, *Money, Interest, and Prices* (2d ed., 1965); Dennis H. Robertson, *Money* (1929); and Dennis H. Robertson, *Essays in Monetary Theory* (1946).

THEORY OF ECONOMIC FLUCTUATIONS

From a macroeconomic point of view, the desired state of the economy is full employment with stable prices. Unfortunately, often the economic situation is different: many countries have experienced periods of inflation and periods of unemployment. Further, it seems that there is a certain regularity in these fluctuations of economic activity and that they have the pattern of a cycle: a period of high economic activity is followed by a period of low activity, and that period, in turn, is followed by a period of high activity.

The regularity of business cycles, and the apparent periodicity they possessed, led some economists to look for nonhuman causes for them. Thus, one explanation for the cycles was that the sunspot cycle caused a cycle of agricultural productivity, and that the agricultural cycle affected the other sectors of the economy, and therefore the whole economy moved in cycles. Because of the regularity of the cycle, many economists thought that the expansion of the economy by itself creates stresses which ultimately cause a collapse and contraction, but that the contraction creates forces which ultimately lead to recovery and expansion. This element appears in theories which explain the cycle through alternations between optimism and pessimism by business leaders, through differences in the rate of growth of production and consumption, and through the effect of changes in the rate of growth of the economy on investment.

A satisfactory theory of business cycles has not yet been found. Nowadays, however, economists prefer to talk about business *fluctuations*, rather than cycles, because it seems that recently these fluctuations have lost some of their regularity. This may be due to the "Keynesian revolution," which led to a better use by government of the tools of fiscal and monetary policy. We may not yet have learned how to avoid fluctuations in a free-enterprise economy completely, but we probably know the way and means of avoiding deep depressions or prolonged recessions and of guarding against runaway inflations.

The following books discuss the different approaches to business fluctuations: John M. Clark, *Strategic Factors in Business Cycles* (1934); Gottfried Haberler, *Prosperity and Depression: A Theoretical Analysis of Cyclical Movements* (1958); Alvin H. Hansen, *Fiscal Policy and Business Cycles* (1941); John R. Hicks, *A Contribution to the Theory of the Trade Cycle* (1950); Wesley C. Mitchell, *Business Cycles: The Problem and Its Setting* (1927); Joseph A. Schumpeter, *Business Cycles* (1939); and Robert A. Gordon, *Business Fluctuations* (2d ed., 1961).

THEORIES OF ECONOMIC GROWTH

The growing concern which the developed countries feel today about the economic problems of the less developed countries has also expressed itself in an ever-expanding literature in the field of economic growth. Theories of economic growth try to explain why some economies, from a certain point on, tend to progress to higher and higher levels of performance. For even though there are depressions and periods of downturn, the subsequent upturn tends to lead to higher levels of income and output than any peak reached before. In other words, many economies have proven that they experience decided secular growth. These economies may be contrasted with others which have stagnated for a long time, which have apparently been unable to overcome their inherently low productivity, and which do not seem to be able to progress to a point of self-sustained economic growth.

If advancing and stagnating economies are contrasted with one another, the crucial question immediately arises as to what factors determine the point of "take-off." This is merely another way of asking what factors differentiate advancing from stagnant economies and is equivalent to pointing to the practical policy problem of what changes must be made in stagnating economies in order to push them to a level of output where self-sustained growth will begin. The debate on this question is by no means resolved. Some writers assign predominant importance to the supply of capital, others to the skill and level of education of the labor force, and still others to noneconomic factors which have their primary basis in the culture, social structure, or political affairs of the societies concerned. The study of economic growth has also prominently concerned itself with the reexamination of the economic history of countries which are among the leaders in the world economy. This has been done in the hope that, by examining this history, often from a new point of view, certain strategic factors could be singled out which would then point to the most appropriate policies poor "underdeveloped" countries could embrace in order to enter the stage of sustained growth.

The study of economic growth represents, in a certain sense, the general state of studies in contemporary economics: it has a theoretical core around which are built considerations stretching into the applied, the historical, and the noneconomic areas. It is concerned primarily not with a static equilibrium, or even a temporary equilibrium in the short run, but with a situation into which change is built in the form of long-run dynamic movement. Finally, it accepts the variability of economic institutions and explicitly recognizes their differentiation in time and space.

The following list is a sample of the large literature on this subject: Colin Clark, *The Conditions of Economic Progress* (1957); Evsey D. Domar, *Essays in the Theory of Economic Growth* (1957); Albert O. Hirschman, *The Strategy of Economic Development* (1958); Bert F. Hoselitz, *Sociological Aspects of Economic Growth* (1960); Simon Kuznets, *Six Lectures on Economic Growth* (1959) and *Modern Economic Growth, Rate, Structure, and Spread* (1966); Harvey Leibenstein, *Economic Backwardness and Economic Growth* (1957); W. A. Lewis, *The Theory of Economic Growth* (1955); Ragnar Nurkse, *Problems of Capital Formation in Underdeveloped Countries* (1957); Walt W. Rostow, *The Stages of Economic Growth* (1960); and Gerald M. Meier, *Leading Issues in Development Economics* (1964).

TIME AND SPACE IN ECONOMIC THEORY

In the theory of value and price, time did not enter explicitly—the problem was one of "comparative statistics": the study of the equilibrium position of the economy and of how an external disturbance (like changes in taxes, changes in tastes, the outbreak of war) calls for a different equilibrium position. However, the theories of income fluctuations and of economic growth—and the empirical evidence in these fields—have shown that the adjustment of the economy is not instantaneous; it takes some time after the external disturbance until prices, income, and the like reach a new stable level. But if the adjustment process is of relatively long duration—measured in months or even in years—then certainly the economist should also study what happens during this adjustment period, what the adjustment path of the economy looks like, how long it takes for the economy to adjust, and how the shape and duration of the adjustment path can be controlled by government policy. The study of these problems is the domain of "economic dynamics."

The study of economic dynamics is relatively new—and so also is the study of the location of economic activity, i.e., the role of space in economics. In early writings, space was almost assumed as being nonexistent, except in theories relating to the international division of labor. Gradually, economic considerations of location were introduced explicitly into general theorizing, and at present they have come to assume such an important role in the eyes of some students that a separate field of inquiry, "regional science," has become crystallized. Interest in regionalism is not confined to economists, but is also found, above all, among geographers and ecologists. Yet the economics of transportation, of differential pricing depending upon the location of the producer and consumer, and the problems arising out of the fact that shipments between two points may require different transport facilities and different quantities of transport equipment, have been combined with regional studies and thus are providing a more rounded picture of the place of space and location in economic theory. Some of the more outstanding monographs on dynamics, static equilibrium theory, and location theory, including regionalism, are listed here: Roy F. Harrod, *Towards A Dynamic Economics* (1948); Walter Isard, *Methods of Regional Analysis* (1960); August Losch, *The Economics of Location* (1954); Harvey Perloff, *Regions, Resources and Economic Growth* (1960); Arthur C. Pigou, *The Economics of Stationary States* (1935); George L. S. Shackle, *Time in Economics* (1958); and Charles E. Lindbolm, *The Intelligence of Democracy* (1965).

THEORIES OF CONSUMPTION

So far, we have been concerned primarily with production and distribution and have paid relatively little attention to consumption. To be sure, the subjective value theories, based on considerations of utility, are concerned with the consumer; so are theories of demand and even theories of business fluctuation. We have seen, for example, that some business cycle theories are based upon assumptions of underconsumption. But, on the whole, consumption and welfare have so far entered into consideration only accidentally or in a subordinate fashion. Yet it may be argued that all production is ultimately destined for the satisfaction of human needs, through consumption either by individuals or by collectivities, e.g., the state. The purchase of armaments and similar objects is also a form of consumption, only these objects are consumed not by private individuals but by a nation, i.e., by its citizens as a collective group.

In the past, not too much explicit attention was given to the economics of consumption. Most of the studies which dealt with consumption were centered around a specific commodity or group of commodities (e.g., food), and their main purpose was to determine the nature of the demand for these commodities and their place in the consumer's budget. Yet, even at a fairly early stage, a number of rather general propositions were made, and quite common relations were discovered. The best known among them is perhaps Engel's law, which states that as the income of a household rises, the proportion of its expenditure on food declines. This generalization was shown to be quite widely applicable by Engel, the German statistician, in the middle of the nineteenth century; since then it has been confirmed numerous times.

More modern research in the field of consumption has gone beyond the problem of expenditure on food, and students have discovered relations between a household's income and its expenditures on various perishable, semidurable (clothes and such) and durable (furniture and other household equipment) consumer goods. These studies tend to be summarized in works dealing with the function of consumption as a whole, in which various generalizations relating to changes in the level and type of consumption and changes in income are discussed. The literature on consumption, both on the theoretical and empirical level, is one of the fastest growing branches of modern economics: Robert Ferber, *A Study of Aggregate Consumption Functions* (1953); Robert Ferber and Hugh G. Wales (eds.), *Motivation and Market Behavior* (1958); Milton Friedman, *A Theory of the Consumption Function* (1957); George Katona and Eva Mueller, *Consumer Expectations* (1957); Margaret G. Reid, *Consumers and the Market* (1942); and Carolyn Bell, *Consumer Choice in the American Economy* (1967).

WELFARE ECONOMICS

Ultimately, the purpose of economics is to find a way to maximize human material welfare. In this context, one has to distinguish between one's own and the welfare of others. However, once one turns from the welfare of the individual to the welfare of the community as a whole, the problem becomes more complicated. Here one question is the optimal income distribution within the population—those who would prefer an egalitarian income distribution face the problem of the possible loss of incentives in such an economy, and hence a lower average standard of living. Another problem lies in the amount of resources which should be allocated to public consumption—those services provided by government and from which the whole community automatically benefits: military and police protection, preventive medicine, and so on.

The difficulty in solving these problems arises from the necessity of finding a balance between the egoistic and the altruistic elements inherent in each person: most people try to maximize their material welfare, but are also ready to sacrifice some of it for the benefit of the poor or for the benefit of some cultural or nationalistic projects undertaken by the community. Thus, a "community welfare" function must be developed which will take into account the different preferences of different citizens. Here economic reasoning comes close to social philosophy and a discussion of the problem of social values and is clearly influenced by the assumptions made about these values. In the field of welfare economics we reach, so to speak, the limits of pure economics and approach politics, philosophy, and the analysis of social psychology. These problems are discussed in Kenneth J. Arrow, *Social Choice and Individual Values* (1951); Ian M. D. Little, *A Critique of Welfare Economics* (1957); Arthur C. Pigou, *The Economics of Welfare* (1938); and Melvin W. Reder, *Studies in the Theory of Welfare Economics* (1947).

INTERNATIONAL ECONOMICS

International economics is an extension of economic theory to the economic relations among nations. Many principles of economics hold both for national and international economies, but there are also some important differences. In international economic relations there is much less mobility of labor and capital than within a country; the different countries have different currencies; and whereas usually each country has a strong central government, no such central government exists for the world community.

The basic works in this field are James W. Angell, *The Theory of International Prices* (1926); Gottfried Haberler, *The Theory of International Trade* (1937); James E. Meade, *Trade and Welfare* (1955); Bertil Ohlin, *Interregional and International Trade* (1933); Frank W. Taussig, *International Trade* (1927); Jacob Viner, *Studies in the Theory of International Trade* (1937); and Harry G. Johnson, *Economic Policies Toward Less Developed Countries* (1967).

THE APPLICATION OF ECONOMIC THEORIES

The previous section described briefly the main branches of economic theory. This theory is applicable for "practical" purposes to many areas of economic activity, and some of those areas are now described.

AGRICULTURAL ECONOMICS

In the area of agricultural economics, a literature has developed which in scope and quantity equals, or perhaps even exceeds, that of all other fields combined. Agricultural economists in the United States have their own professional organization and their own journal, and, in most universities, are organized into their own departments. Hence, there are probably more available data on various aspects of economic matters pertaining to agriculture than to any other sector of production. This proliferation of research and publication in the field of agricultural economics has taken place in spite of the fact that an increasingly smaller percentage of the labor force in the United States is employed in agriculture. It has had the effect, however, of bringing to the attention of many agricultural economists the importance of farming in foreign countries, especially the poorer countries of Asia, Africa, and Latin America. There the majority of the labor force is engaged in agriculture, and a sizable proportion of the total output of these nations is produced in agriculture. Moreover, the techniques of farming are primitive, the organization of agricultural production is backward and clumsy, and the applications of modern methods are lagging behind. Important changes are needed in the structure of landholding and in the patterns of farm management and agricultural marketing. Though the literature does not yet fully represent these problems, there is a growing stream of articles and pamphlets devoted to them, and even the official agencies of the United States Department of Agriculture are becoming increasingly concerned with the problems of the poorer countries.

It would be impossible within a reasonable space to represent all the ramifications of empirical, theoretical, and applied studies in the field of agricultural economics; we therefore list only a few of the monographs which appear to be of most general interest and of widest applicability. But it should be pointed out that such organizations as the U.S. Bureau of Farm Economics, the Food Research Institute at Stanford University, and many agricultural extension stations and departments of agriculture, especially at the land-grant colleges, supply an abundance of valuable special materials on all aspects of farming, land economics, agricultural marketing, and agricultural management. Our list here includes John W. Mellor, *The Economics of Agricultural Development* (1966); A. T. Mosher, *Getting Agriculture Moving* (1966); C. K. Eicher and L. W. Witt (eds.), *Agriculture in Economic Development* (1964); Earl O. Heady, *Economics of Agricultural Production and Resource Use* (1952); D. G. Johnson, *Forward Prices for Agriculture* (1947); Theodore W. Schultz, *The Economic Organization of Agriculture* (1953), *Transforming Traditional Agriculture* (1965) and (ed.), *Food for the World* (1945); and Alvin S. Tostlebe, *Capital in Agriculture: Its Formation and Financing since 1870* (1957).

THE INDUSTRIAL LABOR FORCE

With agriculture declining in importance in the most advanced countries, there has been an increase in the attention given to industrialism and its associated phenomena. At one time, principal attention was paid by or to the standard of living of the laborer, but with the growing capacity of the more highly developed economies to afford a rising degree of comfort for the average worker, the focus has turned to other problems, principally, the question of the size and composition of the labor force, the impact and strategy of trade unions, and the conditions of work on the job, including the problem of labor-management relations.

At first sight, the problem of the determination of the labor force appears easiest and most straightforward. Superficially, one would assume that the study of the labor force turns around a primarily statistical problem, that of counting the number of workers in a series of industries and of determining fluctuations and changes in that number over time. But once one penetrates beneath the reasons for these fluctuations, one observes that many difficult and complex social problems are involved. For example, if we witness a sharp, sudden change in the labor force in a given industry, is this due to technical change, to different social views on the part of the part of the population, to changes in wages or general working conditions, to changes in the requirements of skill in the industry, or to some combination of these forces? What determines the participation of women, especially married women, in the labor force? The income of a household is one factor; its aspirations another; cultural and social attitudes regarding women's work a third; the conditions under which a job may be performed a fourth; hours, wages, and wage differentials a fifth; sixth; and seventh; and so on. Whether we are interested in the participation of women just in industrial work or also in related work, or whether we ask what impact the age of leaving school exerts, or whether we study the consequences of automation or the problem of unemployment, we are concerned with some aspect of the analysis of the labor force. Hence, studies in the field have appeared in growing number and have become oriented toward an increasing variety of questions and problems: Gertrude Bancroft, *The American Labor Force: Its Growth and Changing Composition* (1958); Clarence D. Long, *The Labor Force under Changing Income and Employment* (1958); Herbert S. Parnes, *Research on Labor Mobility* (1954); Lloyd G. Reynolds, *The Structure of Labor Markets* (1951); Richard A. Lester, *Labor* (1965); and Ray Marshall, *The Negro Worker* (1967).

THE ECONOMICS OF TRADE UNIONISM

Of equally great concern as the problems of the size, quality, and composition of the labor force is that of trade unions. Probably little needs to be said in substantiation of the importance of the subject, and so we will list merely a few of the major economic questions associated with the growth and changing structure of labor unionism.

Unions appear most prominently in the public eye as organizations whose internal structure is under scrutiny. When congressional committees investigate unions or racketeering in labor organizations, they are concerned with the degree of internal democracy and representative government within a given local or national trade union. They ask, basically, whether the leadership is autocratic and whether it uses the resources of the union for the proper purposes of the organization. This is not a strictly economic but primarily a political problem.

The proper economic purpose of labor organizations is collective bargaining, and it is this aspect of unionism to which economists have paid most attention. To be sure, the internal structure of a union, the degree of free determination of its policies and objectives by the membership, its centralization, and the weight of its financial control play a role; but the major economic problems relate to the methods the union uses in determining wages and associated working conditions. In this context, there is a whole set of further considerations, since determination of wages and working conditions by unions has extensive effects upon the economy as a whole. We have all heard of the inflationary tendencies inherent in a wage-price spiral, and this development is possible only in an economy in which most wages are subject to negotiation by unions.

Of equal seriousness is the question of negotiations with management. The confrontation between a labor union and the heads of a large enterprise is, economically speaking, an instance of bilateral monopoly. Negotiations under these conditions can best be analyzed by application of principles of the theory of games. Here, again, the nonachievement of consensus may lead to strikes or work stoppages, which in the case of some basic industries may have far-reaching effects upon a country's economy. Hence, it is not surprising that most modern nations have passed extensive legislation designed to regulate the organization, internal structure, and activities of labor unions.

The following works consider the problems outlined above: John T. Dunlop, *Wage Determination under Trade Unions* (1944); Frederick H. Harbison and John R. Coleman, *Goals and Strategy in Collective Bargaining* (1951); Robert F. Hoxie, *Trade Unionism in the United States* (1947); Selig Perlman, *A Theory of the Labor Movement* (1928); Leonard R. Sayles and George Strauss, *The Local Union* (1953); Joel L. Seidman and others, *The Worker Views His Union* (1958); Lloyd Ulman, *The Rise of the National Trade Union* (1955); Sidney and Beatrice Webb, *Industrial Democracy* (1926); and Jack Barbash, *Structure, Government and Politics of American Unions* (1967).

LABOR-MANAGEMENT RELATIONS

Negotiations between management and unions about wages and conditions of work also have an impact upon general labor-management relations. The work situation for an individual is not confined to a day's work in a completely impersonal environment, and departure after work is done without the factory or the office having any impact whatsoever.

It was discovered early, at first by efficiency experts, that the environment in which work was performed has an effect upon productivity. It was learned later that in many instances workers formed informal groups which cooperated, and that if these groups were disturbed productivity declined. In brief, it was shown that the internal organization and layout of the work process, the flow of tasks, and the informal social relations which became established between workers had an effect upon the economic result of an enterprise.

But the relations between management and the workers also played a role. Here such problems as grievance procedures, the possibilities of advancement in pay and in rank, considerations of seniority and rights derived therefrom, and the barriers which exist between the blue-collar and the white-collar portions of the work force are paramount. Labor-management relations have passed through various phases. They begin with emphasis on strong paternalistic features, developed to a point where the two parties faced one another as "enemies" and gradually grew into more or less impersonal business relations. It is becoming ever more apparent that the injection of some added ingredients which will enhance the worker's interest in his job, his company, and his industry may have a beneficial effect upon productivity. A job, it is increasingly recognized, is not merely a means of earning a living: it is part of a man's life.

Some important studies of labor-management relations are Clark Kerr and others, *Industrialism and Industrial Man* (1960); Elton Mayo, *The Human Problems of an Industrial Civilization* (1946); Wilbert E. Moore and Arnold S. Feldman, *Labor Commitment and Social Change in Developing Areas* (1960); Fritz J. Roethlisberger and William J. Dickson, *Management and the Worker* (1960); Sumner H. Slichter and others, *The Impact of Collective Bargaining on Management* (1960); William Foote Whyte, *Industry and Society* (1946); and Frederick Harbison and C. A. Myers, *Education, Manpower and Economic Growth* (1964).

THEORIES OF MANAGEMENT

The trends which have been observed in the study of and research on labor problems have their parallels in the field of management research.

On the one hand, there has been a growth of interest in the social position of persons in management jobs, and studies have been extended to cover the psychological pressures and personality characteristics—creativity, achievement orientation, and others—which contribute to the performance of their jobs. On the other hand, there has been the development of scientific management and the growing interpretation of business administration as a system of decision-making processes. Decisions of varying importance under varying constraints are made on different levels in a management structure, and the organization of a decision-making machinery which entails both vertical and horizontal lines of interconnection has become a fascinating field of study.

At the same time, the place and role of business, its structural aspects, and its evolution have become points of interest. Thus, the literature may be divided into three parts. The first, which will not be discussed here, is the rather old-fashioned set of studies and texts on technical aspects of business administration, such as accounting practice, advertising, salesmanship, and so forth. The second consists of literature devoted to management as a set of decisions and considerations underlying this interpretation. The third is materials for the interpretation of business leadership as the performance of the entrepreneurial function and the history of and present challenge to entrepreneurship. A few of the more important works on management proper are listed here: Adolf A. Berle and Gardiner C. Means, *The Modern Corporation and Private Property* (1932); Sune Carlson, *Executive Behavior* (1951); Eliot D. Chapple and Leonard R. Sayles, *The Measure of Management* (1961); Peter F. Drucker, *The Practice of Management* (1954); Ruth P. Mack, *The Flow of Business Funds and Consumer Purchasing Power* (1911); James C. March and Herbert A. Simon, *Organizations* (1958); and Herbert A. Simon, *The New Science of Management Decisions* (1960).

ENTREPRENEURSHIP

As we have seen, the various studies of the human element in productive activity—labor, management, salaried officials—have begun to stress increasingly the motivational and general psychological background of economic performance in these areas. Of all the types of economic activity, entrepreneurship has been studied most intensively, with the personality angle in view, and it is with primary consideration of the performance of entrepreneurs that some students have written monographs explicitly devoted to both economics and psychology.

Entrepreneurship has been differently defined, i.e., its main characteristics have been given different weight. J. B. Say specified it as the performance of the act of combining productive factors, i.e., of drawing together labor, capital, and science, for purposes of production. Later writers stressed primarily the risk element characteristic of entrepreneurs; but Joseph Schumpeter emphasized the innovating activity of enterprisers, and this interpretation has become more or less generally accepted in a private enterprise economy, it is the entrepreneur who performs the crucial function of pushing the system along higher and better standards of performance, who introduces innovations in technology, organization, and marketing activities. But since not every person has the innate or even acquired propensities for entrepreneurship, it is not strange that researchers should have asked what personality traits were associated with the performance of entrepreneurial functions. The life histories and activities of past entrepreneurs have been examined to determine whether any useful generalizations can be derived.

The list of studies of entrepreneurship includes Miriam Beard, *A History of the Business Man* (1938); Thomas C. Cochran, *The American Business System, A Historical Perspective, 1900–1955* (1957); Arthur H. Cole, *Business Enterprise in Its Social Setting* (1959); Frederic C. Lane and Jelle C. Riemersma, *Enterprise and Secular Change* (1953); David C. McClelland, *The Achieving Society* (1961); and Walter A. Weisskopf, *The Psychology of Economics* (1957).

INVENTION AND INNOVATION

If entrepreneurship is defined as consisting primarily of the introduction of innovations, the role of invention in economics becomes crucial. This is a field which is still too little explored for us to have really useful theories. Yet some work has been done, both along historical lines and in an analytical direction. Here, as in the general field of business management, the haphazard accidental practices of earlier days are shown to have been replaced by the much more orderly procedures of research and development departments and the planned execution of inventive activity. The economics of the modern research laboratory have not yet been explored as exhaustively as those of the family farm or the industrial plant, but the principles applicable to them in terms of performance and profitability differ little, if at all, from those applied to other business entities.

Works here include John Jewkes and others, *The Sources of Invention* (1958); Richard L. Meier, *Science and Economic Development* (1956); National Bureau of Economic Research, *The Rate and Direction of Inventive Activity: Economic and Social Factors* (1962); W. Paul Strassman, *Risk and Technical Innovation* (1959); Jack Stieber (ed.), *Employment Problems of Automation and Advanced Technology* (1966);

and Daniel Hamberg, *R & D: Essays on the Economics of Research and Development* (1966).

BANKING

When speaking of the banking system, one has to distinguish between the commercial banks and the nation's central bank (like the Federal Reserve System in the United States). The commercial banks, like other economic units of the private sector, are profit-motivated. The central bank, on the other hand, is not profit-motivated and should be regarded as a government agency partly in charge of monetary policy.

Banks are an invention of medieval Europe. Since then, they have developed many new techniques and new functions; various banks have specialized in such aspects of business as small loans, mortgage lending, savings deposits, investment trusts, and other financial practices. But the major business of banks has been commercial banking, i.e., the granting of short-term loans and the acceptance of demand deposits against which checks can be drawn.

Today checks are accepted as a means of payment just as much as cash, and hence both cash and demand deposits are counted in the money supply. Since commercial banks can create demand deposits (for example, by making loans), they can thus affect the money supply; and since an excessive creation of money can have very inflationary consequences, it is necessary to limit the capacity of the commercial banks to create demand deposits. This is done by the central bank, which requires the commercial banks to hold certain reserves against their deposits.

The central bank has several tasks. One is the protection of the depositors; this is done by continuous controls to assure the liquidity of the bank. Another major task is the regulation of the money supply: expanding the money supply during recession and reducing its rate of expansion during inflation. The central bank can regulate the money supply in three ways: changing the amount of reserves which have to be held by the commercial banks against each dollar of deposits (reserve ratio requirements), changing the rate of interest at which commercial banks can borrow from the central bank (rediscount rate), and selling or buying government securities from the public (open market operations).

The following books describe the banking system and its impact on the economy: Walter Bagehot, *Lombard Street, A Description of the Money Market* (1873); John G. Gurley and Edward S. Shaw, *Money in a Theory of Finance* (1960); Ralph G. Hawtrey, *The Art of Central Banking* (1932) and *Currency and Credit* (1950); Lloyd W. Mints, *A History of Banking Theory in Great Britain and the United States* (1945); Dennis H. Robertson, *Banking Policy and the Price Level* (1932); Richard S. Sayers,

American Banking System (1948) and *Modern Banking* (1960); Harry G. Johnson, *Essays in Monetary Economy* (1967); and Charles Kindleberger, *Europe and the Dollar* (1966).

PUBLIC FINANCE

The economic role of government is continuously growing—as can be seen from the proportion of a nation's income which is transferred to the government through taxes and from the proportion of national expenditure which is spent by the government. Government intervention is necessary even in societies which believe in the merits of private enterprise—to modify income distribution and to maintain full employment and price stability. Through the budgetary process, the government can withdraw from or add to the purchasing power of the public and can affect the level of employment and prosperity in the community. Deficit financing may be a blessing when the economy at large is sluggish and may be a curse in a situation of full or nearly full employment.

Among all the features of public finance, the problem of taxation is the most hotly debated. It is not so much the fact of taxation, but rather the economic impact of taxes, the kinds of taxes, and the distribution of the burden of taxation which is under discussion. Among the most important and controversial subjects are the question of indirect *versus* direct taxes, the problem of proportionality *versus* progressivity of taxation, and the question of how easy it is to shift taxes onto the shoulders of someone else, e.g., by price changes or by alteration of wage payments. In addition, there are problems of cost of collection, of the possibility of tax evasion and tax avoidance, and above all, of the equity and justice of a tax system. It should be remembered that modern societies all have a multiplicity of taxes and that what affects each person is not the impact of a single selected tax, but of the tax system as a whole. These many related problems are discussed in the following monographs: Roy Blough, *The Federal Taxing Process* (1952); Walter J. Blum and Harry Kalven, Jr., *The Uneasy Case for Progressive Taxation* (1953); John M. Clark, *Economics of Planning Public Works* (1935); Hugh Dalton and others, *Unbalanced Budgets* (1934); Arthur C. Pigou, *A Study in Public Finance* (1947); Henry C. Simons, *Personal Income Taxation* (1938); Henry C. Simons, *Federal Tax Reform* (1950); Ursula K. Hicks, *Development Finance Planning and Control* (1965); and James W. Buchanan, *The Public Finances* (1965).

GOVERNMENT CONSUMPTION

From the previous discussion, it might seem that government

expenditure functions only as a means of stabilization. Actually, a large part of government expenditure is determined almost without any regard to its stabilizing or destabilizing effects. For example, the expenditure on armaments or on education, on the dispensing of justice, and on general administration are autonomous expenses; only such expenses as certain relief payments or expenditures on certain public works have primarily a stabilizing function. It is proper, therefore, to study the general level of government activity as it has developed over time and to look into the problems of such governmental activities as the provision of materials and services for defense, education, and so on. The following books discuss these matters: Solomon Fabricant, *The Trend of Government Activity in the United States since 1900* (1952); Charles J. Hitch and Roland N. McKean, *The Economics of Defense in the Nuclear Age* (1960); and Horst Menderhausen, *The Economics of War* (1940).

ECONOMIC POLICY AND ECONOMIC PLANNING

Fiscal measures, as well as other steps taken by the government, are all part and parcel of the overall economic policy of the government. This policy may have varying objectives: it may be directed primarily toward the welfare of the people, or toward defense, or toward the maximization of the rate of economic growth. In any case there will be efforts to bring about some degree of equity in the distribution of goods and services, at least in the more modern nations. The steps taken toward these ends may be fiscal or regulatory; they usually will be combinations of both.

In all instances in which the intervention of government is not inspired by a general production plan, we customarily speak of economic policy or sets of economic policies. Whenever the quantity or degree of regulation is ordered according to a systematic comprehensive schedule of production, we speak of economic planning. Dahl and Lindblom have shown that the limits between economic policy and economic planning are often blurred, and that certain policies shade into planning and certain plans into measures of somewhat disjointed policies. In the literature, somewhat sharper distinctions are drawn; and one may list separately studies which concern themselves primarily with economic policies, the rationale for certain policies. A few of the more challenging books in this vein are listed here: John M. Clark, *Social Control of Business* (1939); Robert A. Dahl and Charles E. Lindblom, *Politics, Economics, and Welfare* (1953); Anthony Downs, *An Economic Theory of Democracy* (1957); Edward R. Walker, *From Economic Theory to Policy* (1943); Gordon Tullock, *Toward a Mathematics of Politics* (1967); and Friedrich A. Hayek, *Individualism and Economic Order* (1948).

ECONOMICS 285

Other books concentrate on planning. At one point, the possibility of planning as such is questioned, at another its wisdom, and at some points its efficiency. To all these questions answers have been given, but the debate continues: Hayek (ed.), *Collectivist Economic Planning* (1955); Oskar Lange and Fred M. Taylor, *On the Economic Theory of Socialism* (1938); W. A. Lewis, *The Principles of Economic Planning* (1940); and Barbara Wootton, *Freedom under Planning* (1945).

BALANCE OF PAYMENTS AND FOREIGN TRADE

In its economic relations with the rest of the world, the value of a country's exports may differ from the value of its imports. For example, imports may exceed exports because the domestic price level is too high compared to foreign prices, and therefore the locally produced goods cannot compete with foreign-made goods, causing a high level of imports and a low level of exports. Imports may also exceed exports intentionally: when a country wants to develop its economy rapidly or reconstruct it after the damages of war, it may find its own resouces insufficient and hence will resort to imports as a source for the additional goods needed in the economy. If imports exceed exports, the difference has to be paid for. In the short run, the deficit in the balance of payments (the excess of imports over exports) can be financed through borrowing abroad or by paying with gold; but since debts have to be repaid, and a country's gold reserves are limited, ultimately the payment must be made in kind, i.e., by increased exports. Hence, in the long run a country must maintain a balanced foreign trade. Whereas once governments did not intervene much in foreign trade, nowadays all of them do. There are various ways in which the flow of international trade can be regulated: adjustment of the exchange rate, putting restrictions on foreign trade (exchange controls, quotas, and so forth), imposing tariffs on imports, and subsidizing exports. The following books discuss some of the balance-of-payments problems: William H. Beveridge and others, *Tariffs, the Case Examined* (1931); Percy W. Bidwell, *The Invisible Tariff: A Study of the Control of Imports into the United States* (1939); Howard S. Ellis, *Exchange Control in Central Europe* (1941); Carl Iversen, *Aspects of the Theory of International Capital Movements* (1935); Charles P. Kindleberger, *The Dollar Shortage* (1950); John W. Letiche, *Balance of Payments and Economic Growth* (1959); Frank W. Taussig, *Some Aspects of the Tariff Question* (1915); John B. Williams, *International Trade under Flexible Exchange Rates* (1954); Gunnar Myrdal, *An International Economy* (1956); Robert Triffin, *Our International Monetary System* (1964); and Harry G. Johnson, *International Trade and Economic Growth* (1958).

A high level of international trade has its advantages and its disadvantages. One disadvantage is that business fluctuations in one country can easily be transferred, through the mechanism of international trade, to another country. Another disadvantage, from the national point of view, is the greater economic dependence on other countries, since the country is no longer self-sufficient. Against these disadvantages stands the big advantage of the efficiency derived from specialization—the international division of labor. Many governments have realized that cooperation in the field of international trade is preferable to the pursuit of independent national economic policies—hence, the recent attempts to create custom unions or other forms of economic union. The European Economic Community (the so-called "Common Market") is perhaps the most important example and the most far-reaching in its goals, but there exist other regional organizations and economic blocs all over the world.

The main problems of the formation of these unions are political; but, to the extent to which they extend the territory of common trade and related economic actions, they have economic results. It is to these economic results that the most serious literature has been devoted. Most of the more popular treatments do not come to the heart of the economic problem, but discuss mainly or exclusively the political questions involved.

Among the works on economic union are Émile Benoit, *Europe at Sixes and Sevens* (1961); Albert O. Hirschman, *National Power and the Structure of Foreign Trade* (1945); James E. Meade, *Problems of Economic Union* (1953); James E. Meade, *The Theory of Customs Unions* (1955); Jacob Viner, *The Customs Union Issue* (1950); Charles Wolf, Jr., *Foreign Aid: Theory and Practice in Southern Asia* (1960); and Hoselitz (ed.), *Economics and the Idea of Mankind* (1965).

ECONOMIC HISTORY

Economic history is the study of economic institutions (such as those for production, distribution, and exchange) in societies with different cultures and in different time periods in the same society. The study of *economic* history—regarded from the point of view of the economist and not the historian—is the comparison of economic institutions. It relates the changing economic institutions to the historical evolution of society, and the differences between economic institutions of different societies to cross-cultural differences.

It is most convenient to distinguish works on economic history as between ancient, medieval, and modern. In ancient and medieval history there are too few figures in any important field to make it possible to relate economic history to mathematical computations. In a few modern history publications, especially on historical developments of the nineteenth and twentieth centuries, there has developed an emphasis on New Economic History or Cliometrics which makes them different from ordinary economic history texts.

In ancient history we have examples like A. H. M. Jones, *The Later Roman Empire* (1964), Mikhail I. Rostovtsev, *The Social and Economic History of the Roman Empire* (1926) and *The Social and Economic History of the Hellenistic World* (1941), Fritz Heichelheim, *Wirtschaftsgeschichte des Altertums*, Vols. I and II (1938 and 1964), and Arthur E. R. Boak, *Manpower Shortage and the Fall of the Roman Empire in the West* (1955).

The chief advances in medieval history have been both in Western history as well as in the history of the Byzantine Empire. Examples of a new treatment of the Byzantine Empire are books by Georges Ostrogorskij, *History of the Byzantine State* (1956), and Steven Runciman, *The History of the Crusades* (1951-54). Especially in the economic history of the Western world have there been new developments, the main results of which are contained in Vols. II and III of the *Cambridge Economic History of Europe* (1952 and 1963), and in the three-volume *Essays in Economic History*, edited by E. M. Carus-Wilson (1954, 1962, 1962). Some of those results are derived from such books as Marc Bloch's *Feudal Society* (1961), Alfons Dopsch, *The Economic and Social Foundations of European Civilization* (1937), Robert Latouche, *Les Origines de L'Economie Occidentale* (1956), and Henri Pirenne, *Economic and Social History of Medieval Europe* (1937).

With the economic history of the modern age we have arrived at a treatment of economic relations which are, as we have said, taken up in two forms. One form is a continuance of economic history as it has been since W. Cunningham, *The Growth of English Industry and Commerce* (1896). Such historical works are, for example, Karl Bücher, *Industrial Evolution* (1901); John H. Clapham, *An Economic History of Modern Britain* (1959); John U. Nef, *War and Human Progress* (1950); Karl Polanyi, *The Great Transformation* (1944); Werner Sombart, *The Quintessence of Capitalism* (1915), translated and edited by M. Epstein; Max Weber, *General Economic History* (1950); Chester Wright, *Economic History of the United States* (2d ed., 1949); and Alexander Gerschenkron, *Economic Backwardness in Historical Perspective* (1962). Quite different from these are the economic histories in books of New Economic History or Cliometrics. This new form of economic history is treated in, for example, Douglass C. North, *The Economic Growth of the United States 1790-1860* (1961), Robert William Fogel, *Railroads and American Economic Growth* (1964), and Ralph Andreano, *New Views on American*

Economic Development (1965). The final test of the New Economic History is whether or not it has a return in understanding and generalization which is superior to the alternative methods of research and conceptualization. Has the New Economic History yielded results which were not previously available? North, Fogel, and Andreano say yes. Some of the work cited in these three books as well as in a dozen or so doctoral dissertations in final stages shows that the new theory covers a much broader aspect of economic history than the old findings did. Unfortunately, there are no theories yet on some of the fundamental aspects of historic economic development included in some of the older economic histories of the United States. None of these works, for example, gives us a clear description of the economy of the United States as does Charles and Mary Beard's *The Rise of American Civilization* (1930), or the well-known book by Louis Hacker, *The Triumph of American Capitalism* (1940). If Cliometrics will come close to the achievements of the two last-mentioned books, it will have made very consistent progress in its exposition of economic history.

One of the consequences of the research of the German historical school in economics was the development of institutional economics, which experienced its main flowering in the United States in the early twentieth century. Its main representatives were Thorstein Veblen and John R. Commons in the United States and John A. Hobson in Great Britain. The institutionalists had no real quarrel with then-prevailing economic theory, though in some of the less friendly reviews of their ideas this opinion is sometimes expressed. They tried to do what some of the more thoughtful members of the German school of historical economics had already attempted, i.e., they endeavored to examine the social role played by economic institutions and the way in which these institutions exerted a feedback on the functioning of the economic system itself. They tried to provide answers to questions which general theory had not been able to solve. These answers were not to be found in the economic system as such, but in the social relations, in the psychology of the participants in the economic process, and in the distribution of political power throughout a given society.

In its period of flowering, i.e., during the first three decades of this century, institutional economics made a very real contribution; but by now many of the suggestions proffered by the institutional economists have been incorporated into the general body of economics. In the postwar period, this has been facilitated by the growing interest in the economics of underdeveloped countries and the fact that cultural and social conditions, as well as the economic institutions of these countries, were patently different from those of Western nations. Hence, contemporary economics, though still predominantly "theoretical and analytical," has become much more "institutional" than the economics of even a generation ago. Thus, books by the leading institutional economists have more interest as contributions to the history of economic ideas than to the analysis of contemporary economic problems. Some of the important books in institutional economics are Clarence E. Ayres, *The Theory of Economic Progress* (1944); Commons' *Institutional Economics* (1934); Hobson's *Work and Wealth: A Human Valuation* (1914); and Veblen's *The Theory of Business Enterprise* (1904) and *The Theory of the Leisure Class* (1934).

Some of the work which has incorporated suggestions originally made by the institutional economists relates, as already suggested, to cross-cultural comparisons of economic institutions. The number of studies in this field has grown rapidly in recent years, and research in this branch of economics has become very popular. A large number of field reports on the economic institutions of peoples with cultures very different from those of the West has been made available; some steps have been taken to develop a field of "economic anthropology." It would be impossible to provide an adequate listing of all the case studies in this field which are now available.

On the basis of these field studies, and through cooperation among several researchers, some comparative studies have been produced. These tend to incorporate the results of field research from various sources. The economist searching for generalizations of some kind is better served by comparative studies than by special field studies, since the former already contribute a certain effort at generalization. Moreover, comparative studies tend to select the major variables from several field studies and place primary emphasis on them. In an area where institutional variety is so large, this is an important step forward.

In the following, we present a few studies which may properly be said to fall into the area of the comparative cross-cultural study of economic institutions. Some are case studies; others are more genuine comparative studies. Some deal with relatively simple and primitive societies, others with more advanced societies, notably those in which extensive planning of the more socialist variety is practiced. These are merely samples of a rapidly growing literature which in the not-too-distant future is likely to supply us with extensive descriptive and analytical accounts of the economic relations in most countries and societies of the world: Hugh G. J. Aitken (ed.), *The State and Economic Growth* (1959); Cyril S. Belshaw, *In Search of Wealth* (1955); Abram Bergson, *Soviet Economic Growth: Conditions and Perspectives* (1953); Melville Herskovitz, *Economic Anthropology* (1952); Wilbert E. Moore, *Industrialization and Labor* (1951); Sol Tax, *Penny Capitalism: A Guatemalan Indian Economy* (1953); Richard Thurnwald, *Economics in Private*

Communities (1932); and Stanley G. Udy, *The Organization of Work* (1959).

SOURCES OF ECONOMIC DATA

As has already been said, economists often need empirical data upon which to construct their theories or against which to test their theories. Sometimes the interested economist must himself collect the necessary data; often, however, they are already available in the library. Publications by governments and international organizations containing current data have become one of the main sources of the facts upon which economic analysis is based. The forms in which these data are presented vary considerably. Some are compiled in annual serials, such as the *Statistical Abstract of the United States* (1878–) or the *Demographic Yearbook* (1948–) of the United Nations. Others appear in monthly serial publications, as, for example, *Survey of Current Business* (1921–), published by the U.S. Bureau of Foreign and Domestic Commerce, or *International Financial Statistics* (1948–), published by the International Monetary Fund. Finally, factual data are often published in special books or monographs. For example, many of the printed reports on congressional hearings include sections presenting basic economic data, and the United States government and other governments publish frequent studies of economic import.

One of the main producers of works and sponsors of research in international economics is the United Nations and its specialized agencies. The United Nations itself publishes statistical and general works on international economic relations among all countries, such as United Nations Department of Economic and Social Affairs, *World Economic Survey* (1945–). The various regional economic commissions bring out annual reports and additional occasional studies on international economic relations pertaining to the region they serve. The Food and Agriculture Organization publishes works on international aspects of farm production and trade in agricultural commodities, such as Food and Agricultural Organization of the United Nations, *Yearbook of Food and Agricultural Statistics* (annually since 1947), and the International Labor Organization on international migration and comparative studies on wages, and the like, such as International Labor Office, *Yearbook of Labor Statistics* (annually since 1931). In addition, some special agencies, such as the Organization of American States, or NATO, or the Organization for European Economic Cooperation also sponsor international economic research and bring out publications falling into the field of regional or worldwide international economics, such as the Organization for European Economic Cooperation, *The OECD Observer* (six times yearly beginning in 1966).

The quality of these works varies considerably, both as to method of compilation and form of presentation. In general, the governmental publications of the poorer "underdeveloped" countries are less reliable and less skillfully presented than those of the richer, more economically advanced countries. However, even these somewhat less satisfactory data form an important reservoir of the raw statistics on which a good part of economic analysis and research is based.

Because businessmen need current and accurate information upon which to base their decisions, some private firms too have entered into the field of collecting and publishing economic data. The Fuggers, bankers to the Holy Roman Emperors, met this need by collecting letters, dispatches, and news items from many sources and having a selection of them copied, in order that their international banking decisions might be made upon the best information available—an interesting example of an early forerunner of the modern newspaper, or even of the financial or business service. There is a modern compilation edited by Victor Klarwill, published under the title *The Fugger News-Letters* (1924-   ), which illustrates the kind of news about persons, events, and trade that was considered worth reporting.

Examples of more modern sources are the English *The Economist* and the American *Wall Street Journal*. Such weekly or daily economic publications exist in most countries, as do surveys published annually, such as *Moody's Bank & Financial Manual, Industrial Manual, Municipal & Government Manual, Public Utility Manual, Transportation Manual,* and the 104th volume of *The Statesman's Year-Book* (1967-68; annually).

6 Geography

Norton Ginsburg

THE DOMAIN OF GEOGRAPHY

Geography shares with the other social sciences the task of understanding man both in society and as part of the total environment which he has in part created. As a social science, it is anthropocentric and is concerned with questions of human behavior to the same degree, though not necessarily in the same way, that the other social sciences are. Although an ancient field of knowledge, the origins of which lay in the curiosity that men seem always to have had in the world about them, the modern discipline has undergone various conceptual vagaries in the past 100 years and its current character differs markedly from that of, say, fifty years ago. At the same time, geography has suffered from substantial misconceptions as to its purposes and methodology—not only among laymen but also among social scientists—one of the reasons for which is the plethora of definitions with which it has been afflicted. Although all of these, as described below, have some basis in the perceptions various geographers have had of their field, and although all to a degree at least relate to the "four P's" of geographic endeavor—people, places, patterns, and processes—they represent highly divergent and often conflicting views of geographic interests and roles in higher education and scholarly enquiry.

Fortunately, there are several treatments of geography as a research discipline which provide the reader with the background for understanding recent developments in the field. The first of these is Richard Hartshorne's *The Nature of Geography* (1939), first published as an issue of the

Annals of the Association of American Geographers, then published as a separate book, and later reprinted several times both in hard-cover and paperback editions. In 1959, Hartshorne followed this major methodological work with a short monograph entitled *Perspective on the Nature of Geography* (1959) as the first of the Association's *Monograph Series*. Meanwhile, the Association had undertaken a massive collective inventory of status and trends in American geography, which was published under the editorship of P. E. James and C. F. Jones as *American Geography: Inventory and Prospect* (1954). The earlier Hartshorne and the James and Jones books provide valuable benchmarks from which to compare developments in a rapidly changing and developing field. For an historical view of modern geography distinctive from Hartshorne's 1939 work and with a useful bibliographical section, there also is T. W. Freeman's *A Hundred Years of Geography* (1961). More recently, two quite different books have appeared which introduce the reader to the present state of the art. The first of these is a short, thoughtful, retrospective paperback, J. O. M. Broek's *Geography: Its Scope and Spirit* (1965), possibly the best short statement of the origins and recent development of geographic thought. The second volume consists of contributions from nineteen geographers, prepared originally as lectures for the Voice of America and edited by S. B. Cohen as *Problems and Trends in American Geography* (1967). In contrast with the Broek book, which is broadly methodological, the Cohen volume contains much substantive information concerning the major research frontiers along which geographers are moving in their current research. A third reference book, somewhat similar in coverage to Broek's but markedly different in organization and spirit, is W. D. Pattison's *The Geographer's Way* (1968), an attempt to unravel the several major traditions of geographic enterprise from the fabric into which they have been woven. In addition to these books and monographs, there are literally scores of methodological articles and chapters concerning the character of geography. Of these mention should be made of P. E. James's article "Geography," in the *Encyclopaedia Britannica* (1963). Furthermore, there is a convenient and recent basic geographical bibliography prepared for the Association of American Geographers available—M. Church, R. E. Huke, W. Zelinsky (eds.), *A Basic Geographical Library: A Selected and Annotated Book List for American Colleges* (1966).

GEOGRAPHY AS A COMPENDIUM OF FACTS

It generally is acknowledged that modern geographical study developed out of the interests of men about the characteristics of foreign places. A common conception—or misconception—among laymen has followed that geographers compile facts about places, particularly countries. This compilation is assumed to include such items as the areal dimensions, boundaries, cities, rivers, mountains, population, railways, and imports and exports of countries and continents. Geography, as taught in many of the elementary schools of this country at least, has been represented by listings of these uncoordinated "geographical" facts which are memorized by children without explanation or synthesis.

Unfortunately, the idea of geography as uncoordinated areal description has not been restricted to popular or semipopular literature, or even to the elementary schools. Some college textbooks still consist largely of country-by-country descriptions and listings of these "geographical" facts.

The objections to the concept of geography as an encyclopedic compendium are several. The mere listing of facts without a frame of reference cannot lead to generalizations about them. An area is not simply a receptacle full of unrelated phenomena. The lack of organizational principles and a problem focus militates against contributions to scientific knowledge. Furthermore, the selection of facts may vary with each observer, and an emphasis on much that is unique rather than characteristic has been the almost inevitable result. In sum, the geographer is no more concerned with fact accumulation than any of his colleagues in the other sciences.

GEOGRAPHY AS THE STUDY OF ENVIRONMENTAL INFLUENCES

The influence that nature exerts on mankind also has been a focus of attention for centuries. The idea that the "natural environment" directly influences and even dominates man's activities may be found scattered through the writings of the ancients. The most important modern presentation of this viewpoint is in Friedrich Ratzel's *Anthropogeographie* (1882–91). the influence of which has permeated geographic thinking to this day. Ratzel's fundamental thesis was that the elements of the "natural" or "geographic" environment—climate, soils, topography, geologic structure, and water bodies, and their arrangement over the earth—determine or have determined, within rigid bounds, the activities of men. This environmental determinism is found in the writings of Ellen Churchill Semple, Ellsworth Huntington, and the German geopoliticians. It is discussed by Oscar H. K. Spate, in an article, "Toynbee and Huntington: A Study of Determinism," *Geographical Journal* (1952), and questioned by Robert S, Platt in his "Determinism in Geography," *Annals*, Association of American Geographers (1948), and in "Environmentalism Versus Geography," *American Journal of Sociology* (1948). In the works of the environmentalists the history of people and states is interpreted in terms of the dominant influences that natural conditions have exerted through time. Although there are no proponents of this point of view active in geographic work today, the stigma of environmental determinism upon geography has been difficult to remove, and there still are references in the social science literature which identify this deterministic outlook as the core concept of the field.

The major limitations and objections to this definition of geography lie in its basic assumption that natural conditions continuously dominate human events. This assumption cannot be proven, but it permits a simple explanation for an enormous variety of complex social phenomena. Ratzel himself, in later writings, recognized the dangers of such facile explanations and shifted his emphasis from the "natural" to the "cultural" environment. It is possible of course, that a sudden and catastrophic change in nature, water supply for example, may be the immediate cause for a migration of peoples or a radical change in social organization, but causal relations of this kind cannot be assumed and even when proven must be considered episodic, not continuous.

GEOGRAPHY AS THE STUDY OF MAN-NATURE RELATIONSHIPS

The uncompromisingly deterministic view of geographic study gradually was modified, especially by the French geographers, to the point where geography became defined as a kind of human ecology, the study of man and the "natural" environment, in which there was assumed an interplay of forces both natural and cultural. This concept has had numerous supporters in the United States and abroad and is still held as a useful definition by many geographers. The view is well presented by John M. Mogey in *The Study of Geography* (1950). The question arises, however, as to whether a science may deal primarily with assumed relationships not precisely defined, rather than with the reality basic to those relationships. Furthermore, since the relationships are *assumed* to exist, the geographer may in effect be *directed* by his conception of them, even though his conceptions may in fact remain unverified hypotheses. The result has been a kind of determinism which is less apparent but no less strong than environmental determinism itself.

A further difficulty lies in defining the "natural" environment. The "natural" environment is generally divided into elements such as climate, soils, bedrock, landforms, water bodies, vegetation, and animal life. Each of these elements, however, with the exception of climate, may be modified strongly by men, and even climate, particularly microclimate, is not immune to change. A soil under cultivation, for example, becomes both a "natural" and "cultural" element. As for climate, many studies which have claimed to link human events with the "natural" environment have in effect subscribed to the more limited concept of climatic determinism. Therefore, the "natural" environment may be regarded as only a hypothetical construct of limited utility; its use had led to a kind of dualism between a "cultural" environment on the one hand and a "natural" environment, on the other. In reality, however, there is only one physical environment, composed of various elements both natural and cultural. This argument does not propose to minimize the significance of climate, landforms, soils, minerals, and vegetation in the study of societies; rather it opposes grouping them into a "natural" class alone. The artificial separation of the unitary physical environment into two major segments often has led to a substantial distortion of reality, not only in some works of geographers, but commonly also in studies by social scientists. The problems involved in defining environment are brilliantly discussed by P. L. Wagner in his *The Human Use of the Earth* (1960), a major effort to delineate some of the major themes of cultural geography.

GEOGRAPHY AS THE STUDY OF LANDSCAPE

The definition of geography as the study of landscape is associated also with the French school of geography. According to this conception, geographers describe and trace the historical development of the "physical" landscape and thereby explain it. This "physical" landscape is composed of two aspects, the "natural" landscape, which was in existence before man entered the scene, and the "cultural" landscape, which man imposed over the natural base. The existing landscape complex is predominantly cultural and is explained by tracing its evolution from the natural to the present state. A notable American statement of this view is contained in Carl O. Sauer's "The Morphology of Landscape," *University of California Publications in Geography* (1925). To a considerable degree, also, it is associated with studies in historical geography of a sort most characteristic of European geographers, such as, for example, H. C. Darby, "The Changing English Landscape," *Geographical Journal* (1951). More recently, interest has shifted to the *perception* of landscape rather than the material landscape itself, as in D. Lowenthal and H. Prince, "English Landscape Tastes," *Geographical Review* (1965).

Among the difficulties accruing to this definition of geography is the confusion associated with the meanings of the word *landscape*, of which there are at least two: one nearly synonymous with the term "area"; the other pertaining to all the phenomena of the earth surface as viewed from a single point. A second drawback is the maintenance of a "natural"-"cultural" landscape dichotomy, as in the case of the "natural" and "cultural" environments. Furthermore, if the "natural" landscape refers to associations of physical phenomena on the surface of the earth before the coming of man, it can only be reconstructed historically, a difficult task at best. Geography, therefore, would become, in effect, only one aspect of history.

A final objection is the limit placed upon the subject matter of the geographer. If his study is restricted to the material phenomena of the earth's surface, he must ignore those characteristics of area that are not directly visible, although they may be of great significance to regional characterization. Emphasis is placed on form, not function, even though functional relations may be of far greater importance to the understanding of an areal complex than the physical forms that superficially compose it.

GEOGRAPHY AS HUMAN ECOLOGY

One of the more viable definitions of geography is as human ecology, and there have been adherents to this view of geography ever since, and even before, H. H. Barrows delivered his seminal presidential address to the Association of American Geographers, "Geography as Human Ecology" (1924). Although Barrows argued for a dichotomy between man and nature, later advocates of the human ecological approach have avoided it, and regard man as part of a gigantic ecosystem varying in composition and functions from place to place, but amenable to study at various scales and in the context of specifically formulated problems. In recent years, this view of geography has been strengthened by several methodological statements, such as Wagner's (1960), and by a number of publications, many interdisciplinary, such as H. C. Brookfield and P. Brown, *Struggle for Land: Agriculture and Group Territories among the Chimbu of the New Guinea Highlands* (1962), and F. R. Fosberg (ed.), *Man's Place in the Island Ecosystem* (1965). Although there are problems in geography which do not readily fit this definition, it represents, unlike the others thus far cited, one of the mainstreams of current geographic research.

GEOGRAPHY AS THE SCIENCE OF DISTRIBUTIONS

Geographers always have been concerned with the distributions of various phenomena and with the patterns that they form and the processes associated with them. In the abstract, any distributions and their patterns may be examined by the geographer, but in fact not all distributions fall within his purview. Many, both social and otherwise, are of equal concern to other disciplines. Clearly, interest in distributions per se is not restricted to geographers nor is the study of areal distributions their exclusive concern.

However, geographers have been particularly active in recent years in the study of processes of distribution, with regard both to the diffusion of culture traits and to the ecological matrices within which diffusion takes place. These interests are illustrated by the work of the Swedish geographer Torsten Hägerstrand, *The Propagation of Innovation Waves* (1952) and that of C. O. Sauer, *Agricultural Origins and Dispersals* (1952). To these must be added an extensive literature on the distribution of settlements, stemming from the work of the German geographer Walter Christaller, *Central Places in Southern Germany* (1933, 1966), and subsumed under the general heading of "central-place theory," a major bibliography of which is available in B. J. L. Berry and A. Pred, *Central Place Studies: A Bibliography of Theory and Practice* (1961).

Although this definition, too, falls short of satisfying all four of the conditions for a satisfactory definition of the field, it represents a major focus of geographical interest, though one shared with other disciplines.

CAN THERE BE A SATISFACTORY DEFINITION OF GEOGRAPHY?

It is probable that no single definition of geography would be satisfactory to all geographers, but, as indicated in the prior discussion of useful if inadequate or otherwise unsatisfactory definitions, such a one must include the several major strands of geographic thought as well as the factors of population, place, pattern, and process. The key to the problem lies in the multidimensional character of human organization. For most of the social sciences, that organization is tantamount to social organization—the ways in which men in society organize themselves institutionally so as to attain certain ends. Social organization, however, also has an areal aspect and a spatial dimension. The spatial dimension refers to the ways in which men, activities, and institutions display themselves over the surface of the earth. The areal aspect refers to areas which evolve from the interplay of social forces and their spatial concomitants—countries, regions, cities, villages, even farms. All of these are the product of social processes by which human organization is accomplished, but on what might be termed a "horizontal" rather than a "vertical" dimension. It is this dimension that occupies the attention of most geographers. On the other hand, that dimension in turn may be analyzed into three clusters of problems: (1) those that are fundamentally distributional; (2) those that are primarily ecological; and (3) those that are largely historical. Thus, a definition of geography must identify its interests in the areal structure and organization of society, in the distribution and diffusion of elements of culture, broadly interpreted, in the interrelationships within and evolution of ecosystems composed of elements both of society and of nature, and in the ways in which these systems, both distributional and ecological, have evolved over time.

It follows that a geographical problem is one that refers not simply to the natural state of the earth's surface, nor to the relations between natural conditions and men, nor even to the simple distribution of an infinity of phenomena whatever their origins, but one that looks at the processes that bear upon the ways in which men have organized territory; have distributed themselves and their works; have perceived, utilized, or even created resources; and have made of the surface of the earth a dynamic of overlapping, interacting, areally displayed systems that in themselves form appropriate and demanding objects of study.

To be sure, there is interest in other disciplines in some aspects of this type of problem. Human ecology is recognized to be a major field in sociology; ecosystems form part of anthropological research; and locational problems are part of the economist's array of problems; but *all* geographers are primarily concerned with these issues, and all aspects of geographical scholarship focus upon them. On the other hand, the fact that this type of problem has interdisciplinary attributes is entirely in keeping with trends in the evolution of the social science disciplines. After all, all of these disciplines possess a common interest in social—if not all human—organization, and their concern with these aspects changes over time. Inevitably, this means overlapping fields of interest, sharing of research endeavors, the creation of interdisciplinary research groups, and the probable evolution of new disciplines to replace the old.

ON SYSTEMATIC GEOGRAPHY AND THE REGIONAL CONCEPT

The history of geographic thought, as revealed in Hartshorne, is marked with seeming contradictions within dichotomies, as between physical and human geographies and systematic or general and regional geographies. So vigorous was discussion and dissent that geography long appeared to be not one but many, and the field seemed distinguishable less as a discipline than for lack of it. Although discussion continues, its acerbity has been blunted and what has appeared to be two has, in the case of systematic and regional geography, become one, or at least as much one as two sides of a coin.

The traditional division of geographic knowledge developed from two considerations: first, the need to deal with particular phenomena as they are distributed over the earth, and second, the necessity of comprehending the similarities and differences in organization of various areas. For analytical purposes, such a division of knowledge still has its uses, but most geographers realize that it is largely a heuristic convention for attaining the same objectives. The distinction between the two methods of organization is recognized to be primarily a matter of purpose or emphasis than of differing subject matters. Relatively few geographical studies can be classified simply under one or the other categories, although differences in scale or degree of generalization in any geographic study will tend to place it primarily in one of the two categories.

SYSTEMATIC GEOGRAPHY

Systematic geography is concerned with the geographic aspects of particular phenomena—i.e., with the distribution of a phenomenon as it relates to other areally distributed phenomena and as it contributes to an understanding of areal differences in human organization. This is not the same concern that motivates the specialist in a systematic science. For example, the soil scientist, like the geographer, is concerned with the distribution of the various kinds of soils over the earth. He is interested, however, primarily in the distributional study not as a means for understanding areal differentiation in general, but as a way to understanding the nature of soils. The soil geographer on the other hand examines distributions of soils in terms of the part they play in differentiating one area of human activity from another, in their relation to patterns of agriculture, forestry, and transportation. The soil geographer inevitably seeks information from the soil scientist regarding the nature of soils. At the same time his aim is to generalize, if possible, concerning the relations that particular groupings or arrangements of soils have to other areally distributed phenomena.

REGIONAL GEOGRAPHY AND REGIONAL CONCEPT

The regional concept is the logical result of attempts to organize knowledge concerning differences from place to place in the ways men have occupied the surface of the earth and established areally defined systems of organization. It differs from systematic geography in that it emphasizes, first, the complex organization of territory and, second, the localized association of phenomena, rather than the specific elements in such associations. Regional geography, however, deals with the same patterns of distribution as does systematic geography and utilizes the facts and generalizations about distributions, patterns, and processes developed by systematic geography; but its prime function is the welding of these facts and generalizations into systems of areal relationships, either conceptual or functional. The regional geographer, therefore, is a systematizer and integrator of given data into systems of regions—i.e., areas of relative homogeneity on the one hand or of functional organization on the other.

The region based upon specific criteria which recur in more than one place is known as a *generic* region. One type of generic region is a relatively homogeneous area which can be defined in terms of certain characteristics. To take an example from physical geography, the "tropical rain-forest region" can be identified in terms of its associations of vegetation, soils, and climate, and it occurs in several parts of the world. Such a region is, of course, a taxonomic generalization, but on the basis only of selected criteria. No two "tropical rain-forest regions" are identical. The class "tropical rain-forest region" is based upon only a few of the phenomena which exist, in reality, within the areas thus defined. To take another example, in the "region of dairying" in northern Illinois and southern Wisconsin, there are numerous nondairying activities, as evidenced by cash-grain and specialized farms, recreational facilities, and small industries in towns. The dairying region, however, is defined in terms of the dominant activity, as indicated by percentage of land area devoted to dairying uses or percentage of labor force engaged in dairying. As a generalization, however, the generic region of uniformity or homogeneity provides a tool for the solution of certain problems in area, and provides one means for comparing and generalizing about localized associations wherever they may occur.

Each generic region has an additional quality, that of situation. Every portion of the earth's surface is distinct from every other part on the basis of relative location—only one association of elements can occupy a point at any one time. It is perfectly plain, for example, that Chicago is the only metropolis at the southern end of Lake Michigan, that this city is bound to its hinterland by a web of highways and railways following certain known routes, and that it acts as a focus of activities for a commensurable tributary area. In another case, the importance of the Great Lakes to American heavy industry is a characteristic in large part of the locational happenstance of these water bodies. Although certain attributes of the city and the lakes are unique to them, it does not follow that they cannot be studied in terms of their uniqueness. Science demands as its goal an understanding of reality, and the unique aspects of these phenomena are important aspects of their significance to society.

Whenever the unique aspect of a region becomes more significant than its generic aspect, it can be thought of as a *specific region*. The Corn Belt of the United States is a specific region. Insofar as there may be other areas in which the corn-hog association of the Corn Belt may be found, it partakes of certain qualities of the generic region as well.

Another example, the so-called "Chicago region," refers to that point of the United States, the nerve center and focal point of which is the city of Chicago. Not only is this a *specific* region, it also is *generic*; but it is representative of a type of generic region substantially different from those of uniformity or relative homogeneity. That type of region is organizational, functional, and usually nodal. Much work in modern geography relates to regions of organization, especially as related to settlement. There is a vast literature dealing with the form, structure, and functions of such nodal regions, an increasing proportion of which deals with abstract models of areal types and spatial distributions relating to cities, hinterlands, and metropolitan areas.

The concept of the geographic region, therefore, extends from the region based upon its uniformity with regard to a single, areally distributed criterion to the highly complex areal unit defined in terms of its functional organization. As the areal unit becomes increasingly complex, it also becomes increasingly difficult to describe, analyze, and generalize about. Therefore, much regional geographic study retains, perforce, a highly subjective quality, in much the same fashion that many studies of human behavior are highly intuitive in their interpretations.

As a corollary, it should be emphasized that various kinds of regions overlap, and that regional systems suitable for one kind of study may not be suitable for another. Furthermore, the drawing of regional boundaries may be extremely difficult and provides the geographer with one of his major problems, except perhaps where political units act as the basis for a regional system. In some instances a numerical standard provides a relatively simple regional limit, as in the case, say, of population densities. Where nodal regions are being examined, the areal extent of relations between focal point and hinterland varies both with the kind of relationship involved and with time. In such cases, the boundary may be little more than a very broad and fluctuating zone which merges with areas partly associated with other nodal regions; and the identification of the regional focus or core becomes the more pressing and significant geographical task.

Few regional studies, moreover, can be called "complete"; indeed, it is impossible to deal with *all* elements of the occupance pattern and relations within a given area. In fact, all generic regional studies may be described as "systematic" studies as well, since they deal with the areal similarities and differences of certain phenomena only. It is for this reason that the greater number of geographical studies can be described as being *both systematic and regional*, since they tend to concentrate on the regional qualities of certain types of localized associations or elements within those associations. The typical geographical study, then, can seldom be fitted with one or the other of the systematic-regional dichotomy, since it partakes of the qualities of both. A discussion of this question may be found in R. S. Platt, "Regionalism in World Order," *Social Education* (1944).

A more comprehensive treatment of regional geography is given in R. Minshull, *Regional Geography* (1967), a review of definitions, concepts, and research in this aspect of the discipline. Most introductory general geography textbooks use some system of regional division for their organization. Formerly, most such regional divisions were based upon climate, but more recent publications rely either on culture regions *in sensu stricto* or upon traditional reference to continents and countries. Among examples of these are R. J. Russell, F. B. Kniffen, and E. L. Pruitt, *Culture Worlds* (1961); R. Murphey, *An Introduction to Geography* (1966); and J. H. Wheeler, J. T. Kostbade, and R. S. Thoman, *Regional Geography of the World* (1961). The first of these employs regional units akin to the "culture areas" of anthropology.

SYSTEMATIC SUBDIVISIONS OF GEOGRAPHY

Like the other sciences, geography has been divided traditionally into a number of subfields, each with its own literature and each often dealing with problems of relatively peripheral interest to the others. One of these remarkable trends in modern geography has been the transformation of certain of these subfields on the one hand and the development of new specializations overlapping several of the old on the other.

PHYSICAL GEOGRAPHY

Perhaps the most conservative of the major subfields of geography has been physical geography. Furthermore, the history of modern geography both in Europe and America shows the significance of physical geography in the development of various aspects of the discipline. In the United States, for example, the earliest departments of geography either developed from or were developed along with the other earth sciences. Since geographers traditionally worked from the land—in its broadest sense—toward problems of human occupance and organization on that land, physical geography has provided a major base for inquiry into various phases of human geographical enquiry.

Physical geography commonly includes the study of the geography of soils, landforms, water, vegetations, minerals, and climate. In studying these phenomena the geographer is concerned not with their genetic aspects, but with their distributions and interrelations both among themselves and with the occupance features in area. However, it is this geographical interest which has led to the description of geography as a bridge between the natural and social sciences.

Although the orientation of physical geography is toward the "use" aspect of the elements within it, its concentration on natural elements grants it a certain autonomy from the other subdivisions of systematic geography. This autonomy is evidenced by the considerable literature in so-called "pure" physical geography. The literature may be classified into three groups: (1) that which is basically descriptive, (2) that which is concerned with natural processes and the genesis of natural elements, and (3) that which attempts to generalize regarding the areal relations among two or more such elements. The first and second of these are not necessarily geographical; the second may more properly be considered geology, geomorphology, or climatology. The third type of study is geographical in that it is concerned with the nature of localized associations, although when these lack a "use" orientation, they may be considered peripheral to the core of geographical understanding.

The scope of physical geography is well illustrated in two of the standard works in the field, V. C. Finch, G. T. Trewartha, and E. H. Hammond, *Physical Elements of Geography* (1967) and A. Strahler, *Introduction to Physical Geography* (1965). Special interests within physical geography are illustrated by such works as Trewartha's *The World's Problem Climates* (1961), B. T. Bunting, *The Geography of Soil* (1966), and S. R. Eyre, *Vegetation and Soils* (1963), an attempt to describe systematically the ecological relationships between these two factors of environment.

On the other hand, physical geography has been enriched by an increasing literature concerned with, *inter alia*, the relationships between physical environmental factors and culture, past and present, as part of the man-land relationship tradition. Illustrative of this work is K. W. Butzer's classic *Environment and Archeology* (1964), described as a "comprehensive introduction to Pleistocene research, reconstructing the physical environment and man-land relationships of prehistory." Other developments have been associated with the application of mathematical and probability models to the study of elements in nature, both as to their distributions and their interrelations in area, as described in Part II of R. J. Chorley and P. Haggett (eds.), *Models in Geography* (1967).

HISTORICAL GEOGRAPHY

In some respects historical geography has been more conservative than any other of the subfields of geography, but it too is experiencing change, and the problem of describing it is increased by its breadth of interest. In fact, historical geography has been described by Hartshorne in the *Nature of Geography* (1939) as "not a branch of geography comparable to economic or political geography. Neither is it the geography of history, nor the history of geography. It is rather another geography complete in all its branches."* Historical geography, in a phrase, is the study of human occupance and organization of past times, in effect a noncontemporary geography. The reconstruction and evaluation of conditions of geographical significance in particular periods of time thus provides a major problem for the historical geographer. For example, the Domesday Book, with its data on property holdings and land use in the England of the post-Norman invasion period, is the basis for current British studies in the historical geography of that time, as in H. C. Darby, *The Domesday Geography of Eastern England* (1952). An example of this type of literature on the United States is R. H. Brown, *Mirror for Americans: Likeness of the Eastern Seaboard, 1810* (1943). In studies of this kind where historical reconstruction is at issue, the distinction between history and geography may become virtually nonexistent, a problem discussed by Darby, in "On the Relation of Geography and History," *Transactions and Papers*, Institute of British Geographers (1953) and by H. R. Merrens in "Historical Geography and Early American History," *William and Mary Quarterly* (1965). In fact, many studies in "historical geography" have been more often than not geographical interpretations of history, as witness the well-known work of Ellen Semple, *Geography of the Mediterranean Region: Its Relations to History* (1931). On the other hand, studies of this sort usually bear an unmistakable professional geographical stamp, as in the case of J. Gottman, *Virginia at Mid-Century* (1955) or P. Wheatley, *The Golden Khersonese* (1961).

The affinities of historical and cultural geography are particularly great, since one of the major interests in cultural geography concerns the evolution of patterns of occupance and areal organization, as well as the diffusion of culture traits and even entire civilizations. One of the classic exemplars of this genre is A. H. Clark, *The Invasion of New Zealand by People, Plants, and Animals: The South Island* (1949). Another would be D. W. Meining, *On the Margins of the Good Earth* (1962), a study of the expansion of the South Australian wheat frontier between 1869 and 1884. On a more general level, but equally illustrative of the cross-fertilization between historical and cultural geographic enterprise is M. W. Mikesell's review of interdisciplinary research on the history of frontiers, "Comparative Studies in Frontier History," *Annals*, Association of American Geographers (1960). It should be noted, however, that whereas most historical geographic studies focus upon the reconstruction

---

* Pages 184–5.

of past geographical patterns and associations and upon the sequence of events concomitant with them, the cultural geographic approach, as exemplified by the Meining and Clark volumes, is more concerned with process. The standard reference illustrating the less dynamic geographical "stages" rather than processual approach is D. Whittlesey, "Sequent Occupance," *Annals*, Association of American Geographers (1929).

On the other hand, geographers are not above attempting studies in intellectual history, especially as they apply to geographic thought and problems. A remarkable example is seen in C. J. Glacken, *Traces on the Rhodian Shore: Nature and Culture in Western Thought from Ancient Times to the End of the Eighteenth Century* (1967).

CULTURAL GEOGRAPHY

Long a major subfield in geography, cultural geography has been characterized by the broadest interests within the discipline. To some extent, it is to geography in general as, say, anthropology is to the social sciences, but it is not to be confused with human geography in general. Cultural geography has long been associated with work in culture history, with the reconstruction of past landscapes, with movements of people from one region to another, with the development of culture regions, with the diffusion of selected cultural traits, and with the ways different societies have, in the past, organized the territories which they occupied. Many examples of these interests can be found in the doctoral dissertations prepared at the Department of Geography of the University of California in Berkeley. Others are admirably presented and described in Wagner and Mikesell, *Readings in Cultural Geography* (1962).

At the same time, there have been several different trends in cultural geography, the relations among which are only beginning to be elaborated. One important research focus has been on man as a changer of his environment—i.e., on environmental modification in the tradition of G. P. Marsh, *Man and Nature: Or, Physical Geography as Modified by Human Action* (1864; reprinted 1965 with an introduction by David Lowenthal). An interdisciplinary interest, the literature in this field is suggested by the massive volume of essays by W. L. Thomas (ed.), *Man's Role in Changing the Face of the Earth* (1956). In contrast to this focus is the view of man as part of an all-encompassing ecosystem, in short, with a geographical variant of cultural ecology. Here, one must refer again for elaboration to Wagner's *The Human Use of the Earth* (1960) and to the more recent book by G. R. J. Jones and S. R. Eyre, *Geography as Human Ecology* (1956), both of which attempt to relate the landscape transformation interest to a broader perception of the role of men in a world set of ecological relationships. But cultural ecology involves also the comparative study of culture as an areal and distributional phenomenon, and by extension to aspects or elements of culture as well as to the cultural complex itself. To this end, geographers have examined the ecological matrix and distributional vectors of various cultural phenomena, as in David Sopher's *Geography of Religions* (1967), an attempt to relate symbolic values to environments both natural and synthetic; or F. Simoons, *Eat Not This Flesh* (1961) which examines the location, origins, and diffusion of flesh-eating habits and tabus. Moreover, a massive traditional literature exists along the margins of these more pervasive problems in the form of studies of the distribution and spread of selected artifacts, such as house types, fences, barns, and certain types of settlements, examples of which may be found in the Mikesell and Wagner readings volume previously cited.

The interests of cultural geography merge also into that of population geography, a more specialized and less carefully cultivated field, the nature of which is discussed in W. Zelinsky, *A Prologue to Population Geography* (1966) and the literature of which is noted in his *A Bibliographic Guide to Population Geography* (1962).

Especially insofar as these interests relate to movements of people and of culture traits, they have come to identify a new subfield within geography, that relating to *diffusion*, which brings together historical, cultural, and economic geographers. Here, the work of certain Swedish geographers, especially that of Hägerstrand (1952), as previously cited, is particularly important, though much of their work is less retrospective than simulation-oriented and predictive.

Despite internal differences, cultural geography as a subdiscipline of geography is marked by commitment to the concept of culture, the perception of which is shared with anthropologists; by concern with the culture area—i.e., with the areal and spatial dimensions of culture and specific elements in cultures, as well as the areas themselves; by the systematic study of the cultural landscape, that man-created, nature-endowed, culturally relative artifact which reflects man's complex patterns of regional occupance; by interest in culture history as a device for explaining and understanding the nature and evolution of culture areas and landscapes; and by a basic preoccupation with cultural ecology, or the processes by which men in society, and therefore by definition possessing cultures, act as parts of those ecosystems, both large and small, which provide one major aspect of human organization. This wealth of interest could have been crippling; in fact, it has helped make cultural geography exceptionally vital and dynamic. This vitality is captured in the basic text by J. O. M. Broek and J. W. Webb, *A Geography of Mankind* (1968).

ECONOMIC GEOGRAPHY

Traditionally, economic geography has been production-oriented. Numerous textbooks and articles have described the distribution of various types of production, both agricultural and industrial, by commodity and by region. In general, relations with economics and the use of economic theory were minimal. Product distributions were interpreted largely within the context of a simple deterministic framework of natural conditions, of climate in the case of agriculture, of the location of key natural resources in the case of manufactural production. One of the major recent developments in modern geography has been the emancipation of economic geography from these traditional constraints.

One major element in this emancipation has been concern with locational analysis. A major literature has developed within the past twenty years that attempts to account for the location of various types of economic activities, not only those relating to production, but also those relating to marketing and to consumption. This literature is examined and ordered with care and precision by P. Haggett in his *Locational Analysis in Human Geography* (1966). In this volume, Haggett examines a series of models of what he calls "locational structure," models which relate to movement, networks, nodes, hierarchies, and surfaces, and including a variety of gravity and potential models. One of the virtues of this presentation is that it successfully relates the descriptive and empirical literature with the more theoretical, and demonstrates the value of the use of mathematical and statistical techniques in the development of regional systems and in attacking problems of relationships between particular distributions on the one hand and partial ecosystems on the other. Equally intriguing is the overlap of interest with cultural geography in the nature of settlements and therefore landscapes, and with a cultural ecological view of processes of production, distribution, and consumption of goods and services.

One of the important features of the locational analysis syndrome is its concern with the relative value of sites and situation, the classic duo of much of human geography, for various economic purposes. This problem is explored by H. H. McCarty and J. B. Lindberg in their *A Preface to Economic Geography* (1966). It also is the major subject matter of M. Chisholm's *Rural Settlement and Land Use* (1962), in which distance and intensity relationships with regard to agriculture are explored. Chisholm also is author of *Geography and Economics* (1966), an examination of the intellectual relationships between the two disciplines, and a hallmark of the increasing enrichment of economic geographical studies by concepts from the sister discipline.

Basic to the recent work in economic geography is the conception of economic activities as having both spatial and areal components; that is, various elements in an economy are assumed to be distributed according to comprehensible principles of location that can be derived from economic theory; and they are integrated into complex regional systems, such as the metropolitan area, for example, which by definition is amenable to geographical analysis. Thus, regional geographical study is becoming enriched by more rigorous models of the spatial structure economic of organization.

Another focus of interest has been on the geographical aspects of economic growth, as examined in N. Ginsburg (ed.), *Essays on Geography and Economic Development* (1960). At the world scale, this work is illustrated by N. Ginsburg, *Atlas of Economic Development* (1961), a graphic and analytical examination of selected indices to economic development. At the regional scale, one can look to such monographs as D. M. Ray, *Regional Aspects of Foreign Ownership of Manufacturing in Canada* (1967).

The field of resources management is another growth point, which is as much concerned with public policy, however, as it is with economic factors themselves. Studies by G. F. White and his colleagues relate research on perception to the management of resources, thereby further linking the cultural and economic fields, as in his *Choice of Adjustment to Floods* (1964), and White has further carried his long-term interest in water resources into a geographically based appraisal of a long-term water policy for the American people, *Strategies of American Water Management* (1968).

Other special fields in economic geography are illustrated by R. S. Thoman and E. C. Conkling, *Geography of International Trade* (1967) a pioneering study of world and regional trade patterns in a comprehensive taxonomic framework, and B. Berry, *Geography of Market Centers and Retail Distribution* (1967), an analysis of the distributional sector of a space economy as related to models of locational structure, as described in Haggett above. More traditional are G. Alexandersson, *Geography of Manufacturing* (1967) and R. C. Estall and R. C. Buchanan, *Industrial Activity and Economic Geography* (1966), both, however, equally concerned with economic principles for the location of industry and the noneconomic variables which bear upon that location; as well as E. Higbee, *American Agriculture: Geography, Resources, Conservation* (1958).

Several excellent textbooks are available which summarize developments in economic geography, among which are Thoman, *The Geography of Economic Activity* (1962), D. W. Fryer, *World Economic Development* (1965), and J. Alexander, *Economic Geography* (1963).

URBAN GEOGRAPHY

Unlike historical, cultural, and economic geography, but like physical geography, urban geography has been concerned with the characteristics of a particular type of material phenomenon—the city. An enormous literature exists, chiefly in the form of journal articles published not only in geographical periodicals, but also in such nongeographical periodicals as the *American Journal of Sociology*, *Journal of the Regional Science Association*, and *Journal of the American Institute of Planners*. Urban geography has had a particularly interdisciplinary bent, as revealed in the useful book of readings edited by H. M. Mayer and C. F. Kohn, *Readings in Urban Geography* (1959). In addition, a convenient discussion of recent developments in the field can be found in three chapters by H. M. Mayer, B. J. Berry, and N. S. Ginsburg respectively in P. M. Hauser and L. F. Schnore (eds.), *The Study of Urbanization* (1965).

Several subfields in geography converge upon the study of the city, of which economic geography and cultural geography, of course, are the most important, but several significant contributions also have a strong historical bent. A modern classic illustrating this convergence, as well as the strong relations between urban geography on the one hand and urban sociology and urban history on the other, is J. Gottmann, *Megalopolis: The Urbanized Northeastern Seaboard of the United States* (1961), a masterful interpretive synthesis of strands from several disciplines, but focusing nonetheless on the organization and evolution of a unique area, a specific region, with strong generic qualities comparable to other examples of the regional type found in Northwestern Europe and in Japan.

Several geographical traditions are reflected in the emphasis of certain urban geographical studies. One tradition combines both the landscape and processual traditions in cultural geography, and looks at the city as a culturally relative artifact, as in the case of T. G. McGee's *The Southeast Asian City* (1967). Another focuses upon the primarily economic processes which work upon the city and lead to its morphological development, as described in R. E. Murphy, *The American City: An Urban Geography* (1956). A third views the city as a system in interaction with its hinterland and with other urban and metropolitan systems, as dealt with in R. E. Dickinson, *City and Region: A Geographical Interpretation* (1964), and J. Beaujeu-Garnier and G. Chabot, *Urban Geography* (1967). A fourth examines specific urban functions such as residential patterns, land uses, and retail and wholesaling activities, as these are related to each other and to the forces, chiefly economic, which help explain the complex patterns of activities within metropolitan areas. In this case, use is made of the spatial models referred to earlier in Haggett, and are illustrated well in Parts I and II of K. Norborg (ed.), *Proceedings of the IGU Symposium in Urban Geography, 1960* (1962).

Much of the work in urban geography closely resembles that found in human ecology as part of sociology. However, the geographical variant makes greater use of theories and models in locational analysis and of economic principles that help describe comparative advantages for various urban purposes of factors of site and situation. To a degree, therefore, urban geography represents a microcosm of the methodological macrocosm that is the whole of geography, made distinctive by an emphasis on the functions of urban areal entities as part of the study of human organization.

POLITICAL GEOGRAPHY

The traditional involvement of political geography has been with certain politically based phenomena, such as boundaries, and there is an extensive literature on boundaries, as exemplified by S. B. Jones, *Boundary Making: A Handbook for Statesmen, Treaty Editors, and Boundary Commissioners* (1945) and by J. R. V. Prescott, *The Geography of Frontiers and Boundaries* (1965). The contrast between these two works, however, illustrates some of the major changes in the character of political geography over a twenty-year period. Whereas Jones in this work, not later, emphasizes boundary taxonomy and procedures for definition of them, Prescott views boundaries in terms of the functions they perform for the states or other political areas they bound or separate and of their role in influencing landscapes and the relations between areas. The one approach is essentially static and descriptive; the second is dynamic and processual and bears family resemblances in conception, though not in technique, to both the work of the cultural geographer and the economic geographer concerned with processes of areal organization.

Here lies the key to the definition of contemporary political geography, the study of the relations between political systems and political areas, or the spatial concomitants of politics. This conception of the field is borne out in the title of the book of readings by W. A. D. Jackson (ed.), *Politics and Geographic Relationships* (1964), as well as another such volume by R. Kasperson and J. Minghi (eds.), *Readings in Political Geography* (1969), each of which draws upon literature outside of geography to flush out the as yet modest relevant geographical output. A similar perspective is displayed in S. B. Cohen's *Geography and Politics in a World Divided* (1963) which has marked regional inclination.

The Cohen book helps mark a distinctive quality of political geography—to a considerable degree the field partakes of the quality of regional geography, more so than the other systematic fields, in that much of the literature focuses upon the state as a territorial unit, already bounded and organized. Insofar as the state is a regional entity, it is not an abstraction but a real object. Thus, one major object of study in political geography is a given, defined territory, itself a derivative of human organization. Taxonomies of states, based upon sets of morphological and organizational characteristics, thus form one major aspect of political geography, as do certain of the relations among states. Similarly, the relations among subnational political and administrative units form another syndrome in the literature, and increasing use is being made of models similar to those in economic geography for examining hierarchical and functional relations as expressed in territorial terms.

Along the margins of political geography work is on-going in the field of perception as it relates both to decisions concerning resources management and to both domestic and foreign policy, as in N. S. Ginsburg, "On the Chinese Perception of a World Order," in T. Tsou (ed.), *China's Policies in Asia and America's Alternatives* (1968).

Problems relating to the development of new states and the relations between territory and nationalism within various polities also are being examined, usually with an interdisciplinary bent, as in D. Lowenthal (ed.), *The West Indies Federation: Perspectives on a New Nation* (1961). Equally significant is research being done on electoral patterns, some of which is discussed in J. R. V. Prescott, "The Functions and Methods of Electoral Geography," *Annals*, Association of American Geographers (1959); and on the relations between political development and transportation, such as that of R. I. Wolfe, *Transportation and Politics* (1963).

The conclusion is inescapable that much of the work in political geography is of interdisciplinary interest and that the field has yet to develop a body of distinctive theory. Many of its strengths and weaknesses are revealed in the numerous textbooks covering the field, such as N. G. J. Pounds, *Political Geography* (1963), and H. de Blij, *Systematic Political Geography* (1967). Earlier works of general significance, not simply textbooks, include H. M. Mackinder, *Democratic Ideals and Reality* (1919, 1967), I. Bowman, *The New World: Problems in Political Geography* (1921), and D. Whittlesey, *The Earth and the State* (1939). A cross section of work in political geography may also be seen in Van Nostrand's paperback Searchlight Books of which Wolfe, cited above, is one, and David Hooson's *A New Soviet Heartland?* (1964) is another, and almost all of which deal with political geographic problems in particular regions or states.

THE MAP

One of the more distinctive tools of the geographer is the map. Maps serve at least three functions: first, as a record for raw data as they are initially gathered and organized in field and library; second, as a tool for separating out the elements of a given area in the process of a real analysis and putting them together in new areal combinations; finally, as one means for expressing and examining the relations among patterns of phenomena over the earth.

All maps are generalizations, the extent of which varies directly with their scale. As scale increases, the closer the map approaches reality; as it becomes smaller, the distortion of reality increases. Despite this distortion, the map provides a shorthand means for expanding research horizons beyond the limits imposed on direct observation.

The nature of the map varies with the data it portrays and the purpose for which it has been made. No map can show everything in an area no matter how large the scale. Thus, the information shown on maps is selected according to certain criteria. Even the *topographic map*, with its wealth of natural and cultural information, is restricted to certain kinds of phenomena, and the *general maps* which appear in many atlases are even more restricted. In some cases landscape forms are the primary phenomena shown; in others intensity and frequency patterns are shown in a diagrammatic fashion, as on traffic- or commodity-flow maps.

Maps are an ancient means of representing three-dimensional reality on a two-dimensionsional surface. Therefore, all maps are subject to distortions other than those that are scale-induced. The distortion of the earth's surface on a map may be in its shape, direction, or equivalence. Each kind of projection has its uses: one may portray the shapes of areas in middle latitudes with greater faithfulness; another may be characterized by true direction from its center; another will be most accurate about the poles. Any map user must be aware of the properties of maps in order to select the one best suited to the purpose for which it will be used.

For example, the Mercator Projection, which until recent years was the most commonly used of all map projections, distorts the proportions of the extreme latitudes as compared with the equatorial latitudes and does not show the polar areas at all. Its shapes, however, are accurate, and its directions are true. Therefore, its chief value is as a navigation chart; distributions plotted on it are misleading. In recent years, many distributions have been shown on so-called "interrupted projections," of which Goode's Homolosine Equal Areal Projection is perhaps the best known. This projection retains good shape and equivalence of area, but presents difficulties in that the earth's surface is cut into lobes, and sense of continuity may be lost. More detailed explanations of these and other projections may be found in a number of works such as: E. Raisz's *Principles of Cartography* (1962) and A. H. Robinson, *Elements of Cartography* (1960).

Most small-scale maps of the world or large portions of the earth's surface are political maps or political and hypsometric maps. The first show the political divisions of the world and such features as large cities, rivers, and sometimes roads and railways. The second show the general surface configuration of large areas by means of standardized colors denoting elevations in addition to the other information found on political maps. There are also some political and hypsometric sets of maps at medium scales, say, 1 : 4,000,000, covering a hemisphere or some large portion of the globe.

On much larger scales there are sets of maps which emphasize terrain and show differences in landforms by means of contour lines, shading, hachures, or combinations of all three. These maps are known as "*topographic maps*"; and by "topography" is meant all material features on the earth surface, including those man-made. Such maps generally are issued by special mapping agencies of various governments, such as the United States Geological Survey and the British Ordnance Survey. There is, however, a map set covering much of the world and published by various agencies under international agreement at a scale of 1 : 1,000,000, the so-called *International Map of the World*. Most topographic maps, however, are at scales of 1 : 25,000 or larger, the greater number being between 1 : 50,000 and 1 : 100,000. Those of the United States Geological Survey, which cover little more than half of this country, are chiefly at scales of 1 : 24,000 and 1 : 62,000.

The topographic map is not merely a landform and drainage map; a great wealth of other information is shown on each sheet. The symbols used for physical and cultural features are explained on the map itself or in separate instructional materials issued by the publishing agency. Skill in reading and interpreting these maps depends not only upon recognizing the symbolic representation, but also upon general and/or specific knowledge of the area covered by the map.

Much of the accuracy of the topographic map depends on the reliability of the "control" system upon which it is based. Every country possesses some kind of control grid composed of a network of triangles developed from a carefully surveyed baseline, and by which field data can be accurately plotted. In the United States a highly accurate triangulation grid has been completed by the Coast and Geodetic Survey, although increased precision of instruments and observations makes occasional revision necessary. Control in other areas of the world may or may not be equally reliable. Most of Europe is well covered, but most of Latin America, Asia, and Africa is sketchily mapped, if at all.

There are as many kinds of special *distribution maps* as there are distributions. Most are in the form of single sheets, although geological and soil maps, for example, may come in sets. Of great interest to geographers are land utilization maps which classify land in particular areas according to its actual or potential use. In Great Britain, for example, a complete set of land utilization maps has been completed, based on the one-inch-to-one-mile topographic set published by the Ordnance Survey. City plans, maps of cultural phenomena, natural features, earth magnetism, traffic flow, and wholesale and retail service areas, among others, are to be found, each possessing its own characteristics.

The entire world ocean is covered in a series of *charts* published by the U.S. Hydrographic Office, a branch of the Department of the Navy. Territorial waters of the United States and its possessions, however, are charted by the Coast and Geodetic Survey. Many of the USHO charts are compiled from surveys made by American Navy vessels; others are derived from surveys and charts published by hydrographic offices of other countries, particularly by the British Admiralty.

The hydrographic charts show ocean depths and shorelines, which are given with a high degree of accuracy, along with prominent landmarks and seamarks, such as signal lights, buoys, channel markers, and the like. The USHO also publishes *Sailing Directions* for various ocean areas which are to be used in conjunction with the charts.

The sources of maps are innumerable, ranging from governmental agencies, through large and reputable private publishers, to maps of explorers and field workers.

In the United States the major governmental map-producing agencies are the Army Map Service, Coast and Geodetic Survey, Hydrographic Office of the Navy, and Geological Survey. Each of these agencies publishes indexes to its published maps. Other important government map producers are the Soil Conservation Service, Forestry Service, TVA, Corps of Engineers, and Weather Bureau. In other countries, similar agencies perform the same duties.

In addition to government agencies maps are published by private map publishers. In the United States there are, for example, the scholarly American Geographical Society and such commercial agencies as the National Geographic Society, Rand McNally, Hammond, Weber-Costello, General Drafting, and Denoyer-Geppert, which are among the largest firms of this kind.

Although cartography is a field separate from geography, there are close relations between the two, and developments in cartography are watched closely by geographers. Of special interest currently is the progress being made in computer mapping, whereby diagrammatic maps showing distributions and relationships may be produced directly by properly programed electronic computers. Of even greater significance are the efforts to attach grid coordinates to census data in several countries so as to permit direct mapping of those data. It is expected that the 1970 Census of the United States will make use of such coordinates, thereby greatly facilitating the plotting of distributions and developing hypotheses concerning relations among these distributions on the one hand and regional associations or sets of elements on the other.

OTHER REFERENCE MATERIALS

ATLASES AND GAZETTEERS

An atlas is a group of maps bound together into one or more volumes. Atlases can be filed as books according to the areas covered. On the other hand, there are specialized atlases which cannot be fitted easily into an areal classification or which would be more useful if filed according to a subject matter classification. Agricultural, industrial, economic, geological, or linguistic atlases are of this type.

General world atlases differ considerably in quality, just as maps do. The American atlases in common use for general reference fail to approach the quality of many European publications. The handiest American atlases are *Goodes World Atlas* (1966) and the *Aldine University Atlas* (1969). For more detailed coverage the best English-language atlas is the *Times Atlas of the World* (1968). Many nations have published so-called "national atlases," official and unofficial, covering their territories and possessions—Japan, France, India, and Great Britain, among others —and the United States has one in preparation.

Different forms of *place names*, or toponyms, as they occur in various languages, present a special problem in the use of maps. The study of place names, toponymics, has been developing in recent years about the work of the U.S. Board on Geographic Names of the Department of Interior. Although the Board has not prepared a world gazetteer, by 1968 it had published gazetteers for 104 countries; these are available from the Board itself.

Most atlases incorporate a gazetteer within their bindings, but these are seldom up-to-date or standardized among themselves. Nevertheless, they are useful appendices to any atlas. Separate gazetteers also have been compiled, such as the great *Columbia Lippincott Gazetteer of the World* (1952). For desk use the smaller *Webster's Geographical Dictionary* (1955) is more convenient.

RESEARCH AIDS AND PUBLICATIONS

The infinite variety of materials of geographical interest presents a constant challenge to both the geographer and the librarian. A most useful aid to both is J. K. Wright and E. T. Platt, *Aids to Geographical Research: Bibliographies, Periodicals, Atlases, Gazetteers and Other Reference Books* (1947). A valuable 41-page introduction describes the nature and problems of the use of geographical materials.

There are, of course, numerous geographical journals. In the United States the chief ones are the *Annals* (Association of American Geographers), the *Geographical Review*, and *Economic Geography*. Foreign countries are in turn represented by one or more similar journals, many in English or with English-language summaries. *An International List of Geographical Serials* (1960) has been compiled by C. D. Harris and J. D. Fellmann; it lists these journals by country and supplies pertinent information concerning their publication and library holdings in the United States. Harris also has prepared an *Annotated World List of Selected Current Geographical Serials in English* (1964).

Bibliographies concerning geographical materials are, or have been, maintained by agencies in three countries. The American Geographical Society publishes its *Current Geographical Publications* (1938–), which lists accessions of the Society arranged under area and topical headings. In France, there is published the *Bibliographie Geographique Internationale* (1915–), an annual summary by areas and topics of the geographical literature of the world. In Germany before the war there appeared the *Geographisches Jahrbuch* (1866–), covering separate areas or topics in individual volumes which appeared irregularly and covered several years of the pertinent geographical literature.

In addition, several geographical dictionaries are of value, among which are L. D. Stamp (ed.), *A Dictionary Geography* (1966) and F. J. Monkhouse, *A Dictionary of Geography* (1965).

Bibliography and Author Index

Note: The numbers in **boldface** indicate pages where each author is mentioned throughout the book.

Where two dates appear, the later is that of republication.

Sociology

ADORNO, THEODOR W., et al.
   1950 *The Authoritarian Personality.* New York: Harper; paper, Wiley. **34, 119**.

ALIHAN, MILLA
   1938 *Social Ecology.* New York: Columbia University Press. **32**.

ANDERSON, ELIN
   1937 *We Americans.* Cambridge, Mass.: Harvard University Press. **33**.

ARENSBERG, CONRAD, and SOLON KIMBALL
   1940 *Family and Community in Ireland.* Cambridge, Mass.: Harvard University Press. **28, 33, 47, 77**.

ARISTOTLE
   1962 *Ethics.* New York: Barnes & Noble; paper, Penguin. Tr. J. A. K. Thompson. **4, 131, 133, 136–137, 139, 170, 172, 175, 213**.
   1946 *Politics.* New York: Oxford University Press; paper, Oxford. Tr. E. Barker.

BALES, ROBERT F.
   1950 *Interaction Process Analysis.* Reading, Mass.: Addison-Wesley. **24, 27**.

BARNARD, CHESTER I.
   1938 *The Functions of the Executive.* Cambridge, Mass.: Harvard University Press. **37, 157**.

BARNES, HARRY ELMER (ed.)
   1948 *An Introduction to the History of Sociology.* Chicago: University of Chicago Press; paper, Chicago. **39**.

———, and HOWARD BECKER
   1952 *Social Thought from Lore to Science;* 2d ed. Washington: Harren; paper, Dover. **39**.

BENDIX, REINHARD, and SEYMOUR M. LIPSET
   1966 *Class, Status and Power.* New York: Free Press. **20–21, 25–26, 29, 35, 65, 155, 157, 170, 177, 190, 214, 219**.

BIBLIOGRAPHY AND AUTHOR INDEX

BENEDICT, RUTH
  1934 *Patterns of Culture*. New York: Houghton; paper, Houghton. **29, 65**.
BERELSON, BERNARD, PAUL F. LAZARSFELD, and WILLIAM N. MCPHEE
  1954 *Voting*. Chicago: University of Chicago Press; paper, Chicago. **21, 25–26, 30, 115, 169**.
BERGER, J., B. P. COHEN, J. L. SNELL, and M. ZELDITCH, JR. (eds.)
  1962 *Types of Formalization in Small-Group Research*. New York: Houghton. **28**.
BERLE, JR., ADOLF A., and GARDINER C. MEANS
  1937 *The Modern Corporation and Private Property*. New York: Macmillan. **36, 280**.
BETTELHEIM, BRUNO, and MORRIS JANOWITZ
  1964 *Social Change and Prejudice*. New York: Free Press. **34, 130, 134, 168, 170, 185, 208, 219, 221, 233**.
BLALOCK, HUBERT
  1964 *Causal Inferences in Nonexperimental Research*. Chapel Hill, N.C.: University of North Carolina Press; paper, North Carolina. **25**.
BLAU, PETER M.
  1963 *The Dynamics of Bureaucracy*, 2d rev. ed. Chicago: University of Chicago Press. **23, 36, 155, 180**.
  1964 *Exchange and Power in Social Life*. New York: Wiley.
  ———, and OTIS DUDLEY DUNCAN.
  1967 *The American Occupational Structure*. New York: Wiley. **36**.
BOGUE, DONALD
  1949 *The Structure of the Metropolitan Community*. Ann Arbor, Mich.: University of Michigan Press. **30–32**.
BOOTH, CHARLES (ed.)
  1902 *Life and Labour of the People in London* (1892–97). New York: Macmillan. **9**.
BROOM, LEONARD, and PHILIP SELZNICK
  1963 *Sociology*, 3d ed. New York: Harper. **37, 39, 157, 184**.
BUCKLEY, WALTER
  1967 *Sociology and Modern Systems Theory*. Englewood Cliffs, N.J.: Prentice-Hall. **23**.
BURGESS, ERNEST W. (ed.)
  1926 *The Urban Community*. Chicago: University of Chicago Press. **10, 39**.
CAHNMAN, WERNER J., and ALVIN BOSKOFF (eds.)
  1964 *Sociology and History: Theory and Research*. New York: Free Press. **24**.
CAMPBELL, ANGUS, GERALD GURIN, and WARREN E. MILLER
  1954 *The Voter Decides*. New York: Harper. **26, 169, 188**.
CARLSON, GOESTA
  1958 *Social Mobility and Class Structure*. Lund, Sweden: Gleerup. **35**.
CARTWRIGHT, DORWIN, and ALVIN ZANDER (eds.)
  1953 *Group Dynamics*. New York: Harper. **28, 120**.

CENTERS, RICHARD
1949 *The Psychology of Social Classes.* Princeton, N.J.: Princeton University Press. **35.**

CHRISTIE, RICHARD, and MARIE JAHODA (eds.)
1954 *Studies in the Scope and Method of "The Authoritarian Personality."* New York: Free Press. **25, 119.**

COALE, ANSLEY, and MELVIN ZELNIK
1963 *New Estimates of Fertility and Population in the United States.* Princeton, N.J.: Princeton University Press. **31.**

COLEMAN, JAMES S.
1964 *Introduction to Mathematical Sociology.* New York: Free Press. **20, 23, 26, 157, 212, 217.**

COMTE, AUGUST
1953 *Cours de Philosophie Positive* (1830–42). Stanford, Cal.: Academic Reprints. **6–7, 15.** Tr. J. H. Bridges as *General View of Positivism.*

COOLEY, CHARLES H.
1922 *Human Nature and the Social Order* (1902), rev. ed. New York: Scribner; paper, Schocken. **18–19.**
1909 *Social Organization.* New York: Scribner; paper, Schocken.

COSER, LEWIS A.
1956 *The Functions of Social Conflict.* New York: Free Press; paper, Free Press. **23.**

CUBER, JOHN F.
1963 *Sociology,* 5th ed. New York: Appleton. **39.**

DAVIS, ALLISON, B. BURLEIGH, and MARY R. GARDNER
1941 *Deep South.* Chicago: University of Chicago Press; paper, Chicago. **30, 33.**

DAVIS, ALLISON, and ROBERT J. HAVINGHURST
1947 *Father of the Man.* Boston: Houghton. **30, 33.**

DAVIS, JAMES A.
1962 *American Journal of Sociology,* Vol. 67 (1962), p. 458.
1964 *Great Aspirations.* Chicago: Aldine. **22, 26.**

DAVIS, KINGSLEY
1949 *Human Society.* New York: Macmillan. **31, 39.**
1951 *The Population of India and Pakistan.* Princeton, N.J.: Princeton University Press.

DOLLARD, JOHN
1937 *Caste and Class in a Southern Town.* New Haven, Conn.: Yale University Press; paper, Doubleday. **33, 117.**

DRAKE, ST. CLAIR, and HORACE R. CAYTON
1946 *Black Metropolis.* New York: Harcourt. **34.**

DUNCAN, O. D.
1965 "Social Organization and the Ecosystem," in Robert E. L. Faris (ed.), *Handbook of Modern Sociology.* Chicago: Rand. **31–33, 36, 39.**

———, et al.
1960 *Metropolis and Region.* Baltimore: Johns Hopkins University Press.

DURKHEIM, EMILE
1893 *De la Division du travail social.* New York: Free Press, 1947; paper, Free Press. Tr. G. Simpson as *Division of Labor in Society.* **15–17, 18–19, 21, 51–52, 54–55, 68, 71–72, 77, 81.**
1947 *The Elementary Forms of the Religious Life* (1915). New York: Free Press; paper, Free Press. Tr. J. W. Swain.
1950 *The Rules of Sociological Method,* 8th ed. New York: Free Press; paper, Free Press. Tr. S. Solovay and J. H. Mueller; ed. G. E. G. Catlin.
1951 *Suicide* (1897). New York: Free Press; paper, Free Press. Tr. J. A. Spaulding and G. Simpson; ed. G. Simpson.

ELDRIDGE, HOPE T., and DOROTHY S. THOMAS
1964 *Population Redistribution and Economic Growth, United States, 1870–1950,* Vol. III. Philadelphia: American Philosophical Society. S. S. Kuznets, General Ed. **31.**

FARIS, ROBERT E. L.
1964 *Handbook of Modern Sociology.* Chicago: Rand. **32–33, 39.**

——, and HENRY WARREN DUNHAM
1939 *Mental Disorders in Urban Areas.* Chicago: University of Chicago Press; paper, Chicago. **32.**

FESTINGER, LEON
1962 *A Theory of Cognitive Dissonance.* Stanford: Stanford University Press. **28, 124.**

FIREY, WALTER
1947 *Land Use in Central Boston.* Cambridge, Mass.: Harvard University Press. **32.**

FRAZIER, EDWARD FRANKLIN
1949 *The Negro in the United States.* New York: Macmillan. **54, 56, 62, 81.**

FREEDMAN, RONALD, PASCAL K. WHELPTON, and ARTHUR A. CAMPBELL
1959 *Family Planning, Sterility, and Population Growth.* New York: McGraw-Hill. **31.**

FROMM, ERICH
1941 *Escape from Freedom.* New York: Farrar; paper, Avon. **29, 119.**

GANS, HERBERT
1962 *The Urban Villagers.* (New York: The Free Press; paper, Free Press. **24.**

GARFINKEL, HAROLD
1967 *Studies in Ethnomethodology.* Englewood Cliffs, N.J.: Prentice-Hall. **29.**

GERTH, HANS, and C. WRIGHT MILLS (eds. and trs.)
1946 *From Max Weber: Essays in Sociology.* New York: Oxford University Press; paper, Oxford. **12–14, 15, 18, 21, 23, 36, 77, 155, 206, 213, 255, 287.**

GITTLER, JOSEPH B. (ed.)
1957 *Review of Sociology.* New York: Wiley. **39.**

GLASS, DAVID B.
1954 *Social Mobility in Great Britain.* New York: Free Press. **35.**
GLAZER, NATHAN, and D. P. MOYNIHAN
1963 *Beyond the Melting Pot.* Cambridge, Mass.: M.I.T. Press. **34.**
GOFFMAN, ERVING
1961 *Asylums.* New York: Doubleday; paper. **29, 70.**
1959 *The Presentation of Self in Everyday Life.* New York: Doubleday; paper, Doubleday.
1963 *Stigma.* Englewood Cliffs, N.J.: Prentice-Hall; paper, Prentice.
GOODE, WILLIAM J., and PAUL K. HATT
1952 *Methods in Social Research.* New York: McGraw-Hill. **25, 35.**
GORDON, MILTON
1964 *Assimilation in American Life.* New York: Oxford University Press; paper, Oxford. **34.**
GOULDNER, ALVIN W.
1954 *Patterns of Industrial Democracy.* New York: Free Press; paper, Free Press. **37, 177.**
GREBLER, LEO, et al.
America's Second Minority: Los Chicanos (unpublished). **34.**
HADDEN, JEFFREY K., and EDGAR F. BORGATTA
1965 *American Cities.* Chicago: Rand. **24.**
HARE, A. PAUL (ed.)
1962 *A Handbook of Small Group Research.* New York: Free Press, **24, 28.**
———, EDGAR F. BORGATTA, and ROBERT F. BALES
1955 *Small Groups.* New York: Knopf. **24, 27.**
HAUSER, P. M.
1963 *The Population Dilemma.* Englewood Cliffs, N.J.: Prentice-Hall; paper, Prentice. **31, 311.**
———, and OTIS D. DUNCAN
1959 *The Study of Population.* Chicago: University of Chicago Press. **31–32, 35.**
———, and LEO F. SCHNORE
1965 *The Study of Urbanization.* New York: Wiley. **31, 311.**
HAWLEY, AMOS
1950 *Human Ecology.* New York: Ronald. **28, 32.**
HOLLINGSHEAD, AUGUST
1949 *Elmtown's Youth.* New York: Wiley; paper, Wiley. **33.**
HOMANS, GEORGE C.
1950 *The Human Group.* New York: Harcourt. **20–23.**
1961 *Social Behavior.* New York: Harcourt.
HOUSE, FLOYD N.
1936 *The Development of Sociology.* New York: McGraw-Hill. **39.**
HOVLAND, CARL I., ARTHUR A. LUMSDAINE, and FRED D. SHEFFIELD
1949 *Experiments in Mass Communication.* Princeton, N.J.: Princeton University Press; paper, Wiley. **30, 120.**

BIBLIOGRAPHY AND AUTHOR INDEX

HUGHES, EVERETT C.
1943 *French Canada in Transition.* Chicago: University of Chicago Press; paper, Chicago. 33–34.
——, and HELEN M. HUGHES
1952 *Where Peoples Meet.* New York: Free Press. 34.
HUNTER, FLOYD
1953 *Community Power Structure.* Chapel Hill, N.C.: University of North Carolina Press; paper, Doubleday. 33, 167, 207.
HYMAN, HERBERT
1955 *Survey Design and Analysis.* New York: Free Press. 25, 184.
JAHODA, MARIE, MORTON DEUTSCH, and STUART COOK
1951 *Research Methods in Social Relations.* New York: Dryden. 25, 119.
JONES, ALFRED W.
1941 *Life, Liberty and Property.* Philadelphia: Lippincott. 35.
KARDINER, ABRAM
1939 *The Individual and His Society.* New York: Columbia University Press. 29, 54, 65.
——, et al.
1945 *The Psychological Frontiers of Society.* New York: Columbia University Press; paper, Columbia.
KATZ, ELIHU, and PAUL F. LAZARSFELD
1955 *Personal Influence.* New York: Free Press; paper, Free Press. 21, 25, 26, 30, 115, 169.
KELLOGG, PAUL U.
1909–14 *Pittsburgh Survey.* New York: Charities Publishing Committee. 10.
KILLIAN, LEWIS, and CHARLES GRIGG
1964 *Racial Crisis in America.* Englewood Cliffs, N.J.: Prentice-Hall; paper, Prentice. 34.
KIRK, DUDLEY
1946 *Europe's Population in the Interwar Years.* New York: Columbia University Press. 31.
KISER, CLYDE V. (ed.)
1962 *Research in Family Planning.* Princeton, N.J.: Princeton University Press. 31.
LAZARSFELD, PAUL F., BERNARD BERELSON, and HAZEL GAUDET
1944 *The People's Choice.* New York: Duell. 21, 25–26, 30, 115, 169.
LAZARSFELD, PAUL F., and MORRIS ROSENBERG
1955 *The Language of Social Research.* New York: Free Press; paper, Free Press. 21, 25–26, 30, 115, 169.
LAZARSFELD, PAUL F., and WAGNER THIELENS
1958 *The Academic Mind.* New York: Free Press. 21, 25–26, 30, 115, 169.
LENSKI, GERHARD E.
1966 *Power and Privilege.* New York: McGraw-Hill. 35.
LEPLAY, PIERRE FRÉDÉRIC
1872–79 *Les Ouvriers Européens.* Tours, France: A. Mame et fils. 9.

LIKERT, RENSIS
  1961 *New Patterns of Management.* New York: McGraw-Hill. **37.**
LINDESMITH, ALFRED, and ANSELM STRAUSS
  1956 *Social Psychology.* New York: Dryden. **29.**
LINDZEY, GARDINER (ed.)
  1954 *Handbook of Social Psychology.* Reading, Mass.: Addison-Wesley. (2d ed. with E. ARONSON, 1968.) **28, 66, 109–110, 119–120, 170.**
LIPSET, SEYMOUR M.
  1960 *Political Man.* New York: Doubleday; paper, Doubleday. **20–21, 25–26, 35, 157, 170, 177, 190, 214, 219.**
  ———, and REINHARD BENDIX
  1959 *Social Mobility in Industrial Society.* Berkeley, Cal.: University of California Press; paper, California. **35, 155, 214.**
  ———, MARTIN TROW, and JAMES S. COLEMAN
  1956 *Union-Democracy.* New York: Free Press; paper, Doubleday. **20, 23, 26, 157, 212, 217.**
LUNDBERG, GEORGE
  1939 *Foundations of Sociology.* New York: Macmillan. **19.**
LYND, ROBERT S., and HELEN M. LYND
  1929 *Middletown.* New York: Harcourt; paper, Harcourt. **33, 46.**

  1937 *Middletown in Transition.* New York: Harcourt; paper, Harcourt.
MACIVER, ROBERT M., and CHARLES H. PAGE
  1949 *Society.* New York: Holt. **39, 143, 174.**
MALINOWSKI, BRONISLAW
  1948 *Magic, Science and Religion.* Boston: Beacon; paper, Doubleday. Ed. R. Redfield. **19, 72–73, 76–77, 189.**
MALTHUS, THOMAS R.
  1963 *An Essay on the Principle of Population.* Homewood, Ill.: Irwin; paper, Michigan. **7, 247.**
MANNHEIM, KARL
  1936 *Ideology and Utopia.* New York: Harcourt; paper, Harcourt. Tr. L. Wirth and E. Shils. **8, 129.**
MAYO, ELTON
  1945 *The Social Problems of an Industrial Nation.* Boston: Harvard Business School. **37, 157, 279.**
MEAD, GEORGE HERBERT
  1934 *Mind, Self and Society.* Chicago: University of Chicago Press; paper, Chicago. **18, 29.**
MEAD, MARGARET
  1939 *From the South Seas.* New York: Morrow. **29, 54, 65, 80, 88–89.**
MERTON, ROBERT K.
  1956 *Social Theory and Social Structure* (1949). New York: Free Press. **20–21, 155.**

BIBLIOGRAPHY AND AUTHOR INDEX

―――, and PAUL F. LAZARSFELD (eds.)
   1950 *Continuities in Social Research.* New York: Free Press. **21, 25–26, 30, 115, 169.**

MICHELS, ROBERT
   1949 *Political Parties* (1915). New York: Free Press; paper, Dover. **20, 36, 165.**

MILLER, S. M.
   1960 "Comparative Social Mobility," *Current Sociology.* **9, 35.**

MILLS, C. WRIGHT
   1956 *The Power Elite.* New York: Oxford University Press; paper, Oxford. **13, 23, 35, 36, 155, 206.**
   1959 *The Sociological Imagination.* New York: Oxford University Press; paper, Oxford.
   1951 *White Collar.* New York: Oxford University Press; paper, Oxford.

MORENO, JACOB L.
   1953 *Who Shall Survive?* Boston: Beacon; rev. ed. **27.**

MYRDAL, GUNNAR
   1944 *An American Dilemma.* New York: Harper; paper, McGraw-Hill (2 vols.). **34, 285.**

OGBURN, WILLIAM F.
   1922 *Social Change.* New York: Viking; paper, Dell. **10, 39.**

―――, and MEYER F. NIMKOFF
   1940 *Sociology.* Boston: Houghton. **39.**

PARK, ROBERT E., and ERNEST W. BURGESS
   1924 *Introduction to the Science of Sociology.* Chicago: University of Chicago Press; 2d ed. **10, 39.**

―――, and RODERICK D. MACKENZIE
   1925 *The City.* Chicago: University of Chicago Press. **10, 32.**

PARSONS, TALCOTT
   1951 *The Social System.* New York: Free Press; paper, Free Press. **11, 21, 23, 61–63, 72, 155, 180, 181, 213, 227, 249.**
   1937 *The Structure of Social Action.* New York: McGraw-Hill; paper, Free Press (2 vols.).

―――, and EDWARD A. SHILS
   1952 *Toward a General Theory of Action.* New York: Oxford University Press; paper, Harper. **21, 25, 39, 61.**

―――, and NEIL J. SMELSER
   1956 *Economy and Society.* New York: Free Press; paper, Free Press. **21, 249.**

PETERSEN, WILLIAM
   1965 *Population.* New York: Macmillan. **31.**

PLATO
   1966 *The Republic.* New York: Cambridge University Press; paper, Cambridge. Ed. and tr. I. A. Richards. **4, 97, 131, 136–137, 175, 177, 182.**

POWDERMAKER, HORTENSE
   1939 *After Freedom.* New York: Viking. **34.**

RADCLIFFE-BROWNE, ALFRED R.
1952 *Structure and Function in Primitive Society.* New York: Free Press; paper, Free Press. **19, 50, 72–73, 74, 77, 90.**
RAINWATER, LEE
1965 *Family Design.* Chicago: Aldine. **31, 34.**
———, and WILLIAM L. YANCEY
1967 *The Moynihan Report and the Politics of Controversy.* Cambridge, Mass.: M.I.T. Press; paper, M.I.T. **34.**
ROETHLISBERGER, FRITZ J., and WILLIAM J. DICKSON
1939 *Management and the Worker.* Cambridge, Mass.: Harvard University Press; paper, Wiley. **37, 157, 279.**
ROGERS, EVERETT M.
1962 *Diffusion of Innovations.* New York: Free Press. **30.**
ROGOFF, NATALIE
1953 *Recent Trends in Occupational Mobility.* New York: Free Press. **36.**
SELZNICK, PHILIP
1949 *TVA and the Grass Roots.* Berkeley, Cal.: University of California Press; paper, Harper. **37, 39, 157, 184.**
SEXTON, PATRICIA C.
1965 *Spanish Harlem.* New York: Harper; paper, Harper. **34.**
SHAW, CLIFFORD R., and HENRY MCKAY
1942 *Juvenile Delinquency and Urban Areas.* Chicago: University of Chicago Press. **32.**
SHERIF, MUZAFER
1936 *The Psychology of Social Norms.* New York: Harper; paper, Harper. **28, 118.**
SHILS, EDWARD A.
1948 *The Present State of American Sociology.* New York: Free Press. **21, 25, 39, 61.**
SOROKIN, PITIRIM A.
1928 *Contemporary Sociological Theories.* New York: Harper; paper, Harper. **21, 35, 39.**
1941 *Social and Cultural Dynamics.* New York: American Book.
1927 *Social Mobility* New York: Harper.
1966 *Sociological Theories of Today.* New York: Harper.
SPENCER, HERBERT
1928 *First Principles.* London: Williams & Norgate; 6th ed. **7–8, 55.**
1900 *The Principles of Sociology.* New York: Appleton; 3rd ed. **31–32, 35, 252.**
SPENGLER, JOSEPH J., and OTIS D. DUNCAN (eds.)
1956 *Population Theory and Policy.* New York: Free Press.
STANTON, ALFRED H., and MORRIS S. SCHWARTZ
1954 *The Mental Hospital.* New York: Basic Books. **37.**
STOUFFER, SAMUEL A.
1955 *Communism, Conformity and Civil Liberties.* New York: Doubleday; paper, Wiley. **17, 21, 25, 38, 120, 169.**

——, et al.,
1949 *The American Soldier*. Princeton, N.J.: Princeton University Press; paper, Wiley.
1950 *Measurement and Prediction*. Princeton, N.J.: Princeton University Press; paper, Wiley.

SULLIVAN, HARRY STACK
1953 *The Interpersonal Theory of Psychiatry*. New York: Norton. 29, 119.

SUMNER, WILLIAM GRAHAM
1933 *War, and Other Essays*. New Haven, Conn.: Yale University Press. Ed. A. G. Keller. 8–9.
1920 *What Social Classes Owe to Each Other* (1883). New York: Harper; paper, Caxton.

SVALASTOGA, KAARE
1959 *Prestige, Class and Mobility*. Copenhagen, Denmark: Gyldendalske Boghandel. 35.

THIBAUT, JOHN W., and HAROLD H. KELLEY
1959 *The Social Psychology of Groups*. New York: Wiley. 23.

THOMAS, WILLIAM I., and FLORIAN ZNANIECKI
1920 *The Polish Peasant in Europe and America*. Boston: Badger. 10, 17, 119.

UNITED NATIONS DEPARTMENT OF SOCIAL AFFAIRS POPULATION STUDY NO. 17
1953 *The Determinants and Consequences of Population Trends*. New York: United Nations. 31.

WALKER, CHARLES R., et al.
1956 *The Foreman on the Assembly Line*. Cambridge, Mass.: Harvard University Press. 37.

——, and ROBERT GUEST
1952 *The Man on the Assembly Line*. Cambridge, Mass.: Harvard University Press. 37.

WARD, LESTER F.
1920 *Dynamic Sociology* (1883). Appleton, rev. ed. 8–9.

WARNER, W. LLOYD
1955 *Occupational Mobility in American Business and Industry, 1928–1952*. Minneapolis: University of Minnesota Press. 33, 36, 46, 73, 90, 167, 195.

——, and PAUL S. LUNT
1941 *The Social Life of a Modern Community*. New Haven, Conn.: Yale University Press. "Yankee City Series," Vol. I. 33.

——, and LEO SROLE
1945 *The Social Systems of American Ethnic Groups*. New Haven, Conn.: Yale University Press. "Yankee City Series," Vol. III. 33.

WEBER, MAX
1951–52 *Gesammelte Aufsaetze zur Religionssoziologie* (1920–21), partly tr. as *The Religion of China* and *Ancient Judaism*. New York: Free Press; paper, Free Press. (1) Tr. and ed. H. H. Gerth; (2) Tr. and ed. H. H. Gerth and D. Martindale. 12, 14, 15, 18, 21, 36, 55, 77, 155, 213, 255, 287.

1949 *The Methodology of the Social Sciences.* New York: Free Press. Tr. and ed. E. A. Shils and H. A. Finch. **21, 25, 39, 61.**
1930 *The Protestant Ethic and the Spirit of Capitalism.* New York: Scribner; paper, Scribner. Tr. T. Parsons.
1947 *The Theory of Social and Economic Organization.* New York: Oxford University Press; paper, Free Press. Tr. T. Parsons.

WEIDNER, EDWARD W.
1964 *Technical Assistance in Public Administration Overseas.* Chicago: Public Administration Service. **214.**

WESTOFF, CHARLES F., ROBERT G. POTTER, and PHILIP C. SAGI
1963 *The Third Child.* Princeton, N.J.: Princeton University Press, **31.**

WHYTE, WILLIAM F.
1948 *Human Relations in the Restaurant Industry.* New York: McGraw-Hill. **28, 37, 166-167, 279.**
1955 *Street Corner Society* (1943). Chicago: University of Chicago Press; paper, Chicago.

WILLIAMS, JR., ROBIN M.
1960 *American Society.* New York: Knopf. **34, 39.**
———, et al.,
1964 *Strangers Next Door.* Englewood Cliffs, N.J.: Prentice-Hall.

WILSON, EVERETT
1966 *Sociology: Rules, Roles, Relationships.* Homewood, Ill.: Dorsey. **39.**

WIRTH, LOUIS
1928 *The Ghetto.* Chicago: University of Chicago Press; paper, Chicago. **34.**

WOLFF, KURT H. (tr. and ed.)
1950 *The Sociology of Georg Simmel.* New York: Free Press; paper, Free Press. **14.**

ZETTERBERG, HANS (ed.)
1956 *Sociology in the United States of America.* Paris: UNESCO. **39.**

MISCELLANEOUS SOURCES

Administrative Science Quarterly (1956–   ).
American Journal of Sociology (1895–   ).
American Sociological Review (1936–   ).
British Journal of Sociology (1950–   ).
Human Organization (1941–   ).
Human Relations (1947–   ).
Public Opinion Quarterly (1937–   ).
Rural Sociology (1936–   ).
Social Forces (1922–   ).
Social Problems (1953–   ).
Sociological Abstracts (1952–   ).
Sociology and Social Research (1916–   ).
Sociometry (1937–   ).
Survey Research Center, University of Michigan, publications.

Anthropology

ADAMS, ROBERT
1966 *Evolution of Urban Society: Early Mesopotamia and Prehistoric Mexico.* Chicago: Aldine. **64.**

ALBERT, ETHEL M., and CLYDE KLUCKHOHN
1959 *A Selected Bibliography on Values, Ethics, and Esthetics in the Behavioral Sciences and Philosophy, 1920–1958.* New York: Free Press. **48, 50, 62, 66, 220.**

AMMAR, HAMED
1954 *Growing Up in an Egyptian Village: Selwa, Province of Aswan.* London: Routledge. **85.**

ARENSBER, CONRAD
1959 *The Irish Countryman: An Anthropological Study.* Magnolia, Mass.: Smith. **28, 33, 47, 77.**

ATKINSON, J. W. (ed.)
1958 *Motives in Fantasy, Actions and Society.* Princeton, N.J.: Van Nostrand. **67, 116.**

BACHOFEN, JOHANN JACOB
1948 *Das Mutterrecht.* Basel: Schwabe. Mit Unterstützung H. Fuchs, G. Meyer, und K. Schefold; Herausgeber K. Meuli.

BAILEY, FREDERICK GEORGE
1957 *Caste and the Economic Frontier.* Manchester: Manchester University Press. **76.**
1960 *Tribe, Caste and Nation: A Study of Political Activity and Political Change in Highland Orissa.* Manchester: Manchester University Press.
1963 *Politics and Social Changes in Orissa in 1959.* Berkeley, Cal.: University of California Press.

BANTON, MICHAEL P. (ed.)
1965 *Political Systems and the Distribution of Power.* New York: Praeger. **75.**
1965 *Relevance of Models for Social Anthropology.* New York: Praeger.
1966 *Anthropological Approaches to the Study of Religion.* New York: Praeger.
1966 *The Social Anthropology of Complex Societies.* New York: Praeger.

BARNETT, H.
1960 *Being a Palaun.* New York: Holt; paper, Holt. **89.**

BARNOUW, VICTOR
1963 *Culture and Personality.* Homewood, Ill.: Dorsey. **66.**

BARTH, FREDERIK
1960 *Nomads of South Persia.* New York: Humanities. **85.**

BEALS, ALAN, and B. J. SIEGEL
1966 *Divisiveness and Social Conflict: An Anthropological Approach.* Stanford, Cal.: Stanford University Press. **48, 75, 76, 87.**

BEALS, RALPH LEON, and HARRY HOIJER
1965 *An Introduction to Anthropology.* New York: Macmillan; 3rd ed. With the collaboration of V. M. Roediger. **49, 69.**

BEARDSLEY, R. K., JOHN W. HALL, and ROBERT E. WARD
1959 *Village Japan.* Chicago: University of Chicago Press. **88, 212, 236.**

BEATTIE, J.
1964 *Other Cultures: Aims, Methods and Achievements in Social Anthropology.* New York: Free Press. **49.**

BELLAH, ROBERT N.
1957 *Tokugawa Religion: The Values of Preindustrial Japan.* New York: Free Press. **88.**

BELSHAW, CYRIL S.
1955 *In Search of Wealth.* Washington: American Anthropological Association. Memoir No. 80. **77, 89, 289.**
1965 *Traditional Exchange and Modern Markets.* Englewood Cliffs, N.J.: Prentice-Hall; paper, Prentice.

BENEDICT, RUTH
1934 *Patterns of Culture.* Boston: Houghton; paper, Houghton. **29, 65.**

BERNDT, RONALD MURRAY, and CATHERINE H. BERNDT
1964 *The World of the First Australian: An Introduction to the Traditional Life of the Australian Aborigine.* Chicago: University of Chicago Press. **89.**

BERREMAN, GERALD
1963 *Hindus of the Himalayas.* Berkeley, Cal.: University of California Press. **87.**

BOAS, FRANZ
1888 *The Central Eskimo.* Washington: U.S. Bureau of American Ethnology; paper, Nebraska. **49, 50, 54, 56, 59, 69, 82.**
1925 *Contributions to the Ethnology of the Kwakiutl, Based on Data Collected by George Hunt.* New York: Columbia University Press.
1938 *The Mind of Primitive Man.* New York: Macmillan; paper, Free Press.
1940 *Race, Language and Culture.* New York: Macmillan; paper, Free Press.
1966 *Kwakiutl Ethnography.* Boston: Heath. Ed. H. Codere.
1938 (ed.), et al., *General Anthropology.* Boston: Heath.

BOHANNAN, PAUL
1963 *Social Anthropology.* New York: Holt. **49, 54, 74, 77, 84.**
1964 *Africa and Africans.* New York: Doubleday; paper, Doubleday.
1966 (ed.), *Law and Warfare: Studies in the Anthropology of Conflict.* Garden City, N.Y.: Natural History.
———, and G. DALTON (eds.)
1962 *Markets in Africa.* Evanston: Ill.: Northwestern University Press; paper, Doubleday. **77.**

BRAIDWOOD, ROBERT J., and GORDON R. WILLEY
1962 *Courses Toward Life: Archaeological Considerations of Some Cultural Alternates.* New York: Wenner-Gren Foundation for Anthropological Research. **64.**

BURROWS, E. G., and M. E. SPIRO
1957 *An Atoll Culture: Ethnography of Ifaluk in the Central Carolines.* New York: Taplinger. **89.**

BUTZER, KARL W.
1964 *Environment and Archaeology: An Introduction to Pleistocene Geography.* Chicago: Aldine. **65, 305.**

CHANG, KWANG-CHIK
1965 *Archaeology of Ancient China.* New Haven, Conn.: Yale University Press. **64.**

CHICAGO, UNIVERSITY COLLEGE OF
1957 *Introduction to the Civilization of India: Changing Dimensions of Indian Society and Culture.* Chicago: University of Chicago Press.

COHEN, E. (ed.)
1966 *Comparative Political Systems.* Garden City, N.Y.: Natural History.

COLSON, ELIZABETH, and MAX GLUCKMAN (eds.)
1951 *Seven Tribes of British Central Africa.* New York: Oxford University Press. **49, 75.**

COON, CARLETON
1931 *Tribes of the Rif.* Cambridge, Mass.: Peabody Museum. **85.**

COULANGES, FUSTEL DE
1874 *The Ancient City.* Boston: Lothrop; paper, Doubleday. Tr. W. Small. **71.**

COX, EDWARD G.
1949 *A Reference Guide to the Literature of Travel.* Seattle: University of Washington Press. **51.**

CURTIN, PHILIP D.
1964 *The Image of Africa: British Ideas and Action, 1780–1850.* Madison, Wis.: University of Wisconsin Press. **51.**

DALTON, G. (ed.)
1966 *Tribal and Peasant Economies.* Garden City, N.Y.: Natural History: paper, Doubleday.

DANIEL, GLYN EDMUND
1950 *A Hundred Years of Archaeology.* New York: Macmillan. **53.**
1963 *The Idea of Prehistory.* Cleveland: World; paper, Penguin.

DE BARY, WILLIAM THEODORE (ed.)
1958 *Sources of Indian Tradition.* New York: Columbia University Press; paper, Columbia. **87, 88.**

———, et al.,
1960 *Sources of Chinese Tradition.* New York: Columbia University Press; paper, Columbia.

DeLaguna, Frederica (ed.)
1960 *Selected Papers from the American Anthropologist, 1888–1920*. New York: Harper.
De Vore, Irwen
1965 *Primate Behavior: Field Studies of Monkeys and Apes*. New York: Holt. **58.**
Dewey, Alice
1962 *Peasant Marketing in Java*. New York: Free Press. **77.**
Dole, Gertrude E., and Robert L. Carnier (eds.)
1960 *Essays in the Science of Culture: In Honor of Leslie A. White*. New York: Crowell; paper, Crowell. **57.**
Dore, Ronald Philip
1958 *City Life in Japan: A Study of a Tokyo Ward*. Berkeley, Cal.: University of California Press; paper, California. **88.**
1965 *Education in Tokugawa, Japan*. Berkeley, Cal.: University of California Press.
Driver, Harold E.
1961 *Indians of North America*. Chicago: University of Chicago Press; paper, Chicago. **82.**
1964 *The Americas on the Eve of Discovery*. Englewood Cliffs, N.J.: Prentice-Hall; paper, Prentice.
Drucker, Philip
1955 *Indians of the Northwest Coast*. New York: McGraw-Hill. **280.**
DuBois, Cora
1944 *The People of Alor: A Social-Psychological Study of an East Indian Island*. Minneapolis: University of Minnesota Press; paper, Harper.
Durkheim, Émile
1957 *The Elementary Forms of Religious Life*. New York: Free Press; paper, Free Press. Tr. J. W. Swain. **15–17, 18–19, 21, 51–52, 54–55, 68, 71–72, 77, 81.**
———, and Marcel Mauss
1963 *Primitive Classification*. Chicago: University of Chicago Press; paper, Chicago. Tr. R. Needham. **55, 71.**
1938 *Left Handed, Navaho Indian, Son of Old Man Hat: A Navaho Autobiography*. New York: Harcourt; paper, Nebraska. Recorded by Walter Dyk, with intro. by Edward Sapir.
Eggan, Frederick R.
1950 *Social Organization of the Western Pueblos*. Chicago: University of Chicago Press. **73, 83.**
1956 *Selected Bibliography of the Philippines*. New York: Taplinger. Prepared by the Philippines Study Program, Dept of Anthropology, University of Chicago.
1966 *The American Indian: Perspectives for the Study of Social Change*. Chicago: Aldine.
Eisenstadt, S. N.
1963 *Political Systems of Empires*. New York: Free Press. **63, 76, 216.**

ELKIN, A. P.
    1953 *Social Anthropology in Melanesia: A Review of Research.* New York: Oxford University Press. Published under the auspices of the South Pacific Committee. **89, 90.**

EMBREE, JOHN F.
    1939 *Suye Mura: A Japanese Village.* Chicago: University of Chicago Press. **86, 88.**

——, and LILLIAN OTA DOTSON
    1950 *Bibliography of the People and Cultures of Mainland S.E. Asia.* New Haven, Conn.: Yale University S.E. Asia Studies. **86.**

ERASMUS, CHARLES J.
    1961 *Man Takes Control: Cultural Development and American Aid.* Minneapolis: University of Minnesota Press; paper, Bobbs. **80.**

ETTINGHAUSEN, RICHARD
    1954 *A Selected and Annotated Bibliography of Books and Periodicals in Western Languages Dealing with the Near and Middle East, with Special Emphasis on Medieval and Modern Times.* Washington: Middle East Institute. **86.**

EVANS-PRITCHARD, EDWARD EVAN
    1940 *The Nuer.* Oxford: Clarendon. **50, 53, 71, 73–75, 78.**
    Kinship and Marriage Among the Nuer. Oxford: Clarendon.
    1952 *Social Anthropology.* New York: Free Press.
    1956 *Nuer Religion.* Oxford: Clarendon.
    1962 *Essays in Social Anthropology.* New York: Free Press, paper, Free Press,
    1965 *The Position of Women in Primitive Society and Other Essays in Social Anthropology.* New York: Free Press.

——, and M. FORTES
    1940 *African Political Systems.* New York: Oxford University Press. **73, 74.**

FAIRBANK, JOHN KING (ed.)
    1957 *Chinese Thought and Institutions.* Chicago: University of Chicago Press. **86.**

FALLERS, LLOYD A.
    1956 *Bantu Bureaucracy: A Study of Integration and Conflict in the Political Institutions of an East African People.* Cambridge, England: Heffer. **76.**

FEI, HSAIO-T'UNG
    1939 *Peasant Life in China: A Field Study of Country Life in the Yangtze Valley.* New York: Dutton.

FERGUSON, C. A., and JOHN S. GUMPERZ (eds.)
    1960 *Linguistic Diversity in South Asia: Studies in Regional, Social, and Functional Variation.* Bloomington, Ind.: Indiana University Research Center in Anthropological Folklore and Linguistics. Publication 13. **70, 191.**

FIELD, HENRY
    1953– *Bibliography on Southwestern Asia.* Coral Gables, Fla.: University of Miami Press. **86.**

FIRTH, RAYMOND WILLIAM
  1936 *We, the Tikopia: A Sociological Study of Kinship in Primitive Polynesia.* New York: American Book. **49–50, 73–74, 77, 80, 89.**
  1939 *Primitive Polynesian Economy.* London: Routledge.
  1956 *Elements of Social Organization.* London: Watts; paper, Beacon.
  1957 *Man and Culture: An Evaluation of the Work of Bronislaw Malinowski.* New York: Humanities.
  1959 *Social Change in Tikopia: Restudy of a Polynesian Community After a Generation.* London: Allen & Unwin.
  1964 *Essays in Social Organizations and Values.* London: University of London, Athlone Press.
  ———, and B. S. YAMEY (eds.)
  1964 *Capital, Saving, and Credit in Peasant Societies.* Chicago: Aldine. **77.**
FISHER, CHARLES A.
  1964 *South-East Asia: A Social, Economic and Political Geography.* New York: Dutton. **86.**
FORD, CLELLAN S.
  1941 *Smoke from Their Fires: The Life of a Kwakiutl Chief.* New Haven, Conn.: Yale University Press. **67.**
FORDE, C. DARYLL
  1934 *Habitat, Economy and Society: A Geographical Introduction to Ethnology.* London: Methuen; paper, Dutton. **49, 85.**
  ——— (ed.)
  1954 *African Worlds.* New York: Oxford University Press; paper, Oxford.
FORTES, MEYER
  1945 *Dynamics of Clanship Among the Tallensie.* New York: Oxford University Press. **73–74.**
  1949 *The Web of Kinship Among the Tallensie.* New York: Oxford University Press.
  1962 *Marriage in Tribal Societies.* New York: Cambridge University Press.
FORTUNE, REO F.
  1963 *Sorcerers of Dobu: The Social Anthropology of the Dobu Islanders of the Western Pacific.* New York: Dutton; paper, Dutton. **89.**
FOSTER, GEORGE M.
  1960 *Culture and Conquest: America's Spanish Heritage.* New York: Wenner-Green Foundation for Anthropological Research. **80.**
  1962 *Traditional Cultures and the Impact of Technological Change.* New York: Harper.
FRANKENBURG, RONALD
  1957 *Village on the Border: A Study of Religion, Politics and Football in a North Wales Community.* New York: Humanities. **47.** .
FRAZER, SIR JAMES G.
  1951 *The Golden Bough: A Study in Magic.* New York: Macmillan; paper, New American. **54, 56, 62, 81.**

FRIED, MORTON HERBERT
1959 *Readings in Anthropology.* Vol. V. New York: Crowell; paper, Crowell. **49.**

FÜRER-HAMENDORF, ELIZABETH VON (comp.)
1958 *An Anthropological Bibliography of S.E. Asia, Together with a Directory of Recent Field Work.* New York: Humanities; paper, Humanities.

GEDDES, W. R.
1963 *Peasant Life in Communist China.* Ithaca, N.Y.: Cornell University Press. **88.**

GEERTZ, CLIFFORD
1963 *Peddlers and Princes: Social Development and Economic Change in Two Indonesian Towns.* Chicago: University of Chicago Press. **77, 79, 86, 214.**
1960 *The Religion of Java.* New York: Free Press; paper, Free Press.
1965 *Social History of an Indonesian Town.* Cambridge, Mass.: M.I.T. Press.
—— (ed.)
1963 *Old Societies and New States: The Quest for Modernity in Asia and Africa.* New York: Free Press.

GIBB, HAMILTON A. R.
1949 *Mohammedanism.* New York: Oxford University Press; paper, Oxford. **85.**

GIBBS, JAMES L.
1965 *Peoples of Africa.* New York: Holt. **84.**

GLADWIN, T., and S. B. SARASON
1953 *Truk: Man in Paradise.* New York: Wenner-Gren Foundation for Anthropological Research. **89.**

GLUCKMAN, MAX
1965 *Politics, Law and Ritual in Tribal Society.* Chicago: Aldine. **49, 75.**

GOFFMAN, ERVING
1956 *Presentation of Self in Everyday Society.* New York: Doubleday; paper, Doubleday. **29, 70.**
1963 *Behavior in Public Places.* New York: Free Press; paper, Free Press.

GOLDSCHMIDT, WALTER R. (ed.)
1959 *The Anthropology of Franz Boas: Essays on the Centennial of His Birth.* San Francisco: Chandler; paper, Chandler. **59.**

GOODENOUGH, WARD HUNT
1963 *Cooperation in Change: An Anthropological Approach to Community Development.* New York: Russell Sage Foundation; paper, Wiley. **69, 80, 89.**
1964 *Explorations in Cultural Anthropology: Essays in Honor of George Peter Murdock.* New York: McGraw-Hill.
1961 *Property, Kin and Community on Truk.* New Haven, Conn.: Yale University Press. Reprint.

GRAEBNER, FRITZ
1911 *Methode der Ethnologie.* Heidelberg: C. Winter. **63.**

GREENWAY, JOHN
    1963 *Bibliography of the Australian Aborigine and the Native Peoples of the Torres Straits to 1959.* Sydney: Angus & Robertson. **90.**

GULICK, JOHN
    1955 *Social Structure and Culture Change in a Lebanese Village.* New York: Wenner-Gren Foundation for Anthropological Research. **153.**

HADDON, ALFRED CORT
    1910 *History of Anthropology.* London: Watts. **53.**
    —— (ed.)
    1901–35 *Reports of the Cambridge Anthropological Expedition to the Torres Straits.* 6 vols.; New York: Cambridge University Press.

HALL, JOHN W., and RICHARD K. BEARDSLEY
    1965 *Twelve Doors to Japan.* New York: McGraw-Hill. **80.**

HAMMOND, PETER B. (ed.)
    1964 *Cultural and Sociological Anthropology.* New York: Macmillan; paper, Macmillan. **49.**

HAYS, HOFFMAN R.
    1958 *From Ape to Angel: An Informal History of Social Anthropology.* New York: Knopf; paper, Putnam. **53.**

HEATH, DWIGHT B., and R. N. ADAMS
    1965 *Contemporary Cultures and Societies of Latin America: A Reader of the Social Anthropology of Middle and South America and the Caribbean.* New York: Random. **83.**

HERSKOVITS, MELVILLE JEAN
    1938 *Acculturation: The Study of Culture Contact.* New York: Augustin. **49, 59, 76, 79, 289.**
    1952 *Economic Anthropology.* New York: Knopf; paper, Norton.
    1940 *The Economic Life of Primitive Peoples.* New York: Knopf.
    1953 *Franz Boaz.* New York: Scribner.
    1948 *Man and His Works: The Science of Cultural Anthropology.* New York: Knopf.

HERTZ, ROBERT
    1960 *Death and the Right Hand.* New York: Free Press. Tr. R. and C. Needham. **55.**

HICKEY, GERALD
    1964 *Village in Vietnam.* New Haven, Conn.: Yale University Press; paper, Yale. **86.**

HILL, ARCHIBALD
    1965 *The Promises and Limitations of the Newest Type of Grammatical Analysis.* Cincinnati: University of Cincinnati Press. **71.**

HODGE, FREDERICK WEBB
    1959 *Handbook of American Indians North of Mexico.* New York: Pageant. **83.**

HOEBEL, E. A., J. D. JENNINGS, and E. R. SMITH (comps.)
    1955 *Readings in Anthropology.* New York: McGraw-Hill. **49.**

HOIJER, HARRY (ed.)
  1954 *Language in Culture.* Chicago: University of Chicago Press. **49, 69.**
HOWELL, C., and FRANÇOISE BOURLIÈRE (eds.)
  1963 *African Ecology and Human Evolution.* Chicago: Aldine. **58, 65.**
HSU, FRANCIS L. K. (ed.)
  1961 *Psychology and Anthropology: Approaches to Culture and Personality.* Homewood, Ill.: Dorsey. **66–67, 88, 256.**
HSÜ, LANG-KUANG
  1948 *Under the Ancestors' Shadow: Chinese Culture and Personality.* New York: Columbia University Press.
HUNT, ROBERT (ed.)
  Personalities and Cultures: Readings in Psychological Anthropology. Garden City, N.Y.: Natural History; paper, Doubleday. **66.**
HYMAN, STANLEY EDGAR
  1962 *The Tangled Bank: Darwin, Marx, Frazer, and Freud as Imaginative Writers.* New York: Atheneum; paper, Grosset. **54.**
HYMES, DELL
  1964 *Language in Culture and Society: A Reader in Linguistics and Anthropology.* New York: Harper. **70.**
——, and JOHN J. GUMPERZ
  1964 *Ethnography of Communication.* Washington: American Anthropological Association. Special Publication, Vol. LXVI, No. 6, Pt. 2. **70.**
ISAACS, HAROLD
  1965 *India's Ex-Untouchables.* New York: Day. **87.**
JANSEN, MARIUS B. (ed.)
  1965 *Changing Japanese Attitudes Toward Modernization.* Princeton, N.J.: Princeton University Press. **88.**
JARVIE, I. C.
  1964 *Revolution in Anthropology.* New York: Humanities. **62.**
JESUIT RELATIONS AND ALLIED DOCUMENTS
  Travels and Explorations of the Jesuit Missionaries in New France, 1610–1791. Cleveland: Burrows, 1896–1901; New York: Boni 1925. (1) Ed. R. G. Thwaites; (2) Ed. E. Kenton.
KANITKAR, J. M.
  1960 *A Bibliography of Indology.* Calcutta: National Library.
KAPLAN, BERT (ed.)
  1961 *Studying Personality Cross-Culturally.* New York: Harper. **66.**
KARDINER, ABRAM, et al.
  1945 *Psychological Frontiers of Society.* New York: Columbia University Press; paper, Columbia. **29, 54, 65.**
KARVE, D. D.
  1963 *The New Brahmans: Five Marharashtrian Families.* Berkeley, Cal.: University of California Press.
KARVE, IRAWATI
  1958 *Kinship Organization in India.* New York: Taplinger.

KEESING, FELIX MAXWELL
    1953 *Culture Change: An Analysis and Bibliography of Anthropological Sources in 1952.* Stanford, Cal.: Stanford University Press. **79, 89.**
    1953 *Social Anthropology in Polynesia: A Review of Research.* New York: Oxford University Press.

KEIL, CHARLES
    1966 *Urban Blues.* Chicago: University of Chicago Press. **46.**

KENNEDY, RAYMOND
    1955 *Bibliography of Indonesian Peoples and Culture.* (rev. ed.; New York: Taplinger. Ed. T. W. Maretski and H. T. Fischer.

KENNY, MICHAEL
    1961 *A Spanish Tapestry: Town and Country in Castile.* Bloomington, Ind.: Indiana University Press; paper, Harper. **47.**

KLUCKHOHN, CLYDE
    1962 *Culture and Behavior.* New York: Free Press; paper, Free Press. **50, 62, 66, 220.**
    ———, and A. L. KROEBER
    1952 *Culture: A Critical Review of Concepts and Definitions.* Cambridge, Mass.: Peabody Museum; paper, Vintage. **49–50, 61–62, 82.**

KRADER, LAWRENCE (ed.)
    1956 *Handbook of Central Asia.* New York.: Taplinger.

KROEBER, ALFRED LOUIS
    1948 *Anthropology: Race, Language, Culture, Psychology and Prehistory.* New York: Harcourt; paper, Harcourt. **49–50, 61–62, 82.**
    1939 *Cultural and Natural Areas of Native North America.* Berkeley, Cal.: University of California Press.
    1952 *The Nature of Culture.* Chicago University of Chicago Press.

KUNSTADTER, PETER
    Southeast Asian Tribes: Minorities and Nations (unpublished). **86.**

LACH, DONALD F.
    1965 *Asia in the Making of Europe.* Chicago: University of Chicago Press. **51.**

LAMBTON, ANN K. S.
    1953 *Landlord and Peasant in Persia: A Study of Land Tenure and Land Revenue Administration.* New York: Oxford University Press. **86.**

LANG, OLGA
    1946 *Chinese Family and Society.* New Haven, Conn.: Yale University Press. **88.**

LANGNESS, L. L.
    1965 *The Life History in Anthropological Science.* New York: Holt; paper, Holt. **67.**

LASKER, GABRIEL W. (ed.)
    1960 *The Process of On-Going Human Evolution.* Detroit: Wayne State University Press. **48, 58.**

LASLETT, P. and W. G. RUNCIMAN
    1962 *Philosophy, Politics, and Society.* Oxford: Blackwell. **75.**

LAWRENCE, PETER
  1964 *Road Belong Cargo.* New York: Humanities. **89.**
LEACH, EDMUND RONALD
  1960 *Aspects of Caste in Southern India, Ceylon, and Northwest Pakistan.* New York: Cambridge University Press. **47, 50, 74, 76, 87.**
  1954 *Political Systems of Highland Burma: A Study of Kachin Social Structure.* Cambridge, Mass.: Harvard University Press.
  1961 *Pul Eliya, a Village in Ceylon: A Study of Land Tenure and Kinship.* New York: Cambridge University Press.
  1962 *Rethinking Anthropology.* New York: Humanities.
LEBAR, FRANK M., GERALD C. HICKEY, and JOHN K. MUSGRAVE
  1964 *Ethnic Groups of Mainland Southeast Asia.* New York: Taplinger. **86.**
LE PAGE, R. B.
  1964 *The National Language Question: Linguistic Problems of Newly Independent States.* New York: Oxford University Press; paper, Oxford. **70.**
LESSA, WILLIAM ARMAND, and EVON Z. VOGT (eds.)
  1958 *A Reader in Comparative Religion: An Anthropological Approach.* New York: Harper. **46, 78.**
LÉVI-STRAUSS, CLAUDE
  1964 *Mythologiques: Le Cru et le cuit.* Paris: Plon. **50, 53, 68.**
  1966 *The Savage Mind.* Chicago: University of Chicago Press.
  1963 *Structural Anthropology.* New York: Basic Books.
  1963 *Totemism.* Boston: Beacon; paper, Beacon. Tr. R. Needham.
LEVY, MARION
  1949 *The Family Revolution in Modern China.* Cambridge, Mass.: Harvard University Press. **88, 213.**
LEWIS, BERNARD
  1950 *The Arabs in History.* New York: Harper; paper, Harper. **85.**
LEWIS, OSCAR
  1961 *The Children of Sanchez: Autobiography of a Mexican Family.* New York: Random; paper, Random. **47, 83–84.**
  1959 *Five Families: Mexican Case Studies in the Culture of Poverty.* New York: Basic Books; paper, New American.
  1951 *Life in a Mexican Village: Tepotzlán Restudied.* Urbana, Ill.: University of Illinois Press; paper, Illinois.
  1960 *Tepotzlán: A Village in Mexico.* New York: Holt; paper, Holt.
  1958 *Village Life in Northern India: Studies in a Delhi Village.* Urbana, Ill.: University of Illinois Press.
LIENHARDT, GODFREY
  1961 *Divinity and Experience: Religion of the Dinka.* Oxford: Clarendon. **49, 78.**
  1964 *Social Anthropology.* New York: Oxford University Press; paper, Oxford.

ANTHROPOLOGY 341

LINDZEY, GARDNER
1954 *Handbook of Social Psychology*. Reading, Mass.: Addison-Wesley. (2d ed. with E. ARONSON, 1968.) **28, 66, 109–110, 119–120, 170.**

LINTON, RALPH
1936 *The Study of Man: An Introduction*. New York: Appleton; paper, Appleton. **61.**

LONDON UNIVERSITY, SCHOOL OF ORIENTAL AND AFRICAN STUDIES
1958 *Index Islamicus, 1906–1955* (Cambridge, England: Heffer. Comp. J. D. Pearson and J. F. Ashton.

LOWIE, ROBERT HARRY
1935 *The Crow Indians*. New York: Farrar. **50, 53–54, 78, 83.**
1917 *Culture and Ethnology*. New York: Boni; paper, Basic.
1937 *The History of Ethnological Theory*. New York: Farrar.
1954 *Indians of the Plains*. New York: McGraw-Hill; paper, Doubleday.
1960 *Selected Papers in Anthropology*. Berkeley, Cal.: University of California Press. Ed. C. DuBois.

LYND, ROBERT S., and HELEN M. LYND
1959 *Middletown: A Study in Contemporary American Culture*. New York: Harcourt; paper, Harcourt. **33, 46.**

MAINE, SIR HENRY J. S.
1917 *Ancient Law*. New York: Dutton; paper, Beacon. **51–52, 56**

MAIR, LUCY PHILIP
1962 *Primitive Government*. Baltimore: Penguin; paper. **75.**

MALINOWSKI, BRONISLAW
1961 *Argonauts of the Western Pacific: An Account of Native Enterprise and Adventure in the Melanesian Archipelago of New Guinea*. New York: Dutton; paper, Dutton. **19, 72–73, 76–77, 89.**
1935 *Coral Gardens and Their Magic: A Study of Methods of Tilling the Soil and of Agricultural Rites in the Trobriand Islands*. New York: American Book.
1948 *Magic, Science and Religion, and Other Essays*. Boston: Beacon; paper, Doubleday.

MANDELBAUM, DAVID G., G. W. LASKER, and E. M. ALBERT (eds.)
1963 *Resources for the Teaching of Anthropology*. Washington: American Anthropological Association; paper, California (abr.). Memoir 95. **48, 58, 65, 69.**

MARRIOTT, McKIM
1965 *Caste Ranking and Community Structure in Five Regions of India and Pakistan*. Poona, India: Deccan College Postgraduate and Research Institute. **87.**
——— (ed.)
1955 *Village India: Studies in the Little Community*. Chicago: University of Chicago Press.

MAUSS, MARCEL
1954 *The Gift: Forms and Functions of Exchange in Archaic Societies*. New York: Free Press; paper, Norton. Tr. I. Cunnison. **55, 71.**

MAXWELL, GAVIN
 People of the Reeds. New York: Harper; paper, Pyramid. **85.**
MAYER, ADRIAN
 1960 *Caste and Kinship in Central India.* London: Routledge. **87.**
MAYER, PHILIP (ed.)
 1963 *Xhosa in Town: Studies of the Bantu Population of East London.* New York: Oxford University Press.
MEAD, MARGARET
 1956 *Coming of Age in Samoa: A Psychological Study of Primitive Youth for Western Civilization.* New York: Morrow; paper, Apollo, Dell. **29, 54, 65, 80, 88, 89.**
 1953 *Growing Up in New Guinea: A Comparative Study of Primitive Education.* New York: New American; paper; also Apollo; paper.
 1956 *New Lives for Old: Cultural Transformation—Manus, 1928–1953.* New York: Morrow; paper, Apollo.
 ———, and RUTH L. BUNZEL (eds.)
 1960 *The Golden Age of American Anthropology.* New York: Braziller. **54.**
MEGGARS, BETTY J. (ed.)
 Evolution and Anthropology: A Centennial Appraisal. Washington: Anthropological Society of Washington. **58.**
MIDDLETON, JOHN, and DAVID TAIT (eds.)
 1958 *Tribes without Rulers: Studies in African Segmentary Systems.* London: Routledge.
MINTZ, SIDNEY W.
 1960 *Worker in the Cane: A Puerto Rican Life History.* New Haven, Conn.: Yale University Press. **47, 77.**
MOONEY, JAMES
 1965 *Ghost Dance Religion and the Sioux Outbreak of 1890.* Chicago: University of Chicago Press; paper, Chicago. Ed. A. F. C. Wallace. **54.**
MOORE, FRANK W. (ed.)
 1961 *Readings in Cross-Cultural Methodology.* New York: Taplinger. **67.**
MORGAN, LEWIS HENRY
 1959 *Ancient Society: Or, Researches into the Lines of Human Progress from Savagery, Through Barbarism to Civilization.* London: Routledge; paper, World. **51–52, 54, 57–58, 71.**
 1965 *Houses and Houselife of the American Aborigines.* Chicago: University of Chicago Press; paper, Chicago.
 1904 *League of the Ho-dé-no-sau-nee or Iroquois.* New York: Dodd; paper, Corinth.
 1870 *Systems of Consanguinity and Affinity of the Human Family.* Washington: Smithsonian Institution.
MURDOCK, GEORGE PETER
 1949 *Social Structure.* New York: Free Press; paper, Free Press. **50, 75, 83–84, 86.**
 1959 *Africa: Its People and Their Cultural History.* New York: McGraw-Hill.

1965 *Culture and Society.* Pittsburgh: University of Pittsburgh Press.
1960 *Ethnographic Bibliography of North America.* New York: Taplinger.
1960 *Social Structure in S.E. Asia.* Chicago: Quadrangle.

MUSSEN, P. H. (ed.)
1960 *Handbook of Research Methods in Child Development.* New York: Wiley. **67.**

NASH, MANNING
1965 *The Golden Road to Modernity: Village Life in Contemporary Burma.* New York: Wiley. **79, 86.**
1958 *Machine Age Maya: The Industrialization of a Guatemalan Community.* Washington: American Anthropological Association; paper, Chicago. Memoir 87.

NEEDHAM, RODNEY
1962 *Structure and Sentiment.* Chicago: University of Chicago Press. **74.**

NEWMAN, PHILIP
1965 *Knowing the Gururumba.* New York: Holt; paper, Holt. **78.**

O'LEARY, TIMOTHY J.
1963 *Ethnographic Bibliography of South America.* New York: Taplinger. **84.**

OLIVER, DOUGLAS
1962 *The Pacific Islands.* Cambridge, Mass.: Harvard University Press; paper, Doubleday (rev. ed.). **89.**

OTTENBERG, SIMON, and PHOEBE OTTENBERG
1960 *Cultures and Societies of Africa.* New York: Random. **85.**

PARSONS, TALCOTT
1951 *The Social System.* New York: Free Press; paper, Free Press. **11, 21, 23, 61–63, 72, 155, 180–181, 213, 227, 249.**
1966 *Societies: Evolutionary and Comparative Perspectives.* Englewood Cliffs, N.J.: Prentice-Hall; paper, Prentice.
1960 *Structure and Process in Modern Society.* New York: Free Press.

———, and EDWARD A. SHILS
1951 *Toward a General Theory of Action.* Cambridge, Mass.: Harvard University Press; paper, Harper. **21, 25, 39, 61.**

PEARSON, J. D., and J. F. ASHTON (eds.)
1960 *Index Islamicus.* Cambridge, England: Heffer. **86.**

PERISTIANY, J. G. (ed.)
1966 *Honor and Shame: The Values of Mediterranean Society.* Chicago: University of Chicago Press.

PERRY, WILLIAM J.
1927 *The Children of the Sun: A Study in the Early History of Civilization.* London: Methuen. **63.**

PITT-RIVERS, JULIAN A.
1954 *The People of the Sierra.* New York: Criterion. **47.**
——— (ed.)
1963 *Mediterranean Countrymen: Essays in the Social Anthropology of the Mediterranean.* Paris: Mouton.

PLATH, DAVID
1964 *The After Hours: Modern Japan and the Search for Enjoyment.*
Berkeley, Cal.: University of California Press. **88.**
POCOCK, D. F.
1961 *Social Anthropology.* London: Sheed. **49, 87.**
POLANYI, KARL, and CONRAD M. ARENSBERG
1957 *Trade and Market in Early Empires.* New York: Free Press. **28, 33, 47, 77, 287.**
PORTER, ARTHUR T.
1963 *Creoledom: A Study of the Development of Freetown Society.* New York: Oxford University Press.
PREBLE, EDWARD, and ABRAM KARDINER
1961 *They Studied Man.* Cleveland: World; paper, New American. **29, 54, 65.**
PURCELL, VICTOR W. W. S.
1965 *The Chinese in S.E. Asia.* New York: Oxford University Press.
RADCLIFFE-BROWN, ALFRED REGINALD
1948 *Andaman Islanders.* New York: Humanities; paper, Free Press. **19, 50, 72–74, 77, 90.**
1957 *Natural Science of Society.* New York: Free Press.
1931 *Social Organization of Australian Tribes.* New York: Macmillan.
1957 *Structure and Function in Primitive Society: Essays and Addresses.* New York: Free Press; paper, Free Press.
———, and C. DARYLL FORDE (Eds.)
1950 *African Systems of Kinship and Marriage.* New York: Oxford University Press; paper, Oxford. **49, 85.**
RADIN, PAUL
1933 *Method and Theory of Ethnology: An Essay in Criticism.* New York: McGraw-Hill; paper, Basic. **54, 67.**
1960 *Autobiography of a Winnebago Indian.* New York: Dover; paper, Dover.
RATZEL, F.
vide Semple, Ellen C. **51–52, 63, 295, 296.**
REDFIELD, ROBERT
1934 *Chan Kom: A Mayan Village.* Washington: Carnegie Institution. **47, 61, 80, 84.**
1941 *The Folk Culture of Yucatan.* Chicago: University of Chicago Press.
1930 *Tepoztlán, a Mexican Village: A Study of Folk Life.* Chicago: University of Chicago Press.
1950 *A Village That Chose Progress: Chan Kom Revisited.* Chicago: University of Chicago Press; paper, Chicago.
REDFIELD, MARGARET PARK (ed.)
1962 *Human Nature and the Study of Society: The Papers of Robert Redfield.* Chicago: University of Chicago Press.
1963 *The Social Uses of Social Science: The Papers of Robert Redfield,* Vol. II. Chicago: University of Chicago Press.

REISCHAUER, E. O., and JOHN K. FAIRBANK
1960 *History of East Asian Civilization.* (2 vols.) Boston: Houghton, 65. 86.
RICE, F. A. (ed.)
1962 *Study of the Role of Second Languages.* New York: Center for Applied Linguistics. 70.
ROMNEY, ANTONE K., and ROY G. D'ANDRADE (eds.)
1964 *Transcultural Studies in Cognition.* Washington: American Anthropological Association. Special publication, Vol. LXVI, No. 3, Pt. 2. 68–69.
SAHLINS, MARSHALL D.
1958 *Social Stratification in Polynesia.* Seattle: University of Washington Press. 57.
————, and ELMAN R. SERVICE (eds.)
1960 *Evolution and Culture.* Ann Arbor, Mich.: University of Michigan Press. 57.
SAPIR, EDWARD
1949 *Selected Writings of Edward Sapir in Language, Culture and Personality.* Berkeley, Cal.: University of California Press; paper, California. Ed. D. Mandelbaum. 60, 65, 66, 69.
SCHMIDT, FATHER WILHELM
1939 *The Culture History Method of Ethnology: The Scientific Approach to the Racial Question.* New York: Fortuny. 63.
SCHNEIDER, D. M., and K. GOUGH (eds.)
1961 *Matrilineal Kinship.* Berkeley, Cal.: University of California Press. 74.
SCHUSKY, ERNEST
1967 *Manual of Kinship Analysis.* New York: Holt; paper, Holt. 75.
SEBEOK, T., ALFRED S. HAYES, and MARY C. BATESON
1964 *Approach to Semiotics.* The Hague: Mouton. 70.
SEMPLE, ELLEN C.
1911 *Influence of Geographic Environment on the Basis of Ratzel's System of Anthropo-Geography.* New York: Holt.
SIEGEL, BERNARD J. (ed.)
1959– *Biennial Review of Anthropology.* Stanford, Cal.: Stanford University Press. 48, 75–76, 87.
SILBERMAN, BERNARD S. (ed.)
1962 *Japanese Character and Culture: A Book of Selected Readings.* Tucson: University of Arizona Press. 88.
SIMMONS, LEO (ed.)
1942 *Sun Chief.* New Haven, Conn.: Yale University Press; paper, Yale. 76.
SINGER, MILTON B. (ed.)
1959 *Traditional India: Structure and Change.* Philadelphia: American Folklore Society. 66, 87.
SMITH, GRAFTON E.
1927 *The Diffusion of Culture.* New York: Norton. 63.

SMITH, MARY F.
   1955 *Baba of Karo: A Woman of the Muslim Hausa.* New York: Philosophical Library. **67.**

SPENCER, SIR BALDWIN, and FRANCIS J. GILLEN
   1899 *Native Tribes of Central Australia.* London: Macmillan. **81, 89.**

SPICER, E. H. (ed.)
   1961 *Perspectives in American Indian Cultural Change.* Chicago: University of Chicago Press. **83.**

SRINIVAS, MYSORE N.
   1964 *Caste in Modern India, and Other Essays.* New York: Taplinger. **87.**
——— (ed.)
   1960 *India's Villages.* New York: Taplinger.

STACEY, MARGARET
   1960 *Tradition and Change: A Study of Banbury.* New York: Oxford University Press. **80.**

STANNER, W. E. H., and HELEN SHIELS
   1963 *Australian Aboriginal Studies.* New York: Oxford University Press; paper, Oxford. **90.**

STEWARD, JULIAN H.
   1955 *Theory of Culture Change: The Methodology of Multilinear Evolution.* Urbana, Ill.: University of Illinois Press. **57, 84.**
——— (ed.)
   1946–59 *Handbook of South American Indians.* Washington: GPO.
   1955 *Irrigation Civilizations.* Washington: Pan American Union.
———, and LOUIS C. FARON
   1959 *Native Peoples of South America.* New York: McGraw-Hill. **84.**

SUGGS, ROBERT C.
   1960 *The Island Civilizations of Polynesia.* New York: New American; paper. **64–65, 89.**

SWANTON, JOHN R.
   1946 *The Indians of the Southeastern United States.* Washington: GPO. **8.**
   1952 *The Indian Tribes of North America.* Washington: GPO.

SWARTZ, MARC J., VICTOR W. TURNER, and ARTHUR TUDEN
   1966 *Political Anthropology.* Chicago: Aldine. **75, 220.**

TALAYESVA, DON C.
   1942 *Sun Chief: The Autobiography of a Hopi Indian.* New Haven, Conn.: Yale University Press; paper, Yale. Ed. L. Simmons.

TAX, SOL
   1953 *Penny Capitalism.* Chicago: University of Chicago Press. **57, 58, 70, 77, 79, 289.**
——— (ed.)
   1952 *Acculturation in the Americas.* Chicago: University of Chicago Press.
   1960 *Evolution After Darwin.* (3 vols.) Chicago: University of Chicago Press.
   1964 *Horizons in Anthropology.* Chicago: Aldine.

TAYLOR, C. R. A.
   1965 *A Pacific Bibliography.* (rev. ed.) Oxford: Clarendon. **89.**

THULE EXPEDITION, FIFTH (1921–24)
    1927–52 *Report of the Fifth Thule Expedition.* (10 vols.) Copenhagen: Glydendal.
TYLOR, EDWARD B.
    1964 *Researches into the Early History of Mankind* (1878). Chicago: University of Chicago Press; paper, Chicago. **51–52, 54, 56–57, 62.**
UNDERHILL, RUTH
    1953 *Red Man's America.* Chicago: University of Chicago Press. **82.**
VOGT, EVON Z.
    1955 *Modern Homesteaders: The Life of a Twentieth-Century Frontier Community.* Cambridge, Mass.: Belknap. **46, 78.**
    1951 *Navaho Veterans: A Study of Changing Values.* Cambridge, Mass.: Peabody Museum.
VON GRUNEBAUM, GUSTAVE E.
    1961 *Islam: Essays in the Nature and Growth of a Cultural Tradition.* London: Routledge. **85.**
    1953 *Medieval Islam: A Study in Cultural Orientation.* Chicago: University of Chicago Press.
—— (ed.)
    1954 *Studies in Islamic Cultural History.* Washington: American Anthropological Association. Tr. I. Lichtenstadter.
    1955 *Unity and Variety in Muslim Civilization.* Chicago: University of Chicago Press.
WALLACE, ANTHONY F. C.
    1961 *Culture and Personality.* New York: Random. **66, 78.**
    1966 *Religion: An Anthropological View.* New York: Random.
WALLERSTEIN, IMMANUEL
    1966 *Social Change: The Colonial Situation.* New York: Wiley. **79.**
WARNER, WILLIAM LLOYD
    1958 *A Black Civilization: A Social Study of an Australian Tribe.* New York: Harper; paper, Harper. **33, 36, 46, 73, 90, 167, 195.**
WARRINER, DOREEN
    1948 *Land and Poverty in the Middle East.* New York: Oxford University Press. **85.**
    1957 *Land Reform and Development in the Middle East: A Study of Egypt, Syria, and Iraq.* New York: Oxford University Press.
WASHBURN, SHEERWOOD L.
    1961 *The Social Life of Early Man.* New York: Wenner-Gren Foundation for Anthropological Research. **58, 65.**
WATSON, JAMES A. (ed.)
    1964 *New Guinea: The Central Highlands.* Washington: American Anthropological Association. Special publication, Vol. LXVI, No. 4, Pt. 2. **89.**
WAUCHOPE, R. (ed)
    1964– *Handbook of Middle American Indians.* Austin, Tex.: University of Texas Press. **83.**

BIBLIOGRAPHY AND AUTHOR INDEX

WEINREICH, URIEL
    Languages in Contact: Findings and Problems. New York: Linguistic Circle of New York.

WESTERMARCK, EDWARD A.
    1921 *History of Human Marriage.* London: Macmillan. **56.**

WEYER, EDWARD M.
    1962 *The Eskimos: Their Environment and Folkways.* Hamden, Conn.: Shoe String.

WHITE, LESLIE A.
    1963 *The Ethnography and Ethology of Franz Boas.* Austin, Tex.: Texas Memorial Museum of the University of Texas. **56–57, 59.**
    1959 *The Evolution of Culture: The Development of Civilization to the Fall of Rome.* New York: McGraw-Hill; paper, McGraw.
    1949 *The Science of Culture: A Study of Man and Civilization.* New York: Farrar.

WHITING, BEATRICE B. (ed.)
    1963 *Six Cultures: Studies of Child Rearing.* New York: Wiley. **67.**

WHITING, JOHN W. M., and IRVING L. CHILD
    1953 *Child Training and Personality Development: A Cross-Cultural Study.* New Haven, Conn.: Yale University Press; paper, Yale.

WHORF, B. L.
    1956 *Language, Thought, and Reality: Selected Writings.* New York: Wiley. Ed. J. B. Carroll. **69.**

WILLEY, G
    1966 *Introduction to American Archaeology.* Englewood Cliffs, N.J.: Prentice-Hall, 1966.

WINTER, EDWARD H.
    1959 *Beyond the Mountains of the Moon: The Lives of Four Africans.* Urbana, Ill.: University of Illinois Press. **67.**

WISSLER, CLARK
    1922 *The American Indian.* New York: Oxford University Press. **82.**

WITHERS, CARL
    1945 *Plainville, U.S.A.*, by James West (pseud.) New York: Columbia University Press.

WOLF, ERIC R.
    1964 *Anthropology.* Englewood Cliffs, N.J.: Prentice-Hall. **63.**
    1959 *Sons of Shaking Earth.* Chicago: University of Chicago Press; paper, Chicago.

WORSLEY, PETER M.
    1957 *The Trumpet Shall Sound.* London: MacGibbon. **89.**

WRIGHT, ARTHUR F. (ed.)
    1953 *Studies in Chinese Thought.* Chicago: University of Chicago Press; paper, Chicago. **88.**

WYLIE, LAURENCE W.
    1957 *Village in the Vauclase.* Cambridge, Mass.: Harvard University Press; paper, Harper. **47.**

YANG, CH'ING-K'UN
1959 *A Chinese Village in Early Communist Transition.* Cambridge, Mass.: Harvard University Press.

MISCELLANEOUS SOURCES

Africa.
African Bibliographic Center bibliographies.
American Anthropologist.
American Museum of Natural History Source Books in Anthropology.
Anthropological Linguistics.
Association of Social Anthropology, *The Anthropological Study of Religion.*
Australian National University Pacific publications.
Basic Books Classics in Anthropology Series, Stanley Diamond (ed.).
Bishop Museum Facsimile Catalogue.
Case Studies in Anthropology Series, George and Louise Spindler (eds.).
Comparative Studies in Society and History.
Contributions to Indian Sociology.
Economic Development and Cultural Change.
Ethnographic Survey of Africa Monograph Series.
Ethnology.
G. H. Hall Co. catalogues of special collections.
History of the Behavioral Sciences.
Human Organization.
Human Relations Area Files (Taplinger).
International African Institute Ethnographic Bibliography, C. Daryll Forde (ed.).
The International Journal of American Linguistics, Word.
Introduction to the Civilization of India (University of Chicago syllabus).
Journal of African History.
Journal of American Folklore.
Journal of Asian Studies.
Language.
Mankind.
Middle Eastern Review.
Modern African Studies.
Northwestern University African Collection.
Oceania.
Peabody Museum Facsimile Catalogue.
Prentice-Hall Foundations of Modern Anthropology Series.
Royal Anthropological Institute of Great Britain and Northern Ireland, *Index to Current Periodicals* (1963–   ).
Smithsonian Institution publications.
Southwestern Journal of Anthropology.
UNESCO, *International Bibliography of Cultural Anthropology* (1955–   ).
University of Chicago Press Classics in Anthropology Series, Paul Bohannan (ed.).

University of Hawaii Pacific publications.
Yale University Southeast Asia Cultural Report Series.
Yankee City Series, W. Lloyd Warner (ed.).

Psychology

ADLER, DANIEL L.
- 1954 "Some Recent Books on Personality," *Psychological Bulletin*. **107.**

ADORNO, THEODOR, et al.
- 1950 *The Authoritarian Personality*. New York: Harper; paper, Science Eds. **34, 119.**

ALLPORT, FLOYD H.
- 1954 *Social Psychology* (1924). New York: Johnson Reprints. **95, 117.**
- 1955 *Theories of Perception and the Concept of Structure*. New York: Wiley,

ALLPORT, GORDON W.
- 1954 "The Historical Background of Modern Social Psychology," in G. Lindzey (ed.), *Handbook of Social Psychology*. Cambridge, Mass: Addison-Wesley. **109, 119, 123.**
- 1937 *Personality: A Psychological Interpretation*. New York: Holt.

ANASTASI, ANNE
- 1964 *Fields of Applied Psychology*. New York: McGraw-Hill. **106, 123.**
- 1961 *Psychological Testing*. New York: Macmillan; 2d ed.

ASCH, SOLOMON E.
- 1958 "Effects of Group Pressure upon the Modification and Distortion of Judgments," in E. Maccoby, T. M. Newcomb, and E. L. Hartley (eds.), *Readings in Social Psychology*. New York: Holt; 3d ed. **116.**

ATKINSON, JOHN W.
- 1964 *Introduction to Motivation*. Princeton, N.J.: Van Nostrand. **67, 116.**

ATKINSON, RICHARD C., GORDON H. BOWER, and EDWARD J. CROTHERS
- 1965 *An Introduction to Mathematical Learning*. New York: Wiley. **93, 103, 125.**

BEACH, FRANK A., and JULIAN JAYNES
- 1954 "Effects of Early Experience upon the Behavior of Animals," *Psychological Bulletin*. **114.**

BEEBE-CENTER, JOHN G.
- 1932 *The Psychology of Pleasantness and Unpleasantness*. New York: Russell. **111.**

BELLUGI, URSULA, and ROGER BROWN (eds.)
- 1964 *The Acquisition of Language* Purdue, Ind.: Society for Research in Child Development, Purdue University. **99, 120.**

BENNETT, EDWARD, JAMES DEGAN, and JOSEPH SPIEGEL (eds.)
- 1963 *Human Factors in Technology*. New York: McGraw-Hill. **121.**

BERLYNE, DANIEL
- 1965 *Structure and Direction in Thinking*. New York: Wiley. **100.**

BLUM, GERALD S.
   1953 *Psychoanalytic Theories of Personality.* New York: McGraw-Hill; paper, McGraw. **109.**
BORING, EDWIN G.
   1950 *A History of Experimental Psychology.* New York: Appleton; 2d ed. **94.**
   1942 *Sensation and Perception in the History of Experimental Psychology.* New York: Appleton.
BROWN, ROGER
   1965 *Social Psychology.* New York: Free Press. **99, 120.**
BRUNER, JEROME S.
   1960 *The Process of Education.* Cambridge, Mass.: Harvard University Press; paper, Vintage. **97, 99, 119, 123.**
   1966 *Toward a Theory of Instruction.* Cambridge, Mass.: Harvard University Press.
―――, and GORDON W. ALLPORT
   1940 "Fifty Years of Change in American Psychology," *Psychological Bulletin.* **109, 119, 113.**
―――, JACQUELINE J. GOODNOW, and GEORGE A. AUSTIN
   1956 *A Study in Thinking.* New York: Wiley; paper, Science Eds. **97.**
   1966 *Et al., Studies in Cognitive Growth.* New York: Wiley.
BUROS, OSCAR K. (ed.)
   1938 40, 49, 53, 59, 65 *Mental Measurements Yearbook.* Highland Park N.J.: Gryphon. **106.**
BUSH, ROBERT R., and FREDERICK MOSTELLER
   1955 *Stochastic Models for Learning.* New York: Wiley. **97, 125, 169.**
CANNON, WALTER B.
   1929 *Bodily Changes in Pain, Hunger, Fear and Rage.* New York: Appleton; 2d ed.
   1932 *The Wisdom of the Body.* New York: Norton; paper, Norton (rev. ed.).
CARTWRIGHT, DORWIN, and ALVIN ZANDER (eds.)
   1960 *Group Dynamics.* New York: Harper; 2d ed. **28, 120.**
CATTELL, RAYMOND B.
   1950 *Personality: A Systematic, Theoretical and Factual Study.* New York: McGraw-Hill. **106–107, 110.**
   1955 "The Principal Replicated Factors Discovered in Objective Personality Tests," *Journal of Abnormal and Social Psychology.*
   1965 *The Scientific Analysis of Personality.* Chicago: Aldine; paper, Penguin.
CHAUNCEY, HENRY, and JOHN E. DOBBIN
   1963 *Testing.* New York: Harper; paper, Harper. **123.**
CHOMSKY, NOAM
   1965 *Aspects of the Theory of Syntax.* Cambridge, Mass.: M.I.T. Press. **71, 99.**
COFER, CHARLES N., and MORTIMER H. APLEY (eds.)
   1964 *Motivation: Theory and Research.* New York: Wiley. **116.**

COOMBS, CLYDE H.
   1964 *A Theory of Data.* New York: Wiley. **115, 125.**
COULSON, JOHN E. (ed.)
   1962 *Programmed Learning and Computer-Based Instruction.* New York: Wiley. **123.**
CRICK, F. H. C.
   1966 "The Genetic Code: III," *Scientific American.* **93.**
CRONBACH, LEE J.
   1963 *Educational Psychology.* New York: Harcourt; 2d ed. **123.**
DAVIDSON, ERIC H.
   1965 "Hormones and Genes," *Scientific American.* **93.**
DE GROOT, ADRIAAN D.
   1966 *Thought and Choice in Chess.* New York: Basic Books. **98–99.**
DUNLAP, KNIGHT
   1919 "Are There Any Instincts?" *Journal of Abnormal and Social Psychology.* **117.**
EBBINHAUS, HERMANN
   1885 *Uber das Gedachtnis.*
EDWARDS, WARD
   1954 "The Theory of Decision Making," *Psychological Bulletin.* **115–116.**
———, and HAROLD LINDMAN, and LAWRENCE D. PHILLIPS
   1965 "Emerging Technologies for Making Decisions," in F. Barron, *et al., New Directions in Psychology.* New York: Holt. **116.**
ERIKSEN, CHARLES W.
   1957 "Personality," *American Review of Psychology.* **126.**
ERWIN-TRIPP, SUSAN M., and DAN I. SLOBIN
   1966 "Psycholinguistics," Vol. VII, *Annual Review of Psychology.* Ed. P. R. Farnsworth, O. McNemar, and Q. McNemar. **99.**
ESTES, WILLIAM K., et al.
   1954 *Modern Learning Theory.* New York: Appleton. **102, 104, 113.**
EYSENCK, HANS J.
   1953 "The Logical Basis of Factor Analysis," *American Psychologist.* **110.**
   1952 *The Scientific Study of Personality.* New York: Macmillan.
   1960 *The Structure of Human Personality.* New York: Barnes & Noble; 2d ed.
FEIGENBAUM, EDWARD A., and JULIAN FELDMAN (eds.)
   1963 *Computers and Thought.* New York: McGraw-Hill. **98.**
FISKE, DONALD W., and SALVATORE MADDI (eds.)
   1961 *Functions of Varied Experience.* Homewood, Ill.: Dorsey. **113, 121.**
FLAVELL, JOHN H.
   1963 *The Developmental Psychology of Jean Piaget.* Princeton, N.J.: Van Nostrand.
FODOR, JERRY A., and JERROLD J. KATZ (eds.)
   1964 *The Structure of Language.* Englewood Cliffs, N.J.: Prentice-Hall. **99.**
FORGUS, RONALD H.
   1966 *Perception.* New York: McGraw-Hill.
FOURAKER, LAWRENCE E., and SIDNEY SIEGEL
   1963 *Bargaining Behavior.* New York: McGraw-Hill. **125.**

PSYCHOLOGY 353

FOWLER, HARRY
    1965 *Curiosity and Exploratory Behavior*. New York,: Macmillan; paper Macmillan. **113.**

FREEMAN, FRANK S.
    1962 *Theory and Practice of Psychological Testing*. New York: Holt; 3d ed. **106.**

FREUD, SIGMUND
    1959 *Collected Papers* (1948–50). New York: Basic Books; 5 vols. Ed. E. Jones. **29, 54, 65, 81, 108–109, 115, 118, 150.**
    1953–7 *Standard Edition of the Complete Psychological Works*. New York: Macmillan; 24 vols. Ed. J. Strachey.
    1922 *Group Psychotherapy and the Analysis of the Ego*. New York: Liveright; paper, Bantam. Tr. J. Strachey.
    1955 *The Interpretation of Dreams* (1913). New York: Basic Books. Tr. from 3d German ed. and ed. J. Strachey.
    1917 *Psychopathology of Everyday Life* (1914). New York: Macmillan; paper, New American; Norton. Ed. J. Strachey; tr. A. Tyson.

GALTON, SIR FRANCIS
    Inquiries into Human Faculty and Its Development (1883). New York: Dutton's Everyman's. **105.**

GARDINER, HARRY N., RUTH C. METCALF, and JOHN G. BEEBE-CENTER
    1937 *Feeling and Emotion*. New York: American Book. **111.**

GARNER, WENDELL R.
    1962 *Uncertainty and Structure as Psychological Concepts*. New York: Wiley. **125.**

GELLHORN, ERNST
    1953 *Physiological Foundations of Neurology and Psychiatry*. Minneapolis: University of Minnesota Press. **112.**

GLASER, ROBERT (ed.)
    1965 *Teaching Machines and Programmed Learning*. Washington: N.E.A. Audio-Visual Instruction Dept. **123.**

GOLDHAMER, HERBERT, and ANDREW W. MARSHALL
    1953 *Psychosis and Civilization*. New York: Free Press. **92.**

GRAHAM, CLARENCE H.
    1965 *Vision and Visual Perception*. New York: Wiley. **95.**

GREEN, DAVID M., and JOHN A. SWETS
    1960 *Signal Detection Theory and Psychophysics*. New York: Wiley. **95.**

GRINSTEIN, ALEXANDER
    1956–60 *The Index of Psychoanalytic Writings*. New York: International Univ.; 9 vols. **108.**

GUTHRIE, EDWIN R.
    1952 *The Psychology of Learning*. Magnolia, Mass.: Smith; rev. ed. **103.**

HABER, RALPH N. (ed.)
    1966 *Current Research in Motivation*. New York: Holt. **116.**

HALL, CALVIN S.
    1954 *A Primer of Freudian Psychology*. Cleveland: World; paper, New American. **109–110.**

———, and GARDNER LINDZEY
    1954 "Psychoanalytic Theory and Its Applications in the Social Sciences," in G. Lindzey (ed.), *Handbook of Social Psychology*. Cambridge, Mass.: Addison-Wesley. **28, 66, 109–110, 119–120, 170.**
    1957 *Theories of Personality*. New York: Wiley.

HARLOW, HARRY F.
    1952 "Learning," *Annual Review of Psychology*. **102, 113.**

HAYS, WILLIAM L.
    1963 *Statistics for Psychologists*. New York: Holt; paper, Holt. **124.**

HEBB, DONALD O.
    1955 "Drives and the CNS (Conceptual Nervous System)," *Psychological Review*. **112, 114–115.**
    1949 *The Organization of Behavior*. New York: Wiley.

HERON, WOODBURN, et al.
    1957 "The Pathology of Boredom," *Scientific American*. **96.**

HILGARD, ERNEST R.
    1954 HULL'S A Behavior System. *Psychological Bulletin*, **51, 91–96.**

———, and RICHARD C. ATKINSON
    1967 *Introduction to Psychology*. New York: Harcourt; 4th ed. **93, 103, 125.**

———, and GORDON H. BOWER
    1966 *Theories of Learning*. New York: Appleton; 3rd ed. **103–104, 125.**

HOFFMAN, MARTIN, and LOIS MARTIN (eds.)
    1964, 66 *Review of Child Development Research*. New York: Russell Sage Foundation; 2 vols. **106.**

HOLLAND, JAMES G., and BURRHUS F. SKINNER
    1961 *The Analysis of Behavior*. New York: McGraw-Hill. **22, 100, 103.**

HOLLANDER, EDWIN P.
    1967 *Principles and Methods of Social Psychology*. New York: Oxford University Press. **120.**

HOLT, EDWIN B.
    1931 *Animal Drive and the Learning Process*. New York: Holt. **117.**

HOVLAND, CARL I., ARTHUR A. LUMSDAINE, and FRED D. SHEFFIELD
    1949 *Experiments in Mass Communication*. Princeton, N.J.: Princeton University Press.

HUBEL, DAVID H.
    1963 "The Visual Cortex of the Brain," *Scientific American*. **95.**

HULL, CLARK, L.
    1951 *Essentials of Behavior*. New Haven, Conn.: Yale University Press. **102–103, 115, 117.**
    1943 *Principles of Behavior*. New York: Appleton; paper, Appleton.
    1952 *A Behavior System*. New Haven: Yale University Press.

HUMPHREY, GEORGE
    1951 *Thinking: An Introduction to Its Experimental Psychology*. New York: Wiley; paper, Science Eds. **97.**

HUNT, EARL, B.
    1962 *Concept Learning.* New York: Wiley. **97.**
——, JANET MARIN, and PHILIP J. STONE
    1966 *Experiments in Induction,* New York: Academic. **97.**
HUNT, J. MCVICKER
    1961 *Intelligence and Experience.* New York: Ronald. **100.**
JAHODA, MARIE, and RICHARD CHRISTIE
    1954 *Studies in the Scope and Method of "The Authoritarian Personality."* New York: Free Press. **25, 119.**
JAMES, WILLIAM
    1960 *Principles of Psychology* (1890). Magnolia, Mass.: Smith; 2 vols.; paper, Dover. **94, 100.**
JONES, ERNEST
    1953–57 *The Life and Work of Sigmund Freud.* New York: Basic Books. Ed. L. Trilling and S. Marcus. **109.**
JONES, MARSHALL R. (ed.)
    1953–00 *Nebraska Symposium on Motivation.* Lincoln: Psychology Dept., University of Nebraska. **113, 116.**
JUNG, CARL G.
    1954–67 *Collected Works.* Princeton, N.J.: Princeton University Press. **65, 108.**
KELLY, E. LOWELL
    1954 "Theory and Techniques of Assessment," *Annual Review of Psychology.* **121–122.**
KELLY, E. LOWELL, and DONALD W. FISKE
    1951 *The Prediction of Performance in Clinical Psychology.* Ann Arbor: University of Michigan Press.
KELLY GEORGE A.
    1955 *The Psychology of Personal Constructs.* New York: Norton; 2 vols. **110.**
KIMBLE, GREGORY A., ERNEST R. HILGARD, and DONALD G. MARQUIS
    1965 *Conditioning and Learning.* New York: Appleton; 2d ed. **93, 103–104.**
KOCH, SIGMUND
    1954 "Clark L. Hull," in W. K. Estes, *et al., Modern Learning Theory.* New York: Appleton. **102, 127.**
    1962–63 (Ed.), *Psychology: A Study of Science.* New York: McGraw-Hill.
KOFFKA, KURT
    1935 *Principles of Gestalt Psychology.* New York: Harcourt; paper, Harcourt. **96.**
KOHLER, WOLFGANG
    1947 *Gestalt Psychology: An Introduction to New Concepts in Modern Psychology.* New York: Liveright; paper, New American. **96.**
KRECH, DAVID, RICHARD S. CRUTCHFIELD, and EGERTON L. BALLACHEY
    1963 *The Individual in Society.* New York: McGraw-Hill. **118.**

BIBLIOGRAPHY AND AUTHOR INDEX

LASHLEY, KARL S.
    1951 "The Problem of Serial Order in Behavior," in Lloyd A. Jeffress (ed.), *Cerebral Mechanisms in Behavior: The Hixon Symposium*. New York: Wiley. **112.**

LAZARSFELD, PAUL F. (ed.)
    1954 *Mathematical Thinking in the Social Sciences*. New York: Free Press. **21, 25–26, 30, 115, 169.**

LEBON, GUSTAVE
    1925 *The Crowd* (1897). New York: Macmillan; paper, Viking. **116.**

LEWIN, KURT
    1935 *A Dynamic Theory of Personality*. New York: McGraw-Hill; paper, McGraw. **28, 104, 118, 120.**
    1951 *Field Theory in Social Science*. New York: Harper; paper, Harper. Ed. D. Cartwright.

LINDSLEY, DONALD B.
    1951 "Emotion," in S. S. Steyens (ed.), *Handbook of Experimental Psychology*. New York: Wiley. **112.**

LINDZEY, GARDNER, and ELLIOT ARONSON
    1968 *Handbook of Social Psychology*. Cambridge, Mass.: Addison-Wesley. **28, 66, 109–110, 119–120, 170.**

LORENZ, KONRAD Z.
    1952 *King Solomon's Ring*. New York: Crowell; paper, Apollo. **114.**

LUCE, R. DUNCAN, ROBERT R. BUSH, and EUGENE GALANTER
    1963 *Readings in Mathematical Psychology*. New York: Wiley. **97, 98, 125.**

MCCLELLAND, DAVID C.
    1951 *Personality*. New York: Holt. **110, 113, 281.**

MCCORMICK, ERNEST J.
    1964 *Human Factors in Engineering*. New York: McGraw-Hill; 2d ed. **121.**

MACCORQUODALE, KENNETH, and PAUL E. MEEHL
    1954 "Edward C. Tolman," in W. K. Estes, *et al.*, *Modern Learning Theory*. New York: Appleton. **104, 121.**

MCDOUGALL, WILLIAM
    1950 *An Introduction to Social Psychology* (1908). New York: Barnes & Noble; 30th ed.; paper, Barnes. **117.**

MARTIN, EDWIN J.
    1965 "Concept Utilization," in Vol. III of R. D. Luce, R. R. Bush, and E. Galanter, *Handbook of Mathematical Psychology*. New York: Wiley; 2 vols. **97.**

MEEHL, PAUL E.
    1954 *Clinical Versus Statistical Predication*. Minneapolis: University of Minnesota Press,

MELTON, ARTHUR W. (ed.)
    1964 *Categories of Human Learning*. New York: Academic. **104.**

MILLER, GEORGE (ed.)
    1964 *Mathematics and Psychology*. New York: Wiley; paper, Wiley. **98, 125.**

———, EUGENE GALANTER, and KARL H. PRIBRAM
    1960 *Plans and the Structure of Behavior*. New York: Holt. **97–98, 125.**

MILLER, NEAL E., and JOHN DOLLARD
- 1941 *Social Learning and Imitation.* New Haven, Conn.: Yale University Press; paper, Yale. 117.

MORGAN, CLIFFORD T., JESSE S. COOK, ALPHONSE CHAPANIS, and MAX W. LUND (eds.)
- 1963 *Human Engineering Guide to Equipment Design.* New York: McGraw-Hill.

MOSES, LINCOLN E.
- 1956 "Statistical Theory and Research Design," *American Review of Psychology.* 125.

MUNROE, RUTH
- 1955 *Schools of Psychoanalytic Thought.* New York: Holt. 109.

MURPHY, GARDNER
- 1949 *Historical Introduction to Modern Psychology.* New York: Harcourt. 94, 163.

MURRAY, HENRY A.
- 1938 *Explorations in Personality.* New York: Oxford University Press; paper, Science Eds. 109.

NATIONAL SOCIETY FOR THE STUDY OF EDUCATION YEARBOOK
- 1963 *Child Psychology.* Chicago: University of Chicago Press. Ed. H. W. Stevenson.

NEISSER, ULRIC
- 1967 *Cognition.* New York: Appleton. 100.

NEWCOMB, T. M.
- 1950 *Social Psychology.* New York: Dryden; paper, Holt. 28, 116, 119, 113.

OLDS, JAMES
- 1955– "Physiological Mechanisms of Reward," in M. R. Jones (ed.), *Nebraska Symposium on Motivation.* Lincoln: University of Nebraska. 113.
- 1955 "A Physiological Study of Reward," in D. C. McClelland, *Studies in Motivation.* New York: Appleton.

PAVLOV, IVAN P.
- 1955 *Conditioned Reflexes* (1927). Magnolia, Mass.: Smith; paper, Dover. Tr. and ed. G. V. Anrep. 102–103.

PIAGET, JEAN
- 1959 *The Language and Thought of the Child* (1926). New York: Humanities; 3d rev. ed. 18, 99, 106.
- 1932 *The Moral Judgment of the Child.* New York: Free Press; paper, Free Press.

POSTMAN, LEO J.
- 1947 "The History and Present Status of the Law of Effect," *Psychological Bulletin.* 113.

RAPAPORT, DAVID
- 1968 *Emotions and Memory.* New York: International University; paper, Science Eds. 111.

RAPOPORT, ANATOL
- 1960 *Fights, Games and Debates.* Ann Arbor, Mich.: University of Michigan Press. 125, 234.
- 1964 *Strategy and Conscience.* New York: Harper.

358 BIBLIOGRAPHY AND AUTHOR INDEX

REITMAN, WALTER R.
   1965 *Cognition and Thought.* New York: Wiley. **98.**
ROGERS, CARL R.
   1951 *Client-Centered Therapy: Its Current Practice, Implications and Theory.* Boston: Houghton; paper, Houghton. **109.**
ROSENBLITH, WALTER A. (ed.)
   1961 *Sensory Communication.* Cambridge, Mass.: M.I.T. Press.
ROTTER, JULIAN B.
   1954 *Social Learning and Clinical Psychology.* Englewood Cliffs, N.J.: Prentice-Hall. **110.**
SCHULMAN, LEE, and EVAN R. KEISLER (eds.)
   1966 *Learning by Discovery.* Chicago: Rand. **123.**
SHELLY, MAYNARD, W., and GLENN L. BRYAN (eds.)
   1964 *Human Judgments and Optimality.* New York: Wiley. **116.**
SHERIF, MUZAFER
   1936 *The Psychology of Social Norms.* New York: Harper; paper, Harper. **28, 118.**
SHOBEN, EDWARD J.
   1955 "Some Recent Books on Counseling and Adjustment," *Psychological Bulletin.* **122.**
SKINNER, BURRHUS F.
   1938 *The Behavior of Organisms.* New York: Appleton; paper, Appleton. **22, 100, 103.**
   1948 *Walden Two.* New York: Macmillan; paper, Macmillan.
SMITH, KEITH
   1953 "Distribution-Free Statistical Methods and the Concept of Power Efficiency," in L. Festinger and D. Katz (eds.), *Research Methods in the Behavioral Sciences.* New York: Holt.
SMITH, MORTIMER B., JEROME S. BRUNER, and ROBERT W. WHITE
   1956 *Opinions and Personality.* New York: Wiley; paper, Science Eds. **97, 99, 119, 123.**
STELLAR, ELIOT
   1954 "The Psychology of Motivation," *Psychological Review.* **112.**
STOUFFER, SAMUEL A. et al.
   1949 *The American Soldier: Adjustment During Army Life.* Princeton, N.J.: Princeton University Press. **17, 21, 25, 38, 120, 169.**
   1949 *The American Soldier: Combat and Its Aftermath.* Princeton, N.J.: Princeton University Press.
   1950 *Measurement and Prediction.* New York: Science Eds. (paper).
SWETS, JOHN A. (ed.)
   1964 *Signal Detection and Recognition by Human Observers.* New York: Wiley. **95.**
TABER, JULIAN I., et al.
   1965 *Learning and Programmed Instruction.* Cambridge, Mass.: Addison-Wesley. **123.**
TARDE, GABRIEL
   1958 *Les lois de l'imitation* (1890). Magnolia, Mass.: Smith. Tr. from the French. **116.**

TERMAN, LEWIS M.
   1916 *The Measurement of Intelligence.* Boston: Houghton. **105–106.**
   1925– et al. (eds.), *Genetic Studies of Genius.* Stanford, Cal.: Stanford University Press; 5 vols.
THOMAS, WILLIAM I., and FLORIAN ZNANIECKI
   1927 *The Polish Peasant in Europe and America* (1918–20). New York: Knopf; 2 vols. **10, 17, 119.**
THOMPSON, RICHARD F.
   1967 *Foundations of Physiological Psychology.* New York: Harper. **127.**
THOMPSON, WILLIAM R.
   1955 "Early Environment—Its Importance for Later Behavior," in P. H. Hoch and J. Zubin (eds.), *Psychopathology of Childhood.* New York: Grune. **114.**
THORNDIKE, EDWARD L.
   1965 *Animal Intelligence* (1898). New York: Hafner. **101–102.**
THRALL, ROBERT M., CLYDE H. COOMBS, and ROBERT L. DAVIS (eds.)
   1954 *Decision Processes.* New York: Wiley. **115, 125.**
THURSTONE, LOUIS L.
   1947 *Multiple-Factor Analysis.* Chicago: University of Chicago Press. **124.**
TINBERGEN, NIKOLAAS
   1951 *The Study of Instinct.* New York: Oxford University Press. **114.**
TITCHENER, EDWARD B.
   1929 *Systematic Psychology.* New York: Macmillan. **94.**
TOLMAN, EDWARD C.
   1951 *Collected Papers in Psychology.* Berkeley, Cal.: University of California Press; paper, California. **103–104.**
   1932 *Purposive Behavior in Animals and Men.* New York: Appleton; paper, Appleton.
TORGERSON, WARREN S.
   1958 *Theory and Method of Scaling.* New York: Wiley. **125.**
TYLER, LEONA E.
   1966 *The Psychology of Human Differences.* New York: Appleton; 3rd ed. **106.**
UTTAL, WILLIAM R.
   1967 *Real-Time Computers.* New York: Harper. **126.**
VERPLANCK, WILLIAM S.
   1955 "Since Learned Behavior is Innate, and Vice Versa, What Now?" *Psychological Review.* **114.**
WALKER, EDWARD L.
   1957 "Learning," *American Review of Psychology.* **113, 125.**
WATSON, JOHN B
   1914 *Behavior: An Introduction to Comparative Psychology.* New York: Holt. **101.**
WECHSLER, DAVID
   1958 *The Measurement and Appraisal of Adult Intelligence.* Baltimore: Williams; 4th ed. **105.**
WERTHEIMER, MAX
   1912 Experimentelle Studien uber das Sehen von Bewegung. *Zeitschrift fur Psychologie.*

WHITE, ROBERT W.
    1966 *Lives in Progress.* New York: Holt; 2d ed.; paper, Holt. **119.**

WUNDT, WILHELM
    1902 *Outlines of Psychology* (1874). New York: Macmillan. Tr. from 5th German ed. as Principles of Physiological Psychology by E. B. Titchener. **111.**
    1897 Translation by Chas. H. Judd. New York: G. E. Stechert.

MISCELLANEOUS SOURCES

American Psychologist.
Annual Review of Psychology.
Canadian Journal of Psychology.
Contemporary Psychology (1956–).
Educational and Psychological Measurement (1941–).
Journal of Abnormal Psychology (1965–).
Journal of Applied Psychology (1917–).
Journal of Comparative and Physiological Psychology (1921–).
Journal of Consulting Psychology (1937–).
Journal of Counseling Psychology (1954–).
Journal of Educational Psychology (1910–).
Journal of Experimental Psychology (1916–).
Journal of Personality and Social Psychology (1965–).
Journal of Verbal Learning and Verbal Behavior (1962–).
Psychological Abstracts.
Psychological Bulletin (1904–).
Psychological Review (1894–).
Psychometrika (1936   ).
Thirty-Ninth Yearbook of the National Society for the Study of Education.

Political Science

ABERNATHY, GLENN
    1961 *The Right of Assembly and Association.* Columbia, S.C.: University of South Carolina Press. **199.**

AGGER, ROBERT E., DANIEL GOLDRICH, and BERT E. SWANSON
    1964 *The Rulers and the Ruled.* New York: Wiley. **208.**

ALFORD, ROBERT R.
    1963 *Party and Society: The Anglo American Democracies.* Chicago: Rand. **219.**

ALKER, JR., HAYWARD R.
    1965 *Mathematics and Politics.* New York: Macmillan; paper, Macmillan. **219, 234, 236.**

——, and BRUCE M. RUSSETT
    1965 *World Politics in the General Assembly.* New Haven, Conn.: Yale University Press. **219, 229, 234.**

POLITICAL SCIENCE

ALLARET, ERIK, and YRJO LITTUNEN (eds.)
   1964 *Cleavages, Ideologies and Party Systems: Contributions to Comparative Political Sociology.* Helsinki: Academic Bookstore. **224.**

ALMOND, GABRIEL A.
   1960 *The American People and Foreign Policy* (1950). New York: Praeger (paper). **161, 163, 182, 212–213, 220, 223.**
   1954 *The Appeals of Communism.* Princeton, N.J.: Princeton University Press; paper, Princeton.

———, and G. BINGHAM POWELL
   1966 *Comparative Politics: A Developmental Approach.* Boston: Little, Brown; paper. **213.**

ALMOND, GABRIEL A., and JAMES S. COLEMAN
   1960 *The Politics of the Developing Areas.* Princeton, N.J.: Princeton University Press. **161, 163, 182, 212–213, 220, 223.**

———, and SIDNEY VERBA
   1963 *The Civic Culture: Attitudes and Democracy in Five Nations.* Princeton, N.J.: Princeton University Press. **161, 163, 182, 212–213, 220, 223.**

AMERICAN POLITICAL SCIENCE ASSOCIATION, COMMITTEE FOR THE ADVANCEMENT OF TEACHING
   1951 *Goals for Political Science.* New York: Sloane.

ANDERSON, LEE F., *et al.*
   1966 *Legislative Roll-Call Analysis.* Evanston, Ill.: Northwestern University Press; paper, Northwestern. **236.**

ANDERSON, ROBERT W.
   1965 *Party Politics in Puerto Rico.* Stanford, Cal.: Stanford University Press. **217.**

ANDERSON, WILLIAM
   1964 *Man's Quest for Political Knowledge: The Study and Teaching of Politics in Ancient Times.* Minneapolis: University of Minnesota Press. **173, 196.**
   1955 *The Nation and the States: Rivals or Partners?* Minneapolis: University of Minnesota Press.

APPLEBY, PAUL II.
   1949 *Policy and Administration.* University, Ala.: University of Alabama Press. **154, 194.**

APTER, DAVID E.
   1955 *The Gold Coast in Transition.* Princeton, N.J.: Princeton University Press. **134, 212–213, 224.**
   1961 *The Political Kingdom of Uganda.* Princeton, N.J.: Princeton University Press.
   1965 *The Politics of Modernization.* Chicago: University of Chicago Press.
   1964 (ed.) *Ideology and Discontent.* New York; Free Press.

ARISTOTLE
   1946 *Politics.* New York: Oxford University Press; paper, Oxford. Tr. E. Barker. **4, 131, 133, 136–137, 139, 170, 172, 175, 213.**

BIBLIOGRAPHY AND AUTHOR INDEX

ARNOLD, THURMAN
- 1937 *The Folklore of Capitalism.* New Haven, Conn.: Yale University Press; paper, Yale. **146.**
- 1962 *The Symbols of Government* (1935). New York: Harcourt (paper).

BACHRACH, PETER
- 1966 *The Theory of Democratic Elitism: A Critique.* Boston: Little, Brown (paper). **177.**

BAGEHOT, WALTER
- 1933 *The English Constitution* (1867). New York: Oxford University Press; paper, Cornell; Doubleday. **146, 282.**

BAILEY, STEPHEN K.
- 1950 *Congress Makes a Law.* New York: Columbia University Press; paper, Vintage. **148, 201.**

BAILEY, THOMAS A.
- 1964 *The Man in the Street* (1948). Magnolia, Mass.: Smith. **160.**

BANFIELD, EDWARD C.
- 1951 *Government Project.* New York: Free Press. **156–157, 207, 209, 220.**
- 1958 *The Moral Basis of a Backward Society.* New York: Free Press; paper, Free Press.
- 1961 *Political Influence.* New York: Free Press; paper, Free Press.
- ———, and JAMES Q. WILSON
- 1963 *City Politics.* New York: Vintage (paper). **184, 209, 289.**

BANKS, ARTHUR, and ROBERT TEXTOR
- 1963 *A Cross-Country Survey.* Cambridge, Mass.: M.I.T. Press. **219.**

BARBER, JAMES D.
- 1965 *The Lawmakers: Recruitment and Adaptation to Legislative Life.* New Haven, Conn.: Yale University Press; paper, Yale. **186, 191.**
- 1966 *Power in Committees: An Experiment in Government Process.* Chicago: Rand.

BARNARD, CHESTER I.
- 1938 *The Functions of the Executive.* New York: Oxford University Press. **37, 157.**

BAUER, RAYMOND A., ALEX INKELES, and CLYDE KLUCKHOHN
- 1956 *How the Soviet System Works: Cultural, Psychological and Social Themes.* Cambridge, Mass.: Harvard University Press; paper, Vintage. **50, 62, 66, 201, 204, 220.**

BAUER, RAYMOND A., ITHIEL DE S. POOL, and LEWIS A. DEXTER
- 1963 *American Business and Public Policy.* New York: Atherton. **61, 173, 201–202, 204, 236.**

BAY, CHRISTIAN
- 1958 *The Structure of Freedom.* Stanford, Cal.: Stanford University Press; paper Atheneum. **176.**

BEAN, LOUIS H.
- 1940 *Ballot Behavior.* Washington: American Council on Public Affairs. **168.**
- 1948 *How to Predict Elections.* New York: Knopf.

BEARD, CHARLES A.
　1935 *An Economic Interpretation of the Constitution of the United States* (1913). New York: Macmillan; paper, Free Press. **160, 165, 288.**
　1966 *The Idea of National Interest* (1934). Chicago: Quadrangle; paper. Ed. A. Vogts and W. Beard.
BECHHOFER, BERNARD C.
　1961 *Postwar Negotiations for Arms Control*. Washington: Brookings. **233.**
BECK, JAMES M.
　1932 *Our Wonderland of Bureaucracy*. New York: Macmillan. **154.**
BEER, SAMUEL
　1965 *British Politics in the Collectivist Age*. New York: Knopf. **215.**
BENDIX, REINHARD
　1949 *Higher Civil Servants in American Society*. Boulder, Colo.: University of Colorado Press; paper. **35, 155, 214.**
　1964 *Nation and Citizenship Building*. New York: Wiley.
BENOIT, EMILE, and KENNETH E. BOULDING
　1963 *Disarmament and the Economy*. New York: Harper. **233, 286.**
BENSON, GEORGE C. S.
　1941 *The New Centralization*. New York: Farrar. **147.**
BENTHAM, JEREMY
　1948 *An Introduction to the Principles of Morals and Legislation* (1789). New York: Hafner; paper, Hafner. **9, 139, 175, 252.**
BENTLEY, ARNOLD F.
　1967 *The Process of Government* (1908). Cambridge, Mass.: Harvard University Press. Ed. P. H. Odegard. **148–149, 155, 165.**
BERELSON, BERNARD, PAUL F. LAZARSFELD, and WILLIAM N. MCPHEE
　1954 *Voting*. Chicago: University of Chicago Press; paper, Chicago. **21, 25–26, 30, 115, 169.**
BERGER, MORROE
　1957 *Bureaucracy and Society in Modern Egypt*. Princeton, N.J.: Princeton University Press. **216.**
BERKOWITZ, MORTIMER, and PETER G. BOCK
　1965 *American National Security: A Reader in Theory and Policy*. New York: Free Press. **233.**
BERNS, WALTER
　1957 *Freedom, Virtue and the First Amendment*. Chicago: Regnery; paper. **199.**
BERNSTEIN, MARVER H.
　1957 *The Politics of Israel: The First Decade of Statehood*. Princeton, N.J.: Princeton University Press. **155, 214.**
　1955 *Regulating Business by Independent Commission*. Princeton, N.J.: Princeton University Press; paper, Princeton.
BETH, LOREN P.
　1958 *The American Theory of Church and State*. Gainesville, Fla.: University of Florida Press. **199.**

BINDER, LEONARD
1964 *The Ideological Revolution in the Middle East.* New York: Wiley. **212, 224.**
1962 *Iran: Political Development in a Changing Society.* Berkeley, Cal.: University of California Press.
1961 *Religion and Politics in Pakistan.* Berkeley, Cal.: University of California Press.

BINKLEY, WILFRED E.
1963 *American Political Parties: Their Natural History.* New York: Knopf. 4th rev. ed. **147, 166, 193.**
1959 *The Man in the White House: His Powers and Duties.* Baltimore: Johns Hopkins University Press; paper, Harper.
1963 *President and Congress* (1947). 3d rev. ed. Magnolia, Mass.: Smith; paper, Vintage.

BLACHLY, FREDERICK F., and MIRIAM E. OATMAN
1934 *Administrative Legislation and Adjudication.* Washington: Brookings. **154.**

BLACK, DUNCAN
1958 *The Theory of Committees and Elections.* New York: Cambridge University Press. **180.**

BLAU, PETER M.
1956 *Bureaucracy in Modern Society.* New York: Random; paper. **23, 36, 37, 155, 180.**
1963 *The Dynamics of Bureaucracy.* (2d rev. ed.) Chicago: University of Chicago Press.
1964 *Exchange and Power in Social Life.* New York: Wiley.

BLOOMFIELD, LINCOLN P.
1957 *Evolution or Revolution? The United Nations and the Problem of Peaceful Territorial Change.* Cambridge, Mass.: Harvard University Press.
1966 *The United Nations and U.S. Foreign Policy* (rev. ed.). Boston: Little, Brown; paper, Little.

BLUHM, WILLIAM T.
1965 *Theories of the Political System: Classics of Political Thought and Modern Political Thought.* Englewood Cliffs, N.J.: Prentice-Hall. Ed. D. Easton. **178.**

BODIN, JEAN
1936 *Republic* (1576). Chicago: Caxton Club. **138, 243.**

BOLLENS, JOHN C., and HENRY J. SCHMANDT
1965 *The Metropolis: Its People, Politics, and Economic Life.* New York: Harper. **209.**

BONE, HUGH A.
1958 *Party Committees and National Politics.* Seattle: University of Washington Press. **189.**

BOSANQUET, BERNARD
1923 *The Philosophical Theory of the State* (1899) (4th ed.). New York: St. Martins; paper, St. Martins. **133.**

BOULDING, KENNETH E.
1961 *Conflict and Defense.* New York: Harper; paper. **157, 233, 260.**
1953 *The Organizational Revolution: A Study in the Ethics of Economic Organization.* New York: Harper.

BOWIE, ROBERT R., and CARL J. FRIEDRICH (eds.)
1954 *Studies in Federalism.* Boston: Little, Brown.

BOYER, WILLIAM W.
1964 *Bureaucracy on Trial.* Indianapolis: Bobbs; paper, Bobbs. **147.**

BOZEMAN, ADDA B.
1960 *Politics and Culture in International History.* Princeton, N.J.: Princeton University Press. **227.**

BRECHT, ARNOLD
1945 *Federalism and Regionalism in Germany.* Ithaca, N.Y.: Cornell University Press. **145, 175.**
1959 *Political Theory: The Foundations of Twentieth-Century Thought.* Princeton, N.J.: Princeton University Press; paper, Princeton.

BRODIE, BERNARD
1959 *Strategy in the Missile Age.* Princeton, N.J.: Princeton University Press; paper, Princeton. **232.**

BROGAN, DENIS W.
1954 *Politics in America.* New York: Harper; paper, Doubleday. **164.**

BROOKS, GLENN E.
1961 *When Governors Convene: The Governors' Conference and National Politics.* Baltimore: Johns Hopkins University Press. **196.**

BRYCE, JAMES
1950 *American Commonwealth* (1888) (2 vols.). New York: Putnam; paper. Ed. L. M. Hacker. **145, 164.**
1921 *Modern Democracies.* New York: Macmillan.

BRZEZINSKI, Z. K.
1967 *The Soviet Bloc* (rev. ed.). Cambridge, Mass.: Harvard University Press; paper, Praeger. **223, 231.**

———, and SAMUEL HUNTINGTON
1963 *Political Power: USA/USSR.* New York: Viking; paper. **295.**

BUCHANAN, JAMES M., and GORDON TULLOCH
1962 *The Calculus of Consent: Logical Foundations of Constitutional Democracy.* Ann Arbor, Mich.: University of Michigan Press; paper, Michigan.

BUCHANAN, WILLIAM
1963 *Legislative Partisanship: The Deviant Case of California.* Berkeley, Cal.: University of California Press; paper. **191.**

BUCK, PHILIP W.
1963 *Amateurs and Professionals in British Politics.* Chicago: University of Chicago Press. **185.**

BUEL, RAYMOND L.
1925 *International Relations.* New York: Holt. **159.**

BURDICK, EUGENE, and ARTHUR J. BRODBECK
 1959 *American Voting Behavior.* New York: Free Press. **184.**
BURGESS, JOHN W.
 1938 *Political Science and Comparative Constitutional Law* (1891). Boston: Ginn. **136.**
BURKE, EDMUND
 1962 *Reflections on the Revolution in France* (1790). Indianapolis: Bobbs; paper, Bobbs. **139, 164, 177.**
BURNS, ARTHUR L., and NINO HEATHCOTE
 1963 *Peace-Keeping by U.N. Forces from Suez to the Congo.* New York: Praeger. **230.**
BURNS, JAMES M.
 1949 *Congress on Trial.* New York: Harper. **183.**
 1956 *Roosevelt: The Lion and the Fox.* New York: Harcourt; paper, Harcourt.
BUTLER, DAVID E.
 1963 *The Electoral System in Britain, 1918–1951* (2d ed.). New York: Oxford University Press. **167.**
CAHILL, FRED V.
 1952 *Judicial Legislation: A Study of American Legal Theory.* New York: Ronald. **146.**
CAHN, EDMOND
 1961 *The Predicament of Democratic Man.* New York: Dell; paper. **176.**
CAMPBELL, ANGUS, *et al.*
 1960 *The American Voter.* New York: Wiley. **26, 169, 188.**
 1966 *Elections and the Political Order.* New York: Wiley.
———, WARREN E. MILLER, and GERALD GURIN
 1954 *The Voter Decides.* New York: Harper. **26, 169, 188.**
CARALEY, DEMETRIOS
 1966 *The Politics of Military Unification: A Study of Conflict and the Policy Process.* New York: Columbia University Press. **202.**
CARDOZO, BENJAMIN
 1921 *The Nature of the Judicial Process.* New Haven, Conn.: Yale University Press; paper, Yale. **146.**
CARR, CECIL T.
 1921 *Delegated Legislation.* New York: Macmillan. **154.**
CARR, EDWARD H.
 1942 *Conditions of Peace.* New York: Macmillan. **161.**
 1947 *The Soviet Impact on the Western World.* New York: Macmillan.
 1939 *The Twenty Years' Crisis, 1919–1939.* New York: Macmillan; paper, Harper.
CARR, ROBERT K.
 1942 *The Supreme Court and Judicial Review.* New York: Holt.; paper. **146.**
CARROLL, HOLBERT N.
 1966 *The House of Representatives and Foreign Affairs* (rev. ed.). Boston: Little, Brown; paper, Little. **192, 229.**

1966 *The House of Representatives and Foreign Policy* (rev. ed.). Boston: Little, Brown; paper, Little.
CARTER, GWENDOLYN M.
1958 *The Politics of Inequality: South Africa since 1948.* New York: Praeger, 1958. **217.**
CASSSINELLI, G. W.
1965 *The Politics of Freedom: An Analysis of the Modern Democratic State.* Seattle: University of Washington Press. **176.**
CATLIN, GEORGE E. G.
1964 *The Science and Method of Politics* (1927). Hamden, Conn.: Shoe String. **133, 176.**
1962 *Systematic Politics: Elementa Politica et Sociologica.* Toronto: University of Toronto Press.
CHAMBERLAIN, LAWRENCE H.
1966 *The President, Congress and Legislation* (1946). New York: AMS. **147.**
CHAMBERS, WILLIAM N.
1963 *Political Parties in a New Nation.* New York: Oxford University Press; paper, Oxford. **190.**
CHARLESWORTH, JAMES C. (ed.)
1967 *Contemporary Political Analysis.* New York: Free Press; paper, Free Press. **174.**
CLAPP, CHARLES L.
1963 *The Congressman: His Work as He Sees It.* Washington: Brookings; paper, Doubleday. **193.**
CLARK, GRENVILLE, and LOUIS B. SOHN
1966 *World Peace Through World Law* (3d ed. rev.). Cambridge, Mass.: Harvard University Press. **226.**
CLARK, JANE PERRY
1965 *The Rise of a New Federalism* (1938). New York: Russell. **147.**
CLAUDE, INIS L.
1964 *Swords into Ploughshares: The Problems and Progress of International Organizations* (rev. ed.). New York: Random. **226.**
COHEN, ARTHUR A.
1964 *The Communism of Mao Tse-tung.* Chicago: University of Chicago Press; paper, Chicago. **223.**
COHEN, BERNARD C.
1957 *The Political Process and Foreign Policy: The Making of the Japanese Peace Settlement.* Princeton, N.J.: Princeton University Press. **201, 228–229.**
1963 *The Press and Foreign Policy.* Princeton, N.J.: Princeton University Press; paper, Princeton.
COKER, FRANCIS
1966 *Organismic Theories of the State* (1910). New York: AMS. **136.**
COLE, TAYLOR
1953 *European Political Systems.* New York: Knopf. **145.**

COLEMAN, JAMES S.
   1958 *Nigeria: Background and Nationalism.* Berkeley, Cal.: University of California Press. **20, 23, 26, 157, 212, 217.**
   ———, and CARL G. ROSBERG
   1964 *Political Parties and National Integration in Tropical Africa.* Berkeley, Cal.: University of California Press. **217.**
COLTER, CORNELIUS P., and BERNARD C. HENNESSY
   1964 *Politics Without Power: The National Party Committees.* New York: Atherton. **189.**
CORNWELL, JR., ELMER E.
   1965 *Presidential Leadership of Public Opinion.* Bloomington, Ind.: Indiana University Press. **194.**
CORWIN, EDWARD S.
   1965 *The Doctrine of Judicial Review* (1914). Magnolia, Mass.: Smith. **146–147, 193.**
   1957 *The President: Office and Powers* (4th ed. rev.). New York: New York University Press.
   ———, and LOUIS W. KOENIG
   1956 *The Presidency Today.* New York: New York University Press. **147.**
COTTRELL, ALVIN J., and JAMES E. DOUGHERTY
   1964 *Politics of the Atlantic Alliance.* New York: Praeger; paper, Praeger. **230.**
CRABB, JR., CECIL V.
   1957 *Bipartisan Foreign Policy: Myth or Reality?* New York: Harper. **229.**
CRICK, BERNARD
   1959 *The American Science of Politics.* Berkeley, Cal.: University of California Press. **172.**
CROLY, HERBERT
   1965 *The Promise of American Life* (1909). Cambridge, Mass.: Harvard University Press; paper, Dutton. Ed. A. M. Schlesinger, Jr. **152.**
CUMMINGS, JR., MILTON C.
   1966 *Congressmen and the Electorate.* New York: Free Press. **185, 192.**
CUNNINGHAM, NOBLE E.
   1967 *The Jeffersonian Republicans.* Chapel Hill, N.C.: University of North Carolina Press; paper, North Carolina. **190.**
   1967 *The Jeffersonian Republicans in Power.* Chapel Hill, N.C.: University of North Carolina Press; paper, North Carolina.
CUSHMAN, ROBERT E.
   1941 *The Independent Regulatory Commissions.* New York: Oxford University Press. **155.**
DAHL, ROBERT A.
   1964 *Congress and Foreign Policy* (1950). New York: Norton; paper. **141, 158, 163, 181, 206–207, 218, 284.**
   1967 *Pluralist Democracy in the United States: Conflict and Consent.* Chicago: Rand.
   1956 *A Preface to Democratic Theory.* Chicago: University of Chicago Press; paper, Chicago.

1961 *Who Governs? Democracy and Power in an American City.* New Haven, Conn.: Yale University Press; paper, Yale.
——— (ed.)
1966 *Political Oppositions in Western Democracies.* New Haven, Conn. Yale University Press.
———, and CHARLES E. LINDBLOM
1953 *Politics, Economics and Welfare.* New York: Harper; paper. **158, 180–181, 273, 284.**

DANELSKI, DAVID J.
1964 *A Supreme Court Justice Is Appointed.* New York: Random; paper, Random. **199.**

DARLING, FRANK C.
1965 *Thailand and the United States.* Washington: Public Affairs. **229.**

DAUER, MANNING
1953 *The Adams Federalists.* Baltimore: Johns Hopkins University Press. **190.**

DAVID, PAUL T., RALPH M. GOODMAN, and RICHARD C. BAIN
1960 *The Politics of National Party Conventions.* New York: Vintage; paper. **134, 189.**
———, MALCOLM MOOS, and RALPH GOLDMAN
1954 *Presidential Nominating Politics in 1952* (5 vols.). Baltimore: Johns Hopkins University Press. **134, 166.**

DAVIDSON, ROGER H., DAVID M. KOVENOCH, and MICHAEL K. O'LEARY
1966 *Congress in Crisis: Politics and Congressional Reform.* New York: Hawthorn. **193.**

DAVIES, JAMES C.
1963 *Human Nature and Politics.* New York: Wiley; paper, Wiley. **183.**

DAWSON, R. H.
1959 *The Decision to Aid Russia, 1941: Foreign Policy and Domestic Politics.* Chapel Hill, N.C.: University of North Carolina Press. **228.**

DE GRAZIA, ALFRED
1951 *Public and Republic: Political Representation in America.* New York: Knopf. **150, 164, 170.**
1954 *The Western Public, 1952 and Beyond.* Stanford, Cal.: Stanford University Press.

DERTHICK, MARTHA
1965 *The National Guard in Politics.* Cambridge, Mass.: Harvard University Press. **204.**

DEUTSCH, KARL W.
1953 *Nationalism and Social Communication.* Cambridge, Mass.: M.I.T. Press; paper, M.I.T. **163, 181, 214, 219, 231.**
1963 *The Nerves of Government: Models of Communication and Control.* New York: Free Press; paper, Free Press.
———, and WILLIAM J. FOLTZ (eds.)
1963 *Nation-Building.* New York: Atherton; paper. **214.**

DEUTSCH, KARL W. *et al.*
  1957 *Political Community and the North Atlantic Area.* Princeton, N.J.: Princeton University Press. **163, 181, 214, 219, 231.**
DEWEY, JOHN
  1930 *Individualism, Old and New.* New York: Putnam; paper, Putnam. **18, 142, 153.**
  1937 *Liberalism and Social Action.* New York: Putnam; paper, Putnam.
  1927 *The Public and Its Problems.* New York: Holt.
DICKINSON, JOHN
  1927 *Administrative Justice and the Supremacy of Law in the United States.* New York: Russell Sage Foundation. **155.**
DOOB, LEONARD W.
  1964 *Patriotism and Nationalism: Their Psychological Foundations.* New Haven, Conn.: Yale University Press. **224.**
DOWNS, ANTHONY
  1957 *American Economic Theory of Democracy.* New York: Harper; paper, Harper. **179, 195, 284.**
  1967 *Inside Bureaucracy.* Boston: Little, Brown; paper, Little.
DUNNING, WILLIAM A.
  1905 *A History of Political Theories, Ancient and Medieval.* (2 vols.). New York: Macmillan, 20. **136, 140.**
DUVERGER, MAURICE
  1964 *Political Parties* (2d rev. ed.). New York: Barnes & Noble; paper, Science Eds. **167.**
DYE, THOMAS R.
  1966 *Politics, Economics, and the Public.* Chicago: Rand. **201.**
EAGLETON, CLYDE
  1957 *International Government* (3d ed.). New York: Ronald. **159.**
EASTON, DAVID
  1963 *A Framework for Political Analysis.* Englewood Cliffs, N.J.: Prentice-Hall. **75, 133, 140, 172, 175, 178, 181.**
  1953 *The Political System: An Inquiry into the State of Political Science.* New York: Knopf.
  1965 *A Systems Analysis of Political Life.* New York: Wiley.
  ——— (ed.)
  1966 *Varieties of Political Theory.* Englewood Cliffs, N.J.: Prentice-Hall.
ECKSTEIN, HARRY
  1960 *Pressure Group Politics: The Case of the British Medical Association.* Stanford, Cal.: Stanford University Press. **213, 215.**
  ———, and DAVID E. APTER (eds.)
  1963 *Comparative Politics.* New York: Free Press. **134, 212–213, 224.**
EDELMAN, MURRAY
  1964 *The Symbolic Use of Power.* Urbana, Ill.: University of Illinois Press. **174, 202.**
  ———, and R. W. FLEMING
  1965 *The Politics of Wage-Price Decisions: A Four Country Analysis.* Urbana, Ill.: University of Illinois Press. **202.**

EDINGER, LEWIS J.
 1956 *German Exile Politics: The Social Democratic Executive Committee in the Nazi Era.* Berkeley, Cal.: University of California Press. **183, 217.**
 ———, and KURT SCHUMACHER
 1965 *A Study in Personality and Political Behavior.* Stanford, Cal.: Stanford University Press. **183.**
EHRMANN, HENRY W. (ed.)
 1958 *Interest Groups on Four Continents.* Pittsburgh: University of Pittsburgh Press; paper. **203.**
 1957 *Organised Business in France.* Princeton, N.J.: Princeton University Press.
EISENSTADT, S. N.
 1963 *The Political Systems of Empires.* New York: Free Press. **63, 76, 216.**
ELAZAR, DANIEL J.
 1966 *American Federalism: A View from the States.* Chicago: University of Chicago Press. **196.**
 1962 *The American Partnership.* Chicago: University of Chicago Press.
ELDERSVELD, SAMUEL J.
 1958 "American Interest Groups: A Survey of Research and Some Implications for Theory and Method," in H. W. Ehrmann (ed.), *Interest Groups on Four Continents.* Pittsburgh: University of Pittsburgh Press; paper. **130, 134, 168, 189, 203.**
 1956 "Theory and Method in Voting Behavior Research," in H. Eulau, S. J. Eldersveld, and M. Janowitz (eds.), *Political Behavior: A Reader in Theory and Research.* New York: Free Press. **34, 130, 134, 168, 170, 185, 208, 219, 221, 233.**
ELLIOTT, WILLIAM Y.
 1928 *The Pragmatic Revolt in Politics* (1928). New York: Fertig. **141.**
EMERSON, RUPERT
 1960 *From Empire to Nation.* Cambridge, Mass.: Harvard University Press; paper, Beacon. **213.**
ENGLER, ROBERT
 1967 *The Politics of Oil.* Chicago: University of Chicago Press; paper. **203.**
EPSTEIN, LEON D.
 1964 *British Politics in the Suez Crisis.* Urbana, Ill.: University of Illinois Press. **189, 218.**
 1958 *Politics in Wisconsin.* Madison, Wis.: University of Wisconsin Press.
EULAU, HEINZ
 1962 *The Behavioral Persuasion in Politics.* New York: Random; paper. **134, 168, 172, 185, 187–188, 191.**
 1962 *Class and Party in the Eisenhower Years.* New York: Free Press.

——, and JOHN D. SPRAGUE
  1964 *Lawyers in Politics: A Study of Professional Convergence.* Indianapolis: Bobbs; paper, Bobbs. **185.**

EWING, CORTEZ A. M.
  1940 *Presidential Elections: From Abraham Lincoln to Franklin D. Roosevelt.* Norman, Okla.: University of Oklahoma Press. **168.**
  1947 *Congressional Elections, 1896–1944.* Norman, Okla.: University of Oklahoma Press.

FAINSOD, MERLE
  1963 *How Russia is Ruled* (rev. ed.). Cambridge, Mass.: Harvard University Press. **145.**

FARNSWORTH, D. N.
  1961 *The Senate Committee on Foreign Relations.* Urbana, Ill.: University of Illinois Press. **229.**

FAY, SIDNEY B.
  1938 *The Origins of the World War* (2d rev. ed., 2 vols.). New York: Free Press; paper, Free Press. **159.**

FELD, WERNER
  1964 *The Court of European Communities: New Dimensions in International Adjudication.* The Hague: Nijhoff. **231.**

FELLMAN, DAVID
  1958 *The Defendant's Rights.* New York: Holt. **199.**

FENNO, RICHARD F.
  1966 *The Power of the Purse.* Boston: Little, Brown.
  1959 *The President's Cabinet.* Cambridge, Mass.: Harvard University Press; paper, Vintage.

FENTON, JOHN H.
  1960 *The Catholic Vote.* New Orleans: Hauser. **184, 189.**
  1966 *Midwest Politics.* New York: Holt; paper.
  1957 *Politics in the Border States.* New Orleans: Hauser.

FENWICK, CHARLES G.
  1963 *The Organization of American States.* Washington: Pan American Union. **230.**

FIFIELD, RUSSELL H.
  1963 *Southeast Asia in United States Policy.* New York: Praeger. **229.**

FINER, HERMAN
  1961 *The Theory and Practice of Modern Government* (1932) (2 vols.). New York: Barnes & Noble. **143, 145.**

FLATHMAN, RICHARD E.
  1966 *The Public Interest: An Essay Concerning the Normative Discourse of Politics.* New York: Wiley. **175.**

FOLLETT, MARY PARKER
  1960 *The New State* (1918). Magnolia, Mass.: Smith. **157.**

FORD, HENRY J.
  1967 *The Rise and Growth of American Politics* (1898). New York: Plenum. **164.**

FOSS, PHILLIP O.
  1960 *Politics and Grass.* Seattle: University of Washington Press. **203.**

Fox, William T. R.
 1944 *The Super-Powers.* New York: Harcourt. **162.**
Frank, Jerome
 1949 *Courts on Trial.* Princeton, N.J.: Princeton University Press; paper, Atheneum. **146.**
 1963 *Law and the Modern Mind* (1930). Magnolia, Mass.: Smith.
Frankfurter, Felix
 1964 *The Public and Its Government* (1930). Magnolia, Mass.: Smith; paper, Beacon. **153.**
Free, Lloyd A.
 1959 *Six Allies and a Neutral.* New York: Free Press. **220.**
Frey, Frederick W.
 1965 *The Turkish Political Elite.* Cambridge, Mass.: M.I.T. Press. **221.**
Fried, Robert C.
 1963 *The Italian Prefects: A Study in Administrative Politics.* New Haven, Conn.: Yale University Press. **216.**
Friedrich, Carl J.
 1950 *Constitutional Government and Democracy* (rev. ed.). Boston: Ginn. **143, 145, 147, 155, 176, 223.**
 1937 *Constitutional Government and Politics.* New York: Harper.
 1963 *Man and His Government: An Empirical Study of Politics.* New York: McGraw-Hill.
——, and Z. K. Brzezinski
 1956 *Totilitarian Dictatorship and Democracy.* Cambridge, Mass.: Harvard University Press; paper, Praeger. **223, 231.**
Frohock, Fred M.
 1967 *The Nature of Political Inquiry.* Homewood, Ill.: Dorsey. **236.**
Froman, Jr., Lewis A.
 1967 *The Congressional Process.* Boston: Little, Brown; paper, Little. **187, 192.**
 1963 *Congressmen and Their Constituencies.* Chicago: Rand; paper, Rand.
 1962 *People and Politics: An Analysis of the American Political System.* Englewood Cliffs, N.J.: Prentice-Hall, 1962; paper, Prentice.
Fuchs, Lawrence H.
 1956 *The Behavior of American Jews.* New York: Free Press. **184.**
Furnivall, J. S.
 1956 *Colonial Policy and Practice: A Comparative Study of Burma and Netherlands India.* New York: New York University Press. **214.**
Galloway, George B.
 1946 *Congress at the Crossroads.* New York: Crowell. **147.**
 1962 *History of the House of Representatives.* New York: Crowell.
Garceau, Oliver
 1941 *The Political Life of the American Medical Association.* Cambridge, Mass.: Harvard University Press. **149.**
Garfinkel, Herbert
 1959 *When Negroes March.* New York: Free Press. **29.**
Garner, James W.
 1910 *Introduction to Political Science.* New York: American Book. **143.**

GARTHOFF, RAYMOND L.
  1958 *Soviet Strategy in the Nuclear Age.* New York: Praeger. **233.**
GATES, ROBBINS L.
  1964 *The Making of Massive Resistance.* Chapel Hill, N.C.: University of North Carolina Press. **184.**
GAUS, JOHN M.
  1947 *Reflections on Public Administration.* University, Ala.: University of Alabama Press. **154.**
——, and LEON O. WOLCOTT
  1940 *Public Administration and the United States Department of Agriculture.* Chicago: Public Administration Service.
GAUS, JOHN M., L. D. WHITE, and MARSHALL E. DIMOCK
  1936 *The Frontiers of Public Administration.* Chicago: University of Chicago Press. **150, 152–154, 158, 194.**
GEERTZ, CLIFFORD
  1963 *Old Societies and New States: A Quest for Modernity in Asia and Africa.* New York: Free Press.
GEORGE, ALEXANDER L., and JULIETTE L. GEORGE
  1956 *Woodrow Wilson and Colonal House.* Magnolia, Mass.: Smith, paper, Dover. **150, 183.**
GERTH, HANS, and C. WRIGHT MILLS
  1946 *From Max Weber: Essays in Sociology.* New York: Oxford University Press. **13, 35, 36, 155.**
GETTELL, RAYMOND G.
  1922 *Introduction to Political Science* (rev. ed.). Boston: Ginn. **143.**
GILB, CORINNE L.
  1966 *Hidden Hierarchies.* New York: Harper. **204.**
GLASER, WILLIAM H., and DAVID L. SILLS (eds.)
  1966 *The Government of Associations.* New York: Bedminster. **204.**
GOLDWIN, ROBERT A. (ed.)
  1963 *A Nation of States.* Chicago: Rand. **196.**
GOLEMBIEWSKI, ROBERT T.
  1962 *Behavior and Organization.* Chicago: Rand. **186, 195.**
  1962 *The Small Group: An Analysis of Research Concepts and Operations.* Chicago: University of Chicago Press.
GOODNOW, FRANK G.
  1900 *Politics and Administration.* New York: Russell Sage Foundation. **152–153, 156.**
GOODNOW, HENRY F.
  1964 *The Civil Service of Pakistan: Bureaucracy in a New Nation.* New Haven, Conn.: Yale University Press. **216.**
GOODSELL, CHARLES T.
  1965 *Administration of a Revolution: Executive Reform in Puerto Rico under Governor Tugwell, 1941–1946.* Cambridge, Mass.: Harvard University Press. **214.**

GORE, WILLIAM J.
  1964 *Administrative Decision-Making: A Heuristic Model*. New York: Wiley. **195.**
  ———, and J. W. DYSON (eds.)
  1964 *The Making of Decisions*. New York: Free Press. **195.**
GOSNELL, HAROLD F.
  1948 *Democracy: The Threshold of Freedom*. New York: Ronald. **150, 164, 166–168.**
  1927 *Getting Out the Vote*. Chicago: University of Chicago Press.
  1942 *Grass Roots Politics*. Washington: American Council on Public Affairs.
  1937 *Machine Politics: Chicago Model*. Chicago: University of Chicago Press.
  1930 *Why Europe Votes*. New York: Cambridge University Press.
GOTTFRIED, ALEX
  1962 *Boss Cernak of Chicago: A Study of Political Leadership*. Seattle: University of Washington Press. **183.**
GOULDNER, ALAN W.
  1965 *Enter Plato: Classical Greece and the Origins of Social Theory*. New York: Basic Books. **37, 177.**
GRAEBNER, NORMAN A.
  1956 *The New Isolationism: A Study of Politics and Foreign Policy Since 1950*. New York: Ronald. **63.**
GRAVES, W. BROOKE
  1964 *American Intergovernmental Relations*. New York: Scribner. **196.**
GREEN, HAROLD P., and ALAN ROSENTHAL
  1963 *Government of the Atom: The Integration of Powers*. New York: Atherton. **202.**
GREENSTEIN, FRED I.
  1963 *The American Party System and the American People*. Englewood Cliffs, N.J.: Prentice-Hall; paper, Prentice. **184, 189.**
  1965 *Children and Politics*. New Haven, Conn.: Yale University Press; paper, Yale.
GRODZINS, MORTON
  1966 *The American System*. Chicago: Rand. **196.**
GROSS, BERTRAM M.
  1953 *The Legislative Struggle: A Study in Social Combat*. New York: McGraw-Hill. **147, 195.**
  1964 *The Managing of Organizations* (2 vols.). New York: Free Press.
GROSSMAN, JOEL B.
  1965 *Lawyers and Judges: The ABA and the Politics of Judicial Selection*. New York: Wiley. **199.**
GUETZKOW, HAROLD, et al.
  1963 *Simulation in International Relations*. Englewood Cliffs, N.J.: Prentice-Hall. **235.**

GULICK, LUTHER, and LYNDALL URWICK
   1937 *Papers on the Science of Administration.* New York: Institute of Public Administration. **153.**

GUSFIELD, JOSEPH R.
   1963 *Symbolic Crusade: Status Politics and the American Temperance Movement.* Urbana, Ill.: University of Illinois Press; paper, Illinois. **203.**

GUTTSMAN, WILLIAM L.
   1963 *The British Political Elite.* New York: Basic Books. **221.**

HAAS, ERNEST B.
   1964 *Beyond the Nation-State: Functionalism and International Organization.* Stanford, Cal.: Stanford University Press. **231.**
   1958 *The Uniting of Europe: Political, Social and Economic Forces 1950–1957.* Stanford, Cal.: Stanford University Press.

HACKER, ANDREW
   1963 *The Study of Politics: The Western Tradition and American Origins.* New York: McGraw-Hill; paper, McGraw. **175.**

HAINES, CHARLES G.
   1959 *The American Doctrine of Judicial Supremacy.* New York: Russell. **146.**

HALPERIN, MORTIMER H.
   1963 *Limited War in the Nuclear Age.* New York: Wiley; paper, Wiley. **232.**

HAMBURGER, JOSEPH
   1965 *Intellectuals in Politics: John Stuart Mill and the Philosophical Radicals.* New Haven, Conn.: Yale University Press. **176.**
   1963 *James Mill and the Art of Revolution.* New Haven, Conn.: Yale University Press.

HAMILTON, ALEXANDER, JAMES MADISON, and JOHN JAY
   Federalist Papers. New York: Modern Library; paper, Modern. **139, 152, 232.**

HAMMOND, PAUL Y.
   1961 *Organizing for Defense: The American Military Establishment in The Twentieth Century.* Princeton, N.J.: Princeton University Press.

HARGROVE, ERWIN C.
   1966 *Presidential Leadership: Personality and Political Style.* New York: Macmillan; paper. **183.**

HARRIS, JOSEPH P.
   1964 *Congressional Control of Administration.* Washington: Brookings; paper, Doubleday.

HARRIS, ROBERT J.
   1960 *The Quest for Equality.* Baton Rouge, La.: Louisiana State Press. **199.**

HART, JAMES
   1925 *The Ordinance Making Power of the President of the United States.* Baltimore: Johns Hopkins University Press. **147.**

HARTZ, LOUIS
 1955 *The Liberal Tradition in America.* New York: Harcourt; paper, Harcourt. **142.**

HAWKINS, BRETT W.
 1966 *Nashville Metro: The Politics of City-County Consolidation.* Nashville: Vanderbilt University Press. **210.**

HEARD, ALEXANDER
 1960 *The Costs of Democracy.* Chapel Hill, N.C.: University of North Carolina Press; paper, North Carolina. **189.**

HEGEL, GEORG
 1942 *Philosophy of Right.* New York: Oxford University Press. Ed. T. M. Knox. **139.**

HENDERSON, A. M., and TALCOTT PARSONS (trs.)
 1947 *The Theory of Social and Economic Organization* by Max Weber. New York: Oxford University Press. **11, 21, 23, 61–63, 72, 155, 180–181, 213, 227, 249.**

HENKIN, LOUIS
 1958 *Arms Control and Inspection in American Law.* New York: Columbia University Press. **233.**

HENRY, LAURIN L.
 1960 *Presidential Translations.* Washington: Brookings. **193.**

HERO, JR., ALFRED O.
 1965 *The Southerner and World Affairs.* Baton Rouge, La.: Louisiana State Press. **229.**

HERRING, EDWARD P.
 1936 *Federal Commissioners: A Study of Their Careers and Qualifications.* Harvard University Press. **148, 155, 165.**
 1929 *Group Representation Before Congress.* Washington: Brookings.
 1940 *The Politics of Democracy.* New York: Norton.
 1936 *Public Administration and the Public Interest.* New York: McGraw-Hill.

HERZ, JOHN H.
 1951 *Political Realism and Political Idealism.* Chicago: University of Chicago Press. **162.**

HEWART, GORDON
 1929 *The New Despotism.* New York: Farrar. **154.**

HILL, DAVID J.
 1967 *A History of Diplomacy in the International Development of Europe* (1905–14) (3 vols.). New York: Fertig. **159.**

HILSMAN, ROGER
 1967 *To Move a Nation.* New York: Doubleday. **193, 229, 232.**
 1956 *Strategic Intelligence and National Decisions.* New York: Free Press.

HINSLEY, F. H.
 1963 *Power and the Pursuit of Peace: Theory and Practice in the History of Relations between States.* New York: Cambridge University Press; paper, Cambridge.

HITCH, CHARLES J., and ROLAND MCKEAN
   1960 *The Economics of Defense in the Nuclear Age.* Cambridge, Mass.: Harvard University Press. **232, 284.**

HOBBES, THOMAS
   Leviathan. New York: Dutton's Everyman's; paper, Collier. **5, 6, 138, 141, 149, 175.**

HOFFMAN, STANLEY H.
   1960 *Contemporary Theory in International Relations.* Englewood Cliffs, N.J.: Prentice-Hall. **227.**

HOFSTADTER, RICHARD F.
   1948 *The American Political Tradition and the Men Who Made It.* New York: Knopf; paper, Vintage. **166.**

HOLCOMBE, ARTHUR N.
   1965 *The Middle Classes in American Politics* (1940). New York: Russell. **143, 165, 168.**
   1923 *Foundations of the Modern Commonwealth.* New York: Harper.
   1924 *Political Parties of Today.* New York: Harper.

HOLT, ROBERT T., and JOHN E. TURNER
   1965 *The Political Basis of Economic Developments.* New York: Van Nostrand Reinhold; paper, Van Nostrand. **214, 230.**

HOLT, ROBERT T., and ROBERT W. VAN DE VELDE
   1960 *Strategic Psychological Operations in American Foreign Policy.* Chicago: University of Chicago Press. **214, 230.**

HORN, ROBERT A.
   1956 *Groups and the Constitution.* Stanford, Cal.: Stanford University Press; paper. **198.**

HORN, STEPHEN
   1960 *The Cabinet and Congress.* New York: Columbia University Press. **193.**

HOVET, JR., THOMAS
   1963 *Africa in the United Nations.* Cambridge, Mass.: Harvard University Press. **234.**
   1960 *Bloc Politics in the United Nations.* Cambridge, Mass.: Harvard University Press.

HUNTER, FLOYD
   1953 *Community Power Structure.* Chapel Hill, N.C.: University of North Carolina Press; paper, Doubleday. **33, 167, 207.**

HUNTINGTON, SAMUEL P.
   1962 *Changing Patterns of Military Politics.* New York: Free Press. **223, 232–233.**
   1962 *The Common Defense: Strategic Problems in National Politics.* New York: Columbia University Press; paper, Columbia.
   1957 *The Soldier and the State: The Theory and Politics of Civil-Military Relations.* Cambridge, Mass.: Harvard University Press; paper, Vintage.

HYMAN, HERBERT
   1959 *Political Socialization.* New York: Free Press. **25, 184.**

HYNEMAN, CHARLES S.
1950 *Bureaucracy in a Democracy*. New York: Harper, **155, 173, 199.**
1959 *The Study of Politics: The Present State of American Political Science*. Urbana, Ill.: University of Illinois Press.
1963 *The Supreme Court on Trial*. New York: Atherton.

IKLÉ, FREDERICK C.
1964 *How Nations Negotiate*. New York: Praeger. **230.**

INKELES, ALEX, and RAYMOND A. BAUER
1959 *The Soviet Citizen*. Cambridge, Mass.: Harvard University Press. **201, 204, 220.**

JACKSON, ROBERT H.
1941 *The Struggle for Judicial Supremacy*. New York: Knopf; paper, Vintage. **146.**

JACOB, HERBERT
1963 *German Administration since Bismarck: Central Authority vs. Local Autonomy*. New Haven, Conn.: Yale University Press. **197–198, 205, 216.**
1965 *Justice in America*. Boston: Little; paper, Little.
———, and KENNETH N. VINES
1965 *Politics in the American States: A Comparative Analysis*. Boston: Little, Brown. **197–198, 205.**

JACOB, PHILIP E., and J. V. TOSCANO (eds.)
1964 *The Integration of Political Communities*. Philadelphia: Lippincott; paper. **210, 231.**

JANDA, KENNETH
1965 *Data Processing: Applications to Political Research*. Evanston, Ill.: Northwestern University Press; paper, Northwestern. **236.**

JANOWITZ, MORRIS
1964 *The Military in the Political Development of New Nations*. Chicago: University of Chicago Press; paper, Chicago. **34, 130, 134, 168, 170, 185, 208, 219, 221, 233.**
1960 *The Professional Soldier*. New York: Free Press; paper, Free Press.
——— (ed.)
1961 *Community Political Systems*. New York: Free Press.
———, and DWAINE MARVICK
1964 *Competitive Pressure and Democratic Consent* (2d ed.). Chicago: Quadrangle. **155, 170, 185, 221.**

JENNINGS, M. KENT
1964 *Community Influentials: The Elites of Atlanta*. New York: Free Press. **185, 188, 207.**
———, and L. HARMON ZEIGLER (eds.)
1966 *The Electoral Process*. Englewood Cliffs, N.J.: Prentice-Hall. **188, 203.**

JENNINGS, WILLIAM I.
1936 *Cabinet Government*. New York: Macmillan.

JESSUP, PHILIP C.
1948 *A Modern Law of Nations.* New York: Macmillan. **160, 231.**
1956 *Transnational Law.* New Haven, Conn.: Yale University Press.

JEWELL, MALCOLM E., and SAMUEL C. PATTERSON
1966 *The Legislative Process in the United States.* New York: Random. **191.**

KAHN, HERMAN
1960 *On Thermonuclear War.* Princeton, N.J.: Princeton University Press. **232.**

KALVEN HARRY
1965 *The Negro and the First Amendment.* Chicago: University of Chicago Press; paper. **199, 283.**

———, and HANS ZEISEL
1966 *The American Jury.* Boston: Little, Brown. **199.**

KANTOR, HARRY
1966 *The Ideology and Program of the Peruvian Aprista Movement.* New York: Octagon. **224.**

KAPLAN, MORTON
1957 *System and Process in International Politics.* New York: Science Eds.; paper.

KARIEL, HENRY S.
1961 *The Decline of American Pluralism.* Stanford, Cal.: Stanford University Press; paper, Stanford. **177.**

KATZENBACH, NICHOLAS DE B., and M. A. KAPLAN
1961 *The Political Foundations of International Law.* New York: Wiley. **226–227.**

KAUFMAN, HERBERT
1960 *The Forest Ranger.* Baltimore: Johns Hopkins University Press; paper, Johns. **195, 207.**

KAUTSKY, JOHN H.
1962 *Political Change in Underdeveloped Countries: Nationalism and Communism.* New York: Wiley. **224.**

KEEFE, WILLIAM J., and MORRIS, S. OGUL
1964 *The American Legislative Process.* Englewood Cliffs, N.J.: Prentice-Hall. **191.**

KELMAN, HERBERT, et al. (eds.)
1965 *International Behavior: A Social-Psychological Analysis.* New York: Holt. **234.**

KENNAN, GEORGE F.
1951 *American Diplomacy, 1900–1950.* Chicago: University of Chicago Press. **162.**

KETTLER, DAVID
1965 *The Social and Political Thought of Adam Ferguson.* Columbus: Ohio State University Press. **177.**

KEY, JR., VALDIMIR O.
1956 *American State Politics: An Introduction.* New York: Knopf. **150, 165, 168–169, 185, 188–189.**

1942 *Politics, Parties and Pressure Groups.* New York: Crowell; paper.
1960 *Public Opinion and American Democracy.* New York: Knopf.
1966 *The Responsible Electorate.* Cambridge, Mass.: Harvard University Press.
1949 *Southern Politics in State and Nation.* New York: Knopf.

KILPATRICK, FRANKLIN, MILTON C. CUMMINGS, JR., and M. KENT JENNINGS
1964 *The Image of the Federal Service.* Washington: Brookings. **185, 188, 192.**

KINGSLEY, JOHN D.
1944 *Representative Bureaucracy.* Yellow Springs, Ohio: Antioch. **155.**

KIRCHHEIMER, OTTO
1961 *Political Justice: The Use of Legal Procedure for Political Ends.* Princeton, N.J.: Princeton University Press. **200.**

KISSINGER, HENRY A.
1957 *Nuclear Weapons and Foreign Policy.* New York: Harper. **229, 232.**
1965 *The Troubled Partnership: A Reappraisal of the Atlantic Alliance.* New York: McGraw-Hill; paper, Doubleday.

KLINEBERG, OTTO
1950 *Tensions Affecting International Understanding.* New York: Social Science Research Council. **163.**

KNORR, KLAUS
1956 *The War Potential of Nations.* Princeton, N.J.: Princeton University Press. **227, 231.**

———, and SIDNEY VERBA (eds.)
1961 *The International System: Theoretical Essays.* Princeton, N.J.: Princeton University Press. **182, 186, 212, 220, 227.**

KOEBNER, RICHARD, and HELMUT D. SCMHIDT
1961 *Imperialism: The Story and Significance of a Political World.* New York: Cambridge University Press. **228.**

KOFMEHL, KENNETH
1962 *Professional Staffs of Congress.* Purdue, Ind.: Purdue University Press. **193.**

KOLODZIEJ, EDWARD A.
1966 *The Uncommon Defense and Congress 1945–1963.* Columbus: Ohio State University Press. **202.**

KONVITZ, MILTON R.
1957 *Fundamental Liberties of a Free People: Religion, Speech, Press, Assembly.* Ithaca, N.Y.: Cornell University Press. **199.**

KORNBERG, ALLAN
1967 *Canadian Legislative Behavior.* New York: Holt. **217.**

KORNHAUSER, WILLIAM
1959 *The Politics of Mass Society.* New York: Free Press. **177.**

KRISLOV, SAMUEL
1965 *The Supreme Court in the Political Process.* New York: Macmillan; paper. **199.**

LADD, JR., EVERETT C.
  1966 *Political Leadership in the South.* Ithaca, N.Y.: Cornell University Press. **184.**
LAKOFF, SANFORD A.
  1964 *Equality in Political Philosophy.* Cambridge, Mass.: Harvard University Press. **176.**
LANDIS, JAMES M.
  1938 *The Administrative Process.* New Haven, Conn.: Yale University Press; paper, Yale. **155.**
LANE, EDGAR
  1964 *Lobbying and the Law.* Berkeley, Cal.: University of California Press. **204.**
LANE, ROBERT E.
  1962 *Political Ideology: Why the Common Man Believes What He Does.* New York: Free Press; paper, Free Press. **183–184.**
  1959 *Political Life: Why People Get Involved in Politics.* New York: Free Press; paper, Free Press.
LA PALOMBARA, JOSEPH
  1964 *Interest Groups in Italian Politics.* Princeton, N.J.: Princeton University Press. **212, 215.**
  ——— (ed.)
  1963 *Bureaucracy and Political Development.* Princeton, N.J.: Princeton University Press; paper, Princeton.
  ———, and MYRON WEINER (eds.)
  1966 *Political Parties and Political Development.* Princeton, N.J.: Princeton University Press. **212.**
LASKI, HAROLD J.
  1957 *A Grammar of Politics* (4th ed.). New York: Humanities. **133, 143.**
LASSWELL, HAROLD D.
  1948 *The Analysis of Political Behavior: An Empirical Approach.* New York: University Press. **133, 150–151, 162, 173, 182, 186, 219, 231.**
  1941 *Democracy Through Public Opinion.* Menasha, Wis.: Banta.
  1963 *The Future of Political Science.* New York: Atherton.
  1949 *The Language of Politics.* Cambridge, Mass.: M.I.T. Press.
  1936 *Politics: Who Gets What, When, How.* Magnolia, Mass.: Smith; paper, Meridian.
  1948 *Power and Personality.* New York: Norton; paper, Viking.
  1960 *Psychopathology and Politics* (rev. ed.). New York: Viking; paper.
  1965 *World Politics and Personal Insecurity* (1935). New York: Free Press; paper.
  1951 *The World Revolution of Our Time: A Framework for Basic Policy Research.* Stanford, Cal.: Stanford University Press.
  ———, and ABRAHAM KAPLAN
  1950 *Power and Society.* New Haven, Conn.: Yale University Press; paper, Yale. **133, 151.**

LASSWELL, HAROLD D., DANIEL LERNER, and C. EASTON ROTHWELL
1952 *The Comparative Study of Elites.* Stanford, Cal.: Stanford University Press; paper. **133, 150–151, 162, 173, 182, 186, 219, 231.**

LATHAM, EARL
1965 *The Group Basis of Politics* (1952). New York: Octagon. **156, 178.**

LAUTERPACHT, HERSH
1966 *The Function of Law in the International Community* (1933). Hamden, Conn.: Shoe String. **159.**

LAZARSFELD, PAUL F., BERNARD BERELSON, and HAZEL GAUDET
1946 *The People's Choice.* New York: Columbia University Press. **21, 25–26, 30, 115, 169.**

LEE, EUGENE C.
1960 *The Politics of Nonpartisanship.* Berkeley, Cal.: University of California Press. **189.**

LEIGHTON, ALEXANDER H.
1945 *The Governing of Men.* Princeton, N.J.: Princeton University Press. **157.**

LEISERSON, AVERY
1942 *Administrative Regulation: A Study in Representation of Interests.* Chicago: University of Chicago Press.
1958 *Parties and Politics: An Institutional and Behavioral Approach.* New York: Knopf. **150, 156, 188.**

LEITES, NATHAN
1959 *On the Game of Politics in France.* Stanford, Cal.: Stanford University Press. **163, 220.**
1953 *A Study of Bolshevism.* New York: Free Press.
———, and CONSTANTIN MELNIK
1958 *The House without Windows: France Selects a President.* Stanford, Cal.: Stanford University Press. Tr. R. Manheim. **220.**

LERNER, DANIEL
1958 *The Passing of Traditional Society: Modernizing the Middle East.* New York: Free Press; paper, Free Press. **162, 220.**

LERNER, MAX
1939 *Ideas are Weapons.* New York: Viking. **142.**
1941 *Ideas for the Ice Age.* New York: Viking.
1938 *It Is Later Than You Think.* New York: Viking.

LEVI, WERNER
1950 *Fundamentals of World Organization.* Minneapolis: University of Minnesota Press. **163.**

LEVY, MARION J.
1966 *Modernization and the Structure of Societies.* (2 vols.). Princeton, N.J.: Princeton University Press. **88, 213.**

LINDBERG, L. N.
1963 *The Political Dynamics of European Economic Integration.* Stanford, Cal.: Stanford University Press. **309.**

LINDBLOM, CHARLES E.
  1965 *The Intelligence of Democracy.* New York: Macmillan. **158,** **180–181, 273, 284.**
  ———, and DAVID BRAYBROOKE
  1963 *A Strategy of Decision.* New York: Free Press. **180.**
LIPPMANN, WALTER
  1955 *Essays in the Public Philosophy.* Boston: Little, Brown; paper, New American. **142, 149.**
  1965 *An Inquiry into the Principles of the Good Society* (1937). Magnolia, Mass.: Smith; paper, Grosset.
  1967 *A Preface to Morals* (1929). New York: Macmillan.
  1962 *A Preface to Politics* (1913). Ann Arbor, Mich.: University of Michigan Press; paper.
  1965 *Public Opinion* (1922). New York: Pree Press; paper.
LIPSET, SEYMOUR M.
  1963 *The First New Nation.* New York: Basic Books. **20–21, 25, 26, 35, 157, 170, 177, 190, 214, 219.**
  1959 *Political Man.* New York: Doubleday; paper.
  ———, and STEIN ROKKAN (eds.)
  1967 *Party Systems and Voter Alignment.* New York: Free Press.
LIPSET, SEYMOUR M., MARTIN TROW, and JAMES COLEMAN
  1956 *Union Democracy.* New York: Free Press. **20–21, 25, 26, 35, 157, 170, 177, 190, 214, 219.**
LIPSET, SEYMOUR M., *et al.*
  1954 "The Psychology of Voting: An Analysis of Political Behavior," in G. Lindzey (ed.), *Handbook of Social Psychology* (2 vols.). Cambridge, Mass.: Addison-Wesley. **20–21, 25–26, 35, 157, 170, 177, 190, 214, 219.**
LIPSON, LESLIE
  1954 *The Great Issues of Politics* (3d ed.). Englewood Cliffs, N.J.: Prentice-Hall. **142.**
LISKA, GEORGE
  1957 *International Equilibrium: A Theoretical Essay on the Politics and Organization of Security.* Cambridge, Mass.: Harvard University Press. **227.**
LOCKARD, DUANE
  1959 *New England State Politics.* Princeton, N.J.: Princeton University Press. **189.**
LOCKE, JOHN
  1966 *Second Treatise of Civil Government* (3d ed.). New York: Barnes & Noble; paper, Barnes. Ed. J. W. Gough. **5, 6, 138.**
LOEWENBERG, GERHARD
  1966 *Parliament in the German Political System.* Ithaca, N.Y.: Cornell University Press. **217.**
LOWELL, ABBOTT LAWRENCE
  1929 *Government and Parties in Continental Europe* (1897). Cambridge, Mass.: Harvard University Press. **145, 149, 164.**

1926 *Public Opinion and Popular Government* (1913). New York: Longmans.

LOWI, THEODORE J.
1964 *At the Pleasure of the Mayor: Patronage and Power in New York City 1898–1958.* New York: Free Press. **209.**

LUCE, ROBERT
1924 *Legislative Assemblies.* Boston: Houghton. **147.**
1922 *Legislative Procedure.* Boston: Houghton.

LYONS, GENE M., and LOUIS MORTON
1965 *Schools for Strategy: Education and Research in National Security Affairs.* New York: Praeger. **233.**

MAAS, ARTHUR (ed.)
1959 *Area and Power: A Theory of Local Government.* New York: Free Press. **196.**

MCCAMY, JAMES L.
1950 *The Administration of American Foreign Affairs.* New York: Knopf. **163.**

MCCLOSKEY, ROBERT G.
1960 *The American Supreme Court.* Chicago: University of Chicago Press; paper, Chicago.

MCCONNEL, GRANT
1966 *Private Power and American Democracy.* New York: Knopf. **204.**

MCDONALD, NEIL A.
1965 *Politics: A Study of Control Behavior.* New Brunswick, N.J.: Rutgers University Press. **165, 181.**

MACDONALD, ROBERT W.
1965 *The League of Arab States: A Study in the Dynamics of Regional Organization.* Princeton, N.J.: Princeton University Press; paper, Princeton. **230.**

MCDOUGAL, MYRES S., HAROLD D. LASSWELL, and I. A. VLASIC
1963 *Law and Public Order in Space.* New Haven, Conn.: Yale University Press. **117, 133, 150–151, 162, 186, 219, 231.**

MACHIAVELLI
The Prince. New York: Dutton's Everyman's; paper, New American. **131, 137–138, 149, 177.**

MCILWAIN, CHARLES H.
1932 *The Growth of Political Thought in the West.* New York: Macmillan. **140.**
1919 *The Political Works of James I.* Cambridge, Mass.: Harvard University Press.

MACIVER, ROBERT M.
1926 *The Modern State.* New York: Oxford University Press; paper. **39, 143, 174.**
1965 *The Web of Government* (rev. ed.). New York: Free Press; paper, Free Press.

McKean, Dayton D.
1940 *The Boss: The Hague Machine in Action.* Boston: Houghton. **232, 284.**
McKenzie, Robert T.
1964 *British Political Parties: The Distribution of Power within the Conservative and Labour Parties.* New York: Praeger. **217.**
Macmahon, Arthur W. (ed.)
1962 *Federalism: Mature and Emergent* (1955). New York: Russell. **147, 155.**
———, and John D. Millett
1965 *Federal Administrators: A Biographical Approach to the Problem of Departmental Management* (1939). New York: AMS. **155.**
MacRae, Jr., Duncan
1958 *Dimensions of Congressional Voting.* Berkeley, Cal.: University of California Press; paper. **192, 217.**
1967 *Parliament, Parties and Society in France 1946–1958.* New York: St. Martins.
Macridis, Roy C.
1955 *The Study of Comparative Government.* New York: Random; paper. **145.**
Mailick, Sidney, and Edward H. Van Ness (eds.)
1962 *Concepts and Issues in Administrative Behavior.* Englewood Cliffs, N.J.: Prentice-Hall. **195.**
Mann, Dean E., and James W. Doig
1965 *The Assistant Secretaries: Problems and Processes of Appointment.* Washington: Brookings. **185.**
Mannheim, Karl
1936 *Ideology and Utopia.* New York: Harcourt; paper, Harcourt. Tr. L. Wirth and E. Shils. **8, 129.**
Mansfield, Jr., Harvey C.
1965 *Statesmanship and Party Government—A Strategy of Burke and Bolingbroke.* Chicago: University of Chicago Press. **177.**
March, James G., and Herbert A. Simon
1958 *Organizations.* New York: Wiley. **97, 98, 104–105, 150, 156–157, 158, 180, 194, 195, 280.**
Markel, Leslie, et al.
1949 *Public Opinion and Foreign Policy.* New York: Harper. **160.**
Marshall, T. H.
1964 *Class, Citizenship, and Social Development.* New York: Doubleday. **214.**
Martin, Roscoe C.
1965 *The Cities and the Federal System.* New York: Atherton. **194, 196, 210.**
——— (ed.)
1965 *Public Administration and Democracy.* Syracuse, N.Y.: Syracuse University Press.

MARTIN, ROSCOE C., and FRANK J. MUNGER (eds.)
1961 *Decisions in Syracuse.* New York: Doubleday; paper. **194, 196, 210.**

MARVICK, DWAINE
1954 *Career Perspectives in a Bureaucratic Setting.* Ann Arbor, Mich.: University of Michigan Press. **155, 170, 185, 221.**
1961 *Political Decision-Makers: Recruitment and Performance.* New York: Free Press.

MARX, FRITZ (ed.)
1946 *Elements of Public Administration.* Englewood Cliffs, N.J.: Prentice-Hall. **154.**

MARX, KARL, and FRIEDRICH ENGELS
1967 *The Communist Manifesto.* New York: Pantheon; paper, Penguin. **11–12, 23, 139, 175, 205–206, 222–223, 246–247, 252–253, 257.**

MASLAND, JOHN W., and LAWRENCE I. RADCOCEY
1957 *Soldiers and Scholars: Military Education and National Policy.* Princeton, N.J.: Princeton University Press. **233.**

MASON, ALPHEUS T.
1964 *The States Rights Debate: Antifederalism and the Constitution.* Englewood Cliffs, N.J.: Prentice-Hall; paper. **196.**

MASTERS, NICHOLAS A., ROBERT H. SALISBURY, and THOMAS H. ELIOT
1964 *State Politics and the Public Schools.* New York: Knopf. **197, 204.**

MASUR, GERHARD
1966 *Nationalism in Latin America.* New York: Macmillan. **224.**

MATTHEWS, DONALD R.
1960 *U.S. Senators and Their World.* Chapel Hill, N.C.: University of North Carolina Press; paper, Vintage. **185, 191.**

———, and JAMES W. PROTHRO
1966 *Negroes and the New Southern Politics.* New York: Harcourt. **185.**

MAYHEW, DAVID R.
1966 *Party Loyalty among Congressmen.* Cambridge, Mass.: Harvard University Press. **192.**

MAYO, ELTON
1960 *The Human Problems of an Industrial Civilization.* New York: Viking; paper. **37, 157, 279.**

MEEHAN, EUGENE J.
1967 *Contemporary Political Thought: A Critical Study.* Homewood, Ill.: Dorsey. **178, 236.**
1965 *The Theory and Method of Political Analysis.* Homewood, Ill.: Dorsey.

MEISEL, JAMES H.
1958 *The Myth of the Ruling Class: Gaetano Mosca and the Elite.* Ann Arbor, Mich.: University of Michigan Press; paper, Michigan. **177.**

BIBLIOGRAPHY AND AUTHOR INDEX

MELMAN, SEYMOUR (ed.)
    1958 *Inspection for Disarmament.* New York: Columbia University Press. **233.**
MERRIAM, CHARLES E.
    1926 *A History of the Theory of Sovereignty since Rousseau* (1900). New York: Columbia University Press. **131, 136, 149, 167.**
    1925 *New Aspects of Politics.* Chicago: University of Chicago Press.
——, and H. F. GOSNELL
    1924 *Non-Voting.* Chicago: University of Chicago Press; paper, Chicago. **150, 164, 166–168.**
MERRITT, RICHARD L.
    1966 *Symbols of American Community 1735–1775.* New Haven, Conn.: Yale University Press. **190, 219.**
——, and STEIN ROKKAN (eds.)
    1965 *Comparing Nations: The Use of Quantitative Data in Cross-National Research.* New Haven, Conn.: Yale University Press. **219.**
MERTON, ROBERT K., et al. (eds.)
    1952 *A Reader in Bureaucracy.* New York: Free Press; paper, Free Press. **20–21, 155.**
METCALF, HENRY, and LYNDALL URWICK
    1942 *Dynamic Administration.* New York: Harper.
MEYERSON, MARTIN, and EDWARD C. BANFIELD
    1955 *Politics, Planning, and the Public Interest.* New York: Free Press; paper, Free Press. **156–157, 207, 209, 220.**
MICAUD, CHARLES
    1964 *The French Right and Nazi Germany 1933–1939* (1943). New York: Octagon. **160.**
MICHELS, ROBERT
    1958 *Political Parties* (1915). New York: Free Press; paper, Free Press. **20, 36, 165.**
MILBRATH, LESTER W.
    1965 *Political Participation.* Chicago: Rand; paper, Rand. **184, 204.**
MILBRATH, LEWIS
    1963 *The Washington Lobbyists.* Chicago: Rand.
MILL, JOHN STUART
    Utilitarianism, Liberty, and Representative Government. New York: Dutton's Everyman's; paper, Bobbs (*On Liberty*); Regnery (*Considerations on Representative Government*). **139, 149, 177, 182, 247, 249.**
MILLS, C. WRIGHT
    1956 *The Power Elite.* New York: Oxford University Press; paper, Oxford. **13, 23, 35, 36, 155, 206.**
MITCHELL, WILLIAM C..
    1967 *Sociological Analysis and Politics: The Theories of Talcott Parsons.* Englewood Cliffs, N.J.: Prentice-Hall. **181.**

MODELSKI, GEORGE
 1960 *The Communist System.* Princeton, N.J.: Princeton University Center of International Studies. **227.**
 1962 *A Theory of Foreign Policy.* New York: Praeger.

MONTESQUIEU, C. L. DE S.
 1960 *De l'Esprit des loix* (2 vols.). New York: French & European; paper, French & European. **139.**

MOON, PARKER T.
 1926 *Imperialism and World Politics.* New York: Macmillan. **159.**

MOORE, BARRINGTON
 1966 *Social Origins of Dictatorship and Democracy: Lord and Peasant in the Making of the Modern World.* Boston: Beacon; paper, Beacon. **216.**

MOORE, CLEMENT H.
 1965 *Tunisia Since Independence: The Dynamics of One-Party Government.* Berkeley, Cal.: University of California Press. **216.**

MORGENTHAU, HANS J.
 1958 *Dilemmas of Politics.* New York: Knopf. **162, 228, 230.**
 1966 *Politics Among Nations: The Struggle for Power and Peace* (3d rev. ed.). New York: Knopf.
 1960 *The Purpose of American Politics.* New York: Knopf; paper, Vintage.

MORGENTHAU, RUTH S.
 1964 *Political Parties in French West Africa.* New York: Oxford University Press. **217.**

MOSHER, FREDERICK C., and ORVILLE F. POLAND
 1964 *The Costs of American Governments: Facts, Trends, Myths.* New York: Dodd; paper. **195.**

MOSTELLER, FREDERICK, *et al.*
 1949 *The Pre-election Polls of 1948.* New York: Social Science Research Council; paper. **125, 169.**

MURPHY, GARDNER
 1953 *In the Minds of Men.* New York: Basic Books. **94, 163.**

MURPHY, WALTER F.
 1964 *Elements of Judicial Strategy.* Chicago: University of Chicago Press. **199.**

NEUMANN, SIGMUND
 1956 *Modern Political Parties.* Chicago: University of Chicago Press. **166.**

NEUSTADT, RICHARD
 1960 *Presidential Power.* New York: Wiley; paper, Science Eds.; New American. **193.**

NIEBURG, HAROLD L.
 1964 *Nuclear Secrecy and Foreign Policy.* Washington; Public Affairs. **230.**

NORTH, ROBERT C., et al.
   1963 *Content Analysis.* Evanston, Ill.: Northwestern University Press. **236.**
NYE, JR., JOSEPH S.
   1965 *Pan Africanism and East African Integration.* Cambridge, Mass.: Harvard University Press. **231.**
ODEGARD, PETER H.
   1956 "A New Look at Leviathan," in L. T. White, *Frontiers of Knowledge in the Study of Man.* New York: Harper. **148, 170–171, 172.**
   1967 *Pressure Politics* (1928). New York: Octagon.
OLSON, JR., MANCUR
   1965 *The Logic of Collective Action.* Cambridge, Mass.: Harvard University Press. **179.**
OPPENHEIM, FELIX
   1961 *Dimensions of Freedom.* New York: St. Martins. **176.**
ORGANSKI, A. F. K.
   1965 *The Stages of Political Development.* New York: Knopf. **214.**
OSGOOD, ROBERT E.
   1957 *Limited War: The Challenge to American Strategy.* Chicago: University of Chicago Press. **232.**
OSTROGORSKII, MOSEI
   1964 *Democracy and the Organization of Political Parties.* (1902) (2 vols.). Chicago: Quadrangle. **287.**
PALAMOUNTAIN, JOSEPH C.
   1955 *The Politics of Distribution.* Cambridge, Mass.: Harvard University Press. **204.**
PAYNE, JAMES L.
   1965 *Labor and Politics in Peru: The System of Political Bargaining.* New Haven, Conn.: Yale University Press. **219.**
PEABODY, ROBERT L.
   1964 *Organizational Authority: Superior-Subordinate Relationships in Three Public Service Organizations.* New York: Atherton. **191, 195.**
———, and NELSON W. POLSBY (eds.)
   1963 *New Perspectives on the House of Representatives.* Chicago: Rand; paper, Rand. **189, 191, 194, 208.**
PEEL, ROY V.
   1935 *The Political Clubs of New York.* New York: Putnam. **166.**
PENNOCK, J. ROLAND
   1964 *Self-Government in Modernizing Nations.* Englewood Cliffs, N.J.: Prentice-Hall; paper. **214.**
PINNER, FRANK, PAUL JACOBS, and PHILIP SELZNICK
   1959 *Old Age and Political Behavior.* Berkeley, Cal.: University of California Press. **37, 39, 157, 184.**
PITKIN, HANNA F.
   1967 *The Concept of Representation.* Berkeley, Cal.: University of California Press. **175.**

PLATO
1966 *The Republic.* New York: Cambridge University Press; paper, Cambridge. Tr. and ed. I. A. Richards. **4, 97, 131, 136–137, 175, 177, 182.**

POLLOCK, JAMES K.
1939 *Voting Behavior: A Case Study.* Ann Arbor, Mich.: University of Michigan Press; paper. **168.**

———, and SAMUEL J. ELDERSVELD
1942 *Michigan Politics and Transition.* Ann Arbor, Mich.: University of Michigan Press; paper. **130, 134, 168, 189, 203.**

POLSBY, NELSON W.
1963 *Community Power and Political Theory.* New Haven, Conn.: Yale University Press. **189, 191, 194, 208.**
1964 *Congress and the Presidency.* Englewood Cliffs, N.J.: Prentice-Hall; paper.

———, and AARON B. WILDAVSKY
1964 *Presidential Elections* (2d ed.). New York: Scribner; paper, Scribner. **189, 195, 201, 207.**

POMPER, GERALD
1963 *Nominating the President: The Politics of Convention Choice.* Evanston, Ill.: Northwestern University Press; paper, Norton. **190.**

POOL, ITHIEL DE S.
1952 *The "Prestige Papers".* Stanford, Cal.: Stanford University Press. **161, 173, 201–202, 204, 236.**

——— (ed.)
1967 *Contemporary Political Science: Toward Empirical Theory.* New York: McGraw-Hill.

POOL, ITHIEL DE S., ROBERT P. ABELSON, and SAMUEL POPKIN
1965 *Candidates, Issues, and Strategies—A Computer Simulation of the 1960 and 1964 Presidential Elections* (2d rev. ed.). Cambridge, Mass.: M.I.T. Press. **161, 173, 201–202, 204, 236.**

PRESTHUS, ROBERT
1964 *Men at the Top: A Study of Community Power.* New York: Oxford University Press; paper, Oxford. **195, 207.**
1962 *The Organizational Society.* New York: Vintage; paper.

PRICE, DON K.
1965 *The Scientific Estate.* Cambridge, Mass.: Harvard University Press. **204.**

PRICE, HUGH D.
1956 *The Negro and Southern Politics.* New York: New York University Press. **184.**

PRITCHETT, CHARLES H.
1954 *Civil Liberties and the Vinson Court.* Chicago: University of Chicago Press. **146, 150, 197–198.**
1948 *The Roosevelt Court.* New York: Macmillan.

PYE, LUCIAN W.
1965 *Aspects of Political Development.* Boston: Little, Brown; paper, Little.

1956 *Guerilla Communism in Malaya: Its Social and Political Meaning.* Princeton, N.J.; Princeton University Press.
1962 *Politics, Personality, and Nation Building: Burma's Search for Identity.* New Haven, Conn.: Yale University Press; paper, Yale.
—— (ed.)
1963 *Communications and Political Development.* Princeton, N.J.: Princeton University Press; paper, Princeton.

PYE, LUCIAN W., and SIDNEY VERBA (eds.)
1965 *Political Culture and Political Development.* Princeton, N.J.: Princeton University Press. **182–183, 186, 212, 214, 220, 227.**

RANNEY, AUSTIN
1963 *Essays on the Behavioral Study of Politics.* Urbana, Ill.: University of Illinois Press. **173, 185.**
1965 *Pathways to Parliament: Candidate Selection in Britain.* Madison, Wis.: University of Wisconsin Press.

RANSOM, HARRY H.
1958 *Central Intelligence and National Security.* Cambridge, Mass.: Harvard University Press. **232.**

RAPOPORT, Anatol
1960 *Fights, Games and Debates.* Ann Arbor, Mich.: University of Michigan Press. **125, 234.**

REAGAN, MICHAEL D.
1963 *The Managed Economy.* New York: Oxford University Press. **203.**

RICE, STUART A.
1924 *Farmers and Workers in American Politics.* New York: Columbia University Press. **133, 168.**
1928 *Quantitative Methods in Politics.* New York: Appleton.

RICHARDSON, LEWIS F.
1960 *Arms and Insecurity.* Pittsburgh: Boxwood. Ed. N. Rashevsky. **233.**

RICHTER, MELVIN
1964 *The Politics of Conscience: T. H. Green and His Age.* Cambridge, Mass.: Harvard University Press. **177.**

RIESELBACH, LEROY N.
1966 *The Roots of Isolationism.* Indianapolis: Bobbs; paper, Bobbs. **192.**

RIGGS, FREDERICK W.
1964 *Administration in Developing Countries: The Theory of Prismatic Society.* Boston: Houghton. **216.**

RIKER, WILLIAM H.
1964 *Federalism: Origin, Operation, Significance.* Boston: Little, Brown; paper. **180, 197.**
1962 *The Theory of Political Coalitions.* New Haven, Conn.: Yale University Press; paper, Yale.

ROBINSON, JAMES A.
1967 *Congress and Foreign Policy-Making: A Study of Legislative Influence and Initiative* (rev. ed.). Homewood, Ill.: Dorsey; paper. **315.**
1963 *The House Rules Committee.* Indianapolis: Bobbs; paper, Bobbs.

ROETHLISBERGER, FRITZ J., and WILLIAM J. DICKSON
  1964 *Management and the Worker.* New York: Science Eds.; paper. **37, 157, 279.**
ROGERS, LINDSAY
  1949 *The Pollsters.* New York: Knopf. **168.**
ROGOW, ARNOLD
  1963 *James Forrestal: A Study of Personality, Politics and Policy.* New York: Macmillan. **183.**
  ———, and HAROLD D. LASSWELL
  1963 *Power, Corruption and Rectitude.* Englewood Cliffs, N.J.: Prentice-Hall. **133, 150–151, 162, 173, 182, 183, 219, 231.**
ROSECRANCE, RICHARD N.
  1963 *Action and Reaction in World Politics: International Systems in Perspective.* Boston: Little, Brown. **227.**
ROSENAU, JAMES N.
  1961 *International Politics and Foreign Policy.* New York: Free Press. **229, 230.**
  1963 *National Leadership and Foreign Policy: A Case Study in the Mobilization of Public Support.* Princeton, N.J.: Princeton University Press.
  1961 *Public Opinion and Foreign Policy.* New York: Random; paper.
ROSENBLUM, VICTOR G.
  1955 *Law as a Political Instrument.* New York: Random; paper. **146, 198.**
ROSS, JAMES F. S.
  1955 *Elections and Electors: Studies in Democratic Representation.* New York: Duell. **167.**
ROSSI, PETER H., and ROBERT A. DENTLER
  1961 *The Politics of Urban Renewal.* New York: Free Press. **209.**
ROSSITER, CLINTON
  1966 *The American Presidency* (rev. ed.). New York: Harcourt; paper, Harcourt. **142, 147, 190.**
  1955 *Conservatism in America.* (2d ed. rev.). New York: Knopf; paper, Vintage.
  1966 *1787: The Grand Convention.* New York: Macmillan.
ROTHMAN, DAVID J.
  1966 *Politics and Power: The United States Senate 1869–1901.* Cambridge, Mass.: Harvard University Press. **192.**
ROURKE, FRANCIS E.
  1961 *Secrecy and Publicity Dilemmas of Democracy.* Baltimore: Johns Hopkins University Press; paper, Johns. **204.**
ROUSSEAU, JEAN JACQUES
  Social Contract. Chicago: Regnery; paper. Tr. W. Kendall. **5, 6, 138–139.**
ROWAT, DONALD C.
  1965 *The Ombudsman: Citizen's Defender.* Toronto: University of Toronto Press. **216.**

RUBENSTEIN, ROBERT, and HAROLD D. LASSWELL
  1966 *The Sharing of Power in a Psychiatric Hospital.* New Haven, Conn.: Yale University Press. **186.**
RUSSELL, FRANK M.
  1936 *Theories of International Relations.* New York: Appleton. **159.**
RUSSETT, BRUCE M.
  1963 *Community and Contention: Britain and America in the Twentieth Century.* Cambridge, Mass.: M.I.T. Press. **219, 229, 234.**
———, et al. (eds.)
  1964 *World Handbook of Political and Social Indicators.* New Haven, Conn.: Yale University Press.
SABINE, GEORGE H.
  1961 *A History of Political Theory* (3d ed.). New York: Holt. **140.**
SAIT, EDWARD M.
  1938 *Political Institutions.* New York: Appleton.
SAPIN, BURTON M.
  1966 *The Making of United States Foreign Policy.* Washington: Brookings; paper, Praeger. **158, 163, 204.**
SARTORI, GIOVANNI
  1962 *Democratic Theory.* Detroit: Wayne State University Press; paper, Praeger. **176.**
SAYRE, WALLACE S.
  1960 *Governing New York City.* New York: Russell Sage Foundation. **207.**
SCALAPINO, ROBERT
  1953 *Democracy and the Party Movement in Prewar Japan.* Berkeley, Cal.: University of California Press. **145.**
SCHAAR, JOHN H
  1961 *Escape from Authority.* New York: Basic Books; paper, Harper. **176, 183.**
  1957 *Loyalty in America.* Berkeley, Cal.: University of California Press.
SCHATTSCHNEIDER, ELMER E.
  1942 *Party Government.* New York: Holt; paper.
  1963 *Politics, Pressures and the Tariff* (1935). Hamden, Conn.: Shoe String.
  1961 *The Semi-sovereign People.* New York: Holt; paper.
SCHELLING, THOMAS C.
  1960 *The Strategy of Conflict.* Cambridge, Mass.: Harvard University Press; paper, Oxford. **233.**
SCHLESINGER, JOSEPH A.
  1966 *Ambition and Politics: Political Careers in the United States.* East Lansing, Mich.: Governmental Research Bureau, Michigan State University. **185.**
  1957 *How They Became Governor.* East Lancing, Mich.: Governmental Research Bureau, Michigan State University.

SCHMIDHAUSER, JOHN R.
1958 *The Supreme Court as Final Arbiter in Federal-State Relations 1789–1957.* Chapel Hill, N.C.: University of North Carolina Press. **199.**
1960 *The Supreme Court: Its Politics, Personalities, and Procedures.* New York: Holt; paper.

SCHUBERT, GLENDON
1960 *Constitutional Politics: The Political Behavior of Supreme Court Justices and the Constitutional Policies That They Make.* New York: Holt. **177, 193, 198.**
1965 *The Judicial Mind.* Evanston, Ill.: Northwestern University Press.
1957 *The Presidency in the Courts.* Minneapolis: University of Minnesota Press.
1960 *The Public Interest.* New York: Free Press.
1960 *Quantitative Analysis of Political Behavior.* New York. Free Press.
——— (ed.)
1964 *Judicial Behavior: A Reader in Theory and Research.* Chicago: Rand.

SCHUBERT, GLENDON, et al.
1963 *Judicial Decision-Making.* New York: Free Press. **177, 193, 198.**

SCHUMAN, FREDERICK L.
1937 *International Politics.* New York: McGraw-Hill. **150, 159.**

SCHURMANN, FRANZ
1966 *Ideology and Organization in Communist China.* Berkeley, Cal.: University of California Press. **223.**

SCOTT, ROBERT E.
1964 *Mexican Government in Transition* (rev. ed.). Urbana, Ill.: University of Illinois Press; paper.

SELZNICK, PHILIP
1949 *TVA and the Grass Roots.* New York: Harper; paper. **37, 39, 157, 184.**

SEWELL, JAMES P.
1966 *Functionalism and World Politics: A Study Based on United Nations Programs Financing Economic Development.* Princeton, N.J.: Princeton University Press. **231.**

SHAPIRO, MARTIN
1964 *Law and Politics in the Supreme Court.* New York: Free Press. **199.**

SHARP, WALTER R.
1961 *Field Administration in the United Nations System.* New York: Praeger. **145, 230.**
1931 *The French Civil Service.* New York: Macmillan.

SILVERT, KALMAN H.
The Conflict Society: Reaction and Revolution in Latin America (rev. ed.). Washington: American Universities Field Staff. **224.**

SIMON, HERBERT A.
1957 *Administrative Behavior: A Study of Decision-Making Processes in Administrative Organization.* (2d ed.). New York: Free Press; paper, Free Press. **97, 98, 104–105, 150, 156–158, 180, 194–195, 280.**
1957 *Models of Man: Social and Rational.* New York: Wiley.
1955 "Recent Advances in Organization Theory," in *Research Frontiers in Politics and Government.* Washington: Brookings.

SINDLER, ALAN P.
1966 *Political Parties in the United States.* New York: St. Martins; paper. **189.**

SINGER, J. DAVID
1966 *Human Behavior and International Politics.* Chicago: Rand. **230, 234.**
1961 *Financing International Organization: The United Nations Budget Process.* The Hague: Nijhoff.
1968 *Quantitative International Politics: Insights and Evidence.* New York: Free Press.

SKINNER, G. WILLIAM
1958 *Leadership and Power in the Chinese Community in Thailand.* Ithaca, N.Y.: Cornell University Press. **220.**

SKLAR, RICHARD L.
1963 *Nigerian Political Parties: Power in an Emergent African Nation.* Princeton, N.J.: Princeton University Press. **216.**

SMALLWOOD, FRANK
1965 *Greater London: The Politics of Metropolitan Reform.* Indianapolis: Bobbs; paper, Bobbs. **216.**

SMITH, ALICE K.
1965 *A Peril and a Hope: The Scientists' Movement in America, 1945–1947.* Chicago: University of Chicago Press. **204.**

SMITH, JAMES ALLEN
1965 *The Spirit of American Government* (1907). Cambridge, Mass.: Harvard University Press. Ed. C. Strout. **165.**

SMITH, THOMAS V.
1936 *Beyond Conscience.* New York: McGraw-Hill.
1926 *The Democratic Way of Life.* Chicago: University of Chicago Press; paper, New American (rev. ed.).
1936 *The Promise of American Politics.* New York: Cambridge University Press.

SMITHBERG, DONALD W., VICTOR A. THOMPSON, and HERBERT A. SIMON
Public Administration. New York: Knopf.

SNYDER, GLENN H.
1961 *Deterrence and Defense.* Princeton, N.J.: Princeton University Press. **202, 232.**
1966 *Stockpiling Strategic Materials: Politics and National Defense.* Chicago: Science Research Associates; paper, Chandler.

SNYDER, RICHARD C.
- 1955 "Game Theory and the Analysis of Political Behavior," in *Research Frontiers in Politics and Government*. Washington: Brookings. **158, 163, 232.**
———, H. W. BRUCK, and BURTON SAPIN
- 1962 *Foreign Policy Decision Making: An Approach to Study of International Politics*. New York: Free Press. **158, 163, 228.**

SOFEN, EDWARD
- 1963 *The Miami Metropolitan Experiment*. Bloomington, Ind.: Indiana University Press; paper, Doubleday. **210.**

SOKOLOVSKY, V.D.
- 1963 *Military Strategy: Soviet Doctrines and Concepts*. New York: Praeger, 1963.

SOMIT, ALBERT, and JOSEPH TANENHAUS
- 1967 *The Development of American Political Science*. Boston: Allyn. **173, 198.**

SORAUF, FRANK J.
- 1963 *Party and Representation: Legislative Politics in Pennsylvania*. New York: Atherton. **189, 191.**
- 1964 *Political Parties in the American System*. Boston: Little, Brown; paper.

SORENSEN, THEODORE C.
- 1963 *Decision-Making in the White House*. New York: Columbia University Press; paper, Columbia. **193.**

SPANIER, JOHN W., and JOSEPH L. NOGEE
- 1962 *The Politics of Disarmament*. New York: Praeger. **233.**

SPITZ, DAVID
- 1958 *Democracy and the Challenge of Power*. New York: Columbia University Press. **176.**

SPROUT, HAROLD, and MARGARET SPROUT
- 1965 *The Ecological Perspective on Human Affairs, with Special Reference to International Politics*. Princeton, N.J.: Princeton University Press. **228.**

SPYKMAN, NICHOLAS
- 1942 *America's Strategy in World Politics*. New York: Harcourt. **160.**

STANLEY, DAVID T.
- 1964 *The Higher Civil Service*. Washington: Brookings. **185.**

STEIN, HAROLD (ed.)
- 1952 *Public Administration and Policy Development*. New York: Harcourt. **158.**

STEINER, GILBERT Y.
- 1969 *Social Insecurity: The Politics of Welfare*. Chicago: Rand. **202.**

STEINER, KURT
- 1965 *Local Government in Japan*. Stanford, Cal.: Stanford University Press. **217.**

STOESSINGER, JOHN
- 1964 *Financing the United Nations System*. Washington: Brookings. **230.**

STORING, HERBERT J. (ed.)
1962 *Essays on the Scientific Study of Politics.* New York: Holt. **172.**

STOUFFER, SAMUEL A.
1964 *Communism, Conformity, and Civil Liberties* (1955). Magnolia, Mass.: Smith; paper, Science Eds. **17, 21, 25, 38, 120, 169.**

STRAUSS, LEO
1952 *The Political Philosophy of Hobbes: Its Basis and Its Genesis.* Chicago: University of Chicago Press; paper, Chicago. **141, 172, 175.**
1959 *What Is Political Philosophy?* New York: Free Press.

SUSSMANN, LEILA A.
1963 *Dear F.D.R.: A Study of Political Letter Writing.* New York: Bedminster. **184.**

SWARTZ, MARC J., VICTOR W. TURNER, and ARTHUR TUDEN
1966 *Political Anthropology.* Chicago: Aldrine. **75, 220.**

THOMAS AQUINAS
1950 *Summa Theologica.* New York: Benziger. **136–137.**

THOMPSON, LAURA
1950 *Culture in Crisis: A Study of the Hopi Indians.* New York: Harper. **157.**

THOMPSON, VICTOR A.
1961 *Modern Organization.* New York: Knopf. **157, 195.**

THORSON, THOMAS L.
1962 *The Logic of Democracy.* New York: Holt; paper. **176.**

TILMAN, ROBERT O.
1964 *Bureaucratic Transition in Malaya.* Durham, N.C.: Duke University Press. **216.**

TORNEY, JUDITH V., and R. D. HESS
1967 *The Development of Political Attitudes in Children.* Chicago: Aldine. **184.**

TOCQUEVILLE, ALEXIS DE
1965 *Democracy in America.* (2 vols.) New York: Harper; paper, New American; Washington Square, Schocken. **164.**

TRUMAN, DAVID B.
1959 *The Congressional Party.* New York: Wiley; paper. **149, 150, 156, 166, 178, 192.**
1961 *The Governmental Process.* New York: Knopf.

TUCKER, ROBERT W.
1960 *The Just War: A Study in Contemporary American Doctrine.* Baltimore: Johns Hopkins University Press. **177.**

TULLOCK, GORDON
1965 *The Politics of Bureaucracy.* New York: Public Affairs. **179, 195, 284.**

TURNER, JULIUS
1952 *Party and Constituency: Pressures on Congress.* Baltimore: Johns Hopkins University Press; paper.

TUSSMAN, JOSEPH
  1960 *Obligation and the Body Politic.* New York: Oxford University Press; paper, Oxford. 176.
ULAM, ADAM
  1960 *The Unfinished Revolution.* New York: Random; paper, Random. 223.
UNESCO, DEPARTMENT OF SOCIAL SCIENCE
  1950 *Contemporary Political Science: A Survey of Methods, Research, and Teaching.* New York: Columbia University Press.
VALEN, HENRY, and DAVID KATZ
  1964 *Political Parties in Norway.* New York: Barnes & Noble. 218.
VAN DYKE, VERNON
  1960 *Political Science: A Philosophical Analysis.* Stanford, Cal.: Stanford University Press; paper, Stanford. 173, 230.
  1964 *Pride and Power: The Rationale of the Space Program.* Urbana, Ill.: University of Illinois Press.
VERBA, SIDNEY
  1961 *Small Groups and Political Behavior: A Study in Leadership.* Princeton, N.J.: Princeton University Press, 182, 186, 212, 220, 227.
VICO, GIOVANNI BATTISTA
  1960 *Principii d'una Scienza Nuova.* Indianapolis: Bobbs; paper, Bobbs. Tr. E. Gianturco. 139.
VOSE, CLEMENT
  1959 *Caucasians Only: The Supreme Court, the NAACP, and the Restrictive Covenant Cases.* Berkeley, Cal.: University of California Press. 199.
WAHLKE, JOHN C., and HEINZ EULAU (eds.)
  1959 *Legislative Behavior: A Reader in Theory and Research.* New York: Free Press. 134, 168, 172, 185, 187–188, 191.
WAHLKE, JOHN C., et al.
  1962 *The Legislative System: Explorations in Legislative Behavior.* New York: Wiley. 191.
WALDO, C. DWIGHT
  1948 *The Administrative State: A Study of the Political Theory of American Public Administration.* New York: Ronald. 154, 173.
  1956 *Political Science in the United States of America.* Paris: UNESCO.
WALLACE, SCHUYLER
  1941 *Federal Departmentalization: A Critique of Theories of Organization.* New York: Columbia University Press. 154.
WALLAS, GRAHAM
  1962 *Human Nature in Politics* (1908). Gloucester, Mass.: Smith; paper, Nebraska. 149, 165.
WALTZ, KENNETH N.
  1959 *Man, the State, and War: A Theoretical Analysis.* New York: Columbia University Press; paper, Columbia. 228.

WALZER, MICHAEL
   1965 *The Revolution of the Saints.* Cambridge, Mass.: Harvard University Press. **177.**

WARD, ROBERT E.
   1964 *Studying Politics Abroad: Field Research in Developing Areas.* Boston: Little, Brown: paper, Little. **88, 212, 236.**

———, DANIEL KWART, and A. RUSTOV (eds.)
   1964 *Modernization in Japan and Turkey.* Princeton, N.J.: Princeton University Press. **212.**

WARNER, WILLIAM L.
   1949 *Democracy in Jonesville.* New York: Harper; paper. **33, 36, 46, 73, 90, 167, 195.**

———, *et. al.*,
   1963 *The American Federal Executive.* New Haven, Conn.: Yale University Press; paper, Yale.

WEBER, MAX
   1947 *The Theory of Social and Economic Organization.* New York: Oxford University Press. Tr. A. M. Henderson and T. Parsons. **12–14, 15, 18, 21, 36, 55, 77, 155, 213, 255, 287.**

WEINER, MYRON
   1962 *The Politics of Scarcity: Public Pressures and Political Response in India.* Chicago: University of Chicago Press. **212.**

WELDON, THOMAS D.
   1962 *States and Morals* (1947). New York: Barnes & Noble. **141, 161.**
   1953 *The Vocabulary of Politics.* Baltimore: Penguin; paper.

WHITE, LEONARD D.
   1955 *Introduction to the Study of Public Administration.* New York: Macmillan; 4th ed. **150, 152–154, 158, 194.**
   1954 *The Jacksonians.* New York: Free Press; paper, Free Press.
   1951 *The Jeffersonians.* New York: Free Press; paper, Free Press.
   1958 *The Republican Era, 1869–1901.* New York: Free Press; paper, Free Press.
   1933 *Trends in Public Administration.* New York: McGraw-Hill.

WHITING, A. S.
   1960 *China Crosses the Yalu: The Decision to Enter the Korean War.* New York: Macmillan. **229.**

WHYTE, WILLIAM F.
   1955 *Street Corner Society: The Social Structure of an Italian Slum.* Chicago: University of Chicago Press; rev. ed.; paper, Chicago. **28, 37, 166–167, 279.**

WILDAVSKY, AARON
   1962 *Dixon-Yates: A Study of Power Politics.* New Haven: Conn.: Yale University Press. **189, 195, 201, 207.**
   1964 *Leadership in a Small Town.* New York: Bedminster.
   1964 *The Politics of the Budgetary Process.* Boston: Little, Brown; paper, Little.

WILLIAMS, OLIVER P., and CHARLES R. ADRIAN
  1963 *Four Cities: A Study in Comparative Policy Making.* Philadelphia: University of Pennsylvania Press. **209.**
WILLOUGHBY, WESTEL W.
  1930 *The Ethical Basis of Political Authority.* New York: Macmillan. **143.**
  1910 *An Examination of the Nature of the State* (1896). New York: Macmillan.
  1924 *The Fundamental Concepts of Public Law.* New York: Macmillan.
WILLOUGHBY, WILLIAM F.
  1936 *The Government of Modern States.* New York: Appleton; rev. ed. **152.**
WILMERDING, JR., LUCIUS
  1958 *The Electoral College.* New Brunswick, N.J.: Rutgers University Press; paper, Beacon. **190.**
WILSON, FRANCIS G.
  1936 *The Elements of Modern Politics.* New York: McGraw-Hill. **143.**
WILSON, JAMES Q.
  1962 *The Amateur Democrat.* Chicago: University of Chicago Press; paper, Chicago. **184, 189, 209.**
  1960 *Negro Politics: The Search for Leadership.* New York: Free Press; paper, Free Press.
WILSON, WOODROW
  1918 *The State* (1889). Boston: Heath. **136, 150, 152, 161, 183, 205.**
  1887 "The Study of Administration." *Political Science Quarterly.*
WITTFOGEL, KARL A.
  1957 *Oriental Despotism: A Comparative Study of Total Power.* New Haven, Conn.: Yale University Press; paper, Yale. **216.**
WOLF, JR., CHARLES
  1960 *Foreign Aid: Theory and Practice in Southern Asia.* Princeton, N.J.: Princeton University Press. **230, 286.**
WOLFERS, ARNOLD
  1940 *Britain and France Between Two Wars.* New York: Harcourt. **160.**
WOLIN, SHELDON S.
  1960 *Politics and Vision.* Boston: Little, Brown. **175.**
WOLL, PETER
  1963 *American Bureaucracy.* New York: Norton. **195.**
WOOD, ROBERT C.
  1959 *Suburbia: Its People and Their Politics.* Boston: Houghton; paper, Houghton. **210.**
  1961 *1400 Governments.* New York: Doubleday; paper.
WRIGHT, QUINCY
  1964 *A Study of War.* Chicago: University of Chicago Press; paper, Chicago. **150, 163.**
YOUNG, JAMES S.
  1966 *The Washington Community, 1800–1828.* New York: Columbia University Press. **270.**

YOUNG, ROLAND
    1958 *The American Congress.* New York: Harper. **173, 191.**
    1962 *Approaches to the Study of Politics.* Evanston, Ill.: Northwestern University Press; paper, Northwestern.

ZEIGLER, HARMON
    1964 *Interest Groups in American Society.* Englewood Cliffs, N.J.: Prentice-Hall. **188, 203.**

ZINK, HAROLD
    1966 *City Bosses in the United States* (1930). New York: AMS. **166.**

ZOLBERG, ARISTIDE R.
    1964 *One-Party Government in the Ivory Coast.* Princeton, N.J.: Princeton University Press. **212.**

MISCELLANEOUS SOURCES

Major Problems of United States Foreign Policy (series). Washington: Brookings, 1947–54.

Economics

AITKEN, HUGH G. J. (ed.)
    1959 *The State and Economic Growth.* New York: Social Science Research Council. **289.**

ALLEN, ROY G. D.
    1962 *Mathematical Analysis for Economists* (rev. ed.). New York: St. Martins; paper, St. Martins. **265.**

ANDREANO, RALPH
    1965 *New Views on American Economic Development.* Cambridge, Mass.: Schenkman; paper, Schenkman. **287, 288.**

ANGELL, JAMES W.
    1965 *The Theory of International Prices* (1926). New York: Kelley. **275.**

ARROW, KENNETH J.
    1963 *Social Choice and Individual Values* (2d ed.). New York: Wiley. **275.**

ASHLEY, WILLIAM J.
    1965 *An Introduction to English Economic History and Theory* (1893). (2d ed.). New York: Kelley. **243.**

AYRES, CLARENCE E.
    1962 *The Theory of Economic Progress* (1944). New York: Schocken; paper, Schocken. **289.**

BAGEHOT, WALTER
    1921 *Lombard Street: A Description of the Money Market* (1873). New York: Dutton. **146, 282.**

BANCROFT, GERTRUDE
    1958 *The American Labor Force: Its Growth and Changing Composition.* New York: Wiley. **277.**

BARBASH, JACK
    1966 *Structure, Government, and Politics of American Unions.* New York: Random; paper. **278.**

BAUMOL, WILLIAM J.
    1967 *Business Behavior, Value, and Growth* (rev. ed.). New York: Harcourt; paper, Harcourt. **269.**

BAWERK, EUGEN BÖHM VON
    1930 *Capital and Interest* (1890). New York: Kelley. **250, 267.**

BEARD, CHARLES A., and MARY R. BEARD
    1933 *The Rise of American Civilization* (rev. ed.). New York: Macmillan. **160, 165, 288.**

BEARD, MIRIAM
    1938 *A History of the Business Man.* New York: Macmillan. **281.**

BECKERATH, ERWIN V., et al.
    1922–35 *Schriften, Reden, Briefe von Friedrich List.* Berlin: R. Hobbin. **253.**

BELL, CAROLYN
    1966 *Consumer Choice in the American Economy.* New York: Random. **274.**

BELSHAW, CYRIL S.
    1955 *In Search of Wealth.* Washington: American Anthropological Association. **77, 89, 289.**

BENOIT, ÉMILE
    1961 *Europe at Sixes and Sevens.* New York: Columbia; paper, Columbia. **233, 286.**

BENTHAM, JEREMY
    1952–54 *Economic Writings.* Stark, W. (ed.), New York: Franklin. **253.**

BERGSON, ABRAM
    1953 *Soviet Economic Growth: Conditions and Perspectives.* New York: Harper. **258, 289.**

———, and SIMON KUZNETS (eds.)
    1963 *Economic Trends in the Soviet Union.* Cambridge, Mass.: Harvard University Press. **258, 269, 272.**

BERLE, ADOLF A., and GARDNER C. MEANS
    1937 *The Modern Corporation and Private Property* (rev. ed.). New York: Macmillan. **36, 280.**

BEVERIDGE, SIR WILLIAM H.
    1960 *Full Employment in a Free Society* (2d ed.). New York: Hillary. **261, 269, 285.**

———, et al.
    1931 *Tariffs: The Case Examined.* New York: Longmans.

BIDWELL, PERCY W.
    1939 *The Invisible Tariff: A Study of the Control of Imports in the United States.* New York: Council on Foreign Relations. **285.**

BIEL, GABRIEL
    1930 *Treatise on the Power and Utility of Money.* Philadelphia: University of Pennsylvania Press. **243.**

BIENSTOCK, GREGORY, SOLOMON M. SCHWARTZ, and AARON YUGOW
    1944 *Management in Russian Industry and Agriculture.* Ithaca, N.Y.: Cornell University Press. **258.**

BIBLIOGRAPHY AND AUTHOR INDEX

BLOCH, MARC
  1961 *Feudal Society* (2 vols.). Chicago: University of Chicago Press; paper, Chicago. Tr. L. A. Manyon. **287.**

BLOUGH, ROY
  1952 *The Federal Taxing Process.* Englewood Cliffs, N.J.: Prentice-Hall. **283.**

BLUM, WALTER J., and HARRY KALVEN, JR.
  1953 *The Uneasy Case for Progressive Taxation.* Chicago: University of Chicago Press; paper, Chicago. **283.**

BOAK, ARTHUR E. R.
  1955 *Manpower Shortage and the Fall of the Roman Empire in the West.* Ann Arbor, Mich.: University of Michigan Press. **287.**

BODIN, JEAN
  1946 *The Response to the Paradoxes of Malestroit* (1578). Chevy Chase, Md.: Country Dollar. Tr. from 2d Fr. ed. G. A. Moore. **138, 243.**

BOULDING, KENNETH E.
  1966 *Economic Analysis* (4th ed.). New York: Harper. **157, 233, 260.**
  1945 *The Economics of Peace.* Englewood Cliffs, N.J.: Prentice-Hall.

BUCHANAN, JAMES M.
  1965 *The Public Finances* (rev. ed.). Homewood, Ill.: Irwin. **179.**

BÜCHER, KARL
  1901 *Industrial Evolution.* New York: Franklin. **255, 287.**

CANTILLON, RICHARD
  1965 *Essai sur la nature du commerce en général* (1755). New York: Kelley. **245.**

CAREY, HENRY C.
  1959 *Principles of Social Science* (1859). New York: Kelley. **248.**

CARLSON, SUNE
  1951 *Executive Behavior.* Stockholm: A. Strömberg. **267, 280.**
  1939 *Study on the Pure Theory of Production.* London: King.

CARUS-WILSON, E. M. (ed.)
  1954, 62 *Essays in Economic History* (3 vols.). New York: St. Martins. **287.**

CHAMBERLIN, EDWARD
  1962 *The Theory of Monopolistic Competition* (8th ed.). Cambridge, Mass.: Harvard University Press. **268.**

CHAPPLE, ELIOT D., and LEON R. SAYLES
  1961 *The Measure of Management.* New York: Macmillan. **28, 280.**

CLAPHAM, JOHN H.
  1959 *An Economic History of Modern Britain* (2d ed., 3 vols.). New York: Cambridge University Press; paper, Cambridge. **287.**

CLARK, COLIN
  1957 *The Conditions of Economic Progress.* New York: St. Martins. **272.**

CLARK, JOHN M.
  1935 *Economics of Planning Public Works.* New York: Kelley. **267, 271, 283, 284.**

1939 *Social Control of Business.* New York: McGraw-Hill.
1934 *Strategic Factors in Business Cycles.* New York: Kelley.
1923 *Studies in the Economics of Overhead Costs.* Chicago: University of Chicago Press.

COCHRAN, THOMAS C.
1957 *The American Business System: A Historical Perspective, 1900–1955.* Cambridge, Mass.: Harvard University Press. **281.**

COLE, ARTHUR H.
1959 *Business Enterprise in Its Social Setting.* Cambridge, Mass.: Harvard University Press. **281.**

COMMONS, JOHN R.
1934 *Institutional Economics.* Madison, Wis.: University of Wisconsin Press; paper, Wisconsin (2 vols.). **248, 288, 289.**
1960 *Legal Foundations of Capitalism* (1924). Madison, Wis.: University of Wisconsin Press; paper.

COPELAND, MORRIS A.
1952 *A Study of Money Flows in the United States.* New York: National Bureau of Economic Research. **270.**

CUNNINGHAM, WILLIAM
1966 *The Growth of English Industry and Commerce* (1896). (3 vols.). New York: Kelley. **287.**

DAHL, ROBERT A., and CHARLES E. LINDBLOM
1953 *Politics, Economics, and Welfare.* New York: Harper. **141, 158, 163, 180, 181, 206–207, 218, 273, 284.**

DALTON, HUGH, et al. (eds.)
1934 *Unbalanced Budgets.* London: Routledge. **283.**

DOMAR, EVSEY D.
1957 *Essays in the Theory of Economic Growth.* New York: Oxford University Press. **272.**

DOPSCH, ALFONS
1937 *The Economic and Social Foundations of European Civilization* New York: Harcourt. **287.**

DORFMAN, JOSEPH
1946 *The Economic Mind in American Civilization.* New York: Viking. **252.**

DORFMAN, ROBERT, et al.
1958 *Linear Programming and Economic Analysis.* New York: McGraw-Hill. **265.**

DOUGLAS, PAUL H.
1966 *The Theory of Wages* (1930). New York: Kelley. **241, 267.**

DOWNS, ANTHONY
1957 *An Economic Theory of Democracy.* New York: Harper; paper. **179, 195, 284.**

DRUCKER, PETER F.
1954 *The Practice of Management.* New York: Harper. **280.**

DUNLOP, JOHN T.
    1950 *Wage Determination under Trade Unions* (1944). New York: Kelley. **278.**

DUPUIT, JULES
    1844 "De la mesure de l'utilité des travaux publics," *Annales des ponts et chaussées.* **254, 263.**
    1930–35 "Economics," *Encyclopedia of the Social Sciences.* Vol. V, pp. 285–6.

EDGEWORTH, FRANCIS Y.
    1881 *Mathematical Psychics.* New York: Kelley. **267.**

EICHER, C. K., and L. W. WITT (eds.)
    1964 *Agriculture in Economic Development.* New York: McGraw-Hill. **276.**

ELLIS, HOWARD S.
    1941 *Exchange Control in Central Europe.* Cambridge, Mass.: Harvard University Press. **285.**

FABRICANT, SOLOMON
    1952 *The Trend of Government Activity in the United States since 1900.* New York: National Bureau of Economic Research. **284.**

FERBER, ROBERT, and HUGH G. WALES (eds.)
    1958 *Motivation and Market Behavior.* Homewood, Ill.: Irwin. **274.**

FISHER, IRVING
    1965 *The Nature of Capital and Interest* (1906). New York: Kelley. **267, 270.**
    1963 *The Purchasing Power of Money: Its Determination and Relation to Credit, Interest, and Crises* (1922) (2d ed.). New York: Kelley.

FOGEL, ROBERT W.
    1964 *Railroads and American Economic Growth.* Baltimore: Johns Hopkins University Press. **287–288.**

FRIEDMAN, MILTON
    1953 *Essays in Positive Economics.* Chicago: University of Chicago Press; paper, Chicago. **268, 274.**
    1957 *A Theory of the Consumptive Function.* Princeton, N.J.: Princeton University Press.

GEORGE, HENRY
    1938 *Progress and Poverty* (1879). New York: Modern Library. **248.**

GERSCHENKRON, ALEXANDER
    1962 *Economic Backwardness in Historical Perspective.* New York: Praeger; paper, Praeger. **287.**

GERVAISE, ISAAC
    1954 *The System or Theory of the Trade of the World* (1720). Baltimore: Johns Hopkins University Press. **244.**

GOLDBERGER, A. S.
    1964 *Econometric Theory.* New York: Wiley. **266.**

GOLDSMITH, RAYMOND W.
    1955–56 *A Study of Savings in the United States.* Princeton, N.J.: Princeton University Press. **269.**

GORDON, ROBERT A.
: 1961 *Business Fluctuations* (2d ed.). New York: Harper. **271.**

GURLEY, JOHN G., and EDWARD S. SHAW
: 1960 *Money in a Theory of Finance.* Washington: Brookings. **282.**

HAAVELMO, TRYGVE
: 1944 *The Probability Approach in Economics.* (Chicago) *Econometrica,* Vol. XII Suppl. **265.**

HABERLER, GOTTFRIED
: 1958 *Prosperity and Depression: A Theoretical Analysis of Cyclical Movements* (4th ed.). Cambridge, Mass.: Harvard University Press: paper, Atheneum. **271, 275.**
: 1936 *The Theory of International Trade.* New York: Macmillan.

HACKER, LOUIS M.
: 1940 *The Triumph of American Capitalism.* New York: Columbia University Press; paper, McGraw. **288.**

HALÉVY, ELIE
: 1952 *The Growth of Philosophic Radicalism.* New York: Kelley; paper, Beacon. **252.**

HAMBERG, DANIEL
: 1966 *R. & D.: Essays on Economics of Research and Development.* New York: Random. **282.**

HANSEN, ALVIN H.
: 1941 *Fiscal Policy and Business Cycles.* New York: Norton. **251, 271.**

HARBISON, FREDERICK H., and JOHN R. COLEMAN
: 1951 *Goals and Strategy in Collective Bargaining.* New York: Harper. **287, 279.**

HARRISON, FREDERICK H., and C. A. MYERS
: 1964 *Education, Manpower and Economic Growth.* New York: McGraw-Hill. **287, 279.**

HARRIS, SEYMOUR E.
: 1948 *The European Recovery Program.* Cambridge, Mass.: Harvard University Press. **261.**

HARROD, ROY F.
: 1951 *The Life of Maynard Keynes.* New York: Kelley; paper, St. Martins. **249, 273.**
: 1948 *Towards a Dynamic Economics.* New York: St. Martins.

HAWTREY, RALPH G.
: 1932 *The Art of Central Banking* (2d ed.). New York: Kelley. **249, 282.**
: 1950 *Currency and Credit.* New York: Longmans.

HAYEK, FRIEDRICH A. VON
: 1948 *Individualism and Economic Order.* Chicago: University of Chicago Press. **261, 285.**
: 1944 *The Road to Serfdom.* Chicago: University of Chicago Press; paper, Chicago.
——— (ed.)
: 1967 *Collective Economic Planning* (1935). New York: Kelley.

BIBLIOGRAPHY AND AUTHOR INDEX

HEADY, EARL O.
    1952 *Economics of Agricultural Production and Resource Use.* Englewood Cliffs, N.J.: Prentice-Hall. **276.**

HECKSCHER, ELI F.
    1955 *Mercantilism.* New York: Barnes & Noble. **245.**

HEICHELHEIM, FRITZ
    1938 *Wirtschaftsgeschichte des Altertums* (2 vols.). Leyden: A. W. Sijthoff. **287.**

HERSKOVITS, MELVILLE
    1952 *Economic Anthropology.* New York: Norton; paper. **49, 59, 76, 289.**

HICKS, JOHN R.
    1965 *Capital and Growth.* New York: Oxford University Press. **249, 251, 267–268, 271.**
    1950 *A Contribution to the Theory of the Trade Cycle.* New York: Oxford University Press.
    1932 *The Theory of Wages* (2d ed.). New York: St. Martins.
    1946 *Value and Capital* (2d ed.). New York: Oxford University Press.
——, and ALBERT G. HART
    1945 *The Social Framework of the American Economy.* New York: Oxford University Press. **251.**

HICKS, URSULA K.
    1965 *Development Finance: Planning and Control.* New York: Oxford University Press. **283.**

HIGGS, HENRY
    1935 *Bibliography of Economics, 1751–1775.* New York: Cambridge University Press. **245.**

HIRSCHMAN, ALBERT O.
    1945 *National Power and the Structure of Foreign Trade.* Berkeley, Cal.: University of California Press. **272, 286.**
    1958 *The Strategy of Economic Development.* New Haven, Conn.: Yale University Press; paper, Yale.

HITCH, CHARLES J., and ROLAND N. MCKEAN
    1960 *The Economics of Defense in the Nuclear Age.* Cambridge, Mass.: Harvard University Press. **232, 284.**

HOBSON, JOHN A.
    1914 *Work and Wealth: A Human Valuation.* New York: Macmillan. **288, 289.**

HOSELITZ, BERT F. (ed.)
    1965 *Economics and the Idea of Mankind.* New York: Columbia University Press. **252, 272, 286.**
    1960 *Sociological Aspects of Economic Growth.* New York: Free Press.
——, et al. (eds.)
    1960 *Theories of Economic Growth.* New York: Free Press; paper, Free Press. **252, 272, 286.**

HOUTHAKKER, H. S., and L. D. TAYLOR
  1966 *Consumer Demand in the United States, 1927–1970*, Analysis and Projections. Cambridge, Mass.: Harvard University Press. **266.**
HOXIE, ROBERT F.
  1947 *Trade Unionism in the United States*. New York: Russell. **278.**
INTERNATIONAL BANK FOR RECONSTRUCTION AND DEVELOPMENT
  1963 *The Economic Development of Kenya*. Baltimore: Johns Hopkins University Press.
  1966 *The Economic Development of Morocco*. Baltimore: Johns Hopkins University Press.
ISARD, WALTER, et al.
  1960 *Methods of Regional Analysis*. Cambridge, Mass.: M.I.T. Press. **273.**
ISE, JOHN
  1946 *Economics*. New York: Harper. **259.**
IVERSON, CARL
  1936 *Aspects of the Theory of International Capital Movements* (2d ed.). New York: Kelley. **285.**
JEWKES, JOHN, et al.
  1958 *The Sources of Invention*. New York: St. Martins. **281.**
JOHNSON, D. G.
  1947 *Forward Prices for Agriculture*. Chicago: University of Chicago Press. **276.**
JOHNSON, HARRY G.
  1967 *Economic Policies Toward Less Developed Countries*. Washington: Brookings. **275, 283, 285.**
  1967 *Essays in Monetary Economy*. Cambridge, Mass.: Harvard University Press.
  1958 *International Trade and Economic Growth*. Cambridge, Mass.: Harvard University Press.
JOHNSTON, J.
  1963 *Econometric Methods*. New York: McGraw-Hill. **266.**
JONES, A. H. M.
  1964 *The Later Roman Empire* (2 vols.). Norman, Okla.: University of Oklahoma Press. **287.**
KALDOR, NICHOLAS
  1960 *Essays on Value and Distribution*. New York: Free Press. **267.**
KATONA, GEORGE, and EVA MUELLER
  1957 *Consumer Expectations*. Ann Arbor, Mich.: University of Michigan Institute for Social Research. **274.**
KERR, CLARK et al.
  1964 *Industrialism and Industrial Man* (2d ed.). New York: Oxford University Press; paper. **279.**
KEYNES, JOHN MAYNARD
  1936 *The General Theory of Employment, Interest and Money*. New York: Harcourt; paper, Harcourt. **246, 249–250, 260, 265, 268–270.**
  1924 *Monetary Reform*. New York: Harcourt.

KEYNES, JOHN NEVILLE
  1956 *The Scope and Method of Political Economy* (1891) (4th ed.). New York: Kelley.

KINDLEBERGER, CHARLES P.
  1950 *The Dollar Shortage.* Cambridge, Mass.: M.I.T. Press. **283, 285.**
  1966 *Europe and the Dollar.* Cambridge, Mass.: M.I.T. Press.

KLEIN, L. R.
  1950 *Economic Fluctuations in the United States, 1921–1941.* New York: Wiley. **286.**

KNIGHT, FRANK H.
  1935 *The Ethics of Competition and Other Essays.* New York: Harper. **76, 267.**

KOOPMANS, TJALLING
  1957 *Three Essays on the State of Economic Science.* New York: McGraw-Hill. **265.**

K'UAN, HUAN
  1931 *Discourses on Salt and Iron.* Leyden: E. J. Brill. Tr. E. M. Gale.

KUZNETS, SIMON
  1966 *Modern Economic Growth: Rate, Structure, and Spread.* New Haven, Conn.: Yale University Press; paper, Yale. **258, 269, 272.**
  1955–56 *National Income and Its Composiiton, 1919–1938.* New York: National Bureau of Economic Research.
  1959 *Six Lectures on Economic Growth.* New York: Free Press.

LANE, FREDERIC C., and JELLE C. RIEMERSMA (eds.)
  1953 *Enterprise and Secular Change.* Homewood, Ill.: Irwin. **281.**

LANGE, OSKAR, and FRED M. TAYLOR
  1938 *On the Economic Theory of Socialism.* New York: McGraw-Hill; paper, McGraw-Hill. **285.**

LATOUCHE, ROBERT
  1961 *Les Origines de l'Economie Occidentale* (1956). New York: Barnes & Noble; paper, Harper. Tr. E. M. Wilkinson as *The Birth of Western Economy.* **287.**

LAW, JOHN
  1934 *Oeuvres complètes de John Law.* Harsin, Paul (ed.), Paris: Librairie du Recueil Sirey. **253.**

LEIBENSTEIN, HARVEY
  1957 *Economic Backwardness and Economic Growth.* New York: Wiley; paper, Science Eds. **272.**

LEO XIII
  1891 *Rerum Novarum.* **241.**

LEONTIEF, WASSILY W.
  1951 *The Structure of American Economy* (2d enl. ed.). New York: Oxford University Press. **267.**

LERNER, ABBA P.
  1945 *The Economics of Control*. New York: Macmillan. **260, 269.**
  1936 "Mr. Keynes' 'General Theory of Employment, Interest and Money.'" *International Labour Review*. **260, 269**
LESTER, RICHARD A.
  1965 *Labor*. New York: Random; paper. **277.**
LETICHE, JOHN W. M.
  1966 *Balance of Payments and Economic Growth* (1959). New York: Kelley. **285.**
LEWIS, W. A.
  1949 *The Principles of Economic Planning*. London: Dobson. **272, 285.**
  1955 *The Theory of Economic Growth*. Homewood, Ill.: Irwin.
LINDBLOM, CHARLES E.
  1965 *The Intelligence of Democracy*. New York: Macmillan. **158, 180–181, 273, 284.**
LIPSEY, RICHARD G., and PETER O. STEINER
  1966 *Economics*. New York: Harper. **260.**
LIST, FREIDRICH
  1966 *The National System of Political Economy* (1856). New York: Kelley. **248, 252.**
LITTLE, IAN M. D.
  1957 *A Critique of Welfare Economics* (2d ed.). New York: Oxford University Press; paper, Oxford. **275.**
LONG, CLARENCE D.
  1958 *The Labor Force under Changing Income and Employment*. Princeton, N.J.: Princeton University Press. **277.**
LÖSCH, AUGUST
  1954 *The Economics of Location*. New Haven, Conn.: Yale University Press; paper, Science Eds. Tr. from 2d rev. ed. W. H. Waglom. **273.**
LYASHCHENKO, PETER I.
  1949 *History of the National Economy of Russia to the 1917 Revolution*. New York: Macmillan. **258.**
MCCLELLAND, DAVID C.
  1961 *The Achieving Society*. New York: Free Press; paper, Free Press. **110, 113, 281.**
MCCULLOCH, JOHN R. (ed.)
  1963 *The Literature of Political Economy: A Classified Catalogue* (1845). New York: Kelley. **245, 253.**
  1933 *Old and Scarce Tracts on Money*. London: King.
MACK, RUTH P.
  1941 *The Flow of Business Funds and Consumer Purchasing Power*. New York: Columbia University Press. **280.**
MALTHUS, THOMAS ROBERT
  An Essay on the Principle of Population (2 vols.). New York: Dutton's Everyman's; paper, Irwin. **7, 247.**

MARCH, JAMES G., and HERBERT A. SIMON
  1958 *Organizations*. New York: Wiley. **97–98, 104–105, 150, 156–157, 158, 180, 194–195, 280.**
MARGET, ARTHUR W.
  1965 *The Theory of Prices* (1938–42). New York: Kelley. **270.**
MARSHALL, ALFRED
  1940 *Principles of Economics* (1890) (9th ed., 2 vols.). New York: Macmillan. **240, 246, 249–250, 254, 259.**
MARSHALL, RAY
  1967 *The Negro Worker*. New York: Random; paper. **277.**
MARX, KARL
  1867 *Capital*. New York: Dutton's Everyman's; paper, Regnery. Tr. from 4th ed. E. and C. Paul; ed. F. Engels. **11–12, 23, 139, 175, 205–206, 222–223, 246, 247, 252–253, 257.**
MASSIE, JOSEPH
  1967 *Bibliography of the Collection of Books and Tracts on Commerce, Currency and Poor Law, 1557–1763*. New York: Franklin. **245.**
MAYO, ELTON
  1946 *The Human Problems of an Industrial Civilization*. New York: Viking; paper, Viking. **37, 157, 279.**
MEADE, JAMES E.
  1953 *Problems of Economic Union*. Chicago: University of Chicago Press. **275, 286.**
  1966 *The Theory of Customs Unions* (1955). New York: Humanities.
  1955 *Trade and Welfare*. New York: Oxford University Press.
MEIER, GERALD M.
  1964 *Leading Issues in Development Economics*. New York: Oxford University Press. **272.**
MEIER, RICHARD L.
  1956 *Science and Economic Development* (2d ed.). Cambridge, Mass.: M.I.T. Press; paper, M.I.T. **281.**
MELLOR, JOHN W.
  1966 *The Economics of Agricultural Development*. Ithaca, N.Y.: Cornell University Press. **276.**
MENDERSHAUSEN, HORST
  1940 *The Economics of War*. Englewood Cliffs, N.J.: Prentice-Hall. **284.**
MENGER, KARL
  1933–34 *The Collected Works*. London: London School of Economics; paper. **246, 259, 253, 263.**
  1950 *Principles of Economics*. New York: Free Press.
MILL, JOHN STUART
  1965 *The Principles of Political Economy* (1848). New York: Kelley. **139, 149, 177, 182, 247, 249.**
MINTS, LLOYD W.
  1945 *A History of Banking Theory in Great Britain and the United States*. Chicago: University of Chicago Press. **282.**

MITCHELL, WESLEY C.
 1937 *The Backward Art of Spending Money.* New York: Kelley. **248, 271.**
 1927 *Business Cycles: The Problem and Its Setting.* New York: National Bureau of Economic Research.
——, and ARTHUR F. BURNS
 1944 *Measuring Business Cycles.* New York: Columbia University Press.
MOORE, WILBERT E.
 1951 *Industrialization and Labor.* New York: Russell. **279, 289.**
——, and ARNOLD S. FELDMAN
 1960 *Labor Commitment and Social Change in Developing Areas.* New York: Social Science Research Council. **279.**
MOSHER, A. T.
 1966 *Getting Agriculture Moving.* New York: Praeger; paper, Praeger. **195.**
MYRDAL, GUNNAR
 1956 *An International Economy.* New York: Harper. **34, 285.**
NATIONAL BUREAU OF ECONOMIC RESEARCH
 1962 *The Rate and Direction of Inventive Activity: Economic and Social Factors.* Princeton, N.J.: Princeton University Press.
NEF, JOHN U.
 1950 *War and Human Progress.* New York: Russell. **287.**
NEUMAN, JOHN VON, and OSKAR MORGENSTERN
 1964 *Theory of Games and Economic Behavior* (3d ed.). New York: Science Eds.; paper. **265.**
NORTH, DOUGLASS C.
 1961 *The Economic Growth of the United States, 1790–1860.* Englewood Cliffs, N.J.: Prentice-Hall. **287–288.**
NURSKE, RAGNAR
 1957 *Problems of Capital Formation in Underdeveloped Countries.* New York: Oxford University Press; paper, Oxford. **272.**
OHLIN, BERTIL
 1933 *Interregional and International Trade.* Cambridge, Mass.: Harvard University Press. **275.**
OSTROGORSKY, GEORGE
 1956 *History of the Byzantine State.* New Brunswick, N.J.: Rutgers University Press. **164–165.**
PAN KU
 1950 *Food and Money in Ancient China.* Princeton, N.J.: Princeton University Press. Tr. N. L. Swann. **256.**
PARNES, HERBERT S.
 1954 *Research of Labor Mobility.* New York: Social Science Research Council; paper. **277.**
PARSONS, TALCOTT, and NEIL J. SMELSER
 1946 *Economy and Society.* New York: Free Press; paper, Free Press. **11, 21, 23, 61–62, 63, 72, 155, 180–181, 213, 227, 249.**

PATINKIN, DON
 1964 *Money, Interest, and Prices* (2d ed.). New York: Harper. **270.**
PERLMAN, SELIG
 1966 *A Theory of the Labor Movement* (1928) New York: Kelley. **278.**
PERLOFF, HARVEY, et al.
 1960 *Regions, Resources, and Economic Growth.* Magnolia, Mass.: Smith; paper, Nebraska. **273.**
PETTY, WILLIAM
 1966 *Economic Writings* (1899) New York: Kelley. **245.**
PIGOU, ARTHUR C.
 1935 *The Economics of Stationary States.* New York: Macmillan. **249, 273, 275, 283.**
 1938 *The Economics of Welfare* (4th ed.). New York: St. Martins; paper, St. Martins.
 1947 *A Study in Public Finance.* New York: Macmillan.
PIRENNE, HENRI
 1937 *Economic and Social History of Medieval Europe.* New York: Harcourt; paper, Harcourt. **287.**
POLANYI, KARL
 1957 *The Great Transformation* (1944). Boston: Beacon; paper.
REDER, MELVIN W.
 1948 *Studies in the Theory of Welfare Economics.* New York: Columbia University Press. **275.**
REID, MARGARET G.
 1942 *Consumers and the Market.* New York: Appleton. **274.**
REYNOLDS, LLOYD C.
 1951 *The Structure of Labor Markets.* New York: Harper. **277.**
RICARDO, DAVID
 1817 *The Principles of Political Economy and Taxation.* New York: Dutton's Everyman's; paper, Irwin. **247, 253.**
ROBBINS, LIONEL
 1935 *An Essay on the Nature and Significance of Economic Science* (2d ed.). New York: St. Martins. **252, 265.**
 1952 *The Theory of Economic Policy in English Classical Political Economy.* New York: St. Martins.
ROBERTSON, DENNIS H.
 1932 *Banking Policy and the Price Level.* New York: Kelley. **249, 270, 282.**
 1922 *Money.* New York: Harcourt.
ROBINSON, JOAN
 1965 *The Accumulation of Capital* (2d ed.). New York: St. Martins. **260, 267–268.**
 1933 *The Economics of Imperfect Competition.* New York: St. Martins.
 1937 *Introduction to the Theory of Employment.* New York: St. Martins.

ROETHLISBERGER, FRITZ J., and WILLIAM J. DICKSON
   1964 *Management and the Worker* (1960). New York: Science Eds.; paper. **37, 157, 279.**

ROSTOVTSEFF, MIKHAIL I.
   1941 *The Social and Economic History of the Hellenistic World* (3 vols.). New York: Oxford University Press. **287.**
   1957 *The Social and Economic History of the Roman Empire* (2d ed., 2 vols.). New York: Oxford University Press.

ROSTOW, WALT W.
   1960 *The Stages of Economic Growth.* New York: Cambridge University Press; paper, Cambridge. **272.**

RUNCIMAN, STEVEN
   1951–54 *The History of the Crusades* (3 vols.). New York: Cambridge University Press; paper, Harper (3 vols.). **287.**

SAMUELSON, PAUL
   1967 *Economics* (7th ed.). New York: McGraw-Hill. **260, 265.**
   1965 *Foundations of Economic Analysis* (1947). New York: Atheneum; paper, Atheneum.

SAYERS, RICHARD S.
   1948 *American Banking System.* New York: Oxford University Press. **282.**
   1964 *Modern Banking* (6th ed.). New York: Oxford University Press.

SAYLES, LEONARD R., and GEORGE STRAUSS
   1953 *The Local Union.* New York: Harcourt; paper, Harcourt. **278, 280.**

SCHULTZ, THEODORE W.
   1953 *The Economic Organization of Agriculture.* New York: McGraw-Hill. **261, 276.**
   1965 *Transforming Traditional Agriculture.* New Haven, Conn.: Yale University Press.
   —— (ed.)
   1945 *Food for the World.* Chicago: University of Chicago Press.

SCHUMPETER, JOSEPH A.
   1964 *Business Cycles.* (rev. ed.) New York: McGraw-Hill; paper, McGraw. **251, 271, 281.**
   1954 *History of Economic Analysis* (rev. ed.). New York: Oxford University Press. Ed. E. Schumpeter.

SEIDMAN, JOEL L., et al.
   1958 *The Worker Views His Union.* Chicago: University of Chicago Press. **278.**

SHACKLE, GEORGE L. S.
   1938 *Expectations, Investment, and Income.* New York: Oxford University Press. **269, 273.**
   1958 *Time in Economics.* Amsterdam: North-Holland.

SHIMKIN, D.
   1953 *Minerals: Key to Soviet Power.* Cambridge, Mass.: Harvard University Press. **258.**

SIMON, HERBERT A.
  1960 *The New Science of Management Decisions.* New York: Harper. **97, 98, 104, 150, 156–158, 180, 194–195, 280.**
SIMONS, HENRY C.
  1948 *Economic Policy for a Free Society.* Chicago: University of Chicago Press. **251, 283.**
  1950 *Federal Tax Reform.* Chicago: University of Chicago Press.
  1938 *Personal Income Taxation.* Chicago: University of Chicago Press.
SLICHTER, SUMNER H., et al.
  1960 *The Impact of Collective Bargaining on Management.* Washington: Brookings. **279.**
SMITH, ADAM
  The Wealth of Nations (1776) (2 vols.). New York: Dutton's Everyman's; paper, Irwin (2 vols.). **240, 242, 244–246.**
SOMBART, WERNER
  1902 *Der moderne Kapitalismus.* Leipzig: Duncker & Humblot. **255, 287.**
  1967 *The Quintessence of Capitalism* (1915). New York: Fertig. Tr. and ed. M. Epstein.
SPENGLER, JOSEPH J., and WILLIAM R. ALLEN (eds.)
  1960 *Essays in Economic Thought: Aristotle to Marshall.* Chicago: Rand. **31, 252.**
SPIEGEL, HENRY W. (ed.)
  1964 *The Development of Economic Thought: Great Economists in Perspective* (1952). New York: Science Eds.; paper. **251.**
SRAFFA, PIERO, and M. H. DOBB (eds.)
  1951–55 *The Works and Correspondence of David Ricardo.* New York: Cambridge University Press. **253.**
STEPHEN, LESLIE
  1953 *The English Utilitarians* (1900). Magnolia, Mass.: Smith. **252.**
STIGLER, GEORGE J.
  1966 *The Theory of Price.* (3d ed.). New York: Macmillan. **268.**
STIEBER, JACK (ed.)
  1966 *Employment Problems of Automation and Advanced Technology.* New York: St. Martins. **281.**
STRASSMAN, W. PAUL
  1959 *Risk and Technological Innovation.* Ithaca, N.Y.: Cornell University Press. **281.**
STUDENSKI, PAUL
  1958 *A Study of the Income of Nations: Theory, Measurement, and Analysis, Past and Present.* New York: New York University Press. **269.**
TAUSSIG, FRANK W.
  1966 *International Trade* (1927). New York: Kelley. **275, 285.**
  1915 *Some Aspects of the Tariff Question.* Cambridge, Mass.: Harvard University Press.
TAWNEY, RICHARD H.
  1925 "Introduction" to T. Wilson, *A Discourse upon Usury* (1572). New York: Kelley. **243.**

TAX, SOL
   1953 *Penny Capitalism: A Guatemalan Indian Economy*. Washington: Smithsonian Institution. **57-58, 70, 77, 79, 289.**

THEIL, HENRI
   1961 *Economic Forecasts and Policy* (2d rev. ed.). New York: Humanities.
   1954 *Linear Aggregation of Economic Relations*. New York: Humanities.

THURNWALD, RICHARD
   1965 *Economics in Private Communities* (1932). New York: Humanities. **289.**

TOSTLEBE, ALVIN S.
   1957 *Capital in Agriculture: Its Formation and Financing since 1870*. Princeton University Press. **276.**

TRIFFIN, ROBERT
   1940 *Monopolistic Competition and General Equilibrium Theory*. Cambridge, Mass.: Harvard University Press. **268, 285.**
   1964 *Our International Monetary System*. Princeton, N.J.: Princeton University International Finance Section.

TULLOCK, GORDON
   1967 *Toward a Mathematics of Politics*. Ann Arbor, Mich.: University of Michigan Press. **179, 195, 284.**

TURGOT, A. R. J.
   1913-23 *Oeuvres de Turgot et documents le Concernant*. Schelle, Gustave (ed.), Paris: F. Alcan. **253.**

UDY, JR., STANLEY H.
   1959 *The Organization of Work*. New York: Taplinger, 1959; paper, Taplinger. **290.**

ULMAN, LLOYD
   1955 *The Rise of the National Trade Union* (2d ed.). Cambridge, Mass.: Harvard University Press. **278.**

VEBLEN, THORSTEIN
   1965 *The Theory of Business Enterprise* (1904). New York: Kelley; paper, New American. **248, 288-289.**
   The Theory of the Leisure Class (1899). New York: Modern Library; paper, New American; Viking; Crowell.

VINER, JACOB
   1950 *The Customs Union Issue*. New York: Anderson. **244, 275, 286.**
   1965 *Studies in the Theory of International Trade* (1937). New York: Kelley.

WAGNER, ADOLPH H. G.
   1907-09 *Theoretische Sozialoekonomik*. Leipzig: C. F. Winter. **248.**

WALKER, EDWARD R.
   1943 *From Economic Theory to Policy*. Chicago: University of Chicago Press. **113, 125.**

WALRAS, LEON
   1954 *Elements of Pure Economics*. Homewood, Ill.: Irwin. Tr. W. Jaffe. **249, 254, 267.**

WEBB, SIDNEY, and BEATRICE WEBB
  1965 *Industrial Democracy* (1897). New York: Kelley. **241, 278.**
WEBER, MAX
  1950 *General Economic History.* New York: Collier; paper. Tr. F. H. Knight. **12–14, 15, 18, 21, 36, 55, 77, 155, 213, 255, 287.**
  1930 *The Protestant Ethic and the Spirit of Capitalism.* New York: Scribner; paper, Scribner.
  1947 *The Theory of Social and Economic Organization.* New York: Free Press; paper, Free Press.
WEISKOPF, WALTER A.
  1957 *The Psychology of Economics.* New York: Humanities. **281.**
WEULERSSE, GEORGES
  1910 *Le Mouvement physiocratique en France.* Paris: F. Alcan. **252.**
WHYTE, WILLIAM F.
  1946 *Industry and Society.* New York: McGraw-Hill. **28, 37, 166–167, 278.**
WILLIAMS, JOHN B.
  1954 *International Trade under Flexible Exchange Rates.* New York: Kelley. **285.**
WOLF, JR., CHARLES
  1960 *Foreign Aid: Theory and Practice in Southern Asia.* Princeton, N.J.: Princeton University Press. **230, 286.**
WOOTTON, BARBARA
  1945 *Freedom under Planning.* Chapel Hill, N.C.: University of North Carolina Press. **285.**
WRIGHT, CHESTER
  1949 *Economic History of the United States.* New York: McGraw-Hill; 2d ed.

MISCELLANEOUS SOURCES

American Economic Association list of special fields in economics.
American Economic Review (1911–   ).
Bureau of Farm Economics publications.
Cambridge Economic History of Europe. Vols. II, III.
Canadian Journal of Economics and Political Science (1935–   ).
Consumer Reports (1936–   ).
Demographic Yearbook (1948–   ).
Department of Agriculture specialized reports.
Economic Development and Cultural Change (1952–   ).
The Economist.
Food Research Institute (Stanford) publications.
Fortune (1930–   ).

The Fugger News-Letters (1924–), V. Klarwill (ed.).
Goldsmith Library of London School of Economics mercantilist collection.
Handbook of Latin American Studies (1936–).
Index Translatorium (1932–) (UNESCO).
Industrial Manual.
International Economic Papers (1951–).
International Financial Statistics (1948–).
International Labour Review.
Johns Hopkins University Press classical and mercantilist series.
Joint Committee on Slavic Studies of the American Council of Learned Societies and Social Science Research Council, *Current Digest of the Soviet Press* (1949–).
Journal of Farm Economics (1919–).
Journal of Finance (1946–).
Journal of Political Economy (1892–).
Kress Collection, Harvard.
Land Economics (1925–).
Library of the British Museum mercantilist collection.
Monthly Labor Review (1915–).
Moody's Bank and Financial Manual.
Municipal and Government Manual.
National Committee for a Free Europe *News from Behind the Iron Curtain* (1952–).
The OECD Observer (1916–).
Public Utility Manual.
Quarterly Journal of Economics (1886–).
Reprints of Economic Tracts (1903–), J. H. Hollander (ed.).
Scottish Journal of Political Economy (1954–).
Scrittori Classici Italiani di Economia Politica (50 vols., 1803–16), P. Custodi (ed.).
Selig Collection, Columbia.
Social Research (1934–).
Southern Economic Journal (1933–).
Statesman's Year-Book.
Statistical Abstracts of the United States (1878–).
Survey of Current Business (1921–).
Times Sales Financing (1936–).
Transportation Manual.
Wagner Collection, Yale.
Wall Street Journal.
World Economic Survey (1945–).
Yearbook of Food and Agricultural Statistics (1947–).
Yearbook of Labor Statistics (1931–).

Geography

ALEXANDER, J. W.
   1963 *Economic Geography.* Englewood Cliffs, N.J.: Prentice-Hall. 310.

ALEXANDERSSON, G.
   1967 *Geography of Manufacturing.* Englewood Cliffs, N.J.: Prentice-Hall. 310.

BARROWS, H. H.
   1924 "Geography as Human Ecology"; an address. 298.

BEAUJEU-GARNIER, J., and G. CHABOT
   1967 *Urban Geography.* New York: Wiley.

BERRY, B. J.
   1967 *Geography of Market Centers and Retail Distribution.* Englewood Cliffs, N.J.: Prentice-Hall; paper.

BOWMAN, I.
   1922 *The New World: Problems in Political Geography.* New York: Harcourt. 313.

BROEK, J. O. M.
   1965 *Geography: Its Scope and Spirit.* Columbus, Ohio: Merrill. 294, 308.

———, and J. W. WEBB
   1968 *A Geography of Mankind.* New York: McGraw-Hill. 308.

BROOKFIELD, H. C. and P. BROWN
   1962 *Struggle for Land: Agriculture and Group Territories among the Chimbu of the New Guinea Highlands.* New York: Oxford University Press. 298.

BROWN, R. H.
   1943 *Mirror for Americans: Likeness of the Eastern Seaboard, 1810.* New York: Plenum. 206.

BUNTING, B. T.
   1966 *The Geography of Soil.* Chicago: Aldine; paper, Aldine. 305.

BUTZER, K. W.
   1964 *Environment and Archeology.* Chicago: Aldine. 65, 305.

CHISHOLM, M.
   1966 *Geography and Economics.* New York: Praeger. 309.
   1962 *Rural Settlement and Land Use.* New York: Hillary; paper, Science Eds. 309.

CHORLEY, R. J., and P. HAGGETT (eds.)
   1967 *Models in Geography.* New York: Barnes & Noble. 305, 309–311.

CHRISTALLER, W.
   1966 *Central Places in Southern Germany.* Englewood Cliffs, N.J.: Prentice-Hall. 299.

CHURCH, M., R. E. HUKE, and W. ZELINSKY (eds.)
   1966 *A Basic Geographical Library: A Selected and Annotated Book List for American Colleges.* Washington: Association of American Geographers. 294.

CLARK, A. H.
- 1949 *The Invasion of New Zealand by People, Plants, and Animals: The South Island.* New Brunswick, N.J.: Rutgers University Press. **306–307.**

COHEN, S. B.
- 1963 *Geography and Politics in a World Divided.* New York: Random. **294, 312.**
- 1967 *Problems and Trends in American Geography.* New York: Basic Books.

DARBY, H. C.
- 1951 "The Changing English Landscape," *Geographical Journal.* **297, 306.**
- 1952 *The Domesday Geography of Eastern England.* New York: Cambridge University Press.
- 1953 "On the Relation of Geography and History," *Transactions and Papers,* Institute of British Geographers.

DE BLIJ, H. J.
- 1967 *Systematic Political Geography.* New York: Wiley. **313.**

ESTALL, R. C., and R. O. BUCHANAN
- 1966 *Industrial Activity and Economic Geography.* New York: Hillary; paper, Science Eds.

EYRE, S. R.
- 1963 *Vegetation and Soils.* Chicago: Aldine. **305, 307.**

FINCH, V. C., G. T. TREWARTHA, and E. H. HAMMOND
- 1967 *Physical Elements of Geography.* New York: McGraw-Hill. **305.**

FOSBERG, F. R.
- 1965 *Man's Place in the Island Ecosystem.* Honolulu: Bishop. **298.**

FREEMAN, T. W.
- 1961 *A Hundred Years of Geography.* Chicago: Aldine; paper, Aldine. **294.**

FRYER, D. W.
- 1965 *World Economic Development.* New York: McGraw-Hill. **310.**

GINSBURG, N.
- 1961 *Atlas of Economic Development.* Chicago: University of Chicago Press. **310–311, 313.**
- 1960 (Ed.), *Essays on Geography and Economic Development.* Chicago: University of Chicago Press.

GLACKEN, C. J.
- 1967 *Traces on the Rhodian Shore: Nature and Culture in Western Thought from Ancient Times to the End of the Eighteenth Century.* Berkeley, Cal.: University of California Press. **307.**

GOTTMAN, J.
- 1961 *Megalopolis: The Urbanized Northeastern Seaboard of the United States.* New York: Twentieth Century; paper, M.I.T. **306, 311.**
- 1955 *Virginia at Mid-Century.* New York: Holt.

HAGGETT, P.
: 1966 *Locational Analysis in Human Geography.* New York: St. Martins. **305, 309–310, 311.**

HARRIS, C. D., and J. D. FELLMANN
: 1960 *An International List of Geographical Serials.* Chicago: University of Chicago Press. **318.**

HARTSHORNE, R.
: 1939 *The Nature of Geography.* Cambridge, Mass.: Association of American Geographers. **293, 300, 306.**
: 1959 *Perspective on the Nature of Geography.* Chicago: Rand.

HAUSER, P. M., and L. F. SCHNORE (eds.)
: 1965 *The Study of Urbanization.* New York: Wiley. **31, 311.**

HIGBEE, E.
: 1958 *American Agriculture: Geography, Resources, Conservation.* New York: Wiley. **310.**

HOOSON, D.
: 1964 *A New Soviet Heartland?* New York: Van Nostrand Reinhold; paper.

JACKSON, W. A. D. (ed.)
: 1964 *Politics and Geographic Relationships.* Englewood Cliffs, N.J.: Prentice-Hall. **312.**

JAMES, P. E.
: 1963 "Geography," *Encyclopaedia Britannica.* **294.**

———, and C. F. JONES
: 1954 *American Geography: Inventory and Prospect.* Syracuse, N.Y.: Syracuse University Press. **294.**

JONES, G. R. J., and S. R. EYRE
: 1956 *Geography as Human Ecology.* New York: St. Martins. **305, 307.**

JONES, S. B.
: 1945 *Boundary-Making: A Handbook for Statesmen, Treaty Editors, and Boundary Commissioners.* New York: Columbia University Press. **312.**

LOWENTHAL, D. (ed)
: 1961 *The West Indies Federation: Perspectives on a New Nation.* New York: Columbia University Press. **297, 307, 313.**

———, and H. PRINCE
: "English Landscape Tastes," *Geographical Review.* **297.**

MCCARTY, H. H., and J. B. LINDBERG
: 1966 *A Preface to Economic Geography.* Englewood Cliffs, N.J.: Prentice-Hall. **231, 309.**

MCGEE, T. G.
: 1967 *The Southeast Asian City.* New York: Praeger. **311.**

MACKINDER, H. M.
: 1967 *Democratic Ideals and Reality* (1919). New York: Norton; paper.

MARSH, G. P.
   1965 *Man and Nature: Or, Physical Geography as Modified by Human Action* (1864). Cambridge, Mass.: Harvard University Press. Ed. D. Lowenthal. 307.
MAYER, H. M., and C. F. KOHN
   1959 *Readings in Urban Geography*. Chicago: University of Chicago Press. 311.
MEINIG, D. W.
   On the Margins of the Good Earth. Chicago: Rand. 306–307.
MERRENS, H. R.
   1965 "Historical Geography and Early American History," *William and Mary Quarterly*. 306.
MIKESELL, M. W.
   1960 "Comparative Studies in Frontier History," *Annals*, Association of American Geographers. 306–308.
MOGEY, JOHN M.
   1950 *The Study of Geography*. New York: Oxford University Press. 296.
MONKHOUSE, F. J.
   1965 *A Dictionary of Geography*. Chicago: Aldine. 318.
MURPHEY, R.
   1966 *An Introduction to Geography*. Chicago: Rand. 304.
MURPHY, R. E.
   1956 *The American City: An Urban Geography*. New York: McGraw-Hill. 311.
PLATT, R. S.
   1948 "Determinism in Geography," *Annals*, Association of American Geographers. 295, 304.
   1948 "Environmentalism Versus Geography," *American Journal of Sociology*.
   1944 "Regionalism in World Order," *Social Education*.
POUNDS, N. J. G.
   1963 *Political Geography*. New York: McGraw-Hill. 313.
PRESCOTT, J. R. V.
   1959 "The Functions and Methods of Electoral Geography," *Annals*, Association of American Geographers. 312–313.
   1965 *The Geography of Frontiers and Boundaries*. Chicago: Aldine.
RAISZ, E.
   1962 *Principles of Cartography*. New York: McGraw-Hill. 315.
RATZEL, F.
   Vide Semple, E. C. 51–52, 63, 295, 296.
ROBINSON, A. H.
   1960 *Elements of Cartography*. New York: Wiley; 2d ed. 315.
RUSSELL, R. J., F. B. KNIFFEN, and E. L. PRUITT
   1961 *Culture Worlds*. New York: Macmillan. 304.
SAUER, C. O.
   1952 *Origins and Dispersals*. New York: American Geographical Society. 297, 299.

1925 *The Morphology of Landscape.* Berkeley, Cal.: University of California.

SEMPLE, E. C.
1931 *Geography of the Mediterranean Region: Its Relation to History.* New York: Holt. **295, 306.**
1911 *Influence of Geographic Environment on the Basis of Ratzel's System of Anthropo-Geography.* New York: Holt.

SIMOONS, F.
1961 *Eat Not This Flesh.* Madison, Wis.: University of Wisconsin Press; paper. **308.**

SOPHER, D.
1967 *Geography of Religions.* Englewood Cliffs, N.J.: Prentice-Hall; paper, Prentice. **308.**

SPATE, O. H. K.
1952 "Toynbee and Huntington: A Study of Determinism," *Geographical Journal.* **295.**

STAMP, L. D. (ed.)
1966 *A Dictionary Geography.* New York: Wiley. **318.**

STROHLER, A. N.
1965 *Introduction to Physical Geography.* New York: Wiley.

THOMAN, R. S.
1962 *The Geography of Economic Activity.* New York: McGraw-Hill. **304, 310.**

———, and E. C. CONKLING
1967 *Geography of International Trade.* Englewood Cliffs, N.J.: Prentice-Hall; paper. **310.**

THOMAS, W. L. (ed.)
1956 *Man's Role in Changing the Face of the Earth.* Chicago: University of Chicago Press. **307.**

TREWARTHA, G. T.
1961 *The World's Problem Climates.* Madison, Wis.: University of Wisconsin Press. **305.**

WAGNER, P. L.
The Human Use of the Earth. New York: Free Press. **297–298, 307–308.**

———, and M. W. MIKESELL
1962 *Readings in Cultural Geography.* Chicago: University of Chicago Press. **306–308.**

WHEATLEY, P.
1961 *The Golden Khersonese,* New York: Oxford University Press; paper. **306.**

WHEELER, J. H., J. T. KOSTBADE, and R. S. THOMAS
1961 *Regional Geography of the World.* New York: Holt; rev. ed. **304.**

WHITE, G. F.
1964 *Choice of Adjustment to Floods.* Chicago: University of Chicago Dept. of Geography. **310.**

WHITTLESEY, D.
> 1939 *The Earth and the State.* New York: Holt. **307, 313.**
> 1929 "Sequent Occupance," *Annals,* Association of American Geographers.

WOLFE, R. I.
> 1963 *Transportation and Politics.* New York: Van Nostrand Reinhold; paper. **313.**

WRIGHT, J. K., and E. T. PLATT
> 1947 *Aids to Geographical Research: Bibliographies, Periodicals, Atlases, Gazetteers, and Other Reference Books.* New York: Columbia University Press; 2d ed. **318.**

ZELINSKY, W.
> 1962 *A Bibliographic Guide to Population Geography.* Chicago: University of Chicago Dept. of Geography. **294, 308.**
> 1966 *A Prologue to Population Geography.* Englewood Cliffs, N.J.: Prentice-Hall; paper.

MISCELLANEOUS SOURCES

Aldine University Atlas (1969).
American Journal of Sociology.
Annals, Association of American Geographers.
Bibliographie Geographique Internationale (1915–   ).
British Ordnance Survey Maps.
Coast and Geodetic Survey Grids.
Columbia-Lippincott Gazeteer of the World (1952).
Current Geographical Publications (1938–   ).
Economic Geography.
Geographical Review.
Geographisches Jahrbuch (1866–   ).
Geological Survey Maps.
Goode's World Atlas.
Harris Annotated World List of Selected Current Geographical Serials in English (1964).
Hydrographic Office Charts.
IGU Symposium in Urban Geography, *Proceedings* 1960 (1962), K. Norborg (ed.).
International Map of the World.
Journal of the American Institute of Planners.
Journal of the Regional Science Association.
Sailing Directions.
Times Atlas of the World.
Webster's Geographical Dictionary (1955).